Economic and Financial Crises in Emerging Market Economies

A National Bureau
of Economic Research
Conference Report

Economic and Financial Crises in Emerging Market Economies

Edited by **Martin Feldstein**

The University of Chicago Press

Chicago and London

MARTIN FELDSTEIN is the George F. Baker Professor of Economics, Harvard University, and president of the National Bureau of Economic Research.

The University of Chicago Press, Chicago 60637
The University of Chicago Press, Ltd., London
© 2003 by the National Bureau of Economic Research
Chapter 3, Comment 4 © 2003 by George Soros
All rights reserved. Published 2003
Printed in the United States of America
12 11 10 09 08 07 06 05 04 03   1 2 3 4 5
ISBN: 0-226-24109-2 (cloth)

Library of Congress Cataloging-in-Publication Data

Economic and financial crises in emerging market economies / edited
    by Martin Feldstein.
        p.   cm. — (NBER conference report)
    Includes bibliographical references and index.
    ISBN 0-226-24109-2 (cloth : alk. paper)
    1. Financial crises—Congresses.   2. Economic stabilization—
Congresses.   3. Economic policy—Congresses.   4. International
Monetary Fund—Congresses.   I. Feldstein, Martin S.   II. Series.

HB3722 .E25 2002
338.5'42—dc21

2002067528

Since this volume is a record of conference proceedings, it has been exempted from the rules governing critical review of manuscripts by the Board of Directors of the National Bureau (resolution adopted 8 June 1948, as revised 21 November 1949 and 20 April 1968).

Contents

Preface

The financial and currency crises that began in Thailand in 1997 and spread around the world are a warning and a challenge to officials, to private market participants, and to economic researchers. The National Bureau of Economic Research (NBER) responded to this challenge by organizing a major project aimed at understanding how the risk of such crises might be reduced and how the crises that do occur could be managed in a way that does less damage in both the short run and the more distant future.

Our project consisted of three related parts. We held a series of separate day-long meetings that dealt with the experience in each of the crisis countries. These meetings brought together officials and private economists from the crisis countries, economists from the U.S. government and Federal Reserve, officials from the International Monetary Fund (IMF) and World Bank, private bankers, and NBER economists. Brief summaries of the discussions at each meeting are posted on the NBER web site at [http://www.nber.org/crisis].

The second part of the project was two in-depth research projects dealing with the two separate parts of our study. Sebastian Edwards and Jeffrey A. Frankel organized a project on reducing the risk of economic crises. Michael P. Dooley and Jeffrey A. Frankel organized a parallel project on managing the crises that do occur. The two groups of researchers met separately and occasionally together at meetings of the NBER International Finance and Macroeconomics program. The final stage of each project was a conference at which the research papers were discussed with a broader group of economists. The papers summarizing the research in these two projects are published in two NBER volumes by the pairs of organizers. A large number of additional technical studies appear as NBER working papers and can be found at [http://www.nber.org/crisis/#papers].

Finally, the third part of the project brought together a remarkable group of very senior officials, business leaders, and academic economists who were involved in the crises in the United States and in the crisis countries to discuss their personal perspectives on these events. Each participant prepared a personal statement on some aspect of the crises. Six major nontechnical papers, each written by a distinguished economist who is a specialist dealing with these issues, served as a background for the discussions. This volume brings together the background papers, the prepared remarks of those who played important roles, and a summary of the discussion at the meeting, prepared by John McHale. The meeting itself was held at the Woodstock Inn in Woodstock, Vermont, on 20–21 October 2000.

When the crises began, there were many calls for fundamental changes in the international economic architecture. The discussion at the conference left me with the strong feeling that what is needed is not a new architecture but a return to some of the basic principles of economic virtue.

Financial support for the entire project came from the Ford Foundation, the Mellon Foundation, the Starr Foundation, and the Center for International Political Economy. I am grateful to them for making this work possible.

I am grateful also to the authors of the background papers for the extensive research and writing that went into preparing these very useful documents and to the officials, executives, and academics who took time from their very busy schedules to share their insights and experience in the economic crises. I also want to thank several members of the NBER staff for their assistance in the planning and execution of the project, the conference, and this volume, in particular Kirsten Foss Davis and Amy Tretheway of the NBER conference department, Helena Fitz-Patrick, Gerardine Johnson, and Norma MacKenzie. I am grateful to John McHale for preparing the summaries of the fast-moving discussions.

After the conference, financial and currency crises continued to happen around the world. I can only hope that the analyses and ideas presented in this volume will help to reduce the frequency and severity of such crises in the future.

Martin Feldstein

Economic and Financial Crises in Emerging Market Economies
An Overview of Prevention and Management

Martin Feldstein

Financial and currency crises have occurred for as long as there have been financial markets. However, the crises in the emerging market economies since the late 1990s were more global and potentially more damaging to economic and political stability than the crises of the past. The events that began in Thailand in 1997 eventually enveloped several countries of east Asia, as well as Russia, Turkey, and key Latin American economies. Finding ways to reduce the risk of future crises and to improve the management of crises when they do occur is a policy challenge of great importance.

The crises that hit Latin America in the 1980s were significantly different from those of the 1990s. The governments of Latin America had borrowed heavily from foreign commercial banks during the 1970s, encouraged by very low real interest rates and by high prices for their commodity exports. When real interest rates rose sharply at the end of that decade and an Amer-

This volume contains a combination of background papers by economists on various aspects of the financial crises and personal statements of seventeen individuals who have dealt with the recent financial crises as officials of U.S. and foreign governments and of international organizations, private sector executives, and academic analysts. This introductory chapter benefitted from what the author learned at the conference as well as from the papers and discussions at two other NBER conferences, which appear in collected form as *Preventing Currency Crises in Emerging Markets*, edited by Sebastian Edwards and Jeffrey A. Frankel (Chicago: University of Chicago Press, 2002) and *Managing Currency Crises in Emerging Markets*, edited by Michael P. Dooley and Jeffrey A. Frankel (Chicago: University of Chicago Press, 2003). The author also benefitted from the NBER meetings on individual crisis countries; the discussions at those meetings are summarized by John McHale on the NBER web site at The NBER Project on Exchange Rate Crises. Some of the author's earlier views on these issues were presented in "Refocusing the IMF," *Foreign Affairs*, March/April 1998, "A Self-Help Guide for Emerging Markets," *Foreign Affairs*, March/April 1999, and "No New Architecture," *The International Economy*, September/October 1999.

ican recession reduced the demand for Latin American exports, the borrower countries were unable to service their debts. As a result, the major money center banks of the United States and Europe were significantly impaired, causing widespread concern about the possibility of a systemic banking crisis in the industrial world. The Latin American governments were forced to reduce the spending that had been financed by foreign credits and to deflate their economies even further in order to increase net exports so that they could make interest and principal payments on their external debt. The combination of these actions, a general recovery of global demand, a decline of real interest rates, and some forced write-downs of debt eventually brought the crisis to an end. Even after it was resolved, however, incomes in Latin America remained below their precrisis levels for some time.

Governments and banks learned some important lessons from this experience. The Latin American governments financed their subsequent budget deficits in their domestic capital markets to a much greater extent,[1] and the commercial banks of the industrial counties reduced their lending to foreign governments. Although large current account deficits continued in several countries, they were financed primarily by a combination of private borrowing in international bond markets, equity flows, and foreign direct investment.

The late 1980s and 1990s saw a very substantial expansion of the global capital market with rapid increases in private debt and equity flows and in foreign direct investment.[2] This expansion reflected a wide variety of changes in the global political environment, in financial technology, and in investors' preferences. The collapse of the Soviet Union and the general shift to more democratic and market-oriented policies around the world increased the attractiveness of lending and investing in the emerging market countries and the desire of their governments to attract foreign equity capital. Technological developments facilitated global portfolio management and the retail index funds that shifted debt and equity investments to emerging economies. Portfolio investors seized the opportunity to diversify portfolios in pursuit of the higher returns and the lower overall volatility that they believed would follow such diversification.

Avoiding the mistakes of the 1970s did not, however, prevent a return of international financial crises. In retrospect, the crises of the 1990s were due primarily to a combination of unsustainable current account deficits, excessive short-term foreign debts, and weak domestic banking systems. Although the experience in each crisis country was unique, one or more of these adverse conditions was present in each case.

The industrial countries responded to these crises both directly and

1. Argentina was an exception to this, borrowing heavily in dollars in the international markets to finance its government deficits.

2. See the papers and personal commentaries in Feldstein 1999 for analyses of these capital flows.

through the International Monetary Fund (IMF) with substantial packages of financial support and with the imposition of wide-ranging requirements of domestic economic reforms. Now, however, more than four years after the crises began, the major crisis countries have neither returned to their precrisis rates of economic growth nor achieved the structural reforms that the IMF had tried to impose.

What, then, are the lessons to be learned from this experience? What can be done to reduce the risk of recurrent crises in emerging market countries? And how can the crises that will occur in the future be managed in a way that reduces the direct adverse consequences of dealing with those crises and that also discourages behavior by emerging market countries and by foreign creditors that increases the risk of future crises?

Although much has been learned about the answers to these questions, there is no general agreement about all of these issues among economists or among others who have dealt with these problems. Although the research and discussion in the National Bureau of Economic Research (NBER) project has strongly influenced my thinking, what follows is my personal view rather than an attempt to summarize the background and research papers that appear in this and related NBER volumes or in the personal statements and discussion summaries in this volume. They speak eloquently for themselves.

Reducing the Risk of Financial and Currency Crises in Emerging Markets

Fixed Exchange Rates, Current Account Deficits, and Debt Deflation

A primary cause of the crises that began with Mexico in the mid-1990s and continued in East Asia in the late 1990s was a large and growing current account deficit caused by a fixed exchange rate. The experience in Thailand illustrates this very dramatically. Thailand fixed the value of the baht at twenty-five baht to the dollar, a level that initially made Thai exports very competitive. As the dollar fell relative to the Japanese yen, the baht fell with it, increasing the competitiveness of Thai products in Japanese and other markets. The stable dollar-baht exchange rate encouraged Thai companies to finance themselves by borrowing dollars (which had lower interest rates than baht) even when their only sales revenue were in baht, because they were told by the Thai government that the baht-dollar rate would remain unchanged, a statement quite consistent with their observation over several years. Thai banks also borrowed dollars on the world market and lent them to these local companies, comfortable in the knowledge that their dollar assets and liabilities were balanced even though the Thai borrowers did not earn dollars directly but depended on converting their baht incomes into dollars to service their dollar debts.

Eventually, however, the baht became overvalued, reflecting rising domestic prices in Thailand and an appreciating dollar, particularly relative to the Japanese yen. Thailand's current account deficit grew rapidly, reaching 4 percent of gross domestic product (GDP) in the early 1990s and surging to 8 percent of GDP by 1997. This unsustainable current account deficit caused substantial selling of baht by foreign investors. The Thai government responded by defending the baht with their foreign exchange reserves and then used the forward market to support the baht so that they could appear to maintain their foreign exchange reserves even as their true net position deteriorated. Eventually, the negative forward market position equaled the country's net reserves. At that point, the Thai government had no choice but to stop pegging the value of the currency. The baht floated to nearly fifty baht to the dollar, half of its precrisis value.

This fall in the value of the baht caused the baht value of dollar-denominated debt to double. For the many companies that were both highly leveraged in dollars and dependent on baht earnings to pay their dollar liabilities, the doubling of the debt meant bankruptcy. The banks that had made loans to those companies were also bankrupt and unable to pay the foreign creditors who had loaned them dollars during the fixed exchange rate period. The widespread bankruptcies caused a sharp economic downturn.

Thailand was not unusual in experiencing the ravages of debt deflation when its currency devalued. The experience during all of the crises shows that the existence of large amounts of private debt denominated in dollars or other hard currencies is the most serious source of economic hardship facing the economy. When the domestic currency comes down in value, a bank or nonfinancial company that has a large dollar debt sees its indebtedness rise sharply in the local currency. Avoiding large amounts of dollar-denominated debt, and particularly private dollar debt, is probably the most useful thing that a country and corporation can do to reduce the serious consequences of a currency fall. This is true of financial institutions as well as of nonfinancial companies.

Countries adopt fixed (but potentially adjustable) exchange rates[3] for a variety of reasons. A fixed exchange rate can provide a nominal anchor that helps the country to achieve price stability. A fixed exchange rate also encourages an inflow of foreign capital and, by appearing to eliminate exchange rate volatility, can keep interest rates lower than they would otherwise be. However, a fixed exchange rate also brings with it the danger that the real exchange rate becomes overvalued, either because the domestic price level increases more rapidly than that of competing countries or because of a relative decline in the nominal value of the competing currencies

---

3. All so-called fixed exchange rates are potentially adjustable unless the country literally gives up its currency (as the members of the European Economic and Monetary Union have done). Even a currency board country like Argentina has a potentially adjustable exchange rate, a fact supported by the currency risk in the interest rate in excess of the country risk.

to which the home currency is not pegged. Foreign lenders may be induced by higher interest rates to continue financing a growing current account deficit, but eventually the fear of devaluation overcomes the high interest rate reward. At that point, lenders will no longer extend loans when they are due or roll over bond debt that matures. This problem is exacerbated by domestic residents who convert funds and take them out of the country. When these things happen, the currency declines, possibly by a large amount.

Governments that have fixed their exchange rate at an unsustainable level are reluctant to devalue as soon as they should because devaluation is itself painful. Doing so raises domestic inflation and, when domestic debts are written in the foreign currency, causes widespread losses and possible bankruptcies. Those who would lose are often politically well connected. In addition, delaying provides the opportunity for a spontaneous correction of the current account deficit if the real exchange rate of the competing currency appreciates. Unfortunately, waiting longer to devalue often merely exacerbates the trade imbalance and makes the cost of devaluation greater when it does occur.

The obvious alternative to a fixed but adjustable exchange rate is a floating currency. If the currency floats, a growing current account deficit will generally be self-correcting because the value of the currency declines as financial market participants sell the currency in response to the increased current account deficit in order to protect themselves from a potential future currency decline. Although a floating currency introduces volatility that makes business more difficult for exporters and for those companies that compete with imports from abroad, the pain caused to them is much less than the pain of the crises and bankruptcies that occur when an overvalued fixed currency falls in a sharp devaluation. Experience in Brazil, Israel, and elsewhere shows that the potential inflationary effect of a floating exchange rate can be dealt with by tightening monetary policy to achieve the country's desired rate of inflation.

Although there is a growing consensus among economists in favor of floating exchange rates, many countries have "managed floats": exchange rate systems in which they intervene extensively to stabilize the value of the currency. In principle, such a system might be an improvement on a clean float if officials increase the short-term stability of the exchange rate while allowing the exchange rate to adjust in ways that offset current account imbalances and differences in inflation rates. In practice, however, it appears to be too difficult for officials to avoid the temptation to prevent a currency decline even when fundamentals point in that direction. The result is the same problems as those created in a more explicitly fixed-but-adjustable exchange rate regime.

Despite the obvious problems with fixed exchange rates, there is still some professional support for fixed exchange rates that are supported by currency boards. In principle, such exchange rates are not adjustable at all but are permanently fixed by a mechanism that automatically raises interest rates by enough to maintain demand for the currency at its pegged exchange rate. Although Argentina, the leading currency board country, has (as of the time of this writing in October 2001) been able to maintain its fixed exchange rate vis-à-vis the dollar, its situation is precarious. Brazil, Argentina's largest competitor, has a floating exchange rate that has made the Brazilian real increasingly competitive and the Argentine peso increasingly uncompetitive. The result has been to create a growing trade deficit in Argentina, putting significant pressure on the currency that translates into extremely high real interest rates in Argentina. Those high interest rates produce substantial economic weakness and cause a ballooning of the government deficit because of the higher interest on the national debt and the lower taxes caused by the economic downturn.

Domingo Cavallo, the finance minister who established the currency board system in Argentina in order to end the hyperinflation that previously plagued his country, makes it clear in his comment in this volume that he does not see the currency board as a permanent arrangement. Instead, he spoke of looking ahead to a time when the Argentine currency would generally be perceived as undervalued so that its link to the dollar could be ended and the currency could float to a higher value. Since the conference at which he made these remarks, the sharp decline of the Brazilian real has caused a major increase in Argentina's current account deficit, thereby putting substantial downward pressure on its currency.

Argentina's fixed exchange rate system is made even more unstable by a full capital account convertibility that not only allows Argentinians to convert pesos to dollars at a fixed exchange rate of one peso per dollar but that also allows an unlimited export of those dollars. If the time comes when enough Argentinians fear an end of the fixed exchange rate and a peso devaluation, the capital outflow will force that collapse to occur.

In my judgment, the evidence from around the world during the past decade, as well as much evidence from earlier years, points clearly to the conclusion that any form of fixed but potentially adjustable exchange rate, including currency board arrangements, raises the risk of unsustainable current account deficits and a subsequent currency crisis.[4]

This has induced Ecuador to abandon its own currency in favor of using the U.S. dollar and has caused a number of economists to call for dollarization more generally in Latin America and elsewhere. Dollarization differs from a dollar-based currency board in completely abolishing the local currency. There are three serious problems with such an approach. First,

---

4. Despite the adverse experience with fixed-but-adjustable exchange rates, the IMF continues its policy of not advising governments on the choice of exchange rate system. It explicitly supported the Argentinian currency board arrangement by a large loan in 2001.

because the country has a different pattern of imports and exports from that of the United States, the exchange rate between the dollar and other currencies around the world that is suitable for the United States may lead to substantial trade deficits for the dollarizing country unless it is able to achieve a real devaluation by reducing its domestic price level, a difficult task at best. Second, cyclical fluctuations in demand cannot be modulated by automatic or induced interest rate changes since, except for default risk, the interest rate on dollar loans must be the same in the dollarized emerging market country as they are in the United States.

Third, because the central bank of the dollarized country does not have the ability to create dollars it cannot act as a lender of last resort if there is a run on any of the local commercial banks. Although residents use ordinary dollar bills for cash transactions, they also have checking and time deposit accounts that represent claims on dollars from their commercial banks. If residents become nervous about whether these "dollar" deposits can actually be shifted into dollars that can be held as currency or sent out of the country, they may create bank runs that the government cannot manage because it lacks sufficient dollars and the ability to create dollars. Dollarization does not seem any more likely to be a viable long-term strategy than a currency board.

Capital Account Convertibility

The issue of capital account convertibility is important in its own right. Many countries that have current account convertibility (i.e., that allow foreigners and local residents to buy and sell the currency for trade purposes) do not have capital account convertibility (i.e., do not allow the purchase and sale of the currency for portfolio investments). Capital account convertibility can benefit a country by encouraging capital inflows and by permitting domestic residents to enjoy the benefits of international portfolio diversification. However, capital account convertibility brings with it the possibility of much more volatile capital flows that can destabilize domestic financial markets and the exchange rate.

A compromise arrangement that can provide most of the advantages of foreign capital inflows while reducing the volatility that can result from speculative inflows and outflows has been developed in Chile. The Chilean government has from time to time taxed short-term capital inflows (by requiring that financial inflows be held in the country for a period of time without receiving interest), thus discouraging speculative inflows while still having the advantage of foreign direct investment and longer-term debt and equity capital.

Financial Supervision

The gains from an open capital account are more likely to outweigh the potential adverse effects in a country where the domestic financial system is strong and well supervised. The crisis in Thailand was exacerbated by the Thai banks' policy of borrowing dollars from abroad and then lending those dollars to Thai companies. Although this appeared to be a reasonable activity as long as the exchange rate between the Thai baht and the dollar was unchanged, it was in fact a very risky strategy because the Thai businesses generally did not have the ability to earn dollars. When the currency fell sharply relative to the dollar, the Thai banks were unable to collect on their loans. If the banking supervisors had been doing their job correctly, they would never have allowed the banks to accept large dollar liabilities offset by dollar loans that lacked real value because they depended on the fixity of the exchange rate.

The weakness of banking supervision and regulation was also a problem in Korea. When the Korean capital market was opened more broadly, some of the Korean nonbank financial institutions borrowed heavily abroad in dollars and then lent these funds to Korean firms or used them to speculate in high-risk assets like Russian bonds. Even the major Korean banks and corporations borrowed dollars to finance activities in Korea. The crisis in Korea occurred when foreign investors recognized that the sum of the short-term dollar liabilities of the Korean public and private sectors exceeded the country's foreign exchange reserves. They worried correctly that if any of the country's creditors chose not to roll over the loans and the bond debt that were coming due in the next year, the remaining creditors could not all be paid. When they saw that, many gave notice that they would not renew their credit, forcing Korea to use up its foreign exchange reserves and eventually to turn to the IMF for help in dealing with its crisis. Here too a crisis might have been avoided by better banking supervision and by regulation that limited the exposure to foreign currency liabilities.

The soundness of the domestic financial system is important for local depositors as well as for foreign creditors. If depositors come to believe that the volume of bad loans and investments causes the liabilities of the domestic banks to exceed the real value of their assets, depositors will withdraw funds and precipitate a banking crisis. Although the risk of this can be reduced by the government's provision of complete deposit insurance, that encourages more risky lending by banks. Moreover, when large depositors fear that banking failures will lead to a currency depreciation, they will want to shift their funds to foreign banks even if there is deposit insurance in the domestic currency.

It is significant that the banking systems in so many of the crisis countries were weak and now remain insolvent or nationalized or both. Countries with strong banking systems and good bank supervision, like Singapore, avoided the difficulties that happened in the crisis countries. Brazil avoided the banking problems that affected so many of the others because a very large fraction of its total bank assets was in Brazilian government bonds. Argentina had an early crisis in which many banks failed but now has shifted the ownership of most of its banking industry to foreign banks, primarily from the United States and Spain, that provide a much greater professionalism of management. Mexico recently changed its banking law to permit majority foreign ownership of its banks. Although many countries resist such foreign ownership for a variety of reasons, it does appear to be one way of improving banking practice quickly.

Foreign Exchange Liabilities and Reserves

An excess of short-term foreign currency liabilities over a nation's foreign exchange reserves readily precipitates a crisis. Countries find themselves in that situation not only because of the excessive currency risk taken by financial institutions and nonfinancial corporations but also because of the traditional policy of many emerging market countries of having foreign exchange reserves that are too small in the context of the current global capital markets. A traditional approach has been to hold foreign exchange reserves equal to three months of imports. Although that standard might be relevant for countries without capital account convertibility, it is clearly not relevant when the country is exposed to large fluctuations in capital flows.

There is of course no level of reserves that can protect an exchange rate that is fundamentally overvalued (as indicated by a large and growing current account deficit). The purpose of reserves in a floating rate regime is to protect a country's currency against unwarranted speculative attacks. For that purpose the standard for judging the adequacy of reserves is the size of the speculative attack that might be mounted against the country. China, with reserves of more than $150 billion, and Taiwan, with more than $100 billion, do not have to worry about speculative attacks. Korea learned its lesson in 1997 and now also has reserves of more than $100 billion.

A second measure of the adequacy of foreign exchange reserves is the size of reserves relative to the foreign currency liabilities that will be due in a year or less. It was a failure to have adequate reserves by this standard that caused the crisis in Korea. To improve this balance, it is easier and less costly for a country to limit its short-term liabilities than to increase its foreign exchange assets. The government itself can avoid short-term borrowing and extend the duration of its debts as they come close to maturity. The Chilean system of mandatory deposits achieves much the same thing for private capital inflows.

However, the absolute level of foreign exchange reserves, and not just those reserves in relation to short-term liabilities, is important for deterring speculative attacks. Emerging market countries are nevertheless generally reluctant to hold adequate reserves because of the perceived high cost of doing so. Large reserves appear costly because these countries typically hold their reserves in U.S. Treasury bills, which have a yield far below the country's own cost of borrowing dollars and far below the opportunity cost of those reserves as measured by the potential yield on real investments within the economy. Even so, that cost is small relative to the economic damage that would follow a successful speculative attack on the currency.

It is possible, moreover, to reduce the net cost of large reserves by holding reserves in a form that provides immediate liquidity but with a higher yield than Treasury bills. A country that holds a significant portion of its reserves in the form of a broadly diversified portfolio of foreign equities can expect a significantly higher rate of return and therefore a lower net cost of holding reserves. Although such an equity fund would involve greater investment risk than a portfolio invested in U.S. Treasury bills, the overall risk that the country faces may be lower with a larger and riskier foreign exchange portfolio than with a smaller portfolio of safer assets, substituting some investment risk for less risk of speculative attack.

In short, there are five primary ways in which a country can reduce the risk of a currency crisis: (a) avoiding an overvalued currency by allowing the currency's value to float; (b) maintaining a substantial level of foreign exchange reserves; (c) keeping short-term foreign exchange liabilities low relative to reserves; (d) maintaining a sound banking system; and (e) avoiding large amounts of dollar-denominated debt, especially the debt of the private sector.

Although these policies can in principle avoid the fundamental factors that caused the crises of the 1980s and 1990s and discourage purely speculative "contagion" attacks, crises will no doubt continue to happen in the future. The fact that the crises of the 1990s were caused by different conditions than those that caused the crises of the 1980s should, in itself, be a warning that conditions that we do not now anticipate may cause crises in the future. All that countries can do to protect themselves is to avoid the policies that caused crises in the past.

If a crisis does occur, the consequences for the economy will depend on how the crisis is managed and on the structural condition within the economy at the time of the crisis. Before we discuss the management of crises, it is useful to consider how the policies of the industrial countries might be modified to reduce the risk of financial and currency crises in the emerging market economies.

Policies of the Industrial Countries

Although there are in principle a variety of things that the United States and other industrial countries could do to reduce the risk of crises in the emerging markets, there is in fact little likelihood that those things will be done to an extent that will have an appreciable effect on the risk of future crises. It is nevertheless worth reviewing some of the key suggestions that have been made for changes in industrial country policies.

Stabilizing Exchange Rates Among the Industrial Countries

Fluctuations of the exchange rates among the dollar, the yen, and the euro can exacerbate trade deficits of emerging market countries, precipitating balance-of-payment crises. A country that has dollar-denominated liabilities but that earns yen or euros from its exports could see its ability to service its debts suffer if the dollar appreciates relative to the other currencies. The rise of the dollar in the 1980s hurt Latin American economies, the fall of the yen in the mid-1990s hurt the economies of Southeast Asia, and the decline of the euro exacerbated Argentina's trade deficit. Similarly, a country that imports dollar-denominated products (like oil) but exports to Europe or Japan would have difficulty paying for its imports if the dollar appreciates relative to the other Group of Three (G3) currencies. It is not surprising, therefore, that the emerging market countries and several economists have spoken of the advantages of stabilizing the exchange rates among the dollar, yen, and euro.

In reality, there is little prospect that the United States and other countries will pursue deliberate policies to stabilize their exchange rates. To some extent, more stable exchange rates among the three major industrial currencies will occur as a result of policies aimed at low inflation and low budget deficits. However, going beyond that to stop fluctuations would require adopting a common monetary policy, something that none of the governments or central banks would contemplate.[5]

The emerging market countries should therefore act on the assumption that the major exchange rates will vary. That implies a further reason to float and to avoid debt that is denominated in dollars or any other single currency. A country that does borrow abroad might protect itself from currency fluctuations by borrowing in a mix of currencies.

Avoiding High Interest Rates

Countries that borrow in dollars or other hard currencies are directly affected by any increase in the interest rates in the home countries of those currencies. Market participants also believe that an increase in the dollar interest rate causes interest rates on emerging market loans to rise by more than an equal amount. Since there is no prospect that the industrial countries will modify their domestic monetary policy in order to reduce adverse effects on the emerging market countries, private and public borrowers in those countries must take into account the possibility of interest rate moves that are not based on local conditions, making the optimal debt level less than it would otherwise be and increasing the optimal maturity of that debt.

Opening Markets to Emerging market Products

Opening the industrial-country markets to increase imports of textiles and agricultural products from the emerging market countries would raise the standard of living in the export countries as well as among the im-

---

5. Alternatively, without a common monetary policy, attempts to reduce currency fluctuations would lead to fluctuations in interest rates that could be as unsettling to the emerging market economies as the exchange rate fluctuations.

porters. It is an idea widely supported by economists and opposed by the special interests in the industrial countries that would be hurt by the import competition. Progress toward greater market opening will therefore continue to be slow. Moreover, such market opening might do little to reduce the risk of economic crises. The more open markets would provide a permanent improvement in the level of exports but might not change the net balance of trade once imports had adjusted to the new ability to finance increased imports.

Regulating Lending by Private Industrial-Country Creditors

After both the Latin American crisis of the 1980s and the Asian crisis of the 1990s there was widespread agreement that there had been too much borrowing by private and public entities in the crisis countries. When there is too much borrowing, there is also too much lending. Many experts therefore suggest that steps be taken to reduce the amount of lending to emerging market countries and to increase creditors' sensitivity to the risks involved.

Bank supervisors in industrial countries do provide oversight on the amount and concentration of emerging market-country lending by the banks for which they are responsible. This is reinforced by the Basel capital rules that require more capital per dollar of loans or investments in emerging market countries, although these rules were misleading when they treated the sovereign debt of Mexico and Korea as free of credit risk because both countries are members of the Organization for Economic Cooperation and Development (OECD). Requiring banks to mark credit portfolios to market would be another discipline on bank lending and risk taking.

The shift from bank lending to the emerging market countries in the 1980s to the international bond market in the 1990s reduced the role of bank supervision and capital requirements in limiting credit to the emerging market countries. Bond finance generally places assets in less leveraged institutions (pension funds, insurance companies, etc.) and reduces the risk of systemic damage to the industrial-country financial institutions. However, this dispersion of ownership may encourage a greater amount of lending and make it difficult for the creditor countries to track the amount loaned by entities within its borders, let alone the global amount of lending to particular borrowing countries. When conditions look favorable in emerging markets, it is easy for lenders to rush in, unaware of the total amount of debt being incurred by the countries to which they are lending. Even if the credit standing of the borrowers is good, the accumulation of substantial debt may strain foreign exchange availability.

Providing a Lender of Last Resort

A nation's central bank can prevent runs on solvent commercial banks by providing sufficient liquidity to assure depositors and other creditors that they have nothing to fear. They do so by lending against good but illiquid collateral. The very existence of such a lender of last resort helps to reduce the risk of domestic financial crises.

There is no such institution in the international economy that can lend foreign exchange to solvent central banks to assure foreign creditors that they need not fear a collapsing currency. Some have suggested that the IMF or the Bank for International Settlements might play such a role. (The IMF programs since the Thailand crisis of 1997 have involved large amounts of financial assistance, but these payments are conditioned on various structural reforms and are not available immediately—the key requirement of a lender of last resort.) Opponents of creating such a facility note that central banks do not have the illiquid but good collateral that are the key to the domestic lender-of-last-resort transactions. Opponents also worry that the availability of such a lender in the international context would create moral hazard problems, encouraging more commercial lending to the emerging market countries in the expectation that the loans would be repaid with the funds provided by the lender of last resort.

In practice, the potential for an international analog of the domestic central bank as lender of last resort will fail for the simple reason that the IMF does not have the resources to "lend freely" (as Bagehot advised in his classic discussion of the lender of last resort) and because the debtor countries do not have the "good collateral" (against which Bagehot said such lending should be done). Indeed, after a half-decade of unprecedentedly large IMF-led packages, the future is likely to involve much less availability of official funds.

The emerging market countries must therefore be prepared to protect themselves against the unwarranted currency attacks and bank runs associated with "pure contagion" and with deliberate attempts at destabilizing speculation. For those countries that have full capital account convertibility, that means accumulating large enough reserves on their own to deter speculators and reassure domestic and foreign investors.

Managing Financial and Currency Crises in Emerging markets

Although the crisis countries must manage their own recoveries, they have done so in recent years under the close supervision and direction of the IMF. The Fund has itself been guided to a large extent by the preferences of the U.S. government and, to a lesser extent, by the preferences of the other major Group of Seven (G7) countries. The IMF's approach has differed in many ways from its behavior in earlier crises, particularly in the extent to which it has used very large low-interest loans to induce and enforce wide-ranging conditions of structural economic reform. It is important to assess whether the new IMF policies were successful in dealing with the crises of the 1990s and how those policies might be modified in the future.

In doing so, I will arrange my comments as answers to six questions:

1. Have the crises been resolved, permitting the crisis countries to return to solid economic growth and to achieve renewed access to international capital markets?

2. Did the combination of monetary and fiscal policies and IMF loans resolve the crisis with as little economic pain and damage as possible?

3. Did the structural reforms required by the IMF agreements actually occur, and, to the extent that they did, were they successful?

4. How did the experience of the crisis countries affect the incentives of others: the lenders to be more careful in the future, the borrowers to reduce future risks, and countries facing potential future crises to come earlier to the IMF for assistance?

5. Were the actions of the IMF politically legitimate for an international agency dealing with sovereign nations?

6. What were the political consequences of the crises and the policies that followed?

Needless to say, these questions cannot be answered unambiguously, and careful students of the data can reach different conclusions. I offer my own evaluation knowing that readers will consult the views of others in this volume and elsewhere.

It is useful to begin by putting the current crisis management in the context of the IMF's history. When the IMF was established after World War II, the major industrial countries were its main concern. Those countries operated fixed but adjustable exchange rate systems, often with some form of capital control, within the framework of the gold-dollar standard. Balance-of-payments crises arose when excess domestic demand or inflation-induced currency misalignments caused trade deficits that led to unsustainable pressure on the exchange rate. The IMF responded with a combination of short-term balance-of-payments assistance (to allow the crisis country to pay for imports) while advising the crisis country to devalue its currency (to make its exports more competitive and to reduce its imports) and to deflate domestic demand by contractionary monetary and fiscal policy (to reduce imports, create capacity for exports, and end the inflation that was frequently a cause of the currency misalignment). This devalue-and-deflate became a standard part of the IMF prescription for dealing with currency crises even when, as we shall see, such explicit deflation strategy was not necessary. In time, the industrial countries generally abandoned the system of fixed-but-adjustable exchange rates in favor of floating, and the balance-of-payments crises ceased to be a significant problem.

The 1980s saw Mexico and then nearly all of the Latin American countries face serious crises because of an inability to service their foreign debt. That debt generally took the form of borrowing by the governments from the commercial banks of the United States and other major industrial countries. The ability of the governments to continue attracting funds and to service their debts was undermined in the early 1980s by a combination of factors including the sharp appreciation of the dollar, the dramatic rise of real dollar interest rates, and a global recession that reduced the demand for and prices of the products of the Latin American economies. The IMF responded with short-term loans that allowed the debtor countries to meet at least part of their immediate debt service obligations and then focused its efforts on three things: advising the defaulting countries on the fiscal and monetary policies needed to achieve a sustainable current account balance, bringing borrowers and creditors together to negotiate debt restructuring, and monitoring the fiscal and monetary performance on behalf of the creditors.

The next challenge facing the IMF was providing assistance to the countries of Eastern Europe and the former Soviet Union as they sought to move from being communist satellites of Russia to independent market economies. The IMF provided substantial technical assistance on a wide range of subjects including privatization, tax systems, commercial legal structures, central banking, commercial banking, and securities markets.

The crises of the 1990s that began in Thailand and spread among the Southeast Asian countries and to Latin America differed from the earlier crises in two basic ways: the debts were no longer concentrated in the commercial banks of the industrial countries but had been shifted to bonds and securatized loans; and the debtors were no longer the sovereign governments but were the private commercial banks and nonfinancial corporations in those countries. The crises arose, as I noted in the earlier part of this chapter, from three primary sources: current account deficits caused by "fixed but adjustable" exchange rates that had become overvalued; excess amounts of foreign debt that could not be serviced in the short run if creditors were not willing to roll over loans and bonds because the debt due in the short run exceeded the countries' foreign exchange reserves; and weak banking systems that led to bank runs by domestic and foreign creditors.

Although the IMF's response to these crises varied from country to country, the basic approach was the same in each case. The fund prescribed floating the currency, since the old fixed rate could not be defended, but mandated high interest rates and tight fiscal policy to limit the extent of the currency's decline and to reduce the budget deficit. It developed structural reform plans covering a wide range of areas, including reform of commercial and central banking, ending government support for private companies, opening product and capital markets, changing labor laws and corporate governance rules, eliminating subsidies for various products, and so on. These extensive and detailed structural reforms were without precedent in the IMF's dealing with the industrial countries in the 1950s and 1960s or with the Latin American crisis countries in the 1980s. Rather, they were similar in style to the technical assistance given to countries of Eastern European and the former Soviet Union in the early 1990s. These macroeconomic policies and structural reforms were embodied in letters of intent that, in principle, bound the crisis country to comply. In exchange for their agreement, the crisis countries received highly subsidized loans that were larger than anything that had ever been contemplated before in an IMF program. Korea's, for example, was $57 billion. The loans were to be paid out gradually as the country showed that it was living up to its promises and achieving the structural reform goals set by the IMF.

The IMF described the big loan packages as a way to rebuild reserves and to renew market confidence in the crisis country. In practice, they were used to pay creditors and were only made available with such lags and subject to such strong but ambiguous conditions that the future portions of the loans could not provide much comfort to foreign or domestic creditors. Their purpose appeared to be to convince the crisis countries to accept the IMF's terms and to give the political leaders of each country the political cover with its own population.

With that brief description as background, I turn to the six questions listed above as the framework for evaluating the management of the crises and the lessons for the future.

Have the Crises Been Resolved, Permitting the Crisis Countries to Return to Solid Economic Growth and to Achieve Renewed Access to International Capital Markets?

In general, the initial crises have been resolved, exchange rates have rebounded from their worst postcrisis levels and stabilized,[6] and positive growth has resumed. However, there are many ways in which the crises continue to affect the countries. The growth rates have been much lower than they had been for the three decades before the crises, foreign lending has not resumed, stock markets are much lower than they were before the onset of the crisis, domestic lending to the private sector has essentially collapsed, and the domestic financial sector has not been restructured and strengthened.

The balance of payments improved substantially, driven initially by the collapse of import demand when the crisis countries went into deep recessions and continued with improved exports as a result of the sharp fall in the real exchange rate. The countries used the resulting current account surpluses to accumulate foreign exchange reserves, with Korea achieving $50 billion by the end of 2000.

Gross domestic product declined sharply after the crisis began because of the collapse of credit and because the increased value of debt (measured in domestic currencies) impoverished many households and caused widespread business bankruptcies. The sharp decline of the currency, however, brought a sharp upturn in late 1998 and 1999 as exports boomed, but the

---

6. Indonesia is an exception; its currency continues to deteriorate.

year 2000 saw a sharp slowdown again to growth rates roughly half of what they had been from 1970 to the start of the crisis.

It is of course difficult to know whether the recession and subsequent recovery would have been different without the IMF programs or with different policies. It is clear that the growth resumed because of the currency collapse and the resulting rise of exports and not because of anything more fundamental. Also, by late 1999 the IMF had relaxed its tight monetary and fiscal policies.

It is significant that neither domestic lending nor foreign capital has come back to its previous level. Similarly, the low level of real growth represents a failure to reestablish the previous performance of the "Asian tigers." This may be the result of the crisis itself or of the policies that weakened the economies, leaving a trail of corporate bankruptcies and insolvent banks that cannot provide the credit needed to achieve strong growth. The general public and the business community—even in Korea, which might be considered the most successful of the crisis countries—may exhibit depressed levels of demand because of a shattering of confidence in the future and a concern that the economy could return to the same crisis conditions that they have recently escaped.

The IMF spoke of trying to restore confidence by a combination of large loans, tough monetary and fiscal policies, and widespread structural reforms. The combination of IMF statements, the extensiveness of the reforms, and the delayed loan payouts may have had the opposite effect. When the crisis hit, the IMF did not try to argue that the problem was one of illiquidity (a temporary inability to pay) rather than insolvency (a permanent inability to repay), even for a country like Korea, where the total foreign debt was only about one-third of GDP. Instead, the senior IMF officials insisted that all of the crisis countries were fundamentally sick—characterized by political corruption, "crony capitalism," inadequate financial systems, and the like. Foreign lenders and investors who had been happy to lend and invest until mid-1997 were shocked by the crisis and discouraged by the IMF's diagnosis. The extensive structural reforms called for by the IMF and the notion that the countries needed large loans that would only be paid out gradually and conditionally on meeting vague performance targets of structural reform was a further blow to confidence. All of this continues to weigh on the crisis countries' access to funds.

The situation in Indonesia is fundamentally worse than in the other crisis countries. In addition to the problems that affect the other countries, Indonesia is caught in a political crisis. The economic collapse and the IMF policies forced President Suharto's resignation. The small but economically important Chinese minority that Suharto had protected became the object of political and physical attacks and withdrew in part from the economic activities that they had previously performed. The political and military turmoil has depressed foreign lending and direct investment.

Did the Combination of Monetary and Fiscal Policies and IMF Loans
Resolve the Crisis With as Little Economic Pain and Damage as Possible?

I agree with the critics of the IMF policies who claim that they caused unnecessary pain and damage in the early stage of the crisis because of excessively tight monetary and fiscal policies. I suspect that the short-run damage had a continuing adverse effect that depressed growth in 2000 and 2001
and beyond.

The IMF called for increases in taxes to reduce the budget deficits that
would result from the reduced tax collection in the economic downturn and
from the increase in public-sector debt that would result from the government's assumption of some of the liabilities of banks and corporations. It is
hard to understand why the IMF pursued such contractionary policies at a
time when economic activity in the crisis economies was collapsing, with
real GDP growth dropping from more than 5 percent per year to equally
large negative amounts.

I suspect that this reflects a continuation of old IMF policies designed for
different problems. The balance-of-payments crises in the industrial countries in the 1950s and 1960s were often associated with low levels of national
saving caused by excessive government borrowing that needed to be reversed. The Latin American crises in the 1980s were also characterized by
large government budget deficits. In contrast, the Asian tigers had very high
national saving rates, often exceeding 30 percent of GDP, and did not have
large budget deficits.

The tight fiscal and monetary policies may also have been a holdover
from the tradition of "devalue and deflate" as a way of dealing with balance-of-payments crises. Any such explicit policy action to deflate demand
was unnecessary in the Asian crisis countries because of the debt deflation—that is, because the market-driven currency devaluation caused a major deflationary effect by increasing the value of debts in the local currency.
The devalue-and-deflate recipe, first advocated for the industrial countries
by James Meade in the 1950s, was not intended for an economy with substantial international debt denominated in the foreign currency. The debt
deflation in the Asian crisis countries meant widespread bankruptcies and
a collapse of lending by local banks to the few creditworthy borrowers that
remained.

The economic downturn was particularly hard on the urban poor. In addition to widespread job losses, their real incomes were reduced by the rise
in prices of imported products and of local products (especially food) that
could now be sold on world markets for higher prices in the local currency.
The rural poor were less hard hit because they were much less dependent on
the market economy for food and housing and could gain by selling their
agricultural products at higher domestic prices because of the currency devaluation.

The IMF's own self-evaluation now acknowledges that fiscal policy was too tight at the start of its programs but notes in self-defense that it subsequently and repeatedly allowed an easing of fiscal policy (IMF staff 2001). The fact remains, however, that the fiscal policies required by the IMF made the cyclical situation worse. Moreover, whatever the desirability of limiting budget deficits, there was no attempt to balance the contractionary effects of higher tax rates with structural tax incentives to encourage more investment and economic recovery.

The IMF also required the crisis countries to raise interest rates sharply to defend their currencies. Real interest rates jumped to more than 20 percent in Korea and other countries. The Fund argued that this was important for three reasons. First, it believed that each falling currency put downward pressure on the other currencies in the region, leading to a continuing downward spiral of exchange rates. Second, it argued that currency stability was needed to achieve confidence in the country both at home and abroad. Third, currency stability was needed to prevent further debt deflation.

Balanced against this, of course, was the usual direct adverse effect of high interest rates on domestic demand. High debt to capital levels made the rise in interest rates particularly damaging, leading to a great increase in the volume of nonperforming loans and to widespread bankruptcies. This was particularly important because the crisis countries were experiencing not only a currency crisis but also a financial crisis characterized by nonperforming loans and widespread bank failures. Treating that financial crisis by itself would require increasing liquidity and lowering interest rates.

The Fund's argument that currency declines had to be checked by high interest rates to avoid a continuing downward spiral ignored the fact that at some point the currencies would be so undervalued that foreign speculators would want to buy them. A currency can attract investors even with a low interest rate if potential investors believe that it has fallen below its equilibrium level and can therefore be expected to appreciate. At some point, the falling currencies of the crisis countries would attract that kind of speculative buying. Even if all of the currencies in the region fell together, they would still be declining relative to the dollar, the European currencies, and probably the Japanese yen. The improved competitiveness that would result would provide a natural lower limit to their decline.

In using high interest rates to stop the currency decline, the IMF was implicitly setting a target exchange rate for the currency. There is no reason to believe that the IMF actually had any idea of what an equilibrium exchange rate should be after the sharp declines in the exchange rates of some of the competing currencies and the collapse of much of the domestic supply-side capacity. The Korean won, for example, fell from 800 won per dollar at the start of the crisis to 1,800 won per dollar before bouncing back to 1,100 won per dollar.

Even if the IMF was correct in concluding that it was appropriate to use high interest rates to stabilize the currency, it did nothing to offset the adverse effects of those high interest rates on the domestic economy. It would have been possible to use targeted fiscal policies to offset the adverse effects of the high interest rates on the domestic borrowers while maintaining the favorable international effect of high interest rates on the demand for the currency. For example, a corporate tax credit based on the amount of the company's debt in the year before the crisis would offset the destructive effect of the higher interest rate on the ability to service existing debt while not changing the marginal incentive effect to foreign and domestic investors.

The Fund, together with the World Bank and some of the G7 countries, provided large subsidized loans to the crisis countries. These loans permitted the countries to meet their immediate foreign currency obligations to foreign creditors and to provide foreign exchange to private borrowers so that they could meet their obligations. These loans, at very subsidized rates, were a strong incentive to accept the Fund's painful monetary and fiscal policies and the very intrusive structural policies that I discuss below. However, unlike the loans of a domestic lender of last resort, they did not serve to prevent runs by domestic and foreign creditors or otherwise to offset the contractionary effects of the tight monetary and fiscal policies.

A domestic central bank, acting as a lender of last resort, can stop runs by offering to lend without limit but against good collateral at a penal rate. The fact that it is known to be ready to provide such liquidity is enough to stop runs against sound but illiquid banks. The IMF does not have the resources to lend as much as the foreign debt of the crisis countries. The countries themselves do not have good collateral that would make lending safe for the Fund, and theFund lends at a very much subsidized rate to make its loans attractive so that it can trade these subsidized loans for an acceptance of its conditionality.

The loans failed to reassure foreign lenders not only because they were limited in magnitude relative to the size of the country's external debt but also because the funds were not available immediately but could only be drawn over time as the country carried out its agreement with the IMF. Although the agreement was stated in a detailed letter of intent signed by the country, these agreements were frequently revised; Korea signed nine such letters of intent between December 1997 and July 2000. Many of the policies on which payouts were conditioned were unlikely to be done, and others were so ambiguous that they left the Fund with substantial discretion about whether the debtor country had done enough to warrant payment by the Fund.

Some critics of the IMF's policies point to Malaysia as an example of a country that was hit by the crisis but that chose not to go to the Fund for help. It declared a standstill on payments of foreign obligations and closed its international capital account. Although there is some evidence that the decline in Malaysia was less than in other countries, this may be more a matter of timing than of better performance.

Looking ahead, the International Financial Institution Advisory Commission (known also as the Meltzer commission) has suggested that the IMF loans be replaced by Conditional Credit Lines (CCLs), for which countries could prequalify. The IMF has accepted this idea as an additional option rather than as a replacement for its existing programs. The basic idea of the CCL is that a country that has sound macroeconomic and structural policies could apply for prequalification approval. If it is approved, it would have the right to draw funds in case its currency came under attack. The logic is that such an attack would be an unwarranted speculative attack that the country should be able to repulse. It is significant that no country has yet to apply for such CCL prequalification approval. Doing so might be regarded as a negative signal by market participants, an indication that the country expects its currency to be attacked. There is the further problem that the country would presumably have to be re-approved from time to time. If the country failed to be reapproved, that would be a very serious signal to the market, indicating that the credit line is no longer available and that the fund had concluded that the country's policies were such that it no longer met the standard. It seems very unlikely that the CCL will ever be a viable alternative to direct debt workouts.

There is also much discussion about ways to enforce "private-sector involvement," that is, the imposition of some mandatory losses on private lenders. I find it strange that this is thought of as a matter for Fund policy rather than as a natural outcome of a debt workout in a future in which the IMF's funds are more limited than they have been in the past. If the debtor country cannot afford to make the payments that are due and the Fund does not have sufficient funds to permit it to lend that amount to the debtor country, the outcome must be a debt restructuring. Bank creditors will find that they have to roll over loans, delaying principal repayments and accepting lower interest rates. The private bond holders may also find that their bonds are exchanged for new ones with lower interest rates or rescheduled principal payments or both.

One of the serious problems in the debt workouts since 1997 has been the inadequate development of bankruptcy laws and procedures in many of the emerging market countries. When private creditors have made loans to private borrowers in an emerging market country, the usual remedy of the courts should be available. Creditors should be able to take property, including real estate and ongoing businesses, if the debtors cannot make the promised payments.

Special bond provisions that allow actions to be taken by a majority of bond holders, rather than the unanimity rules that now prevail on most bonds, would facilitate such debt restructuring. However, in doing so, they would make the bonds riskier to the creditors and would raise the cost of capital to high-quality borrowers in the emerging market countries. It is not surprising that officials in Mexico and Brazil, for example, have opposed the introduction of such bonds.

Did the Structural Reforms Required by the IMF Agreements Actually Occur, and, to the Extent That They Did, Were They Successful?

In responding to the crises that began in Thailand in 1997, the IMF required structural reforms by the debtor countries that were unprecedented in both range and detail as a condition for its approval and for the substantial funds that would accompany that approval.[7] The specific conditions differed from country to country, but all of the programs had substantially similar elements. The Fund stipulated that it would release successive tranches of its multibillion loans only as these changes were implemented.

Some of the structural reforms were aimed at improving the banking sector and the process of capital accumulation. Among other things, the IMF called upon the debtor country to make its central bank independent of the political authorities and committed to price stability. The Fund also ordered governments to stop interfering in the loans made by the commercial banks to industrial companies. The debtor countries were also told to recapitalize the commercial banks so that they met international capital standards, to consolidate weak banks with stronger ones, and to permit foreign investors to buy troubled banks. Complete deposit insurance was to be eliminated so that depositors would have a greater incentive to monitor the risk-taking by the banks.

A second focus of structural reforms involved corporate finance and governance. The Fund called for substantial reductions in corporate leverage, major changes in accounting practices, and restructuring of corporate board memberships. Restrictions on foreign share ownership were to be eliminated, and government-owned corporations were to be privatized. The legal structure was to be modified in various ways and bankruptcy procedures altered to increase the effective rights of creditors.

Much was made of "crony capitalism," that is, the granting of preferential treatment to favored companies, political allies, and members of the governing family. The fund pointed out that such behavior was not acceptable in countries like the United States and the United Kingdom. Specific practices such as the granting of monopolies to particular companies or individuals were also to end.

The Fund required the end of many government subsidies, even of products—like cooking oil—that were widely purchased by low-income households. Other changes involved labor laws, the provision of unemployment

---

7. The chapter by Morris Goldstein in this volume provides a unique and very detailed analysis of the myriad of changes called for in the different programs.

benefits and other social insurance, and tax reform. Barriers to trade and foreign direct investment were to be eliminated.

It is clear that these "mandatory" changes went far beyond what was necessary to stabilize the individual economies or to allow them to regain voluntary access to the global capital markets. The Fund had gotten into the habit in Eastern Europe and the former Soviet Union of telling countries what it regards as "best practice" in a wide variety of aspects of national economic management. It now used the leverage that it had with the crisis countries to try to force such changes on them. The Fund's managing director, Michel Camdessus, once commented that the crises were a blessing in disguise because they provided the fund with the opportunity to improve the economic structure and governance of these countries.

The Fund sometimes justified the far-reaching structural programs as necessary to regain confidence in the country among foreign investors. In fact, of course, those investors had shown substantial confidence before the crisis, lending and investing large amounts of money. If they now interpreted the crises in the debtor countries as due to more than an overvalued exchange rate, a mismanaged international balance sheet, and an underdeveloped banking system, it was probably because of the IMF's very public criticism of what it regarded as fundamental structural problems.

The demand for detailed changes in so many aspects of the countries' economies created local opposition to the Fund programs, both because they would hurt powerful special interests and because they were widely felt within the countries to be an overreaching by the fund into subjects that should be left to national decision-making. Any attempt to deal with the full range of structural changes while also trying to manage a short-term recovery from the crisis put severe strains on government competence that made economic recovery and foreign debt negotiations more difficult.

The IMF, in an official review of its experience in the crisis countries, has now acknowledged that their structural programs were excessive (IMF staff 2001) and has said that in the future it would try to distinguish between those structural changes that are necessary for the success of the country's recovery from the crisis and those other structural changes that the Fund deems to be useful and desirable but not necessary for the country's recovery. It remains to be seen how well this distinction will work in practice. Moreover, even if the Fund does not insist on certain structural reforms in future crises, if it or the World Bank offers substantial financial incentives to make the change, it is politically very difficult for countries to resist accepting the offer.

At first, the political leaders in Indonesia, Korea, and Thailand said that they would refuse to accept the IMF's conditions. They soon relented, however, saying that they would implement the plans, and signing the agreements with the IMF in exchange for the promise that very large amounts of money would be paid as the program was implemented. In practice, however, the countries did not implement even those mandatory changes that seem most relevant to the success of their programs. They nevertheless generally received the funds that the IMF had said were conditional on adherence to the terms of the program.

In Korea, for example, the Fund placed great emphasis on eliminating the government's role in capital allocation and making the commercial banks fully independent, ending the tradition in which bank lending was subject to detailed Ministry of Finance guidance. What has actually happened is that the government has infused substantial public money as equity in the banks in order to recapitalize them after their widespread losses and thus obtained a new basis for government control over the banks' activities. Although the banks' managements are in principle free to act without consulting their government owners, the actual practice keeps the government very much involved in major lending decisions, particularly to companies that are in trouble. Moreover, since the banks have become owners of many foreclosed nonfinancial corporations, the Korean government is in fact the indirect owner of these companies as well. Although the government of Korea is in principle willing to sell to foreign investors these banks and the nonfinancial corporations that the banks have acquired, there is in fact little desire to sell them at the prices that potential buyers would be willing to pay. There have been many negotiations but relatively few sales. Although the banking sector is improving, it will be a long time before Korea has an adequate number of experienced bankers who are capable of making loan decisions on strictly commercial considerations and evaluating credit risks more generally even if the government is willing to let them do so.

Korea has now graduated from its IMF program and repaid its IMF loans. It has accumulated foreign exchange reserves of more than $100 billion and has an exchange rate that gives it a healthy balance-of-trade surplus. Korea clearly does not want to find itself again under IMF management.

How Did the Experience of the Crisis Countries Affect the Incentives of Others: the Lenders to Be More Careful in the Future, the Borrowers to Reduce Future Risks, and Countries Facing Potential Future Crises to Come Earlier to the IMF for Assistance?

The crises were clearly painful experiences for the debtor countries, and they are taking some steps to avoid a repetition of that pain. Korea's $100 billion of foreign exchange is far more than the IMF has told Korea is adequate and prudent. Korea is nevertheless willing to incur the cost of holding those reserves because it does not want to find itself again under IMF supervision. That surplus and a floating exchange rate that produces large trade surpluses are likely to succeed in keeping Korea away from IMF supervision for as long as those conditions last.

Many of the critics of the IMF's crisis management argue that the Fund's provision of large low-interest loans that can be used to repay foreign creditors creates a "moral hazard" problem in which emerging market countries and their creditors take excessive risk because they know that creditors will be paid relatively quickly in a crisis and without having to take substantial losses of principal. This causes a greater willingness to lend and keeps the interest rates on those loans substantially lower than they would otherwise be. The borrowers and the borrowing countries are then tempted by these relatively low-interest commercial loans to borrow more than they should, particularly in dollars, which causes a serious deflationary problem if the local currency devalues sharply.

There is no doubt that the large low-interest loans provided by the IMF made it easier for the debtor countries to repay their creditors and therefore reduced the cost of the crisis to both debtors and creditors relative to what it would otherwise have been. Whether this effect was large enough to make borrowers and lenders less vigilant than they would otherwise have been is uncertain. Moreover, even if one can presume that some decrease in prudence would inevitably follow the provision of such subsidized lending, it is not clear whether the magnitude of the change in behavior is significant enough to be a problem.

Despite the loans from the IMF, the individuals who were directly involved suffered significant personal losses. The finance ministers in the debtor countries lost their jobs, the business owners in the debtor countries were frequently in bankruptcy, and the bankers involved on both sides of the transactions were often fired. The banks that loaned the money were frequently forced to roll over their loans, taking greater risk without adequate additional compensation. Bondholders were also forced to take some losses. For some while at least, the flow of both debt and equity funds to the emerging market countries as a group declined.

The large losses incurred on loans to Russia may have further reduced the moral hazard problem. Before the Russian default, it was widely assumed that because of Russia's nuclear arsenal and geopolitical importance, it would not be allowed to default. However, the moral hazard risk was increased when the IMF provided Turkey with substantial financial support and gave a major loan to Argentina in 2001 when it was becoming clear that, because of the devaluation of the Brazilian real, Argentina would not be able to maintain its peg to the dollar. Nevertheless, the willingness of private lenders to maintain their loans to Argentina in 2001 shows a continued appetite for risk that some would regard as unwarranted and based on the assumption that the Fund would be there to help in a future crisis.

A quite different incentive effect of the IMF programs is on countries that see a potential crisis looming but do not want to put themselves in the hands of the IMF. Thailand, Indonesia, and Korea all waited as long as they could before coming to the IMF. Their experience after coming to the IMF in 1997 is not likely to do anything to cause future governments in those countries or elsewhere to move more quickly to seek IMF help. There are many reasons why the political leaders of a country put off going to the IMF. Doing so indicates a failure of policy that is likely to be harmful in the next election. If the IMF requires floating the currency or devaluing the exchange rate, many local businesses will be adversely affected, no doubt including many who are close to the governing party. The experience in the recent crises is likely to convince political leaders in countries that face crises in the future that bringing in the IMF may lead to their own ouster and, even if they can stay in office, in a shift of power to the IMF staff. Waiting has the virtue that the crisis may be postponed and may even go away if the real exchange rate declines as a result of changes in the currencies of other trading partners and trade competitors.

If the IMF wants to be actively involved in preventing crises in individual countries as well as in dealing with those countries after crises occur, it cannot continue to be seen as a source of national pain and political embarrassment to the government in power. It must become a helpful resource to the countries that are approaching a crisis point. If it wants to reduce the risk of financial crises, the IMF must change its behavior during crises so that it is called upon at an earlier stage, before a full-scale crisis is inevitable.

Were the Actions of the IMF Politically Legitimate for an International Agency Dealing with Sovereign Nations?

This politically powerful question cannot be given a technical answer. There is no doubt, however, that it is an extremely important question to the debtor countries that are required to accept IMF programs and to all of the countries that contemplate the chance of such an IMF intrusion into their domestic affairs. The United States does not and cannot think about the possibility of being a subject of such a program, but virtually every other country in the world can identify with the countries that have had IMF programs. The legitimacy of those programs themselves is therefore at stake.

It is clear from the experience of the past few years that the IMF is much more than an adviser and a source of credit to which countries are entitled by virtue of their membership in the Fund. When a country begins a program with the Fund, it signs a letter of intent that imposes certain obligations on the country. The extraordinarily large loans that the IMF can bring to a country put its politicians in a position in which it would be very difficult, if not impossible, to reject the IMF's advice if it meant also forgoing the billions of dollars of economic help.

The power of the IMF to force its policies on countries raises the important question of the legitimate role of an international financial institution in dealing with sovereign countries. Even if the technical soundness of the IMF's prescriptions was beyond doubt, is it appropriate for the Fund to impose rules about such things as the role and independence of the central bank or the rights of workers or the nature of social insurance benefits of the country? My own judgment is that all such preemptive actions are inappropriate unless they are necessary to resolve the current crisis and to permit the debtor country to regain access to the international capital market. Extending the scope of mandatory policies to other things that the fund's staff believes is in the long-run interest of the debtor country is not a legitimate part of the IMF's mandate. It is likely to do more harm than good by creating resistance to the program as a whole and by discouraging countries from seeking Fund help at an early stage.

In some cases, the Fund's staff based mandated structural reforms on the suggestions of the political party that was then out of power in the debtor country (and therefore critical of the policies of the existing government). In Korea, for example, significant parts of the structural reforms were designed by the staff of the opposition presidential candidate at the time of the crisis. When he won the election, those policies became the policies of the president. These policies could not, however, have been turned into laws without IMF leverage because the democratically elected parliament had not changed political parties. Although the Fund's staff pointed to the support for those parts of the program by the new Korean president, it remains true that the program had to be imposed because it could not obtain the political support needed to be enacted according to the country's constitutional rules.

The appropriateness of the Fund's imposition of detailed structural policies is made even more questionable by uncertainty about the technical correctness of the Fund's advice. Fashions in economic policy change over the years. A generation ago, the conventional wisdom favored fixed exchange rates, and many economists believed that a country should aim to grow by substituting domestic production for foreign imports. Today the Fund promotes flexible exchange rates, and most economists support the pursuit of comparative advantage in trade. A generation from now, will the policies that the IMF now imposes on countries still be deemed to have been correct?

What Were the Political Consequences of the Crises and the Policies That Followed?

The appropriateness of the IMF's programs cannot be evaluated without considering the political consequences of the Fund's programs on the crisis countries and on the relation of those countries and other emerging market nations to the industrial countries in general and to the United States in particular.

The IMF was originally conceived of as a kind of mutual assistance organization to which countries made financial contributions and from which they could borrow funds in times of temporary financial crisis. With the shift of its activities from the industrial countries to the emerging market economies, the Fund might be seen as a way in which the industrial countries provide assistance to the emerging market nations when they get into trouble. There is a danger, however, that the Fund is instead viewed as the agent of the industrial countries that lends in times of crisis so that the creditor banks and bond holders in the industrial countries can be repaid, using the leverage of the Fund's credit line and approval process to force the debtor countries to make changes that benefit the business community in the G7 countries. The U.S. Congress and other national parliaments in the G7 countries are prepared to vote large sums for the IMF and for bilateral assistance only on the condition that the IMF impose policies that benefit their business and labor constituents.

The statements of officials in the debtor countries are not a useful basis for assessing their true attitudes because they remain dependent on the good will of the Fund and the creditor countries. The actions and statements of the nongovernment organizations that decry globalization and the international financial organizations may be equally misleading in the opposite direction as a true indication of the opinions of the public and the elites in the emerging market countries.

The long-term political effects of the Fund programs within the debtor countries are no less difficult to evaluate. The humiliation of the government and its leaders, the shift of power from the national government to the IMF, and the radical reforms imposed by the Fund can all have powerful effects on domestic politics in both the short run and the longer term. Indonesia is a good example of this process. Indonesia is a large and strategically located country with the second largest Moslem population in the world. The actions of the IMF in Indonesia led to the resignation of President Suharto and the introduction of a series of short-term and weak national leaders. The specific policies were particularly hard on urban workers and the urban poor, politically volatile groups in any emerging market country. Even now, several years later, the political future and stability of Indonesia are unclear and civil war exists in important regions of the country. The eventual dissolution of Indonesia as a single nation cannot be ruled out, and the geopolitical consequences of such a dissolution cannot be foreseen.

Even before Suharto's resignation, the IMF's policies demonstrated that he had lost control of the government. When that occurred, many of the important Chinese minority in Indonesia left out of fear for their personal safety and for the dangers to their businesses. Suharto had protected the Chinese minority because he valued their central role in providing entrepreneurship, capital and global market connections for Indonesia. Suharto's resignation made it much more difficult to achieve economic stability and contributed to the political uncertainty and instability that have characterized Indonesia since then.

The IMF programs also coincided with changes in political leadership in Korea and Thailand. It may be because the conditions that forced the authorities to call in the IMF also caused the local voters to want a different group to govern. However, that did not happen in Malaysia, where the financial crisis also caused economic decline but where Prime Minister Mahathir did not accept an IMF program. There are too many political factors that are specific to each country to draw any firm conclusions. However, there were no doubt officials at the IMF who believed that the fundamental economic restructuring that the Fund wanted could only be carried out if there was a change in the local government leadership. Quite apart from the inappropriateness of an IMF strategy that includes encouraging a change of government, there is the obvious adverse incentive effect that such behavior has on the willingness of any government to seek IMF help at an early stage.

The painful IMF programs antagonized the people of the recipient countries who objected to the policies imposed by the Fund and to the way in which those policies were imposed. The harsh public criticisms by the Fund were a blow to the pride of the people who had seen their countries as the Asian miracle just a few years earlier.

This antagonism was directed not only at the Fund but at the western nations generally and at the United States in particular because it was seen as the power that dictated the Fund's programs. Critics were aware that some of the Fund's "reform conditions" were required by the United States, Japan, and European countries seeking market opening for their products and services. They particularly resented the pressure to sell domestic firms to foreign buyers at what they believed would be "fire sale" prices during the crisis and early recovery years.

It is not easy for the residents of the debtor countries or even for their sophisticated elites to distinguish the painful effects of the crises that they brought upon themselves from the pain of the macroeconomic adjustments and radical structural reforms that the IMF imposed. However, the experience as a whole no doubt contributed to a general distrust of "globalization" and of western institutions in all of the emerging market countries. For many groups in these countries, the experience also increased the distaste for the market system and for capitalism. The long-term consequences of these changes may be the most serious and lasting effects of the crises.

References

Feldstein, Martin, ed. 1999. *International capital flows.* Chicago: University of Chicago Press.

International Monetary Fund (IMF) staff. 2001. Refocusing the IMF: An IMF issues brief. IMF Issues Brief no. 2001/03. Washington, D.C.: IMF, April.

Exchange Rate Regimes

1. Sebastian Edwards
2. Domingo F. Cavallo
3. Arminio Fraga
4. Jacob A. Frenkel

1. Sebastian Edwards

Exchange Rate Regimes, Capital Flows, and Crisis Prevention

1.1.1 Introduction

The emerging markets' financial crises of the 1990s had remarkable similarities.[1] Attracted by high domestic interest rates, a sense of stability stemming from rigid exchange rates, and what at the time appeared to be rosy prospects, large volumes of foreign portfolio funds moved into Latin America, East Asia, and Russia. This helped to propel stock market booms and to finance large current account deficits. At some point, and for a number of reasons, these funds slowed down or were reversed. This change in conditions required significant corrections in macroeconomics policies. Invariably, however, adjustment was delayed or was insufficient, increasing the level of uncertainty and the degree of country risk. As a result, massive volumes of capital left the country in question, international reserves dropped to dangerously low levels, and real exchange rates became acutely overvalued. Eventually the pegged nominal exchange rate had to be abandoned, and the country was forced to float its currency. In some cases—Brazil and

The author has benefited from conversations with Ed Leamer. He thanks Martin Feldstein for comments.

1. I am referring to the crises in Mexico (1997), East Asia (1997), Russia (1998), and Brazil (1999).

Russia are the clearest examples—a severe fiscal imbalance made the situation even worse.

Recent currency crises have tended to be deeper than in the past, resulting in steep costs to the population of the countries involved. In a world with high capital mobility, even small adjustments in international portfolio allocations to the emerging economies result in very large swings in capital flows. Sudden reductions in these flows, in turn, amplify exchange rate or interest rate adjustments and generate overshooting, further bruising credibility and unleashing a vicious circle. Two main policy issues have been emphasized in recent discussions on crisis prevention: First, an increasing number of authors have argued that in order to prevent crises, there is a need to introduce major changes to exchange rate practices in emerging economies. According to this view, emerging economies should adopt "credible" exchange rate regimes. A "credible" regime would reduce the probability of rumors-based reversals in capital flows, including what some authors have called have called "sudden stops." These authors have pointed out that the emerging economies should follow a "two-corners" approach to exchange rate policy: they should either adopt a freely floating regime or a super-fixed exchange rate system (Summers 2000). Second, a number of analysts have argued that the imposition of capital controls—and in particular controls on capital inflows—provides an effective way to reduce the probability of a currency crisis.

The purpose of this paper is to analyze, within the context of the implementation of a new financial architecture, the relationship between exchange rate regimes, capital flows, and currency crises in emerging economies. The paper draws on lessons learned during the 1990s and deals with some of the most important policy controversies that emerged after the Mexican, East Asian, Russian, and Brazilian crises. I also evaluate some recent proposals for reforming the international financial architecture that have emphasized exchange rate regimes and capital mobility. The rest of the paper is organized as follows: In section 1.1.2 I review the way in which economists' thinking about exchange rates in emerging markets has changed in the last decade and a half. More specifically, in this section I deal with four interrelated issues: (a) the role of nominal exchange rates as nominal anchors; (b) the costs of real exchange rate overvaluation; (c) strategies for exiting a pegged exchange rate; and (d) the death of middle-of-the-road exchange rate regimes as policy options. In section 1.1.3 I deal with capital controls as a crisis prevention device. In this section Chile's experience with market-based controls on capital inflows is discussed in some detail. Section 1.1.4 focuses on the currently fashionable view that suggests that emerging countries should freely float or adopt a super-fixed exchange rate regime (i.e., currency board or dollarization). In doing this I analyze whether emerging markets can adopt a truly freely floating exchange rate system, or whether, as argued by some analysts, a true floating system is not feasible in less advanced nations. The experiences of Panama and Argentina with super-fixity, and of Mexico with a floating rate, are discussed in some detail. Finally, section 1.1.5 contains some concluding remarks.

1.1.2   Exchange Rate Lessons from the 1990s Currency Crises

The currency crises of the 1990s have led economists to rethink their views on exchange rate policies in emerging countries. Specifically, these crises have led many economists to question the merits of pegged-but-adjustable exchange rates, both in the short run—that is, during a stabilization program—and in the longer run. Indeed, the increasingly dominant view among experts is that, in order to prevent the recurrence of financial and currency crises, most emerging countries should adopt either freely floating or super-fixed exchange rate regimes. In this section I discuss the way in which policy thinking on exchange rates in emerging countries has evolved in the last decade and a half or so.

Nominal Anchors and Exchange Rates

In the late 1980s and early 1990s, and after a period of relative disfavor, rigid nominal exchange rates made a comeback in policy and academic circles. Based on time-consistency and political economy arguments, a number of authors argued that fixed, or predetermined, nominal exchange rates provided an effective device for guiding a disinflation program and for maintaining macroeconomic stability. According to this view, an exchange rate anchor was particularly effective in countries with high inflation—say, high two-digit levels—that had already tackled (most of) their fiscal imbalances. By imposing a ceiling on tradable prices, and by guiding inflationary expectations, it was said, an exchange rate nominal anchor would rapidly generate a convergence between the country's and the international rates of inflation. This view was particularly popular in Latin America and was behind major stabilization efforts in Argentina, Chile, and Mexico, among other countries. According to this perspective, a prerequisite for a successful exchange rate–based stabilization program was that the country in question had put its public finances in order before the program was implemented in full. This, indeed, had been the case in Chile in 1978–79 and Mexico during the late 1980s and early 1990s, when the so-called Pacto de Solidaridad exchange rate–based stabilization program was implemented (see Edwards and Edwards 1991; Aspe 1993).

However, a recurrent problem with exchange rate–based stabilization programs—and one that was not fully anticipated by its supporters—was that inflation tended to have a considerable degree of inertia. That is, in most episodes, domestic prices and wages continued to increase even after the nominal exchange rate had been fixed. In Edwards (1998c) I used data from the Chilean (1977–82) and Mexican (1988–94) exchange rate–based stabilizations to analyze whether the degree inflationary persistence declined once the nominal exchange rate anchor program was implemented. My results suggest that, in both cases, the degree of persistence did not change significantly and remained very high. I attributed these results to two factors: a rather low degree of credibility of the programs, and, particularly in the case of Chile, the effects of a backward-looking wage-rate indexation mechanism.

If inflation is indeed characterized by a high degree of inertia, a fixed— or predetermined—nominal exchange rate will result in a real exchange rate appreciation and consequently in a decline in exports' competitiveness. Dornbusch (1997, 131) forcefully discussed the dangers of exchange rate anchors in his analysis of the Mexican crisis:

> Exchange rate–based stabilization goes through three phases: The first one is very useful . . . [E]xchange rate stabilization helps bring under way a stabilization . . . In the second phase increasing real appreciation becomes apparent, it is increasingly recognized, but it is inconvenient to do something . . . Finally, in the third phase, it is too late to do something. Real appreciation has come to a point where a major devaluation is necessary. But the politics will not allow that. Some more time is spent in denial, and then—sometime—enough bad news pile[s] up to cause the crash.

An additional complication is that under pegged exchange rates, negative external shocks tend to generate a costly adjustment process. Indeed, in a country with fixed exchange rates the optimal reaction to a negative shock—a worsening of the terms of trade or a decline in capital inflows, for example—is tightening monetary and fiscal policies until external balance is reestablished. A direct consequence of this is that, as a result of these negative shocks, economic activity will decline, and the rate of unemployment will tend to increase sharply. If the country is already suffering from a real exchange rate overvaluation, this kind of adjustment becomes politically difficult. More often than not, countries that face this situation will tend to postpone the required macroeconomics tightening, increasing the degree of vulnerability of the economy. Following this kind of reasoning, and after reviewing the fundamental aspects of the Mexican crisis, Sachs, Tornell, and Velasco (1995, 71) argue that it is "hard to find cases where governments have let the [adjustment process under fixed exchange rate] run its course." According to them, countries' political inability (or unwillingness) to live according to the rules of a fixed exchange rate regime reduces its degree of credibility.

In the mid-1990s, even as professional economists in academia and the multilateral institutions questioned the effectiveness of pegged-but-adjustable rates, policymakers in the emerging economies continued to favor that type of policies. In spite of Mexico's painful experience with a rigid exchange rate regime in the first half of the 1990s, the five East Asian nations that eventually ran into a crisis in 1997 had a rigid—de facto, pegged, or quasi pegged—exchange rate system with respect to the U.S. dollar. Although this system worked relatively well while the U.S. dollar was relatively weak in international currency markets, things turned to the worse when, starting in mid-1996, the dollar began to strengthen relative to the Japanese yen. Naturally, as the dollar appreciated relative to the yen, so did those currencies pegged to it. Ito (2000, 280) has described the role of pegged exchange rates in the East Asian crisis in the following way:

> [T]he exchange rate regime was de facto dollar pegged. In the period of yen appreciation, Asian exporters enjoy high growth contributing to an overall high, economic growth, while in the period of yen depreciation, Asian economies' performance becomes less impressive . . . Moreover, the dollar peg with high interest rates invited in short-term portfolio investment. Investors and borrowers mistook the stability of the exchange rate for the absence of exchange rate risk.

In Russia and Brazil the reliance on rigid exchange rates was even more risky than in Mexico and in the East Asian nations. This was because in both Russia and Brazil the public-sector accounts were clearly out of control. In Russia, for example, the nominal deficit averaged 7.4 percent of gross domestic product (GDP) during the three years preceding the crisis. Worse yet, the lack of accountability during the privatization process, and the perception of massive corruption, had made international investors particularly skittish. In Brazil, the real plan, launched in 1994, relied on a very slowly moving preannounced parity with respect to the U.S. dollar. In spite of repeated efforts, the authorities were unable to rein in a very large fiscal imbalance. By late 1998 the nation's consolidated nominal fiscal deficit exceeded the astonishing level of 8 percent of GDP.

Real Exchange Rate Overvaluation: How Dangerous?
How to Measure It?

The currency crises of the 1990s underscored the need to avoid overvalued real exchange rates—that is, real exchange rates that are incompatible with maintaining sustainable external accounts. In the spring 1994 meetings of the Brookings Institution Economics Panel, Rudi Dornbusch argued that the Mexican peso was overvalued by at least 30 percent and that the authorities should rapidly find a way to solve the problem. In that same meeting, Stanley Fischer, soon to become the International Monetary Fund's (IMF's) first deputy managing director, expressed his concerns regarding the external sustainability of the Mexican experiment. Internal U.S. government communications released to the U.S. Senate Banking Committee during 1995 also reflect a mounting concern among some U.S. officials. Several staff members of the Federal Reserve Bank of New York, for example, argued that a devaluation of the peso could not be ruled out. For example, according to documents released by the U.S. Senate, on 27 October 1994 an unidentified Treasury staff member commented to Secretary Lloyd Bensten that "[rigid] exchange rate policy under the new Pacto [the tripartite incomes policy agreement between government, unions, and the private sector] could inhibit a sustainable external position" (D'Amato 1995, 308).

The overvaluation of the Mexican peso in the process leading to the 1994 currency crisis has been documented by a number of postcrisis studies. According to Sachs, Tornell, and Velasco (1996), for example, during the 1990–94 period the Mexican peso was overvalued, on average, by almost 29 percent (see their table 9). An ex post analysis by Ades and Kaune (1997), using a detailed empirical model that decomposed fundamentals' changes in permanent and temporary changes, indicates that by the fourth quarter of 1994 the Mexican peso was overvalued by 16 percent. According to Goldman Sachs, in late 1998 the Brazilian real was overvalued by approximately 14 percent. Moreover, although the investment houses did not venture to estimate the degree of misalignment of the Russian ruble, during the first half of 1997 there was generalized agreement that it had become severely overvalued.

The East Asian nations did not escape the real exchange rate overvaluation syndrome. Sachs, Tornell, and Velasco (1996), for instance, have argued that by late 1994 the real exchange rate picture in the East Asian countries was mixed and looked as follows: While the Philippines and Korea were experiencing overvaluation, Malaysia and Indonesia had undervalued real exchange rates, and the Thai baht appeared to be in equilibrium. Chinn (1998) used a standard monetary model to estimate the appropriateness of nominal exchange rates in East Asia before the crisis. According to his results, in the first quarter of 1997 Indonesia, Malaysia, and Thailand had overvalued exchange rates, whereas Korea and the Philippines were facing undervaluation.

After the Mexican and East Asian crises, analysts in academia, the multilaterals, and the private sector have redoubled their efforts to understand real exchange rate (RER) behavior in emerging economies. Generally speaking, the RER is said to be "misaligned" if its actual value exhibits a (sustained) departure from its long-run equilibrium. The latter, in turn, is defined as the RER that, for given values of "fundamentals," is compatible with the simultaneous achievement of internal and external equilibrium.[2] Most recent efforts to assess misalignment have tried to go beyond simple versions of purchasing power parity (PPP) and to incorporate explicitly the behavior of variables such as terms of trade, real interest rates, and productivity growth. Accordingly to a recently published World Bank book

---

2. For theoretical discussions on real exchange rates, see Frenkel and Razin (1987) and Edwards (1989).

(Hinkle and Montiel 1999), one of the most common methods for assessing real exchange rates is based on single-equation, time series econometric estimates. The empirical implementation of this approach is based on the following steps:

1. A group of variables that, according to theory, affect the RER is identified. These variables are called the RER fundamentals and usually include the country's terms of trade, its degree of openness, productivity differentials, government expenditure, foreign direct investment, and international interest rates.

2. Time series techniques are used to estimate an RER equation. The regressors are the fundamentals listed above. In most cases, an error correction model is used to estimate this equation.

3. The fundamentals are decomposed into a "permanent" and a "temporary" component. This is usually done by using a well-accepted statistical technique, such as the Hodrick-Prescott decomposition.

4. The permanent components of the fundamentals are inserted into the estimated RER equation. The resulting "fitted" time series is interpreted as the path through time of the *estimated equilibrium* RER.

5. Finally, the estimated equilibrium RER is compared to the actual RER. Deviations between these two rates are interpreted as misalignment. If the actual RER is stronger than the estimated equilibrium, the country in question is considered to face an RER overvaluation.

In the late 1990s Goldman Sachs (1997) implemented an RER model (largely) based on this methodology. The first version of this model, released in October of 1996—almost eight months before the eruption of the East Asian crisis—indicated that the RER was overvalued in Indonesia, the Philippines, and Thailand. Subsequent releases of the model incorporated additional countries and suggested that the Korean won and the Malaysian ringgit were also (slightly) overvalued. In mid-1997, Goldman Sachs introduced a new refined version of its model; according to these new estimates, in June of 1997 the currencies of Indonesia, Korea, Malaysia, the Philippines, and Thailand were overvalued, as were the currencies of Hong Kong and Singapore. In contrast, these calculations suggested that the Taiwanese dollar was undervalued by approximately 7 percent. Although, according to Goldman Sachs, in June 1997 the degree of overvaluation was rather modest in all five East Asian crisis countries, its estimates suggested that overvaluation had been persistent for a number of years: in Indonesia the RER had been overvalued since 1993, in Korea in 1988, in Malaysia in 1993, in the Philippines in 1992, and in Thailand since 1990 (see Edwards and Savastano 1999 for a review of other applications of this model for assessing RER overvaluation).

More recently, JPMorgan (2000) unveiled its own RER model. In an effort to better capture the dynamic behavior of RERs, this model went beyond the "fundamentals" and explicitly incorporated the role of monetary variables in the short run. In spite of this improvement, this model retained many of the features of the single-equation RER models summarized above and analyzed in greater detail in Edwards and Savastano (1999).

Although the methodology described above—and increasingly used by the multilateral institutions and investment banks—represents a major improvement over simple PPP-based calculations, it is still subject to some limitations. The most important one is that, as is the case in all residuals-based models, it assumes that the RER is, on average, in equilibrium during the period under study. This, of course, need not be the case. Second, this approach ignores the roles of debt accumulation and of current account dynamics. Third, the simpler applications of this model ignore the major jumps in the RER following a nominal devaluation. This, in turn, will tend to badly bias the results and to generate misleading predictions. A fourth shortcoming of these models is that they do not specify a direct relationship between the estimated equilibrium RER and measures of internal equilibrium, including the level of unemployment, or the relation between actual and potential growth. Fifth, many times this type of econometric-based analysis generates results that are counterintuitive and, more seriously perhaps, tend to contradict the conclusions obtained from more detailed country-specific studies (see Edwards and Savastano 1999 for a detailed discussion).

An alternative approach to evaluate the appropriateness of the RER at a particular moment in time consists of calculating the "sustainable" current account deficit, as a prior step to calculating the equilibrium RER. The simplest versions of this model—sometimes associated with the IMF—rely on (rather basic) general equilibrium simulations and usually do not use econometric estimates of an RER equation. Recently, Deutsche Bank (2000) used a model along these lines to assess RER developments in Latin America. According to this model, the sustainable level of the current account is determined, in the steady state, by the country's rate of (potential) GDP growth, world inflation, and the international (net) demand for the country's liabilities. If a country's actual current account deficit exceeds its sustainable level, the RER will have to depreciate in order to help restore long-run sustainable equilibrium. Using specific parameter values, Deutsche Bank (2000) computed both the sustainable level of the current account and the degree of RER overvaluation for a group of Latin American countries during early 2000. It is illustrative to compare the estimated degree of RER overvaluation according to the Goldman Sachs, JPMorgan, and Deutsche Bank models for a selected group of Latin American nations. This is done in table 1.1, where a positive (negative) number denotes overvaluation (undervaluation). These figures refer to the situation in March–April 2000. As may be seen, for some of the countries—Brazil being the premier example—the calculated extent of overvaluation varies significantly across models. The above discussion, including the results in table 1.1, re-

Table 1.1   **Alternative Estimates of Degree of Overvaluation in Selected Latin American Countries, March–April 2000 (%)**

Country	Goldman Sachs	JPMorgan	Deutsche Bank
Argentina	7	13	17
Brazil	−11	1	5
Chile	5	−8	0
Colombia	−4	0	10
Mexico	22	3	−2
Peru	−2	−5	5
Venezuela	44	9	n.a.

Sources: Goldman Sachs, "Latin America Economic Analyst" (March 2000). JPMorgan, "Introducing JPMorgan's Emerging Markets Real Exchange Rate Model" (3 April 2000). Deutsche Bank, "Latin America Current Accounts: Can They Achieve Sustainability?" (22 March 2000).
Note: n.a. = not available.

flects quite vividly the eminent difficulties in assessing whether a country's currency is indeed out of line with its long-term equilibrium. These difficulties are more pronounced under pegged or fixed exchange rate regimes than under floating exchange rate regimes.

On Optimal Exit Strategies

In the aftermath of the Mexican peso crisis, the notion that (most) exchange rate anchors eventually result in acute overvaluation prompted many analysts to revise their views on exchange rate policies. A large number of authors argued that in countries with an inflationary problem, after a short initial period with a pegged exchange rate, a more flexible regime should be adopted. This position was taken, for example, by Dornbusch (1997, 137), who, referring to lessons from Mexico, said, "crawl now, or crash later." The late Michael Bruno (1995, 282), then the influential chief economist at the World Bank, said that "[t]he choice of the exchange rate as the nominal anchor only relates to the initial phase of stabilization." Bruno's position was greatly influenced by his own experience as a policymaker in Israel, where, in order to avoid the overvaluation syndrome, a pegged exchange rate had been replaced by a sliding, forward-looking crawling band in 1989.

The view that a pegged exchange rate should only be maintained for a short period of time, while expectations are readjusted, has also been taken by Sachs, Tornell, and Velasco (1995), who argued that "[t]he effectiveness of exchange rate pegging is probably higher in the early stages of an anti-inflation program." Goldstein (1998, 51), maintained that "all things considered, moving toward greater flexibility of exchange rate at an early stage (before the overvaluation becomes too large) will be the preferred course of action."

In 1998 the IMF published a long study on "exit strategies," in which it set forward the conditions required for successfully abandoning a pegged exchange rate system (Eichengreen et al. 1998). This important document reached three main conclusions: (a) most emerging countries would benefit from greater exchange rate flexibility; (b) the probability of a successful exit strategy is higher if the pegged rate is abandoned at a time of abundant capital inflows; and (c) countries should strengthened their fiscal and monetary policies before exiting the pegged exchange rate. This document also pointed out that because most exits happened during a crisis, the authorities should devise policies to avoid "overdepreciation." An important implication of this document is that it is easier for countries to exit an exchange rate nominal anchor from a situation of strength and credibility than from one of weakness and low credibility. That is, the probability of a successful exit will be higher if after the exit, and under the newly floating exchange rate regime, the currency strengthens. In this case the authorities' degree of credibility will not be battered, as the exit will not be associated with a major devaluation and crisis, as has often been the case in the past. Chile and Poland provide two cases of successful exits into a flexible exchange rates in the late 1990s.

The most difficult aspect of orderly exits—and one that is not discussed in detail in the 1998 IMF document—is related to the political economy of exchange rates and macroeconomic adjustment. At the core of this problem is the fact that the political authorities tend to focus on short-term horizons and usually discount the future very heavily. This situation is particularly acute in the emerging economies, where there are no politically independent institutions with a longer time horizon. In many (but not all) industrial countries, independent central banks have tended to take the role of the longer perspective.[3]

Defining an appropriate exit strategy from a fixed exchange rate amounts, in very simple terms, to estimating the time when the marginal benefit of maintaining a pegged rate becomes equal to the marginal cost of that policy. As was pointed out above, the greatest benefit of a nominal exchange rate anchor is that it guides inflationary expectations down at the same time that it imposes a ceiling on tradable goods' prices. There is ample empirical evidence suggesting that these positive effects of a nominal anchor are particularly high during the early stages of a disinflation program (Kiguel and Liviatan 1995). As times goes by, however, and as inflation declines, these benefits will also decline. On the other hand, the more important cost of relying on an exchange rate nominal anchor is given by the fact that, in the presence of (even partial) inflationary inertia, the RER will become appreciated, reducing the country's degree of competitiveness. To the extent that the real appreciation is not offset by changes in fundamentals, such as higher productivity gains, the cost of the exchange rate anchor will tend to

---

3. Interestingly enough, in the few emerging countries with an independent central bank, exchange rate policy tends to be in the hands of the ministry of finance. This was, for instance, the case of Mexico in 1994.

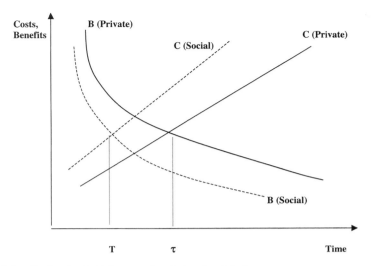

Fig. 1.1   Optimal exit: Private and social optimal timing

increase through time. Figure 1.1 provides a simple representation of this situation of declining benefits and increasing time-dependent costs of an exchange rate anchor (C denotes costs and B refers to benefits). The actual slopes of these curves will depend on structural parameters and on other policies pursued by the country. These include the country's degree of openness, expectations, the fiscal stance, and the degree of formal and informal indexation. In figure 1.1, the two schedules cross at time τ, which becomes the optimal exit time. Three important points should be noted. First, changes in the conditions faced by the country in question could indeed shift these schedules, altering the optimal exit time. Second, it is possible that, for a particular constellation of parameters, the two schedules do not intersect. Naturally, this would be the case where the optimal steady-state regime is a pegged exchange rate. Third, "private" cost and benefits will usually be different from "social" costs and benefits. That would be the case when, due to political considerations, the authorities are subject to "short-termism." In this case, benefits will tend to be overestimated and costs underestimated, resulting in a postponement of the optimal exit. Postponing the exit could—and usually does—result in serious costs, in the form of bankruptcies, major disruptions in economic activity, and, in some cases, the collapse of the banking system (Edwards and Montiel 1989).

The Death of Intermediate Exchange Rate Regimes
and the "Two-Corner" Approach

After the East Asian, Russian, and Brazilian crises, economists' views on nominal exchange rate regimes continued to evolve. Fixed-but-adjustable regimes rapidly lost adepts, while the two extreme positions—super-fixed (through a currency board or dollarization), and freely floating rates—gained in popularity. This view is clearly captured by the following quotation from U.S. Secretary of the Treasury Larry Summers (2000, 8):

> [F]or economies with access to international capital markets, [the choice of the appropriate exchange rate regime] increasingly means a move away from the middle ground of pegged but adjustable fixed exchange rates toward the two corner regimes of either flexible exchange rates, or a fixed exchange rate supported, if necessary, by a commitment to give up altogether an independent monetary policy.

Summers goes on to argue, as do most supporters of the "two-corner" approach to exchange rate regimes, that this policy prescription "probably has less to do with Robert Mundell's traditional optimal currency areas considerations than with a country's capacity to operate a discretionary monetary policy in a way that will reduce rather than increase the variance in economic output" (9).

From a historical perspective the current support for the two-corner approach, is largely based on the shortcomings of the intermediate systems—pegged-but-adjustable, managed float, and (narrow) bands—and not on the historical merits of either of the two-corner systems. The reason for this is that in emerging markets there have been very few historical experiences with either super-fixity or with floating. Among the super-fixers, Argentina, Hong Kong, and Estonia have had currency boards and Panama has been dollarized.[4] This is not a large sample. Among floaters, the situation is not better. Mexico is one of the few countries with a somewhat long experience with a flexible rate (1995 to date), and most of it has taken place during periods of high international turmoil (see, however, the discussion in section 1.1.4 of this paper).

The IMF entered this debate in a rather guarded way. Eichengreen, Masson, Savastano, and Sharma (1999, 6) capture the Fund's view regarding exchange rate regimes quite vividly:

> Experience has shown that an adjustable peg or a tightly managed float with occasional large adjustments is a difficult situation to sustain under high capital mobility. . . . In an environment of high capital mobility, therefore, the exchange regime needs to be either a peg that is defended with great determination . . . or it needs to be a managed float where the exchange rate moves regularly in response to market forces.

Notice that, although these authors reject intermediate regimes, they fall considerably short of endorsing a free float. Indeed, in discussing the most

---

4. Recently Ecuador has gone through a dollarization process, but it is too early to analyze the results of that reform. A number of smaller nations, however, have historically had currency boards. See the discussion in Hanke and Schuler (1994).

appropriate policy action in emerging economies, they argue that market forces should be supplemented with "some resistance from intervention and other policy adjustments" (6).

Current skepticism regarding pegged-but-adjustable regimes is partially based on the effect that large devaluations tend to have on firms' balance sheets and, thus, on the banking sector. As the experience of Indonesia dramatically showed, this effect is particularly severe in countries where the corporate sector has a large debt denominated in foreign currency.[5] Calvo (2001) has offered one of the very few theoretical justifications for ruling out middle-of-the road exchange rate regimes. He has argued that in a world with capital mobility and poorly informed market participants, emerging countries are subject to rumors, runs, and (unjustified) panics. This is because these uninformed participants may—and usually will—misinterpret events in the global market. This situation may be remedied, or at least minimized, by the adoption of a very transparent and credible policy stance. According to Calvo, only two types of regimes satisfy this requirement: super-fixes, and in particular dollarization, and a (very) clean float. In section 1.1.4 of this paper I discuss in great detail the most important issues related to this view.

It is important to note that although the two-corner solution has become increasingly popular in academic policy circles in the United States and Europe, it is beginning to be resisted in other parts of the world, and in particular in Asia. In the recently released report on crisis prevention, the Asian Policy Forum (2000, 4) has argued: "[T]he two extreme exchange rate regimes . . . are not appropriate for Asian economies. Instead, an intermediate exchange rate system that could mitigate the negative effects of the two extreme regimes would be more appropriate for most Asian economies."

1.1.3 Capital Flow Reversals, Capital Controls, and Exchange Rate Regimes

One of the fundamental propositions in recent debates on exchange rate regimes is that under free capital mobility, the exchange rate regime determines the ability to undertake independent monetary policy.[6] A (super) fixed regime implies giving up monetary independence, whereas a freely floating regime allows for a national monetary policy (Summers 2000). This idea has been associated with the so-called "impossibility of the Holy Trinity": it is not possible to simultaneously have free capital mobility, a pegged

5. In 1982 Chile experienced the effects of a major devaluation on a corporate sector that was highly leveraged in foreign currency. For a thorough discussion of the case, see Edwards and Edwards (1991).

6. This, of course, is an old proposition dating back, at least, to the writings of Bob Mundell in the early 1960s. Recently, however, and as a result of the exchange rate policy debates, it has acquired renewed force.

exchange rate, and an independent monetary policy. Some authors have argued, however, that this is a false policy dilemma, since there is no reason that emerging economies have to allow free capital mobility. Indeed, the fact that currency crises are almost invariably the result of capital flow reversals has led some authors to argue that capital controls—and in particular controls on capital inflows—can reduce the risk of a currency crisis. Most supporters of this view have based their recommendation on Chile's experience with capital controls during the 1990s. Joe Stiglitz, the former World Bank chief economist, has been quoted by the *New York Times* (1 February 1998) as saying: "You want to look for policies that discourage hot money but facilitate the flow of long-term loans, and there is evidence that the Chilean approach or some version of it, does this." More recently, the Asian Policy Forum has explicitly recommended the control of capital inflows as a way of preventing future crises in the region. The Forum's policy recommendation number two reads as follows: "If an Asian economy experiences continued massive capital inflows that threaten effective domestic monetary management, it may install the capability to implement unremunerated reserve requirements (URR) and a minimum holding period on capital inflows" (page 5).

In this section I discuss in detail the most important aspect of the controls on capital inflows, and I evaluate Chile's experience with these policies.[7] More specifically, I focus on three issues: First, is there evidence that Chile's capital controls affected the composition of capital flows? Second, is there evidence that the imposition of these restrictions increased Chile's ability to undertake independent monetary policy? Third, did these controls help Chile reduce the degree of macroeconomic instability and vulnerability to externally originated shocks?[8]

Background

Chile introduced restrictions on capital inflows in June 1991.[9] Initially, all portfolio inflows were subject to a 20 percent reserve deposit that earned no interest. For maturities of less than a year, the deposit applied for the duration of the inflow, whereas for longer maturities, the reserve requirement was for one year. In July 1992 the rate of the reserve requirement was raised to 30 percent, and its holding period was set at one year, independently of the length of stay of the flow. Also, at that time its coverage was extended to trade credit and to loans related to foreign direct investment. New changes

7. By now there are numerous pieces dealing with these issues. See, for example, Edwards (1999a,b), De Gregorio, Edwards, and Valdes (2000), and the literature cited therein.

8. Most analyses of the Chilean experience with controls on inflows also analyze their impact on real exchange rate dynamics. Due to space consideration, and because it is only a tangentially relevant issue, I do not deal with it in this paper. See, however, my discussion in Edwards (1998a).

9. Chile had had a similar system during the 1970s. See Edwards and Edwards (1991).

were introduced in 1995, when the reserve requirement coverage was extended to Chilean stocks traded in the New York Stock Exchange (ADRs), to financial foreign direct investment (FDI), and bond issues. In June of 1998, and as a way of fighting off contagion coming from the East Asian crisis, the rate of the reserve requirement was lowered to 10 percent, and in September of that year the deposit rate was reduced to zero. Throughout this period Chile also regulated FDI: until 1992, FDI was subject to a three-year minimum stay in the country; at that time the minimum stay was reduced to one year, and in early 2000 it was eliminated. There are no restrictions on the repatriation of profits from FDI.[10]

In 1991, when the capital controls policy was introduced, the authorities had three goals in mind: First, to slow down the volume of capital flowing into the country, and to tilt its composition toward longer maturities. Second, to reduce (or at least delay) the RER appreciation that stemmed from these inflows. Third, to allow the Central Bank to maintain a high differential between domestic and international interest rates. This, in turn, was expected to help the government's effort to reduce inflation to the lower single-digit level. It was further expected that the controls would reduce the country's vulnerability to international financial instability (Cowan and de Gregorio 1998; Massad 1998a; Valdés-Prieto and Soto 1998).

Chile's system of unremunerated reserve requirements (URRs) is equivalent to a tax on capital inflows. The rate of the tax depends on both the period of time during which the funds stay in the country and the opportunity cost of these funds. As shown by Valdés-Prieto and Soto (1998) and De Gregorio, Edwards, and Valdes (2000), the tax equivalent for funds that stay in Chile for k months is given by the following expression:

$$(1) \qquad \tau(k) = \left[\frac{r * \lambda}{(1 - \lambda)} \right] \left(\frac{\rho}{k} \right),$$

where r^* is an international interest rate that captures the opportunity cost of the reserve requirement, λ is the proportion of the funds that has to be deposited at the Central Bank, and ρ is the period of time (measured in months) that the deposit has to be kept in the Central Bank.

Figure 1.2 contains estimates of this tax equivalent for three values of k: six months, one year, and three years. Three aspects of this figure are particularly interesting: First, the rate of the tax is inversely related to the length of stay of the funds in the country. This, of course, was exactly the intent of the policy, because the authorities wanted to discourage short-term inflows. Second, the rate of the tax is quite high even for a three-year period. During 1997, for example, the average tax for three-year funds was 80 basis points. Third, the tax equivalent has varied through time, both because the

---

10. Parts of this section rely on my previous work on the subject. See also the discussion by Massad (1998a).

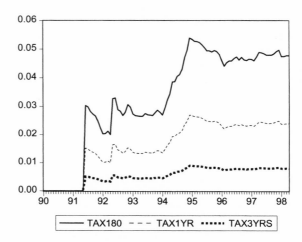

Fig. 1.2   Tax equivalent of capital controls: Stay of 180 days, 1 year, 3 years

rate of the required deposit was altered and because the opportunity cost has changed.

Capital Controls and the Composition of Capital Inflows in Chile

In table 1.2 I present data, from the Central Bank of Chile, on the composition of capital inflows into Chile between 1988 and 1998. As may be seen, during this period shorter-term flows—that is, flows with less than one-year maturity—declined steeply relative to longer-term capital. The fact that this change in composition happened immediately after the implementation of the policy provides some support for the view that by restricting capital mobility, the authorities indeed affected their composition. These data also show that, with the exception of a brief decline in 1993, the total volume of capital inflows into the country continued to increase until 1998. In constructing the figures in table 1.2, the Central Bank of Chile classified inflows as short term or long term on the basis of *contracted* maturity. It is possible to argue, however, that when measuring a country's degree of vulnerability to financial turmoil what really matters is residual maturity, measured by the value of the country's liabilities in the hands of foreigners that mature within a year. Table 1.3 presents data, from the Bank of International Settlements, on residual maturity for loans extended by Group of Ten (G10) banks to Chile and a group of selected of Latin American and East Asian countries. The results are quite revealing. First, once residual maturity is used, the percentage of short-term debt does not look as low as when contracting maturities are considered. Second, the figures in table 1.3 indicate that in late 1996 Chile had a lower percentage of short-term debt to G10 banks than any of the East Asian countries, with the exception of Malaysia. Third, although by end 1996 Chile had a relatively low percent-

Table 1.2   Capital Inflows (Gross) to Chile (US$ millions)

Year	Short-Term Flows	% of Total	Long-Term Flows	% of Total	Total	Deposits
1988	916,564	96.3	34,838	3.7	951,402	n.a.
1989	1,452,595	95.0	77,122	5.0	1,529,717	n.a.
1990	1,683,149	90.3	181,419	9.7	1,864,568	n.a.
1991	521,198	72.7	196,115	27.3	717,313	587
1992	225,197	28.9	554,072	71.1	779,269	11,424
1993	159,462	23.6	515,147	76.4	674,609	41,280
1994	161,575	16.5	819,699	83.5	981,274	87,039
1995	69,675	6.2	1,051,829	93.8	1,121,504	38,752
1996	67,254	3.2	2,042,456	96.8	2,109,710	172,320
1997	81,131	2.8	2,805,882	97.2	2,887,013	331,572

Notes: Deposits in the Central Bank of Chile are due to reserve requirements. n.a. = not applicable.

Table 1.3   Ratio of Short-Term Bank Loans to Total Bank Loans (%)

	Mid-1996	End 1996	Mid-1997	End 1997	Mid-1998
Argentina	53.4	56.3	54.2	57.7	57.4
Brazil	57.7	63.0	62.6	64.3	62.6
Chile	**57.7**	**51.2**	**43.3**	**50.4**	**45.9**
Colombia	45.9	39.3	39.4	40.0	39.6
Mexico	47.8	44.7	45.5	43.7	44.9
Peru	78.3	79.2	67.0	69.3	75.7
Indonesia	60.0	61.7	59.0	60.6	55.0
Korea	70.8	67.5	68.0	62.8	45.8
Malaysia	49.7	50.3	56.4	52.7	48.6
Taiwan	86.4	84.4	87.3	81.6	80.1
Thailand	68.9	65.2	65.7	65.8	59.3

Source: The Bank for International Settlements.

age of short-term residual debt, it was not significantly lower than that of Argentina, a country with no capital restrictions, and it was higher than that of Mexico, another Latin American country without controls. Fourth, Chile experienced a significant reduction in its residual short-term debt between 1996 and 1998.

A number of authors have used regression analysis to investigate the determinants of capital flows in Chile and to determine whether the controls on inflows have indeed affected the composition of these flows. Soto (1997) and De Gregorio, Borenzstein, and Lee (1998), for example, have used vector autoregression analysis on monthly data to analyze the way in which capital controls have affected the composition of capital inflows. Their results confirm the picture presented in tables 1.2 and 1.3 and suggest that the tax on capital movements discouraged short-term inflows. These early studies suggest, however, that the reduction in shorter-term flows was fully compensated by increases in longer-term capital inflows and that, consequently, aggregate capital moving into Chile was not altered by this policy. Moreover, Valdés-Prieto and Soto (1996) have argued that the controls only became effective in discouraging short-term flows after 1995, when the tax-equivalent rate of the deposits had increased significantly.

In a recent study, De Gregorio, Edwards, and Valdes (2000) use a new data set to evaluate the effects of the URR on the volume and composition of capital inflows into Chile. Using semistructural vector autoregressions (VARs), the authors conclude that this policy affected negatively, and quite strongly, short-term flows. More specifically, they estimated that the presence of the URR implied that, on average, quarterly short-term flows were between 0.5 and 1.0 percentage points of GDP below what they would have been otherwise. Their results for total flows, however, show that the capital controls policy had not had a significant effect on this aggregate variable.

A traditional shortcoming of capital controls (either on outflows or inflows) is that it is relatively easy for investors to avoid them. Valdés-Prieto and Soto (1998), for example, have argued that in spite of the authorities' efforts to close loopholes, Chile's controls have been subject to considerable evasion. Cowan and De Gregario (1997) acknowledged this fact and constructed a subjective index of the "power" of the controls. This index takes a value of 1 if there is no (or very little) evasion and takes a value of zero if there is complete evasion. According to these authors, this index reached its lowest value during the second quarter of 1995; by late 1997 and early 1998 this index had reached a value of 0.8.

Capital Controls and Monetary Policy in Chile

One of the alleged virtues of Chile-style capital controls is that, in the presence of pegged exchange rates, they allow the country in question greater control over its monetary policy. That is, in the presence of controls, the local monetary authorities will have the ability to affect domestic (short-) term interest rates. In fact, this greater control over monetary policy has been one of the reasons given in support of the imposition of this type of controls in the Asian nations (Asian Policy Forum 2000).

A small number of studies has used Chilean data to look empirically at this issue. Using a VAR analysis, De Gregorio, Borenzstein, and Lee (1998) and Soto (1997) found that an innovation to the tax had a positive and very small short-term effect on indexed interest rates. In Edwards (1998b), I used monthly data to analyze whether, after the imposition of the controls (and after controlling for other variables), there was an increase in the differential between dollar- and peso-denominated interest rates (properly adjusted by expected devaluation). I tested this proposition by using rolling regressions to estimate the parameters of an AR(1) process for the interest rate differential. I found out that, although the steady-state interest rate differential had actually declined after the imposition of the controls in 1991, it had become more sluggish.[11] That is, after the imposition of the controls—and in particular after their tightening in 1993—it took a longer period of time for interest rate differentials to decline until they reached their steady-state equilibrium. I interpreted this evidence as suggesting that the controls had indeed increased Chile's control over short-run monetary policy. These results largely confirmed those obtained by Laurens and Cardoso (1998).

De Gregorio, Edwards, and Valdes (2000) have recently used monthly data to estimate a series of semistructural VARs. Their main interest was to analyze the way in which a shock to the URR tax equivalent affects a number of macroeconomic variables. In addition to the tax equivalent of the controls, their analysis included the following endogenous variables: domestic (indexed) interest rates;[12] a proxy for the expected rate of depreciation; short- and long-term capital flows; and RER-effective depreciation. In addition, they introduced the six-month Libor interest rate and the JP-Morgan Emerging Markets Bond Index. The results obtained from this analysis suggest that in response to a 1–standard deviation shock to the tax equivalent of the capital controls affected domestic interest rates positively. The effect, however, is quantitatively small—between 10 and 25 basis points—and peaked after six months. This means that the capital controls policy did help Chile's monetary authorities' efforts to target short-term domestic interest rates without unleashing a vicious circle of higher rates followed by higher capital inflows, monetary sterilization, and even higher domestic interest rates.

Controls on Capital Inflows, External Vulnerability, and Contagion

From a crisis prevention perspective, a particularly important question is whether Chile-style controls on inflows reduce financial vulnerability and, thus, lower the probability of a country's being subject to contagion. At a more specific historical level, the question is whether Chile was spared from financial contagion during the period when the controls on capital inflows were in effect (1991–98). In particular, did these controls isolate Chile's key macroeconomics variables—and especially domestic interest rates—from externally generated financial turmoil? In panel A of figure 1.3 I present weekly data on the evolution of Chile's ninety-day deposit interest rates for 1996–99.[13] This figure provides a very interesting (preliminary) picture of the way in which Chile's domestic financial market reacted to externally generated disturbances. The most salient aspects of this figure are

---

11. The decline in the steady-state interest rate differential was attributed to the reduction of Chile's country risk premium.

12. For more than thirty years Chile's financial sector has operated on the bases of inflation-adjusted, or indexed, interest rates. The vast majority of financial transactions of maturities in excess of thirty days are documented in Chile's unit of account, the *Unidad de Fomento* (UF).

13. Although the data for thirty-day rates refer to nominal rates, those for ninety-day deposits are in Chile's "real" (inflation-corrected) unit of account.

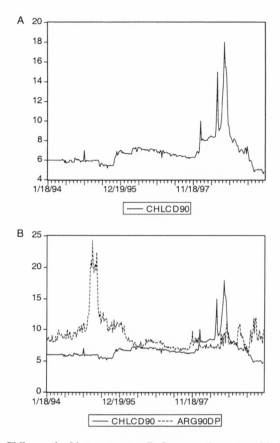

Fig. 1.3 *A,* **Chile nominal interest rates;** *B,* **Comparative rates with Argentina**

- Chile's domestic interest rates reacted very mildly to the Mexican crisis of December 1994. In fact, as may be seen from the figure, there was a very short-lived spike in January of 1995. During the rest of that year— and at a time when most of Latin America was suffering from the so-called Tequila effect—Chile's interest rates remained low and stable. The tranquility in Chile's financial markets at the time is captured clearly in panel B of figure 1.3, where interest rates in Chile and Argentina are depicted (notice Argentina did not have any form of capital controls during this period).
- Until late 1997—that is, even after the Asian crisis erupted—Chile's interest rates continued to be low and relatively stable. Indeed, this great stability in domestic interest rates between 1994 and the first ten months of 1997 contributed greatly to the notion that Chile's controls on capital inflows had been instrumental in reducing the country's degree of vulnerability.

- Throughout the October 1997–September 1998 period, and in spite of the presence of the controls, Chile's domestic interest rates were subject to massive increases. These jumps were largely in response to increased financial turmoil in Asia and to the Russian default of August 1998 and took place in spite of the fact that during this time the controls were tightened.
- Paradoxically, perhaps, financial stability in Chile returned in the last quarter of 1999, *after* the controls had been reduced to zero.

Figure 1.3, on Chile's domestic interest rates behavior, suggests that during the second half of the 1990s there was structural change in the process generating this interest rates. More specifically, it appears that around 1997–98 there was a break in the relationship between Chile's interest rates and emerging countries' risk premia. Although during the early years Chile's domestic financial market was not subject to contagion, the situation appears to have changed quite drastically in 1997–98. What makes this particularly interesting is that this apparent structural break that increased Chile's vulnerability to external disturbances took place at a time when the authorities were *expanding* the coverage of the controls on inflows (see De Gregorio, Edwards, and Valdes 2000 for details).

In order to investigate this issue formally, I analyzed the way in which Chile's interest rates responded to shocks to the emerging markets' "regional" risk premium, as measured by the cyclical component of JPMorgan's EMBI index for non–Latin American countries. I estimated a series of VAR systems using weekly data for a number of subperiods spanning 1994–99.[14] The following endogenous variables were included in the estimation:

1. The cyclical component of the non–Latin American emerging markets' JPMorgan EMBI index.[15] An increase in this index reflects a higher market price of (non–Latin American) emerging markets' securities and, thus, a reduction in the perceived riskiness of these countries. Given the composition of the EMBI index, this indicator mostly captures the evolution of the market perception of "country risk" in Asia and Eastern Europe.[16]

2. The cyclical component of the Latin American emerging markets' JPMorgan EMBI index.

---

14. The use of weekly data permits us to interpret the interest rates' impulse response function to a "regional risk" shock in a structural way. This interpretation requires that changes in domestic interest rates not be reflected in changes in the non–Latin American EMBI index during the same week. In the case of Chile, this is a particularly reasonable assumption, because during most of the period under consideration Chilean securities were not included in any of the emerging market EMBI indexes. The period was chosen in order to exclude the turmoil generated two major crises. For comparative purposes I estimated similar VARs for Argentina and Mexico.

15. The cyclical component was calculated by subtracting the Hodrick-Prescott filter to the index itself.

16. Details on the index can be found in JPMorgan's website.

3. The weekly rate of change in the Mexican peso–U.S. dollar exchange rate.

4. The weekly rate of change in the Chilean peso–U.S. dollar exchange rate.

5. The spread between ninety-day peso and U.S. dollar–denominated deposits in Argentina. This spread is considered as a measure of the expectations of devaluation in Argentina.

6. Argentine ninety-day, peso-denominated deposit rates.

7. Mexican ninety-day, certificate of deposit nominal rates expressed in pesos.

8. Chilean ninety-day deposit rates in domestic currency.[17]

In addition, interest rates on U.S. thirty-year bonds were included as an exogenous variable. All the data were obtained from the Datastream data set. In the estimation a two-lag structure, which is suggested by the Schwarz criteria, was used. In determining the ordering of the variables for the VAR estimation, I considered the (cyclical component of the) EMBI index for non–Latin American emerging markets, and the EMBI for Latin American countries to be, in that order, the two most exogenous variables. The results obtained indicate that Chile's domestic interest rates were affected significantly by financial shocks from abroad. One–standard deviation positive (negative) shock to the non–Latin American EMBI index generates a statistically significant decline (increase) in Chile's domestic interest rates. This effect peaks at 30 basis points after three weeks and dies off after seven weeks.

This exercise also suggests that domestic interest rates in Argentina and Mexico were significantly affected by shocks to the non–Latin American EMBI index. Generally speaking, then, this analysis provides some preliminary evidence suggesting that shocks emanating from other emerging regions were transmitted to the Latin nations in a way that is independent of the existence of controls on capital inflows.

In order to analyze whether the relationship determining Chile's domestic interest rates experienced a break point in the second half of the 1990s, I compared the error variance decomposition for Chile's interest rates for two subperiods. The first subperiod extends from the first week of 1994 through the last week of 1996, whereas the second subperiod covers the first week of 1997 through the last week of October 1999. That is, the first subperiod includes only the Mexican crisis, whereas the second subperiod covers the East Asian, Russian, and Brazilian crises. The results obtained indeed suggest the existence of an important structural break: during the first subperiod the EMBI indexes explained less than 1 percent of the variance

---

17. As pointed out above, these deposit rates are expressed in "real" pesos. That is, they are in terms of Chile's inflation-adjusted unit of account, the so-called UF. During the period under study, Chile did not have a deep market for nominal ninety-day deposits.

of Chile's interest rates; during the second subperiod, however, these two indexes explained almost 25 percent of this variance. These results, then, indicate that toward late 1997 the effectiveness of capital controls in shielding Chile from external disturbances had diminished significantly.

Overall, my reading of Chile's experience with controls on inflows is that they were successful in changing the maturity profile of capital inflows and of the country's foreign debt. Also, the controls allowed the monetary authority to have greater control over monetary policy. This effect, however, appears to have been confined to the short run and was not very important quantitatively. The evidence—and, in particular, the new results reported above—suggests that Chile was vulnerable to the propagation of shocks coming from other emerging markets. Moreover, these results indicate that in late 1997, six years after having controls on capital inflows put in place, the relationship between domestic interest rates and emerging markets' risk experienced a significant structural break that resulted in the amplification of externally originated shocks. In light of this evidence, my view is that although Chile-style controls on inflows may be useful, it is important not to overemphasize their effects. In countries with well-run monetary and fiscal policies, controls on inflows will tend to work, having a positive effect. However, in countries with reckless macroeconomic policies, controls on inflows will have little if any effect. It is important to emphasize that even in well-behaved countries, Chile-style controls on inflows are likely to be useful as a short-run tool that will help implement an adequate sequencing of reform. There are, however, some costs and dangers associated with this policy. First, as emphasized by Valdés-Prieto and Soto (1998) and De Gregorio, Edwards, and Valdes (2000), among others, they increase the cost of capital, especially for small and midsize firms. Second, there is always the temptation to transform these controls into a permanent policy. Third, and related to the previous point, in the presence of capital controls there is a danger that policymakers and analysts will become overconfident, neglecting other key aspects of macroeconomic policy.[18] This, indeed, was the case of Korea in the period leading to its crisis. Until quite late in 1997, international analysts and local policymakers believed that, due to the existence of restrictions on capital mobility, Korea was largely immune to a currency crisis—so much so that, after giving the Korean banks' and central bank's stance the next-to-worst ratings, Goldman Sachs argued that because Korea had "a relatively closed capital account," these indicators should be excluded from the computation of the overall vulnerability index. As a consequence of this, during most of 1997 Goldman Sachs played down the extent of Korea's problems. If, however, it had (correctly) recognized that capital restrictions cannot truly protect an economy from financial weaknesses, Goldman Sachs would have

18. This point has been emphasized by Fraga (1999).

clearly anticipated the Korean debacle, as it anticipated the Thai meltdown.

1.1.4   To Freely Float or to Super-Fix: Is That the Question?

As pointed out in section 1.1.2, an increasingly large number of analysts agrees that, in a world of high capital mobility, middle-of-the-road exchange rate regimes—that is, pegged-but-adjustable and its variants—are prone to generate instability, increasing the probability of a currency crisis. As a result of this view, the so-called two-corner perspective on exchange rate regimes has become increasingly popular. Generally speaking, whether a particular country should adopt a super-fixed or a floating system will depend on its specific structural characteristics, including the degree of de facto dollarization of the financial system, the extent of labor market flexibility, the nature of the pass-through coefficient(s), and the country's inflationary history (Calvo 1999). In this section I discuss, in some detail, some experiences with super-fixed and floating exchange rate regimes in emerging economies. The section is organized in three parts: I first review some of the few experiences with super-fixed regimes—Argentina, Hong Kong, and Panama. Although the analysis is not exhaustive and does not cover every angle of these countries' experiences, it deals with some of the more salient, and less understood, aspects of these regimes. I then deal with the feasibility of floating rates in emerging economies. I do this from the perspective of what has become to be known as "fear of floating," or the emerging countries' alleged proclivity to intervene in the foreign exchange market (Reinhart 2000). My analysis of the feasibility of freely floating rates relies heavily on Mexico's experience with floating rates since 1995. In particular, I address three specific issues: (a) Has Mexico's exchange rate been "excessively volatile" since the peso was floated? (b) To what extent have exchange rate movements affected the conduct of Mexico's monetary policy (that is, can we identify a monetary feedback rule)? (c) What has been the relationship between exchange rate and interest rate movements?

Super-Fixed Exchange Rate Regimes: Myths and Realities

Supporters of super-fixed regimes—currency boards and dollarization—have argued that these exchange rate systems provide credibility, transparency, very low inflation, and monetary and financial stability (Calvo 1999, Hanke and Schuler 1998, Hausmann 2000). A particularly attractive feature of super-fixed regimes is that, in principle, by reducing speculation and devaluation risk, they make domestic interest rates lower and more stable than under alternative regimes.

If, as Calvo (1999) has conjectured, the nature of external shocks is not independent of the exchange rate regime, and countries with more credible regimes face milder shocks, super-fixed economies will tend to be less prone

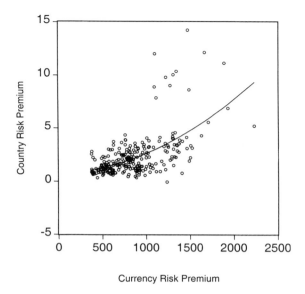

Fig. 1.4   Currency versus country risk premiums: Argentina, 1994–99

to contagion and thus will tend to have lower and more stable interest rates. This, combined with enhanced credibility and financial stability, will, in turn, result in an environment that will be more conducive to long-term growth. This argument would be greatly reinforced if the different risk premiums, and in particular the currency and country premiums, are related among themselves. Indeed, if this is the case a lower exchange rate risk will be translated into a lower country risk premium and a lower cost of capital for the country in question. In figure 1.4 I use weekly data, from 1994 through the end of 1999, to plot Argentina's currency risk premium—measured as the spread between peso- and dollar-denominated deposit rates—against Argentina's country risk premium, measured as the spread of the country's par Brady bonds. As may be seen, this diagram does suggest that these two risk premiums have been positively related.

Even for countries with a super-fixed exchange rate regime achieving credibility is not automatic, however. For this type of regime actually to be credible, some key issues have to be addressed successfully:

- Fiscal solvency. In the stronger version of super-fixed *models* this is taken care of almost automatically, because the authorities understand that they have no alternative but to run a sustainable fiscal policy. This is because the authorities are aware of the fact that the traditional recourse of reducing the real value of the public debt through a surprised devaluation is no longer available. This imposed fiscal responsibility is, in fact, considered to be one of the most positive aspects of the super-fixed regime. However, for the system to be efficient the fiscal requirement also has to include specific operational aspects, including the institutional ability to run countercyclical fiscal policies.

- The lender-of-last-resort function, which under flexible and pegged-but-adjustable regimes is provided by the central bank, has to be delegated to some other institution. This may be a consortium of foreign banks, with which a contingent credit is contracted, a foreign country with which a monetary treaty has been signed, or a multilateral institution.
- Related to the previous point, in a super-fixed regime the domestic banking sector has to be particularly solid in order to minimize the frequency of banking crises. This can be tackled in a number of ways, including implementing appropriate supervision, imposing high liquidity requirements on banks, or having a major presence of first-rate international banks in the domestic banking sector.
- Currency board regimes require that the monetary authority hold enough reserves, an amount that, in fact, exceeds the monetary base. Whether the authorities should hold large reserves under dollarization is still a matter of debate. What is clear, however, is that dollarization does not mean that the holding of reserves should be zero. In fact, it may be argued that in this context, international reserves are an important component of a self-insurance program.

According to models in the Mundell-Fleming tradition—including some modern versions, such as Chang and Velasco (2000)—a limitation of super-fixed regimes is that negative external shocks tend to be amplified. Moreover, to the extent that it is difficult to engineer relative price changes, these external shocks will have a tendency to be translated into financial turmoil, economic slowdown, and higher unemployment. The actual magnitude of this effect will, again, depend on the structure of the economy and, in particular, on the degree of labor-market flexibility. Some authors have recently argued, however, that these costs have been exaggerated and that, in fact, relative price changes between tradable and nontradable goods can be achieved through "simulated devaluations," including the simultaneous imposition of (uniform) import tariffs and export subsidies.[19] Calvo (1999, 21) has gone so far as to argue that the existence of nominal price rigidity may be a blessing in disguise, because it allows adjustment in profits to occur slowly, smoothing the business cycle.

---

19. See Calvo (1999). From a practical perspective, however, there are important limits to this option. In particular, it will violate World Trade Organization regulations. Additionally, the use of commercial policy to engineer relative price adjustments will have serious political economy implications. On the equivalence of this type of commercial policy package and exchange rate adjustments, see Edwards (1988, 31–32).

Argentina's Currency Board

Argentina provides one of the most interesting (recent) cases of a super-fixed regime. In early 1991, and after a long history of macroeconomics mismanagement, two bouts of hyperinflation, and depleted credibility, Argentina adopted a currency board. This program, which was led by Ministry of Economics Domingo Cavallo, was seen by many as a last-resort measure for achieving credibility and stability. After a rocky start—including serious contagion stemming from the Mexican crisis in 1995—the new system became consolidated during the year 1996–97. Inflation plummeted, and by 1996 it had virtually disappeared; in 1999 and 2000 the country, in fact, faced deflation. At the time Argentina adopted a currency board, the public had largely lost all confidence in the peso. In fact, by the late 1980s the U.S. dollar had become the unit of account, and a very large number of transactions was documented and carried on in dollars.

In Argentina, the lender-of-last-resort issue has been addressed in three ways. First, banks are required to hold a very high "liquidity requirement." Second, the Central Bank has negotiated a substantial contingent credit line with a consortium of international banks. Third, there has been a tremendous increase in international banks' presence: seven of Argentina's eight largest banks are currently owned by major international banks.[20]

After the adoption of the currency board and the rapid decline in inflation, the country experienced a major growth recovery, posting solid rates of growth in 1991–94. In 1995, however, and largely as a consequence of the Mexican Tequila crisis, the country went into a severe recession, with negative growth of 3 percent. It recovered in 1996–97, only to fall once again into a recession in 1998–99, this time affected by the Russian and Brazilian currency crises and by increasing doubts about the country's ability to deal with its fiscal and external problems. In 1999 GDP contracted by almost 4 percent, and in 2000 it posted modest growth. The combination of these external shocks and some structural weaknesses—including an extremely rigid labor legislation—resulted in a very high rate of unemployment. It exceeded 17 percent in 1995–96, and it has averaged almost 15 percent during 1999–2000.

Contrary to the simplest version of the model, exchange rate risk did not disappear after Argentina adopted a currency board. This is illustrated in figure 1.5, where a weekly time series of interest rate differential between peso- and dollar-denominated thirty-day deposits paid by Argentine banks from 1993 through October 1999 is presented. As may be seen, this differential experienced a major jump immediately after the Tequila crisis, exceeding 1,400 basis points. Although it subsequently declined, it continued to be very high and volatile. During the first ten months of 1999, for ex-

20. These eight banks, in turn, account for approximately 50 percent of deposits.

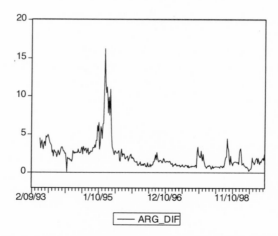

Fig. 1.5   Argentina, interest rate differential between peso- and dollar-denominated deposits (weekly data, 1993–99)

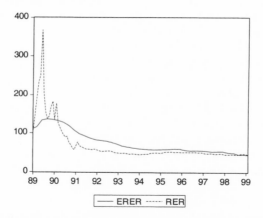

Fig. 1.6   Argentina: Equilibrium and actual trade-weighted real exchange rates, 1985–99 (Goldman Sachs estimates)

ample, the thirty-day peso-dollar interest rate differential averaged 140 basis points.

Since 1996, Argentine (real) domestic interest rates have been relatively high and volatile. Indeed, and as may be seen in figure 1.6, since 1997 the ninety-day deposit rate in Argentina has been higher, on average, than in Chile, a country that has followed a policy of increased exchange rate flexibility. This figure also shows that, except for a short period in 1998, Argentina's ninety-day interest rates have been more volatile than Chile's equivalent rates. Furthermore, during the last three months of 1999 and most of 2000, Argentine real interest rates exceeded those in Mexico, the

Latin American country with the longest experience with floating rates (see the next subsection for a discussion of Mexico). In the last few years, and even after the currency board had been consolidated, Argentina's country risk—measured, for example, by the spread of its Brady Bonds—has also been high and volatile.

Vulnerability and Contagion. As noted above, supporters of super-fixed regimes have argued that to the extent that the regime is credible, the country in question will be less vulnerable to external shocks and contagion. This proposition is difficult to test, since it is not trivial to build an appropriate counterfactual. What can be done, however, is to compare the extent to which countries that are somewhat similar—except for the exchange rate regime—are affected by common international shocks. Such an exercise was described in section 1.1.3 of this paper for the case of domestic interest rates in Argentina, Chile, and Mexico. The results obtained clearly indicate that a 1–standard deviation shock to Latin America's regional risk premium affected Argentina's domestic interest rates significantly. Also, in a recent five-country study on the international transmission of financial volatility using switching ARCH techniques, Edwards and Susmel (2000) found that Argentina has been the country most seriously affected by volatility contagion: the other countries in the study are Brazil, Chile, Mexico, and Hong Kong. Interestingly enough, this study also found that Hong Kong, the most revered of the super-fixers, has also been subject to important volatility contagion during the last five years.

Competitiveness, Fiscal Policy, and Credibility. Analysts have emphasized two factors as possible explanations for Argentina's financial instability during the last few years: an accumulated RER overvaluation and an inability to bring the fiscal accounts under control.

Figure 1.6 presents Goldman Sachs' estimation of Argentina's equilibrium RER as well as its actual (trade-weighted) RER for 1985–99.[21] In this figure, if the equilibrium RER exceeds the actual RER, the currency is overvalued. As may be seen, according to these calculations, Argentina suffered a significant overvaluation until early 1999. Independently of the actual relevance and accuracy of these specific estimates, the belief that Argentina had accumulated a significant RER disequilibrium had a negative effect on expectations and the regime's degree of credibility.

Since 1996 Argentina has run increasingly larger fiscal deficits and has systematically exceeded its own—and successive IMF programs'—deficit targets. This has resulted in a rapidly growing public-sector debt and in swelling external financing requirements. These two factors, plus the slow

21. This equilibrium RER is estimated using a method similar to the one discussed in section 1.1.2 of this paper. For details see Ades and Kaune (1998).

progress in key structural reform areas, such as labor-market legislation and the relationship between the provinces and the federal government, have translated into successive bouts of low credibility and instability.

Panama and Dollarization

In 1998 many analysts and politicians, including Argentina's President Carlos Menem, concluded that Argentina's credibility problems could be tackled by taking an additional step toward exchange rate super-fixity and adopting the U.S. dollar as the sole legal tender. Supporters of this dollarization project pointed to Panama's remarkably low inflation as living proof of the merits of that system. What was surprising, however, was that this early support for dollarization was not based on a serious evaluation of the Panamanian case. More specifically, what admirers of this experience did not know—or did not say—was that Panama's monetary arrangement has survived largely thanks to IMF support. In effect, with the exception of a brief interregnum during the Noriega years, Panama has been almost permanently under the tutelage of the fund. Since 1973 Panama has had sixteen IMF programs, the most recent of which was signed in late 1997, and is expected to run until late 2000. According to Mussa and Savastano (2000), during the last quarter of a century Panama has been the most assiduous user of IMF resources in the western hemisphere; since 1973, only Pakistan has had a larger number of IMF programs. The main factor behind this proliferation of IMF programs has been Panama's inability, until very recently, to control its public finances. Between 1973 and 1998 the fiscal deficit averaged 4 percent of GDP, and during 1973–87—a period of continuous IMF programs— it exceeded a remarkable 7 percent of GDP. In fact, it has only been in the last few years that Panama has been able to put its fiscal accounts in order.

In 1904 Panama adopted the dollar as legal tender. Although there is a national currency, the balboa, its role is largely symbolic. There is no central bank, and the monetary authorities cannot issue balboa-denominate notes. Since 1970 Panama has had no controls on capital mobility and has been financially integrated to the rest of the world. Moreover, for decades Panama has been an important center for offshore banking, with a large number of international banks operating in the country. This, of course, has allowed Panama to face successfully the lender-of-last-resort issue. Panama's most remarkable achievement is its very low rate of inflation. Between 1955 and 1998, it averaged 2.4 percent per annum, and during the 1990s it barely exceeded 1 percent per year. In addition to low inflation, Panama has posted a healthy rate of growth during the last four decades. Between 1958 and 1998, Panama's real GDP expanded at 5.3 percent per year, and during the 1990s, growth has been a full percentage point higher than that of the Latin American countries as a group—4.4 versus 3.4 percent per year.

As pointed out, however, behind these achievements hides Panama's serious historical addiction to IMF financing. In spite of not having a central bank or a currency of its own, for years Panama failed to maintain fiscal discipline. Initially, these large fiscal deficits were financed through borrowing from abroad, and when the foreign debt became too high, the IMF stepped in with fresh resources. When this was not enough, Panama restructured its foreign debt. Panama had its first IMF Stand-By program in 1965. A year later, adjustment was achieved, and the fiscal deficit was brought into check. In 1968, however, the fiscal accounts were again out of hand, and the IMF was called in once more. A remarkable nineteen-year period of uninterrupted IMF programs was thus initiated. Although in some of the early programs there were no withdrawals, the sheer presence of the IMF signaled that, in case of need, the monies would indeed be there.

Year after year, a new IMF program called for the strengthening of public finances. Invariably, year after year, Panama failed to take serious action. After all, the authorities knew that the IMF was there, ready to bail them out. This vicious circle was only broken in 1987, when as a result of General Noriega's confrontational policies and involvement in narcotics trafficking, Panama was subject to severe United States–led economic sanctions. The IMF returned to Panama in September of 1990 with a monitored program. This was followed by lending programs in 1992 (twenty-two months), 1995 (sixteen months), and 1997 (thirty-six months). Significantly, in the last few years the authorities have finally acknowledged the need to maintain a solid fiscal position. Between 1990 and 1996 the country posted public-sector surpluses, and in the last three years it has run modest deficits.

In contrast with Argentina, Panama has successfully eliminated devaluation risk. This has been reflected in a relatively low cost of capital in international financial markets. In that regard, it is illustrative to compare the spreads over U.S. Treasuries of Brady bonds issued by Panama and Argentina. Between January 1997 and December 1998 the average daily spread on Panamanian par bonds was 464 basis points, significantly lower than that of Argentine par Brady bonds, which averaged 710 basis points.

It is very important to note, however, that although there is no devaluation risk in Panama, the country has continued to be subject to sizable country risk and to contagion. In fact, as figure 1.7 shows, the spread over Treasuries of Panamanian Brady bonds has been volatile and has experienced important jumps in response to political shocks—such as the uncertainty over the president's intentions to perpetuate himself in power in 1998—and external developments, including the Russian crisis of 1998. More to the point, the spread over Panamanian bonds has systematically been higher than that of Chile's sovereign bond, and Chile, as has been pointed out, is a country that during the period under discussion experienced an overall increase in the degree of exchange rate flexibility. A careful study of Panama's monetary history suggests that dollarization does not, on its own, assure fiscal solvency and prudence. This has to be accomplished through the creation of budget-related institutions.

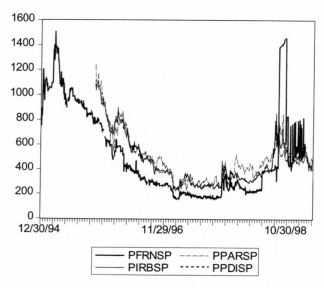

Fig. 1.7   Panama Brady bonds spreads (daily data, December 1994–May 1999)

Until recently, much of the discussion on dollarization has focused on the loss of seigniorage that would result from unilateral dollarization. Supporters of dollarization have argued that the way to deal with the seigniorage issue is to sign a monetary treatise with the United States, under which lost seigniorage would be partially refunded to Argentina. This is not a new idea. In fact, it was proposed in 1972 by Harry Johnson within the context of the Panamanian experience. Such an initiative, however, is likely to face serious political problems. This said, however, it is important to notice that early in the year 2000 legislation aimed at sharing seigniorage in case of dollarization was introduced to the U.S. Senate. The bill, sponsored by Florida's senior senator Connie Mack, establishes specific criteria to be used to calculate what percentage of seigniorage would be transferred to the emerging market in question. In my opinion, however, it is highly unlikely that this bill will be passed any time soon.

On the Feasibility of Floating Exchange Rates in Emerging Economies: Lessons from Mexico

For many years it has been argued that emerging countries cannot successfully adopt a freely floating exchange rate regime. Two reasons have traditionally been given for this position: first, it has been argued that because emerging countries tend to export commodities or light manufactures, a floating exchange rate would be "excessively" volatile. Second, and related to the previous point, it has been argued that emerging countries don't have the institutional requirements to undertake effective monetary policy under purely floating exchange rates (Summers 2000). According to this perspective, emerging markets that float would be unable to implement the type of (rather complex) feedback rule required for implementing an effective inflation targeting system. In particular, it has been argued that countries that float after a currency crisis will be unable to stabilize the value of their currency. This view is expressed by Eichengreen and Masson (1998, 18–19), who, after discussing the merits of floating rates and inflation targeting, state:

> [I]t is questionable whether a freely floating exchange rate and an inflation target objective for monetary policy are feasible, advisable or fully credible for many developing and transition economies . . . [T]hese economies are subject to substantial larger internal and external shocks . . . and the transmission mechanisms through which monetary policy affects the economy and the price level tend to be less certain and reliable.

More recently, a new objection to floating in emerging markets has been raised. Some authors, most notably Calvo (1999), Reinhart (2000), and their associates, have argued that in a world with high capital mobility, incomplete information, fads, rumors, and dollar-denominated liabilities, the monetary authorities will be severely affected by a fear of floating. This is because significant exchange rate movements, and in particular large depreciations, will tend to have negative effects on inflation and on corporate debt. According to this view, floating regimes in emerging markets will be so only in name. In reality, countries that claim to float will be "closet peggers," making every effort, through direct intervention (selling and buying reserves) and interest rate manipulation, to avoid large exchange rate fluctuations. These countries will be in the worst of worlds: they will have de facto rigid exchange rates and high interest rates. Reinhart (2000, 65) has aptly summarized the fear-of-floating view:

> Countries that say that they allow their exchange rate to float mostly do not; there seems to be an epidemic case of "fear of floating." Relative to more committed floaters . . . exchange rate volatility is quite low . . . [T]his low relative–exchange rate volatility is the deliberate result of policy actions to stabilize the exchange rate.

After analyzing the behavior of exchange rate, international reserves, and nominal interest rate volatility, Reinhart concludes that those emerging markets usually considered to be floaters—Bolivia, India, and Mexico— are subject to the fear-of-floating syndrome. She goes on to argue that, under these circumstances, "lack of credibility remains a serious problem," and that the only way to avoid it may be "full dollarization" (69).

In a recent paper, Levy and Sturzenegger (2000) follow (independently) an approach similar to that proposed by Reinhart (2000) to analyze exchange rate policy in emerging economies. These authors use data on the volatility of international reserves, the volatility of exchange rates, and the volatility of exchange rate changes for ninety-nine countries, during the period 1990–98, to determine their true exchange rate regime. Their analysis begins with the well-known fact that the classification system used by the IMF tends to misclassify countries. The authors undertake a series of cluster analysis exercises to classify the countries in their sample into five categories: (a) fixed, (b) dirty float or crawling peg, (c) dirty float, (d) float, and (e) inconclusive. The results from this study tend to contradict the fear-of-floating hypothesis. Indeed, Levy and Sturzenegger find out that for their complete sample, 273 cases out of a total of 955 can be classified as floaters. This, of course, does not mean that a number of countries are wrongly classified according to the IMF. For example, they find that in 1998 there were twelve countries that had been classified as floaters by the fund but that did not really float. Interestingly enough, there were also some fixers that did not fix.

Some of the emerging countries that, according to this study, had a floating regime during 1997–98 (the last two years of their sample) include Chile, Colombia, Ghana, India, and South Africa. A particularly important case is Mexico, a country whose authorities have strongly claimed to have adopted a freely floating rate after the collapse of 1994. The Levy and Sturzenegger analysis indeed suggests that, after a transitional period in the two years immediately following the currency crisis, Mexico has had, since 1997, a freely floating exchange rate regime. According to this study, during 1995 Mexico had a dirty or crawling peg regime. This evolved, in 1996, to a dirty float and, finally, in 1997 to a free float. This means, then, that Mexico's experience can indeed be used as an illustration of the way in which a floating regime will tend to work in an emerging country. Of course, it is not possible to extract general conclusions from a single episode, but in the absence of other experiences with anything that resembles a floating rate, analyses of Mexico's foray into exchange rate flexibility should prove very useful.

Figure 1.8 presents weekly data on the nominal exchange rate of the Mexican peso vis-à-vis the U.S. dollar for the period January 1992 through October 1999. The top panel depicts the nominal peso-dollar rate, and the bottom panel presents the weekly rate of devaluation of the Mexican peso during that period. These figures clearly show the heightened volatility that followed the currency crisis of December 1994. By late 1995, however, Mexico had managed to stabilize the peso-dollar rate. During the second of November, 1995 the peso-dollar rate was at 7.77, and almost two years later, during the second week of October 1997, it was 7.71. At that time, and partially as a result of the East Asian crisis, the peso depreciated significantly.

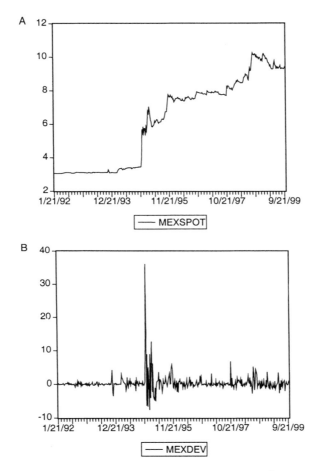

Fig. 1.8   *A,* **Mexican peso-U.S. dollar exchange rate: spot exchange rate (weekly data, January 1992–October 1999);** *B,* **Mexican peso-U.S. dollar exchange rate: rate of depreciation of the peso (weekly data, January 1992–October 1999)**

The peso continued to lose ground until October 1998, when in the midst of the global liquidity squeeze the peso-dollar rate surpassed 10. Once global liquidity was restored the peso strengthened significantly, as the figure shows, and during October-November 1999 it fluctuated around the 9.3 to 9.4 mark. At the time of this writing, September 2000, the peso-dollar rate continues to fluctuate around that level.

Volatility

Tables 1.4 and 1.5 present a series of indicators to compare the volatility of the peso-dollar rate with the rates of the deutsche mark, Japanese yen, British pound, Australian dollar, Canadian dollar, and New Zealand dollar

Table 1.4   Exchange Rate Volatility in Several Countries, 1991–99

Daily Exchange Rates	Australia	Canada	France	Germany	Japan	New Zealand	Mexico	United Kingdom
1991								
No. of obs.	260	260	260	260	260	260	n.a.	260
Mean absolute % change	0.278	0.135	0.575	0.623	0.442	0.286	n.a.	0.532
Standard deviation of % change	0.274	0.131	0.534	0.577	0.407	0.303	n.a.	0.516
Max absolute % change	2.078	0.842	2.720	3.144	2.780	2.005	n.a.	3.058
No. of obs. with zero change	19	17	13	12	13	23	n.a.	17
1992								
No. of obs.	262	262	262	262	262	262	260	262
Mean absolute % change	0.306	0.225	0.686	0.639	0.399	0.268	0.109	0.601
Standard deviation of % change	0.298	0.208	0.677	0.560	0.389	0.279	0.141	0.590
Max absolute % change	1.646	1.471	4.046	2.668	2.988	1.734	1.092	3.081
No. of obs. with zero change	13	14	10	9	11	39	26	13
1993								
No. of obs.	261	261	261	261	261	261	261	261
Mean absolute % change	0.445	0.248	0.498	0.514	0.486	0.308	0.132	0.543
Standard deviation of % change	0.380	0.204	0.432	0.436	0.472	0.327	0.316	0.494
Max absolute % change	1.801	1.070	2.320	2.329	2.871	2.492	4.012	2.746
No. of obs. with zero change	16	14	12	14	11	21	34	21
1994								
No. of obs.	261	261	261	261	261	261	261	261
Mean absolute % change	0.324	0.196	0.400	0.416	0.419	0.248	0.444	0.299
Standard deviation of % change	0.293	0.169	0.359	0.374	0.400	0.238	1.977	0.289
Max absolute % change	1.600	0.905	2.512	2.416	3.353	1.312	19.356	1.762
No. of obs. with zero change	25	12	9	9	12	29	35	12
1995								
No. of obs.	261	261	261	261	261	261	261	261
Mean absolute % change	0.350	0.235	0.466	0.541	0.595	0.292	1.063	0.346
Standard deviation of % change	0.354	0.243	0.488	0.532	0.622	0.248	1.755	0.362
Max absolute % change	1.921	1.674	2.893	3.003	3.328	1.254	10.465	1.975
No. of obs. with zero change	30	17	10	10	11	21	60	16

1996								
No. of obs.	262	262	262	262	262	262	262	262
Mean absolute % change	0.273	0.133	0.276	0.299	0.345	0.280	0.231	0.253
Standard deviation of % change	0.292	0.120	0.252	0.279	0.351	0.264	0.227	0.293
Max absolute % change	2.664	0.645	2.012	2.142	2.235	1.414	1.221	2.539
No. of obs. with zero change	30	18	9	12	13	15	35	18
1997								
No. of obs.	261	261	261	261	261	261	261	261
Mean absolute % change	0.428	0.190	0.457	0.469	0.523	0.357	0.282	0.380
Standard deviation of % change	0.391	0.167	0.381	0.379	0.511	0.351	0.522	0.353
Max absolute % change	3.066	1.052	1.872	1.957	2.868	2.324	6.984	2.151
No. of obs. with zero change	26	16	8	8	11	14	22	11
1998								
No. of obs.	261	261	261	261	261	261	261	261
Mean absolute % change	0.608	0.294	0.413	0.410	0.792	0.673	0.569	0.328
Standard deviation of % change	0.597	0.295	0.367	0.365	0.797	0.643	0.778	0.278
Max absolute % change	4.479	2.096	1.926	1.932	5.495	3.939	4.950	1.718
No. of obs. with zero change	15	14	8	11	8	12	25	9
1999 (–Dec 20)								
No. of obs.	252	252	252	252	252	252	252	252
Mean absolute % change	0.439	0.267	0.422	0.422	0.602	0.510	0.356	0.328
Standard deviation of % change	0.360	0.228	0.372	0.374	0.551	0.457	0.450	0.275
Max absolute % change	1.714	1.382	2.349	2.389	3.118	3.078	3.792	1.452
No. of obs. with zero change	21	9	13	13	7	12	28	10

Source: Constructed from data obtained from Datastream.

Note: n.a. = not available.

Table 1.5 Comparative Exchange Rate Volatility (weekly data)

Weekly Exchange Rates	Australia	Canada	France	Germany	Japan	New Zealand	Mexico	United Kingdom
1991								
No. of obs.	51	51	51	51	51	51	n.a.	51
Mean absolute % change	0.654	0.320	1.348	1.398	0.866	0.678	n.a.	1.257
Standard deviation of % change	0.564	0.253	0.953	0.988	0.856	0.617	n.a.	0.871
Max absolute % change	3.118	1.166	3.519	3.759	3.638	2.708	n.a.	3.482
No. of obs. with zero change	0	0	0	0	1	2	0	0
1992								
No. of obs.	52	52	52	52	52	52	51	52
Mean absolute % change	0.669	0.583	1.726	1.573	0.938	0.530	0.296	1.539
Standard deviation of % change	0.684	0.444	1.367	1.164	0.830	0.544	0.296	1.497
Max absolute % change	3.335	2.158	6.248	4.741	3.393	3.194	1.051	9.906
No. of obs. with zero change	0	0	0	0	1	1	1	1
1993								
No. of obs.	53	53	53	53	53	53	53	53
Mean absolute % change	0.911	0.543	1.183	1.244	1.112	0.631	0.302	1.372
Standard deviation of % change	0.686	0.538	0.829	0.937	0.770	0.567	0.597	0.995
Max absolute % change	2.856	2.203	3.530	3.830	3.037	3.379	3.631	3.897
No. of obs. with zero change	0	2	0	0	0	0	0	1
1994								
No. of obs.	52	52	52	52	52	52	52	52
Mean absolute % change	0.621	0.460	0.924	0.987	0.951	0.584	1.144	0.715
Standard deviation of % change	0.531	0.293	0.706	0.754	0.776	0.400	4.645	0.552
Max absolute % change	3.155	1.272	2.903	3.212	3.325	1.765	33.670	2.093
No. of obs. with zero change	0	0	0	0	2	3	2	0
1995								
No. of obs.	52	52	52	52	52	52	52	52
Mean absolute % change	0.869	0.539	1.089	1.219	1.438	0.595	2.441	0.743
Standard deviation of % change	0.636	0.414	1.053	1.219	1.304	0.464	3.041	0.668
Max absolute % change	3.443	1.653	4.910	5.197	4.660	2.140	17.721	2.284
No. of obs. with zero change	1	1	0	0	0	0	1	0

1996								
No. of obs.	52	52	52	52	52	52	52	52
Mean absolute % change	0.632	0.310	0.681	0.697	0.733	0.584	0.548	0.685
Standard deviation of % change	0.602	0.240	0.607	0.650	0.587	0.440	0.500	0.610
Max absolute % change	2.745	1.267	2.449	2.768	2.285	1.974	2.428	2.643
No. of obs. with zero change	4	0	0	0	0	0	0	1
1997								
No. of obs.	52	52	52	52	52	52	52	52
Mean absolute % change	0.902	0.518	0.902	0.902	1.186	0.744	0.624	0.806
Standard deviation of % change	0.702	0.376	0.694	0.707	1.088	0.732	0.937	0.722
Max absolute % change	4.028	1.882	3.112	3.030	5.049	2.865	6.331	3.020
No. of obs. with zero change	0	0	0	0	1	0	2	1
1998								
No. of obs.	52	52	52	52	52	52	52	52
Mean absolute % change	1.614	0.685	1.073	1.064	2.122	1.460	1.328	0.826
Standard deviation of % change	1.258	0.628	0.694	0.688	2.328	1.300	1.466	0.641
Max absolute % change	5.826	2.818	2.880	2.801	14.908	5.587	7.576	2.614
No. of obs. with zero change	1	0	0	0	0	1	0	0
1999 (~Dec 17)								
No. of obs.	51	51	51	51	51	51	51	51
Mean absolute % change	1.015	0.553	1.119	1.118	1.598	1.103	0.828	0.768
Standard deviation of % change	0.756	0.465	0.689	0.697	1.191	0.864	0.820	0.523
Max absolute % change	3.210	1.704	2.859	2.880	5.620	3.787	3.637	2.612
No. of obs. with zero change	0	1	0	1	0	2	0	0

Source: Constructed from data obtained from Datastream. n.a. = not available.

to the U.S. dollar, as well as the French franc-deutsche mark rate. While table 1.4 deals with daily exchange rate data, table 1.5 presents volatility statistics for weekly data. Generally speaking, the results presented in these tables provide no support for either the idea that the peso-dollar rate has been "excessively" volatile after 1995 nor for the notion that the Mexican peso has been "abnormally" stable. In fact, according to the mean absolute percentage change and the standard deviation of change, the peso-dollar rate was as volatile as the other currencies during 1997. In 1998, its degree of volatility increased significantly but was lower than the yen-dollar rate. In 1999 the extent of volatility declined, and the peso was once again in the middle of the pack. The overall conclusion from the high-frequency volatility analysis is, then, that Mexico does not appear to be different, in terms of volatility, from other floaters.

Monetary Policy, Feedback Rules, and Transparency

The stabilization of the exchange rate at around 7.7 pesos per dollar in 1996 surprised many analysts, for two reasons. First, with a still rapid rate of inflation it was expected that the peso would continue to depreciate at a somewhat rapid pace. Second, the Bank of Mexico stated repeatedly that it was (almost completely) abstaining from intervening in the foreign exchange market. In fact the Bank of Mexico stated that between 1996–97 it never sold foreign exchange, and only on very few occasions it provided signals to the local financial market, suggesting that it would tighten liquidity. No "signals," were provided during 1997.[22]

Market participants, however, were skeptical about the hands-off policy allegedly followed by the Bank of Mexico and believed that, as is often the case in industrial countries, there was a gap between what the Bank of Mexico said and what it actually did. In particular, by mid-1997 market analysts believed that the Bank of Mexico was following a complex monetary policy feedback rule that incorporated exchange rate behavior prominently. The chief economist of Bear Sterns stated in *The Wall Street Journal*: "Mexico stopped its economic and financial deterioration almost overnight [in the aftermath of the 1994 devaluation] by announcing a feedback mechanism between the exchange rate . . . and . . . monetary liquidity" (20 October 1997, A.23). Moreover, JPMorgan's *Emerging Markets Data Watch* of 3 October 1997 (page 6) noted that "It has often been argued in the past year or two that Banxico has been exacerbating upward pressure on the peso by tightening monetary policy." These analysts did not venture to opine on whether the feedback rule was of a Taylor type or whether it was of a looser, and yet more complex, type, such as the ones advocated by supporters of inflation targeting in an open economy (Svensson 1999).

22. See Edwards and Savastano (1999) for a detailed discussion of the bank of Mexico's official description of the way it conducted monetary policy during that period. See also Aguilar and Juan-Ramon (1997).

Between 1995 and 1999, when an inflation-targeting approach was adopted, the Bank of Mexico's official monetary policy consisted of targeting the monetary base on a day-to-day basis.[23] No attempt was made, according to the official view, at targeting interest rates, nor was the exchange rate a consideration in setting liquidity (O'Dogherty 1997). This system was supposed to work as follows: Early in the year the Bank of Mexico announced the day-to-day target for monetary base. This, in turn, was consistent with the official inflation goal, and incorporated expected changes in money demand and seasonality. If, for whatever reason, the Bank decided to alter its stance it did that by sending a signal to the banking sector. This was done by announcing, and thereafter enforcing, a (very) small change in the banking system cumulative balances (O'Dogherty 1997). What puzzled Mexico observers was the small number of episodes in which the Bank of Mexico acknowledged having modified the stance of its monetary policy in response to market developments. By its own reckoning, the Bank of Mexico changed the stance of monetary policy fifteen times between 25 September and 25 December 1995 and eight times between December 1995 and November 1996, and it kept the stance unchanged (at a "neutral" level— i.e., a cumulative balance of zero) during 1997 (Gil-Díaz 1997; Aguilar and Juan-Ramón 1997). According to Mexico's monetary authorities, then, all movements of interest rates and the exchange rate in, say, 1997 (or in any other long period between changes in the Bank of Mexico's objective for the system's cumulative balance) did not justify or elicit a response of monetary policy. Edwards and Savastasno (1998) used weekly data to investigate whether, as stated, the Bank of Mexico followed a mostly hands-off monetary policy, or, as market participants suspected, it followed some type of feedback rule. Their findings suggest, very strongly, that during 1996–97 the Bank of Mexico did follow a monetary policy feedback rule, according to which developments in the exchange rate market were explicitly taken into account when the amount of liquidity made available to the market was determined. More specifically, the authors found that the Bank of Mexico tightened the monetary base, relative to its target, when the peso experienced a "large" depreciation. This analysis indicates that, although monetary policy responded to changes in the peso-dollar exchange rate, the Bank of Mexico did not defend a specific level of the peso.

These results are important for five reasons: First, they clearly indicate that, contrary to the Mexican authorities' claims, the central bank made a concerted effort to stabilize the peso. Second, the results also show that this intervention was not undertaken directly through the foreign exchange market; instead, daily decision on monetary policy were affected by exchange rate developments. Third, the results also suggest that, in spite of the skeptic's view, in emerging economies it is possible for the monetary authority to implement an effective and complex feedback rule, of an aug-

---

23. The discussion that follows is partially based on Edwards and Savastano (1999).

mented Taylor type.[24] Fourth, they suggest that during this period the Bank of Mexico was concerned with the inflationary implications of exchange rate movements. No attempt was made at defending a particular level of the exchange rate. Fifth, these results clearly illustrate that under a floating regime the issue of transparency—and, more specifically, of verifiability—can be serious, and even highly destabilizing. In the case of the Mexican peso discussed above, the *Economist* (14–18 March 1998, 17) pointed out that puzzled investors were not sure how to interpret the relative stability of the peso during 1997:

> [D]istrustful investors have wondered aloud whether the central bank—which lost much credibility with the collapse—really enjoys independence. . . . [T]he doubters have noted that the government's policy on the peso, which is theoretically free to float, has actually been set by a committee.

Calvo (1999) has persuasively argued that, to the extent that there are poorly informed participants in the market for emerging market debt, the lack of transparency and credibility of the authorities will leave these countries open to speculation based on rumors and herd instinct. These, in turn, can easily result in major attacks on the currency. Frankel, Schmukler, and Serven (2000) have recently discussed the issue of exchange rate and monetary policy verifiability. According to them, under most circumstances it is difficult and costly for analysts, even for very sophisticated ones, to actually verify whether a particular country is, in fact, following the policies that it has announced. This view is certainly supported by the work on Mexico discussed above; it took Edwards and Savastano (1999) a substantial amount of time and some detective-type work to unearth the Bank of Mexico reaction function. The above discussion does not mean that emerging countries should avoid complex feedback rules or should abstain from floating. What it underscores, however, is the need to communicate to the public, in as transparent a way as possible, the type of policy that is being followed (see Bernanke et al. 1999 for a discussion of monetary authorities' communication strategies within an inflation-targeting context).

Mexican Lessons and Fear of Floating

As pointed out, according to the fear-of-floating hypothesis, rather than letting the exchange rate fluctuate freely, emerging markets will intervene actively in the domestic financial market, generating a "rigid exchange rate–cum–high interest rates" situation. This point of view has been expressed, very forcefully, by the Inter-American Development Bank's chief economist, Ricardo Hausmann (2000). According to him, depreciations of the Mexican peso have been followed by hikes in interest rates, reflecting mas-

24. Naturally, as pointed out above, it is difficult to make general statements on the basis of one historical case. Nonetheless, Mexico's experience is very useful.

sive government intervention, and thus an intense fear of floating. This situation, Hausman has argued, contrasts with countries such as Australia, where the currency has (recently) depreciated, while domestic interest rates have remained relatively stable.

Although Mexico has indeed adjusted its monetary policy in response to (some) exchange rate developments, there is little evidence suggesting that, since 1997, it has been subject to a significant fear of floating. Figure 1.9 presents weekly data on the peso-dollar nominal exchange rate and on the nominal interest rate on twenty-eight-day government securities (CETES) between 1994 and October of 1999. Table 1.6, on the other hand, presents correlation coefficients between these two variables for different subperiods. As may be seen from this table, the alleged strong positive relationship between the peso-dollar exchange rate and the nominal interest rate on government securities is confined to a rather short subperiod. In effect, between January 1996 and October 1997—when Mexico, as well as the rest of Latin America, was affected by the East Asian crisis—these two variables were

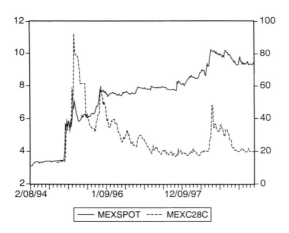

Fig. 1.9   Mexico exchange rate and twenty-eight-day nominal interest rate (cetes; weekly data, 1994–99)

Table 1.6   **Correlation Coefficients Between Mexico's Exchange Rate and Nominal Interest Rate: Weekly Data, 1996–99**

Period	Correlation Coefficient
January 1996–October 1997	−0.60
November 1997–May 1998	0.04
June 1998–April 1999	0.83
May 1999–October 1999	0.08
January 1996–October 1999	0.08

Source: Computed by the author using data from the Datastream database.

negatively correlated. Between November 1997 and May 1998, Mexico looked a lot like Australia, as the peso depreciated significantly (an accumulated 15.4 percent) with stable interest rates. During this period, which corresponds to the first five months in office of a new Central Bank governor, the correlation between the two variables was virtually zero.

After the Russian crisis of August 1998 and the subsequent dry-up of global liquidity, the peso and Mexican domestic interest rates did, indeed, exhibit a positive correlation. At that time, due to a severe attack on the currency, the Mexican authorities decided that this was a temporary situation and that allowing the peso to weaken further would compromise the inflation target. This type of reaction is indeed what a modern and forward-looking inflation-targeting model would indicate (Bernanke et al. 1999). Indeed, in an elegant recent paper Svensson (1999) has developed an inflation-targeting framework that allows for this type of nonlinear, threshold-triggered reaction and judgment-aided reaction to occur.

In retrospect, it is difficult to believe that, had Mexico had a super-fixed exchange rate regime, it would have been able to face the 1998 global liquidity squeeze more effectively. After all, during 1999 the economic recovery continued, inflation was on target, employment grew at healthy rates, and interest rates declined significantly. Moreover, broadly speaking, the exchange rate has gone back to approximately its precrisis level. It should be emphasized, however, that Mexico's successful experience of the last few years does not mean that every country that floats will behave in this way. It does mean, however, that the fear of floating is not as pervasive as claimed. It does also mean that not every monetary policy feedback rule is detrimental to the country's well-being. If implemented correctly, and supported by the right type of fiscal policy, these rules can be very useful in improving macroeconomic management.

1.1.5 Concluding Remarks

The emerging markets' financial crises of the second half of the 1990s have changed economists' views with respect to exchange rate policies. An increasing number of analysts in academia as well as in the official and private sectors argue that pegged-but-adjustable exchange rate regimes are unstable and invite speculation. This view has been taken by the U.S. secretary of state, as well as by the Metzler Commission Report. According to this perspective, in order to reduce the probability of financial crises countries should move to one of the two-corner exchange rate systems: freely floating exchange rates or super-fixed regimes. In this paper I have analyzed the problems and challenges associated with this policy perspective, including issues related to optimal exit policies and exchange rate feedback rules under floating regimes. Although it is too early to make a definitive statement, the evidence discussed in this paper suggests that, under the appropriate conditions and policies, floating exchange rates can be effective and efficient. Indeed, much of the criticism of floating rates in the emerging economies seems to be based on a small number of historical episodes, or has misread the difficulties associated with super-fixed systems. Having said that, I will add that it appears to be reasonable to expect that in the years to come the number of currencies in the world will decline. Many countries are likely to realize that they satisfy the "optimal currency area criteria." This, however, is not likely to be an appropriate solution for every emerging nation.

Some analysts have argued that the control of capital inflows is an effective way of helping to prevent currency crises. In section 1.1.3 of this paper I have evaluated Chile's experience with this type of policy. My conclusion is that, although these controls were useful in Chile, their effectiveness has been exaggerated. In particular, there is no guarantee that they will work in the same way as in Chile in other nations that adopt them.

References

Ades, Alberto, and Federico Kaune. 1997. GS-SCAD: A new measure of current account sustainability for developing countries. New York: Goldman Sachs.

Aguilar, A., and Victor Hugo Juan-Ramón. 1997. Determinantes de la Tasa de Interes de Corto Plazo en Mexico: Efecto de las Senales del Banco Central. Instituto Technologico Autonomo de Mexico *Gaceta de Economia* 3 (5).

Asian Policy Forum. 2000. Policy recommendations for preventing another capital account crisis. Tokyo: Asian Development Bank Institute.

Aspe, Pedro. 1993. *Economic transformation the Mexican way.* Lionel Robbins Lectures. Cambridge: MIT Press.

Bernanke, Ben S., Thomas Laubach, Frederic S. Mishkin, and Adam S. Posen. 1999. *Inflation targeting: Lessons from the international experience.* Princeton: Princeton University Press.

Bruno, Michael. 1995. Currency crises and collapses: Comments. *Brookings Papers on Economic Activity,* Issue no. 2:278–85. Washington, D.C.: Brookings Institution.

Calvo, Guillermo A. 1999. Fixed vs. flexible exchange rates: Preliminaries of a turn-of-millennium rematch. University of Maryland, Department of Economics. Mimeograph.

———. 2001. Capital markets and the exchange rate with special reference to the dollarization debate in Latin America. *Journal of Money, Credit, and Banking* 33 (2): 312–24.

Chang, Roberto, and Andres Velasco. 2000. Exchange rate policy for developing countries. *American Economic Review* 90 (May): 71–75.

Chinn, Menzie. 1998. Before the fall: Were East Asian currencies overvalued? NBER Working Paper no. 6491. Cambridge, Mass.: National Bureau of Economic Research, March.

Cowan, Kevin, and José De Gregorio. 1998. Exchange rate policies and capital account management. In *Managing capital flows and exchange rates: Perspectives from the Pacific Basin,* ed. Reuven Glick, 465–88. Cambridge: Cambridge University Press.

D'Amato, Alfonse. 1995. Report on the Mexican economic crisis. United States Senate, June 29.

De Gregorio, José, Eduardo Borenzstein, and J. W. Lee. 1998. How does foreign direct investment affect economic growth? *Journal of International Economics* 45 (1): 115–35.

De Gregorio, José, Sebastian Edwards, and Rodrigo Valdes. 2000. Controls on capital inflows: Do they work? *Journal of Development Economics* 63:59–83.

Deutsche Bank. 2000. Current accounts: Can they achieve sustainability? London: Deutsche Bank, Global Markets Research.

Dornbusch, Rudiger. 1997. The folly, the crash, and beyond: Economic policies and the crisis. In *Anatomy of an emerging market crash: Mexico 1994*, ed. Sebastian Edwards and N. Naim. Washington, D.C.: Carnegie Endowment.

Edwards, Sebastian. 1988. *Real exchange rates, devaluation, and adjustment: Exchange rate policy in developing countries.* Cambridge: MIT Press.

———. 1989. Structural adjustment policies in highly indebted countries. In *Developing countries debt and economic performance.* Vol. 2, ed. Jeffrey Sachs. Chicago: University of Chicago Press.

———. 1998a. Capital flows, real exchange rates, and capital controls: Some Latin American experiences. NBER Working Paper no. 6800. Cambridge, Mass.: National Bureau of Economic Research.

———. 1998b. Capital inflows into Latin America: A stop-go story? NBER Working Paper no. 6441. Cambridge, Mass.: National Bureau of Economic Research.

———. 1998c. Two crises: Inflationary inertia and credibility. Economic Journal 108 (448): 680–702.

———. 1999a. A capital idea? *Foreign Affairs* 78 (3): 18–22.

———. 1999b. How effective are capital controls? *Journal of Economic Perspectives* 13 (4): 65–84.

Edwards, Sebastian, and Peter J. Montiel. 1989. The price of postponed adjustment. *Finance and Development* 26 (3): 34–37.

Edwards, Sebastian and Alejandra Cox Edwards. 1991. *Monetarism and liberalism: The Chilean experiment.* Chicago: University of Chicago Press.

Edwards, Sebastian, and Miguel A. Savastano. 1999. Exchange rates in emerging economies: What do we know? What do we need to know? NBER Working Paper no. W7228. Cambridge, Mass.: National Bureau of Economic Research.

Edwards, Sebastian, and Raul Susmel. 2000. Interest volatility in emerging markets: Evidence from the 1990s. NBER Working Paper no. 7813. Cambridge, Mass.: National Bureau of Economic Research.

Eichengreen, Barry J., and Paul Masson. 1998. Exit strategies: Policy options for countries seeking greater exchange rate flexibility. IMF Occasional Paper no. 168. Washington, D.C.: International Monetary Fund.

Eichengreen, Barry J., Paul Masson, Miguel Savastano, and Sunil Sharma. 1999. Transition strategies and nominal anchors on the road to greater exchange-rate flexibility. Princeton Essays in International Finance no. 213. Princeton University, Department of Economics, International Economics Section.

Fraga, Arminio. 1999. Capital flows to Latin America: Comment. In *International Capital Flows,* ed. Martin Feldstein, 48–52. Chicago: University of Chicago Press.

Frankel, Jeffrey, Sergio Schmukler, and Luis Serven. 2000. Verifiability and the vanishing intermediate exchange rate regime. NBER Working Paper no. W7901. Cambridge, Mass.: National Bureau of Economic Research.

Frenkel, Jacob A., and Assaf Razin. 1987. *Fiscal policies and the world economy: An intertemporal approach.* Cambridge: MIT Press.

Gil-Diaz, Francisco. 1997. La Politica Monetaria y sus Canales de Transmision en Mexico. Instituto Tecnologico Autonomo de Mexico *Gaceta de Economia* 3 (5).

Goldman Sachs. Various issues. *Emerging markets economic research.* New York: Goldman Sachs.

————. 1997. *The foreign exchange market.* New York: Goldman Sachs, September.

Goldstein, Morris. 1998. The Asian financial crisis: Causes, curses, and systematic implications. Policy Analyses in International Economics, no. 55. Washington, D.C.: Institute for International Economics.

Hanke, Steve H., and Kurt Schuler. 1994. Currency boards for developing countries: A handbook. International center for Economic Growth, Sector Study 9. San Francisco, Calif.

————. 1998. Currency boards and free banking. *Money and the nation state: The financial revolution, government, and the world monetary system,* ed. Kevin Dowd and Richard H. Timberlake Jr., 403–21. Independent Studies in Political Economy. New Brunswick, N.J.: Transaction.

Hausmann, Ricardo. 2000. Latin America: No fireworks, no crisis? In *Global financial crises: Lessons from recent events,* ed. J. R. Bisignano, W. C. Hunter, and G. G. Kaufman. Boston: Kluwer Academic.

Hinkle, Lawrence E., and Peter J. Montiel. 1999. *Exchange rate misalignment: Concepts and measurement for developing countries.* Oxford, England: Oxford University Press.

Ito, Takatoshi. 2000. Capital Flows in Asia. In *Capital flows and the emerging economies,* ed. Sebastian Edwards, 255–98. Chicago: University of Chicago Press.

JPMorgan. 2000. An introduction to J. P. Morgan's emerging markets exchange rate model: Theory and econometrics. New York: J. P. Morgan.

Kiguel, Miguel A., and Nissan Liviatan. 1995. Stopping three big inflations: Argentina, Brazil, and Peru. In *Reform, recovery, and growth: Latin America and the Middle East,* ed. Rudiger Dornbusch and Sebastian Edwards, 369–408. Chicago: University of Chicago Press.

Laurens, Bernard, and Jaime Cardoso. 1998. Managing capital flows: Lessons from the experience of Chile. IMF Working Paper no. WP/98/168. Washington, D.C.: International Monetary Fund.

Levy Yeyati, Eduardo, and Federico Sturzenegger. 2000. Classifying exchange rate regimes: Deeds vs. words. Working Paper no. 2. Buenos Aires, Argentina: Universidad Torcuato Di Tella.

Massad, Carlos. 1998a. The liberalization of the capital account: Chile in the 1990s. In *Should the IMF pursue capital account convertibility?* Ed. Stanley Fischer et al., 34–46. Essays in International Finance no. 207. Princeton, N.J.: Princeton University.

————. 1998b. La Política Monetaria en Chile. *Economía Chilena* 1 (1): 7–27.

Mussa, Michael, and Miguel Savastano. 2000. The IMF approach to economic stabilization. In *NBER macroeconomics annual 1999,* ed. Ben S. Bernanke and Julio Rotemberg, 79–128. Cambridge: MIT Press.

O'Dogherty, Pascual. 1997. La Instrumentacion de la Politica Monetaria en Mexico. Instituto Tecnologico Autonomo de Mexico *Gaceta de Economia* 3 (5).

Reinhart, Carmen. 2000. The mirage of floating exchange rates. *American Economic Review* 90 (May): 65–70.

Sachs, Jeffrey, Aaron Tornell, and Andres Velasco. 1995. The collapse of the Mexican peso: What have we learned? NBER Working Paper no. 4142. Cambridge, Mass.: National Bureau of Economic Research, June.

————. 1996. Financial crises in emerging markets: The lessons of 1995. *Brookings Papers on Economic Activity,* Issue no. 1:147–217. Washington, D.C.: Brookings Institution.

Soto, Claudio. 1997. Controles a los Movimientos de Capitales: Evaluación Empírica del Caso Chileno. Banco Central de Chile.

Summers, Larry H. 2000. International financial crises: Causes, preventions, and cures. *American Economic Review* 90 (2): 1–16.

Svensson, Lars E. O. 1999. Inflation targeting: Some extensions. *Scandinavian Journal of Economics* 101 (3): 337–61.
Valdés-Prieto, Salvador, and Marcelo Soto. 1998. The effectiveness of capital controls: Theory and evidence from Chile. *Empirica* 25 (2): 133–64.

2. Domingo F. Cavallo

Thank you. I prefer to start talking about money as an institution. As a politician who has had to deal with practical issues in government, I came to the conclusion that economic growth is related much more to the quality of institutions, particularly monetary institutions, than to exchange rate regimes.

In adopting rules of the game for an economy, it is very important to think in terms of the institution's ability to generate the appropriate incentives for growth. Of course, once a particular institution is created, it is very important to maintain it over time. As an institution remains and functions, people's understanding of its purpose increases, and the effectiveness of the institution increases as well. Good institutions are those that provide assurance that property rights of people will be defended as well as the rights of human and financial capital. Good institutions are those that create the appropriate incentives for the efficient use of capital and generate higher productivity levels over time.

Money is very important as an institution. What I see as very important about money is its ability to inspire confidence, its ability to reassure that those property rights that are written and documented in monetary terms will be preserved over time. I would like to speak about the quality of money in order to refer to the ability of a particular money to offer reassurance to somebody who has chosen that currency to write contracts that his or her property rights will be defended. The quality of money can be observed by looking at the existence of long-term contracts. If the interest rate is more or less similar to the expected rate of growth of the economy, that means that a particular money does not embody long-term inflationary expectations, that long-term inflationary expectations have been removed, and therefore people will use that money, for example, for long-term lending or borrowing.

In my country, after forty-five years of inflation, originated by the use and abuse of the government's power to print money to finance public fiscal deficits and even private deficits, the people were convinced that our currency was not a good one and that the government would continue printing money and taxing people's savings. That is why, during the 1980s, Argentines decided to repudiate the Argentine currency, the austral, and they started to use the dollar. Therefore dollarization is not something that a particular government advocated for Argentina in those days. Dollarization was a decision made by the Argentine people during the 1980s, at a time of high inflation and even hyperinflation. By then, there was more than $20 billion circulating in Argentina. People started to use the dollar for everyday transactions, and of course for saving, because they did not want the government or the Central Bank to tax away their saving and their income.

In order to inspire confidence in the monetary system, we set new rules of the game for the economy and created a new monetary regime. We decided that we had to allow Argentines to continue using the dollar. We could not prohibit the use of the dollar, because if we had said "now, it is obligatory to sell all the dollars you have to the authorities, and it is forbidden to use the dollar any more," no Argentine would have believed in our commitment to maintaining a sound Argentine currency. That is why I explain that our monetary system is not a permanent currency board, nor is it a permanent fixed exchange rate regime. Our system is a system of *competitive currencies.* We have at least two currencies, the dollar and the peso. The fixed rate of the Argentinean currency to the dollar is a temporary one, and the currency board is a temporary arrangement, to create confidence in our currency. In order to encourage Argentines to use our currency, we created what we call a convertibility plan, which is different from a fixed exchange rate plan. We called it a convertibility plan because what Argentines demanded was convertibility for the currency that they use. The demand for convertibility for a particular currency in the past came mainly from the negative effects of inflation. Argentines did not want to be in a trap; they wanted to be able to convert their currency, and therefore their wealth—their financial property—from one currency to other currencies. Otherwise, they reasoned, the government would eventually continue to tax away their financial wealth.

In the future, however, the demand for convertibility for a particular currency will come increasingly from globalization. In a globalized world, capital flights will be available to everyone, and individual portfolios will allow for the easy reallocation from one currency to another. If a government tries to force its people to use a particular currency, that will no longer be acceptable to citizens, at least in countries where there is no tradition of respect for property rights.

Thus, in Argentina we have the system that we call "convertibility," and we will maintain the system of allowing the changing of one currency for another forever. If the central bank, the economy minister, the president, or even the congress were to decide that the Argentine currency should be nonconvertible, that saving in the system should be in the local currency or that everyone would be forced to use the local currency exclusively, that would be repudiated by the people.

Now, why fix the value of this newly created currency? At the beginning, you create the currency and you want it to be convertible. There is no other alternative but to create that currency through a currency board: that is, fully backing the new currency to a high-quality currency (let's say the dollar) in order to assure that the currency that is being created will preserve its value in terms of the "tutor" currency. If you look at history, most currencies that now inspire confidence were created this way. That is, they were backed by gold and convertible into gold. Also, high-quality younger currencies, such as the Singapore dollar, were created through a currency board. It was a currency board that used the pound sterling as its support; then it shifted to the dollar when the sterling became weaker, and then it abandoned the use of a tutor. Also, remember that when the Singapore dollar was floated it appreciated rather than depreciating.

The whole idea that you are in a totally fixed system and you cannot abandon it is wrong. It is perfectly possible to move from a fixed system to a floating system, if at the time of adopting a floating system there are no forces generating a sharp devaluation, but, on the contrary, there are forces generating the appreciation of the currency. Market forces driving a currency appreciation are likely to happen in a country that has set up a good set of rules of the game and has set up good new institutions, because normally a country that adopts this decision starts with a very low level of productivity in all the sectors of its economy. Thus, over a period of ten or twenty years, productivity growth in that country should be higher than in the country that provides the tutor currency. Therefore, there will be a time when the market will call for an appreciation rather than a depreciation of the domestic currency, and that is the time for exiting the fixed exchange rate but preserving its convertibility, which is a key property that people demand from a currency.

We expect favorable market conditions, and this is why we consider convertibility very important and why the fixed exchange rate of the currency is a temporary phenomenon. When the currency inspires enough confidence, we will have a floating exchange rate, but the currency will still be convertible, and people will have the freedom to choose that currency, the national currency, or other currencies.

Now, has this system served Argentina well and prevented crisis? Of course. Look at the figures of the last decade. Since the creation of the new monetary regime, there was no currency crisis in Argentina in comparison with the five decades previous to convertibility. The financial crises were mild, and we overcame them easily and without big losses for the government. In general, the growth that we achieved during the decade was fairly high. Argentina between 1990 and the year 2000, in a period of ten years, expanded its economy 54 percent. Of course, Chile had a larger expansion, 88 percent, but Chile had implemented many more reforms at an earlier stage in time, and I will explain some differences in a moment. However, compared with Mexico, which expanded its economy 36 percent, and Brazil which expanded by 30 percent, there is no doubt the growth performance of Argentina was very good. Sometimes people say that a fixed exchange rate is bad for exports because it restricts export growth. Look at the figures. Of course, Mexico had a huge expansion of exports, 274 percent, but this was not due to the exchange rate regime: it was due to the North American Free Trade Agreement. Argentina had 118 percent, even more than Chile (at 103 percent), and much more than Brazil, which had a 78 percent increase in total exports. So exports did increase during the decade.

In addition to that, we eliminated inflation. Of course, now we are suffering from deflation, and that is what people perceive as a serious problem, and no doubt it is a problem. It would have been very good if Argentina could have floated its currency before the crisis in Brazil or the devaluation of the euro. However, we could not have floated it during the 1990s, because the peso's flotation would have caused a currency crisis in Argentina because of economic circumstances. In the future, though, we expect that there will be such a moment.

Let me make a final comment. What is the problem now in Argentina? Some people say the currency is overvalued. Argentina is not growing and may face a long period of stagnation and deflation. I think such statements are wrong. Exports are expanding in Argentina. Last year, exports expanded 12 percent. The problem in Argentina is that during the last three or four years investment opportunities have fallen, for two reasons. First, tax increases—very distortive tax increases—affected the cost of capital. Second, rumors of changes to the rules of the game threatened to reduce the profitability of investments in the future. Therefore, investors decided to postpone investments. A business is like a typical family, which, when faced with uncertainty about future income, does not demand loans for purchasing a home or a car. My point is that investment was discouraged in Argentina because of the government's tax increases, not because of the value of the currency itself. Thus, we should not introduce changes to our monetary system, but we should remove these disincentives for investment that deter investment and produce a significant burst of new investments that will generate productivity increases. This way, the Argentine economy will reinitiate a vigorous growth at the same pace it grew in the early 1990s.

3. Arminio Fraga

We are talking here this weekend about exchange rate crises and financial crises in emerging markets. I will give you a brief summary of what I believe are the main factors that one should look for in understanding such crises based on my academic, policy, and market experience.

My view is that most crisis situations have as a basic feature weak balance sheets. The weakness can be found at the government level or in the private sector, and it typically includes situations in which countries or banking sectors borrow short-term to finance development or long-term investments. The interesting question, therefore, is what causes weak balance sheets? The answer can be split into micro and macro reasons. On the micro side—the topic of our next session, with Frederic S. Mishkin's paper—we must discuss financial regimes, including banking, corporate governance issues, and so on. On the macro side, the range of topics covered includes weak fiscal regimes, which are the root cause of many crises, and also problems with monetary regimes and exchange rate regimes. (I will use the last two terms to refer to the same thing.) In the end, there can only be one nominal anchor, as we know.

Let me begin with a classification of exchange rate regimes. I will use the word *fixed* for super-fixed. Fixed to me means that there is a clear commitment, perhaps institutionalized through a currency board or a regional agreement. This differs from what Domingo Cavallo was saying. His emphasis was more on convertibility, and I think the policy debate in the literature has tended to focus more on fixity, rather than convertibility. *Managed* will be the second of three regimes, one in which there is a target. It can be a target rate or band or path or whatever. *Floating* will then be everything else where there is no target, but where some degree of intervention or leaning against the wind may be allowed, provided there is no target. There must really be no target, whether it be announced or not, which is something that is not easy to verify.

I tend to believe with Jeffrey Frankel, who gave a beautiful lecture at the Central Bank of Brazil just this past week, that it is possible to manage something between the extremes. It is not a theoretical impossibility. One could, for example, have a target zone or band. When the exchange rate is inside the band, there may be more room to run an independent monetary policy than when the rate is close to the band, where it becomes more like a fixed exchange rate. The problem is, and as this little example shows, that it gets to be complicated, a notion I will get back to. Also, I believe running an intermediate regime requires a lot of virtue. By that I mean, for example, Asian saving rates, which allow for a lot of flexibility in the conduct of policy, allowing for more room for mistakes.

Let me now be a bit provocative: my view on exchange rate regimes is not that we cannot run intermediate regimes, but that we should not. The reason is, basically, that they lead to two kinds of trouble. One problem is that they lead to *confusion*, and by that I mean confusion by private agents, by society, particularly when they structure their balance sheets. In an intermediate regime, it isn't clear what sort of risk one is subject to (e.g., interest rate risk in a fixed exchange rate regime or exchange rate risk in a floating regime). This may lead to temporarily overoptimistic or pessimistic beliefs, which are part of human nature and part of markets and therefore may lead to a crisis-prone environment. A second problem with intermediate regimes is that they lead to *temptation*. Here I am mainly thinking about governments and the temptation to postpone adjustment, to hide things, to, in a way, avoid facing reality. The problem is related to something I alluded to when I was here three years ago, which is the typically short horizon with which many governments tend to work, due to electoral cycles and so forth, or what academics would call a time-consistency problem. Thus, to summarize, confusion and temptation are good reasons in my view to avoid the intermediate regimes.

The recent Brazilian crisis illustrates some of the points discussed above, which suggest that one is better off with clean, transparent policies. Immediately after the crisis and the floating of the real, the main questions we asked ourselves were whether to float—to which the answer was yes—and how to go about it.

First of all, it was crucial to make sure that a floating exchange rate would not be inconsistent with our goal of providing a long-term, stable environment for the development and growth of our economy. That meant we had to provide a new nominal anchor. We chose inflation targeting, given the unreliable nature of running monetary policy with money aggregates. Inflation targeting goes beyond just having a target for inflation. We think about it almost as a ritual, a routine, a methodical pursuit of a transparent goal, along the lines discussed by Mishkin in his book with Bernanke and coauthors (Bernanke et al. 1999). Inflation targeting requires explaining very carefully and on a timely basis what the central bank does and having long-term objectives to avoid the typical time-consistency problems. It is interesting to note that, as it relates to the exchange rate, inflation targeting introduces an automatic response to volatility. For example, a depreciation of the exchange rate increases expected inflation, and, ceteris paribus, induces a tighter monetary policy (a form of automatic leaning against the wind).

Second—and here I'd like to make one brief point—when we talk about fixed exchange rates, we tend to say that, in order to support the fixed exchange rate, we need a very strong fiscal regime, very strong banking, and so on, as if we didn't need them with a float. There is no real difference, however. Both regimes do well or not depending on the consistency of the overall conduct of macroeconomic policy. For instance, with a weak fiscal regime, I do not think one can run a proper floating exchange rate either. Oftentimes we heard in the political debate back home that floating was a way to run a looser budget. That is just not the case. Indeed, I believe the key factor behind Brazil's recent recovery was the fiscal turnaround that actually started before the crisis and luckily has stayed in place and is being deepened as we move along.

Another issue worth mentioning here belongs to the micro side. In striving to avoid recurrent crises we must be very careful to design policies that are volatility-reducing rather than volatility-suppressing policies, and this is a concept that I heard first from Carlos Massad, my counterpart in Chile, in a recent seminar at the Bank of England. I like that definition: you want to do things that help you reduce and not hide volatility. Here the sequencing of policies and reforms plays a key role. It is important to strengthen the prudential regime before liberalizing the financial sector. We started the process in Brazil with new provisioning rules, new accounting rules, the introduction of market risk as part of capital requirements, and so on. I won't go into detail.

Just to conclude, let me note that since the floating of the real in the crisis of early 1999 we are often asked whether we are afraid of floating. The answer to that is clear when we look at the data: interest rate volatility has declined and exchange rate volatility has increased substantially since the floating, reaching levels similar to those found in countries that traditionally float.

Reference

Bernanke, Ben S., Frederic S. Mishkin, Adam S. Posen, and Thomas Laubach. 1999. *Inflation targeting: Lessons from the international experience.* Princeton, N.J.: Princeton University Press.

4. Jacob A. Frenkel

I'd like to join the previous speakers in thanking and complementing Sebastian Edwards on his paper on exchange rates and exchange rate systems in the context of risk avoidance and risk management. Of course, the issue of exchange rates and exchange rate regimes, or monetary policy and its implications for exchange rates, is not a new one. As a matter of fact, looking back at the programs of the American Economic Association for the past twenty years, there was not a single year without a session on these issues. Nevertheless we come back to them, not because we did not have answers, but because the answers change. The answers change, of course, because the circumstances change. Several key concepts that will come up in the discussion today were completely absent in the past. Therefore, our attitude is indeed legitimately changing. Notions of capital flows as being the sine qua non within which we have to discuss these issues simply did not exist. Credibility, balance sheet tests, the issue of pricing of risks, moral hazards, distinction between nominal and real exchange rates, the role of short-run versus long-run when time is moving relatively fast, and so on—obviously, once those issues are on the table, our approach to exchange rate analysis differs. Let me cover several basic points here.

First, in the context of this new reality, which you can call "globalization" or "integrated capital markets," what are the implications for issues that were at the fore just a few years ago: intervention policies, stabilization policies, pass-through from exchange rates to prices, and Phillips-curve relationships and their relationship to exchange rate systems? Let me begin by saying that I truly believe that the issue of "corners" is a complex one. Because we all live in the intermediate period, an intermediate regime should be all right. However, if there is anything that capital market integration shows us, it is that what we thought was a very simple mechanism of being an in-between regime, having neither clean float nor fully fixed rates, is much more complicated. It is also likely to be much less attractive.

At the end of the day, one needs to gravitate to one of those extremes. Look at my own country's experience. I don't think there is a single exchange rate regime that Israel did not go through. It had a peg to the dollar, a peg to the basket, a horizontal band, a sloped band, a widening slope, a parallel-to-boundaries band, and a nonparallel-to-boundaries band. If one needed a lesson, or an example, of a case in which there is no single exchange rate regime that is the cure for all ills, that's a good one. However, are there some key lessons that have been learned?

In terms of the fear of floating that Edwards speaks about: in Israel, there was a new government in 1977 that thought it had to liberalize everything. Indeed, overnight there was a complete liberalization of the foreign exchange markets, and within a very short period of time the seeds of hyperinflation were sown. We had a stable economy; still, the movement was toward hyperinflation in 1985. Paradoxically, or interestingly enough, it ended because of an exchange rate anchor. The question was, why did the regime fail? The answer is that it jumped from a plane without a parachute. The parachute, in this context, is the creation of markets. I believe it is not a question of which exchange rate policy or which exchange rate regime one has, but rather whether one has the necessary institutional setting. And I think *that* is a major lesson. One must have a well-functioning market to allow the luxury of choosing the best regime. This particular episode in Israel created a twenty-year drama that had to be resolved only in a much later stage when practical floating came into being. When you deal within a political milieu, occasionally you must introduce measures of progress very gradually. Unless, of course, you are pushed into change by crisis. In Israel, we introduced a band, and the band was upward sloping, and we gradually removed foreign exchange controls. Unless you remove foreign exchange controls, you must have "wider roads," because you are allowing faster traffic. Therefore, there was in fact a formal link between exchange rate variability that was allowed by the regime and the openness of the capital account. As you open the capital account, you must allow larger variability of exchange rates to become an integral part of the system. However, if you have larger variability of exchange rates, and you need to avoid the cost of variability, then it becomes essential to develop the market mechanisms and the instruments that are capable of dealing with such variability. Thus the distinction between suppressed volatility and reduced volatility comes into being. You need to actually price volatility properly. So, at least in our context, it becomes an integral part of financial market developments, rather than exchange rate policies.

But then, what does monetary policy do? Here I think that, within the framework of having the tendency toward less schizophrenic monetary authorities all over the world, that is, a much crisper target or objective, we adopt inflation targeting. Once you adopt inflation targeting, however, it is much simpler and almost necessary to have more flexibility in exchange rates. Here perhaps there is a distinction between countries that come into the game from a legacy of less credible financial systems and monetary policy and countries, like the industrial countries, that have had a lot of credibility. A nominal anchor does not have to be tested by actually stopping the boat.

Rather, you can ask: could I lift the anchor when I need to move the boat? As you introduce the anchor, as we did in the stabilization program in the shape of a nominal exchange rate anchor, the key question is what happens when you lift the anchor? Does it mean a collapse of stability? Or does it mean a graduation in stability that allows you to lift the anchor and go to the open sea? Indeed, once you have inflation targeting, you are much clearer in the domestic political debate about your responsibilities. You are not in charge of fixing the competitiveness of the export sector. And that's key, because time and again, monetary authorities that have not been fully independent—not in the legal sense but in the practical sense—have been put under tremendous pressure from interest groups within the industrial sector or the political sector, all of them pointing to the lack of competitiveness. Real exchange rate changes, and hence monetary policy, can affect nominal exchange rates. Ergo, it becomes the responsibility of the Central Bank to deal with competitiveness. Thus there are multiple implicit objectives, and none of them is achieved.

I think that once you are inflation targeting, this is the true anchor, because you operate through expectations. And if you operate through expectations, if you have credible inflation targeting, you can allow the exchange rate to be determined at the correct level. The responsibility for its value also rests in the market, which is where it belongs. I would say that the ability to achieve sustainable disinflation, or maintenance of low inflation, in countries with legacies like those of which we have been speaking, rests on ensuring that the Central Bank can focus on what it does best.

I notice in Domingo Cavallo's remarks something very interesting—a new twist, as far as I can see. In the world of two corners, which says that you have either completely fixed (meaning "throw away the key" and adopt foreign currency, or the equivalent thereof) or completely floating, you appear to have a symmetric choice. For Cavallo, though, what is truly the long-run state is flexibility. You must first gain entry into the Darwinian competition by having credibility acquired through long-term price stability. If it is acquired through currency purchases, so be it. However, when the purchased currency moves into a flexible rate regime, this is not a collapse but, rather, a graduation. And I think that lifting the anchor is part of the anchor strategy. If you don't have a very well defined mechanism to lift the anchor without losing credibility, you had better not start using the anchor but, instead, leave it wherever it belongs.

On capital controls, Edwards has made some remarks, talking a bit about the Chilean experience. It is no accident that the Chilean experience is always mentioned, because it failed dramatically in many, many cases. At least in Israel's case, where we tried to impose capital controls, we learned very well that "water seeps through the cracks." You really cannot have long-term capital controls.

Let me mention here the moral hazard problem. When a government is committing itself to a nominal exchange rate—that is, pegging—it enters into an implicit contract with the industrial sector. And many, many times, when we need to change the peg, we again face the industry saying, "you broke the rules of the game. We planned according to what you promised us, and now you're changing the exchange rate." Obviously, this means that if an exchange rate needs to be changed, it always will have to be a little later than when it is required; and if it is a little later, then we are back to the problems that were mentioned earlier.

The same is true for intervention. In order to succeed with intervention, you had better be able to stabilize. In order to succeed with stabilization, you had better be able to manage the quantities at hand. If indeed the environment is an open capital account, there is simply no way that you can do it successfully. I remember very well the 1998 crisis, when the appetite for investment in emerging markets declined after Russia and other problems: everyone wanted to cash in their emerging markets holdings. Suddenly, on the same day, all finance ministers and governors in practically all emerging markets felt the same mechanism: investors wanted to cash out and leave the country with the pressures of the foreign exchange market. Basically, we had three choices. One was to intervene and prevent the exchange rate changes that were actually about to occur. Another was to close the window: put in capital controls or something of that type. Third, we could allow the exchange rate to adjust, not because we loved that option, but because we had no other choice but to use monetary policy very fiercely in order to deal with the inflationary consequences of the exchange rate change. The reality was that when the exchange rate depreciated, we noticed what the inflationary consequences were likely to be. That's when we raised interest rates. That's when we ended up with this type of scenario. What was the outcome? We raised interest rates quite dramatically, and within an extremely short period of time—we are talking about weeks—the process reversed itself, and someone looking before and after could not see the difference. As a matter of fact, exactly in the period when emerging markets contemplated imposing controls, we publicly eliminated the final traces of controls, making the point that, indeed, our markets are open. Indeed, it was no accident that when money left emerging markets, it came to us. But we *were* emerging markets, and therefore we realized that the concept called "emerging markets," which is based on a color-blind investor, is also part of the past. The countries are involved in beauty contests, and selectivity is the name of the game. It is not the exchange rate regime that will carry the day in these beauty contests, but rather the ability to carry out the right economic policies.

What did we see at the end of the day? We saw that the Phillips curve can be positively sloped, that inflation is now holding solidly enough for two years in a row at the range of 1.5 percent. Growth this year is about 6 percent, and basically this is the payoff for the period of slow growth from before. The fact is, however, that the credibility of monetary policy has been enhanced very strongly. Now you can say, well, that's an esoteric objective for a monetary policymaker, to have credibility. But that's not true, because with this enhanced credibility, the credibility of the inflation-targeting strategy also has been enhanced, and thus the pass-through from exchange rates to prices disappears. In the past, countries with inflationary legacies knew that whenever the exchange rate changes by 5 percent, prices at home would change by 5 percent immediately. And because you know that will happen, the markup occurs instantaneously, and that is basically the self-defeating mechanism of "flexible exchange rates." However, in the inflation-targeting approach, the monetary authorities have the credibility that they will not allow the inflation consequences of the exchange rate to take place, because they use interest rates properly. Then there is no reason that when the exchange rate changes, one is wiped out from its real implications of inflationary changes. This is the case because the inflation will not take place, since everyone knows that it will not be allowed. Therefore, what we have noticed is that when there was a depreciation of the currency, it did not mark the start of inflation and real exchange rate changes, but, rather, it marked the start of improved competitiveness. Suddenly, in this regard, what you observe is that the disinflation process has been accompanied by enhanced rather than declining competitiveness.

Let me conclude by noting one more general statement: If the environment within which we operate is one of capital markets that are integrated, then one implication is that time passes very quickly because this mechanism enables what one anticipates will happen tomorrow to instead happen today through the capital markets. This means that the distinction between short run and long run is getting blurred; all the policy debates and justifications for short-run policies that are not sustainable in the long run cannot stand any more, because the long run is much closer than it used to be. Thus, we have stabilization policies that are not sustainable in the long run and should not be started in the short run. So, although I am not dogmatic about the notion of a "don't be in-between regime," because I realize that you cannot jump to a corner in one day, I do say that it is important to notice where are you going to gravitate, and to recognize that this is a graduation from where you are now; and if it is a graduation, then the movement is not reflecting a collapse and loss of credibility but, rather, progress and a gain in credibility.

Discussion Summary

Guillermo Ortiz began on the theme of whether floating rate regimes are feasible for emerging markets. He recalled that when Mexico began floating in 1995 it was not because the government had studied exchange rate models and decided that the optimum regime was a float. Instead, the country had completely run out of reserves and had no choice but to let the exchange rate go. At the time he felt a float was not a feasible long-term policy. In his capacity as minister for finance he wrote a blueprint for economic policy in early 1995 called the National Development Plan. This plan stated the intention to return to a more predictable exchange rate regime once enough reserves had been accumulated.

Why was the government so afraid the float would not function well? Ortiz said that they had no prior experience with floating and believed that the exchange rate would be unstable. Mexico lacked institutional prerequisites such as a futures market and the capacity to conduct an independent monetary policy. The actual experience has been much more positive than expected, however. First, futures markets have been established domestically and in Chicago, and the volatility of the exchange rate has been comparable to the experience of other floaters. Second, the rate has also changed the composition of capital flows, with 80 percent now being foreign direct investment and 20 percent portfolio investment—the reverse proportions of what Mexico had before. Third, it has allowed Mexico to grow at an average of 5.5 percent in the five years after the crisis. He said he is now "fully converted to this world of floating rates."

Ortiz then turned to the question of whether Mexico is "really floating." To provide an answer, he suggested that we look at how Mexico is conducting monetary policy. Mexico adopted inflation targeting in 1998. He said that the authorities are constantly grappling with the "leaning against the wind" problem posed by Arminio Fraga. He concluded, however, "that the real object of the Central Bank is to get inflation down," adding that in doing so "we do look at exchange rates but we don't worry too much about exchange rates."

Continuing on the theme of "fear of floating," Ortiz drew a distinction between fear of volatility and fear of misalignment. He said, "volatility is something we can live with," adding that the authorities should pursue policies that reduce volatility, not policies that suppress it. On the misalignment question, he said you must believe in the market to align a misaligned exchange rate.

Sounding a more negative note on freely floating exchange rates, *Paul Volcker* observed that in an integrated capital market the foreign exchange market responds like an asset market, and asset markets are inherently volatile. Volcker said he is not too concerned about day-to-day or month-to-month volatility, but about something that comes close to what Ortiz called misalignment. He pointed out that the major economies had "misalignments" of 50 percent running over periods of a couple of years under floating rates. Volcker asked if this is consistent with the efficient international division of labor that we learn about in the textbooks. He said that we learn about the importance of prices and comparative advantage, but when we see the exchange rate move by 50 percent over two or three years, we say, "who cares?" Whatever the impact on large economies, Volcker thinks that such volatility has a big impact on smaller economies. Close to 90 percent of transactions take place with a fixed exchange rate in large economies such the United States and Euroland. Smaller, more internationally open economies are much more exposed.

Turning to what to do about this volatility, Volcker said that if you are going to have open capital markets, the ultimate logic of an efficient international system is a single currency, but he added that he doesn't expect to see this in his lifetime. Regarding the small emerging market economies, he asked if there are intermediate approaches. He recalled Arminio Fraga's point about confusion under pegged rates, adding, "you can't be any more confused than me about the current floating regime." Addressing Guillermo Ortiz, Volcker pointed out that although the Mexican government might be happy with the floating peso, Mexican businessmen say they want him to convince the Mexican government to adopt the dollar to bring about some certainty.

Volcker finished with the stark prediction that Mexico will adopt the dollar after one more big currency crisis, adding that he is "convinced that within a decade we will have such a crisis, judging from experience." *Sebastian Edwards* said that Mexico will adopt the dollar when it becomes truly integrated with the United States, and he joked that that will not happen before the United States has at least one major league baseball team operating in Mexico. *Volcker* noted after the meeting that he had been working toward precisely that aim with the commissioner of major league baseball!

Takatoshi Ito commented on the debate going on in Asia about the appropriate exchange rate regime now that there has been a successful recovery from the crisis and foreign reserves have been built back up. He added that there is some indication that Asian economies are again pegging to the dollar. They are going back to a de facto dollar peg that many consider to have been mistaken. As an alternative, he said, "many of us" are advocating an intermediate regime for Asia, especially the basket band crawl (BBC) proposed by John Williamson. The basket idea makes sense because of Asia's diversified trade structure. The proposal is to give one-fourth weight to Japan, one-fourth to the United States, less than one-fourth to Europe, and slightly more than one-fourth to neighboring non-Japan countries. The band and crawl are needed to have the flexibility to respond to supply shocks. Ito pointed out one problem with getting such a regime established: if your neighbor is adopting a de facto dollar peg, you will want to do likewise, given the strong trade links with neighboring countries. For this reason there has to be a joint decision to adopt the basket system, Ito said.

On the issue of confusion and temptation in intermediate rate systems, Ito said that Asian countries did not have the hyperinflationary experience suffered elsewhere. Thus, even after the crisis the populations have more confidence in their central banks. Temptation can be controlled by International Monetary Fund (IMF) surveillance and peer pressures within the region. Ito concluded by saying that the details of intermediate regimes should be explored rather than dismissed out of hand.

In response to a request for clarification, Ito agreed that this proposal was for Asian countries other than Japan.

Lin See Yan addressed what he regarded as the unfair treatment of Malaysia as a pariah following its imposition of selected capital exchange controls. The Malaysian case must be viewed in the context of its critical need to maintain stable growth with equity, given the vast differences in race, culture, religion, language, occupation by race, and economic status of its diverse population. To keep racial, social, and religious tensions at bay, "the economic pie" has to grow in a sustainable fashion, he said. Malaysia has been remarkably stable following this strategy for the past thirty years. In the early months, things even looked good as the crisis persisted. The managing director of the IMF praised Malaysia's management of the economy shortly before and for months after the crisis. Once the controls were instituted, Lin complained, he was saying that Malaysia was the worst country in the world. Lin went on to describe the devastating impact of sharp exchange rate volatility, large outflows of portfolio capital, and the exceptionally deep fall in stock market prices on businesses and expectations in a small open economy such as Malaysia. Not even a reasonably well managed and well structured economy like Malaysia could withstand, within a very short period of crisis, a 40 percent devaluation of its currency and a 60 percent diminution of its stock market capitalization at a time when the region was engulfed in panic, euphoria, and contagion, without any reasonable prospect of an early recovery. He concluded by saying that the adoption of a reasonable exchange rate regime for any economy must take account of its specific circumstances, in particular the political and social mission of public policy. With hindsight, timely intervention to reestablish stability enabled Malaysia to avoid the political and social unrest experienced by the other crisis-affected nations, notably Indonesia.

Jeffrey Frankel observed that it is remarkable how the "corners hypothesis" has become conventional wisdom five years after if was first proposed following the exchange rate mechanism crisis. What is especially remarkable, he said, is that it has become so widespread without much of a theoretical justification. Various justifications have been mentioned—the impossible trinity, the danger of unhedged dollar liabilities, procrastinating on exit, and the difficulties of transparency and verifiability. However, if you look at each of these in detail, none of them can be written down in a model with the result that you want to go to either a firm-fixed or freely floating corner. Frankel added that each captures a difficult trade-off, but the trade-off does not go away when you go to a corner.

Sebastian Edwards commented on the difficulty of measuring exchange rate misalignment. He pointed out the large differences that exist between the major financial institutions'—Goldman Sachs, JPMorgan, and Deutsche Bank—estimates of misalignments in Latin American economies in early 2000. The models, he concludes, need to be improved. Regarding the debate about the corners hypothesis, he said he agrees with Frankel that it is amazing how popular it has become with essentially no model. As a profession, we have ruled out the middle because it has not worked well in the last five years, without taking a longer historical perspective. Edwards also thinks that we are being naïve about the political difficulties of going to either of the two corners. Most countries will be in the middle, and so, from a technical point of view, we must work on rules to make managed regimes less prone to crisis.

Arminio Fraga predicted that there will be gravitation to the extremes. Based on what he has heard about the Asian experience, he concludes that it takes a lot of virtue to run an intermediate regime. It can be done, he said, but it is risky. He prefers systems that are less demanding of virtue.

Financial Policies

1. Frederic S. Mishkin
2. Andrew Crockett
3. Michael P. Dooley
4. Montek S. Ahluwalia

1. Frederic S. Mishkin

Financial Policies and the Prevention of Financial Crises in Emerging Market Countries

2.1.1 Introduction

In recent years, financial crises have been a common occurrence in emerging market (and transition) countries, with devastating consequences for their economies. For example, the financial crises that struck Mexico in 1994 and the East Asian countries in 1997 led to a fall in the growth rate of gross domestic product (GDP) on the order of ten percentage points. The financial crises in Russia in 1998 and Ecuador in 1999 have had similar negative effects on real output. These crises led not only to sharp increases in poverty, but to political instability as well.

Given the harmful effects and increased frequency of financial crises in emerging market countries in recent years, an issue that is now high on the agenda of policymakers throughout the world is the prevention of these crises. Specifically, what financial policies can help make crises less likely?

This paper examines this question by first developing a framework for understanding what a financial crisis is in emerging market countries and the dynamic process through which these crises occur. It then uses this

Any views expressed in this paper are those of the author only and not those of Columbia University or the National Bureau of Economic Research.

framework to examine what particular financial policies may help to prevent financial crises.

2.1.2   What is a Financial Crisis?

A financial system performs the essential function of channeling funds to those individuals or firms that have productive investment opportunities. To do this well, participants in financial markets must be able to make accurate judgments about which investment opportunities are more or less creditworthy. Thus, a financial system must confront problems of asymmetric information, in which one party to a financial contract has much less accurate information than the other party. For example, borrowers who take out loans usually have better information about the potential returns and risk associated with the investment projects they plan to undertake than lenders do. Asymmetric information leads to two basic problems in the financial system (and elsewhere): adverse selection and moral hazard.

Adverse selection occurs before the financial transaction takes place, when potential bad credit risks are the ones who most actively seek out a loan. For example, those who want to take on big risks are likely to be the most eager to take out a loan, even at a high rate of interest, because they are less concerned with paying the loan back. Thus, the lender must be concerned that the parties who are the most likely to produce an undesirable or adverse outcome are most likely to be selected as borrowers. Lenders may thus steer away from making loans at high interest rates because they know that they are not fully informed about the quality of borrowers, and they fear that someone willing to borrow at a high interest rate is more likely to be a low-quality borrower who is less likely to repay the loan. Lenders will try to tackle the problem of asymmetric information by screening out good from bad credit risks. However, this process is inevitably imperfect, and fear of adverse selection will lead lenders to reduce the quantity of loans they might otherwise make.

Moral hazard occurs after the transaction takes place. It occurs because a borrower has incentives to invest in projects with high risk in which the borrower does well if the project succeeds, but the lender bears most of the loss if the project fails. A borrower also has incentives to misallocate funds for personal use, to shirk and not work very hard, and to undertake investment in unprofitable projects that serve only to increase personal power or stature. Thus, a lender is subjected to the hazard that the borrower has incentives to engage in activities that are undesirable from the lender's point of view: that is, activities that make it less likely that the loan will be paid back. Lenders do often impose restrictions (restrictive covenants) on borrowers so that borrowers do not engage in behavior that makes it less likely that they can pay back the loan. However, such restrictions are costly to enforce and monitor and inevitably somewhat limited in their reach. The potential conflict of interest between the borrower and lender stemming from moral hazard again implies that many lenders will lend less than they otherwise would, so that lending and investment will be at suboptimal levels.

The asymmetric information problems described above provide a definition of what a financial crisis is:

> A financial crisis is a disruption to financial markets in which adverse selection and moral hazard problems become much worse, so that financial markets are unable to channel funds efficiently to those who have the most productive investment opportunities.

A financial crisis thus results in the inability of financial markets to function efficiently, which leads to a sharp contraction in economic activity.

2.1.3   Factors Promoting Financial Crises

To flesh out how a financial crisis comes about and causes a decline in economic activity, we need to examine the factors that promote financial crises and then go on to look at how these factors interact dynamically to produce financial crises.

There are four types of factors that can lead to increases in asymmetric information problems and thus to a financial crisis: (a) deterioration of financial-sector balance sheets, (b) increases in interest rates, (c) increases in uncertainty, and (d) deterioration of nonfinancial balance sheets due to changes in asset prices.

Deterioration of Financial-Sector Balance Sheets

The literature on asymmetric information and financial structure (see Gertler 1988 and Bernanke, Gertler, and Gilchrist 1998 for excellent surveys), explains why financial intermediaries (commercial banks, thrift institutions, finance companies, insurance companies, mutual funds, and pension funds) play such an important role in the financial system. They have both the ability and the economic incentive to address asymmetric information problems. For example, banks have an obvious ability to collect information at the time they consider making a loan, and this ability is only increased when banks engage in long-term customer relationships and line-of-credit arrangements. In addition, their ability to scrutinize the checking account balances of their borrowers provides banks with an additional advantage in monitoring the borrowers' behavior. Banks also have advantages in reducing moral hazard because, as demonstrated by Diamond (1984), they can engage in lower-cost monitoring than individuals, and because, as pointed out by Stiglitz and Weiss (1983), they have advantages in preventing risk-taking by borrowers since they can use the threat of cutting off lending in the future to improve a borrower's behavior. Banks' natural advantages in collecting information and reducing moral hazard explain why banks have such an important role in financial markets throughout the world. Indeed, the greater difficulty of acquiring information on private firms in emerging market countries explains why banks play a more important role in the financial systems in emerging market countries than they do in industrialized countries (Rojas-Suarez and Weisbrod 1994).

Banks (and other financial intermediaries) have an incentive to collect and produce such information because they make private loans that are not traded, which reduces free-rider problems. In markets for other securities, like stocks, if some investors acquire information that screens out which stocks are undervalued and then they buy these securities, other investors who have not paid to discover this information may be able to buy right along with the well-informed investors. If enough free-riding investors can do this and the price is bid up, then investors who have collected information will earn less on the securities they purchase and will thus have less incentive to collect this information. Once investors recognize that other investors in securities can monitor and enforce restrictive covenants, they will also want to free-ride on the other investors' monitoring and enforcement. As a result, not enough resources will be devoted to screening, monitoring, and enforcement. However, because the loans of banks are private, other investors cannot buy the loans directly, and free-riding on banks' restrictive covenants is much trickier than simply following the buying patterns of others. As a result, investors are less able to free-ride off of financial institutions making private loans like banks, and since banks receive the benefits of screening and monitoring they have an incentive to carry it out.

The special importance of banks and other financial intermediaries in the financial system implies that if their ability to lend is impaired, overall lending will decline and the economy will contract. A deterioration in the balance sheets of financial intermediaries indeed hinders their ability to lend and is thus a key factor promoting financial crises.

If banks (and other financial intermediaries making loans) suffer a deterioration in their balance sheets, and so have a substantial contraction in their capital, they have two choices: either they can cut back on their lending, or they can try to raise new capital. However, when these institutions experience a deterioration in their balance sheets, it is very hard for them to raise new capital at a reasonable cost. Thus, the typical response of financial institutions with weakened balance sheets is a contraction in their lending, which slows economic activity. Recent research suggests that weak balance sheets led to a capital crunch that hindered growth in the U.S. economy during the early 1990s (e.g., see Bernanke and Lown 1991; Berger and Udell 1994; Hancock, Laing, and Wilcox 1995; Peek and Rosengren 1995; and the symposium published in Federal Reserve Bank of New York 1993).

If the deterioration in bank balance sheets is severe enough, it can even lead to bank panics, in which there are multiple, simultaneous failures of banking institutions. Indeed, in the absence of a government safety net, there is some risk that contagion can spread from one bank failure to another, causing even healthy banks to fail. The source of the contagion is again asymmetric information. In a panic, depositors, fearing the safety of their deposits and not knowing the quality of the banks' loan portfolios, withdraw their deposits from the banking system, causing a contraction in loans and a multiple contraction in deposits, which then causes other banks to fail. In turn, the failure of a bank means the loss of the information relationships in which that bank participated, and thus a direct loss in the amount of financial intermediation that can be done by the banking sector. The outcome is an even sharper decline in lending to facilitate productive investments, with an additional resulting contraction in economic activity.

Increases in Interest Rates

Asymmetric information and the resulting adverse selection problem can lead to "credit rationing," in which some borrowers are denied loans even when they are willing to pay a higher interest rate (Stiglitz and Weiss 1981). This occurs because as interest rates rise, prudent borrowers are more likely to decide that it would be unwise to borrow, whereas borrowers with the riskiest investment projects are often those who are willing to pay the highest interest rates, since if the high-risk investment succeeds, they will be the main beneficiaries. In this setting, a higher interest rate leads to even greater adverse selection; that is, the higher interest rate increases the likelihood that the lender is lending to a bad credit risk. Thus, higher interest rates can be one factor that helps precipitate financial instability, because lenders recognize that higher interest rates mean a dilution in the quality of potential borrowers, and lenders are likely to react by taking a step back from their business of financial intermediation and limiting the number of loans they make.

Increases in interest rates can also have a negative effect on bank balance sheets. The traditional banking business involves "borrowing short and lending long"; that is, taking deposits that can be withdrawn on demand (or certificates of deposit that can be withdrawn in a matter of months) and making loans that will be repaid over periods of years or sometimes even decades. In short, the assets of a bank typically have longer duration than its liabilities. Thus, a rise in interest rates directly causes a decline in net worth, because in present value terms, the interest rate rise lowers the value of assets, with their longer duration, more than it raises the value of liabilities, with their shorter duration.

Increases in Uncertainty

A dramatic increase in uncertainty in financial markets makes it harder for lenders to screen out good credit risks from bad. The lessened ability of lenders to solve adverse selection and moral hazard problems renders them less willing to lend, leading to a decline in lending, investment, and aggregate activity. This increase in uncertainty can stem from a failure of a prominent financial or nonfinancial institution or from a recession, but, of even more importance in emerging market countries, it can result from uncertainty about the future direction of government policies.

Deterioration of Nonfinancial Balance Sheets

The state of the balance sheet of nonfinancial firms is the most critical factor for the severity of asymmetric information problems in the financial system. If there is a widespread deterioration of balance sheets among borrowers, it worsens both adverse selection and moral hazard problems in financial markets, thus promoting financial instability. This problem can arise in a variety of ways.

For example, lenders often use collateral as an important way of addressing asymmetric information problems. Collateral reduces the consequences of adverse selection or moral hazard because it reduces the lender's losses in the case of a default. If a borrower defaults on a loan, the lender can sell the collateral to make up for at least some of the losses on the loan. However, if asset prices in an economy fall, and the value of collateral falls as well, then the problems of asymmetric information suddenly become more severe.

Net worth can perform a similar role to collateral. If a firm has high net worth, then even if it defaults on its debt payments, the lender can take title to the firm's net worth, sell it off, and use the proceeds to recoup some of the losses from the loan. High net worth also directly decreases the incentives for borrowers to commit moral hazard, because borrowers now have more at stake, and thus more to lose, if they default on their loans. The importance of net worth explains why stock market crashes can cause financial instability. A sharp decline in the stock market reduces the market valuation of a firm's net worth and thus can increase adverse selection and moral hazard problems in financial markets (Bernanke and Gertler 1989; Calomiris and Hubbard 1990). Because the stock market decline that reduces net worth increases incentives for borrowers to engage in moral hazard, and because lenders are now less protected against the consequences of adverse selection because the value of net assets is worth less, lending decreases and economic activity declines.

Increases in interest rates not only have a direct effect on increasing adverse selection problems, as described earlier, but they may also promote financial instability through both firms' and households' balance sheets. A rise in interest rates will increase households' and firms' interest payments, decrease cash flow, and thus cause a deterioration in their balance sheets, as pointed out in Bernanke and Gertler's (1995) excellent survey of the credit view of monetary transmission. As a result, adverse selection and moral hazard problems become more severe for potential lenders to these firms and households, leading to a decline in lending and economic activity.

There is thus an additional reason that sharp increases in interest rates can be an important factor leading to financial instability.

Unexpected changes in the rate of inflation can also affect balance sheets of borrowers. In economies in which inflation has been moderate for a long period of time, debt contracts with long duration have interest payments fixed in nominal terms for a substantial period of time. When inflation turns out to be less than anticipated, which can occur either because of an unanticipated disinflation, as occurred in the United States in the early 1980s, or by an outright deflation, as has occurred in Japan more recently, the value of firms' liabilities in real terms rises, and its net worth in real terms declines. The reduction in net worth then increases the adverse selection and moral hazard problems facing lenders and reduces investment and economic activity.

In emerging market economies, a decline in unanticipated inflation does not have the unfavorable direct effect on firms' balance sheets that it has in industrialized countries. Debt contracts are of very short duration in many emerging market countries, and because the terms of debt contracts are continually repriced to reflect expectations of inflation, unexpected inflation has little real effect. Thus, one mechanism that has played a role in industrialized countries to promote financial instability has no role in many emerging market countries.

On the other hand, emerging market economies face at least one factor affecting balance sheets that can be extremely important in precipitating financial instability that is not important in most industrialized countries: unanticipated exchange rate depreciation or devaluation. Because of uncertainty about the future value of the domestic currency, many nonfinancial firms, banks, and governments in emerging market countries find it much easier to issue debt if the debt is denominated in foreign currencies. With debt contracts denominated in foreign currency, when there is an unanticipated depreciation or devaluation of the domestic currency, the debt burden of domestic firms increases. Since assets are typically denominated in domestic currency and so do not increase in value, there is a resulting decline in net worth. This deterioration in balance sheets then increases adverse selection and moral hazard problems, which leads to financial instability and a sharp decline in investment and economic activity.

2.1.4   Dynamics of Financial Crises

Financial crises in emerging markets undergo several stages. There is an initial stage during which a deterioration in financial and nonfinancial balance sheets occurs and which promotes the second stage, a currency crisis. The third stage is a further deterioration of financial and nonfinancial balance sheets that occurs as a result of the currency crisis, and this stage is the one that tips the economy over into a full-fledged financial crisis, with its devastating consequences.

Initial Stage: Run-Up to the Currency Crisis

The first stage leading up to a financial crisis in emerging market countries has typically been a financial liberalization, which involved lifting restrictions on both interest rate ceilings and the type of lending allowed and often privatization of the financial system. As a result, lending increased dramatically, fed by inflows of international capital.

Of course, the problem was not that lending expanded, but rather that it expanded so rapidly that excessive risk-taking was the result, which led to an increase in nonperforming loans. For example, in Mexico and the East Asian crisis countries, the estimated percentage of loans that were nonperforming increased to over 10 percent before the financial crisis struck (Mishkin 1996b; Goldstein 1998; and Corsetti, Pesenti, and Roubini 1998), and these estimates were probably grossly understated. This excessive risk-taking occurred for two reasons. First, banks and other financial institutions lacked the well-trained loan officers, risk-assessment systems, and other management expertise to evaluate and respond to risk appropriately. This problem was made even more severe by the rapid credit growth in a lending boom, which stretched the resources of the bank supervisors, who also failed to monitor these new loans appropriately. Second, emerging market countries such as Mexico, Ecuador, the East Asian crisis countries, and Russia were notorious for weak financial regulation and supervision. (In contrast, the noncrisis countries in East Asia—Singapore, Hong Kong, and Taiwan—had very strong prudential supervision.) When financial liberalization yielded new opportunities to take on risk, these weak regulatory/supervisory systems could not limit the moral hazard created by the government safety net, and excessive risk-taking was one result. Even as the government failed in supervising financial institutions, it was effectively offering an implicit safety net that these institutions would not be allowed to go broke, thus reassuring depositors and foreign lenders that they did not need to monitor these institutions, since there were likely to be government bailouts to protect them.

It is important to note that banks were not the only source of excessive risk-taking in the financial systems of crisis countries. In Thailand, finance companies, which were essentially unregulated, were at the forefront of real estate lending, and they were the first to get into substantial difficulties before the 1997 crisis (Ito 1998). In Korea, merchant banks, which were primarily owned by the *chaebol* (conglomerates) and were again virtually unregulated, expanded their lending far more rapidly than the commercial banks and were extremely active in borrowing abroad in foreign currency (Hahm and Mishkin 2000). Banks in these countries also expanded their lending and engaged in excessive risk-taking as a result of financial liberalization and weak prudential supervision, but the fact that they received more scrutiny did put some restraints on their behavior.

A dangerous dynamic emerged. Once financial liberalization was adopted, foreign capital flew into banks and other financial intermediaries in these emerging market countries because they paid high yields in order to attract funds to rapidly increase their lending, and because such investments were viewed as likely to be protected by a government safety net, either from the government of the emerging market country or from international agencies such as the International Monetary Fund (IMF). The capital inflow problem was further stimulated by government policies of keeping exchange rates pegged to the dollar, which probably gave foreign investors a sense of lower risk. In Mexico and East Asia, capital inflows averaged over 5 percent of GDP in the three years leading up to the crises. The private capital inflows led to increases in the banking sector, especially in the emerging market countries in the Asia-Pacific region (Folkerts-Landau et al. 1995). The capital inflows fueled a lending boom, which led to excessive risk-taking on the part of banks, which in turn led to huge loan losses and a subsequent deterioration of banks' and other financial institutions' balance sheets.

The inflow of foreign capital, particularly short-term capital, was often actively encouraged by governments. For example, the Korean government allowed *chaebol* to convert finance companies they owned into merchant banks, which were allowed to borrow freely abroad as long as the debt was short-term. A similar phenomenon occurred in Thailand, which allowed finance companies to borrow from foreigners. The result was substantial increases in foreign indebtedness relative to the country's holding of international reserves: Mexico, Thailand, Korea, and Indonesia all ended up with ratios of short-term foreign debt relative to reserves exceeding 1.5. The high degree of illiquidity in these countries suggests that they were vulnerable to a financial crisis (Radelet and Sachs 1998).

This deterioration in financial-sector balance sheets, by itself, might have been sufficient to drive these countries into financial and economic crises. As explained earlier, a deterioration in the balance sheets of financial firms can lead them, at a minimum, to restrict their lending or can even lead to a full-scale banking crisis, which forces many banks into insolvency, thereby nearly removing the ability of the banking sector to make loans. The resulting credit crunch can stagger an economy.

Another consequence of financial liberalization was a huge increase in leverage in the corporate sector. For example, in Korea, debt relative to equity for the corporate sector as a whole shot up to 350 percent before the crisis, and it was over 400 percent for the *chaebol*. The increase in corporate leverage was also very dramatic in Indonesia, where corporations often borrowed directly abroad by issuing bonds, rather than borrowing from banks. This increase in corporate leverage increased the vulnerability to a financial crisis, because negative shocks would now be far more likely to tip corporations into financial distress.

Stock market declines and increases in uncertainty were additional factors precipitating the full-blown crises in Mexico, Thailand, and South Korea. (The stock market declines in Malaysia, Indonesia, and the Philippines occurred simultaneously with the onset of the crisis.) The Mexican economy was hit by political shocks in 1994 that created uncertainty, specifically the assassination of Luis Donaldo Colosio, the ruling party's presidential candidate, and an uprising in the southern state of Chiapas. By the middle of December 1994, stock prices on the Bolsa (stock exchange) had fallen nearly 20 percent from their September 1994 peak. In January 1997, a major Korean *chaebol,* Hanbo Steel, collapsed; it was the first bankruptcy of a *chaebol* in a decade. Shortly thereafter, Sammi Steel and Kia Motors also declared bankruptcy. In Thailand, Samprosong Land, a major real estate developer, defaulted on its foreign debt in early February 1997, and financial institutions that had lent heavily in the real estate market began to encounter serious difficulties, requiring over $8 billion of loans from the Thai central bank to prop them up. Finally, in June, the failure of a major Thai finance company, Finance One, imposed substantial losses on both domestic and foreign creditors. These events increased general uncertainty in the financial markets of Thailand and South Korea, and both experienced substantial declines in their securities markets. From peak values in early 1996, Korean stock prices fell by 25 percent and Thai stock prices fell by 50 percent.

As we have seen, an increase in uncertainty and a decrease in net worth as a result of a stock market decline increases asymmetric information problems. It became harder to screen out good from bad borrowers, and the decline in net worth decreased the value of firms' collateral and increased their incentives to make risky investments, because there is less equity to lose if the investments are unsuccessful. The increase in uncertainty and stock market declines that occurred before the crisis, along with the deterioration in banks' balance sheets, worsened adverse selection and moral hazard problems and made the economies ripe for a serious financial crisis.

Second Stage: Currency Crisis

The deterioration of financial- and nonfinancial-sector balance sheets is a key factor leading to the second stage, a currency crisis. A weak banking system makes it less likely that the central bank will take the steps to defend a domestic currency, because if it raises rates, bank balance sheets are likely to deteriorate further. In addition, raising rates sharply increases the cost of financing for highly leveraged corporations, which typically borrow short-term, making them more likely to experience financial distress. Once investors recognize that a central bank is less likely to take the steps to successfully defend its currency, expected profits from selling the currency will rise, and the incentives to attach the currency have risen. Also, the recognition that the financial sector may collapse and require a bailout that would produce substantial fiscal deficits in the future also makes it more likely that the currency will depreciate (Burnside, Eichenbaum, and Rebelo 1998).

The weakened state of the financial and nonfinancial balance sheets, along with the high degree of illiquidity in Mexico and East Asian countries before the crisis, then set the stage for their currency crises. With these vulnerabilities, speculative attacks on the currency could have been triggered by a variety of factors. In the Mexican case, the attacks came in the wake of political instability in 1994, such as the assassination of political candidates and an uprising in Chiapas. Even though the Mexican central bank intervened in the foreign exchange market and raised interest rates sharply, it was unable to stem the attack and was forced to devalue the peso on 20 December 1994. In Thailand, the attacks followed unsuccessful attempts of the government to shore up the financial system, culminating in the failure of Finance One. Eventually, the inability of the central bank to defend the currency because the required measures would do too much harm to the weakened financial sector meant that the attacks could not be resisted. The outcome was therefore a collapse of the Thai baht in early July 1997. Subsequent speculative attacks on other Asian currencies led to devaluations and floats of the Philippine peso and Malaysian ringgit in mid-July, the Indonesian rupiah in mid-August, and the Korean won in October. By early 1998, the currencies of Thailand, the Philippines, Malaysia, and Korea had fallen by over 30 percent, with the Indonesian rupiah falling by over 75 percent.

Third Stage: Currency Crisis to Full-Fledged Financial Crisis

Once a full-blown speculative attack occurs and causes a currency depreciation, the institutional structure of debt markets in emerging market countries—the short duration of debt contracts and their denomination in foreign currencies—now interacts with the currency devaluation to propel the economies into full-fledged financial crises. These features of debt contracts generate three mechanisms through which the currency crises increase asymmetric information problems in credit markets, thereby causing a financial crisis to occur.

The first mechanism involves the direct effect of currency devaluation on the balance sheets of firms. As discussed earlier, the devaluations in Mexico and East Asia increased the debt burden of domestic firms that were denominated in foreign currencies. This mechanism was particularly strong in Indonesia, the worst hit of all the crisis countries, which saw the value of its currency decline by over 75 percent, thus increasing the rupiah value of foreign-denominated debts by a factor of four. Even a healthy firm is likely to be driven into insolvency by such a shock if it had a significant amount of foreign-denominated debt.

A second mechanism linking the financial crisis and the currency crisis arises because the devaluation of the domestic currency led to further deterioration in the balance sheets of the financial sector, provoking a large-scale banking crisis. In Mexico and the east Asian countries, banks and many other financial institutions had many liabilities denominated in foreign currency, which increase sharply in value when a depreciation occurs. On the other hand, the problems of firms and households meant that they were unable to pay off their debts, also resulting in loan losses on the asset side of financial institutions' balance sheets. The result was that banks' and other financial institutions' balance sheets were squeezed from both the assets and liabilities side. Moreover, many of these institutions' foreign currency–denominated debt was very short-term, so that the sharp increase in the value of this debt led to liquidity problems because this debt needed to be paid back quickly. The result of the further deterioration in banks' and other financial institutions' balance sheets and their weakened capital base is that they cut back lending. In the case of Indonesia, these forces were severe enough to cause a banking panic in which numerous banks were forced to go out of business.

The third mechanism linking currency crises with financial crises in emerging market countries is that the devaluation can lead to higher inflation. The central bank in an emerging market country may have little credibility as an inflation fighter. Thus, a sharp depreciation of the currency after a speculative attack leads to immediate upward pressure on import prices, which can lead to a dramatic rise in both actual and expected inflation. This is exactly what happened in Mexico and Indonesia, where inflation surged to over a 50 percent annual rate after the currency crisis. (Thailand, Malaysia, and South Korea avoided a large rise in inflation, which partially explains their better performance relative to Indonesia.) The rise in expected inflation after the currency crises in Mexico and Indonesia led to a sharp rise in nominal interest rates, which, given the short duration of debt, led to huge increases in interest payments by firms. The outcome was a weakening of firms' cash flow position and a further weakening of their balance sheets, which then increased adverse selection and moral hazard problems in credit market.

All three of these mechanisms indicate that the currency crisis caused a sharp deterioration in both financial and nonfinancial firms' balance sheets in the crisis countries, which then translated to a contraction in lending and a severe economic downturn. Financial markets were then no longer able to channel funds to those with productive investment opportunities, which led to devastating effects on the economies of these countries.

Note that the 1999 Brazilian crisis was not a financial crisis of the type described here. Brazil experienced a classic balance-of-payments crisis of the type described in Krugman (1979), in which concerns about unsustainable fiscal policy led to a currency crisis. The Brazilian banking system was actually quite healthy before the crisis because it had undergone substantial reform after a banking crisis in 1994–96 (see Caprio and Klingbiel 1999). Furthermore, Brazilian banks were adequately hedged against exchange rate risk before the devaluation in 1999 (Adams, Mathieson, and Schinasi 1999). As a result, the devaluation did not trigger a financial crisis, although the high interest rates after the devaluation did lead to a recession. The fact that Brazil did not experience a financial crisis explains why Brazil fared so much better after its devaluation than did Mexico or the East Asian crisis countries.

Russia's financial crisis in 1998 also had a strong fiscal component but was actually a symptom of widespread breakdown of structural reform and institution-building efforts (see IMF 1998). When the debt moratorium/restructuring and ruble devaluation were announced on 17 August, Russian banks were subject to substantial losses on $27 billion face value of government securities and increased liabilities from their foreign debt. The collapse of the banking system and the negative effects on balance sheets on the nonfinancial sector from the collapse of the ruble then led to a financial crisis along the lines outlined above.

2.1.5 Financial Policies to Prevent Financial Crises

Now that we have developed a framework for understanding why financial crises occur, we can look at what financial policies can help prevent these crises from occurring. We examine twelve basic areas of financial reform: (a) prudential supervision, (b) accounting and disclosure requirements, (c) legal and judicial systems, (d) market-based discipline, (e) entry of foreign banks, (f) capital controls, (g) reduction of the role of state-owned financial institutions, (h) restrictions on foreign-denominated debt, (i) elimination of too-big-to-fail policies in the corporate sector, (j) sequencing financial liberalization, (k) monetary policy and price stability, and (l) exchange rate regimes and foreign exchange reserves.

Prudential Supervision

As we have seen, banks play a particularly important role in the financial systems of emerging market countries, and problems in the banking sector have been an important factor promoting financial crises in recent years. Deterioration in banks' balance sheets, which can lead to banking crises, increase asymmetric information problems, which bring on financial crises. Furthermore, problems in the banking sector make a foreign exchange crisis more likely, which, by harming nonfinancial balance sheets, leads to a full-blown financial crisis. Because banking panics have such potentially harmful effects, governments almost always provide an extensive safety net for the banking system to prevent banking panics. The downside of the safety net is that it increases moral hazard incentives for excessive risk-taking on the part of the banks, which makes it more likely that financial crises will occur. To prevent financial crises, governments therefore need to pay particular attention to creating and sustaining a strong bank regulatory/supervisory system to reduce excessive risk-taking in their financial systems.

Because the government safety net in emerging market countries has invariably been extended to other financial intermediaries—for example, the Thai central bank provided liquidity assistance to insolvent finance companies—these other financial institutions also have strong incentives to engage in excessive risk-taking. Indeed, deterioration in the balance sheets of these financial institutions played an important role in the financial crises in East Asia. Effective prudential supervision of these nonbank financial institutions is also critical to promote financial stability.

Encouraging a strong regulatory/supervisory system for the financial system takes seven basic forms.

Prompt Corrective Action

Quick action by prudential supervisors to stop undesirable activities by financial institutions and, even more importantly, to close down institutions that do not have sufficient capital is critical if financial crises are to be avoided. Regulatory forbearance that leaves insolvent institutions operating is disastrous because it dramatically increases moral hazard incentives to take on excessive risk, because an operating but insolvent institution has almost nothing to lose by taking on colossal risks. If they get lucky and the risky investments pay off, they get out of insolvency. On the other hand, if, as is likely, the risky investments don't pay off, insolvent institutions' losses will mount, weakening the financial system further and leading to higher taxpayer bailouts in the future. Indeed, this is exactly what occurred in the savings and loan (S&L) industry in the United States when insolvent S&Ls were allowed to operate during the 1980s and was a feature of the situation in Mexico, East Asia, and Japan in the 1990s.

An important way to ensure that bank supervisors do not engage in regulatory forbearance is through implementation of prompt corrective action provisions that require supervisors to intervene earlier and more vigorously when a financial institution gets into trouble. Prompt corrective action is crucial to preventing problems in the financial sector because it creates incentives for institutions not to take on too much risk in the first place, knowing that if they do so, they are more likely to be punished.

The outstanding example of prompt corrective action is the provision in the Federal Deposit Insurance Corporation Improvement Act (FDICIA) legislation implemented in the United States in 1991. Banks in the United States are classified into five groups based on bank capital. Group 1, classified as "well capitalized," consists of banks that significantly exceed minimum capital requirements and are allowed privileges such as insurance on brokered deposits and the ability to do some securities underwriting. Banks in group 2, classified as "adequately capitalized," meet minimum capital requirements and are not subject to corrective actions but are not allowed the privileges of the well-capitalized banks. Banks in group 3, "undercapitalized," fail to meet risk-based capital and leverage ratio requirements. Banks in groups 4 and 5 are "significantly undercapitalized" and "critically undercapitalized," respectively, and are not allowed to pay interest on their deposits at rates that are higher than average. Regulators still retain a fair amount of discretion in their actions to deal with undercapitalized banks and can choose from a smorgasbord of actions, such as restricting asset growth, requiring the election of a new board of directors, prohibiting acceptance of deposits from correspondent depository institutions, prohibiting capital distributions from any controlling bank holding company, and terminating activities that pose excessive risk or performing divestiture of nonbank subsidiaries that pose excessive risk.[1] On the other hand, FDICIA mandates that regulators must require undercapitalized banks to submit an acceptable capital restoration plan within forty-five days and implement the plan. In addition, the regulatory agencies must take steps to close down critically undercapitalized banks (whose tangible equity capital is less than 2 percent of assets) by putting them in receivership or conservatorship within ninety days, unless the appropriate agency and the Federal Deposit Insurance Corporation (FDIC) concur that other action would better achieve the purpose of prompt corrective action. If the bank continues to be critically undercapitalized, it must be placed in receivership, unless specific statutory requirements are met.

A key element of making prompt corrective action work is that bank supervisors have sufficient government funds to close down institutions when they become insolvent. It is very common that politicians and regulatory authorities engage in wishful thinking when their banking systems are in trouble, hoping that a large injection of public funds into the banking system will be unnecessary.[2] The result is regulatory forbearance, with insolvent institutions allowed to keep operating, which ends up producing disastrous consequences. The Japanese authorities have engaged in exactly this kind of behavior, but this was also a feature of the American response to the S&L crisis up until 1989.

Not only must weak institutions be closed down, but it must be done in the right way: funds must not be supplied to weak or insolvent banking institutions to keep them afloat. To do so will just be throwing good taxpayer

---

1. See Sprong (1994) for a more detailed discussion of the prompt corrective action provisions in FDICIA.

2. In addition, banking institutions often lobby vigorously to prevent the allocation of public funds to close down insolvent institutions because this allows them to stay in business and they hope, get out of the hole. This is exactly what happened in the United States in the 1980s, as is described in Mishkin (2001).

money after bad. In the long run, injecting public funds into weak banks does not deliver a restoration of the balance sheets of the banking system because these weak banks continue to be weak and have strong moral hazard incentives to take on big risks at the taxpayers' expense. This is the lesson learned from the U.S. experience in the 1980s as well as other countries more recently. The way to recapitalize the banking system is to close down all insolvent and weak institutions and sell off their assets to healthy institutions with public funds used to make the assets whole. If this is not possible, a public corporation, like the Resolution Trust Corporation (RTC) in the United States or KAMCO in Korea, can be created that will have the responsibility to sell off the assets of these closed banks as promptly as possible, so that the assets can be quickly put to productive uses by the private sector.

To prevent financial crises, it is also imperative that stockholders, managers, and large uninsured creditors be punished when financial institutions are closed and public funds are injected into the financial system. Protecting managers, stockholders, and large uninsured creditors from the consequences of excessive risk-taking increases the moral hazard problem immensely and is thus highly dangerous, although it is common.

Focus on Risk Management

The traditional approach to bank supervision has focused on the quality of the bank's balance sheet at a point in time and whether the bank complies with capital requirements. Although the traditional focus is important for reducing excessive risk-taking by banks, it may no longer be adequate. First is the point that capital may be extremely hard to measure. Furthermore, in today's world, financial innovation has produced new markets and instruments that make it easy for financial institutions and their employees to make huge bets quickly. In this new financial environment, an institution that is quite healthy at a particular point in time can be driven into insolvency extremely rapidly from trading losses, as has been forcefully demonstrated by the failure of Barings in 1995, which, although initially well capitalized, was brought down by a rogue trader in a matter of months. Thus an examination that focuses only on a bank's or other financial institution's balance sheet position at a point in time may not be effective in indicating whether a bank will in fact be taking on excessive risk in the near future.

For example, bank examiners in the United States are now placing far greater emphasis on evaluating the soundness of bank's management processes with regard to controlling risk. This shift in thinking was reflected in a new focus on risk management in the Federal Reserve System's 1993 guidance to examiners on trading and derivatives activities. The focus was expanded and formalized in the Trading Activities Manual issued early in 1994, which provided bank examiners with tools to evaluate risk management systems. In late 1995, the Federal Reserve and the comptroller of the currency announced that they would be assessing risk management processes at the banks they supervise. Now bank examiners give a separate risk management rating from 1 to 5, which feeds into the overall management rating as part of the CAMELS system (the acronym is based on the six areas assessed: capital adequacy, asset quality, management, earnings, and sensitivity to market risk). Four elements of sound risk management are assessed to come up with the risk management rating: (a) the quality of oversight provided by the board of directors and senior management, (b) the adequacy of policies and limits for all activities that present significant risks, (c) the quality of the risk measurement and monitoring systems, and (d) the adequacy of internal controls to prevent fraud or unauthorized activities on the part of employees. Bank examiners get to see what best practice for risk management is like in the banks they examine, and they can then make sure that best practice spreads throughout the banking industry by giving poor rankings to banks that are not up to speed.

Bank supervision in countries outside the United States would also help promote a safer and sounder financial sector by adopting similar measures to ensure that risk management procedures in their banks are equal to the best practice in financial institutions elsewhere in the world.

Limiting Too-Big-To-Fail Policies

Because the failure of a very large financial institution makes it more likely that a major, systemic financial disruption will occur, supervisors are naturally reluctant to allow a big financial institution to fail and cause losses to depositors. The result is that most countries either explicitly or implicitly have a too-big-to-fail policy, in which all depositors at a big bank, both insured and uninsured, are fully protected if the bank fails. The problem with the too-big-to-fail policy is that it reduces market discipline on large financial institutions and thus increases their moral hazard incentives to take on excessive risk. This problem is even more severe in emerging market countries because their financial systems are typically smaller than those of industrialized countries and so tend to be dominated by fewer institutions. Furthermore, the connections with the government and political power of large financial institutions are often much greater in emerging market countries, thus making it more likely that they will be bailed out if they experience difficulties. Indeed, not only have uninsured depositors been protected in many emerging market countries when large institutions have been subject to failure, but other creditors and even equity holders have been also.

Limiting moral hazard that arises from financial institutions that are too big or too politically connected to fail is a critical problem for prudential supervision in emerging market countries. Thus, in order to reduce increased incentives to take on excessive risk by large institutions, prudential supervisors need to scrutinize them even more rigorously than smaller ones and, at a minimum, must impose losses on shareholders and managers when these institutions are insolvent. However, supervisors still have to face the quandary of not wanting to allow a failure of a large financial institution to destabilize the financial system, while keeping the moral hazard problem created by too-big-to-fail institutions under control.

One proposal, outlined in Mishkin (1999), is for the supervisory agencies to announce that there is a strong presumption that when there is a bank failure, uninsured depositors would not be fully protected unless this is the cheapest way to resolve the failure. It is important to recognize that although large banking institutions may be too big to liquidate, they can be closed, with losses imposed on uninsured creditors. Indeed, this is exactly what FDICIA suggests should be done by specifying that, except under very unusual circumstances when the a bank failure poses "serious adverse effects on economic conditions or financial stability," a least-cost resolution procedure will be used to close down the bank. Ambiguity is created about the use of this systemic-risk exception to the least-cost resolution rule because to invoke it requires a two-thirds majority of both the board of governors of the Federal Reserve System and the directors of the FDIC, as well as the approval of the secretary of the treasury.

An important concern is that the systemic-risk exception to least-cost resolution will always be invoked when the failing bank is large enough because the government and central bank will be afraid to impose costs on depositors and other creditors when a potential financial crisis is looming. Thus, too-big-to-fail policies will still be alive, with all the negative consequences for moral hazard risk-taking by the largest institutions. One way to cope with this problem is for the authorities to announce that although they are concerned about systemic risk possibilities, there will be a strong presumption that the *first* large bank to fail will not be treated as too big to fail and that costs will be imposed on uninsured depositors and creditors when the bank is closed. Rather than bailing out the uninsured creditors at the initial large bank that fails, the authorities will stand ready to extend the safety net to the rest of the banking system if they perceive that there is a serious systemic risk problem.

The advantage of announcing such a stance is that uninsured depositors and creditors now have to worry that if this bank is the first one to fail, they will not be bailed out. As a result, these depositors and creditors will now have an incentive to withdraw their funds if they worry about the soundness of the bank, even if it is very large, and this will alter the incentives of the bank away from taking on too much risk. Clearly, moral hazard still remains in the system, because the authorities stand ready to extend the safety net to the rest of the system after the initial large institution fails if its failure creates the potential for a banking crisis. However, the extent of moral hazard is greatly reduced by the use of this form of constructive ambiguity. Furthermore, the cost of this remaining moral hazard must be balanced against the benefits of preventing a banking crisis if the initial bank failure is likely to snowball into a systemic crisis.

Adequate Resources and Statutory Authority for
Prudential Regulators/Supervisors

In many emerging market countries, prudential supervisors are not given sufficient resources or statutory authority (the ability to issue cease and desist orders and to close down insolvent banks) to do their jobs effectively. For example, in many emerging market countries, including even middle-income countries such as Argentina and the Philippines, supervisors are subject to lawsuits for their actions and can be held personally liable. Their salaries are typically quite low and are much smaller relative to private-sector salaries than in industrialized countries. Without sufficient resources and incentives, not surprisingly, supervisors will not monitor banks sufficiently in order to keep them from engaging in inappropriately risky activities, to have the appropriate management expertise and controls to manage risk, or to have sufficient capital so that moral hazard incentives to take on excessive risk are kept in check. Indeed, sufficient monitoring of banking institutions, not surprisingly, has been absent in many emerging market and transition countries (Mexico, Ecuador, and East Asia being recent examples), and this has also been a very serious problem in industrialized countries. The resistance to providing the S&L supervisory agencies with adequate resources to hire sufficient bank examiners by the U.S. Congress was a key factor in making the S&L crisis in the United States in the 1980s much worse. The inadequacy of bank supervision in Japan and the problems it has caused are well known, with the lack of resources for bank supervision being exemplified by the fact that the number of bank examiners in Japan is on the order of 400, in contrast to around 7,000 in the United States.

Giving supervisors sufficient resources and statutory authority to do their jobs is thus crucial to promoting a safe and sound financial system that is resistant to financial crises. Ruth Krivoy (2000), an ex-supervisor from Venezuela during its banking crisis, has put the point very nicely by saying that supervisors in emerging market countries must be given respect. If they are paid poorly, the likelihood that they can be bribed either directly or through promises of high-paying jobs by the institutions they supervise will be very high. Making them personally liable for taking supervisory action also makes it less likely that they will take the appropriate actions. Furthermore, if they do not have sufficient resources, particularly in information technology, to monitor financial institutions, then they will be unable to spot excessive risk-taking.

Independence of Regulatory/Supervisory Agencies

Because prompt corrective action is so important, the bank regulatory/ supervisory agency requires sufficient independence from the political process so that it is not encouraged to sweep problems under the rug and engage in regulatory forbearance. One way to ensure against regulatory forbearance is to give the bank supervisory role to a politically independent central bank. This has desirable elements, as pointed out in Mishkin (1991), but some central banks might not want to have the supervisory task thrust upon them because they worry that it might increase the likelihood that the central bank would be politicized, thereby impinging on the independence of the central bank. Alternatively, bank supervisory activities could be housed in a bank regulatory authority that is independent of the government.

Supervisory agencies will also not be sufficiently independent if they are starved for resources. If supervisory agencies have to come hat in hand to the government for resources or funds to close down insolvent institutions, they will be more subject to political pressure to engage in regulatory forbearance. Supervisors must have adequate financial resources at their fingertips to prevent this from occurring.

Accountability of Supervisors

An important impediment to successful supervision of the financial system is that the relationship between taxpayers on the one hand and the supervisors on the other creates a particular type of moral hazard problem, the principal-agent problem. The principal-agent problem occurs because the agents (the supervisors) do not have the same incentives as the principal (the taxpayer they ultimately work for) and so act in their own interest rather than in the interest of the principal.

To act in the taxpayer's interest, regulators have several tasks, as we have seen. They must set restrictions on holding assets that are too risky, impose sufficiently high capital requirements, and close down insolvent institutions. However, because of the principal-agent problem, supervisors have incentives to do the opposite and engage in regulatory forbearance. One important incentive for supervisors that explains this phenomenon is their desire to escape blame for poor performance by their agency. By loosening capital requirements and pursuing regulatory forbearance, supervisors can hide the problem of an insolvent bank and hope that the situation will improve, a behavior that Kane (1989) characterizes as "bureaucratic gambling." Another important incentive for supervisors is that they may want to protect their careers by acceding to pressures from the people who strongly influence their careers, the politicians.

Supervisors must be accountable if they engage in regulatory forbearance in order to improve incentives for them to do their job properly. For example, as pointed out in Mishkin (1997), an important but very often overlooked part of FDICIA that has helped make this legislation effective is that there is a mandatory report that the supervisory agencies must produce if the bank failure imposes costs on the FDIC. The resulting report is made available to any member of Congress and to the general public upon request, and the general accounting office must do an annual review of these reports. Opening up the actions of bank supervisors to public scrutiny makes regulatory forbearance less attractive to them, thereby reducing the principal-agent problem. In addition, subjecting the actions of bank supervisors to public scrutiny reduces the incentives of politicians to lean on supervisors to relax their supervision of banks.

In order for supervisors to do their jobs properly, they must also be subject to criminal prosecution if they are caught taking bribes and must also be subject to censure and penalties if they take jobs with institutions that they have supervised recently. This entails a change in culture for supervisors in many emerging market countries, where some are allowed to get too close to the institutions they supervise.

Restrictions on Connected Lending

A particular problem in the financial sector, particularly in emerging market countries, is connected lending, lending to the financial institutions' owners or managers or their business associates. Financial institutions clearly have less incentive to monitor loans to their owners or managers, thus increasing the moral hazard incentives for the borrowers to take on excessive risk, thereby exposing the institution to potential loan losses. In addition, connected lending in which large loans are made to one party can result in a lack of diversification for the institution, thus increasing the risk exposure of the bank.

Prudential supervision to restrict connected lending is clearly necessary to reduce banks' risk exposure. It can take several forms. One is disclosure of the amount of connected lending. Indeed, one prominent feature of New Zealand's disclosure requirements is that the amount of lending to connected persons is mandatory. Another is limits on the amount of connected lending as a share of bank capital. Indeed, although New Zealand has gotten rid of many of the traditional regulatory guidelines, it still has chosen to have prudential limits on the amount of connected lending. Most countries have regulations limiting connected lending, and many emerging market countries have stricter limits than in industrialized countries. However, a key problem in emerging market and transition countries is that connected lending limits are often not enforced effectively. Folkerts-Landau et al. (1995) have pointed out that bank examiners in Asia were often unable to assess the exposure of banks to connected lending because of the use of dummy accounts or the lack of authority for the examiners to trace where the funds are used. Strong efforts to increase disclosure and increased authority for bank examiners to examine the books of the banks to root out connected lending are crucial if this source of moral hazard is to be kept under control.

Having commercial businesses owning large shares of financial institutions increases the incentives for connected lending. A prominent feature of the Korean financial crisis was that the *chaebol* were allowed large ownership stakes in merchant banks, which were virtually unsupervised. The merchant banks were then used as a conduit for greatly increasing the *chaebol*'s leverage by supplying them with large amounts of funds by borrowing abroad and then lending the proceeds to them. The excessive risk-taking by the merchant banks eventually resulted in insolvency for most of them and was an important factor that led to the Korean financial crisis (Hahm and Mishkin 2000). Preventing commercial enterprises from owning financial institutions is crucial for promoting financial stability in emerging market countries.

Accounting Standards and Disclosure Requirements

Accounting standards and disclosure requirements for financial institutions are often particularly lacking in emerging market and transition countries but also in a number of industrialized countries (Japan being the most prominent example). Without the appropriate information, both markets and supervisors will not be able adequately to monitor financial institutions to deter excessive risk-taking.[3] One prominent example is that accounting and supervisory conventions in many countries allow banks to make nonperforming loans look good by lending additional money to the troubled borrower, who uses the proceeds to make the payments on the nonperforming loan, thus keeping it current, a practice known as "evergreening." The result is that nonperforming loans are significantly understated, which makes it harder for the markets to discipline financial institutions or for supervisors to decide when banks are insolvent and need to be closed down. Many countries also do not require the reporting of key financial data by individual financial institutions, including their consolidated financial exposure, which makes it hard to sort out healthy from unhealthy institutions. Implementing proper accounting standards and disclosure requirements is an important first step in promoting a healthy financial system.[4]

An interesting example of an attempt to beef up disclosure requirements and raise their prominence in prudential supervision is the system put in place in New Zealand in 1996 (see Mortlock 1996 and Nicholl 1996). New Zealand scrapped its previous system of regular bank examinations and replaced it with one based on disclosure requirements that uses the market to police the behavior of the banks. Every bank in New Zealand must supply a comprehensive quarterly financial statement that provides, among other

3. The importance of disclosure is illustrated in Garber and Lall (1996), which suggests that off-balance-sheet and offshore derivatives contracts were used by Mexican banks before the Tequila crisis to get around regulations that were intended to prevent them from taking on foreign exchange risk, and this played an important role in the Mexican crisis.
4. See Goldstein and Turner (1996) and Goldstein (1997) for a further discussion of what steps need to be taken to beef up accounting standards and disclosure requirements.

things, information on the quality of its assets, capital adequacy, lending activities, profitability, and its ratings from private credit-rating agencies and whether it has a credit rating. These financial statements must be audited twice a year, and not only must they be provided to the central bank, but they must also be made public, with a two-page summary posted in all bank branches. In addition, bank directors are required to validate these statements and state publicly that their bank's risk management systems are adequate and being properly implemented. A most unusual feature of this system is that bank directors face unlimited liability if they are found to have made false or misleading statements.

The New Zealand example illustrates that disclosure requirements can be strengthened appreciably. However, suggesting that sole reliance on disclosure requirements to police the banking system is a workable model for other countries is going too far. Depositors are unlikely to have the sophistication to understand fully the information provided and thus may not impose the necessary discipline on the banks. Furthermore, unlimited liability for directors might discourage top people from taking these positions, thereby weakening the management of the banks. Although disclosure requirements might be sufficient in New Zealand because almost all New Zealand banks are foreign-owned, so that bank supervision has been in effect outsourced to the supervisors of the foreign banks that own the New Zealand banks, it is unlikely to work in countries where most of the banking system is domestically owned.

Legal and Judicial Systems

The legal and judicial systems are very important for promoting the efficient functioning of the financial system, and the inadequacies of legal systems in many countries are a serious problem for financial markets. If property rights are unclear or hard to enforce, the process of financial intermediation can be severely hampered. Collateral can be an effective mechanism to reduce adverse selection and moral hazard problems in credit markets because it reduces the lender's losses in the case of a default. However, in many developing countries, the legal system prevents the use of certain assets as collateral or makes attaching collateral a costly and time-consuming process, thereby reducing the effectiveness of collateral to solve asymmetric information problems (Rojas-Suarez and Weisbrod 1996). Similarly, bankruptcy procedures in developing countries are frequently very cumbersome (or even nonexistent), resulting in lengthy delays in resolving conflicting claims. Resolution of bankruptcies in which the books of insolvent firms are opened up and assets are redistributed can be viewed as a process to decrease asymmetric information in the marketplace. Furthermore, slow resolution of bankruptcies can delay recovery from a financial crisis, because only when bankruptcies have been resolved is there enough information in the financial system to restore it to healthy operation.

Encouraging Market-Based Discipline

There are two problems with relying on supervisors to control risk-taking by financial institutions. First, financial institutions have incentives to keep information away from bank examiners so that they are not restricted in their activities. Thus, even if supervisors are conscientious, they may not be able to stop institutions from engaging in risky activities. Second, because of the principal-agent problem, supervisors may engage in regulatory forbearance and not do their jobs properly.

An answer to these problems is to have the market discipline financial institutions if they are taking on too much risk. We have already mentioned that disclosure requirements can help provide information to the markets that may help them monitor financial institutions and keep them from taking on too much risk. Two additional steps may help increase market discipline. One is to require that financial institutions have credit ratings. Part of the bonds, auditing, supervision, information, and credit ratings (BASIC) supervisory system implemented in Argentina in December 1996 is the requirement that every bank have an annual rating provided by a rating agency registered with the central bank.[5] Institutions with more than $50 million in assets are required to have ratings from two rating agencies. As part of this scheme, the Argentine central bank is responsible for performing an after-the-fact review of the credit ratings to check if the rating agencies are doing a reasonable job. As of January 1998, these credit ratings must be published on billboards in the banks and must also appear on all deposit certificates and all other publications related to obtaining funds from the public. As part of New Zealand's disclosure requirements, all banks must prominently display their credit ratings on their long-term senior unsecured liabilities payable in New Zealand or, alternatively, indicate if they do not have a credit rating. Clearly, the lack of a credit rating or a poor credit rating is expected to cause depositors and other creditors to be reluctant to put their funds in the bank, thus giving the bank incentive to reduce its risk-taking and boost its credit rating. This has a higher likelihood of working in Argentina and New Zealand because both countries do not have government deposit insurance.

Another way to impose market discipline on banks is to require that they issue subordinated debt (uninsured debt that is junior to insured deposits, but senior to equity). Subordinated debt, particularly if it has a ceiling on the spread between its interest rate and that on government securities, can be an effective disciplining device. If the bank is exposed to too much risk, it is unlikely to be able to sell its subordinated debt. Thus, compliance with the subordinated debt requirement will be a direct way for the market to

5. See Banco Central de la Republica Argentina (1997) and Calomiris (1998) for a description of the Argentine BASIC system.

force banks to limit their risk exposure. Alternatively, deposit insurance premiums could be charged according to the interest rate on the subordinated debt. Not only would the issuance of subordinated debt directly help reduce incentives for banks to engage in risky activities, but it could also provide supplemental information to bank examiners that could help them in their supervisory activities. In addition, information about whether banks are successful in issuing subordinated debt and the interest rate on this debt can help the public evaluate whether supervisors are being sufficiently tough on a particular banking institution, thus reducing the scope of the principal-agent problem.

Argentina has implemented a subordinated debt requirement in its BASIC program, although without an interest rate cap, which took effect on January 1998. As reported in Calomiris (1998), initially about half of the banks have been able to comply with this requirement. Interestingly, as expected, it is the weakest banks that have had trouble issuing subordinated debt. Furthermore, banks that compiled with the requirement had lower deposit rates and larger growth in deposits. Thus, the subordinated debt requirement looks like it has had the intended effect of promoting discipline on the banks (Calomiris and Powell 2001).

Entry of Foreign Banks

Many countries have restrictions on the entry of foreign banks. The entry of foreign banks should be seen not as a threat but as an opportunity to strengthen the banking system. In all but a few large countries, domestic banks are unable to diversify because their lending is concentrated in the home country. In contrast, foreign banks have more diversified portfolios and also usually have access to sources of funds from all over the world through their parent company. This diversification means that these foreign banks are exposed to less risk and are less affected by negative shocks to the home country's economy. Because many emerging market and transition economies are more volatile than industrialized countries, having a large foreign component to the banking sector is especially valuable, because it helps insulate the banking system from domestic shocks. Encouraging entry of foreign banks is thus likely to lead to a banking and financial system that is substantially less fragile and far less prone to crisis.

Another reason for encouraging the entry of foreign banks is that this can encourage adoption of best practice in the banking industry. Foreign banks come with expertise in areas like risk management. As mentioned earlier, when bank examiners in a country see better practices in risk management, they can spread these practices throughout their country's banking system by downgrading banks that do not adopt these practices. Having foreign banks demonstrate the latest risk management techniques can thus lead to improved control of risk in the home country's banking system. Clearly, there are also benefits from the increased competition that foreign bank entry brings to the banking industry in the home country. The entry of foreign banks will also lead to improved management techniques and a more efficient banking system.

Encouraging the entry of foreign banks also makes it more likely that uninsured depositors and other creditors of banks will not be bailed out. Governments are far less likely to bail out the banking sector when it gets into trouble if many of the banks are foreign-owned because it will be politically unpopular. Thus uninsured depositors and other creditors will have greater incentives to monitor the banks and pull out funds if these institutions take on too much risk. The resulting increase in market discipline is therefore likely to encourage more prudent behavior by banking institutions.

Capital Controls

In the aftermath of the recent financial crises in Mexico and East Asia, in which the crisis countries experienced large capital inflows before the crisis and large capital outflows after the crisis, much attention has been focused on whether international capital movements are a major source of financial instability. The asymmetric information analysis of the crisis suggests that international capital movements can have an important role in producing financial instability, but as we have seen this is because the presence of a government safety net with inadequate supervision of banking institutions encourages capital inflows, which lead to a lending boom and excessive risk-taking on the part of banks.[6] Consistent with this view, works by Gavin and Hausman (1996) and Kaminsky and Reinhart (1999) do find that lending booms are a predictor of banking crises, yet it is by no means clear that capital inflows will produce a lending boom that causes a deterioration in bank balance sheets. Indeed, Kaminsky and Reinhart find that financial liberalization, rather than balance-of-payments developments inflows, appears to be an important predictor of banking crises.

Capital outflows have also been pointed to as a source of foreign exchange crises, which, as we have seen, can promote financial instability in emerging market countries. In this view, foreigners pull their capital out of country, and the resulting capital outflow is what forces a country to devalue its currency. However, as pointed out earlier, a key factor leading to foreign exchange crises are problems in the financial sector that lead to the speculative attack and capital outflows. With this view, the capital outflow associated with the foreign exchange crisis is a symptom of underlying fundamental problems rather than a cause of the currency crisis. The consensus from many empirical studies (see the excellent survey in Kaminsky, Lizondo, and Reinhart [1997]) provides support for this view because capital flow or current account measures do not have predictive power in forecast-

6. See Calvo, Leiderman, and Reinhart (1994) for a model of this process.

ing foreign exchange crises, whereas a deeper fundamental such as problems in the banking sector helps predict currency crises.

The analysis here therefore does not provide a case for capital controls such as the exchange controls that have recently been adopted in Malaysia. Exchange controls are like throwing out the baby with the bathwater. Capital controls have the undesirable feature that they may block funds from entering a country that will be used for productive investment opportunities. Although these controls may limit the fuel supplied to lending booms through capital flows, over time they produce substantial distortions and misallocation of resources as households and businesses try to get around them. Indeed, there are serious doubts as to whether capital controls can be effective in today's environment, in which trade is open and there are many financial instruments that make it easier to get around these controls.

On the other hand, there is a strong case to improve bank regulation and supervision so that capital inflows are less likely to produce a lending boom and excessive risk-taking by banking institutions. For example, banks might be restricted in how fast their borrowing could grow, and this might have the impact of substantially limiting capital inflows. These prudential controls could be thought of as a form of capital controls, but they are quite different from the typical exchange controls. They focus on the sources of financial fragility, rather than the symptoms, and supervisory controls of this type can enhance the efficiency of the financial system rather than hampering it.

Reduction of the Role of State-Owned Financial Institutions

A feature of many countries' financial systems, particularly in emerging market and transition countries, is government interventions to direct credit either to themselves or to favored sectors or individuals in the economy. Governments do this either by setting interest rates at artificially low levels for certain types of loans, by creating development finance institutions to make specific types of loans, by setting up state-owned banks that can provide funds to favored entities, or by directing private institutions to lend to certain entities. Private institutions clearly have an incentive to solve adverse selection and moral hazard problems and lend to borrowers who have productive investment opportunities. Governments have less incentive to do so because they are not driven by the profit motive, so their directed credit programs or state-owned banks are less likely to channel funds to those borrowers who will help produce high growth of the economy. This type of government intervention in the credit markets is therefore likely to result in less efficient investment and slower growth. Curtailing this government activity is therefore important for promoting economic growth (Caprio and Honohan 2000).

The absence of a profit motive also means that state-owned banks are less likely to manage risk properly and be efficient. Thus it is not surprising that state-owned banks usually end up having larger loan loss ratios than private institutions, and countries with the highest share of state-owned banks, on average, are also the ones with a higher percentage of nonperforming loans and higher operating costs (Goldstein and Turner 1996; Caprio and Honohan 2000). Thus, the presence of state-owned banks can substantially weaken the banking system. The inefficiency of state-owned banks and their higher loan losses strongly argue for privatization of the banking sector. However, even privatization must be managed properly or it can lead to disaster. If purchasers of banks are those who are likely to engage in excessive risk-taking or even fraud, the possibility that banking problems will arise in the future is high. Also, if purchasers of banks are allowed to put very little of their own capital into the bank, they may also have strong incentives to engage in risky activities at the depositors' and taxpayers' expense. These potential downsides of privatization do not indicate that privatization should be avoided, but rather suggest that the chartering or licensing process be sufficiently stringent to screen out bad owners, making sure that bank ownership goes to individuals who will improve bank performance over the previous government managers.

Restrictions on Foreign-Denominated Debt

The asymmetric information view of financial crises indicates that a debt structure with substantial foreign-denominated debt, which is typical in many emerging market countries, makes the financial system more fragile. Currency crises and devaluations do trigger full-fledged financial crises in countries with foreign-denominated debt, whereas this is not the case for countries whose debt is denominated in domestic currency.

The presence of foreign-denominated debt also makes it far more difficult for a country to recover from a financial crisis. Industrialized countries with debt denominated in domestic currency can promote recovery by pursuing expansionary monetary policy by injecting liquidity (reserves) into the financial system. Injecting reserves, either through open-market operations or by lending to the banking sector, causes the money supply to increase, which in turn leads to a higher price level. Given that debt contracts are denominated in domestic currency and many are often of fairly long duration, the reflation of the economy causes the debt burden of households and firms to fall, thereby increasing their net worth. As outlined earlier, higher net worth then leads to reduced adverse selection and moral hazard problems in financial markets, undoing the increase in adverse selection and moral hazard problems induced by the financial crisis. In addition, injecting liquidity into the economy raises asset prices such as land and stock market values, which also causes an improvement in net worth and a reduction in adverse selection and moral hazard problems. Also, as discussed in Mishkin (1996a), expansionary monetary policy promotes economic recovery through other mechanisms involving the stock market and the foreign exchange market.

A second method for a central bank to promote recovery from a financial crisis is to pursue the so-called lender-of-last-resort role, in which the central bank stands ready to lend freely during a financial crisis. By restoring liquidity to the financial sector, the lender of last resort can help shore up the balance sheets of financial firms, thereby preventing a systemic shock from spreading and bringing down the financial system. There are many instances of successful lender-of-last-resort operations in industrialized countries (see, e.g., Mishkin 1991); the Federal Reserve's intervention on the day after the 19 October 1987 stock market crash is one example. Indeed, what is striking about this episode is that the extremely quick intervention of the Federal Reserve not only resulted in a negligible impact on the economy of the stock market crash, but also meant that the amount of liquidity that the Federal Reserve needed to supply to the economy was not very large (see Mishkin 1991).

However, if the financial system has a large amount of foreign-denominated debt it may be far more difficult for the central bank to promote recovery from a financial crisis. With this debt structure, a central bank can no longer use expansionary monetary policy to promote recovery from a financial crisis. Suppose that the policy prescription for countries with little foreign-denominated debt—that is, expansionary monetary policy and reflation of the economy—were followed in an emerging market country with a large amount of foreign-denominated debt. In this case the expansionary monetary policy is likely to cause the domestic currency to depreciate sharply. As we have seen before, the depreciation of the domestic currency leads to a deterioration in firms' and banks' balance sheets because much of their debt is denominated in foreign currency, thus raising the burden of indebtedness and lowering banks' and firms' net worth.

The net result of an expansionary monetary policy in an emerging market country with a large amount of foreign-denominated debt is that it hurts the balance sheets of households, firms, and banks. Thus, expansionary monetary policy has the opposite result to that found in industrialized countries after a financial crisis: it causes a deterioration in balance sheets and therefore amplifies adverse selection and moral hazard problems in financial markets caused by a financial crisis, rather than ameliorating them, as in the industrialized country case.

For similar reasons, lender-of-last-resort activities by a central bank in an emerging market country with substantial foreign-denominated debt may not be as successful as in an industrialized country. Central bank lending to the financial system in the wake of a financial crisis that expands domestic credit might lead to a substantial depreciation of the domestic currency, with the result that balance sheets will deteriorate, making recovery from the financial crisis less likely. The use of the lender-of-last-resort role by a central bank is therefore much trickier in countries with a large amount of foreign-denominated debt because central bank lending is now a two-edged sword.

The above arguments suggest that the economy would be far less prone to financial crises and could recover far more easily if the issuance of foreign-denominated debt was discouraged. Because much foreign-denominated debt is intermediated through the banking system, regulations to restrict both bank lending and borrowing in foreign currencies could greatly enhance financial stability. Similarly, restrictions on corporate borrowing in foreign currency or tax policies to discourage foreign-currency borrowing could help make the economy better able to withstand a currency depreciation without undergoing a financial crisis. Krueger (2000) has also suggested that restrictions should be placed on financial institutions in industrialized countries to limit lending to emerging market countries using industrialized-country currencies.

Elimination of Too-Big-To-Fail in the Corporate Sector

We have already discussed why a too-big-to-fail policy leads to increased risk-taking by financial institutions. The same incentives clearly apply to corporations if they are considered to be too big to fail (or too politically influential) by the government. Lenders, knowing that they are unlikely to be subjected to losses if the corporation gets into trouble, will not monitor the corporation and withdraw funds if it is taking on excessive risk. In many emerging market countries, governments have propped up large and politically connected corporations when they suffer financial distress, and this has been a source of increased risk-taking by these companies, especially when they face difficult times. For example, as pointed out in Hahm and Mishkin (2000), the Korean government was perceived to have a too-big-to-fail policy for the *chaebol*, whose profitability dropped in the 1990s. Given the resulting lack of market discipline, they proceeded to try to grow out of their problems by borrowing, frequently in foreign currency, and dramatically increasing their leverage. This increase in risk-taking then was a key factor generating the financial crisis in Korea.

To contain incentives for the corporate sector to increase leverage and take on too much risk that leaves them extremely vulnerable to adverse shocks, it is imperative that too-big-to-fail policies be eliminated. This implies a greater separation between the corporate sector and the government, something that also requires a change in business culture in many emerging market countries.

Sequencing Financial Liberalization

Deregulation and liberalization of the financial system have swept through almost all countries in recent years. Although deregulation and liberalization are highly desirable objectives, the analysis of financial crises in this paper indicates that if this process is not managed properly, it can be disastrous. If the proper bank regulatory/supervisory structure, accounting and disclosure requirements, restrictions on connected lending, and well-functioning legal and judicial systems are not in place when liberalization comes, the appropriate constraints on risk-taking behavior will be far too weak. The result will be that bad loans are likely, with potentially disastrous consequences for bank balance sheets at some point in the future.

In addition, before liberalization occurs, banks may not have the expertise to make loans wisely, so opening them up to new lending opportunities may also lead to poor quality of the loan portfolio. We have also seen that financial deregulation and liberalization often lead to a lending boom, because of both increased opportunities for bank lending and financial deepening, in which more funds flow into the banking system. Although financial deepening is a positive development for the economy in the long run, in the short run the lending boom may outstrip the available information resources in the financial system, helping to promote a financial collapse in the future.

The dangers in financial deregulation and liberalization do not imply that countries would be better off by not pursuing a liberalization strategy. To the contrary, financial liberalization is critical to the efficient functioning of financial markets so that they can channel funds to those with the most productive investment opportunities. Getting funds to those with the most productive investment opportunities is especially critical to emerging market countries because these investments can have especially high returns, thereby stimulating rapid economic growth. However, proper sequencing of financial deregulation and liberalization is critical to its success. It is important that policymakers put in place the proper institutional structure before liberalizing their financial systems, especially if there are no restrictions on financial institutions' seeking funds abroad or issuing foreign-denominated debt. Before financial markets are fully liberalized, it is crucial that the precepts outlined above be implemented: provision of sufficient resources and statutory authority to bank supervisors, adoption of prompt corrective action provisions, an appropriate focus on risk management, independence of bank regulators/supervisors from short-run political pressure, increased accountability of bank supervisors, limitations on too-big-to-fail policies, adoption of adequate accounting standards and disclosure requirements, sufficient restrictions on connected lending, improvements in the legal and judicial systems, encouragement of market-based discipline, and encouragement of entry of foreign banks.

Because the above measures are not easy to install quickly and because of the stresses that rapid expansion of the financial sector puts on both managerial and supervisory resources, restricting the growth of credit when financial liberalization is put into place makes a lot of sense. This can take the form of putting upper limits on ratios of loans to value, or, for consumer credit, setting maximum repayment periods and minimum down payment percentages. Banks could also be restricted in how fast certain types of their loan portfolios are allowed to grow. In addition, at the beginning of the lib-

eralization process, restrictions on foreign-denominated debt and prudential controls that might limit capital inflows may be necessary to reduce the
vulnerability of the financial system. As the appropriate infrastructure is
put into place, these restrictions can be reduced. The bottom line is that, although eventually a full financial liberalization is a worthy goal, to avoid financial crises financial liberalization needs to proceed at a measured pace,
with some restrictions imposed along the way.

Monetary Policy and Price Stability

It is also important to recognize that, although it is only indirectly a financial policy, monetary policy can play an important role in promoting financial stability. Price stability is a worthy goal in its own right. Not only do
public opinion surveys indicate that the public is very hostile to inflation,
but there is also mounting evidence from econometric studies that inflation
is harmful to the economy.[7]

The asymmetric information analysis of financial crises provides additional reasons why price stability is so important. As was mentioned earlier,
when countries have a past history of high inflation, debt contracts are often denominated in foreign currencies. As we have seen, this feature of debt
contracts makes the financial system more fragile because currency depreciation can trigger a financial crisis. Achieving price stability is a necessary
condition for having a sound currency, and with a sound currency, it is far
easier for banks, nonfinancial firms, and the government to raise capital
with debt denominated in domestic currency. Thus, another method for reducing an economy's dependence on foreign-denominated debt and en-
hancing financial stability is the successful pursuit of price stability.

Furthermore, central banks that have successfully pursued price stability
have sufficient credibility that expansionary monetary policy or a lender-of-
last-resort operation in the face of a financial crisis is less likely to result in
a rise in inflation expectations and a sharp depreciation of the currency that
would harm balance sheets. Thus countries that have successfully pursued
price stability have an enhanced ability to use monetary policy tools to promote recovery from a financial crisis.

Exchange Rate Regimes and Foreign Exchange Reserves

Although we have seen that the pursuit of price stability can enhance financial stability and is thus desirable, some methods of pursuing price stability can unfortunately promote financial instability. One commonly used
method to achieve price stability is to peg the value of currency to that of a
large, low-inflation country. In some cases, this strategy involves pegging

---

7. Inflation, particularly at high levels, is found to be negatively associated with growth. At
lower levels, inflation is found to lower the level of economic activity, although not necessarily
the growth rate. See the survey in Anderson and Gruen (1995) and Fischer (1993), one of the
most cited papers in this literature.

the exchange rate at a fixed value to that of the other country's currency so that its inflation rate will eventually gravitate to that of the other country. In other cases, the strategy involves a crawling peg or target in which one country's currency is allowed to depreciate at a steady rate against that of another country so that its inflation rate can be higher than that of the country to which it is pegged.

Although adhering to a fixed or pegged exchange rate regime can be a successful strategy for controlling inflation, the analysis of financial crises in this paper illustrates how dangerous this strategy can be for an emerging market country with a large amount of foreign-denominated debt. Under a pegged exchange rate regime, when a successful speculative attack occurs, the decline in the value of the domestic currency is usually much larger, more rapid, and more unanticipated than when a depreciation occurs under a floating exchange rate regime. For example, during the Mexican crisis of 1994–95, the value of the peso fell by half in only a few months time, whereas in the recent Southeast Asian crisis, the worst-hit country, Indonesia, saw its currency decline to less than one-quarter of its precrisis value, also in a very short period of time. The damage to balance sheets after these devaluations was extremely severe. In Mexico, the net debtor position of business enterprises increased several times from before the devaluation in December 1994 until March 1995, whereas in Indonesia the greater than fourfold increase in the value of foreign debt arising from the currency collapse made it very difficult for Indonesian firms with appreciable foreign debt to remain solvent. The deterioration of nonfinancial firms' balance sheets leads to a deterioration in bank balance sheets because borrowers from the banks are now less likely to be able to pay off their loans. The result of this collapse in balance sheets was sharp economic contractions. In Mexico, real GDP growth in the second and third quarters of 1995 fell to rates around –10 percent, whereas Indonesia experienced an even worse rate of decline, with GDP falling by close to 15 percent in 1998, and has an economy still in shambles.

Another potential danger from an exchange rate peg is that, by providing a more stable value of the currency, it might lower risk for foreign investors and thus encourage capital inflows. Although these capital inflows might be channeled into productive investments and thus stimulate growth, they might promote excessive lending, manifested by a lending boom, because domestic financial intermediaries such as banks play a key role in intermediating these capital inflows (Calvo, Leiderman, and Reinhart 1994). Indeed, Folkerts-Landau et al. (1995) found that emerging market countries in the Asia-Pacific region with large net private capital inflows also experienced large increases in their banking sectors. Furthermore, if the bank supervisory process is weak, as it often is in emerging market and transition countries, so that the government safety net for banking institutions creates incentives for them to take on risk, the likelihood that a capital inflow will produce a lending boom is that much greater. With inadequate bank supervision, the likely outcome of a lending boom is substantial loan losses, a deterioration of bank balance sheets, and a possible financial crisis.[8]

A flexible exchange rate regime has the advantage that movements in the exchange rate are much less nonlinear than in a pegged exchange rate regime. Indeed, the daily fluctuations in the exchange rate in a flexible exchange rate regime have the advantage of making clear to private firms, banks, and governments that there is substantial risk involved in issuing liabilities denominated in foreign currencies. Furthermore, a depreciation of the exchange rate may provide an early warning signal to policymakers that their policies may have to be adjusted in order to limit the potential for a financial crisis.

The conclusion is that a pegged exchange rate regime may increase financial instability in emerging market countries. However, this conclusion does not indicate that fixing or pegging an exchange rate to control inflation is always inappropriate. Indeed, countries with a past history of poor inflation performance may find that only with a very strong commitment mechanism to an exchange rate peg (as in a currency board or full dollarization) can inflation be controlled (Mishkin 1998; Mishkin and Savastano 2001). However, the analysis does suggest that countries using this strategy to control inflation must actively pursue policies that will promote a healthy banking system. Furthermore, if a country has an institutional structure of a fragile banking system and substantial debt denominated in foreign currencies, using an exchange rate peg, particularly one with a weak commitment mechanism, to control inflation can be a very dangerous strategy indeed.[9] This is one reason that countries, like Korea, that in the past year have de facto pegged their exchange rate by allowing it to fluctuate only within very narrow bounds may be leaving themselves more exposed to future financial crises than they realize.

Another feature of recent currency and financial crises is that countries with low amounts of international reserves relative to short-term foreign liabilities seemed to be more vulnerable to crises. This has led some researchers (e.g., Radelet and Sachs 1998) to advocate increased holdings of international reserves to insulate countries from financial crises. Indeed, many emerging market countries have taken this recommendation to heart by accumulating large amounts of reserves after their financial crises. For example, Korea currently has accumulated international reserves near the $100 billion level. Although the accumulation of large amounts of interna-

---

8. Gavin and Hausman (1996) and Kaminsky and Reinhart (1999) do find that lending booms are a predictor of banking crises, yet it is less clear that capital inflows will produce a lending boom that causes a deterioration in bank balance sheets. Kaminsky and Reinhart (1999), for example, find that financial liberalization appears to be a more important predictor of banking crises than balance-of-payments developments inflows.

9. See Obstfeld and Rogoff (1995) for additional arguments as to why pegged exchange rate regimes may be undesirable.

tional reserves may make emerging market countries less vulnerable to currency crises, it is unlikely to insulate them from a financial crisis if the financial sector is sufficiently weakened. A large accumulation of international reserves has the potential to lull an emerging market country into complacency about taking the steps to ensure a safe and sound financial system and thus could have a hidden danger.

2.1.6 Concluding Remarks

The bad news is that in recent years we have seen a growing number of banking and financial crises in emerging market countries, with great costs to their economies. The good news, however, is that we now have a much better understanding of why banking and financial crises occur in emerging market countries and so have a better idea of how these crises can be prevented. This paper has outlined a set of financial policies that can help make financial crises less likely. If the political will to adopt these policies in emerging market countries grows, then we should see healthier financial systems in these countries in the future, with substantial gains both from higher economic growth and smaller economic fluctuations.

References

Adams, Charles, Donald J. Mathieson, and Gary Schinasi. 1999. *International capital markets: Developments, prospects, and key policy issues.* Washington, D.C.: International Monetary Fund.

Anderson, P., and David Gruen. 1995. Macroeconomic policies and growth. In *Productivity and growth*, ed. Palle Anderson, Jacqui Dwyer, and David Gruen, 279–319. Sydney: Reserve Bank of Australia.

Banco Central de la Republica Argentina. 1997. Main features of the regulatory framework of the Argentine financial system. Mimeograph, April.

Berger, Allen N., and Gregory Udell. 1994. Do risk-based capital requirements allocate bank credit and cause a "credit crunch" in the United States? *Journal of Money, Credit, and Banking* 26:585–628.

Bernanke, Ben S., and Mark Gertler. 1989. Agency costs, collateral, and business fluctuations. *American Economic Review* 79:14–31.

———. 1995. Inside the black box: The credit channel of monetary policy transmission. *Journal of Economic Perspectives* 9 (Fall): 27–48.

Bernanke, Ben S., Mark Gertler, and Simon Gilchrist. 1998. The financial accelerator in a quantitative business cycle framework. NBER Working Paper no. 6455. Cambridge, Mass.: National Bureau of Economic Research, March.

Bernanke, Ben S., and Cara Lown. 1991. The credit crunch. *Brookings Papers on Economic Activity,* Issue no. 2:205–39. Washington, D.C.: Brookings Institution.

Burnside, Craig, Martin Eichenbaum, and Sergio Rebelo. 1998. Prospective deficits and the Asian currency crisis. Federal Reserve Bank of Chicago Working Paper no. 98-5. September.

Calomiris, Charles W. 1998. Evaluation of Argentina's banking sector, 1991–1998. Columbia University, Graduate School of Business. Mimeograph.

Calomiris, Charles W., and R. Glenn Hubbard. 1990. Firm heterogeneity, internal finance, and "credit rationing." *Economic Journal* 100:90–104.

Calomiris, Charles W., and Andrew Powell. 2001. Can emerging market bank regulators establish credible discipline? The case of Argentina, 1992–99. In *Prudential supervision: What works and what doesn't,* ed. Frederic S. Mishkin, 147–91. Chicago: University of Chicago Press.

Calvo, Guillermo A., Leonardo Leiderman, and Carmen M. Reinhart. 1994. The capital inflows problem: Concepts and issues. *Contemporary Economic Policy* 12 (July): 54–66.

Caprio, Gerald, and Patrick Honohan. 2000. *Finance in a world of volatility.* Washington, D.C.: World Bank. Mimeograph.

Caprio, Gerald, and Daniela Klingbiel. 1999. Episodes of systemic and borderline financial crises. Washington, D.C.: World Bank. Mimeograph, October.

Corsetti, Giancarlo, Paolo Pesenti, and Nouriel Roubini. 1998. What caused the Asian currency and financial crisis? Part I and II. NBER Working Papers no. 6833 and 1844. Cambridge, Mass.: National Bureau of Economic Research.

Diamond, Douglas. 1984. Financial intermediation and delegated monitoring. *Review of Economic Studies* 51: 393–414.

Federal Reserve Bank of New York. 1993. The Role of the Credit Slowdown in the Recent Recession: Federal Bank of New York *Quarterly Review* 18 (Spring), special issue.

Fischer, Stanley. 1993. The role of macroeconomic factors in growth. *Journal of Monetary Economics* 32:485–512.

Folkerts-Landau, David, Gary J. Schinasi, M. Cassard, Vincent K. Ng, Carmen M. Reinhart, and M. G. Spencer. 1995. Effect of capital flows on the domestic financial sectors in APEC developing countries. In *Capital flows in the APEC region,* ed. Moshin Khan and Carmen M. Reinhart, 31–57. Washington, D.C.: International Monetary Fund.

Garber, Peter M., and Subir Lall. 1996. The role and operation of derivative markets in foreign exchange market crises. Brown University, Department of Economics. Mimeograph, February.

Gavin, Michael, and Ricardo Hausman. 1996. The roots of banking crises: The macroeconomic context. In *Banking crises in Latin America,* ed. Ricardo Hausman and Liliana Rojas-Suarez, 27–63. Baltimore, Md.: Interamerican Development Bank and Johns Hopkins University Press.

Gertler, Mark. 1988. Financial structure and aggregate economic activity: An overview. *Journal of Money, Credit, and Banking* 20 (2): 559–88.

Goldstein, Morris. 1997. *The case for an international banking standard.* Washington, D.C.: Institute for International Economics.

———. 1998. *The Asian financial crisis: Causes, cures, and systemic implications.* Washington, D.C.: Institute for International Economics.

Goldstein, Morris, and Philip Turner. 1996. *Banking crises in emerging economies: Origins and policy options.* BIS Economic Paper no. 46. Basel, Switzerland: Bank for International Settlements, October.

Hahm, Joon-Ho, and Frederic S. Mishkin. 2000. The Korean financial crisis: An asymmetric information perspective. *Emerging Markets Review* 1 (1): 21–52.

Hancock, Diana, A. J. Laing, and James A. Wilcox. 1995. Bank capital shocks: Dynamic effects on securities, loans, and capital. *Journal of Banking and Finance* 19 (3–4): 661–77.

International Monetary Fund. 1998. *World economic outlook and international capital markets: Interim assessment.* Washington, D.C.: International Monetary Fund, December.

Ito, Takatoshi. 1998. The development of the Thailand currency crisis: A chronological review. Hitotsubahi University, Department of Economics. Mimeograph, September.

Kaminsky, Graciela, Saul Lizondo, and Carmen M. Reinhart. 1997. Leading indicators of currency crises. IMF Working Paper no. WP/97/79. Washington, D.C.: International Monetary Fund.

Kaminsky, Graciela L., and Carmen M. Reinhart. 1999. The twin crises: The causes of banking and balance-of-payments problems. *American Economic Review* 89 (3): 473–500.

Kane, Edward J. 1989. *The S&L insurance mess: How did it happen?* Washington, D.C.: Urban Institute Press.

Krivoy, Ruth. 2000. Challenges in reforming national bank supervision. In *Building an infrastructure for financial stability.* Federal Reserve Bank of Boston Conference Series no. 44, ed. John S. Jordan and Eric Rosengren, 113–33. Boston: Federal Reserve Bank of Boston.

Krueger, Anne O. 2000. Conflicting demands on the International Monetary Fund. *American Economic Review* 90 (2): 38–42.

Krugman, Paul. 1979. A model of balance of payment crises. *Journal of Money, Credit, and Banking* 11:311–25.

Mishkin, Frederic S. 1991. Asymmetric information and financial crises: A historical perspective. In *Financial markets and financial crises,* ed. R. Glenn Hubbard, 69–108. Chicago: University of Chicago Press.

Mishkin, Frederic S. 1996a. The channels of monetary transmission: Lessons for monetary policy. *Banque De France Bulletin Digest* no. 27 (March): 33–44.

———. 1996b. Understanding financial crises: A developing country perspective. In *Annual World Bank conference on development economics,* 29–62. Washington, D.C.: World Bank.

———. 1997. Evaluating FDICIA. In *FDICIA: Bank reform five years later and five years ahead,* ed. George Kaufman, 17–33. Greenwich, Conn.: JAI Press.

———. 1998. The dangers of exchange rate pegging in emerging market countries. *International Finance* 1 (1): 81–101.

———. 1999. Financial consolidation: Dangers and opportunities. *Journal of Banking and Finance* 23 (2–4): 675–91.

———. 2001. *The economics of money, banking, and financial markets.* 6th ed. Reading, Mass.: Addison Wesley Longman.

Mishkin, Frederic S., and Miguel A. Savastano. 2001. Monetary policy strategies for Latin America. *Journal of Development Economics* 66 (October): 415–44.

Mortlock, Geoff. 1996. A new disclosure regime for registered banks. Reserve Bank of New Zealand *Bulletin* 59 (1).

Nicholl, Peter. 1996. Market-based regulation. Paper presented at International Bank for Reconstruction and Development Conference on Preventing Banking Crises, April.

Obstfeld, Maurice, and Kenneth Rogoff. 1995. The mirage of fixed exchange rates. *Journal of Economic Perspectives* 9 (4): 73–96.

Peek, Joe, and Eric S. Rosengren. 1995. Bank regulation and the credit crunch. *Journal of Banking and Finance* 19 (2–4): 679–92.

Radelet, Steven, and Jeffrey Sachs. 1998. The onset of the East Asian crisis. NBER Working Paper no. 6680. Cambridge, Mass.: National Bureau of Economic Research, August.

Rojas-Suarez, Liliana, and Steven R. Weisbrod. 1994. Financial market fragilities in Latin America: From banking crisis resolution to current policy challenges. IMF Working Paper no. WP/94/117. Washington, D.C.: International Monetary Fund, October.

———. 1996. Building stability in Latin American financial markets. In *Securing stability and growth in Latin America,* ed. Ricardo Hausmann and Helmut Reisen. Paris: Organization for Economic Cooperation and Development Center and Inter-American Development Bank.

Sprong, Kenneth. 1994. *Banking regulation.* Kansas City, Mo.: Federal Reserve Bank of Kansas City.

Stiglitz, Joseph E., and Andrew Weiss. 1981. Credit rationing in markets with imperfect information. *American Economic Review* 71:393–410.

———. 1983. Incentive effects of terminations: Applications to credit and labor markets. *American Economic Review* 73:912–27.

2. Andrew Crockett

Mishkin's paper defines a financial crisis as a breakdown of financial intermediation due to an intensification of asymmetric information problems. Although this definition may not capture all elements of all financial crises, it has several important merits.

1. It focuses on the ways in which financial crisis impairs the performance of the real economy, and not just the fiscal or resolution costs.

2. It forces us to ask what causes moral hazard and adverse selection and thus to see more clearly the danger signals of impending crisis as well as the possible remedies.

3. It is a helpful framework for interpreting the feedback mechanisms between currency and financial crises.

The heart of Mishkin's paper is the analysis of twelve features of the financial system, through which actions could usefully be taken to limit the scope for moral hazard and adverse selection, and thus reduce the likelihood of crisis. To simplify, I will group his proposals into five broad families and comment on each. The five families are

1. The macroeconomic environment
2. Competition and market discipline
3. The infrastructure for financial activity
4. Prudential supervision
5. Restrictions and controls

The Macroeconomic Environment

A stable financial environment is obviously important for the effective pricing and management of risk. Financial intermediaries can do a better job, and are less likely to get into trouble, if inflation is low and stable and the budgetary position is sustainable. There is little dispute about this.

More controversial is the exchange rate regime. For the same reason that financial intermediation benefits from internal price stability, it also benefits from stability in the exchange rate. The question is what regime delivers the greater degree of stability. Our discussion this morning covered this matter extensively.

Here, I want to make only one additional observation. The least satisfactory regime is one of the fixed-but-adjustable rates in which the authorities invest political credibility in defending an announced rate but are not prepared to accept the full discipline of a currency board. Almost without exception, such regimes have encouraged resistance to market pressures beyond the point at which such resistance could be justified.

Fixed-but-adjustable rates contribute to the buildup of financial imbalances by encouraging the mispricing of risk while the rate is fixed. And when a peg is broken, the balance sheet consequences can severely impair financial intermediation. I conclude, therefore, that exchange rate flexibility (not necessarily free floating) is for most countries a part of the sustainable macroeconomic environment. This *does not* mean that countries should not hold views about their exchange rates and even direct some policies toward stabilizing it. It *does* mean that they should avoid declaring a rate and using intervention to defend it.

Competition and Market Discipline

Competition and market discipline are important mechanisms for improving the efficiency of financial systems. Mishkin makes a number of sensible suggestions that are not less important for being fairly familiar. They include encouraging the entry of foreign-owned financial institutions; privatization and the withdrawal of state intervention in the financial system; eschewal of "too-big-to-fail" policies, in both the financial and the corporate sector; and greater use of the issue of subordinated debt.

Still, a cautionary note is needed. Although these measures are useful, their introduction in emerging markets is not straightforward. Opening financial sectors to foreign participation is politically sensitive in a number of countries, sometimes for deep-seated historical and psychological reasons. The withdrawal of the state cannot be unconditional, unless the spontaneous emergence of private-sector substitutes for certain activities can be ensured; the abandonment of too-big-to-fail policies requires an assurance that alternative mechanisms for the orderly resolution of distress are available and that the means to protect depositors exist. And subordinated debt may be less effective as a mechanism in countries where banks are small and debt markets underdeveloped.

The Financial Infrastructure

Mishkin draws attention to the importance of sound accounting standards, robust legal systems, and impartial law enforcement. To this one could add a number of other features, such as effective corporate governance and strong payments and settlement systems.

The fact is that financial activity takes place within a broad context that we, in advanced industrial countries, have come to take for granted. The absence of a stable infrastructure for financial transactions has consequences that can be seen, in their most extreme form, in Russia. However, they were also an important contributory cause to the problems of Asian economies, and in Mexico before that.

Accounting is of course a key element. Accounting lapses are the basis of forbearance. To put it bluntly, they allow bad loans to be classified as good right up to the point of failure. The need is for accounting standards that allow changes in real economic value to be properly reflected in management accounts and in published income and balance sheet statements. I have no dispute with Mishkin's view on this, but it will not be easy to put this simple-sounding prescription into effect.

Much accounting in banking is done on the basis of historical or book costs, and for some quite good reasons. It is hard, and judgmental, to assess a "market" value for a non-marketable asset. Moreover, that value will change through time (up and down) as the borrowers' prospects change. Trying to track the varying value of loan portfolios will introduce greater volatility into the profitability, and the balance sheets, of banks. To dramatize this point, recall that the major U.S. banks would mostly have been insolvent on a mark-to-market basis in 1982. The same could probably have been said about most Japanese banks and insurance companies at various times in the 1990s. Would their prompt liquidation have added to the stability of the system?

Still, I am persuaded that a greater focus on market value accounting is appropriate and probably inevitable. For banks, this would involve provisioning against loans that have not yet become nonperforming. The task will be to persuade other relevant parties, including the accounting profession, tax authorities, and securities regulators, all of whom have varying degrees of principled reservation about the proposal. Beyond that, we will also need to deal with the issues created by greater recorded volatility in banks' balance sheets.

Prudential Supervision

Although I am mentioning this only fourth, improved prudential supervision comes first in Mishkin's list, and for understandable reasons. There can be little dispute about much of what he has to say concerning the need to ensure the independence and accountability of regulators, to provide adequate resources for supervision, to encourage forward-looking risk management, and to close troubled institutions. I will not comment further on these points here.

Rather, I want to make an observation on "prompt corrective action" and then to reflect more generally on the relationship between the *microprudential* and *macroprudential* tasks of supervision.

Prompt corrective action is clearly appropriate when a single institution gets into difficulties as a result of misjudgment and poor risk management. The knowledge that such action will be applied acts as a spur to prudent behavior and avoids the compounding of mistakes. But what about a situation when all institutions get into trouble more or less simultaneously, as a result of a shared problem? Closing down all institutions may not be an attractive option, and neither is imposing generalized restraints on incremental lending.

This problem is one manifestation of the difficulty of reconciling the micro and macro aspects of prudential supervision. The quintessential microprudential dictum is that "the financial system is sound when each of its constituent institutions is sound." At one level, this statement is a truism. But at another level, it is both too broad and too narrow: too broad because it is not the failure of individual institutions that is the problem, and too narrow because it does not recognize adequately endogeneities within the financial system.

The fact is that the problems we are most concerned with are not the result of idiosyncratic mistakes. More usually, a systemic crisis occurs because of common exposures to cyclically induced problems. Banks and their supervisors are reasonably good at assessing *relative* risks in portfolios. They are less good at capturing undiversifiable risks associated with the economic cycle. So we fall back on risk management paradigms that tell us, in effect, that risk falls during booms and rises in recessions. Yet we all know that the worst loans are made in the best times. A more accurate assessment of underlying risk would be to say that it *rises* during upswings and *materializes* during recessions.

I draw three conclusions from this. First, it is naïve to think that introducing "best practice" risk assessment will by itself deal with the fundamental causes of systemic crisis. Second, although "forbearance" is generally a mistake, the problem it is designed to solve is real. The real objective should be to create a situation in which the system is strong enough that forbearance is not necessary. Third, we need to think of supervisory instruments that better address the buildup of systemic risk. Possible approaches include preprovisioning, cyclically adjusted capital requirements, and special capital requirements for systemically significant institutions. More generally, a system with multiple channels of financial intermediation (especially, effective capital markets) is more easily able to countenance the prompt closure of troubled institutions.

Moreover, the actions of individual institutions feed back onto the condition of others. If a large bank fails, its counterparties may be weakened as a result. In addition, an apparently prudential retrenchment of lending, if generalized, may indirectly damage the quality of existing credits. In other words, *individually* rational behavior can be collectively destabilizing.

Restrictions and Controls

The issue of whether capital controls or other restrictions can play a role in crisis avoidance has made a comeback in recent years. Part of the reason has been the effects of capital flow volatility in generating recent crises. The experiences of Malaysia and Chile have also played a role.

My reading of the evidence suggests there is broad consensus that capital controls are *not* a desirable long-term feature of the landscape. First, they limit a country's access to international capital markets. Second, it is difficult to distinguish beneficial flows from volatile ones. Third, financial markets generally find ways to get around controls. Fourth, controls frequently breed corruption. For all these reasons, the removal of capital account controls seems to be still a legitimate long-term aspiration.

Yet a number of qualifications need to be made. First, sequencing is important. There is now general recognition that to remove controls before the domestic supervisory structure for the financial system is in place is asking for trouble. Second, measures that serve a genuine prudential purpose have a legitimate function. Regulatory restraints on mismatching of currency and maturity fall into this category. Third, measures that restrain inflows are more effective and desirable than those that restrain outflows. The experience of Chile, while not clear-cut, shows that effective inflow controls can be designed. Fourth, and last, "market-friendly" controls do less damage than administrative restrictions. Once again, the Chilean regime can be cited. It acts as a sliding scale tax on inflows, with the highest effective tax being levied on the shortest-term inflows.

Codes and Standards

In discussing these various aspects of the financial system that are important in helping avoid crises, I have so far said nothing about *how* the suggested improvements are to be brought about. It is worth noting, however, that the international community now has a strategy for achieving this. It revolves around the articulation and implementation of codes and standards of best practice in the financial area.

It is easy to poke fun at the fact that there are now sixty-six standards on the website of the Financial Stability Forum. But, sarcasm aside, this is simply a reflection of the complexity of a well-functioning financial system. It needs not just sound management of the variety of different intermediaries in the system, but effective transparency, corporate governance, payment and settlement systems, accounting practices, and so on. Certainly, the sixty-six standards call for prioritization and sequencing, and countries committed to introducing them will need help. But those that criticize the sheer number of standards would be more convincing if they showed more evidence they were aware of their content.

How are standards to be drawn up and implemented? The strategy calls for appropriate standards to be developed by committees of national experts (the Basel Committee is the best example), then for implementation to be encouraged through official assessment and market forces.

So far, the strategy is not much more than that—a strategy. Filling in the details will be laborious and time-consuming. However, I believe it presents the best hope of the goal that this conference is designed to promote: helping reduce the incidence and severity of future financial crises.

3. Michael P. Dooley

When Martin Feldstein asked me to participate in this session, he asked that I draw on my experience at the International Monetary Fund (IMF) and the Federal Reserve. I've been an academic for nine years now but will try to lean more on experience than theory in commenting on the issues raised in this morning's discussion and in Frederic S. Mishkin's excellent paper.

I believe that a quite new and important element has influenced recent discussions of exchange rate regimes for emerging markets. What I would call the political economy approach is based on the idea that exchange rate regimes create incentives both for the private sector and for the central bank. This approach is very hostile to the "middle" because managed regimes become adjustable pegs and, in practice, have created very bad incentives for central bankers and private investors in emerging markets. All three central bankers emphasized this point this morning, and I think we need to consider this point of view very carefully.

I will focus on one incentive problem, namely, the association between banking crises and exchange rate regimes. In particular, I think we need to ask why repressed financial systems in emerging markets that were so stable for so long, suddenly become a source of vulnerability for currencies.

The historical evidence suggests that repressed banking systems have been stable as long as they remained repressed. Before liberalization, residents of emerging markets had no choice but to keep their money at home, and repressed banking systems "worked" from a macroeconomic point of view. From a micro point of view, however, they were terribly inefficient. Repressed banking systems are characterized by assets that have little or no market value. This is no secret. Every IMF report on such countries had a standard paragraph warning that losses in the domestic banking system were a threat to the solvency of the banks and the government. Yet the predicted run on the banks never materialized, and governments became less and less likely to pay attention to such warnings.

The key to this puzzle is, I think, that repressed banking systems are similar to pay-as-you-go pension schemes. As long as each generation expects to "tax" the next generation by selling them deposits, the value of banks' assets is not crucial for the value of banks' liabilities. Liberalization of the financial system allows the next generation to buy alternative foreign or domestic assets, breaking this chain. As soon as liberalization becomes a sure thing, the repressed banking system is doomed.

But it does not go quietly. As Mishkin explains in his paper, banks that have lost their franchise value reach for risk. Liberalization also provides a much larger international market for banks' liabilities, and this makes an all-or-nothing play profitable. Finally, the regulatory structure needed to blunt these incentives is not likely to develop overnight.

Why do nonresidents lend? My guess is that the exchange rate regime has contributed to the expectation that their investments in these exploding banking systems are insured by governments. Prior to liberalization, particularly in Asia but also in other emerging markets, governments accumulated reserves in order to stabilize nominal exchange rates. This search for security has had the unintended effect of creating of a very well funded lender of last resort that does not know how to regulate a banking system in an open economy. The result in my view is a capital inflow that is unrelated to the quality of the investments in the emerging market. The capital inflow is related to bank's incentives to reach for risk and nonresident investors' incentives to take advantage of a substantial insurance fund. A financial or exchange market crisis is the natural result of these incentives.

This story is quite simple and should leave its tracks in the data. Inseok Shin and I have taken a careful look at the events leading up to the recent crisis in Korea (Dooley and Shin 2000). We document a clear deterioration in the equity value of Korean banks after 1991, following liberalization. In spite of this, foreign deposits grew rapidly and, in fact, grew more rapidly in individual banks that were known to have the weakest balance sheets. There was also an obvious deterioration in the quality of banks' assets during this rapid growth. We conclude that foreign investors must have been comforted by the expectation that the Korean government would use its reserves and lines of credit to bail them out; and our reading of events following the crisis is that those expectations were largely justified. The Bank of Korea deposited $20 billion in offshore branches of Korean banks and $10 billion in domestic branches. To be sure, not all foreign investors in Korea were bailed out, but that is not important for our story. Those who took uninsured risks received very high rates of return before the crisis.

What can we conclude about the political economy of exchange rate regimes? I think Arminio Fraga hit the nail right on the head this morning when he argued that the traditional arguments about fixed versus floating may someday be relevant for emerging markets but are not crucial now. In virtually every case, emerging markets drag behind a banking system with such a large hole in the balance sheet that it is politically difficult for the government to clean it up by recognizing and the socializing the loss. This generates serious incentive problems both for the private sector, which will view a fixed exchange rate and reserves as a guarantee for its balance sheets, and for the government, which will be tempted to accumulate reserves and grow out of debt with an undervalued exchange rate. Greater exchange rate flexibility will not cure the problem in the banking system, but it will eliminate the most obvious way for the private sector to make matters worse.

Reference

Dooley, Michael P., and Inseok Shin. 2000. Private capital inflows when crises are anticipated: A case study of Korea. NBER Working Paper no. 7992. Cambridge, Mass.: National Bureau of Economic Research, November.

4. Montek S. Ahluwalia

I would like to join the other panelists in complimenting Frederic Mishkin on an excellent paper. The twelve areas of financial policy he has identified reflect the current international consensus on how to avoid financial crises, and most developing countries are moving broadly in the directions indicated. Martin Feldstein has asked me to comment on the paper from the Indian perspective, so I will focus on how India's financial policies measure up against the template provided in the Mishkin paper.

A few words on recent economic developments in India may be useful by way of background information. India experienced a severe foreign exchange crisis in 1991, which led to the adoption of a program of economic stabilization and structural reforms. The reforms were similar to those attempted by several other countries and involved a basic reorientation of economic policy toward economic liberalization and greater integration with the global economy. They were broad based, in the sense of covering several areas such as industrial policy, trade policy, price decontrol, foreign investment policy, and financial liberalization. However, the pace of reforms in India was much more gradualist than in most other countries, reflecting the difficulty in generating a political consensus in a large and highly pluralist democracy. The slow pace has taxed the patience of many otherwise sympathetic observers, but it is important to note that the reforms have yielded positive results. The economy stabilized very quickly after the crisis of 1991, and the average growth in the postreforms period 1992–2000 was about 6.5 percent, making India one of the five or six fastest-growing countries in this period.

An interesting feature of India's experience is the change from its fragile position in 1991, when it was overcome by a crisis, to the much stronger position in 1997 and 1998 when it was able to escape the East Asian contagion. It is relevant to ask how far this was due to India's policies having been brought in line with the prescriptions of the Mishkin paper, and I hope I can throw some light on this question.

Prudential Norms and Supervision

Reforms in the banking sector were an integral part of India's reform program, and some steps were taken even before the East Asian crisis to improve prudential norms and to strengthen supervision. The process acquired a new urgency after East Asia, when financial-sector weaknesses came to be seen as one of the principal causes of crises in emerging markets and there was a growing consensus that prudential norms and supervision standards should be raised to internationally accepted levels.

There has been a significant improvement in capital adequacy requirements and prudential norms in recent years. Banks are currently expected to maintain a minimum ratio of capital to risk assets of 9 percent, and this is expected to be increased to 10 percent in the near future. The norms for income recognition, classification of nonperforming assets, and provisioning have also been tightened. However, since international norms are being implemented in a phased manner, Indian norms remain below the Basel Committee's minimum standards in some important respects. Loans are classified as substandard only when debt service payments become overdue for 180 days, whereas the international norm is 90 days. The extent of provisioning for different categories of assets is also below the international level. The ultimate objective is to align the norms with international levels, but a firm deadline has not been specified.

A number of steps have also been taken to improve accounting standards and disclosure by the banks and to strengthen supervision. Traditional onsite supervision is being supplemented by a system of offsite supervision based on a regular flow of information from the banks and this is expected to allow closer and more continuous monitoring of asset quality, capital adequacy, large exposures, connected lending, and so on.

The need to strengthen regulation by establishing a system for prompt corrective action, which is specifically mentioned in the Mishkin paper, has been recognized. The Reserve Bank of India (RBI) has circulated a discussion paper on this subject, proposing a system that establishes objective trigger points in three different dimensions of bank performance—capital adequacy, percentage of nonperforming assets, and return on assets. If a bank's performance in any dimension deteriorates to a defined trigger point, it will automatically invite a set of mandatory actions by RBI. In addition, there are certain types of discretionary action that may be taken to improve performance. Implementation of this system will definitely improve the quality of supervision.

It is relatively easy to prescribe new norms and even to introduce new supervisory systems, but this does not automatically ensure an improvement in the functioning of banks. That requires institutional changes in the internal functioning of banks, including especially improvements in the systems of credit evaluation and risk assessment, the quality of human resources, and the quality of internal controls and governance. These changes can only be achieved over a period of time. I fully agree with the speaker who said that even after we decide to go down this route, it may take ten years to get there! This is especially so when reforms are being introduced in a noncrisis environment, where the need for change may not be evident to all concerned.[1]

This is well illustrated by the position regarding capital adequacy in the Indian banking system. At present, 97 out of the 101 banks operating in India are above the 9 percent minimum level of capital to risk-weighted assets. However, an independent credit rating agency has pointed out that the position would look much less comfortable if the norms for classifying loans as substandard were immediately set at international levels and provisions had to be made accordingly. The problem would be further aggravated if the banks followed international practice in making provisions wherever loans are expected to deteriorate based on recent trends. The study found that most banks might fall below the 9 percent minimum.

The dilemma facing the regulatory authority is evident. A faster transition to international norms would have pushed many more banks below the accepted capital adequacy level, effectively restricting their ability to expand credit and possibly having a contractionary impact on economic activity. However, it would have strengthened the banking system faster. All banks would have been under greater pressure to improve performance, and the better capitalized and more efficient banks would have gained market share relative to the weaker banks.

A peculiar feature of the Indian experience is that the benefits expected from better norms in terms of improved lending quality may be greatly reduced because the macroeconomic environment is characterized by a high fiscal deficit.[2] The high deficit has produced high interest rates and has had the expected adverse selection consequence of discouraging high-quality low-risk borrowers. The crowding-out on the side of demand for credit is reinforced on the supply side by the fact that banks have to meet high capital adequacy requirements for commercial assets whereas government securities are treated as zero risk assets, which creates a strong regulatory incen-

---

1. A financial crisis, with a visible collapse of some financial institutions, creates a sense of urgency about the need for restructuring, and the process is facilitated if failed institutions are taken over by foreign banks with large-scale replacement of management systems and changes of senior personnel.

2. The need to reduce the fiscal deficit was recognized as a priority objective from the very beginning of the reforms, but progress in this area has been disappointing, and the consolidated deficit of the central and state governments is almost 10 percent of gross domestic product—about the same as just before the 1991 crisis.

tive for investing in government securities. The net result is that banks are encouraged to invest in government securities, effectively crowding out bank credit to the private sector. The fact that Indian banks hold substantial volumes of government securities contributes to the financial stability of the system, but only at the cost of crowding out credit to the private sector, with a resulting loss in efficiency.

Reducing Government Ownership of Banks

The area in which India's financial policies differ most distinctly from the international consensus relates to the role of public ownership of the banking system. The mainstream view, reflected in the Mishkin paper, is that government ownership of financial institutions is fundamentally inconsistent with sound banking and the role of government should therefore be drastically reduced, if not completely eliminated. However, public-sector banks account for 82 percent of the total assets of the banking system in India, and privatization is not on the agenda.

Government policy toward public ownership is being modified to allow public-sector banks to raise equity capital from the market, but this dilution is being driven not by the desire to reduce the government's role in management but by the desire to meet capital adequacy requirements without having to provide capital from the budget. Initially, the reforms permitted dilution provided government equity remained at least 51 percent. More recently, the government has announced its intention to reduce its shareholding to a minority position (33 percent) in order to meet the additional capital needs of the banks, but it has also stated that although the government's shareholding will be reduced to a minority position, the "public-sector character" of the banking system will be maintained. The exact meaning of this phrase has not been clarified, but it clearly implies that government will remain significantly involved in management.

Skeptics doubt whether any significant improvement can be achieved as long as the government remains the largest single (albeit minority) owner, with the rest of the equity dispersed over a large number of shareholders. There are also doubts about whether sufficient private equity could be attracted to recapitalize the banks on these terms, because the shares issued by the public-sector banks in the first stage of equity dilution are currently trading at a substantial discount on the issue price. However, the political resistance to privatization of the banking system is very strong.[3] In this situation, the best that can be expected is that reducing government equity to a minority position would enable the government to give bank manage-

3. Part of the problem is rooted in historical experience with private-sector banking, before the nationalization of the major banks in 1969. The banks were seen as captive banks of industrial houses with a great deal of connected lending. Lending to agriculture and small enterprises was minimal. The experience of privatization of the banks in many developing countries in the past twenty years is also not particularly encouraging.

ments a degree of flexibility and autonomy that would substantially improve their functioning.

It is difficult to judge how much autonomy is really possible. Reducing government equity to a minority will certainly enable the government to free the banks from many of the cumbersome rules and procedures that are otherwise automatically applied to any institution in which the government has more than 50 percent equity. They could be given much greater flexibility in hiring and promotion, and their salary structure could be delinked from the salary structure of the government and the rest of the public sector. In principle, the public-sector banks could be allowed to function as board-managed institutions, in which the board would include some government representatives but would also include independent, professionally competent persons to represent private shareholders. It has been argued that if the top management team in such banks is appointed by the board, and not by the government as at present, the banks could achieve a significantly higher degree of management autonomy, and therefore of efficiency, even if it is less than is possible in a fully private-sector bank.

Whatever happens to the public-sector banks, India's financial reforms will definitely reduce the dominance of the banking sector by the public-sector banks because the private-sector segment (consisting of Indian private-sector banks and foreign banks) is likely to expand very rapidly. An essential part of banking reforms was the grant of banking licenses to new Indian private-sector banks and a more liberal policy for expansion of branches of foreign banks. As a result, the share of the private-sector segment in total assets of the banking system, which was only 8 percent in 1990–91, increased to 18 percent in 1999–2000. The new private-sector banks and the foreign banks do not have as large a branch network as the public-sector banks, but they have other competitive advantages: they are less burdened with excess staff, have a high degree of managerial and operational flexibility, and are adopting information technology much more rapidly, enabling them to offer better services and also a wider range of products. Besides, the advantages of a very large network of brick and mortar branches are likely to diminish over time as information technology makes it possible to access quality clients without a larger number of branches. With continued financial liberalization, the share of the private-sector segment could easily expand to 30 percent over the next five years.

Competition from efficient private-sector banks and foreign banks will put pressure on the public-sector banks to improve their performance, and the stronger public-sector banks can achieve much higher levels of efficiency if given operational flexibility. There is some evidence that they are making an effort. Several banks have attempted to reduce excess staff by offering generous voluntary retirement packages. Although strongly opposed by the unions, this initiative has received a very positive response, with more than 10 percent of the employees opting for retirement. Further cost saving could be achieved by closing down loss-making branches, which have tended to proliferate. Reduction in government equity to a minority position will make it easier for the government to allow bank managements to explore these options without having the issues politicized.

The real challenge will be how to deal with the weak public-sector banks, which will be squeezed between the private-sector banks, which are expanding market share, and the stronger public-sector banks, which will fight to maintain their share. Several public-sector banks have been identified as being weak on the basis of capital adequacy and various efficiency-related criteria. Of these, three were identified as the weakest, calling for one of three options: (a) closure or merger with another public-sector bank, (b) change of ownership (i.e., privatization), or (c) comprehensive restructuring with a one-time cleanup of the balance sheet and continued operation as a public-sector bank. The government has ruled out the first two options and indicated that it will recapitalize these banks, provided a restructuring plan is drawn up by the banks' managements that is acceptable to the government and the RBI.

The credibility of this approach depends upon the extent of restructuring and cost reduction that can be brought about. There will have to be a substantial reduction in staff, possible acceptance of a freeze on wages, and also closure of a sufficient number of loss-making branches to create a smaller, leaner bank, which could become profitable. Without radical restructuring it will be difficult for these banks to survive in the more competitive environment they are likely to face in future.

The worst outcome for the future of public-sector banks would be one in which regulatory forbearance—always a danger when there are public-sector banks—allows these banks to continue to operate despite inadequate capital and without any significant restructuring. If closure or restructuring and privatization is not found to be politically acceptable, the regulatory system should at least insist on compliance with capital adequacy norms so that banks that fail to perform become "narrow banks," functioning as deposit-taking institutions investing mainly in government securities, which does not require a strong capital base and does not pose any threat to financial stability. This would at least allow more efficient banks (both public-sector and private-sector banks) to expand and fill the space vacated by the weak banks, sending the right signal to other banks for the future.

The Indian banking system is also burdened with another feature that is not in line with mainstream views on good banking, although it exists in other countries also in one form or another. This is the practice of directed credit. All Indian banks are required to ensure that 40 percent of their loans and advances portfolio is directed towards what is called the "priority sector": agriculture, small-scale industry, small transport operators, and the like. Banks are not directed to lend to specific borrowers, but only to ensure sufficient allocation of funds to broadly defined sectors, and the banks are expected to use normal credit assessment criteria to identify creditworthy borrowers within these sectors. However, this is clearly a quasifiscal activity. A large portion of priority-sector lending is to small farmers and microenterprises, and the interest rate for these loans is capped at the prime lending rate, which implies a significant subsidy, given the high administrative costs and higher default risk of such loans. Strict adherence to sound banking principles calls for a removal of quasifiscal burdens. If subsidies have to be given, they should be given explicitly through the budget, a process that would automatically be subject to demands for scrutiny, transparency, and, most of all, effectiveness.

Legal and Judicial Issues

The legal and judicial system, which is listed as one of the twelve critical areas, is indeed a major problem area for banks in India, as in many emerging market countries. Indian banks are greatly hampered by legal procedures that make it difficult to attach collateral (especially real estate) and realize its sale value. The procedures regarding bankruptcy are also extremely cumbersome, and liquidation of insolvent companies can take several years. This is undoubtedly one of the principal reasons for the relatively high level of nonperforming assets in the banking system.

The government initially sought to deal with the problem by establishing specialized Debt Recovery Tribunals designed to enable banks to take action for debt recovery within the existing laws through specialized courts empowered to use simpler procedures. This has helped to some extent, but the real lacuna is the lack of a modern bankruptcy law that would represent an appropriate balance between the rights of debtors and creditors and would allow creditors to force liquidation in the event of default after giving debtors a reasonable time to find a mutually acceptable solution. The government has announced its intention to amend the existing legislation along these lines, and this would represent a major improvement in the situation.

Capital Controls

India's policy toward capital controls differs from the view advocated in the paper that controls on capital movement are not only inefficient but also infeasible in the longer run because of leakages and therefore should be avoided. This was also the view advocated by the IMF before the East Asian crisis, but its approach has become more nuanced since then. Free mobility of capital is still regarded as a first best policy, but the IMF now recognizes that it may be risky to move to full capital mobility until the financial sector has been sufficiently strengthened.[4] An alternative view, articulated by Jagdish Bhagwati (1998) and John Williamson (1992), holds that although there may be efficiency gains from liberalizing capital movements, the benefits are small and also uncertain. Bhagwati has argued that whereas there is a very strong empirical basis for asserting significant benefits from liberalization of trade and foreign direct investment (FDI), there is much less evidence of similar benefits from liberalization of capital movements generally. On this view, emerging market countries should liberalize inflows of FDI, but they should continue to be cautious in liberalizing other capital flows. It is sometimes argued that full capital mobility is necessary to enable countries to attract much-needed FDI. This argument is not particularly convincing because China does not allow full capital mobility and yet is clearly the most successful country in attracting FDI. Foreign investors clearly need the assurance of being able to repatriate their capital at will, but full capital mobility may not be necessary.

India's policies are in line with the Bhagwati-Williamson prescriptions. Both FDI and portfolio investment in Indian stock markets have been greatly liberalized, and these investors are also allowed to liquidate their investments and exit at will. Debt flows, on the other hand, are strictly controlled. Borrowing abroad requires government permission, and the system is managed to ensure that total foreign borrowing in any year stays within some predetermined "prudent" level. Furthermore, there are minimum maturity requirements that rule out short-term borrowing, except for normal trade credit.

This policy paid dividends at the time of the East Asian crisis because India's external debt indicators had improved considerably compared to the situation in 1991, and this was surely one factor explaining why India did not suffer from contagion. Most important, India's short-term foreign debt was only 25 percent of total foreign exchange reserves, compared with well over 100 percent for some of the crisis-hit countries. This made India much less vulnerable to a cessation of commercial bank lending, which was the principal cause of the massive reversal of capital flows in East Asia.

India's capital control regime not only restricts short-term capital inflows but also controls capital outflows by Indian residents. Although residents can obtain foreign exchange to make payments abroad for all current transactions, they are not allowed to transfer funds abroad for capital transactions other than for repayment of external debt. In recent years, the system

---

4. It is interesting to note that the IMF position is somewhat asymmetric, because countries that have liberalized the capital account but do not have strong financial systems are not being advised to reimpose controls. This would be understandable if financial systems could be strengthened very quickly, but as we have seen this is not a practical possibility. If strengthening the financial systems is indeed a process that could take ten years, then there is a case for considering whether countries that have liberalized capital controls prematurely should not reimpose some form of control. However, there are no takers for this point of view in the fund.

has operated more liberally to allow Indian firms to create or acquire production or marketing capacity abroad as part of the firm's global expansion plans or in support of an export drive. However, the transfer of funds from India to hold financial assets abroad as an act of portfolio diversification is not allowed.

The original rationale for controlling capital outflows was that it will increase the resources available for investment domestically, and this was perhaps justifiable at a time when foreign investment was not welcome and capital controls were seen as a way to maximize the availability of resources for domestic investment. With foreign investment now welcome, this argument is no longer applicable, since any capital outflow for investment abroad only vacates investment space at home, which in principle could be filled by foreign investment provided productive investment opportunities exist. In other words, the liberalizing of capital controls need not reduce the total level of investment but may only alter its composition, with foreign investors acquiring domestic assets while domestic residents diversify their portfolio by investing abroad.

Indian policymakers are also keen to retain controls on capital outflows for another reason. In the absence of capital controls it is feared that a speculative attack on the currency could create expectations of devaluation that might trigger capital flight, which would prove self-fulfilling. It is of course recognized that controls are porous and significant leakages take place over time, but it is felt that controls can be effective in preventing sudden outflows in a crisis situation. This is not to say that capital outflows should not be allowed under any circumstances. On the contrary, it is argued that the existing system can be operated to achieve whatever level of capital outflow is felt to be manageable in normal times, but the system of controls should be retained so that a sudden outflow can be prevented.

India is likely to continue with its present cautious policy on capital controls, and a measure of caution in this area is perhaps justified on sequencing grounds. It would be better to get the fiscal deficit under control and have more progress on financial reforms before liberalizing the capital account. However, there can be little doubt that the compulsions of globalization will inevitably push India toward allowing greater flexibility. Indian firms will certainly need much greater freedom to invest abroad. Foreign investors locating production facilities in India will also demand greater freedom. At present, they have full freedom to take out their investment and exit at will, but they are subject to the same restrictions in their day-to-day operations that apply to other Indian companies (e.g., they cannot borrow abroad without permission, and such borrowings must conform to minimum maturity requirements even if they are from the parent company to its subsidiary in India). They are likely to demand flexibility for capital transactions comparable to that available in other countries. As the financial sector deepens, there will also be demands from institutions such as mutual funds and insurance companies to diversify their investments by holding some foreign assets.

India is likely to respond to these pressures by loosening existing restrictions in steps as it gains confidence in how to handle macroeconomic shocks in an open economy. However, as capital flows are liberalized, India's vulnerability on this account will also increase, and with it the compulsion to bring other financial policies in line with the requirements of crisis prevention.

Exchange Rate Policies

On exchange rate policies, India's practice compares well with the flexible exchange rate approach recommended in the Mishkin paper. The RBI has stated on many occasions that the exchange rate will be determined by market fundamentals (which it has been careful not to define), and there is certainly no commitment to maintaining a particular exchange rate. Past experience shows that the rupee has depreciated steadily against the U.S. dollar (around 5 percent per year for the period 1996–2000), and no reasonable investor would have any grounds for believing that there is any kind of implicit exchange guarantee.

The exchange rate regime is not a completely free float in which the authorities abstain from any intervention, nor can this be expected, given the thinness of the foreign exchange market. The Reserve Bank intervenes (either through direct intervention in foreign exchange markets or through interest rate interventions) whenever it feels that the movement of the rupee is being driven by "temporary imbalances of demand and supply" or by "speculative pressure." It is of course difficult to tell whether a movement at any particular time reflects these factors or a change in fundamentals, and this judgment necessarily must be left to the RBI. However, it is clear that the RBI's interventions are in the nature of "leaning against the wind" to calm markets, rather than fighting against all odds to maintain a particular rate.

The RBI has been criticized for asymmetric behavior because it is seen to fight much harder to prevent a nominal appreciation of the rupee than a depreciation. This happened during the period 1994 to 1996, when there were substantial inflows of portfolio capital. The rupee would have appreciated vis-à-vis the dollar if left to market forces, but this was effectively prevented by the RBI's active intervention, which led to a substantial buildup of foreign exchange reserves. In retrospect, the RBI's action seems entirely justified. The buildup of reserves cannot be said to have been excessive, especially in the light of the East Asian crisis and the increased importance now accorded to maintaining high levels of reserves. Besides, the resistance to an appreciation in the nominal rate in that period also seems justified since the real effective exchange rate (REER) had already appreciated because the rupee was stable against the dollar, which had appreciated against other currencies in this period. Further appreciation against the dollar would only have worsened the situation. Because the inflation rate in India exceeded the inflation rate in its major trading partners by 3 to 4 percent per year in this period, maintenance of the REER required a nominal depreciation, not appreciation.

The relevance of the REER as a guide for exchange rate policy in India has varied. In certain periods, especially 1994–96, the objective of stabilizing the REER was officially stated on several occasions but the RBI never officially adopted an announced REER target. More recently, the RBI has described the REER as only one of the many factors that are relevant in determining what the exchange rate should be. This "constructive ambiguity" is perhaps unavoidable when operating a managed floating exchange rate regime.

India's exchange rate policies certainly helped to avoid problems that affected many other countries at the time of the East Asian crisis. The rupee came under pressure on several occasions in 1998, but the absence of a rigid exchange rate target meant that it was able to adjust in a series of small steps without attracting much criticism from foreign investors, including portfolio investors. Between June 1997 and October 2000 the rupee depreciated against the dollar by around 23 percent, which was about half of the depreciation in Thailand and Malaysia and only a little lower than Korea (which rebounded strongly in 2000). At no stage, however, did India look as if it was facing a currency crisis.

The logical development of exchange rate policy in future would be to learn to allow greater exchange rate flexibility with less frequent intervention by the RBI. The need for such flexibility will undoubtedly increase as capital controls are progressively liberalized, increasing the possible pressure in foreign exchange markets from this source. The fact that import tariffs are still high, and the government has indicated that they will be lowered to East Asian levels in the medium term, suggests that there must be room for compensating depreciation to accompany tariff reductions. This adjustment would be much easier to achieve in a flexible exchange rate regime.

One consequence of allowing greater flexibility in the exchange rate is that the need for hedging instruments will expand. This in turn will put pressure on the system to liberalize capital transactions, because it is not possible to develop an efficient market for hedging foreign exchange risk with the restrictive capital controls. Banks in particular will have to be given more flexibility to take positions in forward markets subject to reasonable risk limitations.

To summarize, India's financial policies are moving in the direction indicated in the Mishkin paper in many respects, but important gaps remain in some areas. Some of these gaps, especially those relating to prudential norms, will be closed in a phased manner. There are important differences in certain areas, such as, for example, the role of government ownership in the financial system and the policy toward capital controls. Some of these differences (e.g., on capital controls) can be justified on sequencing grounds. On the whole, policies are converging toward those that are currently seen to be necessary to avoid financial crises.

References

Bhagwati, Jagdish. 1998. The capital myth: The difference between trade in widgets and dollars. *Foreign Affairs* 77 (May/June): 7–12.
Williamson, John. 1992. On liberalizing the capital account. In *Finance and the international economy 5: AMEX bank review prize essays 1991,* ed. Richard O'Brien. N.p.: Oxford University Press.

Discussion Summary

Sebastian Edwards stressed the importance of distinguishing between controls on capital inflows and controls on capital outflows. The Chilean experience with its controls, which are market-based and designed to deter short-run inflows, has been largely positive. He said that the controls operated like a tax—which was as high as 600 basis points for short-term flows—and thus shifted the composition of flows toward the longer end. Edwards went on, however, to say that the success of the Chilean flows had been oversold. Chile was significantly affected by the Asian and Russian crises. Thus, he said, certain things needed to be kept in mind when judging the effectiveness of Chilean-type controls. First, they are a temporary solution and must be abandoned at some point. Chile has already abandoned its controls. Second, they can lead to complacency. Edwards gave the example of Korea in 1997, where the existence of controls led international investors to downplay the poor shape of the banking system.

On the relative merits of inflow and outflow controls, *Jacob Frenkel* thinks there is nothing to debate. There is a consensus, he said, that if you control outflows, inflows will not come. He agreed with Edwards that the Chilean success with inflow controls is oversold, remarking that the Chileans did not abandon their controls because they worked so well. He also agreed with Michael P. Dooley that problems are not exposed until you are part of the "stormy ocean" of global capital markets. But this does not mean that robustness is enhanced if you are sheltered by controls. Rather, it means that the distortions are there, and when corrections take place they do so "in a very noisy way." Turning to an example of how the business sector will self-insure in more turbulent markets, he pointed out that, prior to the removal of foreign exchange controls in Israel, there were practically no transactions in the nonspot foreign exchange market. Within a short period after the removal of controls, 40 percent of transactions were in the nonspot market, as the businesses began hedging against exchange rate risk.

Montek S. Ahluwalia agreed with Frenkel's point that you can't have controls on outflows unless you are willing to give up any hope of inflows. In India's case, inflows are welcomed and repatriation is allowed. The preoccupation in India is with controlling outflows by domestic residents. The authorities know that steady leakage will occur as people try to avoid excessive regulation. But a regime that controls outflows by domestic residents prevents sudden flights, so that it is not possible for several billion dollars to leave in one week. He said that this belief holds them back in liberalizing outflows. Another problem with the differential treatment of domestic and foreign investors is that the ease of exit of the latter creates more volatility for the former. But domestic investors don't have the instruments to hedge against this volatility, because the hedging markets do not exist and will only exist when the capital market is opened up. One solution would be Chilean-style controls applying to outflows. This could be done symmetrically—everybody is entitled to exit, but based on unremunerated deposits for one year. This might be politically feasible because domestic regulatory authorities are mostly afraid of short-term outflows.

Stanley Fischer said the International Monetary Fund has not supported the removal of controls until there are signs of financial strengthening. On reimposing controls when the system is weak, he agreed that is difficult short of a major crisis. On inflow controls, he said Chile is not the only country to have used them. They have been used in other countries—for example, Brazil and Columbia—and the empirical results have been more encouraging than the critics have allowed. These results show that the presence of controls does not affect the overall level of inflows, but they alter their composition, moving them to the long end. Turning to measures to strengthen the financial system, he said he agrees with most of what Andrew Crockett said, but he doesn't agree that it takes ten years and thus controls have to be in place for ten years. He said that the incentive effects might be such that you will fix the system less rapidly if controls are in, but that still does not mean that you need ten years to do it.

John Crow said that, like Mexico, Canada adopted a floating rate because of the infeasibility of controls given its proximity to the United States. He also agreed with the concern that controls would turn into an excuse for delaying financial-sector reform.

Karen Johnson expressed concern about the way risk management is addressed. Too much focus is placed on the liability side to the neglect of the asset side. We should really talk about "portfolio management" rather than "liability management," recognizing that every country has assets as well as liabilities and covariances between them. She also complained about how issues are compartmentalized: banking regulations, fiscal policy norms, monetary policy norms, and so on. The relevant issues are allocated to different parts of the public or private sectors to take care of, again ignoring important covariances. She added that what she is advocating is a monumental task—"we don't have a government bureau of risk management," she said—but some progress needs to be made in getting away from thinking of the various elements as separable issues.

Mervyn King drew an analogy between the discussion of "corner solutions" for exchange rate regimes and such solutions for capital controls. Capital controls might provide temptations to follow suboptimal policies, he said, but added: "if you leap naked into this world of free capital movements, you may need superoptimal policies to avoid the sorts of crises that have hit countries." The "middle ground" puts enormous pressure on the quality of policy making, he said, adding that it is not a trivial task to strengthen financial systems and implement better banking supervision. As evidence, he pointed to the experience of banking crises in the industrialized countries over the last 200 to 300 years. He said that the industrial countries still did not deal with these crises very well. The Group of Ten (G10) has collectively spent vast sums of money bailing out their own financial systems, and he added that if he were in Ahluwalia's position, he would be cautious about the speed at which to proceed in this area.

Staying with problems in the G10, King pointed out that creditors are also subject to moral hazard created by the G10 governments themselves. Those who finance the banking flows into emerging markets are often totally unaware of the risks being taken. The reason they can ignore the risks is that industrial country governments underwrite them. He agrees with Fischer that this does not mean that you can easily reimpose capital controls, but it does suggest some natural caution in removing controls when the costs of getting it wrong are expensive crises.

Anne O. Krueger advised Ahluwalia to push for financial strengthening, and if opening up the capital market forces this, she would "push it even harder." Drawing on the Korean experience, she stressed that the argument for financial strengthening is primarily a growth argument. Although Korea had a very high return on capital in the 1960s (a real rate of return of 37 percent per year), in later years the financial system severely misallocated capital through such mechanisms as the evergreening of accounts. Given the importance of the banking system in countries that haven't developed other financial markets, it is crucial that banks move capital to where it has a high rate of return, and this requires banking-sector reform. In India fiscal deficits also draw crucial funds away from real investment. Krueger concluded by reiterating that financial strengthening and fiscal control are long-run growth issues as well as crisis prevention issues.

Peter Garber addressed a trade-off inherent in mark-to-market accounting practices. Previously banks didn't mark to market so as not to impose severe liquidity problems on borrowers. But the practice of carrying borrowers for a long time led to enormous problems when the system eventually broke down. Although the new trend toward marking to market might prevent major solvency problems, it makes liquidity problems much more frequent. This can be good to the extent it heads off insolvencies, but some hold the view that liquidity problems cause insolvencies by creating "multiple equilibria," and so it might not be desirable to "impose these liquidity-hungry methodologies on emerging market countries." Regarding the issue of subordinated debt, Garber believes that such requirements are highly manipulable. Banks can enter the market in undetected ways, effectively buying up their own debt.

Roberto Mendoza continued on the issue of mark-to-market accounting. While recognizing that banks are nowhere near as important to the financial system as they used to be, he notes that their application of historical cost accounting creates enormous distortions from the first day the assets are booked. Banks routinely book assets at cost even when they are worth significantly less than that on the first day. Moreover, derivative markets would allow for quite accurate pricing (individually or in aggregate) of bank assets. One implication of such cost-based accounting is that banks lend at too low a rate—as they did in Thailand—and with cheap funding the recipient engages in overly risky behavior. Since the consequences of such loans will eventually become clear, the single best preventative mechanism would be to force banks to have fair market value accounting immediately.

Domingo F. Cavallo emphasized the link between capital controls and capital account inconvertibility. Local financial institutions cannot directly intermediate using foreign exchange when people do not have the right to convert their money into foreign currencies. This leads to the phenomenon of capital flight as savers insist on being protected by holding foreign currency assets. At the same time there is lending from abroad in foreign currencies. These funds are intermediated through local institutions, with the lending taking place in domestic currency. This leads to fragile balance sheets. There would be better quality intermediation if the banks could take deposits and lend in domestic and foreign currencies.

Larry Summers said that the presence of foreign financial institutions in emerging markets is good on grounds of "diversification, risk sharing, and deep pockets." One aspect of capital controls that must be considered is the adverse impact they have on the presence of foreign institutions. Regarding the distinction between what he called the "macroeconomic-cheat-the-traditional-trade-off" and the "prudential" rationales for capital controls, he said the latter was more compelling. He asked: "If you limit short-term foreign currency–denominated assets in your banking system, is that a capital control or is it a prudential control?" His answer is that a great deal of what is defensible is defensible as prudential policy, without making reference to the notion of capital controls, per se.

Next, drawing an analogy with the policy wisdom that you should eliminate all the energy subsidies before you start putting on energy taxes, Summers said that inappropriate subsidies and incentives to short-term capital are an enormous problem. Most of the countries that got overwhelmed turned out to be those that did a lot of things to keep those flows coming. Finally, he said that a country's receptivity to short-term capital is not something in which those outside the country have a compelling interest. Thus, it would be a mistake for the international community to seek to try to impose views like the ones he has just expressed through either trade policy or the IMF as a broad systematic matter. One substantial exception to this stance, however, is that it is reasonable to ask countries receiving official-sector money to think about removing their barriers to private-sector money.

Yung Chul Park raised the issue of what exactly is meant by a foreign bank. He reported that in Korea foreigners own more than 35 percent of the major commercial banks, but they are all "financial investors, not interested in controlling management." Foreigners own 70 percent of one bank, but still are not interested in controlling management. "Is this bank foreign or is it domestic?" he asked. He noted that the foreign owners are not interested in sharing their risk management techniques with Koreans, but that he does not find this surprising given that they are competing with domestic banks. On credit risk management, he said that the domestic banks actually have an advantage given the importance of local knowledge.

Finally, Park pointed out that when financial problems developed in Korea, the foreign banks left even before the investors in Korea. Yet, he said, we are being constantly reminded that foreigners own practically the entire banking system in Mexico, and it is still doing well. *Martin Feldstein* noted that the issue of the role of foreign ownership is central to the discussion, and asked Cavallo about the experience of other countries with foreign banks. *Cavallo* said that the entry of foreign banks did give more stability to the Argentine financial system.

Nouriel Roubini expressed five concerns about foreign banks. First, these banks might "cherry pick" the best credits, leaving the worst for domestic institutions. Second, there is evidence that foreign banks are more inclined to lending in good times but not in bad times than are domestic banks. Third, although an advantage of foreign banks is supposed to be that they can rely on their headquarters for support in a crisis, we do not see evidence of this. Fourth, it may be that home country regulations force the banks operating abroad to retrench more than is desirable. Finally, although it can be argued that these banks should rely on the home country for any bailouts, the reality is that there is political pressure for the local authority to provide the bailout.

Martin Wolf summed up what he had heard in the session as: "postliberalization crises are virtually inevitable, even desirable." Huge changes are being demanded of developing countries, changes that we know from experience are typically made because of a crisis. The list of past financial crises in the industrial countries is a long one. Wolf said that what we seem to be saying to the developing countries is: "We think you ought to reform and become more like us, and incidentally, along the way, you're going to have a few absolutely staggering crises, and the result is that you will have a better financial system and this is good for you."

Frederic S. Mishkin sought to make the political economy issues that Michael Dooley saw as implicit in his paper more explicit. Taking an example from Korea, he recalled political pressures to introduce legislation to allow the conversion of finance companies into essentially unregulated merchant banking corporations that were owned by the *chaebol*. These pressures came from the need by *chaebol* for foreign funds to keep growth out of their problems (despite a 30 percent national saving rate). The merchant banks were allowed to borrow short-term. This, he said, is an example of exactly what Summers had talked about—there was encouragement of short-term foreign borrowing.

Continuing on the political economy theme, Mishkin noted that, from his conversations with Korean officials, it is clear they know exactly what needs to be done. When he asks, "what should you do?" they list exactly the kinds of things he wrote in his paper. Why doesn't it happen? Mishkin stressed that we need to think about the political incentives needed to bring about these changes. Finally, he returned to the discussion of exchange rate and monetary regimes from the first session, saying that there was no such thing as a free float in a small open economy. If you are going to respond to the exchange rate, however, he said you are better off doing it through a more transparent monetary regime such as inflation targeting. Again, this conclusion is driven by political economy considerations. Good policies and institutions are "not going to come out of thin air," he concluded, so political economy is "implicitly . . . behind a lot of things I talk about in the paper."

Industrial Country Policies

1. Jeffrey A. Frankel and Nouriel Roubini
2. Mervyn King
3. Robert Rubin
4. George Soros

1. Jeffrey A. Frankel and Nouriel Roubini

The Role of Industrial Country Policies in Emerging Market Crises

A search for the causes and solutions of crises in emerging markets must begin with the policies of the countries themselves. Nevertheless, policies of the industrialized countries are relevant as well. That is the topic of this chapter. It covers everything from the macroeconomic policies of the Group of Seven (G7) countries themselves, to their role via the G7 and International Monetary Fund (IMF) in managing international crises when they break out, to their role in seeking to reform the international financial architecture so as to reduce to whatever extent possible the frequency and severity of future crises. A theme throughout the chapter will be the moral hazard question: the tension between the desirability of reducing the adverse consequences of any given crisis, on the one hand, and the danger that such efforts will in the longer term encourage capital flows that are larger, more careless, and more likely to result in future crises, on the other hand.

3.1.1 G7 Macroeconomic Policies

Nothing that the industrialized countries do, at least in the short run, has as big an effect on economic developments in emerging market countries as

The authors wish to thank Ronald Mendoza for research assistance, and Gordon de Brouwer, Martin Feldstein, Mervyn King, Allan Meltzer, Robert Rubin, and George Soros for comments. The usual disclaimers apply with stronger force.

their macroeconomic policies. U.S. monetary contractions, for example, were among the important causes, in a proximate sense, of the international debt crisis that began in 1982 and the Mexican peso crisis of 1994. A global easing of monetary policy in the fall of 1998 helped bring that 1997–98 round of crises to an end. Indeed, there is evidence that asset prices in emerging markets are more sensitive to short-term U.S. interest rates than are comparable asset prices in the United States itself.

Three macroeconomic variables among industrialized countries that have major short-term impact on developing countries are growth rates, real interest rates, and exchange rates. Trade policy in industrialized countries is very important as well. We consider each in turn.

Monetary Policy, Fiscal Policy, and Growth

This paper will not generally try to explain growth rates and interest rates in the industrialized countries but, rather, in this section, will look at their effects on emerging markets. Nevertheless, we begin with a parenthetical aside regarding the sources of growth. Monetary and fiscal policies are traditionally viewed as affecting real growth rates in the short run. They cannot fully explain rapid U.S. growth in the 1990s, however, or rapid Japanese growth in earlier decades. Longer-term supply or productivity determinants are clearly important. In the 1980s, many observers thought that the Japanese brand of capitalism had proven its superiority. In the 1990s, many considered that, to the contrary, the U.S. model had proven its superiority. Perhaps the attractions of Japan as a role model in the 1980s, followed by the United States in the 1990s, have had effects on developing country thinking that are ultimately more important than the immediate economic effects of growth rates in these and other industrialized countries. In any case, it is the latter topic that concerns us here.

Business Cycles

Incomes in developing countries are procyclical, rising when growth rates in the industrialized countries are strong, falling when they are not. The most visible channel of transmission is trade. When incomes in the rich world fall, their imports from developing countries fall as well. This is important because export revenue is key to the ability of poor countries to service debts. Demand for the types of goods that developing countries produce tends to be unusually procyclical (Goldstein and Khan 1985). The impact of Organization for Economic Cooperation and Development (OECD) slowdowns hits in three ways: lower quantities demanded, lower prices on world markets, and the raising of import barriers.

To take an example, the recession among industrialized countries in 1980–82 depressed prices and volumes for exports from developing countries, reversing a preceding period of boom. This, in turn, contributed to the international debt crisis of the 1980s. To take another example, Mexico's 1995 recovery from the peso crisis was aided by rapid U.S. economic growth. With the North American Free Trade Agreement (NAFTA) in place in 1994, Mexican exports to the United States—which were 85 percent of its total exports—were able to grow 92 percent from 1994 to 1999.[1] When East Asia was hit by its currency crises in 1997–98, by contrast, recovery was hampered by the absence of economic growth in the leading regional economy, as Japan remained mired in recession. Japan's G7 partners at the time urged reflation in Tokyo; among other reasons was the need to promote growth in the rest of East Asia. For all the talk of globalization and of the irrelevance of geography, economic prospects in each region of the world are affected particularly strongly by the growth rate of the largest industrialized countries in that region.

A simple regression estimate illustrates the dependence of emerging market economies on the cyclical position of the bigger countries. Every 1 percentage point increase in G7 growth raises the growth rate among market borrowers an estimated 0.78 percentage points.[2]

National Saving Rates

Also critical to emerging markets, even for any given global growth rate, is the availability of capital, as reflected in global interest rates. The best indicator of the availability of capital is the real interest rate, that is, the nominal rate adjusted for expected inflation. An increase in the global inflation rate can for a time actually be good for developing countries. (This is true even if they are fully reflected in nominal interest rates.) The real value of preexisting debt is reduced, relative to the prices of the commodities that they produce.

More broadly, the availability of capital is determined by the balance of saving and investment. The usual presumption is that there is an excess of potentially profitable investment opportunities in the developing world, attributable to its low capital-labor ratio, relative to available domestic saving. At least, this is the presumption for those countries that have put into place the necessary preconditions for growth, such as a market economy and monetary stability, which are generally those countries that warrant the title "emerging markets." The usual presumption is also that the situation is the other way around in the industrialized world: an excess of saving over investment opportunities. As a result, the opening of capital markets results in the flow of capital from low–interest rate rich countries to high–interest rate emerging markets, to the benefit of both.

1. In current dollars. The source is IMF *Direction of Trade* (various issues).
2. Statistically significant at the 95 percent level. The R^2 is 0.23. The period of estimation is 1977–99.

Table 3.1   **Trade and Current Account Balances of Developing Countries (annual average in US$ billions)**

Region	1977–82	1983–90	1991–96	1997–99
Trade balances				
Developing countries	42	34	−14	27
Africa	3	5	5	2
Asia	−14	−2	−24	47
Middle East and Europe	54	5	12	4
Western hemisphere	−1	26	−7	−26
Current account balances				
Market borrowers	−44	−9	−58	−36
Developing countries	−28	−35	−93	−61
Africa	−15	−7	−10	−15
Asia	−15	−3	−28	33
Middle East and Europe	29	−14	−18	−10
Western hemisphere	−28	−10	−38	−69

Source: IMF, *World Economic Outlook* (various years).

Table 3.1 shows that developing countries have indeed been able to run current account deficits, financed by net capital inflows. However, this general pattern varies, depending on circumstances. Inflows are cut off in the aftermath of crises. As the table shows, Latin American countries were obliged to switch to large trade surpluses in 1983–90 and Asian countries in 1997–99.

Demographically, the rapid aging of the population in most industrialized countries, particularly relative to the young populations in poor countries, implies that saving rates will fall in the former over the coming decades. Logically, baby boomers in the rich countries should have been saving at high rates in recent years, and investing part of those savings in high-return emerging markets, in order to develop a good portfolio of assets to draw down in their retirement years. However, the trend in the 1980s and 1990s was in reality something quite different. National saving rates have not risen to prepare for the needs of social security deficits in the twenty-first century, but the reverse.

U.S. national saving, never high, fell sharply in the 1980s, due to an increase in the federal budget deficit, exacerbated by a fall in private saving. This kept real interest rates high in the United States, and to some extent globally, and was a negative factor in the international debt situation of that decade (e.g., Dornbusch 1985, 346–47). One view at the time was that the United States was deliberately pushing up its real interest rates (by a mix of tight money and loose fiscal policy) in order to attract capital, appreciate the dollar, and thereby put downward pressure on import prices and inflation. A particular version of this view was that the United States and Europe were involved in a competition to appreciate their currencies and that the outcome of this ultimately futile race was high world real interest rates. The developing countries, although innocent bystanders, were said to be the victims hardest hit. The claim was that the G7 countries should enter a cooperative agreement to refrain from attempts to appreciate their currencies, and thereby lower world real interest rates, as the biggest possible contribution to helping solve the international debt problem (Sachs 1985; McKibbin and Sachs 1988, 1991). Others pointed out, however, that the relevant government officials had not in fact raised real interest rates deliberately (e.g., Feldstein 1994).

In the late 1990s the United States solved its budget deficit problem. Record deficits were converted to record surpluses. As a direct consequence, national saving rose. The overall outlook for the saving-investment balance remains a concern, however. Investment in the United States in the 1990s rose even more rapidly than national saving. The "New Economy" offers a ready explanation for booming investment. In any case, the result of the investment boom has been an ever-increasing current account deficit, financed by capital on net flowing into the United States, rather than out. The United States in essence is competing with the developing world to attract capital. The U.S. current account deficit is far larger than those of all developing countries combined.

It is possible that over the next decade a depreciation of the dollar against the euro and yen will reduce the U.S. current account deficit. However, such a trend would probably also symmetrically reduce the current account surpluses of Europe and Japan. This would mean a rearrangement of the flow of funds among industrialized countries, rather than making more capital available for developing countries.

The outlook is for low availability of saving everywhere, not just in the United States. The reason is that the demographic problem is even worse in other industrialized countries than in the United States. European progress in reducing budget deficits under the Maastrict Treaty in the 1990s is small compared to the looming liabilities represented by unfunded national retirement programs. Japan has the most rapidly aging population of all, and the fiscal expansion of the late 1990s has already pushed up previously low budget deficits and debt levels in that country. Nowhere are industrialized countries fully taking advantage of the opportunity to prepare for the coming retirement boom by saving heavily in their high-earning years and investing at substantial levels in younger developing countries (e.g., B. Fischer and Reisen 1994).

The Role of Interest Rates in the United States and Other Major Countries

On a yearly or monthly basis, fluctuations in interest rates (whether real or nominal) do not reflect changes in long-term fundamentals such as demographics but, rather, reflect shorter-term factors. These include monetary policy and changes in attitudes toward liquidity and risk. Easy monetary policy among the industrialized countries in the 1970s meant low real interest rates; developing countries thus found it easy to finance their current account deficits, for example, by borrowing petrodollars recycled through banks in London and New York. The U.S. monetary contraction of 1980–82, although it was eventually successful at reversing the high inflation rates of the 1970s, initially pushed up nominal and real interest rates sharply. This, as already noted, helped precipitate the international debt crisis of the 1980s.

In the early 1990s, interest rates in the United States and other industrialized countries were once again low. Investors looked around for places to earn higher returns and discovered the emerging markets. There began what was in many ways the greatest flow of capital to developing countries in history. (The pre–World War I flow of finance from capital-rich Great Britain to land-rich Argentina, Australia, and Canada still holds the record when expressed as a percentage of income. However, the flows of the 1990s were far larger in absolute terms, and more of a global phenomenon.)

During 1992–94, Calvo, Leiderman, and Reinhart (1993, 1994)—and some other authors at the World Bank and IMF—produced a series of research papers examining the new capital flow phenomenon. They enumerated the possible underlying factors, attempted econometric estimation, and generally came to a surprising conclusion: the most important identifiable factors behind the flows were U.S. interest rates and other macroeconomic variables external to the emerging market countries. Capital was heading South because low rates of return were on offer in the North.

This was a surprising conclusion because the more common belief at the time was that domestic factors within the emerging market countries were responsible, particularly promarket policy reforms: monetary stabilization, privatization, deregulation, and the opening of economies to both trade and capital flows. Other candidate explanations were reduction of the existing debt burden under the Brady Plan, which had been launched in 1989 with Mexico as the first case, and institutional innovations in the investor community that made diversification into emerging markets more convenient, such as country funds, American Depository Receipts, and Global Depository Receipts. However, the econometric studies reached the rough consensus that external macroeconomic factors were a major cause, perhaps *the* major cause, of the increased demand for assets in emerging countries.

Calvo, Leiderman, and Reinhart (1993, 136–37) found that "foreign factors account for a sizable fraction (about 50 percent) of the monthly forecast error variance in the real exchange rate . . . [and] . . . also account for a sizable fraction of the forecast error in monthly reserves." Chuhan, Claessens, and Mamingi (1998) estimated that U.S. factors explained about half of portfolio flows to Latin America (although less than country factors in the case of East Asia). Fernandez-Arias (1994) found that the fall in U.S. returns was the key cause of the change in capital flows in the 1990s. Dooley, Fernandez-Arias, and Kletzer (1994), in a study of the determinants of the increase in secondary debt prices among eighteen countries, concluded that "International interest rates are the key factor." It is worth emphasizing that all these papers were written before the Mexican crisis of December 1994, during a period when most analysts in the investment community believed that the capital inflows were likely to continue because they were based on local promarket reforms.[3]

One study of early warning indicators among 105 countries over the period 1971–92 found that foreign variables were among those statistically significant in predicting the probability of a currency crash. Short-term world interest rates were important.[4] A 1 percentage point increase in interest rates was estimated to raise the probability of a currency crash by about 1 percentage point per year. The combination of high indebtedness (ratio of debt to gross domestic product [GDP]) and an increase in world interest rates was particularly likely to lead to trouble. (OECD output growth had an effect on the crash probability that was less clearly significant.) Similarly, Eichengreen and Rose (2001) found that foreign real interest rates were significant in predicting banking crises as well among emerging market countries.

Calvo, Leiderman, and Reinhart (1993)—two years before the Mexican peso crisis—warned that "The importance of external factors suggests that a reversal of those conditions may lead to a future capital outflow." The warning was little heeded at the time. Nevertheless, the prediction came true in 1994, when the Federal Reserve raised interest rates seven times, a total of 3 percentage points (starting 4 February, and counting the last one on 1 February 1995). Foreign purchases of peso assets came to a halt. The assassination of Mexican presidential candidate Luis Donaldo Colosio and a period of other political disturbances also began in early 1994, so it is difficult to disentangle the causes. Both sets of factors undoubtedly played a role, along with domestic macroeconomic policies. In the absence of do-

3. A summary of details regarding the data and statistical techniques used in these four studies appears in Frankel and Okongwu (1996). (That paper also presents more econometric evidence of a heavy influence of U.S. interest rates on portfolio capital flows and local interest rates; these results go up to December 1994 and thus include the adverse effects of U.S. interest rates in 1994 on the Mexican peso crisis.) For a more recent study that finds a significant role of U.S. interest rates in determining capital flows to emerging markets, see Mody, Taylor, and Kim (2001). They, like the authors of some of the other studies, find that the U.S. real growth rate may be at least as important a determinant as U.S. interest rates.

4. Computed as an average of interest rates in six industrialized countries, with weights determined by shares in the debt of the developing country in question (Frankel and Rose 1996). Other variables were also statistically significant in predicting currency crises. Some of the most important concerned the composition of the preceding capital inflows, a topic relevant for the reform of the international financial system.

mestic adjustment during the course of the year, reserves hemorrhaged in December, leading to the collapse of the peso. Regardless of what one thinks of the deeper causes of the problem, or of the need for vigilance by the Federal Reserve on inflation, the increases in U.S. interest rates were among the proximate causes of the Mexican crisis.

There are a number of channels whereby foreign interest rates affect emerging markets. First, high global real interest rates tend to depress, not just real economic activity in general, but the prices of the basic commodities produced by many developing countries in particular. Second, high interest rates directly raise debt service costs. Particularly where debt is short-term, or with floating interest rates tied to London Interbank Offered Rate (LIBOR) or the U.S. treasury bill rate, an increase in world interest rates translates immediately into a higher interest bill for debtor countries. Thus, the ratio of debt service to exports suffers as a result of both an increase in the numerator and a decline in the denominator.

In recent years the emphasis has shifted from the ability of debtors to service bank loans out of export receipts—or to roll them over—to the ability of emerging markets to retain investor confidence and thereby attract enough new inflows to meet maturing bonds. High interest rates in industrialized countries make investments in emerging markets less attractive. At first, diminished capital inflows may show up as only a gradual loss of reserves. In a speculative attack, however, the country loses the confidence of the international financial markets unless it raises interest rates sharply, and sometimes even if it does.

The new abundance of data on securities prices in emerging markets over the last fifteen years makes it easier to examine statistically the sensitivity to financial conditions in the industrialized countries. Table 3.2 shows the sensitivity of emerging market securities prices and growth to G7 interest rates. An increase in the G7 real interest rate (weighted average of the countries' lending rates, adjusted for one-year lagged inflation) has a negative effect on the composite index of emerging market equities. The effect of a 1 percentage point increase in the real interest rate is an estimated 0.17 drop in the log composite index (17 percent). The effect on Latin America considered alone is higher, an estimated 0.42 drop, and on Asia is lower, an estimated 0.11.[5] An increase in the real U.S. federal funds rate has an effect on emerging equity markets that is comparable in magnitude—greater in magnitude, in the case of Latin America—than the effect on U.S. equity markets. The Emerging Market Bond Index (EMBI) Global, which tracks returns for U.S. dollar-denominated debt instruments issued by emerging market sovereign and quasi-sovereign entities, also appears to fall as G7 lending rates

5. These effects at first appear significant statistically, but the significance levels drop sharply when one corrects for high serial correlation. The equations were estimated from annual IFC global data, compiled by the Standard & Poor's Corporation, over the period 1984–99.

Table 3.2   **Sensitivity of Emerging market Securities Prices and Growth to G7 Interest Rates**

	Coefficient	Standard Error	R^2
IFC global index of equities regressed against the G7 real lending rate			
Composite	−0.17	0.02	0.28
Asia	−0.11	0.03	0.09
Europe, Middle East, and Africa	0.03	0.06	0.00
Latin America	−0.42	0.03	0.58
IFC global index of equities regressed against the U.S. real Federal funds rate			
Composite	−0.11	0.02	0.19
Asia	−0.07	0.02	0.08
Europe, Middle East, and Africa	0.15	0.05	0.15
Latin America	−0.29	0.02	0.50
U.S. Standard & Poor's 500 Index regressed against the U.S. real Federal funds rate	−0.16	0.11	0.04
Emerging Markets Bond Index (EMBI) global composite regressed against G7 real lending rate	−0.34	0.03	0.63
EMBI global composite regressed against the U.S. real Federal funds rate	−0.23	0.07	0.14
Developing country growth regressed against the G7 real interest rate			
Market borrowers	−0.39	0.27	0.09
Africa	−0.35	0.19	0.14
Asia	−0.04	0.21	0.00
Middle East and Europe	−0.20	0.22	0.04
Western hemisphere	−0.77	0.23	0.35

Source: IFCG from Standard & Poor's, EMBI from JPMorgan, and interest rates from the IMF (*International Financial Statistics* [various years] and *World Economic Outlook* [various years]).

Notes: All interest rates are expressed in terms of real percentage points, and all indexes are expressed in log form. Regressions with EMBI use monthly data from January 1995 to December 1999 (60 observations). Regressions with IFCG use monthly data from January 1985 to December 1999 (180 observations), except for regressions on EMEA which use monthly data from January 1996 to December 1999 (48 observations). Regressions with S&P 500 use monthly data from January 1996 to December 1999.

increase. A 1 percent increase in the G7 real interest rate coincides with an estimated 34 percent decline in the EMBI.

Real interest rates may also have a negative effect on real growth rates in emerging markets. The effect is only statistically significant in the case of Western Hemisphere countries, however: an effect estimated at 0.77 percent in lost growth for every one percentage point increase in G7 real interest rates.

There is much less reason to think that foreign interest rates played an important role in the arrival of the East Asian currency crisis in Thailand in July 1997 as compared to earlier crises. There had been a quarter-point increase in the federal funds rate on 25 March 1997,[6] and later came the first hints of a possible end to the Bank of Japan's policy of low nominal interest rates. However, these developments were relatively minor.[7]

The *passing* of the crises of 1997–98, on the other hand, can be associated with monetary *easing* in the industrialized countries. August 1998 saw a second round of crises, with the Russian devaluation and default, and subsequent widespread contagion, including trouble for the real in Brazil and trouble for Long-Term Capital Management (LTCM) in New York. The G7 responded in a multifaceted manner (to be discussed below). The most potent arrow in the G7 quiver was interest rates. One view is that each country's central bank would have been reluctant to cut interest rates on its own, for fear of capital outflows and currency depreciation. U.S. leadership could signal the move to a new easier-money global equilibrium. President Clinton, in a speech on the emerging market crises at the Council on Foreign Relations in September, said that the balance of risks in the global economy had shifted from inflation to deflation.[8] The Federal Reserve Board subsequently voted to lower the federal funds rate three times in the fall of 1998 (end-September, mid-October, and mid-November). Virtually every major central bank in the world followed suit. Within a few months the financial crisis had passed. There can be little doubt that the monetary easing played an important role. (Admittedly, it took longer for the real economies to recover in many of the emerging markets.)

Indeed, it is possible that the monetary easing of late 1998 is the answer to a puzzle that the case of Brazil otherwise poses. The conventional wisdom to come out of the crises of 1994–98 was that the worst thing a country can do, once capital inflows turn to capital outflows, is to delay an inevitable devaluation. Vulnerable emerging markets must choose between rigid institutional fixes for the exchange rate, for those countries willing to give up monetary autonomy, or else increased flexibility (see Edwards, chap. 1 in this volume). If they stubbornly cling to a peg or other exchange rate target until they have lost most of their reserves, the devaluation when it comes will be very costly, resulting in a loss of confidence and a severe recession. This is what happened to Mexico, Thailand, and Korea. Brazil stalled throughout the second half of 1998, hoping that capital outflows

---

6. A few observers, apparently including some at the New York Federal Reserve, have implicated the Federal Reserve's one-quarter point move (which could have been the beginning of a new trend, even though it turned out not to be) in the subsequent withdrawal of international investors from Thailand (Woodward 2000, 188).

7. World interest rates do not figure prominently in the more recent statistical studies of crisis predictors, probably because they were not close to the scene of the crime in 1997 when it came time to round up the suspects (e.g., Goldstein, Kaminsky, and Reinhart 2000).

8. Waldman (2000, 231). This was the one time that the administration came close to commenting on monetary policy.

would abate and postponing the devaluation in precisely the way that conventional wisdom warned against. However, when the Brazilian devaluation materialized in January 1999, the feared adverse effects did not. Brazil's growth increased in 1999, led by newly competitive exports, as in the traditional textbook view, but in contradiction to the new conventional wisdom. Furthermore, unlike the contagions of the preceding two years, the Brazilian devaluation had no serious repercussions outside the region. Why the contrast with the preceding crises? There are a number of possible explanations, but one major factor was the easing of liquidity by the major central banks and the restoration of global confidence that had taken place over the intervening five months.

Between the spring of 1999 and the spring of 2000, the Federal Reserve once again raised interest rates, in response to fears of overheating in the U.S. economy. Spreads on some emerging market debt, along with spreads on low-rated U.S. corporate debt, subsequently rose to levels reminiscent of the fall of 1998. This renewed flight of investors away from risk contributed to tremendous financial pressure on Argentina and Turkey in November 2000. It is possible that the movement in U.S. interest rates again contributed to these events.

As with the preceding crises in other countries, macro policies in the industrialized countries were not the most important cause of the problems in Argentina and Turkey. In Argentina an overvalued currency, together with fiscal imbalances and large domestic and external debt refinancing needs, made investors nervous about the economic prospects of the country. In Turkey, structural weaknesses and scandals in the banking system were particularly relevant. In both cases, the turmoil in the currency and domestic bond markets was controlled in late 2000 through a combination of a stronger program of policy adjustment joint with packages of exceptional financing from the IMF (activation of the Supplemental Reserve Facility) and other official creditors; but the peg in Turkey collapsed in February 2001.

G7 Exchange Rates

Regardless of what choices they make for their own currencies, even if they opt for a fixed exchange rate, small countries can do nothing about variability in the exchange rates among the dollar, yen, euro, and other major currencies. To peg to one currency is to float against the others. At a minimum, this variability complicates their lives. However, some observers would protest that this description understates the problem. They attribute crises in emerging markets, in part, to fluctuations in G7 exchange rates, and they propose international plans to stabilize them.

The strong appreciation of the dollar in the early 1980s raised the value of the debt obligations of Latin American countries relative to their export proceeds. The destinations of the exports were more diversified geographically (especially in Europe) than were the origins of the loans, which were mostly denominated in dollars. Thus the dollar appreciation was another of the contributing factors that precipitated the debt crisis.

Did a Rise in the Yen-Dollar Rate Cause the East Asia Crisis?

Standard accounts of the origins of the East Asia crises that began in mid-1997 also feature prominently the 40 percent appreciation of the dollar against the yen over the preceding two years.[9] The East Asian countries are said to have lost international competitiveness because they were pegged to the dollar, which led to large current account deficits, loss of reserves, and ultimately the crises.

This argument is in some ways overstated. In the first place, the appreciation of the dollar against the yen was only a reversal of a sharp depreciation of the dollar that had preceded it in the early 1990s.[10] In the second place, although the competitiveness effects were real enough, there was also a debt denomination effect that could go the other way. Not all foreign debt is denominated in dollars. The use of the yen in Asian finance increased sharply in the 1980s and was widely heralded at the time. The southeast Asian countries, in particular, doubled the share of their debt denominated in yen from 1980 to 1987, surpassing the share denominated in dollars. For this reason, when Southeast Asians in the late 1980s pleaded for a reduction in yen-dollar volatility, citing fears of severe financial stress, they were worried about appreciation of the yen, not depreciation![11]

Admittedly, the currency denomination of Asian debt reversed to some extent in the 1990s. By 1996, the dollar share had reached 41.5 percent, and the yen share had declined to 24.0 percent for the region overall. However, the situation varies substantially from country to country. Toward one end of the spectrum, two of the three crisis countries, Thailand and Indonesia, still had more yen debt in 1996 than dollar debt. For Thailand and the Philippines, the importance of the Japanese market in exports was well below the importance of the yen in their debt. For Indonesia, the debt shares corresponded roughly to the trade shares. Toward the other end of the spec-

---

9. 120/85 = 1.41.

10. The yen-dollar rate, which peaked near 147 in 1998, had also been at that level in 1990, and far higher than that before 1986.

11. It should also be noted that these figures apply only to long-term debt. Figures on the currency denomination of short-term loans are not available for all countries, but they were probably more often dollar-denominated than was long-term debt. (For Korea, short-term debt denominated in dollars represented 91 percent of the $19.9 billion total, yen debt 7 percent, and DM debt 1 percent. The data include debt for all banks or countries that participated in the January 1998 rollover agreement.) It should also be noted that a comparison of debt shares and export shares tells the direction of effect on the debt-export ratio only if export quantities are fixed in terms of the partner's currency. It ignores, for example, competition with Japanese producers in other markets.

trum, Malaysia and, especially, China had dollar debt shares that were higher than their yen debt shares and higher than the relative importance of the dollar area (taken to be the western hemisphere) in their exports. Consequently, these may be the countries that had the most to lose from yen depreciation. This may help explain why China opposed further depreciation of the yen against the dollar in June 1998. A desire to placate China was reported to be the motive behind yen purchases at that date, the first time the Clinton Administration had intervened to resist dollar strength. (Other reasons were important as well, however.)

As recently as the mid-1990s, fears of the consequences in Asia of a yen appreciation were associated with the "yen carry" trade. When Japanese interest rates fell almost to zero, speculators began borrowing heavily in yen and investing the proceeds in dollar-denominated securities that paid higher interest rates, the practice known as yen carry trade. The difference in interest rates is pure profit if the exchange rate remains unchanged, but some were concerned that Asian speculators were underestimating the dangers of future yen appreciation, which could impose huge losses if it occurred. It is ironic that during the two years leading up to the Asia crisis, the yen-dollar movement was in the opposite direction, and the yen carry trade was temporarily very profitable.[12]

To summarize the point, the depreciation of the yen between 1995 and 1997 helped the Southeast Asian debtors on the debt side, by reducing debt service costs and improving their balance sheet, even while it hurt them on the trade side. If the debt service ratio is a relevant indicator, then the depreciation of the yen against the dollar was actually good for countries like Thailand, where the share of debt denominated in yen exceeded the share of exports going to Japan, but bad for countries like China, where the reverse was true. We emphasize the implications for yen-denominated debt only because it has been completely neglected in most commentary.[13]

One interpretation is that large swings of the yen-dollar rate in *either* direction generate stress in the region, that volatility per se is the problem. If exchange rates among the major industrialized countries were stabilized, it would no doubt simplify the lives of everyone else. The key question, then, becomes whether this stabilization can be accomplished in practice, or at what sacrifice.

---

12. Such fears indeed became relevant in the fall of 1998, when the yen appreciated sharply.

13. The Frankel and Rose (1996) study looked for evidence of the debt exposure effects. The question was whether the probability of a currency crash increases in a country when there is an appreciation of the major currencies in which a high proportion of that country's debt is denominated. Even though other measures of the composition of capital inflows or external conditions showed up as significant indicators (e.g., the share of short-term debt and foreign interest rates), this measure of currency composition and movements in G3 exchange rates did not show up with the sign expected. Perhaps the trade composition channel on average outweighs the debt composition channel.

The Proposal for a Group of Three Target Zone

Such commentators as Bergsten, Williamson, and Volcker have urged the Group of Three (G3) countries to stabilize exchange rates, for example, through a target zone arrangement. One of their arguments is precisely that excessive exchange rate volatility among the dollar, yen, and euro plays a role in emerging market crises.[14] Most economists, however, believe that exchange rates reflect monetary conditions in the corresponding countries and other economic fundamentals such as productivity, that the G3 countries have no means for stabilizing their exchange rates other than devoting monetary policy to the task, and that they neither should nor will subordinate domestic priorities to such international goals (e.g., Clarida 2000).

We believe that the view that all exchange rate fluctuations are attributable to monetary policy and other economic fundamentals is too simple. Sometimes the exchange rate moves for reasons unrelated to fundamentals, and sometimes governments can combat such moves by public statements or intervention in the foreign exchange market, even if these actions do not change monetary policy (Dominguez and Frankel 1993). Intervention in support of the dollar in mid-1995 was instrumental in reversing the preceding depreciation of the dollar, and intervention in support of the yen in mid-1998 may also have played a role in reversing the depreciation of the yen.

Nevertheless, the majority's policy conclusion stands. If the G3 or G7 countries were to proclaim an explicit target zone for the major currencies, it would not be long before speculators were testing the limits, a challenge in which they would eventually be successful. We do not view a target zone among the G3 currencies as a practical reform to help avert crises in emerging markets.

Industrial Country Trade Policies

International trade is an important engine of economic development even in the best of times.[15] When a developing country undergoes a balance-of-payments crisis, the ability to increase exports rapidly (or, more generally, to increase production of internationally traded goods) is critical to its resolution. For many of the recovering victims of recent emerging market crises, an improvement of the trade balance led the stabilization of confidence on the part of international investors. These countries succeeded in switching from large deficits to surplus in the span of a couple of months. Unfortunately, this initial "improvement" in the trade balance usually takes the form of a sharp drop in imports due to domestic recession. It takes

14. See, for example, the dissenting statement "On Target Zones for the G-3 Currencies," by Paul Allaire, C. F. Bergsten, and others including George Soros and Paul Volcker, in Council on Foreign Relations (1999), pages 125–29. They believe there can be no serious reform of the architecture regarding emerging markets without a plan to stabilize the dollar, yen, and euro.

15. Econometric evidence and further references are available in Frankel and Romer (1999).

longer before the devaluations have the intended effect of promoting exports. Only over the subsequent few years does growth in exports lead the recovery of economic activity.

In the past, the highest barriers to international trade have been those put in place by the developing countries themselves. However, most of these countries, at least most that qualify as emerging markets, went a long way in the 1990s toward reducing trade barriers. Industrialized countries retain substantial barriers to exports from developing countries, and there is little evidence of a downward trend. True, the rich countries in the Uruguay Round of multilateral negotiations to liberalize trade promised to phase out over time their quotas on apparel and textiles, two of the most important sectors for developing countries, and to end the previous exemption of agriculture from multilateral negotiations. The phasing-out has yet to begin, however, and there is even less sign of any intention to liberalize with respect to those agricultural products, such as sugar and rice, that are of particular interest to developing countries.

In fact, many rich-country politicians, in the wake of both the 1982 and 1997 crises, responded to increases in their constituents' purchases from developing countries by supporting new protection of domestic markets. They either did not realize or did not care that shutting off these exports was inconsistent with calls on emerging market countries to obey the rules of the marketplace and to generate the foreign exchange needed to service their debts. Barriers to the export of steel from Brazil, Korea, and Russia were perhaps the strongest examples.

What are the chances that a future World Trade Organization (WTO) round will address the export interests of the developing countries? Even though decisions in the General Agreement on Tariffs and Trade (GATT) and WTO are technically made by consensus, with each country having an equal vote, it is inevitable that some players in practice count far more than others. The pattern in past GATT rounds has been that cut-and-thrust exchange between the United States and Europe has dominated the negotiations, and when those two powers have come to some agreement, the rest of the world generally falls into line. Other countries have had little influence over the agenda. Little vote was given to the developing countries, largely because they had little in the way of lucrative concessions to offer the rich countries.

Increasingly, however, the developing countries are important players, at least collectively. Asia and Latin America now constitute major markets. Under the new rules agreed upon in the Uruguay Round, they, like other WTO members, are generally no longer able to opt out of aspects of an agreement[16] or to block decisions by panels under the dispute settlement

16. Bhagwati (1998). The requirement that WTO members must adhere to all negotiated obligations as a "single undertaking" still has exceptions for the poorest developing countries. Also, two areas, government procurement and civil aviation, remain under "plurilateral accords" of the WTO (Schott 1998, 3).

mechanism. Furthermore, in the Uruguay Round developing countries were asked in the area of Intellectual Property Rights to put energy into enforcement of a set of rules that, whatever their economic justification, benefit rich-country corporations and not them. For all these reasons, in the next round of WTO negotiations their interests will have to be taken into account. In addition to liberalization of textiles trade, this would also mean protection against arbitrary antidumping measures, if the United States would agree (and liberalization in agriculture, if Europe would agree). If a new round has nothing to offer the developing countries, they might this time try to block it.

Textiles and apparel are typically the first rung of manufacturing exports for poor countries seeking to climb the ladder of development. Rich countries agreed in 1995, under the Uruguay Round, to phase out over the next ten years the quotas that under the Multi Fiber Agreement (MFA) have long kept the textile sector highly protected. An acceleration of the schedule is the simplest concession to offer the poor countries in exchange for the many demands being placed on them. But little liberalization has occurred to date. The difficult time the U.S. administration had in 1998–99 in convincing Congress to support the elimination of barriers to apparel exports even from Africa and the Caribbean is revealing. China's accession to the WTO alarms some with the prospect of a huge increase in the global supply of inexpensive textiles and apparel. There are grounds for skepticism, given domestic politics in the United States and other rich countries, regarding whether the MFA phase-out that was promised in 1995 will actually happen. If rich countries fail fully to deliver on this promise, it is hard to see what incentive developing countries have to go along with a new round or even to carry out their Uruguay Round commitments in the area of Intellectual Property Rights (Wang and Winters 2000; Subramanian 1999).

Antidumping (AD) measures are on the upswing. In 1999, 328 AD cases were launched, up 41 percent from 1998, and more than double the rate in 1995 (*The Economist,* 22 April 2000). The name *antidumping* makes the measure sound like it has something to do with antitrust enforcement against predatory pricing; thus it gives the press and public the impression that these measures are a tool to combat trade distortions and increase competition. On the contrary, they have nothing to do with predatory pricing: they suppress competition rather than defending it, and they are among the costliest of trade barriers.[17]

The use of AD measures increased rapidly in the United States in the 1980s and 1990s, because firms hit by increased imports found it much easier to gain protection under the AD laws than under the safeguard laws.

---

17. The enactment of antidumping duties means import quantities on average fall by almost 70 percent and import prices rise by more than 30 percent (Prusa 2000).

Their use has subsequently increased rapidly in other countries as they emulate and retaliate against the United States. An attempt to rein in the indiscriminate use of AD would rank near the top of the economist's wish list of priorities for the next round of multilateral negotiations. (It could be coupled with some steps toward a multilateral competition policy, to reassure those who are under the illusion that the AD laws have some procompetition value.) Unfortunately, the United States is unlikely to agree to the inclusion of this issue.

Nothing requires waiting for a new WTO round to reduce trade barriers against emerging markets. In the aftermath of the 1997–98 crises, the major industrialized countries could have committed collectively to keeping their markets open to exports from other countries. However, even an initiative to commit the rich countries to end quotas and duties on their imports from the poorest countries, at the IMF and World Bank meetings in the spring of 2000, ran into the inevitable political roadblocks (e.g., "Spring Meetings Fail to Burst into Blossom," *Financial Times,* 19 April 2000).

To recapitulate the conclusions of section 3.1.1, movements among the industrialized countries in interest rates and, to a lesser extent, exchange rates, can have important influences on emerging markets. Inflationary monetary policies among industrialized countries might temporarily help emerging markets but would also do substantial damage to the industrialized countries. Sustaining their own growth and keeping their trade barriers low may be the most important things that industrialized countries can do to maximize growth in emerging markets and minimize the frequency and severity of crises. At the end of the day, providing open markets for goods and services may be more important than all the institutional reforms that have been proposed regarding the financial architecture.

3.1.2   Crisis Management

There is a vast array of organizations and venues where national representatives deliberate over measures that affect emerging markets, whether the measures are in the category of short-term macroeconomic policy coordination or long-term reform of the international financial architecture to reduce the frequency of future crises and resolve more efficiently those crises that do occur. When a crisis breaks out, these mechanisms become particularly important as a mode of crisis management, that is, as a means to minimize adverse effects.

Modalities of Coordination

The governments of the industrialized countries dominate the discussions in these meetings. One defense against wider inclusion is that speed and decisiveness are important in crisis management, which requires a small number of participants. Moreover, groupings of small countries receive a voice through proportionate representation, as on the IMF Board of Executive Directors, with votes roughly proportionate to economic importance. One rationale for participation by the IMF managing director in G7 finance ministers' meetings is as a representative of the smaller countries. (The Russian president is now included in Group of Eight (G8) summit meetings; but the country is not invited to participate in G7 meetings on financial topics.)

Some emerging market countries are large. By 1996, China and Brazil had in economic size surpassed Canada, the seventh largest country in the G7, even when their GDPs are valued at current exchange rates. In addition, India, Mexico, and Indonesia had done so if one evaluates GDPs by purchasing power parity (PPP).[18] Switzerland, Belgium, and Sweden are in the Group of Ten (G10), but by 1996 China, Brazil, Korea, Russia, India, Argentina, and Mexico had passed Sweden, even at current exchange rates (as had many others, if one evaluates GDPs at PPP rates). After the crises of 1997–99, the emerging markets all slipped in the rankings. In 1999 only China remained ahead of Canada, by the PPP measure; Brazil, Mexico, India, Korea, Taiwan, and Argentina remained larger than the smaller members of the G10.

The fact that the G7 (United States, Japan, Germany, France, United Kingdom, Italy, and Canada) and G10 economies are overall larger than the developing countries does not explain the membership in the G7 or G10.[19] Another relevant principle that explains these power relationships is that creditors generally have influence over debtors.[20] While the United States (and Italy) are net debtors internationally, in the context of crises they are net lenders to crisis countries and to the international financial institutions. Perhaps the most succinct description of the membership of the G7 is that it represents the victors in the Cold War, much as the membership of the United Nations (UN) Security Council was chosen to represent the victors of World War II. Moreover, the growing economic importance of systemically important emerging market economies is behind the recent drive to create international groupings, such as the Group of Twenty (G20; to be

18. National incomes are properly evaluated at purchasing power parity rates if one is interested in the real incomes of the population. For purposes of evaluating weight in international power relationships and responsibilities, it is more appropriate to evaluate at actual exchange rates. For example, one might care how many F-16s a country can buy, how much money it can offer a small island nation for the right to put a naval base there, or how much it can contribute to a multilateral peacekeeping operation, famine relief, debt forgiveness, or the New Arrangements to Borrow. In each case, current exchange rates are the right measure, as variable as they are.

19. This group has actually eleven members: the G7 plus the Netherlands, Belgium, Sweden, and Switzerland.

20. This truism is somewhat at odds with another favorite and wise aphorism: "If you owe your banker a million dollars, you have a problem. If you owe your banker a billion dollars, he has a problem."

discussed below), that include these countries along with the advanced industrialized countries.

Finance Ministers and Deputies

The G7 finance ministers, their deputies, and deputies' deputies play a crucial and central role in crisis management. This role takes three central forms:

1. Consultations and cooperation during crises of systemically important countries to resolve such crises (Mexico, Thailand, Korea, Indonesia, Russia, Brazil);

2. Joint work to develop G7 policies and doctrine on how to prevent and resolve financial crises (as in the work on the reform of the international financial architecture);

3. Crisis management for nonsystemic countries requiring external debt rescheduling or restructuring (Pakistan, Ukraine, Ecuador, Romania) and formulation of official doctrine on private-sector involvement in crisis resolution.

Crisis management and resolution as well as formulation of policies regarding private-sector involvement (PSI) involves a number of other institutions, namely, the IMF, the Paris Club, the Bank for International Settlements (BIS) and G10 central bank governors, national security agencies and heads of state and, more recently in a more limited consultative forum for discussing general PSI policies, the G20 group. The role of these other players will be discussed below, after the G7.

There are a variety of views among the G7 on how to deal with these three sets of issues, but the G7 has been able to reach a solid consensus on most questions. Indeed the work on crisis management and architecture reform has been very cooperative. On the question of how to deal with systemic liquidity cases, Europeans have been slightly more wary than the United States of providing large packages of official money out of concerns about moral hazard. Some Europeans have also correspondingly been somewhat more hawkish in support of more coercive ways to involve the private sector in crisis resolution, including stronger sympathy for the idea of debt standstills. The United States has stressed the importance of maintaining some degree of flexibility to address each case on its own merits rather than relying on rigid or formal rules, including using large official packages when appropriate. The United States has shown greater support for the idea of corner solutions in exchange rate regimes (either a firm fixed or flexible one, as opposed to intermediate regimes) than the Europeans and the Japanese, and less sympathy for some suggestions to restrict international capital flows (both inflows and outflows). Some Europeans and Japanese are also more sympathetic toward ideas regarding direct rather than indirect regulation of highly leveraged institutions such as hedge funds in the context of the work of the Financial Stability Forum. There has also been a broad related discussion among the G7 members on how to reform the IMF. In spite of the different nuances and differences, the G7 has been able to reach a significant and constructive consensus about the various elements of architecture reform, including PSI, as shown by the G7 Koln summit report and the Fukuoka summit report, as well as other G7 finance ministers reports and communiqués at the IMF-World Bank meetings.

The G7 dialogue has included issues such as the following: how to reform IMF facilities with Europeans more sympathetic to the Extended Fund Facility (EFF) and the United States wanting to provide a greater role to the Contingent Credit Line (CCL); how much emphasis to give in country programs to traditional macroeconomic policies relative to structural ones; how to reform the governance structure of the IMF (with Europeans pushing to turn the former Interim Committee into a stronger and more powerful executive body; the eventual compromise turned it into the International Monetary and Financial Committee [IMFC]); and how to reform the current country quotas (because, according to some criteria, the European countries are currently overrepresented and emerging market economies are underrepresented).[21] Again, this dialogue has been constructive and led to the development of a consensus as represented by the G7 April 2000 Finance Ministers Communiqué at the time of the IMF-World Bank annual meetings. At the annual IMF-World Bank meetings in Prague in September 2000, agreement was reached on how to operationalize the reform of IMF lending facilities and broader reform of the IMF.[22]

Developing countries believe that they should be better represented in the decisions that affect them. The issue of the representation of significant emerging market economies in international bodies has emerged not only in the context of the discussion about IMF quotas but also in the U.S. position, viewed with some concern by some European G7 countries, that the views of such emerging markets should be more broadly represented in global affairs. Europeans know that any such shift in power will come largely or entirely at their expense. The U.S. push to involve emerging market countries began with a proposal by President Clinton in November 1997, at the Vancouver Leaders Summit of the Asia-Pacific Cooperation forum. It took the form of support for the inclusion of important emerging market governments in the ensuing Group of Twenty-Two and Group of Thirty-Three (G22 and G33) process, support that led to three early reports in late 1998 on international architecture reform. These groups were followed by the creation of the Group of Twenty (G20) as a regular forum of

21. See IMF (2000c) for the report of the official "Cooper Commission" on how to reform the country quotas.
22. The details of this agreement are described later in the "Recent G7 Initiatives to Reform the International Monetary Fund" section.

dialogue among advanced industrial economies and a group of systemically significant emerging markets. The transformation of the Interim Committee into the IMFC balanced some European concerns about the creation of new groups such as the G20.

Coordination among Central Bankers and the Bank for International Settlements

G10 central bankers and the BIS have also been involved in crisis management and resolution. A particularly significant role in crisis response and management has been played by the U.S. Federal Reserve given the lead role of the United States in international financial policies. The role of G10 central banks has been more prominent in the large systemic liquidity cases than in the smaller, nonsystemic countries' cases. In the former cases (Mexico, Thailand, Indonesia, Korea, Russia, Brazil), G10 central banks have been directly involved in the formulation of official policy: consultations on how to deal with systemic countries and on the size of official rescue packages and involvement in lining up second lines of defense financial support.

G7 finance ministries have been most directly in charge of the design of official G7 policy regarding the reform of the international financial architecture (the Koln and Fukuoka summit reports), but central banks have been widely consulted in this process.

G10 central banks' direct involvement in the formulation of official policy for PSI in crisis resolution has been more limited (relative to that of treasuries and finance ministries), although G10 central banks have run some seminars and activities in the debate on PSI. Their involvement in nonsystemic debt restructuring cases has also been more consultation than direct crisis management even if some central banks (the U.S. Federal Reserve and the regional New York Federal Reserve) play a larger role in such cases as well.

G10 central banks and the BIS play a larger role in addressing global systemic risk issues and in questions of international financial regulation (the Financial Stability Forum work). The Federal Reserve was deeply involved in the management of the LTCM crisis. The Basel Eurocurrency Committee (now the Committee on Global Financial Stability [CGFS]) has been involved in discussing and managing the response and formulation of policies to address episodes of global financial turmoil, global liquidity shocks, and systemic financial crises.

G10 central banks have also been deeply involved in the work of the Financial Stability Forum and its formulation of recommendations on highly leveraged institutions, short-term capital flows, offshore financial centers, implementation of codes and standards, and reform of deposit insurance.

Also, the formulation of monetary policy by G10 central banks has been affected by episodes of systemic crises. The reductions of interest rates by the Federal Reserve and many other central banks in the fall of 1998 (following the Russian default, the LTCM crisis, the seizure of global liquidity, and the spillover of financial turmoil from emerging markets to U.S. and other G7 capital markets) were not coordinated but were successful in stemming the risk of a global financial meltdown.

Also, the work on the reform of the Basel Accord (the BIS capital standards) has seen a central role for the central banks and other institutions that supervise and regulate the banking and financial system.

Paris Club

The Paris Club (PC) is a major forum for crisis management and resolution, because it is in charge (in consultation with the IMF) of the rescheduling of official bilateral credits to emerging markets. The PC has become a lightning rod for complaints of the private sector against the official policy for PSI in crisis resolution. Complaints emerged from recent policy debates and private financial-sector views on official PSI policy in general and bonded debt restructuring in Pakistan, Ukraine, Russia, Ecuador, and Nigeria specifically. The club has been accused of a number of ills: being a secretive organization, arbitrary and unfair in its decisions; forcing the private sector to be the residual claimant (deciding first how much the official creditors are paid in cash when there are external financing gaps and letting the residual be paid to private creditors); expecting private debt reduction when it does not provide any itself; lacking transparency, predictability, and openness; being unwilling to engage the private sector in negotiations and dialogue; being politically biased in its decisions; and imposing comparability (the restructuring of private claims on terms comparable to the restructuring of official claims) while not accepting reverse comparability (the restructuring of official claims on terms comparable to those of private claims in cases—like that of Russia—when private claims are restructured before PC ones).

Many of these critiques suggest a significant misunderstanding in the financial community of the role and functions of the PC.

The first misconception about the PC is the belief that its claims are senior to those of the private sector. Although official bilateral claims are perceived to have legal seniority over private ones, the reality of international finance is that PC claims are always effectively junior to private ones. When a country experiences debt-servicing difficulties, the first payments that are suspended are those to PC creditors. Debtors know that going into arrears to PC creditors has little consequence (because such claims are eventually rescheduled), whereas nonpayment to private creditors has consequences (formal default, acceleration, litigation risk, etc.). Thus, debtors are most eager to stop paying official bilateral creditors well before they stop paying private creditors. Indeed, strategic nonpayment to the PC has long been used by debtors as a way to continue paying in full and on time to private creditors. The accumulation of arrears to PC creditors is a systematic and endemic phenomenon that has allowed continued payments to private claims. For example, Nigeria accumulated over $23 billion of arrears to the PC and has so far paid in full its private debts. This is a distorted system of incentives: no private creditors would be willing to provide credits to a sovereign at the terms, risk features, and spreads provided by official bilateral creditors. Indeed, the fact that countries were still able to have market access in spite of rising PC arrears (as in the case of Ecuador's issuance of Eurobonds in the mid-1990s) implied that investors believed that the financing burden would be shifted to the official creditors and they would not be "bailed in." However, recent applications of the PSI framework (discussed below) have changed this perception: investors do now realize that countries with significant PC arrears are more likely to be involved in PSI, when private claims are material.

Second, PC claims not only are the first to go into arrears, but they are immune from litigation risk; they are not subject to rollover risk because they effectively have a rollover option given to the debtor, in that the latter can always stop paying with little consequence; and they are not subject to liquidity risk driven by any panic from creditors withdrawing lines of credit. Also, such claims are restructured at terms that are often quite generous and at interest rates that do not truly reflect repayment risk. Note that if the market had to provide similar claims not subject to rollover, liquidity, and litigation risk, the pricing of such debt (in terms of spread over risk-free assets) would be most expensive. Consequently, the treatment of PC claims is more beneficial in most dimensions for the debtor than that of private claims.

Third, the PC does not systematically provide debt reduction apart from cases in which the country qualifies for debt reduction, such as qualification under the Highly Indebted Poor Countries (HIPC) initiative or other criteria. However, the terms of PC rescheduling are generous and imply some significant effective reduction in the net present value (NPV) of such claims. In fact, the PC fiction of rolling over claims at the contractual original low interest rate and discounting the present value of restructured claims with a discount rate equal to this rollover rate allows the accounting fiction of maintaining NPV neutrality. The use of a more economically appropriate discount rate reflective of the actual expected repayment probability would imply some significant NPV reduction. Finding the appropriate discount rate for PC claims is not easy. It is likely to be smaller than market rates but much higher than the officially used rate. Nevertheless, the terms of PC claims and their restructuring (systematic arrears; no rollover, liquidity, and litigation risk; generous restructurings with long grace periods and low interest rates; and eventual debt writedowns for some qualifying debtors) suggest that, in most cases, PC claims are effectively reduced rather than just restructured even though not formally subject to face-value reduction.

Arguments that PC restructurings are unfair to private creditors when, as in the case of Ecuador, the private sector is asked to provide for debt reduction while the official sector is not, miss the point: PC restructuring is usually not NPV-neutral. Thus, PC restructuring can be "comparable" to private claims debt reduction even when formal face-value reduction is not immediately provided by PC creditors.

Fourth, the rules followed by the club are quite clear and the criteria, amounts, and terms of restructurings quite forecastable, given the track record and procedures of the PC (normal terms for middle-income countries, Houston terms for poor ones, HIPC terms for those who qualify for HIPC, etc.). Thus, the private sector is normally able to infer how much finance will be provided by the PC creditors. The current process is not much different from that in the 1980s by which PC restructurings were followed by London Club restructurings on "comparable" terms. (The London Club represents private banking creditors in the same way that the PC represents government creditors.) The main difference is that now bonded debt may also be subject to comparability because it is no longer "de minimis"—a consequence of the rising importance of securities markets in international capital flows that were once dominated by bank loans.

Fifth, the PC could do better in terms of providing more information and transparency about its activities. There are limits to what can be done, because the PC is not a structured formal organization but rather an ad hoc group of rotating creditors. In this sense, there is not an official PC view, spokesperson, or common view; any external view would have to be cleared by all relevant creditors. However, the PC has recently made some progress on this front by committing to the creation of a website that will provide information to markets and investors about its activities, rules and procedures.

Sixth, the idea that "reverse comparability" would be used in deciding how to fill a financing gap would create many problems. Some clear burden-slicing rules such as a proportionality principle (whenever there are external financing gaps to make cash payments on debt servicing due and to restructure private and official claims according to the proportion of private and public claims coming to maturity) would provide a simpler, more predictable, and, some would say, fairer distribution of the burden than a formal negotiating process. Moreover, the nature, motivation, and terms of the official bilateral claims are very different from those of the private claims; thus, attempts to negotiate a "fair" distribution of the burden are burdensome and add to uncertainty rather than reducing it. In addition, the current structure of the distribution of the financing burden (country adjustment first, senior status for new International Financial Institution money, more junior status for PC claims with clear and established rules for their restructurings, and residual financing by the private sector) provides a clear and mostly predictable system of adjustment and financing. It is not clear that a system in which the financing burden on the private sector is negotiated would improve on this system.

Seventh, although private-sector participants concentrate on the contribution of the PC creditors, the effective contribution of the official sector to PSI also includes the new money provided by the multilateral creditors. This contribution is often significant and may even be larger than that of bilateral creditors. Conceptually, the larger the combined support of official creditors (both bilateral and multilateral), the smaller the amount of private claims that are subject to PSI. Indeed, often the private-sector response to requests for PSI has been to ask the official creditors as a whole to fill in the entire financing gaps, to avoid nonpayment on private claims so as to shift the full adjustment burden onto the official sector.

Eighth, some confusion derives from the fact that the PC does "flow restructurings" while the private sector does "stock restructuring." The origin of this distinction goes back to the 1980s. The PC would restructure all the claims (including arrears) that came due during the consolidation period; thus, only current payment flows are restructured, rather than the total stock of outstanding debt to official creditors. This also means that repeated flow restructurings of PC claims are necessary, because the stock of debt is not dealt with once and for all, but only the consolidation-period flow payments. The London Club instead would take a stock approach, given the nature of the claims rescheduled (i.e., syndicated bank loans), and restructure the entire stock of claims that were due in the consolidation period, both interest and full principal. Once the doctrine of PSI was applied to bonds starting in 1999, it was logical to take a stock approach for the bonded debt. Although restructuring only payments due in the consolidation period could be technically feasible, dealing with the full stock makes more sense because bond restructurings require bond exchanges of the full stock of debt. It would be extremely cumbersome and inefficient to have only flow restructurings of bonded debt and to do bond exchanges over and over again every few years. Thus comes the rationale of dealing with the stock of bonded debt once and for all and restructuring it according to terms that ensure medium- to long-term viability of the debtor.

Ninth, formal negotiations of the private sector with the PC to discuss the "slicing of the pie" are not likely to be productive, for several reasons. First, PC rules for restructuring versus upfront cash payments are clear and known for a long time. Second, negotiations may lead to endless delays beneficial to none. Third, the current system is effectively close to the proportionality distribution of the debt burden described above. Also, once the up-front cash payment distribution has been figured out, there is little to negotiate because the constraint of medium-term debt sustainability and standard PC rules for the terms of the restructuring of the remaining liabilities determine clear parameters of what is comparable and what is sustainable.

Finally, although the original PC claims against a sovereign may be financing projects that are not motivated on strict commercial terms, this does not mean that all PC loans are strictly "political." If there is a political element in such loans, the effectively subsidized terms of the loans (that is, interest rates that are submarket, adjusted for repayment risk) also price that subsidy transfer. Also, some of the financed projects are either formally or informally of a tied-aid nature and provide benefits to private-sector firms of the creditor country. Thus, the private sector often significantly benefits from such "politically" motivated loans.

Other Government Agencies and Heads of State

Other government agencies, such as national security agencies, ministries of foreign affairs, and defense ministries, as well as heads of government, are also involved in crisis management in important countries even if finance and treasury ministries have had a central role. Quite naturally, geopolitical, strategic, and military considerations play some role in deciding the response to crises. A naive view would argue that the introduction of noneconomic considerations in crisis response represents an interference with sound economic judgment. However, decisions about international financial policy are inherently political in the positive political-economy sense of the word. Countries are "of systemic importance" not only because their size implies systemic contagion effects to other economies in the region or around the world; they are also systemic for geostrategic reasons. For example, Indonesia is the largest Muslim country in the world; its stability has economic and strategic implications for the entire Asian region. Russia is also systemically important, for both the United States and Europe, in part because of geostrategic reasons even though its GDP is smaller than that of the Netherlands. To consider these political factors need not imply compromising sound economic judgment on whether and how much support should be given. It means instead that the policy process considers the political economy of stabilization and reform: how much a country can adjust given its political constraints, and the strategic implication of providing or not providing financial support.[23] The concern that consideration of extraeconomic issues may lead to moral hazard (expectations of bailout of systemically important countries) has a valid basis. Rarely, however, do such considerations dominate more narrow economic criteria for supporting adjustment in a crisis country. In the dialogue between finance ministries and agencies for national security, the former usually play the role of guardians of fiscal and monetary orthodoxy and stress the importance of

23. Some critics of the IMF as not being "independent" of its leading members (De Gregorio et al. 1999) miss the point. In a positive sense, the IMF is a "political" institution that is accountable to its shareholders while at the same time maintaining its standards, following its mandate, and rigorously applying its articles of agreement. As in any other efficient principal-agent relation and corporate governance issue, the appropriate balance between goals and objectives of major shareholders (G7 and other industrial countries) and minority shareholders (emerging market economies) has to be found. However, independence, by itself, has little meaning.

sound politically unbiased decisions on whom and by how much to support financially. The latter are, obviously, more concerned about the strategic effects of letting a systemically important country go. Sometimes the finance ministries explain to the others that there may be no way the West can help a crisis victim that isn't willing or able to help itself, no matter how politically sensitive the country is.

National security agencies and foreign affairs ministries are also quite involved in consultations with finance ministries on the proper response to crises in non–systemically important countries. Some of them (Pakistan, Ukraine, Ecuador, Romania, Nigeria) have political importance that goes beyond their economic size. Generally, finance ministries are more "hawkish" (less willing to provide support to poorly managed economies where there is a poor track record of commitment to stabilization and reform), whereas other agencies, ministries, and departments are generally more "dovish."

Heads of state get involved in crisis management in large systemic cases (Mexico, Thailand, Indonesia, Korea, Russia, and Brazil), during episodes of severe global financial turmoil (as in the fall of 1998) and as a part of the G7 summitry. The speech at the Council on Foreign Relations by U.S. president Clinton in the fall of 1998 showed—at the highest level—the concern about the risks of a global financial meltdown and engagement in trying to design policy responses to such a risk. Progress on architecture reform has been achieved in preparation for various G7 heads-of-state summits (Halifax, Kohln, Okinawa). Even the formation of the G20 was a partial response to heads of state interest in getting involved in a broad dialogue on global issues, although the eventual G20 group was centered around finance ministries rather than heads of state.

The Role of the G3

The G7 club is already sufficiently exclusive to expose it to charges of elitism. However, even this exclusive club of richest countries can be effectively reduced to the G3: the United States, the European Union (EU), and Japan. Furthermore, it is commonly believed that the United States has disproportionate power in the deliberations of the G7 and IMF. The complaint that the global system is essentially run by the Group of One (G1) is well represented by the following quotation.

> [C]ertain national governments—and the United States in particular—exercise a disproportionate influence over the decisions taken by the Fund. In this view, the Fund too often pursues policies that serve the interests of Wall Street and the U.S. State Department rather than the world as a whole. . . . [T]he IMF is too responsive to the agendas of national governments (the governments of its principal shareholders in particular). . . . The U.S. government's prominence in international financial markets and large voting share in the Board enable it to exercise a disproportionate influence over decision-making in the Fund. (De Gregorio et al. 1999, 1–4)

These authors propose that the IMF be given independence, in the manner of an independent central bank, in order to insulate it against pressure from the United States and other large shareholders.

It is unquestionably true that the United States has an influence on global governance that is more than proportionate to its economic size, let alone to its population. Three of many instances in which it is widely believed that the U.S. Treasury wielded heavy influence in the IMF include February 1995, when the United States persuaded Managing Director Michel Camdessus to ram through emergency financial support for its neighbor, Mexico, despite opposition from some other major shareholders; December 1997, when a U.S. assistant secretary of the treasury went to Seoul to tell the Korean government what would be the conditions of its IMF program; and several instances during the 1990s when the IMF was arm-twisted to make a lenient interpretation of Russian compliance with the terms of past programs, to prevent the world's number two nuclear power from going into default. This record has been accompanied by steady grumbling, and worse, on the part of other industrialized countries, especially in Europe, as well as developing countries.

If one wished to pass judgment on this state of affairs, much would depend on how well one thought the United States has used its power—intelligently or incompetently, benevolently or selfishly. It is the view of the authors that the power was used well in the emerging market crises of the 1990s, when one considers the policy choices that had to be made and avoids comparing the actual outcomes with unattainable alternatives. Consider the example of the policy toward Russia, much maligned on account of corruption in that country and the ultimate failure of the IMF program in August 1998. There simply did not exist an option that read "first end corruption and establish rule of law; then support enlightened economic reform." The IMF has to work with the government in place, especially if it is democratically elected. It is not the United States alone, but everyone, that has a high stake in a stable and happy Russia. On the one hand, not to have supported Yeltsin when the best reformers in a century were in the Russian government would have been to say that the West was never prepared to help Russia. This is true even when one knows full well Russia's corruption and other problems. On the other hand, to have continued supporting Yeltsin in August 1998 would have been reliably to throw good money after bad. This is true even when one knows full well that the alternative was default and devaluation. The combination of support when there was a chance that reform would work, and pulling the plug in 1998 when the moral hazard had become severe, sent the right combination of signals. Either a policy of never helping or a policy of always helping would have sent much worse signals.

The considerable power of the U.S. Treasury may not always be wielded as wisely as we feel that it was in the crises of 1995–2000. There are broader issues of international political economy at stake, however, that would be relevant even aside from the quality of personnel in any future U.S. administration.

The most important argument in favor of the U.S. role is the classic argument of international relations theory that the world needs a leader to organize the delivery of "public goods" such as international monetary stability. In a world of many small or medium-sized powers, the free-rider problem would prevent effective collective action: it does not pay for any one country to organize or sustain multilateral cooperation. Charles Kindleberger has argued that Great Britain was the hegemon before World War I—the guarantor of free trade, the gold standard, and the Pax Brittanica. In this view, the fundamental reason for the economic, political, and military horrors of 1919–44 was that Britain had lost the capacity to act as hegemon and the United States had not yet gained the will to play the role. The fundamental reason for the relative harmony and prosperity of the postwar period is that the United States did play that role, in part through the IMF and other multilateral institutions, and has continued to do so in the management of recent crises in emerging markets.

Although the United States has played a leadership role in international financial affairs and the management of recent crises, one should not overstate the hegemonic role of the United States. The G7 process, at the level of both heads of state and finance ministers, works on a consensus basis. The United States may have provided leadership in crisis management, in proposals for the reform of the international financial architecture, for PSI in crisis resolution, and in reform of international financial institutions (IFIs: IMF and multilateral development banks [MDBs]), but the process that has led to the implementation of these reforms has operated through a broader consensus. For example, on architecture reform, PSI reform, and IFI reform, initial U.S. and other countries' proposals lead to an intra-G7 dialogue and eventually to a G7 consensus on these policies and reforms. Next, other emerging market countries were involved in the process (in a number of forums: G22, G33, G20, FSF, etc.) so as to reach a global consensus and decisions to approve the reforms were made within the IMF executive board, where all member countries are directly or indirectly represented.

A valid question is whether the United States is up to the role of global leadership. It showed that capacity after the end of World War II; but can it now, fifty years later? In one way, the United States is well suited for hegemony: its domestic economic and political system sets a good example for the rest of the world, a model that is attractive and overall beneficial. In another way it is ill suited to be global leader: many in the public, and especially in Congress, have lost interest in the role. We consider this latter problem.

Lack of Domestic U.S. Support for Internationalism

Many Americans are now reluctant to pay the price for global leadership, even when the price is small. There is a lack of interest in internationalism.

The United States has won the Cold War, as well as the international economic competition, but it may not be sufficiently interested in collecting its winnings to put down the small deposit required for the job of hegemon.

Examples come readily to mind. As recently as thirty years ago, it would have seemed a great "deal" for the United States to be able to exercise influence in the IMF that is more than proportionate to the size of its quota; in 1998 Congress was very reluctant to approve the U.S. share of the quota increases. Thirty years ago the United States criticized the Russians for neglecting to pay their UN dues; in the 1990s, the United States was the nation chronically in arrears. Ever since 1974 the U.S. Congress has given presidents authority to negotiate trade agreements on a fast-track basis, but Congress continued to deny this authority to President Clinton. The United States seems unconcerned that it is almost completely isolated in its position in international negotiations over such issues as the land mines treaty, International Criminal Court, Kyoto Protocol, Comprehensive Test Ban Treaty, and the antiballistic missile treaty.

Ten years ago, much of this reluctance on the part of the American Congress and public to play an active role in the world had already become evident. However, in the 1980s the fear was that the U.S. economy was in decline, particularly compared to Japan and other East Asian countries. It was said that the United States could no longer afford the cost of leadership as it could have when it had the world's strongest economy. Even at that time, there were serious flaws in this argument. The decline in U.S. economic performance was only relative to others, the natural result of gradual economic catch-up in GDP per capita on the part of many countries. If in the immediate postwar period the United States could afford the vast sums involved in the Marshall Plan, it is hard to see why it could not afford in the 1980s to remain the leading aid-giver (for example) at a time when its income was considerably higher than in the 1950s.

However, it is perhaps more surprising that the reluctance of the U.S. Congress to exercise global leadership continued, even deepened, in the 1990s—surprising because U.S. economic performance was so spectacular, whether measured by the length of the expansion (ten years, an all-time record), the average growth rate (4 percent in the late 1990s), the swing from budget deficit to surplus (records in both cases), or the low rates of unemployment and inflation (to the levels of the 1950s).

The lack of domestic support for internationalism is a serious minus for U.S. leadership. Poll results show a higher level of support among the general public than one might think. A poll by the Chicago Council on Foreign Relations found that 61 percent of the public (and 96 percent of leaders) support an active U.S. role in world and that 54 percent think globalization has been good for America. A poll by the Program on International Policy Attitudes found that 61 percent of Americans favored globalization, almost 80 percent of respondents supported more international cooperation, and a plurality even supported a stronger IMF. However, evidently few people feel strongly about foreign affairs issues, except when they think their economic interests are specifically at stake or when they have relevant ethnic ties. The poll results do not translate into support in Congress.

An amateur political scientist can think of five interrelated reasons for a decline in political support for international initiatives:

1. The end of the Cold War. When the United States was in a global contest with the Soviet Union, many in Congress were willing to support initiatives that they were told would contribute. This ended with the breakup of the Soviet Union.

2. Reversion to pre-1941 isolationism. During most of its history, the United States avoided "entangling alliances." It was a reluctant entrant into the two world wars. The period of strong support for international engagement was a deviation from the normal, attributable to the experience of those wars and to a conviction that the Europeans could evidently not be trusted to manage their own affairs.

3. The passing of the World War II generation. By now, those who had the experience of living through and fighting the war have retired from the ranks of senators and presidential candidates. Perhaps those who have taken their place have less appreciation for the long-term dangers of staying out of international affairs. One is tempted to make an analogy with stock market crashes and with the theory that tolerance for risk in the stock market has been rising since the generation of investors who witnessed the crash of 1929 passed from the scene.

4. Lack of trust in elites. Until recently, most voters would accept the word of experts and leaders that fast-track negotiating authority or International Development Association replenishment was necessary, even if they did not understand them. In the wake of Vietnam, Watergate, and so on people no longer trust elites on any issue. Thus they are unwilling to take their word for it in the area of international finance.

5. A general feeling that money is wasted by international bureaucracies. Polls show that voters think the United States spends far more on foreign aid than it actually does. Apparently they would be willing to allocate more than we currently do if they thought the money would be spent efficiently.[24]

The U.S. Congress

The relevance of America's constitutional separation of powers is not a mere abstraction. The government has been substantively divided in most recent years. For example, the executive and legislative branches have been in the hands of different parties since January 1995. In 1998, at the height of

---

24. Most measures relevant for emerging market crises are not foreign aid. Even the quota contributions to the International Monetary Fund are not budgetary costs but rather asset exchanges.

the emerging market crises, Congress initiated proceedings to impeach the president.

Throughout the postwar period, the American executive has generally been committed to international engagement. This was as true of President Clinton as of his predecessors. In the economic sphere, the biggest international accomplishments in the first Clinton Administration were probably the passage of the WTO and North American Free Trade Agreement (NAFTA) legislation and the Mexican rescue program, and in the second administration, the management of the East Asia crisis.

Congress has been much less supportive. Congress showed its resistance to the Clinton Administration's activist approach to emerging market crises in a number of ways. Two of the most important were its opposition to the use of government funds in the Mexican peso crisis and its initial opposition to an increase in resources for the IMF in 1997–98.

In January 1995, the first attempt by the administration to put together a Mexican support package would have required congressional approval. Notwithstanding that the senate majority leader and the speaker of the house, the newly installed Newt Gingrich, agreed in a White House meeting to support the request, the rank and file in Congress rebelled. By the end of February, the administration was forced to give up on Congress and use the Treasury's exchange stabilization fund (ESF) instead. Use of the ESF is at the discretion of the secretary of the treasury (Henning 1999). The Mexico policy worked well: financial confidence quickly stabilized, the Mexican economy (after an admittedly severe recession) recovered in the second year, and the U.S. Treasury loan was repaid ahead of schedule, at a profitable interest rate. (We consider in the next section the argument that this policy, by posing a moral hazard of "bailout," sowed the seeds for the East Asia crisis three years later.) In any case, many in Congress showed anger that the administration had gone ahead. The D'Amato amendment retaliated by putting severe restrictions on the Treasury's use of the ESF.

When the Thai crisis broke in July 1997, the United States was not one of the countries that contributed bilateral funds to the rescue package. In retrospect this was probably a mistake, in light of the ensuing contagion to much of the world. Certainly the Thais were offended that the United States did not contribute, whereas American funds were made available as part of the "second line of defense" in the Korean and Indonesian rescue packages a few months later. However, a key difference was that the D'Amato amendment expired between the dates of the Thai rescue and the subsequent crises, freeing up the ESF. Thus, if it was indeed a mistake for the United States not to participate, at a time when the Thais were prepared to make needed policy reforms and the systemic crisis arguably might have been nipped in the bud, the mistake could be attributed to Congress.

Many in Congress continued to be hostile to administration efforts, whether out of genuine concerns regarding moral hazard or with the motive of seizing an opportunity to make political hay. Congress refused to approve the administration's request that the United States contribute its $18 billion share of an increase in IMF resources—which was to consist of an increase in members' capital quotas and the establishment of the New Arrangements to Borrow. Sentiment in Congress did not begin to change until the Russian default in July 1998 ushered in round two of the crisis. Many market observers were caught by surprise, having expected the G7 and IMF to continue to bail Moscow out under the logic that it was "too important to fail."

For better or worse, some market observers concluded from the Russian default that the IMF might have run out of resources. (Others drew the lesson that unilateral sovereign defaults on bonds had suddenly become more respectable. The most important of the three possible lessons that could have been drawn, that the IMF and G7 were after all serious about conditionality, was the slowest to win acceptance.) In any case, investors everywhere fled from risk and loaded up on liquidity. An unprecedented contagion spread to Brazil and throughout the western hemisphere. Sovereign spreads on emerging market debt rose to 15 percentage points above treasuries in September. The excess demand for liquidity affected U.S. financial markets, most notably in the form of the near collapse of LTCM. Spreads on corporate bonds rose. News magazines put aside their New Economy or Overheating Economy cover stories and instead began to ask if a global economic meltdown was imminent.

President Clinton's speech on the subject of the crisis in September 1998, before the Council on Foreign Relations in New York, implicitly responded to fears that he and other G7 leaders had been too preoccupied with domestic matters to pay attention. He made evident that there was indeed "someone minding the store" (Waldman 2000, 230–36). There, and at the IMF annual meetings the following month, the White House laid out a series of initiatives to address the current crisis and as well to reform the financial architecture so as to avoid future repeats. (The signal of a change in global monetary policy was discussed in the first section of the chapter.) The president also, for the first time, used the word "irresponsible," in describing congressional foot-dragging on IMF funding. Some congressmen began to worry that if a global recession were really to take place, they would be blamed.

Finally in October Congress responded by passing the funding package for the IMF, opening the way for about $90 billion of usable resources to be provided by all IMF members. The financial refueling of the IMF, in conjunction with the easing of monetary policy and various G7 initiatives, probably contributed substantially to the subsequent weathering of the stresses on Brazil and the easing of the crisis worldwide.

There is one sense in which the low and variable level of congressional support for American international engagement generally, or for bailouts in particular, is useful, however. That is the doctrine of constructive ambiguity in bailout policy.[25] Consider the analogy of the domestic lender of last resort. The Federal Reserve does not admit to having a policy that some banks are automatically "too big to fail." To reduce moral hazard, it seeks to maintain ambiguity as to whom it would bail out. In the case of the largest banks, this coyness is not credible. They are too important to the payments system and thus to the entire economy to be allowed to fail. This is a moral hazard problem with no good solution. At the international level, American claims that in the future the G7 will not necessarily bail out troubled debtors are more credible. In the event of a repeat crisis, it may be that a future executive will seek once again to put together a rescue package for suitably deserving and systemically important countries.[26] However, nobody can be confident that Congress will go along. Thus the constructive ambiguity is credible.

Moral Hazard and Private-Sector Involvement in Crisis Resolution[27]

The problem of moral hazard and attempts to address it by involving private investors in a rescue package are relevant to any attempt at crisis management.

Introduction

The issue of the appropriate ways to involve the private sector in crisis resolution has been one of the most hotly debated and contested policy questions to emerge since the onset of currency and financial crises in the 1990s.[28] It is one of the core issues in the current debate on the reform of the international financial architecture.

Even the definition of the problem is controversial. The issue under consideration has been defined by different authors as the "bail-in" issue (as opposed to "bailout"), the "burden-sharing" issue, the "private-sector in-

---

25. See the longer discussion in the section "International Lender of Last Resort."

26. This is equally true whether the president is a Democrat or Republican. It is only after they leave office that policymakers such as former Secretary of State George Schultz decide that the IMF should be abolished (Schultz, Simon, and Wriston 1999). The first Reagan Administration made full use of the IMF and U.S. funds to bail out countries in Latin America and elsewhere that had more profligate fiscal and monetary policies, larger state sectors, and less liberalized economies than the emerging market countries that the IMF rescued in 1995–98.

27. See Roubini (2000) for a more detailed discussion of the bail-in, burden sharing, and PSI debate and issues.

28. Recent official-sector views and policy on PSI can be found in Rubin (1998), Köhler (2000), Fischer (2000), Summers (2000), Geithner (2000), Group of Seven (1999, 2000) and IMF (1999). Private-sector views include IIF (1999a,b), Corrigan (2000), Bucheit (2000), Cline (2000), Dallara (1999), Kahn (2000), and Independent Task Force (1999). Some academic views include Roubini (2000), Eichengreen (1999b, 2000), Eichengreen and Portes (1995), Eichengreen and Ruhel (2000), Dooley (2000a), Portes (2000), Friedman (2000), Haldane (1999), Kenen (2001) and Rogoff (1999). See Cline (1984) for an analysis of crisis resolution during the 1980s debt crisis.

volvement" question, and, most recently, the "constructive engagement" of the private sector question.[29] The definitional semantics are themselves loaded with the views of different actors (creditors, debtors, and the official sector) of what such involvement should be. The issue of PSI remains highly contentious and complex.

In a sense, PSI is not new at all. The evolving strategy to deal with the international debt crisis of the 1980s already implied a significant, and somewhat coercive, involvement of the private sector in crisis resolution: sovereigns stopped payments on their syndicated loans to international banks; significant debt servicing difficulties emerged; bank loans were first rescheduled, then restructured and rolled over; new money was at times put on the table; and eventually debt reduction came via the Brady plan workouts.[30]

What was new in the 1990s was not PSI but the nature of the debt instruments, creditors, and debtors. As for instruments, bonded debt, short-term interbank loans, other structured debt securities, and derivative instruments have increasingly supplanted syndicated medium-long-term bank loans. As regards creditors, commercial banks have been increasingly supplanted by a whole host of other creditors, such as small and large bondholders, investment banks, hedge funds, and real money investors (such as mutual funds and pension funds). Among debtors, although sovereigns are still important, private-sector debtors in emerging markets (such as financial institutions and corporations) are increasing their share of cross-border borrowing.

Whereas in the 1980s the challenge was to restructure and reschedule the loans of a limited set of commercial banks, the challenge in the 1990s became one of rescheduling and restructuring bonded instruments (as well as cross-border short-term interbank loans). Bond rescheduling was not an issue in the former period because bonded debt was mostly "de minimis" compared to bank loans. Initial attempts by the public sector to include

29. A first term used to discuss this issue was "bail-in" as a way to connote the need to avoid systematic "bailouts" of private-sector creditors during crises. This term was deemed a bit too coercive by some, who preferred instead "burden sharing." However, even the latter phrase was contested as suggesting equity considerations rather than the need to fill a financing gap; the term also had coercive connotations that appear at odds with the goal of constructively involving the private sector in crisis prevention and resolution. Thus, the increasing use by the official sector of the term "private sector involvement in crisis resolution" (often referred to as PSI policy) with the adjective "appropriate" often added in front of PSI to stress the view that such involvement should be as voluntary, constructive, and cooperative as possible. Most recently, the new IMF Managing Director Köhler (as well as the outgoing Deputy Managing Director, Stanley Fischer) has suggested a new phrase, "constructive engagement," that emphasizes the need for voluntary and market-based solutions, as opposed to forced or coercive approaches, to PSI. Unfortunately, this series of increasingly less explicit terms has made it harder and harder for the nonspecialist to know what is meant.

30. A detailed discussion of PSI in the 1980s, from payment suspensions on syndicated loans in the early 1980s to the implementation of the Brady plan in the late 1980s and 1990s, is beyond the scope of this paper. Cline (1995) presents a comprehensive discussion of this issue.

bonded debt into PSI were received with skepticism by the private sector as well as the debtors. It was argued that although in the 1980s it was relatively easy to convince a small set of homogenous creditors subject to regulation and pliant to forbearance (commercial banks) to reschedule a set of homogenous instruments (syndicated bank loans), it would have been impossible to restructure some instruments that were more common in the 1990s. This applies particularly to bonds that did not have collective action clauses, that were heterogeneous in their legal and economic features (Eurobonds, Brady bonds, and other bonded securities) and that were held by thousands of creditors who were marking to market, not heavily regulated, and neither willing to engage nor expert in bonded debt instrument restructuring. The collective action problem of coordinating the actions of such a disparate and large group of creditors without creditor committees or majority and sharing clauses was deemed to make it all but impossible to restructure bonds. Also, it was argued that the short-term nature of the interbank loans would make them hard to restructure: creditors would stop rolling them over and would close their positions before the debtors could even start thinking about a possible partially involuntary rollover. The reality of PSI in the 1990s turned out to be quite different from these pessimistic assessments.

For one thing, the collective action problems were also quite serious in the 1980s: there were hundreds of commercial banks with different exposures and interests; the free-rider or holdout problem was as serious then as now; and the debt instruments were quite heterogenous, because hundreds of very different syndicated loans had to be repackaged and restructured.[31] Moreover, as the recent restructuring of the bonded debt of Pakistan, Ukraine, Russia, and Ecuador suggests, restructuring is feasible even in the absence of ex ante collective action clauses (CACs). Also, with the emergence of short-term interbank loans in the 1990s, in part a reaction to the bail-in of longer-term bank loans in the 1980s, a bail-in of such instruments to prevent liquidity-driven runs became a feature of the strategy. In different ways and with different degrees of coercion or voluntarism, the restructuring or monitored rollover of cross-border interbank loans in Korea, Brazil, Russia, Indonesia, and Turkey became part of the PSI policy of the 1990s.

Even the rationales for PSI have been contested and hotly debated. The official G7 doctrine on PSI stresses the following rationales. First, a balance of payments crisis creates an external financing gap. Even after the debtor makes domestic adjustments to policy and reduces domestic absorption as part of its policy adjustment process, a financing gap may remain because the amount of capital outflows and debt that has to be serviced exceeds the foreign reserve resources of the country avail-

---

31. Collective action problems were partly solved by having creditor committees where some financial institutions took a leadership role and prodded creditors to play ball with carrots and stick. The term "Rhodes Rolodex" has been used to characterize the central role played by Citicorp's Bill Rhodes in providing such a coordinating and leadership role. Interestingly, he played a similar role in some of the 1990s' restructuring episodes, namely in the case of Korea.

able for external debt service. Second, involvement of official creditors may contribute to filling this external financing gap but cannot fill it altogether. Even generous PC restructurings of official bilateral debt and normal access by multilateral creditors to financial support from the IMF, the World Bank, and other MDBs still leave a financing gap. In other words, official money, unless it is exceptionally large (a hotly contested issue) cannot in most cases fill in the debtor's entire financing gap. Third, exceptional financing is not only infeasible given political, financial, and other constraints to large-scale official support, but also undesirable, apart from a few special cases. It is undesirable because expectations of official-sector bailout of creditors would lead to severe moral hazard distortions of cross-border borrowing and lending.[32] Thus, financing gaps, the limited availability of official money, and moral hazard considerations are the basis of the need for "appropriate" PSI in crisis resolution.[33]

32. Throughout this section we use the term "bailout" interchangeably with "large official support." However, the term "bailout" has specific positive and normative connotations. When large-scale official finance is provided to a debtor country, this is not technically a bailout if the funds are eventually repaid to the IMF and official creditors. Indeed, in the recent episodes of large-scale support IMF loans have been repaid or have been serviced according to the terms of the lending. Some argue that these official loans have some subsidy component, but this alleged subsidization is far from a "bailout." One could argue that this official lending is a bailout in that it bails out international creditors of the sovereign or its private firms. However, even in this case the term "bailout" may be inappropriate: as long as the debtors (sovereign or private firms such as banks) are solvent, the creditors would be eventually repaid in full, and the IMF support only changes the timing of their receipts. Preventing the postponement of debt payment servicing that would have occurred if official funds were not available is of value to international creditors (because effective restructuring/rollover/restretching of payments may have a net present value cost to them), but it is not, again, a full bailout. In cases in which the debtor is not solvent and a debt write-down would occur in the absence of official support, policies of PSI may effectively bail in creditors and provide burden sharing. Although the term "bailout" may thus be imprecise, in the following discussion we will use it in the loose form that has been used in the debate on bailouts versus bail-ins.

Note also that the degree of coercion in PSI will vary a lot depending on the specific cases. At one extreme are cases of "soft" PSI, where international investors commit to maintain exposure (as international banks in the cases of Brazil and Turkey) or when debt restructuring occurs on voluntary and market terms (as in the megaswap in Argentina in 2001). More coercive forms of PSI are the case of Korea where international banks agreed to turn short-term lines to Korean banks into medium-term government guaranteed claims under the effective threat of a Korean default. Similarly, the restructuring of the sovereign bonded debt of Ukraine and Pakistan, although not implying a reduction in the principal value of the claims, occurred at below market interest rates and thus implied some NPV reduction. At the other extreme are cases in which the country has effectively defaulted—by suspending payments—on its domestic or foreign liabilities and the restructuring implies a reduction in the principal value of the claims (Russia, Ecuador).

33. Other goals of PSI have been mentioned from time to time. For example, the "unfairness" of bailing out private investors and having the official creditor sector fill in the full financing gap is behind the references to burden sharing. However, fairness and burden sharing can also be seen as being motivated by the lack of enough official money ("there is not going to be enough money to fill in all the gaps") and the moral hazard distortions of large scale bailouts ("creditors and debtors would be reckless if they knew that the official sector stands ready to bail them out systematically").

The basic logic behind the official approach to PSI was thus the need to finance external gaps, the limited availability of official money, and the need to avoid moral hazard distortions. The initial private-sector rejection of PSI in the financial community looks perplexing. Indeed, although the logic of PSI may have been quite uncontroversial, and even the private sector has reluctantly come to accept it, the application of PSI to specific cases has remained complex and controversial. The remainder of this section of the paper will make a broad assessment of the logic of PSI, the evolution of the official doctrine, its application to specific cases, and a wide range of open and controversial issues.[34]

First, note that the type of creditors, debtors, and instruments involved in crisis management and resolution and the degree of coerciveness of PSI has been very different in different crises in the 1990s (Mexico, Thailand, Korea, Indonesia, Malaysia, Russia, Brazil, Ecuador, Ukraine, Pakistan, Argentina, Turkey). At one extreme, there is the case of the 1994–95 Mexican crisis, in which there was no meaningful PSI of foreign investors because the amount of official resources provided by the IMF and the United States to Mexico was sufficient to allow all the foreign holders of short-term government debt (*tesobonos*) who were unwilling to roll over their instruments to exit from Mexico at maturity and with no losses. Very soft forms of PSI were implemented in the Brazilian case; in addition to a large package of official support, private cross-border interbank lines were first monitored (starting in the fall of 1998), and, next, international creditors committed to maintain interbank exposure to February 1999 levels. A similar but even softer form of PSI was implemented in Turkey, where the December 2000 IMF package was accompanied by a soft monitoring of cross-border interbank lines and a generic commitment by international investors to maintain such lines. In the case of Argentina there was no meaningful PSI of foreign investors in the IMF package of December 2000 because the amounts of official support committed to the country were sufficient for the government to avoid, if necessary, borrowing new funds from international

---

34. The discussion will concentrate on the role of PSI in *crisis resolution* while touching only marginally on the use of PSI for *crisis prevention* (which will be discussed in section 3.1.4). Appropriate PSI for crisis prevention partly overlaps with crisis resolution. If a rollover of interbank loans is arranged—maybe through ex ante coordination mechanisms such as creditors' committees—before asset prices such as exchange rates, stock prices, and sovereign debt prices have collapsed, one can think of this as crisis-preventing PSI. After the crisis is triggered, it becomes crisis-resolving PSI, but the substance of the problem is quite similar. Many proposals for crisis prevention could be discussed: capital controls, standstills, creditor committees, voluntary rollovers, private contingent credit lines. We will touch on these as part of our discussion of crisis resolution rather than crisis prevention, but a serious, difficult issue remains open. Ideally, one would want to involve constructively the private sector *before,* rather than *after,* the free fall of currency and other asset prices has caused recession, significant financial distress, and bankruptcy of sovereigns, corporations, and financial institutions. Thus, PSI for crisis prevention is preferable to that for crisis resolution. However, knowing how to avoid the crisis in the first place remains difficult.

capital markets for most of 2001. However, there was some soft form of involvement of the domestic private sector as domestically based banks and pension funds committed in principle to purchase in 2001 determined amounts of government debt.

More coercive forms of PSI were implemented in Korea, Thailand, and Indonesia. In Korea, in December 1997, foreign bank creditors of Korean banks were trying to repatriate most of the short-term cross-border inter-bank lines amounting to about $20 billion. However, faced with the risk of an imminent suspension of payments given that Korea and its banks did not have enough foreign reserves to finance such a roll-off, international banks first agreed to roll over such lines and then, in March 1998, to turn them into medium-term claims. This was a semicoercive form of PSI, formally a form of concerted rollover facilitated by the actions of the U.S. Treasury and the New York Federal Reserve. They helped to coordinate the collective action problem faced by the international creditors: international banks were effectively forced to accept the rollover and maturity transformation of their claims because of the country's lack of reserves to finance a roll-off of such lines. Restructuring of short-term international bank claims against the sovereign was implemented in Thailand and Indonesia even though the amounts at stake were much smaller than in Korea. In Indonesia the severe financial distress of corporates and banks also led to an effective standstill of private-sector liabilities to foreign investors (mostly corporate debtors given the larger exposure of the corporate sector to international banks).

In Asia, sovereign bonded debt issued internationally was minimal; thus, the PSI in these countries did not involve bonded debt. Sovereign bonded debt restructurings, instead, were part of the PSI policy in Pakistan, Ukraine, Russia, and Ecuador. Although the restructuring of these claims was, in the end, voluntary in the sense that unilateral exchange offers were made by the sovereign and accepted by a large fraction on bond creditors, there was a significant amount of coerciveness because these restructurings were preceded by effective default (nonpayment on the old instruments), as in Ecuador and Russia, or threat of default, as in Pakistan and Ukraine. Also, although Mexico, Korea, Indonesia, Thailand, Brazil, Argentina, and Turkey involved large official support packages together with policy adjustment and different degrees of PSI, the four bonded debt restructurings occurred in the context of smaller official support and large financing gaps. In Russia, the initially committed IMF package was large, but, given the country's inability to implement conditionality requirements, actually disbursed amounts were smaller and the country decided to default on a broad range of its claims against foreign investors.

The case of Malaysia was the only one not involving official creditors' support, because the country did not request an IMF package. Thus, the country's own decision to impose capital controls in September 1998 was not formally an application by the IMF and G7 of the official PSI doctrine.[35] Such controls were, however, a form of standstills on some payments to foreign investors and will be discussed below in the section on standstills.

The official PSI doctrine has evolved over time. As discussed above, PSI was part and parcel of the official strategy to deal with the 1980s debt crisis including the Baker plan of 1985 and culminating in the Brady plan and its implementation in the early 1990s. The Mexican peso crisis of 1994–95, the first major capital account–based crisis of the 1990s, brought back the issue of whether and how appropriately to involve the private sector in crisis resolution. The effective bailout of private investors was ex post successful in that Mexico had been close to a liquidity run and that its economy rapidly and successfully recovered after official support. However, it led to the now familiar concerns about moral hazard, political limits to the size of official support packages, and the need for PSI. The G10 Rey Report came out in 1996 with recommendations about the need for CACs, IMF lending into arrears, and appropriate PSI. These recommendations were not implemented at that time, but the debate resurged in the aftermath of the Asian crisis. The crisis brought back the question of PSI, both in practice and as a doctrine. Before official doctrine was formally fleshed out, dealing with the crisis cases led to effective private-sector burden sharing in Korea, Indonesia, and Thailand. These cases were limited to cross-border bank loans (to financial institutions and corporates) and did not address the issue of restructuring bonds that were de minimis in these episodes. The official PSI doctrine was next developed as part of the attempt to reform the international financial architecture. The October 1998 reports of the G22 included one on PSI in crisis prevention and resolution. The formal G7 doctrine was fleshed out in early 1999 in preparation for the July 1999 Koln G7 summit, where PSI was addressed as one of the building blocks of the new international financial architecture. The Koln document on architecture reform included a large section on the new G7 PSI framework and doctrine.

This official doctrine can be characterized as a case-by-case approach with principles and tools. While the approach was case by case, a series of clear principles and tools were provided to clarify the process to be used in implementing PSI. Although some suggested the need for more precise rules to guide PSI, rigid rules were in the end deemed by the G7 as unrealistic. In this view, the complexity and novelty of the issues to be addressed did not allow a rigid set of rules. For example, under what circumstances would PSI be implemented? What kind of PSI would be appropriate in different cases: soft, semicoercive, concerted, coercive? What claims are to be included in PSI: bonded debt, short-term interbank flows, other short-

---

35. Formally, even the Russian case was not part of the official PSI policy because involving the private sector was not a requirement of the IMF program. The country decided on its own to default on some of claims.

term credits, Eurobonds, Brady bonds, domestic debt (local and foreign currency–denominated)? What class of creditors is to be included: foreign, domestic, bondholder, bank creditors? How much adjustment and how much filling of external gaps are required? And how would the financing gap be filled between multilateral creditors (IFIs), bilateral official creditors (PC creditors), and the private sector? How is PC comparability to be defined? How is the financing pie to be divided among different creditors? Is PSI to come before or after a PC rescheduling? What about reverse comparability? How to restructure sovereign bonds: via a market soundings process followed by unilateral debt exchange offers, or by relying on committees and formal negotiations between debtors and creditors? Should CACs be used or not? How much to micromanage the restructuring process? What to do in liquidity cases? How to distinguish insolvency from illiquidity?[36] This is only a partial list of the very difficult questions that the official sector had to address in designing its PSI policy. Because many of these questions did not have a simple answer, in the view of the G7 the case-by-case approach-cum-principles and tools for PSI provided the correct balance between the need to provide clear guidelines to market participants and the need to maintain the flexibility of the policy to address specific cases.

The official doctrine has also stressed two other points that are of paramount importance. First, PSI should be "as appropriate." This bland word is intended to signify that, in the G7 view, whether and what type of PSI was needed would have to be considered by case-by-case study. Blanket rules suggesting PSI for all countries in crisis or for all countries that may have an IMF program would be avoided. In each case, the merit of appropriate PSI would have to be carefully assessed. Second, strong preference should be given to cooperative and voluntary solutions relative to more coercive solutions. Given the importance of enforcing international debt contracts and ensuring a steady flow of capital to emerging markets, semicoercive or coercive solutions would be considered only in extreme situations, and strong preference would be given to crisis resolution processes that are as noncoercive and as cooperative as possible. In the G7 view, the aim of PSI is not to punish or inflict losses on private-sector investors. It is rather to resolve, ensuring appropriate financing of external financing gaps and creating conditions that facilitate stable flows of capital to emerging markets and support long-run economic growth. At times, the private sector has perceived actions of the official sector as unfair, punitive, and unpredictable, but the G7 has argued that the whole PSI policy has been guided by an awareness of the importance of maintaining sound international capital markets and avoiding actions and policies that may disrupt flows of capital in undesirable ways.

---

36. Many of these questions are discussed in more detail in Roubini (2000).

The difficult trade-off in official PSI policy was between the official desire to limit large money packages, while maintaining the option of having them when appropriate, and the desire to implement PSI policies that are as voluntary and cooperative as possible. This difficult trade-off is, for example, apparent from the first remarks of the new IMF managing director on the issue of PSI (Köhler 2000). On one hand, he suggested a preference for limiting large official packages; on the other hand, he strongly supported "constructive engagement" with the private sector, which implies, among other things, a preference for cooperative and voluntary, as opposed to semicoercive, solutions to crises. The two goals, while separately valid, are at times in dialectic tension with each other. Less official money might mean more PSI (and at times more coercive forms of PSI when voluntary ones are not feasible), whereas more voluntary forms of PSI or of constructive engagement might require more, rather than less, official money. This basic tension between the desire to limit official finance and the goal of having constructive and voluntary forms of PSI has not been fully resolved in official doctrine and practice.

During the same period that the official PSI policy was being fleshed out, developments in the policy arena led to the first cases of bonded debt restructuring.

First, the PC extended the comparability principle to bonded debt for the case of Pakistan in January of 1999. Although the principle was not new, it had not been applied before to bonds because they were de minimis in most cases. The restructuring of Pakistan's Eurobonds and other bonded claims was then successfully performed in the fall of 1999.

Second, the pressures on the Brazilian currency in the fall of 1998 that eventually led to the devaluation and float of this currency in January 1999 posed again the issue of whether and how to involve appropriately the private sector in crisis resolution. Cross-border short-term bank lines were, again as in Korea, at stake and in risk of no rollover. Moreover, a large stock of very short term domestic debt was also subject to rollover risk. Eventually, the form of PSI in Brazil turned out to be very mild with a system of monitoring of bank lines followed by a mild commitment in March 1999 to maintain exposures to February levels. Such mild PSI worked as the catalytic role of the official package, and the adjustment efforts of the country prevented a destabilizing loss of confidence and eventually restored economic growth without the need to resort to coercive outcomes.

Third, large external financing gaps and debt-servicing difficulties in 1999 by Romania and Ukraine led to attempts to restructure their bonded liabilities.[37] Such attempts were ad hoc and only partially successful: PSI in

---

37. Strictly speaking, the first restructuring case was that of Ukraine in 1998. In that case, the instrument was not a classic bond but a structured financing (a local currency claim packaged with guaranteed access to foreign exchange from the central bank). This was not strictly a bond restructuring but certainly a restructuring of something that was not a bank line.

Romania was attempted (the official policy was to consider bond restructuring but then to back down and let Romania pay its maturing instruments in return for a promise to raise new money) but eventually abandoned. The debt and bond restructurings in Ukraine (the structured note in 1998, the Dutch ING structured note in the summer of 1999, and a European Currency Unit–based claim in the fall of 1999) were first partial, ad hoc, and unsustainable over the medium term, as the strict market approach led to restructurings that were of very short maturity and at interest rates that were unsustainable in the medium term. Only later in 2000, did Ukraine take a comprehensive approach to its bonded debt restructuring (restructuring of Eurobonds and an assortment of Eurobond-like instruments created in earlier restructurings).

Fourth, the effective default of Russian debt following the August 1998 crisis led to a process that would eventually in 2000 restructure its bank and bonded liabilities.[38]

Fifth, the effective decision by Ecuador to stop payments on its external debt in August 1999 represented the first episode in which the previously restructured Brady bonds were effectively defaulted upon. This led to the need to restructure them (as eventually was successfully implemented in July/August 2000).

Sixth, the drive to restructure bonds via market-based debt exchanges was successfully implemented in 1999 and 2000 in Russia and Ukraine (a comprehensive deal for Ukraine in 2000 rather than the ad hoc deals in 1998–99) after the successful Pakistani episode. And Ecuador's bonded debt exchange was successfully launched and completed in July/August 2000.

As these test cases played themselves out, the official doctrine evolved as well. Although the case-by-case approach was maintained and deemed appropriate given the complexity and differences of cases, the G7 agreed in April 2000 on a set of "operational guidelines" for PSI, in part as a response to private-sector requests for greater clarity. These guidelines were reaffirmed as part of the Finance Ministers Communiqué prepared for the July 2000 G7 summit in Fukuoka, Japan, and approved at the September 2000 IMF annual meetings in Prague.

One other general point is worth discussing at this stage. The form of PSI will depend on where a debtor country stands in the broad spectrum that goes from pure "liquidity" cases to pure "insolvency" cases. This is a most complex issue. First, deciding whether a country is insolvent or not is very hard, given that debt servicing depends on both ability to pay and willingness to pay. Second, the spectrum of cases is not limited to corners of pure

---

38. First, there was the default on GKO and nondeliverable forwards in August 1998. Then, cascading defaults on Ministry of Finance bonds (Min Fins), Prins, Ians, and other Soviet-era debt eventually lead to a restructuring of a broad range of external and domestic London Club and bonded obligations.

illiquidity and pure insolvency cases but is more gray and continuous. Often, countries that are mostly illiquid have significant policy problems (such as Mexico in 1994 and Korea in 1997), so that a simple solution such as full unconditional large official support without any PSI may not be feasible. At the other end, countries that look insolvent (for example, Ecuador) may eventually be able to service their restructured—rather than reduced—debt if they implement enough policy adjustment. In between the cases of liquidity (with or without policy problems) and the pure cases of insolvency, there are many cases of countries with significant macro and structural adjustment problems whose debt burden may not be unsustainable in the long run but who do face significant payment humps in the short run (Pakistan, Ukraine, Romania). In these cases some form of PSI short of outright debt reduction may be adequate to solve the payment problems of these countries.

One could argue that the severity of the PSI policy will depend on where a country stands within this spectrum. Debt reduction is inevitable for clear cases of insolvency subject to a country's effort to adjust its underlying problems. Debt restructuring, rescheduling, and rollovers that do not formally touch the face value of principal payments may be warranted in cases in which severe policy problems exist and the debt burden is not unsustainable but payment humps and lack of market access do not allow the country to service its debt in full and on time in the short run.[39] A solution closer to large official support packages (full bailout) may be warranted because of favorable externalities in cases of pure illiquidity, especially if the country is large and of systemic importance. However, as we will discuss in detail in section 3.1.6, the role of PSI in such liquidity cases is a more complex issue than this simple logic suggests.

Moral Hazard

The issue of moral hazard in international capital flows has been hotly debated. Moral hazard in this context has to do with the potential distortions deriving from implicit or explicit official guarantees of debts and the potential effects of official creditors' support packages. Because one of the fundamental rationales for PSI is the idea that excessive official support may lead to moral hazard, it is important to assess the importance of this distortion in international capital markets.

Some definitional distinctions are important. One can be concerned

---

39. Even in such cases, the restructuring will imply some NPV reduction of the debt as interest rate and principal payments will be rescheduled at rates that are below current market rates. Thus, some real debt reduction will occur and does occur even in cases without formal reduction of face value. As official bilateral claims are also rescheduled at rates that do not truly reflect repayment risk, PC debt is also subject to effective NPV reduction even if it is not formally written down. This was discussed in more detail in the section "Modalities of Coordination."

about the debtor's moral hazard or the creditor's moral hazard. The debtor's moral hazard arises if official money (in the form of multilateral and bilateral lending and support) reduces the incentive of a debtor to follow sound policies in the first place and affects its incentives regarding payments on its external liabilities to foreign private investors. Even within the class of debtor moral hazard, one may want to distinguish between the moral hazard of the sovereign and the moral hazard of domestic private agents. The latter refers to the case in which implicit or explicit government guarantees lead domestic agents in emerging markets (financial institutions, corporations, and households) to borrow excessively (directly or indirectly from foreign creditors) relative to what would be optimal and to make distorted investment decisions. The debtor government's moral hazard derives instead from expectations that some external official agent (multilateral or bilateral official creditors) will provide bailout support to the country, thus leading ex ante the sovereign to follow loose economic policies that may eventually cause economic and financial problems. The creditor's moral hazard refers to the distortions in the lending decisions of international creditors that derive either from expectations that the official creditor sector will bail out a sovereign or from expectations that a sovereign will ex post guarantee liabilities of its private sector that have been incurred with private international creditors.[40]

There is a broad range of views on the analytical and practical importance of moral hazard distortions in international capital flows. Some, such as McKinnon and Pill (1997), Calomiris (1998b), Schwartz (1998), Dooley (2000b), Chinn, Dooley, and Shrestha (1999) and Corsetti, Pesenti, and Roubini (1999a,b) believe that such distortions are critical, whereas others, such as Summers (2000) and the Institute of International Finance (IIF; 1999c), think that such distortions are less important than others have made out. The issue is obviously one of quantitative degree rather than absolutes. Official response to crisis always has the potential to lead to moral hazard; the issue is how important the distortion is.

The different views on moral hazard and the determinants of the flows to emerging markets in the 1990s are hard to test.[41] Formal and systematic evidence is scarce. There are, however, a few recent econometric studies. A paper from the IIF (1999c) attempts to test formally for moral hazard by trying to assess whether the significant reduction in sovereign spreads in the period before the Asian crisis can be explained by fundamentals or could be

---

40. Even when governments have declared ex ante that they will not guarantee private claims, they are often nonetheless forced to take responsibility when the time comes. Chile in the early 1980s was a case in point. Korea's guarantee of cross-border banks' liabilities in late 1997 is another example from the recent Asian crisis. More recently during the November-December 2000 turmoil in its markets, Turkey decided to guarantee all bank liabilities, including cross border.

41. See Roubini (2000) for a more detailed discussion of these arguments.

related to bailout expectations following the Mexican rescue. This study does not find evidence of moral hazard. Lane and Phillips (2000) consider whether IMF programs are a source of moral hazard. They find that this type of moral hazard is difficult to detect in market reactions to various IMF policy announcements, and there is no evidence that such moral hazard has recently been on the rise. Dell'Ariccia, Goedde, and Zettelmeyer (2000) have also tested for moral hazard by considering sovereign spreads and their variance before and after the Russian crisis; they find partial, and mixed, evidence of moral hazard in this episode. More circumstantial evidence suggests that investors may have expected large official support packages for systemically important countries in recent episodes of financial turmoil such as Russia in 1998, Brazil in 1998–99, and Argentina and Turkey in 2000.

Both debtor moral hazard and creditor moral hazard deriving from expectations of bailout via official support are important enough to be a concern for the design of an efficient international financial system. Moral hazard affects issues such as the desirability of an international lender of last resort, the optimality of official support packages, and the issue of whether and what form of PSI is appropriate. The overall analytical and empirical evidence suggests that the moral hazard rationale for PSI is a valid argument for appropriate forms of PSI in crisis resolution.

Issues with Standstills

Several authors have suggested that some broad debt standstills (suspension of debt payments) may at times be necessary, either to prevent a period of turmoil from turning into a full-blown crisis or to prevent further overshooting of asset prices and the risk of an outright default once a crisis has occurred. This is certainly a most controversial issue. Support for the idea of standstills comes not only from academic economists but also, cautiously, from some official-sector representatives within the G7 (see, e.g., King 1999).[42]

A standstill, if temporary, can be seen as a radical form of bailing in the private sector, and, according to some, it is a better and more orderly way to gain time and restore confidence than a disorderly rush to the exits. A standstill could be the right policy response both in liquidity cases when there is an "irrational" rush to the exits and in other crisis situations, when serious policy problems are afflicting the debtor country but the rush to the exits of creditors is disorderly and threatening to create a worse outcome.

Standstills pose a lot of complex questions. What are the risks and benefits of standstills? Would they include only sovereign payments or payments on all the debtor country's claims, including by the private sector? Do

---

42. See IMF (2000a,b) for a discussion of standstills and the debate on them at a recent IMF board meeting.

standstills require systematic capital and exchange controls? Should they be sanctioned by the IMF or the official sector? Could they be associated with a stay of litigation?

Consider the potential benefits of standstills. In pure liquidity cases in which there is uncertainty and no risk aversion, the threat of a standstill is enough to support the good equilibrium: that is, ex post there is no need to implement the threat, and agents will avoid rushing to the exits if they know that everyone would be locked in.[43] In reality, uncertainty, risk aversion, and policy problems make this first best equilibrium unlikely, and standstills would have to be introduced (rather than just threatened) to prevent investors from rushing to the exits.

If standstills have to be imposed, what are their benefits? The main benefit may be to prevent a disorderly rush to the exits when, even allowing that the country may have serious policy problems, investors panic and overreact to the negative developments. Such a disorderly rush is inefficient for two reasons: First, it may force the debtor into effective default (inability to make debt payments) when, even if solvency is not at stake, the stock of foreign reserves is below the short-term claims that are coming to maturity and are not being rolled over. Second, when the exchange rate is allowed to float rather than being fixed, the rush to the exits may lead to severe overshooting of the exchange rate. That, in turn, may be extremely costly if it leads to financial distress and bankruptcy of a large set of debtors, sovereign and private.

Take, for example, the cases of Korea and Indonesia. If the concerted rollover of cross-border interbank loans in Korea had occurred by Thanksgiving 1997 rather than a month later at Christmas, widespread financial distress would have been limited. The difference between the two dates is that, at the former, the exchange rate of the won to the U.S. dollar had fallen from 900 to 1,100 (beneficial in terms of competitiveness), whereas by Christmas it had fallen to over 1,800 (causing widespread financial distress). Although many *chaebol* were already distressed earlier in 1997 before the fall of the won, 1,800 was a rate at which many more foreign currency debtors, financial firms, and corporates were effectively distressed if not bankrupt. Thus, the implication of the delay in the concerted rollover was a significant worsening of the financial conditions of Korea and a worsening of the real output effects of the exchange rate shock.

In the case of Indonesia, some have argued that the lack of an early standstill on payments by the local corporates to their international creditors contributed to the free fall of the currency. The collapse in the value of the currency, particularly the move of the exchange rate of the rupiah to the U.S. dollar from 4,000 to 8,000 and then 12,000 (and above) led to the wide-

---

43. See the section "International Lender of Last Resort" for a broader discussion of standstill and other issues in liquidity cases.

spread effective bankruptcy of most financial institutions and firms in the country. At the end, the burden of foreign debt was so high, given the fall in the value of the currency, that these corporates effectively stopped payments. An informal standstill of corporate liabilities occurred by default in a situation of complete financial distress of these firms.

The above arguments suggest that an early standstill might have helped to minimize the costs of further turmoil that derived from a lack of orderly workouts. The reality, however, is more complex. In the case of Indonesia one could argue that the depreciation of the rupiah had less to do with the attempt of corporates to hedge their foreign currency positions than with government failures that shook confidence in the country. The lack of commitment to structural reform, the political uncertainty, the health of Suharto, his crumbling power regime, the monetization policy of Bank of Indonesia, and the capital flight of the ethnic Chinese who were exposed to violent attacks were all more important than hedging demand in driving the rupiah into free fall. In the absence of a more serious and credible adjustment program, it is likely that a standstill would not have worked out and would have failed to stem the fall of the rupiah and the generalized panic that enveloped domestic and foreign investors. Flight and asset stripping might have continued even under strict capital and exchange controls, given the many sources of leakage in capital flows. Thus, it is not obvious that a standstill on private payments would have worked. Also, standstills on payments by private firms are harder to arrange than on sovereign payments. The difficult issues include who will declare one and how to enforce it.

Again, in the case of Korea, it is not clear that a standstill would have worked. The won started to fall precipitously in early December when, in spite of an IMF program, a series of bad news hit markets: the low level of reserves was revealed, the extra offshore liabilities of Korean financial institutions and *chaebol* emerged, the upcoming election and the policy uncertainty around it became important sources of uncertainty and of concern about the willingness of the government to implement reforms credibly. Also, all the players in the game—international creditors, the Korean government, and official creditors—were not ready early on to go for a concerted rollover. It was only when—at the end of December—it became clear that Korean banks were on the verge of defaulting on their liabilities that a concerted rollover became feasible and acceptable to creditors.

The case of the Malaysian capital controls in September 1999 was not formally a case of implementation of PSI as part of a package of official support, because the country did not request an IMF package and did not rely on official creditor financial support. Instead, the country decided to impose capital controls as a way to regain monetary autonomy in the presence of large pressures on its currency. Some of the capital control measures (such as closing down the offshore ringgit market) did not formally represent PSI; others, such as the temporary restrictions to foreign investors' ability to repatriate portfolio investments in Malaysia, were a clear form of coercive bailing in of foreign investors. Note that Malaysia did not impose a standstill on sovereign debt payments, but these liabilities were negligible to begin with.

Standstills have a number of other potential drawbacks that need to be considered.

First, standstills may reduce in the medium to long run the amount of capital flowing to emerging markets if they are perceived to be a tool used by debtors to opportunistically default on their debt obligations.

Second, as in the case of anticipated capital controls, anticipations of a standstill may lead to an earlier crisis (as all investors rush to the doors in expectation that the doors will be shut); or, worse, they can even trigger a crisis that otherwise would not have occurred. This is the main drawback, one that cannot be avoided if there are clear rules that imply some automatic standstills in some circumstances. Constructive ambiguity in place of rules may help, but if investors fear that standstills will be imposed with some probability (even without mechanical rules), the rush to the exits may occur anyway. Proponents of standstills have not seriously addressed this main shortcoming of the tool. For example, it is clear that the Korean concerted rollover in December 1997 led investors to believe that such semicoercive policy might be imposed on Brazil as well. The sharp reduction in interbank exposures to Brazil in the summer and fall of 1998 was clearly affected by the experience of Korea—and that of Malaysia in September 1998—and expectations that similar coercive solutions might be imposed in Brazil. In the case of Malaysia, capital controls of the type that were eventually imposed in September 1998 were widely predicted throughout 1998 as being likely to be implemented. Thus, some of the capital flight and pressures on the currency in 1998 were caused by the expectation of controls. However, the breadth and extent of these controls somewhat surprised investors once they were imposed.

Third, and related, standstills risk international contagion. Contagion may occur either because investors start to expect that such standstills may be imposed on other countries or via the financial contagion channels that the literature has highlighted (common creditor effects, proxy hedging and cross-country hedging, proxy plays, increase in risk aversion of investors, portfolio adjustment effects). The Russian default and imposition of capital controls by Malaysia clearly produced a severe contagion effect in the summer and fall of 1998.

Fourth, partial standstills may not work. They may have to be extensive and widespread. A standstill on sovereign payments probably has to be comprehensive to be effective; otherwise, claims not included will be tempted to flee. Similarly, standstills on sovereign claims alone may not be enough, for several reasons. First, as in Korea and Indonesia, the claims of domestic banks and corporates can be the source of reserve loss and currency depreciation. Second, standstills on sovereign payments may not close the financing gap if private claims can also flee and the existence of a sovereign standstill leads private investors to worry that a broader stay of payments will soon be imposed on them.

Fifth, as a consequence of the point above, broad capital controls and exchange controls may have to be imposed that restrict the payment ability of private agents in the economy.[44] Under fixed exchange rates, since all liquid claims—even those in domestic currency—can be turned into foreign assets, widespread capital controls may be necessary to reduce the pressure on official reserves. Under flexible rates, the same attempt of the private sector to turn domestic assets into foreign ones will lead to a sharp currency depreciation that is potentially very harmful if there are many foreign currency liabilities. Thus, again, broad capital and exchange controls may be necessary to prevent an overshooting of the currency and other asset prices.

Sixth, standstills on payments of domestic private agents, especially corporates, are difficult to arrange; they effectively imply the imposition of capital and exchange controls. The controls may lead, as the experience of Indonesia shows, to perverse effects such as "asset stripping." It is one thing to impose controls to avoid a destabilizing rush to the exits; however, if such controls are used for strategic avoidance of sustainable debt payments or to strip the assets of the underlying firms, the effects may be perverse. Thus, some form of standstill may make sense in countries where there is an efficient and functioning insolvency and corporate restructuring legal system. But it can have perverse effects in countries where, because of inadequate institutions, corruption, and archaic legal systems, creditors cannot seize firm assets and prevent asset stripping.

Seventh, formal standstills present complex legal issues. The main problem is whether a standstill can prevent litigation aimed at seizing the assets of the debtor. One solution would be to provide such a power to the IMF—the power to sanction broad standstills. It is, however, agreed that providing such a power to the IMF would require amending Article VIII.2.b of the fund's Articles of Agreement. There is significant political resistance among the main fund creditors to take a route that would provide the IMF with such authority. All sorts of economic and institutional concerns have been expressed even though several influential voices have expressed support for such a change (including that of former IMF Managing Director Camdessus and other official sources).[45]

---

44. Malaysia is an example of the imposition of capital controls as way to prevent domestic residents' capital flight and as a way to lock in foreign investors trying to exit from their long local portfolio investments.

45. In the absence of a legal mechanism to provide the IMF the power to sanction a standstill, debt suspensions by a sovereign or private-sector entities (whether within or outside official PSI policies) are subject to litigation risk. For example, creditors accelerated their claims once Ecuador defaulted on its Bradies, but then they did not pursue legal action to enforce their claims.

In the absence of such an amendment, the issue is whether, in the presence of a standstill informally sanctioned by the IMF with a policy of lending into arrears, a court would provide a stay of litigation (preventing litigation aimed at seizing the assets of the debtor), especially if the debtor is cooperatively working to work out its payments with some of its creditors. Although there is some limited legal precedent in the United States for courts' imposing such stays, it is an open issue whether such a stay could be legally imposed as a temporary tool aimed at allowing an orderly workout. Also, while threat of litigation is an issue, occurrences of litigation in practice may be limited, especially because the ability of creditors to seize the assets of sovereign and private debtors in emerging markets is limited. The costs of litigation may effectively reduce the occurrences of such a problem.

In spite of serious shortcomings with formal debt standstills, one cannot rule out the possibility that, in some circumstances, their benefits may outweigh their costs. Thus, although having formal rules that determine when a standstill may be introduced would be counterproductive if they triggered the rush to the exit that one wants to avoid in the first place, one cannot rule out their use in extreme situations. Some degree of constructive ambiguity may be helpful in this regard even if the uncertainty over whether, how, and how widespread a standstill is likely to be would in other respects be counterproductive. Temporary, targeted standstills in situations in which a real commitment to policy reform exists (but is not fully credible to market participants) may be a useful part of the tool kit of crisis prevention and resolution.[46] However, such a tool needs to be used with extreme care to prevent consequences worse than the problems that it is aimed to cure.

The G7 PSI Framework and Its Application to Bonded Debt Restructurings

We discuss next the many aspects of the PSI official doctrine and practice as emerged in a number of recent case studies (Pakistan, Ukraine, Romania, Ecuador, and Russia)[47] of sovereign bonded debt restructurings. These recent episodes have involved countries that are small (nonsystemic, with perhaps the exception of Russia) and where restructuring of bonded debt has become an element of the PSI in crisis resolution. Indeed, bonded debt restructuring is a relatively new, controversial, and complex issue. Thus, we will discuss the many issues that have emerged in applying PSI to the case of bonded debt and other similar securities. The official PSI doctrine can be

46. Korea's concerted rollover could be seen as such a targeted standstill in the context of a credible adjustment program, whereas Malaysia's capital controls were much more coercive in their nature and implementation and not linked to an explicit policy adjustment plan.

47. Strictly speaking, the Russian debt restructuring in 2000 was not a case of application of the PSI doctrine but resulted from the decision of the country to restructure again its old restructured London Club bank claims, the Prins (bonds issued in exchange for old 1997 London Club principal) and Ians (bonds issued in exchange for interest arrears on 1997 London Club debt) and the past due interest claims.

characterized as a case-by-case approach–cum–principles and tools. Note that such doctrine applies not only to bonds but also to overall claims of a debtor country (including bank claims). However, the framework has been recently applied to many bonded debt restructuring cases.

Collective Action Clauses and Voluntary Debt Exchanges

All of the recent episodes of sovereign bonded debt restructurings (Pakistan, Ukraine, Ecuador, and Russia) have made a very limited use of CACs before such bonded debt restructurings occurred (via voluntary exchange offers). But strong arguments were made that bonded debt restructurings would not be feasible without CACs such as collective representation mechanism for creditors, majority clauses to change the terms of bond contracts, and sharing clauses. The arguments in favor of and against CACs are by now familiar and the views on CACs of official creditors, the private sector, and debtors quite known. Collective action clauses were first proposed in the Rey Report as a way to facilitate the restructuring of bonded debt. Next, both the official sector in its expressions of PSI doctrine (see Koln G7 Summit Architecture Communiqué) and academics (such as Eichengreen, Portes, and many others) extolled their benefits. It was argued that the lack of such CACs would make it very hard, if not impossible, to restructure bonds. Lack of collective representations mechanisms (such as bondholder committees, trustees, and similar coordination mechanisms) would make it hard to coordinate actions of a multitude of dispersed bondholders and implement restructurings. Lack of majority clauses would require unanimity in the decision to change the terms of the bond contract and would hold a possible large majority of bondholders willing to restructure hostage to a possible miniscule minority of holdouts and vulture creditors. Lack of sharing clauses—which require the sharing among *all* creditors of proceedings obtained by the litigation action of a *subset* of creditors—would open up room for disruptive litigation by a small group of litigious holdout creditors.[48]

The differences between bonds issues under U.K. law and those issued under New York law were also highlighted by many: the former effectively had collective representation, majority, and sharing clauses (especially trustee bonds), whereas the latter did not. Collective action clauses (especially their being mandatory in international bonds) were first strongly resisted by the private sector. In this view they would make restructuring too easy and would thus tip the bargaining power balance in favor of debtors

---

48. Note that London Club debt—syndicated bank loans—implied implicit and explicit forms of collective action clauses: syndicated loans required the formation of creditor committees to represent the interests of creditors, thus solving the collective action problem of coordinating creditors' action; they included effective majority clauses because a majority of creditors could decide to restructure their claims while such actions were not necessarily binding on minority holdout banks; and, often, they included formal sharing clauses.

with the risk of making defaults more frequent (strategic opportunistic defaults based on unwillingness to pay rather than inability to pay) and thus eventually undermining new debt flows to emerging markets. Borrowing countries too were concerned that such clauses would taint their reputations. Emerging market economies were wary of CACs' being forcibly imposed on their debt contracts under the concern that spreads on such instruments would be higher. On the other hand, it was argued that spreads would instead be higher for instruments where restructuring was very hard, because the costs of necessary restructuring would be too high. Next, some academic research (Eichengreen and Mody 2000a,b) suggested that, actually, spreads for good credit countries are lower on bonds with CACs, but higher for poorer credit countries.[49] Thus, the benefits of reducing restructuring costs outweigh the penalty for possible opportunistic default for good credits. Academics (Eichengreen and Ruhel 2000; Eichengreen 2000; Portes 2000) also sharply criticized the ad hockery of the case-by-case approach to PSI and argued that CACs would have provided a much more transparent and simple approach to all PSI problems.

In spite of these arguments in favor of CACs, recent experience with bonded debt restructurings suggests that, although CACs may be marginally helpful in facilitating such restructurings, their usefulness has been somewhat exaggerated. In all recent cases of bond restructurings (Pakistan, Ukraine, Russia, and Ecuador) CACs have had a very marginal role. First, note that all these debt restructurings have occurred through unilateral "debt exchange offers" rather than via the formal use of CACs even in cases in which, as in Pakistan and Ukraine, the instruments included CACs. The use of unilateral debt exchange offers obviates the need for CACs because such an offer is voluntary and can be made regardless of the existence of a majority clause or other CACs. Thus, one can envision a system in which debt exchanges are the norm and the CACs are neither needed nor used when available. Collective action clauses have been marginally helpful only in two cases: in Ukraine, where three out of four restructured instruments had CACs, such clauses allowed the ex post "binding in" of holdout creditors after a vast majority of bondholders (over 90 percent) had accepted the terms of the offer. Thus, they were used ex post rather than ex ante to lock in holdouts and prevent disruptive litigation. In the case of Pakistan, where restructured bonds all had CACs, such clauses were not used either ex ante or ex post. However, one could argue that they were somehow useful, in that the possible threat of their use may have convinced some undecided creditors to accept the exchange offer. In Russia and Ecuador, debt restructurings were performed without any CACs because the underlying instrument did not have such clauses. In the case of Ecuador, however, legal ways were

---

49. Some recent work by Becker, Richards, and Thaicharoen (2000) finds even stronger results that CACs do not increase spreads for either better or worse credit issuers.

found to dilute the litigation benefits of holdouts by the use of "exit consent" amendments. Thus, worse terms were "crammed down" on holdouts.

Thus, exchange offers have been the norm in bond restructurings so far, and CACs have not been used ex ante to force the restructuring even when instruments including them were available. Why didn't CACs turn out to be essential for successful restructurings in the way that had been suggested by many?[50]

One first answer is that exchange offers allow a restructuring of bonded debt even in the absence of any CACs. Litigation risk by holdouts is an issue to be considered in these cases, but experience, so far, has been that such risk has been limited, for reasons to be discussed in more detail below. Thus, exchange offers provide an effective alternative to CACs as a tool to implement bonded debt restructuring. Also, when available ex ante, CACs can be used in a second round if an exchange offer were to fail; so they are an instrument of second resort rather than first resort in bond restructurings even when available.

Second, debtors and debt agents (such as trustees) are obviously wary of the idea of using collective representation clauses (such as creditor committees) and majority clauses because they are concerned that even just calling a meeting of bondholder creditors may lead to undesirable outcomes. Such meetings may start a protracted negotiation process that may take too long; it may allow creditors to coordinate their decisions and take legal action against a debtor. In reality, no debtor or trustee would want to call a meeting of creditors unless previous market soundings and bilateral meetings with creditors have allowed these agents to figure out all the details of a possibly successful debt exchange offer. Thus, the model of debt exchanges without use of CACs—in which financial and legal advisors of the debtor make broad market soundings before the offer is launched to figure out which terms will maximize the probability of a successful offer—can avoid a potentially disruptive, long-delaying formal negotiation under creditor committees and via the use of CACs.

As suggested above, the model of "debt exchanges–cum–market soundings" has successfully worked so far in all bond restructuring cases, and the role of CACs has been either to provide a tool to bind in holdouts ex post or to threaten credibly their use in case an exchange offer does not work. This experience also suggests that academic critiques of the current PSI process as being ad hoc and inferior to one with CACs turned out to be a bit off the mark. Collective action clauses are only an empty shell that may or may not facilitate a restructuring process. They are not, by themselves, a tool that provides ex ante the answer to the complex set of questions (when, how, how much, which assets, which creditors, in which sequence) that have to be addressed when trying to restructure bonds. Collective action clauses

---

50. See Eichengreen and Mody (2000b) for a recent defense of CACs.

do not provide ex ante an easy tool through which these questions can be answered and solved in practice.

Lessons from Recent Cases of Bonded Debt Restructuring

Bonded debt restructurings have occurred since 1999 as the direct outcome of the adoption of the new G7 official PSI policy. Successful recent case studies include Pakistan (the first case of an application of the PSI policy, because the PC requested a restructuring of the private bonded claims of Pakistan on comparable terms to the restructuring of PC claims), Ukraine (where the official sector nudged the country to restructure its sovereign bonded claims as an implicit condition for an IMF program), and Ecuador (where the official sector effectively sanctioned the country's decision to suspend payments on its Brady bonds in the face of an unsustainable external debt-servicing path). In all these episodes, bonded debt restructuring was the effective outcome of the G7 policy to include bonded debt among claims to be restructured when a country suffered severe debt servicing problems. Russia successfully restructured its Principal Interest Notes (Prins) and Interest Accrual Notes (Ians), but this was not formally part of the official PSI policy (but, rather, the result of the country's decision to restructure its liabilities). In Romania, PSI was attempted but eventually abandoned as the country made payment on maturing debt and then was unable to raise new money as required by the PSI components of its IMF program.

What are the lessons learned from these restructuring cases? Although the sample of cases is limited (Ukraine, Ecuador, Pakistan, Russia, and the failed attempt to impose PSI in Romania), one can suggest a number of tentative lessons.

First, debt exchanges (following extensive market soundings) are an operational alternative to the use of CACs or formal negotiations. In all these episodes CACs were not used ex ante, and the benefit of their existence was only the ex post ability to "cram down" new terms on holdouts (as in Ukraine) or threaten their use (as in Pakistan). Even in the case of Ecuador, where there were no formal CACs in the old restructured instruments, the legal advisor found legal ways to cram down new terms on the holdouts to make the old bonds less appealing to the holdouts. Note that although Ecuador's bonds required unanimity to change payment terms, only a simple majority of 51 percent is required to change nonfinancial terms. Thus, "exit consent" for those who accepted the deal were used to change the terms of the old bonds and make them less appealing to potential holdouts.

Second, all these deals provided mark-to-market gains to investors, in that the terms of the deals were generous and included various sweeteners. Such sweeteners included financially favorable terms for creditors, informal upgrade in the seniority of the claims (in Russia), substantial up-front cash payments (Ukraine, Ecuador, Russia), and Brady collateral release (Ecuador). Indeed, some have argued that such deals were very generous to investors because they led to sharp gains evaluated at market prices relative to the predeal prices of the restructured bonds. Such gains were equivalent to over 20 percent for Ukraine, 32 percent for Russian Prins and 18 percent for Russian Ians, 3.5 percent for Pakistani bonds, and averaging over 30 percent (based on the jump in the price of Brady Bonds, PDIs, and euros after the deal was announced) for the case of Ecuador.

Third, the reasons for the mark-to-market gains after the deals were announced are not fully clear. Some argue that the gains were due to the better-than-expected terms of the deals, but if a country's debt price depends on its ability to pay, it is not clear why unexpectedly generous terms would affect that price. Some explanations are that a better-than-expected deal signals something about the country's desire to make more adjustment than otherwise or more commitment to attempt to keep the new payment profile (as debt prices depend not only on the ability but also on the willingness to pay). Other explanations are that the deal implies that the official bilateral creditors will bear a greater burden and the private sector will thus bear a smaller burden; the new instruments have or are perceived to have a greater seniority than other instruments, although this effect on the price is rational only if official creditors or other private creditors who are not in the bond deal are worse off as a consequence of the deal; the up-front cash in most of these deals (very significant in Ecuador as the Brady principal collateral was to be released to creditors) was a positive surprise that effectively gave senior payment treatment to investors who took the deal because cash today is much more valuable than a promise of payments down the line. But if this is the case, whoever gets cash first does so at the expense of future creditors (probably official ones), who are likely to be hurt by the deal. Thus, in most cases, the jump in price signals a deal that made some creditors better off, most likely at the expense of official creditors.

Fourth, it is not obvious that in all cases medium-term debt sustainability has been restored. For cases of countries such as Pakistan or Ukraine where the overall external debt burden was not unsustainable (i.e., the country was not insolvent), a restretching of payment terms allowed avoiding the payment humps and, subject to successful economic reform, the debt profile may become sustainable. Similarly, the default by Russia and restructuring of its external and domestic debt is likely to have put the country on a path of solvency. The same may not be said of the Ecuador deal, whose terms were quite favorable to creditors. Even after the deal is concluded, and even assuming the most optimistic scenarios for domestic adjustment, the country is likely to end up in the medium run with a debt-GDP ratio of around 100 percent and a debt-exports ratio and a debt–government revenues ratio that are well above the official HIPC criteria for significant debt reduction. Although the country's GDP does not allow it to qualify for

HIPC relief, it is likely that the country will remain with debt ratios that are possibly unsustainable. Moreover, considering that the assumptions about fiscal adjustment and trade balance adjustment embedded in the IMF program are the most optimistic in terms of intensity of the country's policy adjustment, any slippage in performance will make such ratios much worse. One could argue that the country has only delayed for a few years its debt-servicing problems and that further debt restructurings will occur as the current debt profile may keep the country insolvent.

Fifth, as the unsuccessful experience with PSI in Romania suggests, attempts to expect "new money" at below market rates from creditors as a form of PSI do not work if the country has lost market access and is allowed to make large debt payments that are coming to maturity. In 1999, Romania, facing $720 million of payments, was allowed by the IMF to use dwindling reserves to make such payments under the condition of raising 80 percent again in new money ($600 million). Once the payment had occurred, the country lost any leverage (nonpayment threat) over creditors, and the IMF and G7 lost their ability to nudge the country to an involvement of the private sector in sharing the burden of external debt adjustment. The subsequent attempts to raise $600 million were sequentially diluted in the face of the country's lack of market access; thus, eventually the IMF waived the PSI requirement in an obvious failure to implement the PSI policy for that country.

The country then bore the consequences of its decision to make the payments on its external debt. The domestic adjustment was deeper than necessary, with output falling in 1999 and early 2000 more than otherwise possible. The subsequent buildup of reserves in 2000—earlier depleted by the large 1999 debt payments—was made at the cost of a substantial and sharp contraction of imports that was feasible only with a sharp contraction of output. Thus, the decision of the country not to restructure its external debt (which was sustainable in terms of its size but characterized by a very lumpy payments profile in the short run) was thus paid for with high real costs.

Stated official PSI doctrine is that the official sector should not force a country into nonpayment but should rather make clear to the country the consequences of continuing to pay when restructuring may be warranted according to the IMF. That is, the official PSI doctrine implies that continuing debt payments in these cases will imply a greater amount of domestic adjustment, not greater amounts of official support. In reality, however, debtor countries may still make decisions—continue payments—that eventually shift some of the debt burden onto official bilateral creditors (PC claims) or lead to greater-than-otherwise-planned multilateral support. In practice, official bilateral and multilateral support may effectively grow ex post in spite of ex ante official statements to the contrary, or the terms of the IMF program may become effectively more lax to allow breathing space to the country.

Sixth, the official sector has indicated that bonded debt restructurings should be evaluated by the IMF to ensure that their terms are comparable to PC restructurings and consistent with medium-term debt sustainability. This means for the IMF to assess the financial terms of these deals, the amount of up-front cash, the upgrade in seniority terms, and the implications for medium-term sustainability in deciding whether such deals are consistent with an IMF program. Note that the current system of incentives and the financial interests of advisors and debtors result in deals that turn to be financially beneficial to private creditors (as suggested by the jump in prices of the old debt in all recent exchanges) but may imply some burden shifting to official-sector claims. Financial advisors are interested in generous deals because they maximize the probability of success (reduce "deal risk"), increase the fees and commissions that are conditional on a successful deal, and reduce the burden sharing for the buy side of their firms (which hold the old bonds) while the sell side is involved in underwriting and successfully placing the new bonds.

Thus, although the official doctrine suggests that the official sector should not "micromanage" debt restructuring, some systematic way to assess whether a deal is appropriate should be developed. It is true that the generosity of the deal may be required at times to ensure its success. In Ukraine, up to 100,000 creditors had to be convinced to accept the new bonds. In Ecuador, up-front cash, on top of the collateral release, was necessary to give incentives to PDI and euro bond holders because such claims did not have collateral. Upgrade of seniority made the Russian Ians and Prins deal more palatable to creditors, and so on. However, the issue that the IMF is mandated to assess is whether the terms of such deals are consistent with the overall adjustment program of the country and the medium-term sustainability of its external debt.

Seventh, an alternative strategy has been to reduce the face value of debt, as in Ecuador, where the judgment was made that the country was insolvent. In other cases (Ukraine, Pakistan, Romania) where it was not clear whether the country was insolvent or rather facing illiquidity given the lumpy debt payments coming due, a rescheduling/restructuring rather than face-value reduction was attempted. Even in such cases, the restructuring did imply some NPV reduction of the debt as interest rate and principal payments were rescheduled at rates that were below current market rates. Thus, some real debt reduction occurred even in cases in which face-value reduction was not formally performed. As official bilateral claims are also rescheduled at rates that do not truly reflect repayment risk, PC debt is also subject to effective NPV reduction even if it is not formally written down. Comparable treatment of official bilateral and private claims is thus possible only in approximate terms because exact comparability is hard to define. In this regard, the Pakistan exchange was broadly comparable to the

PC deal. Other cases (Russia, Ukraine, Ecuador) cannot be assessed because private claims rescheduling preceded PC rescheduling.

Eighth, while a normal or standard restructuring sequence would have seen, as in the 1980s, an IMF program followed by PC rescheduling of official claims followed by London Club rescheduling on comparable terms of private claims, only the Pakistan deal followed this sequence. In the other cases (Ukraine, Russia, Ecuador, and possibly Nigeria in the future), the IMF program was followed by debt exchanges of private claims with PC rescheduling to follow next. This reverse sequencing complicates the application of the comparability principle and may create strategic incentives in the private sector to impose "reverse comparability" or to stake ex ante limits to the amount of private-sector burden sharing. This reverse sequencing also confirms why a case-by-case approach to PSI was followed: simple rules, even for the sequencing process (such as a debt exchange to follow PC rescheduling), appeared to be difficult to implement given the limited and very recent case history in debt restructurings.

The reasons for the reverse sequencing in these episodes are varied: in Russia creditors may have tried to lock in the amount of debt relief they were willing to provide before the PC imposed comparable terms. However, since conditions for Russia (oil prices, current account, fiscal situation) improved significantly after the private deal, the PC ended up offering a restructuring deal that did not imply any debt reduction, only generous restructuring. Thus, the private sector ended up complaining that they did it more than the PC in going first with its deal. In Ukraine, delays and suspensions in the IMF program that delayed a PC deal led investors to try to lock in the best deal they could in spite of the lack of a PC deal. In Ecuador, the PC deal was repeatedly delayed, given the time it took to negotiate an IMF program and, next, the country's inability to reach an agreement with its official bilateral creditors. Thus, in the summer of 2000 the country went ahead with its exchange offer in spite of the lack of a PC deal.

Ninth, differences among classes of creditors and conflicts of interests among them have to be addressed. Short-term investors (such as highly leveraged institutions, hedge funds, vulture funds, and other similar players) willing to buy distressed debt at low market prices have received hefty returns when, following exchange offers, the price of debt has rebounded. Longer-term investors, such as real money funds, asset management firms, and other investors with longer-term horizons, have at times disposed of their holdings of distressed emerging market debt when restructuring became likely and prices of such debt have plunged. Having short-term investors who bought low and who obtained significant capital gains made the chances of a successful exchange deal more likely in that such investors obtained significant mark-to-market gains. But the losses incurred by more dedicated and longer-horizon investors on their holdings of emerging market debt may reduce the core longer-term demand for this class of debt and lead to lower flows and higher spreads for this category of debt.[51] In general, official policy has tried to avoid having a negative effect on the longer-term prospects for emerging market debt. These conflicts of interest among creditors are also one of the reasons why the model of creditors committees as a way to restructure debt may not work: such creditors may have very different interests and agendas, and the collective action problem of finding a common creditor position may be as difficult as the problem of negotiating with the debtor.[52] Also, serious issues about whether Chinese walls are too leaky in a world where mark-to-market investors are buying and selling distressed debt may limit the possibility of having a representative creditor group; the actual composition of the holding group may change due to trading. Also, some investors may be actually shorting the distressed debt rather than holding significant long position in the asset.

Tenth, litigation risk has been, so far, limited. Acceleration and cross-default occurred in the case of Ecuador, but no legal action was taken by creditors to enforce their rights.[53] The usual limits to litigation were at work: it is costly, it takes a long time, and debtor assets are relatively hard to attach (even in cases, such as that of Nigeria, when the waiver of sovereign immunity is quite broad). Also, CACs have been successfully used—for example, in Ukraine—to bind in holdouts, cram down new terms on such dissenting minorities, and dilute their potential legal claims; even in cases, such as that of Ecuador, when the ex ante availability of CACs was quite limited, creative legal clauses such as exit consent clauses have been created to achieve the same result. Also, the generous terms of recent exchange offers, together with the sweetener of significant up-front cash, has effectively helped to bribe possible holdouts.

51. In this sense the interests of sell-side agents in financial firms that manage the restructuring of debt may be at odds with the interests of buy-side agents that manage dedicated emerging market portfolios for these firms. The impression that emerging market creditors' and buy-side interests are not fully represented is behind recent buy-side efforts to be involved in the PSI debate and the creation of the Emerging Markets Creditors Association.

52. Although in the 1980s creditors found ways to solve this collective action problem, the situation today is somewhat different, for several reasons: syndicated loans provided a mechanism for the collective representation of creditors; explicit and implicit majority and sharing clauses were available in those loan contracts, whereas they are often absent in bond contracts; some financial institutions and individuals, namely Bill Rhodes of Citicorp, provided leadership to the group of creditors; the interests of the creditors were more homogeneous because they were all commercial banks, whereas in the case of bonds there is a wide range of creditors with very different interests. Thus, although coordinating creditors may not be impossible in the case of bonds, it appears to be harder than in the 1980s.

53. The recent Peru-Elliott case, in which a "vulture" creditor—Elliott Associates—successfully sued Peru and was able to get payment in full for its pre-Brady claims, may have changed the likelihood that creditors may successfully litigate in court sovereign debtor claims. However, how far-reaching this case will be is open to question because the legal issues were not tested in court, given Peru's decision to pay rather than end up in technical default before a court decision on the case.

In the absence of exit consent clauses in the new bonds or clauses that allow ex post to bind in potential holdouts, the debtor has to decide how to deal with such holdouts.[54] A credible threat not to provide holdouts with better terms than those of the exchange offer is the only way a debtor can ensure that the offer will be accepted; otherwise, many creditors would be better off waiting and trying their luck. Once the offer has been successfully accepted by the minimum threshold of the deal (a minimum 85 percent acceptance rate for the Ecuador case, for example), the debtor has to decide whether to keep its threat and risk litigation or to appease the holdouts and pay them on terms that will lead them to settle. The former solution is a way to ensure that the ex ante threat is not time inconsistent; otherwise, the game would unravel at the next debt-restructuring episode. However, buying off some marginal holdouts may, at times, be better for the debtor than engaging in costly and lengthy litigation.

The risks of litigation in future bonded restructuring cases should not, however, be underestimated. The recent Peru-Elliot case and the lessons learned by investors from previous restructuring cases may imply that creditors aggressively pursuing their claims may become more successful in the future.

Concluding Remarks on PSI

The official G7 and IMF PSI policy ("a case-by-case approach with principles, criteria, tools and guidelines") has been applied in the last few years to cases of bonded debt restructurings and cross-border bank lines (cases such as Korea, Thailand, Indonesia, Brazil, Pakistan, Ecuador, Ukraine and Turkey, and, indirectly, Russia and Argentina). The application of this policy has not led to the dire consequences and negative outcomes predicted by some a couple of years ago. Not only has the international capital market not been destroyed, but there is also little evidence so far that the flows of debt (and their pricing) to emerging market economies have been affected by this policy in ways that are jeopardizing long-term flows to such economies. Moreover, a combination of official money and case-specific PSI minimized the cost of crises in a number of large systemic countries and thus supported their rapid resumption of economic growth. Also, moral hazard distortions have been somewhat reduced, and there is evidence of healthy greater discrimination by creditors between better and worse sovereign debtors: average spreads do not seem to have been affected by the PSI policy, whereas the distribution of such spreads appears to be more reflective of underlying credit or repayment risk. Finally, the G7 PSI policy led to several cases of bonded debt restructuring that were successfully implemented even in the absence of an ex ante use of CACs.

---

54. See Bucheit and Gulati (2000) for a more detailed discussion of such exit consent clauses.

The official PSI framework—as described in the relevant G7 and IMF documents—provided a balance between the benefits of rules (to reduce the uncertainty and unpredictability of policy) and the advantages of discretion to deal with each individual and complex case study. The overall balance of principles, criteria, considerations, and tools in a PSI framework where a case-by-case approach has been shaped by basic principles and operational guidelines seems to have provided a trade-off between rules and discretion. Maybe, over time, case history will allow the development of clearer rules even if some degree of constructive ambiguity may remain as a component of an efficient PSI regime.

Many complex issues are still to be addressed in both the "liquidity" cases and the "insolvency" cases. They are difficult, complex, and not prone to simplistic answers and solutions. But the overall official PSI strategy in the 1990s ensured that the flows of capital to emerging markets continued to be the main source of finance to such countries while not being distorted by expectations of systematic bailouts of investors.

Such PSI policy may lead to endogenous financial engineering to create new classes of claims that are not as easily restructurable. In the 1990s, the emergence of interbank loans and bonded debt was partially—but only partially—the result of the bail-in of syndicated loans in the 1980s. Similarly, one can expect that new structured instruments embedded with complex derivative features may emerge as a strategy to avoid the bail-in of current debt instruments.

However, there are limits to how this PSI avoidance process can go. Eventually, a country's repayment of its debts depends more on its ability to pay than its willingness to pay because there are enforcement mechanisms (reputation and market discipline and punishment) to reduce the risk of opportunistic default. Thus, if a country will face a debt-servicing problem because of either an unsustainable debt burden or a profile of burden that is incompatible with short-term liquidity resources, some rollover, restructuring, rescheduling or, at the extreme, reduction of the debt payments will become unavoidable, however sophisticated the new instruments are.[55] Such

55. When considering the issues of debt restructurings, one should be careful to distinguish between inability to pay and unwillingness to pay. As the theory of sovereign debt clearly suggests, the latter is an important issue. The latter phenomenon, that is, strategic defaults and opportunistic nonpayments, can be avoided via intertemporal and static market discipline. Punishments include trade sanctions, cutoffs from lending in international capital markets, and the output costs that creditors can inflict on defaulting sovereigns. Indeed, some punishment should be, and is, in the system to avoid strategic defaults. Some (e.g., Dooley 2000a), however, go so far as to argue that the rationale behind PSI policy and the IMF's lending into arrears policy is faulty because it will reduce the costs of strategic defaults. In Dooley's view, the output costs of default are the only meaningful punishment that prevents default in a world where the IMF or other agents cannot distinguish between nonpayment due to inability to pay and nonpayment due to unwillingness to pay. In his view, anything that reduces such debt renegotiation costs and makes it easier to restructure sovereign debt (such as CACs, IMF lending into arrears, or official sanctioning of defaults) will make the current system of international capi-

instruments may shift the burden from some secured creditors to others (and the official sector is concerned that their result is not to shift the burden to the official sector), or they may just make the costs of renegotiating debt claims higher and thus make more difficult and more delayed such restructurings.

As long as the debt-servicing problems derive from true inability to pay or avoidable liquidity humps that lead to liquidity runs, a system that makes it very hard or costly to restructure debts may not be efficient and may impose severe costs not only on debtors but also on creditors. Creditors do not internalize the negative externalities or collective action effects of their unilateral attempts to stake seniority at the expense of other actors or the overall system. Thus, the official sector has been concerned about the development and widespread use of instruments that provide effective seniority to some private claims relative to other private claims or official claims or that make it harder to restructure debts.

3.1.3   The Architecture to Reform the International Architecture

Just as we began our discussion of crisis management with a survey of the institutional arrangements by which it is done, so we precede our discussion of more fundamental reform of the international financial architecture with a survey of the additional institutions and forums in which these issues have been discussed.

Halifax Summit and Rey Report

A broad debate on the steps needed to strengthen the international financial system was already under way when the Mexican peso was devalued in December 1994. The ensuing peso crisis gave the debate considerable impetus and pertinence. The annual summit of G7 nation leaders in 1995 held in Halifax, Nova Scotia, initiated work in a number of areas. They

---

tal flow more inefficient and will cause a reduction in the flows of capital to emerging markets. Dooley's basic point (that there must be costs to opportunistic default) is sensible, but the argument is taken to the extreme in ways that are not sensible. First, some countries will stop paying because of inability to pay; thus, in these cases it is in the interests of both the debtors and the creditors to renegotiate the debt contract and restructure, roll over, or reduce the debt. Making it very costly to do this restructuring will only hurt both creditors and debtors. Thus, a system in which the output punishment is as high as possible and the renegotiation costs are as high as possible is not efficient or optimal from a global welfare point of view. Second, in case of pure liquidity runs, there is a collective action problem that needs to be solved. Part of the solution (which is welfare beneficial to all) can be at times concerted rollovers of short-term debts that are coming to maturity. Thus, a system in which the costs of renegotiating debt claims and making reschedulings or rollovers are prohibitively high is also going to be welfare inferior to a system in which renegotiation is possible. Thus, a sound system is one in which the trade-off between the need to avoid strategic default (via punishments) and the need to renegotiate efficiently contracts when liquidity runs or insolvency requires it are balanced. A system in which the costs of renegotiation are too high is inefficient and of no benefit to either debtors or creditors.

called for additional study of means to prevent future crises and to promote their orderly resolution when they do occur. The finance ministers and central bank governors of the G10 countries were asked to review ideas. The G10 group established a working party that submitted a report—informally known as the Rey Report, after its chairman—to the ministers and governors in May 1996.

The Rey Report noted recent changes that have altered the characteristics of currency and financial crises in emerging markets. It indicated that neither debtor countries nor their creditors should expect to be insulated from adverse financial consequences in the event of a crisis. It also called for better market-based procedures for the workout of debts when countries and firms are under financial distress. Specific reforms of bond contracts were proposed to encourage the cooperation and coordination of bondholders when the financial distress of a country or corporation requires the restructuring of the terms of a bond contract. It also suggested a review of IMF rules on lending into arrears in order to extend the scope of this IMF policy to include new forms of debt. Previously the power of the IMF had been used to support creditors' interests in the sense that it would cut off lending to any debtor that was not meeting its private debt service obligations. Lending into arrears would allow the IMF to continue lending, in certain circumstances, to countries that had temporarily suspended debt service payments but had continued to maintain a cooperative approach toward their private creditors and to comply with IMF adjustment policies.

A number of important innovations came out of this reform process: international standards for banking supervision, the so-called Basel core principles for banking supervision (Goldstein 1997); the development of international standards for making economic data publicly available, under the IMF's Special Data Dissemination Standard; an emergency financing mechanism in the IMF, the Supplemental Reserve Facility, to help members cope with sudden and disruptive loss of market confidence with financing significantly larger than traditional quotas; and the decision to expand the IMF's backup source of financing under the New Arrangements to Borrow.[56]

G22 and Reports

Despite some progress in strengthening the system, the eruption of the Asian crisis in 1997 demonstrated the need for further efforts. In November 1997, on the occasion of the Asia Pacific Economic Cooperation (APEC)

56. Twenty-five potential participants to the NAB agreed to make loans to the IMF when supplementary resources are needed to forestall or cope with an impairment of the international monetary system or to deal with an exceptional situation that poses a threat to the stability of the system. The twenty-five include many outside the traditional circle of member countries of the G10 or of the original General Arrangements to Borrow.

Leaders Summit in Vancouver, a number of Asian leaders proposed a meeting of finance ministers and central bank governors to discuss the crisis and broader issues regarding the functioning of the international monetary system. They suggested that the meeting be global, that is, that it should include emerging market countries, and not just the usual small group of major industrialized countries. U.S. President Clinton responded by calling on Secretary Rubin and Chairman Greenspan to convene such a meeting. Finance ministers and central bank governors from twenty-two systemically significant countries (informally dubbed the G22) accordingly gathered in Washington on April 16 to explore ways to reform the international financial system that could help reduce the frequency and severity of crises.[57] Ministers and governors created three working groups to consider measures to increase transparency and openness, potential reforms to strengthen domestic financial systems, and mechanisms to facilitate appropriate burden sharing between the official and private sectors in times of crisis.

The United States was strongly supportive of the creation of the G22 group, because it included systemically important emerging market economies, whereas other G7 members, especially the Europeans, remained slightly wary of a new group that might crowd out some functions traditionally performed by other groups or institutions in which they had more influence and leverage (the IMF executive board, the Interim Committee, the G10). The three working groups of the G22 presented their reports in October 1998, on the occasion of the annual meetings of the IMF and World Bank.

The report of the G22 working group on transparency and accountability recommended that national authorities publish timely, accurate, and comprehensive information on the external liabilities of private financial and corporate sectors as well as their own foreign exchange positions; it recommended adherence to existing international standards for transparency; it called for better monitoring of countries' compliance with such standards, including through IMF reporting on countries' adherence to internationally recognized standards. It also recommended that the potential for greater transparency of the positions of investment banks, hedge funds, and institutional investors should be examined. Finally, the IMF and other IFIs were called upon to be more open and transparent. Unnecessary secrecy was deemed particularly inappropriate in institutions telling others to be more transparent.

Because weaknesses in the financial sector were at the core of the Asian and global crisis of 1997–98, the report of the G22 working group on strengthening financial systems included the following recommendations:

---

57. The group ended up being effectively composed of twenty-six members, the usual size creep in these types of international groupings.

strong prudential regulation and supervision of banks and other financial institutions; the design of explicit and effective deposit insurance schemes to protect bank depositors; the design and implementation of bankruptcy and foreclosure laws for insolvent firms; development of liquid and deep financial markets, especially markets in securities (bonds and equities); national implementation of the Basel core principles of banking supervision and of the objectives and principles of securities regulation set by the International Organization of Securities Commissions (IOSCO); coordination and cooperation among international organizations and international supervisory entities in strengthening financial systems; technical assistance for and training of government officials and regulators; improvement of corporate governance in both the financial and nonfinancial sectors, so that investment decisions respond to market signals rather than to personal relationships; implementation of efficient insolvency and debtor-creditor regimes that would facilitate workouts for corporations in financial distress. These may include procedures for systemic bank and corporate restructuring and debt workouts.

The report of the G22 working group on international financial crises identified policies that could help promote the orderly resolution of future crises, including both official assistance and policies and procedures that could facilitate appropriate PSI in crisis resolution. The work of this working group was a continuation of the development of official PSI policy that started with the Rey Report and continued in 1999 and 2000 with the development of the G7 framework for PSI (see section 3.1.2 for details).

At two subsequent meetings in March and April 1999, an enlarged group, the G33, discussed issues related to reform of the global economy and international financial system. The experience with the ad hoc G22 and G33 groups, which led to a broad dialogue on many important aspects of the international architecture reform, next led the United States to suggest in 1999 that a more permanent group, including advanced economies and systemically important emerging economies, the G20, be created.

The Road to the Koln and Kyushu-Okinawa Summits of the G7

The work of the G22 group laid the foundation for subsequent work on reforming the "international financial architecture" (a term first introduced by U.S. Treasury Secretary Rubin). The G7 took the main lead on this project, but emerging markets and other advanced economies were involved in the dialogue via the G22, G33, and G10 groupings.

In the fall of 1998, the Asian crisis became global with the collapse of Russia in August 1998, the contagious effects of this crisis to other emerging markets (Brazil and the rest of Latin America), the near collapse of LTCM, and the ensuing liquidity seizure in the capital markets of the United States and other advanced economies. By October 1998, the risk of a global financial meltdown had become significantly greater. The United

States and the other G7 countries responded to this threat through a series of joint initiatives, outlined in the 30 October 1998 statement of the G7 finance ministers and central bank governors. The G7 committed to a number of reforms consistent with the recommendations of the G22 working groups as well as a great deal of additional work on architecture reform in areas previously not dealt with. At the same time, a series of uncoordinated reductions in interest rates in the fall of 1998 by the U.S. Federal Reserve, other G7 central banks, and a large number of other monetary authorities helped to restore liquidity in financial markets, reduce the panic that had enveloped financial markets following the Russia and LTCM episodes, and restore investors' confidence in the stability of the international financial system.

The G7 effort to reform the international financial architecture took momentum in the winter of 1998 and spring of 1999. The G7 agreed to come up with a specific architecture reform proposed by the time of the G7 Koln Summit in June 1998. This cooperative effort led to the report of the G7 finance ministers to the Koln Economic Summit ("Strengthening the International Financial Architecture"), where a broad range of proposals to strengthen crisis prevention and crisis resolution were agreed.

The G7 agreed to measures to strengthen and reform the IFIs (i.e., the IMF and MDBs), enhance transparency and the promoting of best practices (specifically, the strengthening of financial regulation in industrial countries), and strengthen macroeconomic policies and financial systems in emerging markets. The last measure included appropriate choice of exchange rate regimes for emerging markets, ways to improve their financial systems, ways to ensure that the benefits of international capital flows are maximized, and appropriate management of external and domestic debt to reduce liquidity and balance sheet risks.

The G7 also agreed on policies to improve crisis prevention and management. The latter included a formal framework for PSI in crisis resolution that became the core of the G7 PSI doctrine. This doctrine can be described as a "case-by-case" approach to PSI constrained by principles, considerations, and tools.

Following in part the private-sector demands for greater transparency, clarity, and rules and to provide clearer guidelines to the IMF, the case-by-case approach to PSI was refined in April 2000 through a set of "operational guidelines" providing more details on the process and substance of PSI. These operational guidelines were agreed by the G7 at the ministerial meeting around the IMF-World Bank spring meeting and were later formally adopted in the G7 finance ministers and central bank governors communiqué prepared for the July 2000 G7 summit.

The July 2000 Kyushu-Okinawa G7 Summit (preceded by the meeting of the G7 finance ministers at Fukuoka that produced the report on "Strengthening the International Financial Architecture" from G7 finance ministers to the heads of state and government) also saw the emergence of further G7 consensus on two other major issues—first, on how to reform the IMF and MDBs. The consensus on IMF reform at Fukuoka fleshed out the agreements previously reached by the G7 at the time of the IMF spring meetings in April 2000. Operationalization of the agreements on IMF reform (especially the reform of facilities approved by the IMF Board) was achieved by September 2000 in coincidence with the Fall Annual meetings of the IMF/World Bank in Prague (see section "Recent G7 Initiatives to Reform the International Monetary Fund" for details). Second, the G7 also agreed on policies towards HLIs (Highly Leveraged Institutions), Capital Flows, and OFCs (Offshore Financial Centers) that were supportive of the recommendations of the working groups of the Financial Stability Forum (see subsection below, "New Groups," for details).

New Groups

The International Monetary and Financial Committee

The International Monetary and Financial Committee (IMFC) came into being on 30 September 1999, when the IMF's board of governors approved a proposal of the IMF executive board to transform the Interim Committee into the IMFC and strengthening its role as the advisory committee of the board of governors; the committee usually meets twice a year.

The IMFC mandate and role are outlined by the IMF as follows:

> Like the Interim Committee, the IMFC has the responsibility of advising, and reporting to, the board of governors on matters relating to the board of governors' functions in supervising the management and adaptation of the international monetary and financial system, including the continuing operation of the adjustment process, and in this connection reviewing developments in global liquidity and the transfer of resources to developing countries; considering proposals by the executive board to amend the Articles of Agreement; and dealing with disturbances that might threaten the system.[58]

The creation of the IMFC was the result of an elaborate diplomatic dialogue between the United States and Europe (especially France) regarding which international bodies to strengthen. The United States supported trying to involve more systemically important emerging markets in the dialogue on international financial issues that eventually led to the creation of the G20. The European nations, especially France, wanted instead to strengthen existing institutions and pushed for turning the IMF Interim

---

58. The committee, whose members are governors of the IMF, reflects the composition of the IMF's executive board: each member country that appoints, and each group that elects, an executive director, appoints a member of the committee, which, like the executive board, has twenty-four members.

Committee into a stronger and permanent political body that would give guidance to the IMF board on major policy issues. The creation of the IMFC turned the longstanding previously "temporary" Interim Committee (IC) into a permanent one. However, the functions and roles of the IMFC effectively ended up being equivalent, with minor nuances, to those of the previous IC; certainly, the new IMFC, currently headed by U.K. Chancellor Gordon Brown, does not have the broad political mandate and power that the French wanted it to have.

The G20

The G20 was created at the urging of the United States, out of a desire for a forum where major emerging market economies would have a voice and participate in a dialogue on global financial issues. The positive experience with the G22 (and G33) process suggested a need to better involve these emerging markets.

The finance ministers of the G7 leading industrialized nations announced the creation of the G20 in September 1999. This new international forum of finance ministers and central bank governors represents nineteen countries, the EU, and the Bretton Woods Institutions (the IMF and the World Bank).[59] The mandate of the G20 is to promote discussion and to study and review policy issues among industrialized countries and emerging markets with a view to promoting international financial stability.[60]

The first ministerial meeting of the G20 was held in Berlin in December 1999, and the second took place in Montreal in October 2000. So far, the G20 has been mostly a forum for dialogue (some belittlingly call it a "talk shop") on exchange rate regimes, national balance sheets management and prudent debt management, PSI and global financial issues, financial-sector regulation and supervision, and international codes and standards. Between ministerial meetings, the G20 work in 2000 continued at the deputies level with a broad dialogue and papers on three crucial issues in international financial architecture: exchange rate regimes, national balance sheets and vulnerabilities, and PSI in crisis resolution.

The October 2000 meeting of the G20 reviewed the global economic outlook, the challenges posed by globalization, and issues related to financial

---

59. Member countries include Argentina, Australia, Brazil, Canada, China, France, Germany, India, Indonesia, Italy, Japan, Mexico, Russia, Saudi Arabia, South Africa, South Korea, Turkey, the United Kingdom, the United States, and the European Union. The managing director of the IMF and the president of the World Bank, as well as the chairpersons of the International Monetary and Financial Committee and Development Committee of the IMF and World Bank, participate fully in the discussions. The first meeting was chaired by Minister Martin in Berlin in December 1999. The second meeting took place in Montreal in October 2000.

60. Finance Minister Paul Martin of Canada was selected to be the inaugural chairperson of the G20.

crime and money laundering and discussed ways to make the world less vulnerable to financial crises, especially the issues discussed at the deputies level. The G20 finance ministers and central bank governors agreed on a series of measures aimed at "reducing vulnerability to financial crises" that included appropriate exchange rate regimes (supporting consistent and credible exchange rate regimes while not endorsing corner solutions to exchange rates), prudent liability management, PSI in crisis prevention and resolution (endorsing the principles and tools agreed by the IMF's IMFC at the 2000 spring and annual meetings), and implementation of international standards and codes.

In the view of some, the G20 should become over time an institution with greater importance and influence than the G7 because it is more representative of systemically important countries. Although over time the views of important emerging market economies might be more represented in international affairs, it is unlikely that in the short run the leadership role of the G7 will be reduced. However, the G20 is a forum where a serious dialogue between advanced economies and emerging markets can be pursued.[61]

The Financial Stability Forum

The Asian and global financial crisis suggested shortcomings to the pattern of national supervision and regulation of financial institutions in a world where such institutions operate globally and financial markets are becoming increasingly integrated. Although proposals for international financial regulation (such as Kaufman's global superregulator, discussed in section 3.1.6) are regarded as unrealistic, greater international coordination of policies of financial regulation and supervision has been deemed most useful and necessary. This need for coordination led to the creation in 1999 of the Financial Stability Forum (FSF).

In the winter of 1998, Bundesbank's President Tietmeyer worked on a proposal to establish an FSF to improve policy coordination among national financial authorities, the IFIs, and international regulatory bodies to promote international financial stability. Another aspect of the FSF is that its membership has been broadened beyond the G7 industrial countries and now includes eleven advanced economies (G7 plus Australia, Hong Kong, Singapore, and the Netherlands); additional emerging market economies (such as Malaysia) participate in the various working groups of the forum.

The FSF was first convened in April 1999, as its website notes, "to promote international financial stability through information exchange and international co-operation in financial supervision and surveillance. The Fo-

---

61. Some—for example, de Brouwer (2000)—go so far as to suggest that new international groups such as the G20 may replace or augment the policy function of the IMF. In this view, the IMF is too bureaucratic an organization and new international groups do not have the additional layer of interference in international policy making. These are, however, minority views.

rum brings together on a regular basis national authorities responsible for financial stability in significant international financial centers, international financial institutions, sector-specific international groupings of regulators and supervisors, and committees of central bank experts. The FSF seeks to co-ordinate the efforts of these various bodies in order to promote international financial stability, improve the functioning of markets, and reduce systemic risk." The forum is chaired by Andrew Crockett, general manager of the BIS, in his personal capacity.

Initially, the FSF formed three working groups on capital flows, offshore financial centers, and highly leveraged institutions. They presented their reports and recommendations in the spring of 2000.

The working group on capital flows recommended that national authorities put in place a risk management framework, or national balance sheet, for monitoring and assessing the risks faced by their economies arising from large and volatile capital flows. The group, recognizing the vulnerabilities associated with sovereign debt that is too short term, recommended that the IMF and World Bank develop a set of guidelines for sound practices in sovereign debt and liquidity management, which they are now doing. The guidelines include, for example, addressing gaps in available statistics, encouraging greater transparency, and eliminating laws and regulations that inadvertently encourage imprudent behavior. The group also pointed to other important ways in which national authorities and international bodies should support the process of addressing the national balance sheet approach to assessing the risks from capital flows.

The working group on offshore financial centers (OFCs) concluded that it was essential for OFCs to implement international standards as soon as possible, especially in the areas of regulation and supervision, disclosure and information sharing, and anti–money laundering, and that such implementation would help address concerns about some OFCs. The group's recommendations spell out a process for assessing OFCs' adherence to international standards, identify standards for priority implementation and assessment, and propose a menu of incentives that could be applied to enhance their adherence to international standards. This led to the publication by the FSF in the summer of 2000 of a "blacklist" of twenty-five financial centers that have poor supervision and are not internationally cooperative. The decision to publish this list was based on the view that OFCs that are unable or unwilling to adhere to internationally accepted standards for supervision, cooperation, and information sharing create a potential systemic threat to global financial stability. The importance of the issue of OFCs was stressed by the G7 finance ministers' report at the Fukuoka Summit. The G7 and FSF consensus has put strong heat on these "deviant" jurisdictions to improve their supervision and be more cooperative.

The highly leveraged institution (HLI) working group considered issues of systemic risk and market dynamic in small and medium sized economies.

Details on the progress in this HLI area are presented in the subsection "Highly Leveraged Institutions and Hedge Funds."

The FSF also began discussion of implementation of international standards to strengthen financial systems. The forum agreed that attention should focus on twelve key international standards, which will be highlighted in a compendium of standards. Also, a study group on deposit insurance made some progress and has asked the group to consult widely in the development of international guidance for deposit insurance arrangements.

In the future, it is likely that the FSF work will be less focused on policy recommendations and will be more of a "talk shop" about issues, providing discussion papers on matters of policy relevance. Also, the existence of the FSF has led to some healthy degree of competition, in addition to cooperation and dialogue, among international agencies such as the IMF and the Basel Committee on Banking Supervision. For example, the work by the FSF on the implementation of international codes and standards has led the IMF to renewed efforts to lead the way on these issues, as exemplified by its work on the Report on the Observance of Standards and Codes (ROSC).

3.1.4   Reforms for Better Crisis Prevention

Two of the most important pillars of the international financial architecture are exchange rate regimes (how flexible should they be?) and capital account regimes (how open should they be?). The attitudes of the G7 countries on these issues are important. Moreover, reform of the world monetary system that was fundamental enough to qualify as a "new architecture" or a "new Bretton Woods" would properly include these questions. However, these two topics fall inside the mandate of another of the chapters for this conference (Edwards, chap. 1 in this volume). In this part of our chapter, we look at other reforms to help prevent crises.

One of the central elements of architecture reform has been designing better policies for crisis prevention. Although crisis resolution is also central to the reform process, prevention is even more important to the extent that stronger policies and institutions can reduce the probability that financial crises will occur in the first place.

The efforts of the G7 and other international institutions and bodies to design policies for better crisis prevention have been comprehensive. Their broad scope includes a vast series of initiatives and actions:

1. Transparency and accountability of emerging markets, their economic agents, and the IFIs (such as the IMF), and greater disclosure and reporting by banks and other financial institutions in advanced economies

2. Greater attention given by the IMF and emerging markets to indicators of vulnerability to crises

3. Greater attention to national balance sheet analysis and risk management, especially liquidity and balance sheet risks

4. Optimal public debt management to reduce liquidity risk, exchange rate risk, and balance sheet risk

5. Prudential regulation and supervision of financial systems in emerging markets

6. Policies to maximize the benefits of international capital flows

7. Work on highly leveraged institutions (including hedge funds)

8. Work on OFCs (see the subsection "New Groups")

9. Reform of the Basel capital adequacy standards

10. Private contingent credit lines

11. Implementation of international standards and codes

12. Better governance of the financial and corporate systems

It is not possible to discuss in great detail all the initiatives, programs, and actions in the above areas. Instead we will concentrate on some of the main issues and open questions.

Transparency

There has been a lot of support for greater transparency by emerging market economies and IFIs. The arguments are familiar: greater information, transparency, and openness on the part of emerging markets, IFIs and even advanced economies' institutions will allow private investors and the entire international financial community to better assess risks, reduce the chances of irrational rushes to the exits, and improve the efficiency of international capital markets. It is usually said that transparency is like motherhood and apple pie (i.e., everyone likes it) with the caveat that it may not be enough by itself to prevent crises.

Things are, however, more complicated. Resistance to greater transparency is still widespread among emerging market economies. For example, some resistance has been presented to the new SDDS (Special Data Dissemination Standard) reserve templates (i.e., the provision within the IMF's SDDS of much more detailed data about the foreign exchange reserves of member countries) and to the effort to expand the SDDS to external debt data disaggregated by economic sector, maturity, and currency composition. Many emerging markets still do not allow the publication of their IMF Article IV reports. Many countries still resist or have not gone through the ROSC exercise. The IMF reports on the state of the banking and financial systems of its member countries (the Financial System Stability Assessments) are still in the experimental stage, and many countries oppose their publication. The IMF effort to develop "macro financial prudential indicators" (which are indicators more of the health of the financial system than macro vulnerability) is somewhat stalled because many data on the financial-sector soundness are not available and there is some political resistance by emerging markets to such assessment. Progress on developing indicators of vulnerability to liquidity and currency risk is positive (as more country documents provide assessments and measures of such vulnerabilities) but still incomplete; regular publication by the IMF of vulnerabilities indicators for emerging markets may be a useful addition to this effort. Moreover, the February 2001 decision by the IMF to create a new international capital markets department will support—among other functions of this new department—the monitoring of vulnerabilities in emerging market economies.

Thus, although a lot of progress has been made in the area of transparency and the IMF has been quite open to the reforms in this area of crisis prevention, a lot of work still needs to be done. One issue that still remains somewhat sticky and is a matter of concern to IMF staff is whether greater transparency (such as, for example, publication of Article IV consultations reports) may lead emerging market officials to be less open, frank, and willing to share confidential information with IMF missions. Some have argued that the great emphasis on transparency has already had some chilling effect on IMF interactions with such officials. The issue is similar to the question of how much bank and financial regulators should disclose of the information they have access to on the health of financial institutions. On the one hand, good supervision and regulation requires, at times, discretion and withholding of some information. On the other hand, financial markets need as much information as possible to make rational assessment of the true valuations of firms and financial institutions. Thus, in general, more information and transparency may be useful, but there are limits to how far one could go in this area.

BIS Capital Adequacy Standards and Their Implications for Crisis Prevention

Many issues in the reform of the Basel Capital Accord, which set guidelines for minimum capital levels to be maintained by countries' banks, are open. The initial draft of the consultative paper on how to reform the accord was issued in June 1999, and the comment period had closed by March 2000. Two of the major proposals in the initial consultative paper were to tie capital weights to ratings by credit rating agencies and to use banks' internal credit ratings as a basis for the capital weights.

The reform of the Capital Accord is a most complex issue with many dimensions. One question is the relative importance to be given to three pillars—market discipline, supervisory review, and capital regulation—in the capital adequacy framework. But some of the sticking points in the debate on this reform have an important bearing for the specific issue of international crisis prevention. First, if you allow some banks to use their internal models of risk, what criteria do you use to decide which banks, and in what countries, as opposed to requiring a more traditional standardized approach? For example, Europeans believe that most of their banks should qualify to use internal models of risk, but some observers, especially in the United States, are skeptical that many European banks have the capacity to do so. Thus, it is important to set benchmarks on what institutions are going to be allowed to use such models.

Second, what is the best way to build compliance with international codes and standards into the capital adequacy ratios? The FSF and other official institutions (especially finance ministries) support this approach as a way to give incentives to emerging markets to implement such codes and standards. However, there is resistance on the part of bank regulators and the Basel Committee; in their view, bank capital charges should not be used as a tool to achieve goals not directly related to appropriate risk assessment. However, compliance with standards and codes does affect capital risk of financial institutions. Also, there is some concern that bank regulators look at the issue of the capital standards in too narrow terms (the risk of individual banks) and do not appreciate enough the importance of systemic risk. Incentives to implement codes and standards may reduce financial contagion, the risk of systemic banking crises, and the likelihood of systemic risk to the international financial system.

The Basel Committee issued a new draft of the consultative paper in January 2001, seeking comments from interested parties by May 2001. The initial draft proposal to link banks' capital to ratings produced by external credit rating agencies was dropped in the new draft. Also, although the January 2001 draft reaffirmed the support for internal risk models, concerns have been expressed that reliance on internal ratings may aggravate economic cycles, because loan standards may be relaxed during economic booms and tightened during recessions.

Highly Leveraged Institutions and Hedge Funds

Concerns about the role of HLIs, and hedge funds in particular, emerged in the wake of the Asian crisis for two reasons. First, the collapse of a large hedge fund, LTCM, provides a vivid example of how high leverage contributes to systemic risk. Second, actions of some hedge funds in small and medium-sized economies led to concerns about the aggressive trade practices of such funds and to allegations of market manipulation. Hong Kong and Australia, in particular, argued that hedge funds had engaged in manipulative practices in their foreign exchange and other asset markets. Accordingly, one of the three initial working groups of the FSF, set up in the spring of 1999, addressed the question of the role of HLIs in systemic risk and market dynamics in small and medium-sized economies.

Regarding the issue of systemic risk, the recommendations of the report of this working group resemble, with some differences, the eight recommendations of the report of the U.S. President's Working Group on Capital Markets (April 1999). It was agreed to emphasize indirect regulation of hedge funds, for the time being, and to avoid direct regulation.[62] The recommendations included measures aimed at better risk management by HLIs and their counterparties (better credit assessments, better exposure measurement, establishment of credit limits, collateral management techniques), better creditor oversight (greater intensity on firms that are falling short, periodic reaffirmation of compliance with sound practices), and enhanced public disclosure and reporting to authorities.

Regarding market dynamics, the HLI working group[63] formed a subgroup that performed a study of the role of HLIs (both hedge funds and proprietary desks) in the currency turmoil experienced by six economies (Hong Kong, Australia, New Zealand, South Africa, Singapore, and Malaysia) during 1998. The results of this study[64] were somewhat different from those of the IMF study on the role of hedge funds in the currency turmoil in East Asia in 1997. The latter considered the role of hedge funds only in the initial stages of the crisis (up to November 1997), whereas the FSF's HLI market dynamics study group considered the continuing turmoil in the six small and medium-sized economies under study during 1998. Whereas the IMF study had come to the conclusion that hedge funds had played only a minor role (being at the back of the herding pack in 1997 rather than as the leaders of it), the HLI study group found a more significant role of hedge funds and proprietary desks (which trade for their own account) of international financial firms in the latter episodes of turmoil in 1998 in the six economies studied. For example, circumstantial evidence was found of some aggressive trade practices (rumors, false information, and placing large trades at less liquid times of the day, such as lunch).[65]

Although it was hard to reach a consensus on controversial issues of market destabilization and manipulation, the group concluded that

- From time to time, HLIs may establish large and concentrated positions in small and medium-sized markets. When this is the case, HLIs have the potential to influence market dynamics, especially in periods of market turmoil.
- The judgment as to whether HLI positions are destabilizing has to be made on a case-by-case basis. Some members of the group took the position that the largest hedge funds exacerbated the macroeconomic difficulties of several economies in 1998 and even manipulated their

62. Options other than indirect regulation, such as a credit register and direct regulation, although rejected for the time being, will be reconsidered by the FSF if implementation of the other recommendations proves ineffective.

63. The HLI group included officials from finance ministries, central banks, and financial regulatory agencies of major industrial countries and some emerging market economies.

64. The report of this group ("Report of the Market Dynamics Study Group") can be found at [http://www.fsforum.org/Reports/RepHLI.html].

65. For a recent theoretical and empirical study of the role of large players in currency crises, see Corsetti, Pesenti, and Roubini (2001).

currencies, whereas others believe that, provided the economic fundamentals are strong, hedge funds are unlikely to present a threat.

The HLI report made a series of recommendations to address the issue of
market dynamics even though most of its policy recommendations were in
the area of systemic risk. First, the report noted that enhanced risk management practices could also address some of the concerns raised by emerging markets by constraining excessive leverage. Second, the HLI group also
noted that where trading takes place on organized exchanges, requiring
market participants to report to regulators, and possibly requiring position
limits as well, could alleviate some of the pressures caused by large and concentrated positions. Third, the FSF recommended that market participants
themselves articulate guidelines for market conduct in the area of foreign
exchange trading. These market guidelines would address the concerns of
smaller and medium-sized economies about the aggressive trading practices that might have contributed to exacerbating market pressures in period of market turmoil.

Progress in implementing the President's Working Group recommendations, and those of the HLI working group, has been slow, because they require both regulatory and legislative actions that have been hard to achieve.
Some who had favored the idea of direct regulation but accepted the indirect regulation approach (hoping for a rapid implementation of the recommendations) feel frustrated that more rapid progress has not been made in
implementing measures to reduce the risks posed by hedge funds and other
HLIs; several of the eight recommendations of the President's Working
Group remain to be implemented.

However, the nature of the hedge fund industry has changed rapidly, with
some significant deleveraging occurring over time. Some major hedge fund
players have effectively closed shop, especially those (LTCM, the Tiger
funds, the Soros funds) that were alleged to be behind the episodes of systemic risk and destabilizing market dynamics. Emphasis on the role of
hedge funds may be now misplaced in that they do not play the same leading role that they did a few years ago. The size of the assets managed by
hedge funds is small (less than $1 trillion), even after controlling for lever-
age, relative to that of the mutual fund or insurance sectors, each of which
manages more than $5 trillion of assets. Although such players are regu-
lated and may be less leveraged than other players, they command large financial resources, and their investment decisions can significantly affect
currencies and asset prices. Thus, such new players may emerge as more relevant for future systemic crises and the efforts to avoid them. Moreover, recent evidence about reduced liquidity in financial markets (the forex market and other G7 financial markets) and the concerns expressed about them
may have to do with the disappearance of large leveraged players in these
markets. As some financial institutions have closed—or scaled down the ac-

tivities of—their proprietary desks, and as some large macro hedge funds have closed shop or significantly reduced the size of their positions, capital and liquidity available for market-making and contrarian positions may have fallen, thus leading to reduced liquidity and greater asset price volatility.

Private Contingent Credit Lines

Another possible tool for emerging market countries to prevent crises is facilities for CCLs from private international banks. These could take two forms, either the contingent repo facilities that Argentina has or loan facilities secured with collateral as suggested by Feldstein (1999b). The issue of collateralized facilities relates to the question of credit enhancements, an issue discussed later in the "Collateral and Credit Enhancements" section. Private CCLs, like those of Argentina, were also set up in Mexico and Indonesia. Although private CCLs may become an element of the toolkit for crisis prevention, one could be somewhat skeptical of their overall effectiveness for a number of reasons:

1. It is not obvious whether these facilities provide additional financing resources to an emerging market economy in periods of pressure and turmoil. The creditors may want to reduce risk when such pressures emerge and can always reduce their exposure to the debtor in a number of ways, either through direct reduction of other long positions in the country or through the use of financial derivatives to hedge the country risk and exposure.

2. The experience with private CCLs has so far been disappointing. They were unable to stem the crisis in Indonesia and were not even used, probably because of their small size relative to the amount of capital flight.

3. Mexico drew on its facility in 1999 when the global turmoil spread to its economy. Because the borrowing rate was well below the higher spreads on Mexican debt, however, Mexico's bank creditors were upset about what they perceived to be an inappropriate use of a cheap facility in periods of pressure. This peculiar attitude of creditors (reluctance to provide the insurance agreed upon on low terms in good times when hard times come) shows that the reality of private CCLs is partially at odds with how they are supposed to work in principle. However, there may be more efficient ways to design private CCLs, such as setting them with a spread relative to LIBOR rather than with a fixed interest rate and thus reducing the incentives of the borrower to capture an arbitrage gain in periods of pressure.

Thus, private CCLs have been so far a mixed bag. There are significant doubts about their true effectiveness as a crisis prevention tool.

Vulnerability Indicators

Emphasis has been given to national balance sheet management at both the aggregate and sectoral (government, financial sector, and corporate sector) levels and the importance of managing liquidity and balance sheet risk. One aspect is the development of better indicators of vulnerability to risk of crisis. Although early warning systems may be a component of this better monitoring of risks, this task is best left to the private sector and academic research.

There is some consensus that the IMF should not be in the business of providing to the markets estimates of the probability of currency and financial crises; it should instead provide the data and indicators (various measures of financial and debt ratios) that allow private investors to make their own assessment of such risks. In fact, having the IMF issue "yellow cards" or "red flags" in the form of specific quantitative assessments of the risk of a crisis would be dangerous. It would be subject to Type I and Type II errors (failing to predict a crisis that then occurs, or predicting one that does not materialize—or, worse, triggering one that would not have otherwise occurred). However, the development of better data and indicators of external vulnerability is an essential public good that the IMF should be able to provide to markets. One problem during the Asian crisis was confusion and lack of data even on basic measures of external debt. The recent agreement by the IMF members to extend the SDDS to external debt data (ideally disaggregated by currency, maturity, sectoral breakdown, and residency of the holder of the claim) will go a long way in the direction of better information about exposure and will be a good basis for the development of more sophisticated indicators of vulnerability.

3.1.5   Policy Regarding Reform of the International Monetary Fund

Because the large industrialized countries dominate the IMF, any discussion of their policies must consider their attitudes toward reform of the IMF. There is no shortage of suggestions to the effect that reform is needed.[66]

The Nature of International Monetary Fund Critiques

Let us consider some of the arguments that have been made in the debate over reform of the IMF.[67] We will not elaborate in detail on each one or try to make a judgment among them; that is the task of other chapters in this conference volume. The arguments are of interest here as inputs to the U.S. and G7 positions on reform of the IMF.

Most evaluations begin with a sentence along the lines of, "The IMF has made serious mistakes—what better evidence than the severity of the 1997–99 crises in emerging markets?" But what comes next? Sometimes the crit-

---

66. Reviews include Krueger (1997). We do not have space here to consider in detail the World Bank and other MDBs.

67. Many of the critiques, and a few defenses, are collected in McQuillan and Montgomery (1999).

ics go into sufficient detail to specify exactly what they think it is that the IMF has been doing wrong and what sort of reforms are necessary. Here are some of the most frequently suggested reforms.

1. The IMF should encourage more exchange rate flexibility. Reluctance to abandon currency targets and to devalue in the face of balance-of-payments disequilibria led to the crises of 1994–99.

2. The IMF should encourage more exchange rate stability, including firm institutional commitments such as currency boards or dollarization that will restore monetary credibility, rather than government manipulation of the exchange rate to gain competitive advantage at the expense of people's living standards.

3. The international community needs to make more official resources available for emergency programs, bailouts, debt forgiveness, and new loans. There was no good reason based in economic fundamentals for the East Asians to suffer the sudden reversal of capital inflows in 1997; under such circumstances it is the role of the IMF to plug the gap and restore confidence with large official packages of financial support. Thus, the IMF should become a quasi-international lender of last resort.

4. We need to address the moral hazard problem more seriously, because it is the ultimate source of the crises. Investors and borrowers alike are reckless when they know they will be bailed out by the IMF and G7. Thus, big bailout packages should be avoided, and whenever there is a run-off (no rollover) on private claims, semicoercive forms of burden sharing, such as concerted rollovers, standstills, and capital controls, should be introduced to bail in the private sector.

5. Countries need to adopt capital controls to insulate themselves from the vagaries of fickle international investors.

6. Countries need financial openness and capital account liberalization so they can take advantage of international capital markets (e.g., to finance investment more cheaply than from domestic savings and to provide some discipline on domestic policies).

7. Country programs need easier monetary and fiscal targets; recent IMF programs have had too much macroeconomic conditionality, inflicting needless recessions.

8. Country programs need tighter macroeconomic discipline, since monetary and fiscal profligacy is the source of most balance-of-payments problems, and private investors cannot be persuaded to keep their money invested in the countries without sound macro policies that restore investors' confidence during a crisis.

9. The IMF needs to customize conditionality to individual countries' circumstances. East Asia did not have the macro problems so familiar from Latin America.

10. The IMF needs to require standardized and strict rules-based pre-certification in order for a country to qualify for IMF assistance.

11. The IMF, along with the World Bank, should pay more attention to the needs of poor countries, rather than those that are successfully developing and able to attract private capital, and should place more emphasis on poverty reduction in each country program.

12. The IMF should remove any subsidy component in loans and charge higher interest rates, close to private market rates. In any case, it should leave poverty reduction to the World Bank.

One could continue, but the point is clear. Some want more exchange rate flexibility; some want less. Some want more macroeconomic austerity and conditionality; some want less. Some want more bailouts, some less. Some want more capital controls, some less. Each odd-numbered point above contradicts each corresponding even-numbered point. But one cannot have both more and less exchange flexibility, both larger and smaller bailouts, both more open and more closed financial markets, both looser and tighter macro policies, both more and less customization of conditionality.

The principle is thus that "for every critique of the IMF there exists an equally forceful critique that is the diametric opposite." This of course does not refute the fact that some number of these attacks could be justified: it does not let the IMF off the hook. Each argument should be considered on its merits. The point, however, is that most of the public debate is conducted at a level of sufficient generality that critics can give the impression of sharing a common viewpoint when they actually have contradictory points in mind. This can give politicians the very misleading illusion that reforms are straightforward to determine and easy to implement.

Critics on the right can give politicians the impression that the desirable reform is a simple matter of reining in the excessive interventionism of the G7 and IMF. They conclude that all unbiased analysts agree that it is sufficient to let the private market work on its own, to refrain from bailouts. The danger is that when such politicians get into office, they will soon discover a need to rescue important and sensitive countries, as their predecessors have done, after having made a point of saying explicitly that they would not.

Critics on the left make a strong case when they argue that the United States and other rich countries are currently devoting a very small level of resources to attempts to help poor countries.[68] However, the political obstacle to greater U.S. support for multilateral institutions is the perception that most such funds have in the past not been well spent. This perception

---

68. For reasons of space, we do not cover in this paper important questions regarding how to deal with poverty, what developmental policy should be, and the status of the HIPC initiative to reduce the debt burden of the poorest developing countries.

has some basis in reality: some international agencies have been inefficient in the past. However, the IMF has been one of the more efficient and cost-effective multilateral institutions.[69] The danger is that the critics will succeed in tearing down the IMF and then be disappointed when no new and improved institution is substituted in its place.

The Meltzer Commission Report

Although proposals for the reform, and even abolition, of the IMF abound (see, e.g., De Gregorio et al. 1999; Feldstein 1999a; Meltzer 1998; Schultz, Simon, and Wriston 1998; Calomiris 1998a), some have had a particularly political high profile. Specifically, the recommendations of the Meltzer Commission—formally the International Financial Institution Advisory Commission created by the U.S. Congress in 1999 to provide suggestions for reform of the IMF and MDBs—have received the most attention. Some of the recommendations of the commission subsume, in one form or another, other proposals for IMF reform. Thus, consideration of the commission recommendations provides an opportunity to analyze a number of other suggestions for the reform of the IFIs and the international architecture (the role of ex ante and ex post conditionality, the need for an international lender of last resort, the use of collateral in IMF loans, market discipline, and the opening up of emerging economies to foreign financial institutions).

The main recommendations of the commission, presented in its report, were as follows:[70]

1. The IMF should become a quasi–international lender of last resort that provides large-scale, essentially unconditional support only to prequalifying countries that are sound in their financial system and fiscal affairs (ex ante conditionality) but that suffer from international contagion nonetheless.

2. The IMF should avoid ex post conditionality and lending to countries in crisis that lack sound economies or policies and thus do not prequalify. It should provide only "counsel" and "advice," no loans or support, to such economies. This would effectively terminate existing lending programs, such as Stand-By Arrangements (SBAs), of the IMF (and MDBs) in a wide range of emerging market economies.

---

69. One would think it would be easier to explain to the public the merits of an organization that has nothing to do with foreign aid but, rather, lends money in time of crisis, in return for countries' commitments to needed reforms, and is almost always repaid.

70. International Financial Institution Advisory Commission (2000). The commission also made recommendations about MDB reform, such as taking the World Bank out of the development finance business and relying mostly on grants for World Bank support. We will not discuss here, given space limits, reform of the World Bank and other MDBs. We briefly touch upon these issues, especially the division of labor between IMF and World Bank, in the later section "Mission Creep."

3. IMF loans to prequalifiers should be short-term (a term of four to eight months was mentioned), set rising penalty interest rates to encourage early repayment, and rely on security by means of a clear priority claim on the borrower's assets.

4. Conditions for prequalification by IMF borrowers include the following: (a) a sound banking system, including the opening of emerging markets' financial systems to foreign banks; (b) regular and timely publication of the maturity structure of a country's outstanding sovereign and guaranteed debt and off–balance sheet liabilities; (c) adequate capitalization of commercial banks either by a significant equity position, in accord with international standards, or by subordinated debt held by nongovernmental and unaffiliated entities; (d) establishment by the IMF of a proper fiscal requirement to assure that IMF resources would not be used to sustain irresponsible budget policies.

To understand the main differences between the current structure of the IMF and that proposed by the commission, one may think as the current IMF structure as being based on four pillars, each requiring some degree of ex ante or ex post conditionality. The commission instead effectively recommends an IMF with only one pillar that relies strictly on ex ante conditionality.[71] Let us consider briefly each of the four pillars.

First is a new CCL facility that is similar in some aspects to the one proposed by the commission in that it relies on prequalification criteria (sound financial and fiscal and data transparency) and stresses ex ante conditionality (prequalifiers would have access with little ex post conditionality to relatively large IMF resources in case of contagion).

Second are regular conditionality-based loans (Stand-By Arrangements) for countries that are small and nonsystemic and have serious macro and financial problems and that therefore do not prequalify for large support. The idea of this pillar is that program conditionality provides the sticks to ensure reform while access to normal quota IMF resources provides financial support for policy adjustment by the country in difficulty. The majority of IMF programs—currently and historically—have been of this type, for countries that do make mistakes and do have crises but who would not prequalify under the stringent conditions of the first pillar, given macro and financial or structural shortcomings.

Third, the current system allows exceptional financing (i.e., financing in excess of normal quotas) to countries that would not prequalify for a CCL because of their policy imperfections but that are deemed to be systemically important and to require large amounts of support to adjust to severe crises, thereby preventing contagious effects on other emerging markets. These ex-

---

71. The commission would also accept the exceptional and transitory use (before the switch to the new long-run regime) of a pillar of large financing for systemically important countries that are in crisis and do not prequalify for the large unconditional financing.

ceptional funding arrangements are the recently created Supplemental Reserve Facility (SRF) or other arrangements that provide loans in significant excess of normal quotas. The SRF was used in recent large support packages for the first time in Korea in 1997, and then in Brazil, Argentina, and Turkey. The commission's view is that this third pillar should be phased out over time. However, the commission added an escape clause that would allow—in a transition period to this new long-run regime—for IMF large lending in exceptional cases in which significant contagion may occur.

Fourth, the last pillar of the current IMF system is the existence of subsidized lending facilities to very poor countries (the Extended Structural Adjustment Facility and now the Poverty Reduction and Growth Facility) and multiyear lending at slow repayment rates to countries with serious structural problems or in transition to a market economy (the Extended Fund Facility [EFF]). The commission argued instead that the IMF should cease lending to countries for long-term development assistance (eliminate ESAF and PRGF while writing off all debt to HIPC countries) and for long-term structural transformation (as in the post-Communist transition economies, i.e., elimination of the EFF). Such functions should instead be moved to the World Bank and other MBDs.

The commission's report argues that IMF packages, especially the large loans to countries having serious problems, exacerbate both creditor and debtor moral hazard; that ex post conditionality is not effective and may even be harmful; and that a sensible long-run regime is one in which crises are prevented in the first place. It urges that a system of inducements (IMF support to sound economies) and sticks (no IMF support to unsound economies) will provide the right strong incentives for countries to implement reforms that will prevent crises from occurring in the first place. In addition, the commission recommends that lending to poor countries and to countries that have structural problems or are in transition should not be the business of the IMF, which should concentrate on avoiding panics, runs, and crises in sound economies that are subject to contagion. The World Bank and MDBs should instead deal with the structural and macro problems of these poor and transition economies.

The publication of the commission report led to a public debate on its recommendations. Critics included minority members of the commission, the U.S. Treasury Department, and others (see Bergsten 2000; Levinson 2000; and U.S. Treasury 2000). We will here summarize some of these critiques and relate them to the arguments made by the commission.

Consider first the CCL. With the recent changes made to this facility, it is similar in some ways to that suggested by the commission: countries would prequalify based on macro and structural criteria, and exceptional financing would be quickly available for them. Although this facility may play a role in the new international financial system, critics (for example, U.S. Treasury 2000) believe that one should not overestimate its importance or place it at the center of a reformed IMF. For one thing, no country has applied (or qualified) for this facility yet, even after the reform of the facility. (Members of the commission would argue that this is because the countries believe that if necessary they will be bailed out on more attractive terms.) Second, while it is possible that very sound economies may be subject to contagion from time to time, the likelihood of this happening may be limited. The history of banking crises suggests that sound banks rarely experience runs and bank runs are almost always triggered by poor financial conditions and policies of particular banks: poor lending, little capitalization, high and growing nonperforming loans, and so on. For the same reason, the possibility that contagion would lead to a run on a very sound country is relatively small: Even if a country qualified for the CCL (or the similar facility proposed by the commission), chances are that this facility would rarely be needed and used. If the above argument is correct, a CCL type of facility could not be the central element of a system of crisis resolution: its importance would, in practice, be limited to preventing occasional extreme episodes of contagion to otherwise sound countries.

Is there a role for the third pillar of the current system, exceptional financing for crisis countries that do not prequalify for the CCL? Critics (again, U.S. Treasury 2000) argue that the commission recommendations—if narrowly interpreted—would have disallowed financial support to most of the large and systemic economies enveloped in the financial crises of the 1990s (Mexico, Thailand, Indonesia, Korea, Brazil, Russia, Argentina, and Turkey). They probably would not have prequalified for IMF support given macro weaknesses (poor fiscal positions in Mexico, Brazil, Russia, Argentina, and Turkey) or structural policy weaknesses (weak financial sectors in Mexico, Thailand, Indonesia, Korea, Russia, and Turkey). The third pillar of the current system, the SRF or other facilities allowing exceptional financing, was used in all these cases. The commission would allow an escape clause in limited, transitory, and exceptional circumstances in which systemic problems are at stake and exceptional financing would be allowed. However, a generous interpretation of this caveat would still imply that most of these large-scale packages would not have occurred in a new regime in which the IMF had been reformed along the lines of the commission recommendations.

To understand the logic of the commission's views, one should note that the commission sees its suggested reforms as leading, over time, to a world where countries "get their act together" in the knowledge that large-scale support would not be available unless the economy is sound. Thus, the commission is aiming at creating a long-run regime in which large-scale packages would not be made available to countries with unsound financial and fiscal policies. Also, according to the commission, the recommendations would be phased in over a period of five years, thus allowing countries the time to adjust their policies to this new regime of "no bailouts or support unless sound." Still, in the new long-run regime, countries that are systemically important but fail to adhere fully to the sound economy criteria for unconditional support would not receive financial support.

The commission supporters rebut that, in the new long-run regime of a reformed IMF, countries would know that failure to satisfy the criteria for CCL-type support would lead to no support at all and that this would provide a large incentive to clean up the economy and the financial system and thus prevent the kind of crises that afflicted these economies. However, supporters of the current system, in which exceptional SRF-style support for countries that do not otherwise prequalify for a CCL facility is maintained even in the long run, make various arguments: these crises may have systemic effects, and thus the international community has to deal with them even if they were partly caused by poor policies. Although poor policies and weak financial systems may trigger a crisis, the case of Asia suggests that an element of panic and self-fulfilling runs prevails even in cases in which fundamentals were not fully sound. Thus, allowing large support to systemically important economies in exchange for a serious program of reform constrained by tight conditionality may be beneficial to the country and its creditors and help maintain the stability of the international financial system. Indeed, in cases such as those of Mexico, Korea, Thailand, and Brazil, this exceptional support to countries that would have not prequalified for a CCL allowed macro and structural reform that benefited all relevant parties.

The terms of the commission recommendation for large-scale unconditional support to prequalifiers were inspired by—and founded on—the Bagehot principles for lender-of-last-resort (LOLR) support. Nevertheless, they have also been debated and criticized by some commentators.

First, the implied scale of the support seems to be extremely large given the resources available to the IMF: the commission suggested that such support might be as large as one year of a country's government revenues. Based on current data, U.S. Treasury (2000) argued that this would have implied lending to Brazil equal to $139 billion. This is far in excess not only of the country's quota in the IMF ($4.5 billion) but even of the size of the recent IMF program ($14.5 billion). In this view, such large packages would be well beyond the financing capacity of the IMF and would increase the moral hazard involved.

The second controversy regards the commission's support for securing IFI loans by means of a clear priority claim on the borrower's assets. There are two substantial issues with this proposal.

1. In practice, IFIs already have quasi-preferred creditor status. Therefore, the extra gain may be small. If it is contemplated to use resources of the government as outright collateral for IFI lending, this may worsen the creditworthiness of the country in the eyes of the private sector.

2. The historical practice of LOLR has been very different from the Bagehot principles that the commission cites. Recent studies show that little real hard collateral has historically been used in LOLR lending.[72]

Third, regarding the idea of lending at penalty rates, note first that, as suggested by Giannini (1999), the Bagehotian principle calling for "lending at a penalty rate" and lending to "solvent but temporarily illiquid banks" has not been usually applied in historical cases of banking crises. Moreover, based on data from recent historical crises showing large and protracted spikes in sovereign spreads after a crisis, U.S. Treasury (2000) argued that lending at penalty rates would "entail in most cases interest rates so high that these loans would worsen the underlying financial position of the borrowing country." Thus, although penalty rates may make some sense—and, indeed, the SRF comes with penalty rates that are 3 percentage points above short-term riskless market rates—systematic use of market rates on a country's debt would imply very high, and possibly unsustainable, borrowing rates. Also, given the seniority of IMF lending (which would be even stronger one if collateral is used), it does not make sense to use market rates that reflect default probabilities on less senior debt.

Fourth, the short-term maturity of the loans recommended by the commission would have forced repayment prematurely relative to what was needed by these economies in crisis. (The report mentioned four months, with only one further four-month extension.)[73] Even in successful large-scale IMF programs (Mexico, Korea, Thailand, Brazil), actual repayment lasted more than eight months. In this regard, note that even the short-term SRF facility allows at least two years for repayment. Given the spikes in sovereign spreads occurring after crises or the effective cutoff of a country from access to international capital markets, excessively short repayment periods may end up being destabilizing.

The commission would also eliminate altogether the second pillar of the current system. It would eliminate all lending to countries that experience a crisis because of their own policy shortcomings and that thus do not prequalify for support. They will have to adjust on their own without any IMF conditional support. These cases, regular SBAs to countries in macro and financial difficulties, represent the bulk of the program activities of the IMF. Thus, the commission would drastically reduce the number of countries and cases for which access to IMF lending is allowed. The IMF would provide only "counsel," not funding, to countries with complex and deep-seated problems. This recommendation is based on several arguments.

---

72. Giannini (2000). Charles Calomiris tells us that the commission support for this type of security is not support for collateral. Members of the commission do not necessarily agree with the language we use to characterize their positions, in general.

73. In congressional testimony, however, one of the commission members—Calomiris—suggested a more flexible interpretation of the maximum maturity of these loans.

First, the argument against funding with only ex post conditionality is the moral hazard argument. Countries believe that the IMF will rescue them if a crisis occurs. Hence they have less of an incentive to strengthen their financial systems until it is demanded by the fund. If strengthening their financial system were instead made a precondition for receiving IMF credit, the argument goes, weaker countries would rush to adopt reforms that would secure their access to IMF resources. Ex ante conditionality is therefore believed by some to be more useful in limiting the incidence of crises or limiting the scope and duration of crises that do occur. Second, the commission argues that ex post IMF conditionality is ineffective in practice, judging by historical experience.

Critics (U.S. Treasury 2000) of the proposal to eliminate standard ex post conditionality lending programs make several arguments. First, they argue that IMF conditionality works both in theory and empirically. Conditionality works in theory because the IMF would not have much of an impact if it could provide only counsel to countries with complex and deep-seated problems. The same is true if it lent to countries without any desire or commitment to change. Leverage comes from money, because the carrot of financial support is an incentive for policy adjustment and reform. These countries often need the catalytic financial support of the IMF, which, in addition to conditionality and commitment to policy stabilization and reform, is crucial to restoring investors' confidence. In recent financial crisis episodes, IMF involvement and ex post conditionality made the key difference, providing incentives for policy adjustment that was eventually successful in restoring economic growth.

Critics also argue that, empirically, IMF conditionality is more effective than argued by the commission. Indeed, there is a broad empirical literature on the effectiveness of conditional IMF lending. Most studies have instead relied on large cross-country samples that allow for the application of standard statistical techniques to test for program effectiveness, avoiding the difficulties associated with trying to generalize from the finding of a few case studies. The overall conclusion of such studies is that IMF programs and IMF conditionality have on balance a positive impact on key measures of economic performance. Such assessments show that IMF programs result in improvements in the current account balance and the overall balance of payments. This result is robust across a range of different methodologies. Haque and Khan (1999) provide a recent survey.[74]

The impact of IMF programs on growth and inflation is less clear. The first round of studies failed to find any improvement in these variables. More recent studies suggest that IMF programs result in lower inflation,

74. Kenen (2001, 53) criticizes the commission report for a selective quoting of Haque and Khan.

but these studies do not consistently establish that this result is statistically significant.[75] The impact of IMF programs on growth is more ambiguous. Results on short-run growth are mixed; some recent studies found that implementation of IMF programs led to an immediate improvement in growth (Dicks-Mireaux, Mecagni, and Schadler 1997), whereas other studies (Bordo and Schwartz 2000) found a negative short-run effect.[76] Studies that look at a longer time horizon, however, tend to show a revival of growth (Conway 1994). This is to be expected: countries entering into IMF programs will often implement policy adjustments that have the immediate impact of reducing demand but could ultimately create the basis for sustained growth. The structural reforms embedded in IMF programs inherently take time to improve economic performance. Finally, the crisis that led to the IMF program, not the IMF program itself, is often responsible for an immediate fall in growth.

Finally, there is a debate on the necessity of the final pillar of the current system, IMF support of macro adjustment and reform in very poor countries and transition economies. One view, espoused by the commission, is that any support to very poor countries should be transferred to the World Bank or MDBs, because the problems of these countries are too structural and complex. The view supported by the G7 and the IMF, instead, is that a proper division of labor between IFIs implies that the many macroeconomic problems of very poor and highly indebted countries should still be dealt with by the IMF in the context of a coordinated program of adjustment, reform, and growth with the World Bank.

This division of labor and coordination is at the center of the recently designed Poverty Reduction and Growth Facility (PRGF). In the PRGF, IMF concessional lending for macro adjustment was broadened to include an explicit focus on poverty reduction in the context of a growth-oriented strategy. The alternative of taking out of the IMF all the macroeconomic components of programs for poor countries has, in the view of critics, several shortcomings. First, these countries would effectively be nonmembers of the IMF and, as such, would feel excluded from the international financial system. Who would be "kicked out" of the IMF, and who would be readmitted, would be a politically charged issue. Second, it is not obvious that the World Bank has the appropriate expertise in the macroeconomic area and the effectiveness to enforce macro conditionality credibly in its pro-

75. Conway (1994) found that inflation fell following an IMF program, and the result was statistically significant. Bagci and Perrudin (1997) also found a statistically significant reduction in inflation. Dicks-Mireaux, Mecagni, and Schadler (1997) found that programs do reduce inflation, but the result was not statistically significant.

76. Bordo and Schwartz (2000) compare countries receiving IMF assistance during crises in the period 1973–98 with countries in the same region not receiving assistance and find that the real performance (for example, GDP growth) of the former group was possibly worse than the latter.

grams.[77] Other objections to the proposal include that the IMF, in phasing out its longer-term facilities such as the EFF, would not be able to deal with the problems of transition economies.

In general, the issue of whether the IMF should make loans to very poor countries or provide long-term facilities to countries with structural problems remains controversial. One can make arguments both ways.

A set of reforms of the IMF was agreed by the member countries at the time of the IMF meetings in Prague in September 2000. The reforms did reflect parts of the Meltzer Commission recommendations that were consistent with the views of the United States and the other G7 countries. Indeed, the IMF reform proposals advanced by the U.S. Treasury, although developed before the commission presented its report, were partly aimed at deflecting criticism of the IMF in congressional circles and preempting possible recommendations of the commission. The U.S. Treasury's reply to the commission report found a series of common reform goals that were shared by the commission and the U.S. administration. These included agreement that the IMF should continue to have an important role in crisis prevention and a strong capacity to respond to financial crises; a radical change in the transparency of the operations of IFIs and of member countries; the development of new mechanisms for strengthening incentives for countries to reduce their vulnerabilities to crises; a focus within the IMF on the importance of sound financial systems, better debt and liability management policies, and appropriate exchange rate regimes; and the need for a clear division of labor between the MDBs and the IMF.

Despite these broad common objectives, however, the U.S. administration remained "in fundamental disagreement with the Report's core recommendations for further reform" (U.S. Treasury 2000). Thus, although the reforms agreed upon by the G7 were consistent with the spirit of the commission goals, their detailed substance was substantially at odds with the more radical recommendations of the commission. The reforms agreed upon by the G7 and the IMFC at the time of the Prague meetings are discussed in more detail later, in the section "Recent G7 Initiatives to Reform the International Monetary Fund."

Mission Creep

Perhaps the most widely held criticism of the IMF is that it has exhibited "mission creep," a term borrowed from the history of military interventions that eventually expand beyond their originally stated aim. There is some truth to this critique.[78] The fund has undergone significant role changes, roughly once a decade.

---

77. Some even argue that existing structural conditionality in World Bank programs is too soft and thus that IMF macro requirements and monitoring effectively become a useful cross-conditionality for World Bank programs and loans.

78. See Feldstein (1999a) for a critique along these lines.

The IMF's original mandate, under the Articles of Agreement negotiated at Bretton Woods, New Hampshire, in 1944, was to help countries with balance-of-payments difficulties, so as maintain a stable system of pegged exchange rates. A majority of members were industrialized countries. The goal of restoring convertibility among most industrialized countries had been achieved by the end of the 1950s. When the Bretton Woods system of fixed exchange rates broke up in the early 1970s, some charged that the IMF had lost its mission but, in good bureaucratic tradition, refused to go out of business; instead, it was filling the gap by turning its attentions to the developing countries, most of which had become independent over the preceding fifteen years (Niehans 1976). This seemed an unfair criticism. The newly independent countries had as much right to belong to the fund as anyone, and most of them maintained some type of exchange rate peg long after the major industrialized countries had given them up. (There were plenty of problems to keep policymakers busy in the 1970s, with the need after the oil crises to recycle surpluses in oil-importing countries to deficit oil importers.) Thus, even a narrow interpretation of the fund's role includes balance-of-payments problems in developing countries.

The role expanded in the international debt crisis of the 1980s. From its inception in 1982, Managing Director Jacques de Larosiere was active in the strategy to manage the crisis. It was a case-by-case approach (much as in the more recent episode), consisting of country programs that each featured three elements: policy adjustments by the country in question, loans from the IMF and industrialized-country governments, and agreement by private bankers to roll over loans or provide new money.

The next big change in the fund's role occurred with the unraveling of the Soviet Bloc. The formerly Communist countries—now transition economies—joined (or, in a few cases, re-joined) the IMF. Clearly the problems in their transition extended far behind the standard IMF issues of macroeconomic policy, exchange rates, and the balance of payments. Here, however, the IMF faced the first of its big cases of "damned if you do, damned if you don't." It is universally agreed that a necessary condition for economic success in the transition economies is the establishment of property rights, the rule of law, and other well-functioning institutions. A common critique is that the G7 and the IMF did not appreciate the importance of these factors, and the extent and importance of corruption in Russia in particular, and failed to do anything about them. At the same time, an equally common critique is that the IMF engaged in mission creep in the transition economies, by taking on tasks of structural reform that are more properly left to the World Bank. One could argue that a clearer division of labor and coordination between IMF and World Bank would have solved these opposite claims, but such an ideal outcome was certainly not easy to achieve.

The most recent evolution came with the emerging market crises of 1997–

98. The IMF did not simply apply the same approach to East Asia that it had applied in the past to Latin America or other problem debtors (even if some of the macro components of these plans—tight fiscal policy and tight money—were initially similar). The new country programs emphasized structural reform more than macroeconomic austerity. This was appropriate, in that these countries have historically followed good monetary and fiscal policies. Restructuring of the banking system and strengthening of prudential supervision are prescriptions that are closely related to the roots of the crisis, and thus they are appropriate subjects for IMF attention and conditionality, even if it means having to hire new personnel with expertise in this area. Issues of corporate governance or trade liberalization are also relevant, although they could be viewed as a bit more afield. At the extreme, issues of the environment, labor rights, and human rights, although extremely important in the wider scheme of things, are clearly not relevant for the IMF's mandate.[79]

To include issues of banking supervision and corruption in the IMF purview certainly represents a relocation of the boundary line that separates the legitimate territory of multilateral governance from the inviolable territory of national sovereignty. How can this be justified? For years, the word "corruption," like the words "military spending," was virtually taboo at the IMF, because the governments of the member countries, who own and run the fund, did not want either of them discussed. The inability to look at issues of military spending and corruption undermined the effectiveness of IMF programs, increasing the burden of austerity on the local population and decreasing the financial effectiveness of the programs. Perhaps the strongest argument for including such structural conditionality in IMF programs is that it is impossible for the international community to justify sending additional resources to a crisis country if everyone believes that the money will end up in the bank accounts of government cronies. As national economies become more highly integrated, it is not surprising if an accounting of costs and benefits results in some moving of the boundary, pushing back national sovereignty, in some well-chosen areas. Where the integration is financial, attempts by the international financial community to address any resulting crises may end up including structural conditions that, although going beyond macroeconomics, are nonetheless relevant to the origin of the crises and to their effective solution.

Macroeconomic conditionality alone could not solve the Indonesia crisis of 1997–98, because neither an overvalued currency nor excessive budget deficits were the original problem. Even best efforts to address problems of the banking sector would probably not have been able to solve the crisis.

---

79. Thus, recent U.S. congressional mandates that force the administration to push issues of trade liberalization, labor and union rights, and environmental issues on the IMF agenda and condition U.S. votes on IMF programs on IMF consideration of such issues are seriously misguided.

The ultimate origins of the Indonesian financial crisis were deeply rooted in corruption, the uncertainties of presidential succession, and the lack of commitment to policy adjustment and reform and the vulnerability of the Chinese minority. Many criticized the IMF program for a list of conditions that was so detailed as to include a dismantling of the clove monopoly; they miss the point that precisely such steps were deemed to be necessary to signal to investors that the economic interests of the president's family would no longer be allowed so fundamentally to distort the national economy. Many criticize the fund and the G7 for failing to realize that the president would never deliver on such promises; they miss the point that his failure to try to deliver is what led to his removal, in favor (eventually) of someone who might. Many criticize the fund, the United States, and the entire international financial community for having supported Suharto all those years. They miss the point that it is neither feasible nor proper for the international community to remove local rulers, leaving aside extreme cases of egregious military threats, but that rulers may be forced by domestic constituencies to leave office as the result of a financial crisis that is in turn the consequence of their bad policies.

The fund is arguably intruding on the traditional territory of the World Bank in three ways. The first, as just discussed, is the expansion beyond macroeconomic conditionality to include structural conditionality. The second is the increased emphasis on poverty reduction, embodied in the renaming of what is now the PRGF. The third is the drift toward programs with longer terms, or toward a pattern of programs that are repeatedly renewed.

It is on the topic of poverty that the IMF is most thoroughly damned by critics either way. Expert assessments from across the political spectrum recommend a clearer division of responsibility between the two agencies, including a decision to leave poverty fighting to the World Bank. On the other hand, critics hit the target with as much punch as the charge that the IMF serves the interest of wealthy capitalists, in both creditor and debtor countries, and that it is the poor who suffer the most unpleasant consequences of adjustment programs. A division of labor may be sensible as a matter of good public policy. Political considerations are also relevant, and protestors concerned with the poor will not like to be told "that is the World Bank's job." However, they don't react much better when they are told "we are working on it," so the fund may not have much to lose by giving the World Bank exclusive rights to the topic of poverty.

Finally comes the question of the length of time that patients are hooked up to the IMF support system. Not long ago, most programs ended in a few years, and the borrower repaid the fund. It is still true that defaults to the fund are exceedingly rare. However, programs that are designed to be long term became more common in the 1990s (the EFF for countries with longer-term macro and structural problem or in transition to a market economy and the Extended Structural Adjustment Facility [ESAF] for very poor and highly indebted countries), as did cases where programs are repeatedly extended or rolled over. There is an open debate over whether the fund should engage only in very short-term financing or be involved in longer-term funding to support structural adjustment.

Some argue that the division of labor between the IMF and the World Bank may need to be restored toward its traditional balance. In this view, the World Bank's proper role is more extensive attention to structural issues, with special attention to poverty reduction, carried out through long-term lending programs. The fund's proper role would instead be addressing shorter-term issues, particularly including financial or currency crises. Thus, in additional to traditional macro issues, IMF surveillance would also cover the soundness of financial systems, whose weaknesses were at the root of many recent crises. Even here, a division of labor could be implemented: the specific financial system reforms necessary to the restoration of confidence, macro stability, and growth may remain under the IMF realm; those regarding the medium restructuring of the banking, financial, and corporate sectors could be taken over by the World Bank. Moreover, given the partial overlap of issues in the financial area, the two institutions could cooperate and coordinate their action in this area. However, this is only one of the ways in which the division of labor between the two institutions could be arranged.

Of course, a large percentage of IMF members, and a still larger percentage of users of IMF programs, is and will continue to be developing countries. And as the World Bank continues to place greater emphasis on the important goals of poverty reduction and environmental protection in its longer-term development programs, it is important to coordinate closely with the fund. The warning that monetary stability is a precondition both for increasing aggregate income and for equitable income distribution is as true as it ever was.

Recommendations that the fund turn some responsibilities back over to the World Bank are not necessarily the same as agreeing with the argument that it has been guilty of a self-serving expansion of authority. In the heat of a crisis, actors scramble to cover whatever positions need covering. Perhaps it is inevitable that a smaller, more nimble institution, as the fund is, will be quicker to step into a gap that opens up in such areas as banking regulation or corporate governance. However, even supporters of the IMF's broadened role in the past few years say that it is now appropriate for the actors to return to their assigned positions.

Recent G7 Initiatives to Reform the International Monetary Fund

The drive to reform the IMF picked up speed in the fall of 1999 for a number of reasons. First, the IMF had been subject to a number of critiques in the wake of the Asian crisis, and it was useful to reassess its role and functions. Second, the recovery of the Asian and world economy from its crisis mode allowed attention to concentrate on how to improve the international financial system and its main constituent bodies. Third, in the United States the congressional resistance to IMF refunding in 1998 showed the need to address some of the concerns expressed regarding the role of the IMF. Congressional action to set up the Meltzer Commission, congressional legislative mandates on areas where the United States should press the IMF in program design (labor issues, trade questions, etc.), and the need to receive congressional support for initiatives such as HIPC funding were also factors. Fourth, the G7 dialogue on architecture reform that started in 1998 suggested that the G7 would look at the issue of the reform of the IFIs.

The United States again took a leadership role in this debate. U.S. Treasury Secretary Summers presented in a December 1999 speech (Summers 1999) the U.S. view on how to reform the IMF. The ensuing dialogue among the G7 countries led first to a consensus on the main outlines of IMF reform by the time of the spring annual meetings of the IMF and World Bank (April 2000) and then to a more detailed consensus and approval by the IMF board of specific proposals by the time of the fall annual meetings (September 2000 in Prague).

The main elements of the U.S. proposals, which were largely adopted by the G7, were as follows:

- Promotion of the flow of information to markets, that is, a shift of IMF surveillance to promoting the collection and dissemination of information for investors and markets. This took the following operational form: (a) IMF encouragement of more countries to adopt and comply with the SDDS, including its new provisions relating to the reporting of reserves and addition to the SDDS of greater reporting of external debt data; (b) encouragement of countries to implement international standards and codes for sound policies; and public release of these assessments (the ROSCs); and (c) a request that independent external audits of central banks and other relevant government entities be done and published.
- Emphasis on assessment of financial vulnerabilities, not just macroeconomic fundamentals, that is, a greater focus on the strength of national balance sheets to reduce liquidity and balance sheet risk at the aggregate and sectoral level through greater use of indicators of external vulnerability and better collection of data on external debt (via the SDDS) and via the development of guidelines for optimal public debt management. The United States also supported highlighting more clearly the risks of unsustainable exchange rate regimes by supporting corner regimes. Although the IMF has placed renewed emphasis on the importance of sustainable exchange rate regimes, the overall G7 consensus on this is not as radical as the U.S. position. Other G7 mem-

bers agree that exchange rate regimes should be sustainable but do not fully endorse the U.S. support for corner regimes in most cases.[80]

- A focus of the IMF's attention on its core competencies (macroeconomic and financial-sector stability) and a focus of its finance on emergency situations. This meant a more limited financial involvement of the IMF with countries, lending selectively and on shorter maturities. It also meant an IMF on the front line of the international response to financial crises, but not as a source of low-cost financing for countries with ready access to private capital, or long-term support for IMF "addicts"—countries that cannot break the habit of bad policies and repeatedly depend on IMF financial support. In the U.S. view, this implied a reform of IMF facilities to streamline and eliminate some longer-term facilities (such as the EFF and other smaller, narrowly designed funds and facilities). It would also change the pricing of the remaining three main facilities (CCL, SBA, and SRF) to charge higher interest rates and limit the duration of most loans for the SBA and SRF and reduce the charges on the CCL to give incentives for its use by sound economies. On one side was the strong U.S. support of easier conditions for CCL access (given its support of this facility and the lack of countries applying to it after its design in 1998) and skepticism of the longer-term EFF. On the other side was the European view that the EFF should be maintained (especially for transition economies and poorer countries) and the CCL not eased too much (out of concerns about moral hazard and excessive large financial packages). The eventual G7 consensus ratified in September 2000 by the IMF executive board eased the conditions for the CCL but maintained a role for the EFF (and eliminated most of the smaller facilities) while limiting and concentrating its use for transition economies and countries graduating from the PRGF program (the new successor to the ESAF program for poor and highly indebted countries). The relative pricing of the three main facilities was also changed to incentivate CCL use and discourage longer-term use of SBAs and SRFs. Measures to reduce IMF "addiction" (repeated use of IMF support) and strengthen postprogram monitoring were also agreed upon.
- Modernization of the IMF as an institution. This was to take place via greater transparency (publication of a large number of official documents) and openness (dialogue with civil society and nongovernmental organizations [NGOs] and with the private financial sector through the new Market Conditions Consultative Group), including regular publication of the IMF's operational budget. The United States also

---

80. We did not discuss the very important issue of the appropriate exchange rate regime for emerging markets because it is discussed in another paper from this conference (chap. 1 in this volume). The views of one of the coauthors of this paper can be found in Frankel (1999).

supported a governing structure that is more representative and a relative reallocation of member quotas. However, reform of IMF quotas has remained highly controversial and a consensus has so far eluded the G7 and emerging market countries. An increase in the quotas of emerging markets is envisioned in most reform solutions (for example, those of the official Quota Formula Review Group or "Cooper Group" after the name of its chair). However, this would also imply a shrinkage of European countries' quotas (which currently compose one-third of the executive director positions within the IMF board), a solution strongly resisted by the European countries.

- A new focus on growth and poverty reduction in the poorest countries via efforts to translate debt relief for the HIPC into concrete reductions in poverty through the PRGF.

The above reforms of the IMF proposed by the G7 at the time of the G7 summit were endorsed by the IMFC at the time of the IMF meetings in Prague in September 2000 and operationalized during the fall of 2000, especially the reform of the IMF facilities. Regarding the latter, the CCL was enhanced by reducing the surcharge on the use of credit under the CCL and the commitment fee and by increasing the amount of funds available for borrowing at the time of activation. The use of the longer-term EFF was restricted and the time period for repayment of EFF loans reduced. Similarly, the repayment period for standby loans (purchases in the credit tranches) was also reduced to incentivate faster repayment of IMF loans. Conversely, the interest rate on exceptionally sized loans, such as those in the SRF, was increased based on an increasing scale. Finally, postprogram monitoring by the IMF of economic developments and policies after the end of a program was operationalized.

3.1.6 Proposals for Alternative Institutions and Tools for Crisis Prevention and Resolution

In this part we discuss a number of proposals for an international LOLR and alternative institutions and mechanisms and tools to deal with international financial crises, both in the crisis prevention and crisis resolution areas.[81]

International Lender of Last Resort

There has been a wide debate on how liquidity crises are to be addressed: full bailout by an international lender of last resort (ILOLR) or bail-in (appropriate PSI)? In cases in which there is a pure liquidity crisis the case for

---

81. Eichengreen (1999a) and Rogoff (1999) consider a broad range of plans, including a global lender of last resort facility, an international bankruptcy court, an international debt insurance corporation, and unilateral controls on capital flows.

an ILOLR might have a stronger basis. At the national level, the central bank can carry out the LOLR function when there is a liquidity run on domestic banks. There is no international equivalent of an LOLR, however. The IMF comes closest, but it does not have the capacity to provide unlimited funds to countries in crisis or to print or create international liquidity at will. Thus, several authors (e.g., Fischer 1999) have suggested that an ILOLR function should be bestowed on the IMF or on some equivalent international institution (a global central bank, as proposed by Jeffrey Garten in "In This Economic Chaos, A Global Bank Can Help," *International Herald Tribune,* 25 September 1998, 8).

Indeed, some argue that in pure liquidity cases, large bailout packages are justified and no PSI (bail-in) of private investors is warranted. Thus, the debate on whether an ILOLR is necessary in liquidity cases has been strongly linked to the debate on whether PSI is necessary in liquidity cases. As the discussion below suggests, the issue is much more complex than the simple argument that a full bailout via an ILOLR is appropriate in pure liquidity cases.

Full Bail-out (an ILOLR Function) or Full Bail-in in Liquidity Cases?
Some Conceptual Issues

An official G7 doctrine for pure liquidity cases has not been fully articulated because of the complexity of such cases. Indeed, even the official PSI framework as elaborated by the G7 only partially addresses the question of what to do, if anything, in liquidity cases, especially if the country is large and has systemic effects.[82]

The issues in these liquidity cases are very difficult. First, it is not obvious whether there are "pure" liquidity cases. Formally, a crisis country may not be insolvent but rather illiquid in the sense that its debt-servicing problems are caused by sudden illiquidity; however, even such a country may have weak fundamentals and serious policy shortcomings. Indeed, it is hard to believe that a country with fully sound fundamentals and policies would become illiquid and subject to self-fulfilling speculative runs and panic. For one thing, even in theory, if fundamentals are strong enough such multiple-equilibria runs may be ruled out: that is, weak fundamentals are necessary for an economy to be in the multiple-equilibria region. Also, empirically all

---

82. The PSI framework is meant to cover both liquidity cases and semi-insolvency or insolvency cases, but it emphasizes the latter and de-emphasizes the former. The preamble of the G7 operational guidelines suggests two approaches to liquidity cases: catalytic financing and voluntary arrangements that recognize the collective interest in staying in. The overall approach to liquidity cases is case-by-case but constrained by the PSI framework, as for the other cases. However, the G7 has not addressed head-on the role that restructurings or reprofilings should play in liquidity cases. For example, one should not lump the PSI approach to Korea with that to Brazil, because the commitment to stay in Korea was much firmer and led to formal extension of maturities via rescheduling. Moreover, the G7 guidelines for restructuring do not explicitly apply to liquidity cases. Thus, there is still a lot of room for fleshing out the G7 views on liquidity and systemic cases.

observed cases, in which something close to an illiquidity problem was the proximate cause of the crisis, were characterized by some fundamentals or policy weaknesses. In cases like those of Mexico, Korea, Thailand, and Brazil, which are conceptually closer to the illiquidity problem, some serious macroeconomic, structural, or policy shortcomings certainly played a role in triggering the crisis. Thus, talking of pure liquidity cases and what, if any, PSI to implement in such cases is somewhat unrealistic.

However, for the sake of the conceptual argument, let us consider first "pure" liquidity cases. Some argue that a solution closer to very large official support packages (full bailout via an ILOLR) may be warranted in cases of pure illiquidity. It is also argued that this full bailout solution might be necessary if the country is not only illiquid but also large and of systemic importance.[83]

Although in such pure liquidity cases one could conceptually make the argument that a full bailout is the efficient policy, one could also argue that the alternative policy of a full bail-in (i.e., a combination of wide standstills, capital controls, and other measures to lock in all investors that are rushing to the exits) is as efficient and optimal. Indeed, if there is no uncertainty and no risk aversion, and there is a pure liquidity problem or run, both the full bailout and the full bail-in are equivalent solutions to the collective-action problem faced by investors (the coordination failure) that is the cause of the liquidity-driven run. So, paradoxically, the full bail-in solution is optimal even in the cases in which the full bailout solution appears warranted.

Paradoxically, in these pure liquidity cases, the bail-in solution may be superior to the bailout one because the ex ante threat of a full bail-in solution is sufficient to sustain ex ante the good equilibrium of "no run" without having to resort to such a threat ex post. In fact, if all agents know that if and when a run occurs the official sector or debtor will introduce standstills

---

83. A complex issue to be discussed below is what to do if the country is large and systemic but its crisis is not purely due to illiquidity: that is, what to do if serious macro and policy shortcomings are at the root of the crisis. The current IMF/G7 doctrine for both systemic and nonsystemic cases suggests that, when catalytic IMF financing, policy adjustment, and soft or voluntary forms of PSI are expected to restore market access and investors' confidence, this route could be followed, but should be substantially justified when exceptional financing is involved—not precluding the use of stronger forms of PSI if such catalytic approach does not succeed. The recent use of exceptional financing in the cases of Argentina and Turkey could have been rationalized by arguing that these may be cases in which catalytic financing and policy adjustment were deemed to be likely to restore market access and investors' confidence. However, the use of stronger forms of PSI cannot be ruled out in case this catalytic approach were not to succeed as indeed became the case in Argentina. Moreover, the Turkish package includes a soft form of PSI à la Brazil and in the spirit of voluntary approaches to PSI: the Turkish authorities met in mid-December with their bank creditors and received commitments that such creditors will maintain their cross-border exposure to the country. The expectation that such exposure would be maintained was reaffirmed by the IMF even when the Turkish peg broke in February 2001. Thus, the large packages for Turkey and Argentina in late 2000 cannot not be interpreted as cases in which PSI was neglected or ruled out altogether. However, in the Turkish case, the significant roll-off of cross-border interbank lines since the February 2001 devaluation makes doubtful the argument that soft and voluntary commitments to maintain exposure can be credible or effective.

or capital controls to avoid the run, the incentive to run will disappear because everyone will know that no one will have the incentive and desire to rush to the door and no real losses will be incurred. In the domestic analogue, no one will want to stand first in the line at the bank if a bank holiday prevents the run from occurring. Thus, the threat of a full bail-in could be sufficient to rule out the bad equilibrium: ex post, no run will occur and the threat will not be exercised, thus avoiding the need to implement the threat in the first place.

This conceptual superiority of the full bail-in solution is, however, extremely fragile in practice. In fact, if (a) the case under consideration is not one of pure illiquidity but one in which some policy shortcomings are behind the illiquidity, (b) there is some uncertainty about the fundamentals and the policy response to the crisis, and (c) creditors are risk-averse, the dominance of a full bail-in solution will break down. When fundamentals are weak and uncertain and agents are risk-averse, they will react to the expectation or threat of a bail-in by rushing to the front of the line because the threat of a bail-in may actually be implemented. Consequently, this bail-in may imply real costs and financial losses to investors when the country is subject to shortcomings of policy and fundamentals rather than being purely illiquid.

What, then, is to be done in liquidity cases, especially considering that some policy shortcomings imply that these are not going to be "pure" liquidity cases? A full bail-in, a full bailout, or something in between? One view is that, if one were to apply the logic of PSI (i.e., that some external financing gaps may occur) that official money will not be enough to fill such gaps and that a solution based only on official money (full bailout) is not appropriate because of moral hazard distortions, then the official sector would want to do a combination of things. Specifically, part of the solution would be policy adjustment by the debtor country if macro, structural, and policy shortcomings caused the crisis. Part of the solution would be official money: the larger the package, when one is closer to a pure liquidity case, and the smaller when shortcomings are important. Additionally, part of the solution might be appropriate forms of PSI that are more or less "voluntary" depending on the circumstances and the nature of the problem being addressed. These bail-ins may take the form of "partial" bail-in (i.e., they may include only a subset of instruments and creditors that may be running).

Indeed, in recent liquidity cases (Mexico, Korea, Brazil), the response has been a combination of policy adjustment, official money, and PSI, with the relative weights being different in different circumstances. Mexico was a case closer to that of full bailout of investors (cum domestic policy adjustment). Korea was closer to a semicoercive rollover of interbank lines because the loss of foreign reserves had put the country close to the brink of default in the face of the attempt of foreign banks to reduce their exposures. Brazil was in between with a mild form of PSI (a monitoring of bank exposure followed by a commitment to maintain exposure at reduced levels).

This, combined with policy adjustment and significant official support, was successful in avoiding a wider loss of confidence and prevented a disruptive loss of market access.

The official-sector response to these liquidity cases has been based on the view that a combination of adjustment, catalytic official money, and appropriate PSI (partial rather than a full bail-in) can be successful in preventing a wider crisis, restoring confidence and market access, and returning the country to a path of recovery and growth.

Conceptually, however, the "middle" solution, as opposed to the corner solutions of full bailout or full bail-in, has been challenged as not being feasible. Observers (such as Paul Krugman) have argued that only corner solutions are feasible in these liquidity cases:[84] either there is an ILOLR with enough resources to engineer a full bailout and avoid a disruptive run, or, at the other extreme, a full bail-in (that locks in all assets and domestic and foreign creditors trying to turn short-term claims into foreign assets) is necessary. In fact, in this view a partial bail-in would not work because, as long as the economy is in the multiple-equilibria region, locking in some creditors and assets, but not all, would lead all the others to run to avoid being locked in next. Conversely, a partial bailout would not work either because, as long as the financing gap is not eliminated, the multiple-equilibria problem is not solved and agents will rush to the exits and trigger a default by claiming all the limited foreign reserves, including those provided by the partial official support. Thus, conceptually, it is argued that the middle solution may not be feasible.

Indeed, the Krugman hypothesis is supported by some theoretical work. Zettelmeyer (2000) formalizes this hypothesis by showing that partial bailouts are bound to fail in models in which illiquidity may lead to self-fulfilling speculative attacks. Such partial bailouts (or bail-ins) would not avoid the possibility of a bad equilibrium because, as long as the size of the support is not large enough to fill the financing gap, the possibility that agents will coordinate on the bad equilibrium cannot be ruled out. Worse, a partial bailout implies that the greater is the official support, the larger is the reserve loss if a run occurs. Indeed, if a partial package cannot avoid a run, the operating constraint on the size of the run is the amount of official reserves (including those provided by the bailout package); thus, more support in this case means only a larger run on reserves.

This theoretical ineffectiveness of middle solutions (partial bailouts and partial bail-ins) is in contrast to the official-sector PSI doctrine that catalytic official money, domestic policy adjustment, and partial and appropriate bail-in might indeed succeed and avoid the bad equilibrium even

---

84. King (1999) is substantially in favor of "middle way" solutions but also suggests that corner-type solutions (such as broad standstills on debt payments) may at times be necessary to stem a crisis. The issue of standstills has been discussed in more detail in section 3.1.2.

when such a three-pronged solution does not formally fill *all* of the external gap. The middle solution is predicated on the view that this combination of actions will restore confidence and lead investors who are not bailed in, and who could thus run for the exit, to avoid running even if the remaining external financing gap is large enough that if they were to decide to run the bad equilibrium could not be avoided.

The gap between the theoretical analysis (which supports the corner solutions) and the actual policies and case studies (which support the view that middle solutions can be successful) can be bridged as follows. In multiple-equilibria models, as long as the financing gap is not completely filled via full bail-in or full bailout, the possibility of a self-fulfilling run cannot be ruled out completely: The economy may end up in the bad equilibrium if those who are not bailed in do decide to rush to the exits. Moreover, in the multiple-equilibrium region, there is nothing (apart from "sunspots") that can nail down the probability that the economy will end up in the bad equilibrium as opposed to the good equilibrium. Since the bad equilibrium requires that enough agents decide to focalize on that equilibrium (i.e., decide to run), the question is how much fundamentals and policy actions can affect such decision. In existing models, this probability is indeterminate, and the economy may be as likely to end up in one equilibrium as the other.

In reality, however, domestic policy choices, official support, and the amount of bail-in *do* affect the probability, even if they do not do so in current analytical models. Indeed, the argument for a middle solution is based on the view that domestic policy adjustment will reduce the probability of a run as the debtor government credibly commits to reduce the imbalances that created the risk of a run in the first place. Also, the amount of official support can also affect the probability of a run because more official money means that the size of the remaining gap is proportionally reduced. And appropriate PSI may also reduce the probability of a run by leading some investors and asset classes to stay in (resulting in a voluntary or concerted rollover) and leading the others who are not subject to bail-in not to run as the domestic adjustment, the official money, and the bail-in of other investors help to restore the confidence of the remaining ones. Thus, although a theoretical understanding for middle solutions (with different degrees of partial PSI) has not been developed, they do appear to work in practice, as recent episodes (in Mexico, Korea, and Brazil) seem to suggest.

In practice, this has led the G7 and the IMF to conclude that liquidity and systemic cases should be dealt with on a case-by-case basis: no simple or rigid rules can be applied, and all relevant factors may have to be considered to decide whether and how much PSI should be applied. Moreover, some argue that some degree of "constructive ambiguity" might have to be maintained in this regime to provide the appropriate response to specific cases and avoid expectations of systematic bailouts.

This view that middle solutions may work in practice does not go unchallenged. Some argue that recent episodes, such as those in Mexico, Korea, and Brazil, are consistent with the view that only corner solutions can work. Indeed, the evidence from these three case studies is ambiguous on whether middle solutions are feasible. All cases had some middle-solution component because official assistance was well below the size of assets that could have been run upon, but a careful analysis suggests that these cases are also, in some dimensions, closer to the corners.[85]

Moreover, corner solutions have a number of practical shortcomings: a full bail-in, as discussed above and as we discussed in more detail when we considered standstills ("Moral Hazard and Private-Sector Involvement in Crisis Resolution"), may lead to a rush to the exits and contagion in a world of uncertainty and risk-averse investors. At the other extreme, a full bailout solution also implies the existence of an ILOLR that might be problematic for reasons that will be discussed next.

ILOLR, Too-Big-to-Fail Doctrine, and Appropriate PSI

What can a full bailout solution achieve, and does it require the existence of an ILOLR? Because countries suffering illiquidity often do so because of some fundamental or policy weakness, if unlimited resources were available to a country with fundamental weaknesses, the funds lent by an ILOLR facility would be used by domestic and foreign investors to liquidate domestic assets and turn them into foreign ones, eventually exacerbating the crisis rooted in weak fundamentals. This is also the reason why, in a domestic context, it would be destabilizing to give extensive and unconditional LOLR support to banks that are in serious financial distress or bankrupt. Allocating more funds to such banks leads to moral hazard (i.e., "gambling for redemption"), as the savings and loan crisis and many other episodes suggest. This is also why the response of a central bank to a banking crisis caused by poor behavior of the banking system is to provide emergency support (to avoid panic) in exchange for very strict controls and restructuring of the financial institution under distress.

In an international context, there are three implications of the above observations.

First, if a country in severe distress because of fundamental weaknesses received unconditional ILOLR support, such support would bail out investors and eventually fail to prevent a crisis, because the country is in serious fundamental distress in the first place. Second, if support is aimed at providing incentives for reform and adjustment, then the support is likely to be of the conditionality form that comes with IMF packages. Third, if bailing in private investors is motivated by the goal of reducing moral hazard, the amount of support would have to be lower than the amount of total domestic assets that could be potentially converted into foreign currency; that

---

85. See Roubini (2000) for a discussion.

is, official financing support that is only partial would contribute to reducing such moral hazard distortions.

What about the issue of big money packages? How large should IMF packages be, and under which conditions should exceptional finance be provided? In the early decades of the life of the IMF, when international capital mobility was not widespread and restrictions to capital flows dominant, it historically was not allowed to provide large and exceptional support for crises generated by capital account problems. The IMF was restricted to providing financing limited to current account problems. Capital account liberalization and the growing size of international capital flows led to the emergence of financial crises driven by capital account problems, the type of liquidity crises associated with the existence of large stocks of short-term foreign debt that may not be rolled over when confidence was lost. Hence, the trend to develop facilities such as the SRF, the General Agreements to Borrow (GAB), the New Agreements to Borrow (NAB), and the CCL, which would allow these capital account crises to be addressed.

Consider now the issue of exceptional packages. Assume that a country experiencing a crisis because of weak fundamentals is large, suffers from a liquidity problem, is systemically important, is a potential source of contagion to other countries, and suffers a capital account crisis (due to creditors' unwillingness to roll over bank loans and other short-term claims); a large financial package significantly in excess of quota may be able to stem default due to illiquidity and avoid further international contagion.

In this respect, such big packages for systemically important countries are the international equivalent of the too-big-to-fail (TBTF) doctrine in the domestic LOLR context. Just as governments do not usually let big banks fail even if not all of their liabilities are covered by deposit insurance because of concerns of systemic effects and contagion to other sound banks, so the international community may act to prevent big countries from defaulting for the same reasons.

A domestic TBTF doctrine may increase the risk of moral hazard. However, in a domestic context there are a number of mechanisms that limit such a risk; also, there are differences between the domestic and international economy context that may exacerbate the moral hazard problem in the international context.

First, in a domestic economy both large and small banks are subject to ex ante direct regulation and supervision, reserve requirements, capital adequacy standards, deposit insurance with risk-adjusted premia. Thus, supervisors and regulators have broad powers to control the behavior of such banks before financial distress forces the authorities to bail them out.

Second, although the FDICIA provides an out for systemically important institutions, such a doctrine was never formally embraced by the Federal Reserve and there are a number of hurdles to such TBTF rescues: the Federal Board has to take a major vote and there has to be concurrence by the secretary of the treasury. Moreover, some constructive ambiguity is used to prevent expectations that large institutions will be systematically rescued on a regular basis.

Third, once a TBTF institution is rescued, the authorities have a broad range of powers to dispose of it: it may be cleaned up, recapitalized, merged with other institutions, or even closed down and liquidated. Also, although an institution may be rescued to avoid systemic contagion, its managers and shareholders may be replaced. Thus, the moral hazard problems of rescuing the institution are reduced, even if there is still the issue of covering the depositors, including the uninsured depositors.

In an international context, the idea of taking over countries, closing them down and merging them with others, or replacing their shareholders is quite meaningless (in an era when, fortunately, debtor's prison and gunboat diplomacy are no longer options). Moreover, the kind of preventive regulation and supervision that are imposed on TBTF institutions in a domestic context is also severely limited in an international context. Sovereignty issues as well as the lack of leverage of the IMF over countries that are not yet in a crisis, and thus do not have an IMF program, limits the ability to provide such ex ante supervision and regulation. Thus, although in a domestic context moral hazard deriving from expectations of TBTF support may be tempered with adequate supervision and regulation, the same cannot easily be done in an international context.

In general, although TBTF arguments for big money packages for systemically important countries have some merit, the potential moral hazard distortions created by such programs have to be carefully addressed. In an ideal world, one would provide relatively large money packages mostly to sound economies without any substantial weaknesses (the type of economies that qualify for the IMF's CCL support). One would want to minimize the use of big money packages for the many cases in which serious fundamental fragilities interacted with illiquidity to generate financial crises. If one had to design a long-term regime from scratch, big money packages would not normally be part of the rules of the games, apart from very clear liquidity cases and cases in which significant contagion is due to systemic effects.[86] A credible commitment to avoid big money would force borrowers and creditors to be more cautious in their investment and borrowing decisions; and, if crises did occur because of a loss of confidence, adequate market mechanisms to avoid a generalized financial meltdown (orderly workouts, concerted market-based rollovers, insurance schemes based on private credit lines) would be found.

This purely market-based solution with no big money bailouts may not be feasible or credible in the current regime, and even in an historic perspective banking crises and international financial crises were messy and protracted when domestic and international financial LOLRs were missing.

---

86. This is the logic of having a facility like the IMF's SRF.

However, if investors, debtors, and the official sector will continue to live in a world where the TBTF doctrine will be at times implemented for countries that are systemically too important and contagious, there is a need to design mechanisms that will minimize the moral hazard and the distortionary effects of such doctrine.

In a domestic banking context, the FDICIA increased the likelihood that uninsured depositors and other creditors would suffer losses when their bank fails. The fix was incomplete, however, because regulators can provide—subject to a board decision with which the Treasury department must concur—full protection when they determine that a failing bank is TBTF—that is, when its failure could significantly impair the rest of the industry and the overall economy. Some, for example, the Minneapolis Federal Reserve, have argued that the TBTF exception is too broad; there is still much protection. Consequently, the Minneapolis Federal Reserve has proposed amending FDICIA so that the government cannot fully protect uninsured depositors and creditors at banks deemed TBTF.[87] The proposed reform attacks the problem of 100 percent coverage by requiring uninsured depositors of TBTF banks to bear some losses when their bank is rescued. Such reforms, by increasing market discipline, may make bank runs and panics more likely.

Consider now how such proposals to limit TBTF-related moral hazard could be applied in an international context. The answer is that some form of private-sector burden-sharing would replicate the type of incentives suggested by the Minneapolis Federal Reserve to limit the perverse effects of an international TBTF. This means that, even (or especially) in cases of liquidity crises, investors would be expected to participate in burden sharing (commitment to rollovers, concerted semivoluntary rollovers, and even small haircuts depending on the circumstances) when a TBTF country is receiving a big money package. The need to limit moral hazard would thus be a fundamental reason for including meaningful PSI for large countries that are receiving big money packages. Indeed, systematically rescuing such large international investors—cross-border bank activities of international banks and highly risky investments of sophisticated international investors—on the basis of the risk of a run on a systemically important illiquid country would exacerbate the moral hazard problem of large rescue packages.[88]

87. This Federal Reserve proposal was first advanced in the Minneapolis Federal Reserve 1997 annual report; see [http://www.mpls.frb.org/pubs/ar/ar1997.html].

88. Avoiding these ex post bailouts of cross-border interbank creditors is easier said than done. As the recent crisis in Turkey in December 2000 suggests, such uninsured creditors may panic when there are problems in the banking system and they are worried about serious losses. Thus, they are likely to run if expectations of a serious banking crisis emerge; consequently, the monetary authorities might be forced, ex post and at the cost of moral hazard distortions, to extend deposit insurance to these uninsured cross-border liabilities to prevent a run. However, this provision of ex post insurance was provided under the proviso that international banks commit to maintain their exposure level to the level existing at the time of the crisis (December 2000). This was the main, but export failed, PSI component of the IMF rescue package in Turkey. A similar quid quo pro was implemented in Korea in 1997; the banks agreed to roll over their exposure into medium-term bonds in exchange for a government guarantee of such lines.

In conclusion, the appropriate form of PSI in liquidity and systemic cases is a complex issue. The G7 and IMF approach has been to deal with these on a case-by-case basis, considering all factors in the case in deciding whether and how much PSI would be applied. Some degree of constructive ambiguity has been maintained in official doctrine and justified as necessary to provide the appropriate response to specific cases and minimize the moral hazard problem of TBTF expectations. Ideally, some combination of significant—but not systematically exceptional—official finance, domestic adjustment, and cooperative, semivoluntary, and least-coercive PSI of some categories of debt could restore confidence, prevent a wider crisis, and provide a middle solution to a crisis. Such a "middle-solution-cum-constructive-ambiguity" may address the trade-off between the need to avoid moral hazard deriving from systemic expectations of bailout and the risk that self-fulfilling runs occur in cases closer to the illiquidity corner.

Some Specific Proposals for New Institutions or Mechanisms/Tools to Prevent and Resolve Financial Crises

In the aftermath of any general crisis comes a variety of proposals for entirely new institutions or mechanisms to prevent and resolve crises.

The Asian Monetary Fund

The idea of an Asian Monetary Fund (AMF) was first advanced by Japan as a way to contain the emerging Asian financial turmoil in late 1997. The idea was that such a fund could pool regional resources to be used by countries in the region to defend their currencies against speculative attacks. The issue of an AMF became contentious as the United States successfully rejected this idea. It argued that it would compete with and duplicate the IMF and that there was a danger that the conditionality attached to the lending of this fund would be soft, undermining IMF conditionality and weakening the discipline to follow appropriate macro and financial policies. As the Asian crisis worsened, some lingering resentment remained among the Japanese and other Asians who argued that such a fund could have successfully stemmed or limited the Asian crisis and contagion throughout the region.

Such a fund might not have been successful in its short-run goal of ending the crises, even leaving aside the longer-run moral hazard issues. For example, Thailand almost exhausted its foreign reserves in the spring and summer of 1997 in spite of attempts to control the outflow of capital. It is not obvious that another $10 or $20 billion of borrowed reserves would have made any difference. Most likely it would have been lost and the eventual currency adjustment merely delayed. History suggests that when parities are unsustainable, sterilized intervention is ineffective and may just feed the short positions taken by speculators. Unsterilized intervention is more effective, but the same results on interest rates can be obtained through domestic open-market operations. One might argue that it may be better to save precious reserves that are a dam against liquidity risk and rather use domestic interest rate policy (domestic open-market operations) if a defense of the peg is deemed to be appropriate. Note, however, that policies of soft pegs before the crisis contributed to overvaluation, large current account deficits, lack of foreign exchange hedging, and moral hazard–related distortions to borrow in foreign currency. Thus, many believe that a currency adjustment was unavoidable in several crisis-affected economies in Asia and that neither unsterilized intervention nor interest rate defense could have prevented the eventual break of the currency pegs.

There are other motivations behind the Japanese push for an AFM, a push that has been later resurrected in the form of an initiative for closer monetary cooperation in the Asian region. For one thing, with the beginning of the European Monetary Union (EMU) and the emergence of the euro, the Japanese are concerned about the potential long-run marginalization of the yen as an international currency and the emergence of a world where the U.S. dollar and the euro are the only two major international currencies. Thus, closer monetary cooperation is one way to stimulate the development of a yen region and the international role of Japan's currency. Whether the yen is the right regional currency for Asia is not clear, however, because the patterns of trade and financial flows of the countries in the region show the western hemisphere (and Europe as well) and their currencies as major trade and financial partners. Furthermore, many Asians would prefer U.S. leadership in the region to Japan's, out of lingering historical resentment against the latter.

Asian countries and Japan have shared an aversion to purely floating exchange rates. The view of the United States Treasury after the Asian crisis, that middle regimes are unstable and that corner solutions may be better than intermediate middle regimes, has not been really accepted by Japan and other countries in the region that still see some form of managed rates as possible and desirable. Indeed, some countries in the region (Korea and Thailand) appear to have used intervention in foreign exchange markets in 1999–2000 to prevent excessive appreciation or depreciation of their currency, a move in the direction of managed exchange rates such as those prevalent before the Asian crisis. In that context, an AMF or other forms of monetary cooperation (such as the recent decision of some countries in the region to increase and extend their forex swap lines) can be seen as a way to ensure that exchange rate stability is maintained in the Asian region. In the view of some, the European Exchange Rate Mechanism (ERM) or EMU appears as a model of how Asian monetary cooperation should evolve over time.[89] But whether Asia is an optimal currency area is a com-

---

89. At the January 2001 meeting of the European and Asian Finance Ministers a joint French and Japanese paper was presented supporting the idea of limiting the degree of exchange rate flexibility in the Asian region; the paper argued that in some circumstances it might be appropriate for countries to peg their currencies to a basket of different currencies or seek to keep their currency within a fixed band (a target zone idea along the lines of the European monetary system).

plex issue that has to be analyzed separately (e.g., Frankel and Wei 1993; McKinnon 2000).

Global Financial Superregulator (Kaufman)

Kaufman (*Washington Post,* 27 January 1998; 1998) has proposed the creation of a global superregulator: a new international institution that would regulate financial markets and institutions. This institution would supervise and regulate the activities of both traditional banks and non-banking financial intermediaries. The logic of this proposal is that financial regulation is still at the national level, but financial institutions now operate globally, and financial markets are globally integrated. Thus, supervision solely at the national level may not be appropriate for firms that do business globally and in markets that are becoming more and more integrated internationally. Indeed, lack of global supervision and regulation may be one cause of the phenomenon of financial contagion.

There are tremendous obstacles—both political and regulatory and economic—to the idea that sovereign governments around the world would give up their right to supervise and regulate their domestic financial institutions. Also, there are issues of the accountability of such a global regulator: to whom would it be accountable and how? However, as the process of financial integration and globalization continues, the case for more coordination among national regulators is becoming more widely accepted. Indeed, the FSF was created in part as a mechanism of coordination of national regulatory policies in financial markets, in light of the international nature of many regulatory problems. Thus, although the idea of a global superregulator is farfetched, the idea of greater international coordination of national policies of supervision and regulation will gain ground, as the experience with the FSF suggests.

Also, greater integration may lead, over time, to supernational regulation of financial markets. For example, in Europe, the process of monetary and financial integration has opened the issue of whether banking supervision and regulation should be left to national monetary authorities or transferred to the European Central Bank. It is possible that the latter solution might eventually emerge.

One major obstacle to international supervision and regulation of banking systems derives from the safety net function played by national monetary authorities. Such services are provided by domestic monetary authorities only to financial institutions (be they domestic or foreign banks and their branches) that do operate within a country's borders. In exchange for this provision of a safety net (access to the discount window, LOLR liquidity support, deposit insurance, and even bailout in case of financial distress) the banking institutions subject themselves to supervision and regulation. If supervision and regulation were made by an international institution, however, who would provide the safety net to banking institutions? Moreover, if a systemic banking crisis in a country leads to significant fiscal costs of bailing out that financial system, who would pay the costs? In the current regime of national regulation, each country (i.e., its taxpayers) bears this cost. However, if regulation is international and if banking crises occur in spite of such regulation (or because of mistakes in such regulation), who should be bearing the fiscal costs, the domestic taxpayer or the international taxpayer? One could make a case in principle for the latter, but the political resistance to such a solution appears currently insuperable.[90] These are complex and difficult questions that have no easy answer.

Soros Proposal for International Deposit Insurance

Soros (*Financial Times*, 31 December 1997; 1998) has proposed the creation of a public international deposit insurance agency that would insure international investors' claims against default. The logic of this proposal is to reduce the risk of self-fulfilling runs when investors panic and fail to roll over short-term claims coming to maturity. Insured claims would not be run on, as they would be safe. To reduce risk of moral hazard, Soros suggests that the amount of insurable claims of each country should be limited to a maximum, with the ceiling set by the IMF based on the soundness of a country's fundamentals. Debtor countries would pay the cost of this insurance scheme by paying an insurance fee when issuing loans, bonds, and other claims.

This proposal raises a number of issues.[91] Specifically, if the insurance fee is actuarially fair and there are no informational failures, the debtor does not gain anything relative to issuing uninsured bonds. An insured bond would be riskless and have no spread relative to other riskless international bonds (say, U.S. treasuries) but the insurance fee would be equal to the spread of that country's debt relative to riskless assets. Thus, after paying the fee, the cost of external borrowing for the country would remain the same.[92]

Also, such schemes are usually not a free lunch. If some claims are insured, others are not. Moreover, because a country's ability to pay—that is, to service its external debt—is given (by its resources and expected future

90. For example, in the debate on dollarization, the United States has made clear that the Federal Reserve safety net would not be extended under any circumstance to the financial system of a dollarizing country and that the U.S. would not accept responsibility for the supervision and regulation of the financial system of a dollarizer. Taking control of supervision and regulation would imply accepting responsibility for problems of the financial system and would put pressure on the Federal Reserve to provide safety net services to a foreign financial system: hence the U.S. unwillingness to supervise other countries financial system. For a review of dollarization, from a faction in the U.S. Senate that wishes to encourage it, see Schuler (1999).

91. See also Eichengreen (1999a) for a thoughtful discussion.

92. If market prices are different from actuarially fair prices, the debtor may gain or lose. Differences in the relative knowledge or ignorance about fundamental risks between the debtor and market providers of insurance may be a channel through which value is created. However, one has to recur to externalities or informational failures to make such an argument.

foreign exchange receipts), giving seniority to some insured claims means that the spread on the uninsured ones will go up, with no overall benefit for the country in terms of reduced average spread on its external debt. For the same reason, the risk of a run on uninsured claims will go up. Thus, the risk of liquidity runs might be increased rather than reduced. Also, if insurance is such a good idea, why wouldn't private markets be providing such services? Why should a public agency provide it? One needs to argue that externalities and informational asymmetries and failures are very important to derive a rationale for the public provision of such services. Such externalities and asymmetries may be important in practice, but designing an international deposit insurance scheme that is incentive-compatible and minimizes moral hazard distortions may be quite challenging.

*Collateral and Credit Enhancements: Creation of Value
or Redistribution of Value?*

Several authors have suggested the usefulness of collateral or credit enhancements as instruments of crisis prevention and crisis resolution (Feldstein 1999b, 2000; Corrigan 2000). Indeed, various types of sweeteners and credit enhancements have been part of recent restructuring episodes.

In general, sweeteners (such as collateral and other enhancements) create different levels of formal or informal seniority among private claims that negatively affect other claims (whether private or official) that do not have the same features. Because a country's ability to pay, while uncertain, is given, there is usually no free lunch here, and provision of greater seniority to some claims comes at the cost of less seniority for other claims.[93] This burden-shifting game, often at the expense of official creditors' claims, can distort debt flows. Deals in which new claims are provided collateral in the form of future exportable receipts are particularly notable and may not be legal (because they may clash with current "negative pledge clauses" in World Bank and MDB loans). They are a case of burden shifting. Milder forms of seniority upgrades (such as the sovereign taking responsibility for claims of semisovereign entities) are also examples of burden shifting. Other seniority upgrades are embedded in the fine print of the new bonds. For example, the Ecuador deal's reinstatement of the original principal (i.e., recession of the haircut on principal payments) in the case that the new bonds are restructured down the line is an example of this indirect attempt to provide seniority to the new instruments.

The arguments presented to justify such reinstatement clauses and general seniority upgrades are as follows: (a) they are necessary to maximize the chances of a successful deal; (b) it is unfair to creditors that instruments that have, as Bradies, already experienced one or more haircuts will experience another one in the future. However, there are several objections to

93. We discuss below the cases in which credit enhancements may create value.

these views. First, investors who want to lock in the value of the new bonds (inclusive of any mark-to-market gains) can do so by selling these new bonds at current market prices; holding them over time implies accepting the credit risk (potential gains and losses) embedded in the underlying claims. Second, as long as such new instruments trade at significant spreads over risk-free assets, it means that they are not risk-free or senior relative to other instruments. If they were formally treated as effectively senior, they would trade at much lower spreads relative to risk-free rates. Third, creating degrees of grayness with some restructured claims being informally more senior (but not fully risk-free) than other private and public claims may add to the confusion and lack of transparency and predictability of the claims. Either new claims have clear collateral (as the Bradies had) and whatever seniority is embedded in them is formally agreed upon so that absolute and relative pricing of different claims can be clearly made, or, otherwise, one creates a new system of pseudo senior claims that adds to the pricing uncertainty and unpredictability of the system of debt flows to emerging markets.

More generally, some—like Corrigan (2000)—have suggested that credit enhancements and broad guarantees should be used as an alternative to large official packages of money. In principle, if one wanted to avoid large official packages and minimize the use of semicoercive PSI schemes, one could think of a world where countries, subject to a run or whose currency is under pressure, could get temporary loans from the private sectors that are guaranteed by the official sector. This, in Corrigan's view, could be a useful alternative to PSI and big official packages. It is, however, not clear whether this solution is truly different from a large official package. Conceptually, however, there is little difference between the IMF's directly borrowing from its official shareholders at risk-free rates and lending the proceeds in big packages at approximately risk-free rates to a country in crisis, and the private sector's lending the same amount of money to the country in crisis under a full guarantee of the loan.

The broader conceptual question is whether such enhancements provide any "value" to debtors beyond the direct benefit or transfer to the debtor deriving the implicit subsidy involved in the guarantee. It is not obvious that this is usually the case. Credit enhancements can create value when there is an externality or some informational asymmetry. For example, in a situation with the risk of a liquidity run, official money, either directly or indirectly through private loans that have guarantees, may improve welfare by avoiding self-fulfilling runs not justified by fundamentals (such as a run that is a clear case of a negative externality and market coordination failure). Thus, enhancements may not imply any subsidy cost to the official sector when they prevent avoidable crises. In those cases, however, the optimal choice is a large package of official money; the alternative of a fully guaranteed loan is not, in any substantial terms, different from the big official package. Political constraints and resistance to official money apply to the first scheme as easily as the latter.

Informational asymmetries may also create value. In general, the broad analytical literature on securitized credit (see, e.g., Klapper [2000] for a review) finds that secured loans occur at the expense of unsecured loans: pledging collateral or providing seniority to one lender subordinates the claims of other creditors. However, secured lending may have a rationale if there are informational asymmetries (if the borrower is unable to otherwise "signal" that its likelihood of defaulting is lower than the one perceived by the market and thus requires collateral for credible signaling) or other agency problems (as in the Jensen and Meckling [1976] case, in which collateral controls for the agency problem of asset substitution, i.e., borrowers substitute for riskier than for less risky assets). It is not, however, obvious that these cases systematically apply to sovereign borrowers. Specifically, signaling from the use of collateral may exacerbate the distortions from asymmetric information rather than reducing them. For example, a highly indebted sovereign who is likely and willing to default and is currently unable to borrow more may use the enhancement or collateral to receive new nondefaultable loans. But this new secured lending occurs at the expense of the previous unsecured loans, and the shift of collateral (the sovereign or country's assets) to the new loans means that, in the default state, unsecured creditors receive even less than they would have if such collateral had not been provided to the new loans.

However, apart from these very specific cases in which value is created, credit enhancements do not generally provide value either in theory or in practice. For example, take a loan that is enjoying a partial guarantee (such as a rolling interest rate guarantee in the 1999 Thailand Electricity Generating Authority of Thailand loan, one of the first cases of a formal World Bank guarantee of a semisovereign loan). Conceptually, investors will price this loan correctly; the component that is guaranteed will have a value equivalent to a risk-free loan, whereas the uncollateralized or unguaranteed part would have a "stripped" spread equal to that of other unguaranteed loans to the debtor. Thus, although the loans provide a financial benefit to the debtor, the subsidy value of the guaranteed part, there is no extra value created. The private sector could have, as well, given the debtor a loan that was not guaranteed at all, and the official sector could give the debtor a grant equal to the subsidy value of the guarantee. Generally, the guarantee cannot create extra value beyond this subsidy or transfer.

Some have argued that value can be created in these enhancements, but the arguments are not fully convincing. Specifically, the argument that is often made is that, while the guarantee is limited to only part of the cash flow (say, a rolling interest payment), the "halo" of safety of the official creditor (an MDB or the World Bank) that is providing the guarantee will fall on the entire loan; as a "pixie dust" effect, the spread on the uncollateralized component of the loan will also be reduced because, it is argued, it is unlikely that the debtor would want to default (and thus trigger the guarantee) on the payments that are guaranteed. However, this halo effect is most likely nonexistent in practice. First, Brady bonds did not benefit from such a halo for the uncollateralized component of their payment stream. Second, the pricing of the Thai EGAT loan suggests that the "halo effect" was minis-cule: the spread on the uncollateralized part of the loan was ex-post similar to that on other nonguaranteed Thai borrowings. Thus, there is little evi-dence that such enhancement provided value.

Finally, there may be an indirect channel through which value is created, but if so, this is a distortionary and moral hazard–biased channel. The nonenhanced component of the loan could have a lower (stripped) spread than that on other nonguaranteed instruments only if investors truly per-ceived the instrument to have lower repayment or default risk than other in-struments because of the official-sector "halo" on the enhanced component of the loan. If this is the case, however, the holders of the nonguaranteed part of the partially guaranteed loan benefit only because this relative sen-iority occurs at the expense of other creditors, those holding nonguaranteed claims. Thus, again, no real value is created: you only get a transfer of value from some creditors to others. Regimes in which such fuzzy hierarchies of seniority are created are not efficient. If relative seniority has to be provided, it is efficient if it is explicit with clear collateral or definition of the position of the asset in the pecking order of claims, not implicit and couched in "halo effects." Otherwise, incentives are distorted, transparency is reduced, and creative financial engineering is used to stake seniority.

Similar concerns can be expressed for debt-restructuring deals in which some of the cash flow payments are collateralized with some future foreign currency resources of the country (such as future oil receipts or other export receipts). Such deals do not usually increase the creditworthiness of the country because the ability—as opposed to the willingness—to pay de-pends on the country's debt relative to its assets, inclusive of the discounted values of any future stream of foreign currency receipts. They usually shift seniority to those creditors who get such deals at the expense of other cred-itors (both private unsecured or official creditors). These collateralized deals may also violate "negative pledge clauses" on World Bank and other MDB loans.

Alternative Ideas for the Process of Debt Restructuring

Many investors and creditors have expressed unhappiness with the cur-rent process of bonded debt restructurings (i.e., the model of "debt exchange offers preceded by market soundings") in spite of the success of recent re-structurings based on this model (see the section on "The Role of the G3"). In their view, the current process is unfair: it does not include enough of their input, it does not allow for a meaningful negotiation with the debtor and official creditors on the distribution of the burden sharing, and it biases the negotiating power in favor of the debtor, thus undermining the incentives to service in full and on time debt payments. Some (for example, a group that was sponsored by the Council on Foreign Relations [CFR]) accordingly suggest that an alternative process should be followed in such restructurings based on creditor committees and more formal negotiations.[94] In this alternative process, an ad hoc group of bondholders (and possibly other creditors) would be formed and a formal negotiation with the debtor would take place. Some also suggest that the negotiations should be extended to official creditors to ensure that the private sector is not a residual claimant but rather has a say in how much of the burden will be borne by private creditors compared to public creditors. To sweeten this shift in bargaining power to private creditors, it has been suggested that creditors may be willing, in exchange for formal committees and negotiations, to accept a voluntary debt standstill accompanied by a legally enforceable stay of litigation.

In contrast to this proposal, critics argue that it is not clear that, in debt exchanges, too much bargaining power is shifted to debtors. In fact, such offers are voluntary in the sense that the debtor has to offer terms that maximize the probability that a large fraction (often formally over 85 percent) of creditors accept it. Thus, if one looks at recent bond restructuring episodes (in Ukraine, Pakistan, Russia, and Ecuador) one can observe that the terms of the restructured bonds have been extremely generous and have provided significant mark-to-market gains to creditors who accepted such offers. Advisors make extensive market soundings before the offer is launched to figure out the preferences of creditors for the type, terms, and conditions of the restructured instruments. It is thus not clear that an alternative process based on formal negotiations would provide a smaller slice of the burden pie to creditors.

Second, formal negotiations with debtors run the risk of dragging on indefinitely and inflicting "delay losses" on both creditors and debtors. A situation in which debts are in default for protracted periods of time is highly disruptive to debtors as cutoff from market access, output losses, and other real costs accumulate over time. Such losses eventually hurt the debtor's ability to pay and are thus costly to creditors as well.

---

94. This is a different group from the task force that, under the CFR umbrella, proposed a framework for the reform of the international financial architecture. For reasons of space, we do not discuss the proposals of this group presented in a report (Independent Task Force 1999). These proposals are conceptually in between the radical reforms of the Meltzer Commission and the gradualist changes agreed upon by the G7 and the IMF. For example, the CFR suggests a smaller use of large IMF packages and a greater reliance on more coercive forms of PSI, but it does not go as far as the Meltzer Commission in restricting the ability of the IMF to provide lending in crisis episodes. Also, the CFR task force expressed some sympathy for a more structured restructuring process (creditor committees, negotiations, and collective action clauses) that is consistent with some of the views of the other CFR group initiative discussed in the text.

Third, there are serious obstacles and disadvantages to the idea that creditors could be involved in the decision on how much adjustment the debtor would make, how much official multilateral support would be provided, and how much of the sharing burden would be borne by the PC creditors.[95]

Fourth, bilateral market soundings between debtors and creditors appear to have worked satisfactorily in Pakistan, Ukraine, and Russia. If anything the experience of the Ecuador Consultative Group in which the debtor regularly met with a broad representation of bondholders has been criticized as unproductive and unsuccessful. It became, at times, an unconstructive forum where frustrated creditors vented their unhappiness with the slowness of the adjustment and restructuring process rather than a productive procedure to accelerate the restructuring. Sometimes bilateral soundings are more efficient than large public forums where both sides posture to stake their claims.

Fifth, it is not obvious that one restructuring process provides more incentive for strategic nonpayments or defaults than another. In the debt exchange offer model, the debtors are usually wary of stopping payments to private creditors and would rather avoid nonpayment for as long as possible because the economic (and legal) costs of such a formal default can be very high: loss of output, loss of market access, trade sanctions, and so on. It is not clear why a formal negotiating process (especially one in which standstills are sanctioned and stays of litigation imposed) would provide lower bargaining power to the debtor. It is ambiguous in theory and in practice whether either process has a systematic effect on the relative bargaining power of debtors versus creditors. Indeed, some processes that would lead to delay in negotiations may be negative-sum games in which inefficient costs of delay impose welfare losses on both debtors and creditors. Thus, a system of debt exchange with market soundings may be beneficial to all.

In conclusion, it is not obvious that an alternative process based on negotiations and formal creditor committees would be in the interest of creditors.[96] It would certainly be worthwhile, however, to study alternative process schemes and improve on existing ones. For example, the current system of "market soundings" has been somewhat unstructured. Maybe a more structured process would contribute to providing financial advisors with the information necessary to design successful debt exchanges. Also, although negotiations between private and official creditors are not likely to

95. See Roubini (2000) for a detailed discussion of these objections. In general, most private-sector participants agree that their involvement in the first two steps, design of macro policy adjustment effort and amount of multilateral support, is not likely to occur; but they would like to be involved in the last step, the discussion of the relative role of official bilateral creditors (PC) and the private sector in burden sharing and a direct negotiation with the debtor on the terms of a restructuring.

96. However, the official sector remains open to the idea that creditors' committees and negotiations between creditors and debtors may be at times an appropriate mechanism to restructure sovereign bonded debt liabilities; see Geithner (2000).

occur, there may be ways to improve the flow of information to the private sector. Official creditors could be more clear about the PSI doctrine and its application; the PC could become somewhat more transparent and better explain its procedures and terms for restructuring;[97] the debtor country should provide information to creditors in good and bad times and keep them fully informed of economic prospects, external debt and payment stream data, economic forecasts, and possible external financing problems and plans to address these problems; and the IMF could have a closer dialogue with the private sector and more regularly brief investors on program developments for a debtor country with external debt-servicing problems. All these steps would increase transparency, openness, and predictability of PSI and reduce the impression that the process is arbitrary and unpredictable. Constructive ideas along these lines could improve the current system and support the cooperative goals of the PSI policy.

3.1.7 Conclusions

The emerging market countries might have reacted to the crises they suffered in the late 1990s by challenging the legitimacy of the world financial system, charging that it was rigged to benefit rich-country investors. For the most part this has not happened. True, they complain that they deserve better representation in the governance structure than they have received in the past. True, the crises made it more difficult to claim that free financial markets operate with perfect efficiency. True, improvements in the system are both desirable and possible. Nevertheless, most countries everywhere now agree that a global capitalist system best promotes growth. Furthermore, few can deny the practical realities that give heavy weight to the United States and other G7 countries as a steering committee in the governance of that system—the logistical advantages of small numbers and the power dynamics of creditor-debtor relationships.

This chapter has reviewed the role of the major industrialized countries in three areas: (a) their own macroeconomic policies, which determine the global financial environment; (b) their role in responding to crises when they occur, particularly through rescue packages with three components—reforms in debtor countries, public funds from creditor countries, and PSI; and (c) efforts to reform the international financial architecture, with the aim of lessening the frequency and severity of future crises. The latter two topics are closely intertwined, due to tension between mitigating crises in the short run and the moral hazard that rescues create in the longer term.

The phrase "new Bretton Woods," or even "new financial architecture," may be too grand to connote the reform initiatives that have been under-

97. The PC has indeed recently opened a website [http://www.clubdeparis.org/] where information is provided to investors about its activities, rules, procedures, and decisions.

taken for the future. These reforms are modest and incrementalist, rather than sweeping and revolutionary—perhaps more like redoing the plumbing and electricity in the house than redesigning the architecture from the ground up. However, they may nonetheless contribute to crisis prevention and resolution. If all the PSI reforms are successfully implemented, crises when they occur may be better managed and resolved at lower costs. If all the crisis prevention reforms are successfully implemented, the system may become less prone to crises in the first place. This will take years. It would be foolish to think that reforms already in progress will eliminate the risk of crises in emerging markets. Some degree of volatility is inevitable—perhaps even a higher degree of volatility at early stages of a poor country's liberalization and industrialization than would prevail if it remained economically isolated and undeveloped. The United States had severe financial and economic crashes during its period of industrialization. Perhaps the rest of the world will settle down to a stable and tranquil path only when its markets and institutions are as well developed as those of the United States today.

References

Bagci, Pinar, and William Perraudin. 1997. The impact of IMF programmes. Institute for Financial Research Working Paper no. 35. London: Birkbeck College, February.

Bhagwati, Jagdish. 1998. Fifty years: Looking back, looking forward. Paper presented at the Symposium on the World Trading System. 30 April, Geneva, Switzerland.

Becker, Torbjorn, Anthony J. Richards, and Yungong Thaicharoen. 2000. Collective action clauses for emerging market bonds: Good news for lower rated borrowers too. Washington, D.C.: International Monetary Fund. Unpublished manuscript.

Bergsten, C. Fred. 2000. Minority dissent on the Report of the International Financial Institution Advisory Commission ("Meltzer Commission"). Washington, D.C.: Institute of International Economics.

Bird, Graham, and Dane Rowlands. 1997. The catalytic effects of lending by the international financial institutions. *World Economy* 20 (7): 967–91.

Bordo, Michael D., and Anna J. Schwartz. 2000. Measuring real economic effects of bailouts: Historical perspectives on how countries in financial distress have fared with and without bailouts. NBER Working Paper no. 7701. Cambridge, Mass.: National Bureau of Economic Research, May.

Bucheit, Lee, and G. Mitu Gulati. 2000. Exit consents in sovereign bond exchanges. *UCLA Law Review* 48 (October): 59–84.

Calomiris, Charles. 1998a. Blueprints for a new global financial architecture. Columbia University, Graduate School of Business. Unpublished manuscript.

———. 1998b. The IMF's imprudent role as lender of last resort. *Cato Journal* 17: 275–95.

Calvo, Guillermo, Leonardo Leiderman, and Carmen Reinhart. 1993. Capital inflows and real exchange rate appreciation in Latin America: The role of external factors. *IMF Staff Papers* 40 (March): 108–50.

———. 1994. The capital inflows problem: Concepts and issues. *Contemporary Economic Policy* 12 (July): 54–66.

Chinn, Menzie D., Michael P. Dooley, and Sona Shrestha. 1999. Latin America and East Asia in the context of an insurance model of currency crises. NBER Working Paper no. W7091. Cambridge, Mass.: National Bureau of Economic Research, April.

Chuhan, Punam, Stijn Claessens, and Nlandu Mamingi. 1998. Equity and bond flows to Latin America and Asia: The role of global and country factors. *Journal of Development Economics* 55:439–63.

Clarida, Richard. 2000. *G3 exchange rate relationships: A recap of the record and a review of proposals for change.* Essays in International Economics no. 219. Princeton, N.J.: Princeton University Press.

Cline, William. 1984. *International debt: Systemic risk and policy response.* Washington, D.C.: Institute for International Economics.

———. 1995. *International debt reexamined.* Washington, D.C.: Institute for International Economics.

———. 2000. The role of the private sector in resolving financial crises in emerging markets. Washington, D.C.: Institute of International Finance. Mimeograph, October.

Conway, Patrick. 1994. IMF lending programs: Participation and impact. *Journal of Development Economics* 45 (December): 365–91.

Corrigan, E. Gerald. 2000. Two international financial stability issues: Asset price inflation and private sector participation in financial crisis stabilisation. *Financial Stability Review* (June): 136–41.

Corsetti, Giancarlo, Paolo Pesenti, and Nouriel Roubini. 1999a. Paper tigers? A model of the Asian crisis. *European Economic Review* 43 (July): 1211–36.

———. 1999b. What caused the Asian currency and financial crisis? *Japan and the World Economy* 11 (September): 305–73.

———. 2001. The role of large players in currency crises. NBER Working Paper no. 8303. Cambridge, Mass.: National Bureau of Economic Research, May.

Council on Foreign Relations. 1999. *Safeguarding prosperity in a global financial system: The future international financial architecture.* Washington, D.C.: Institute for International Economics.

Dallara, Charles. 1999. Letter to the chairman of the Interim Committee. Available at [http://www.iif.com]. 16 September.

de Brouwer, Gordon. 2000. Improving the bureaucracy of international economic cooperation. Australian National University.

De Gregorio, José, Barry Eichengreen, Takatoshi Ito, and Charles Wyplosz. 1999. An independent and accountable IMF. In *Geneva report on the world economy.* London: Centre for Economic Policy Research.

Dell'Ariccia, Giovanni, Isabel Goedde, and Jeromin Zettelmeyer. 2000. Moral hazard in international crisis lending: A test. Washington, D.C.: International Monetary Fund. Manuscript, November.

Diaz-Alejandro, Carlos. 1985. Good-bye financial repression, hello financial crash. *Journal of Development Economics* 19:1–24.

Dicks-Mireaux, Louis, Mauro Mecagni, and Susan Schadler. 1997. Evaluating the effect of IMF lending to low-income countries. Washington, D.C.: International Monetary Fund, Unpublished manuscript.

Dominguez, Kathryn, and Jeffrey Frankel. 1993. *Does foreign exchange intervention work?* Washington, D.C.: Institute for International Economics.

Dooley, Michael. 2000a. Can output losses following international financial crises be avoided? NBER Working Paper no. 7531. Cambridge, Mass.: National Bureau of Economic Research, February.

———. 2000b. A model of crises in emerging markets. *Economic Journal* 110 (460): 256–72.

Dooley, Michael, Eduardo Fernandez-Arias, and Kenneth Kletzer. 1994. Recent private capital inflows to developing countries: Is the debt crisis history? NBER Working Paper no. 4792. Cambridge, Mass.: National Bureau of Economic Research, July.

Dornbusch, Rudiger. 1985. Policy and performance links between LDC debtors and industrial nations. *Brookings Papers on Economic Activity,* Issue no. 2:303–56. Washington, D.C.: Brookings Institution.

Eichengreen, Barry. 1999a. *Toward a new financial architecture: A practical post-Asia agenda.* Washington, D.C.: Institute for International Economics.

———. 1999b. Is greater private-sector burden sharing impossible? University of California, Berkeley, Department of Economics. Manuscript, May.

———. 2000. *Can the moral hazard caused by IMF bailouts be reduced?* Geneva Reports on the World Economy, Special Report no. 1. Geneva: International Center for Monetary and Banking Studies.

Eichengreen, Barry, and Ashoka Mody. 2000a. Would collective action clauses raise borrowing costs? NBER Working Paper no. 7458. Cambridge, Mass.: National Bureau of Economic Research. January.

———. 2000b. Would collective action clauses raise borrowing costs? An Update and Additional Results. Policy Research Working Paper no. 2363. Washington, D.C.: World Bank, June.

Eichengreen, Barry, and Richard Portes. 1995. *Crisis? What crisis? Orderly workouts for sovereign debtors.* London: Center for Economic Policy Research.

Eichengreen, Barry, and Andrew Rose. 2001. Staying afloat when the wind shifts: External factors and emerging market banking crises. In *Money, Factor Mobility, and Trade: Essays in Honor of Robert Mundell,* ed. Guillermo Calvo, Rudiger Dornbusch, and Maurice Obstfeld, 171–205. Cambridge: Massachusetts Institute of Technology Press.

Eichengreen, Barry, and Christof Ruhel. 2000. The bail-in problem: Systematic goals, ad hoc means. NBER Working Paper no. W7653. Cambridge, Mass.: National Bureau of Economic Research. April.

Feldstein, Martin. 1994. American economic policy in the 1980s: A personal view. In *American economic policy in the 1980s,* ed. Martin Feldstein, 1–79. Chicago: University of Chicago Press.

———. 1999a. Refocusing the IMF. *Foreign Affairs* 78 (2): 93–109.

———. 1999b. Self-protection for emerging market economies. NBER Working Paper no. 6907. Cambridge, Mass.: National Bureau of Economic Research, January.

———. 2000. Aspects of global economic integration: Outlook for the future. NBER Working Paper no. 7899. Cambridge, Mass.: National Bureau of Economic Research, September.

Fernandez-Arias, Eduardo. 1994. The new wave of private capital inflows: Push or pull? World Bank Policy Research Working Paper no. 1312. Washington, D.C.: World Bank, Debt and International Finance Division, International Economics Department, June.

Fischer, Stanley. 1999. Learning the lessons of financial crises: The roles of the public and private sectors. Speech to the Emerging Market Traders' Association Annual Meeting. 9 December, New York. Available at [http://www.imf.org/external/np/speeches/1999/120999.HTM].

———. 2000. Managing the international monetary system. Address given at the International Law Association Biennial Conference. 26 July, London.

Fischer, Bernhard, and Helmut Reisen. 1994. Pension fund investment from aging to emerging markets. OECD Development Centre Policy Brief no. 9. Paris: Organization for Economic Cooperation and Development.

Frankel, Jeffrey. 1999. *No single currency regime is right for all countries or at all times.* Essays in International Finance no. 215. Princeton, N.J.: Princeton University Press.

Frankel, Jeffrey, and Chudozie Okongwu. 1996. Liberalized portfolio capital inflows in emerging markets: Sterilization, expectations, and the incompleteness of interest rate convergence. *International Journal of Finance and Economics* 1 (1): 1–23.

Frankel, Jeffrey, and David Romer. 1999. Does trade cause growth? *American Economic Review* 89 (3): 379–99.

Frankel, Jeffrey, and Andrew Rose. 1996. Currency crashes in emerging markets: An empirical treatment. *Journal of International Economics* 41 (3/4): 351–66.

Frankel, Jeffrey, and Shang-Jin Wei. 1993. Is Japan creating a yen bloc in East Asia and the Pacific? In *Regionalism and rivalry: Japan and the U.S. in Pacific Asia,* ed. Jeffrey Frankel and Miles Kahler, 53–85. Chicago: University of Chicago Press.

Friedman, Benjamin. 2000. How easy should debt restructuring be? In *Managing financial and corporate distress: Lessons from Asia,* ed. Charles Adams, Robert Litan, and Michael Pomerleano, 21–46. Washington, D.C.: Brookings Institution.

Geithner, Timothy. 2000. Resolving financial crises in emerging market economics. Remarks before the Securities Industry Association and Emerging Markets Trades Association. 23 October, New York, N.Y.

Giannini, Curzio. 1999. *Enemy of none but a common friend of all: An international perspective on the lender-of-last-resort function.* Essays in International Finance, no. 21. Princeton, N.J.: Princeton University Press.

Goldstein, Morris. 1997. *The case for an international banking standard.* Policy Analyses in International Economics no. 47. Washington, D.C.: Institute for International Economics.

Goldstein, Morris, Graciela Kaminsky, and Carmen Reinhart. 2000. *Assessing financial vulnerability: An early warning system for emerging markets.* Washington, D.C.: Institute for International Economics.

Goldstein, Morris, and Mohsin Khan. 1985. Income and price effects in foreign trade. In *Handbook of International Economics,* vol. 2, ed. R. Jones and Peter B. Kenen, 1041–105. Amsterdam: Elsevier.

Group of Seven (G7). 1999. *Strengthening the international financial architecture.* Washington, D.C.: G7.

———. 2000. Strengthening the international financial architecture. Report from G7 Finance Ministers to the Heads of State and Government. 21 July, Kyushu-Okinawa, Japan.

Haldane, Andy. 1999. Private sector involvement in financial crisis: Analytics and public policy approaches. Bank of England *Financial Stability Review* (November): 184–202.

Haque, Nadeem Ul, and Mohsin Khan. 1999. Do IMF-supported programs work? A survey of the cross-country empirical evidence. IMF Working Paper no. WP/98/169. Washington, D.C.: International Monetary Fund, December.

Henning, C. Randall. 1999. *The exchange stabilization fund: Slush money or war chest?* Policy Analyses in International Economics no. 57. Washington, D.C.: Institute for International Economics.

Independent Task Force. 1999. Safeguarding prosperity in a global financial system: The future international financial architecture. Report of an Independent Task Force sponsored by the Council on Foreign Relations. New York: Council on Foreign Relations.

Institute of International Finance (IIF). 1999a. Global private finance leaders stress the importance of voluntary approaches to crisis resolution in emerging markets. Available at [http://www.iif.com/PressRel/1999pr9.html]. 24 June.

————. 1999b. Summary report on the work of the IIF steering committee on emerging markets finance. Washington, D.C.: IIF.

————. 1999c. Testing for "moral hazard" in emerging markets lending. IIF Research Papers no. 99-1. Washington, D.C.: IIF, August.

International Financial Institution Advisory Commission (IFIAC). 2000. Report of the International Financial Institution Advisory Commission ("Meltzer Commission"). Washington, D.C.: IFIAC.

International Monetary Fund (IMF). Various issues. *Direction of trade.* Washington, D.C.: IMF.

————. Various years. *International financial statistics.* Washington, D.C.: IMF.

————. Various years. *World economic outlook.* Washington, D.C.: IMF.

————. 1999. Involving the private sector in forestalling and resolving financial crises. Washington, D.C.: IMF, Policy Development and Review Department, April.

————. 2000a. *International capital markets: Developments, prospects, and key policy issues.* World Economic and Financial Surveys. Washington, D.C.: IMF, September.

————. 2000b. Involving the private sector in the resolution of financial crises: Standstills, preliminary considerations. Washington, D.C.: Policy Development and Review Department and Legal Department, September.

————. 2000c. Report to the IMF executive board of the Quota Formula Review Group. Washington, D.C.: IMF, April.

Jensen, Michael, and William Meckling. 1976. Theory of the firm: Managerial behavior, agency costs, and ownership structure. *Journal of Financial Economics* 3: 305–60.

Kahn, Robert. 2000. The role of the private sector in the prevention and resolution of international financial crises. Paper presented at the Conference on the Governance of the Global Capital Market. 23 October, Montreal.

Kaufman, Henry. 1998. Proposal for improving the structure of financial supervision and regulation. Remarks before the Brookings Institution Symposium on Limiting Moral Hazard in Financial Rescues. 4 June, Washington, D.C.

Kenen, Peter. 2001. *The international financial architecture: What's new? What's missing?* Washington, D.C.: Institute for International Economics.

King, Mervyn. 1999. Reforming the international financial system: The middle way. Speech delivered to a session of the money marketeers at the Federal Reserve Bank of New York. 9 September.

Klapper, Leora. 2000. The uniqueness of short-term collateralization. World Bank Working Paper no. 2544. Washington, D.C.: World Bank.

Köhler, Horst. 2000. Toward a more focused IMF. Address to International Monetary Conference. 30 May, Paris, France. Available at [http://www.imf.org/external/np/speeches/2000/053000.htm].

Krueger, Anne. 1997. Whither the World Bank and the IMF? NBER Working Paper no. 6327. Cambridge, Mass.: National Bureau of Economic Research, December.

Lane, Timothy, and Steven Phillips. 2000. Does IMF financing result in moral hazard? IMF Working Paper no. WP/00/168. Washington, D.C.: International Monetary Fund, October.

Levinson, Jerome. 2000. Dissent on the report of the International Financial Institution Advisory Commission ("Meltzer Commission"). Washington, D.C.

McKibbin, Warwick, and Jeffrey Sachs. 1988. Coordination of monetary and fiscal policies in the industrial economies. In *International aspects of fiscal policies,* ed. Jacob Frenkel, 73–120. Chicago: University of Chicago Press.

———. 1991. *Global linkages: Macroeconomic interdependence and cooperation in the world economy.* Washington, D.C.: Brookings Institution.

McKinnon, Ronald. 2000. After the crisis, the East Asian dollar standard resurrected. Stanford University, Department of Economics. Manuscript, August.

McKinnon, Ronald, and Huw Pill. 1997. Credible economic liberalizations and overborrowing. *American Economic Review Papers and Proceedings* 87: 189–93.

McQuillan, Lawrence, and Peter Montgomery, eds. 1999. *The International Monetary Fund: Financial medic to the world?* Stanford, Calif.: Hoover Press.

Meltzer, Allan. 1998. Asian problems and the IMF. Testimony prepared for the Joint Economic Committee, U.S. Congress. 24 February, Washington, D.C.

Mody, Ashok, Mark Taylor, and Jung Yeon Kim. 2001. Modelling fundamentals for forecasting capital flows to emerging markets. *International Journal of Finance and Economics* 6 (3): 201–16.

Niehans, Jurg. 1976. How to fill an empty shell. *American Economic Review Papers and Proceedings* 66 (2): 177–83.

Petas, Peter, and Rashique Rahman. 1999. Sovereign bonds: Legal aspects that affect—Default and recovery. *Global emerging markets: Debt strategy.* London: Deutsche Bank.

Portes, Richard. 2000. Sovereign debt restructuring: The role of institutions for collective action. London Business School. Mimeograph, March.

Prusa, Thomas. 2000. On the spread and impact of antidumping. NBER Working Paper no. 7404. Cambridge, Mass.: National Bureau of Economic Research.

Rogoff, Kenneth. 1999. International institutions for reducing global financial instability. *Journal of Economic Perspectives* 13 (4): 21–42.

Roubini, Nouriel. 2000. Bail-in, burden-sharing, private sector involvement (PSI) in crisis resolution and constructive engagement of the private sector. A primer: Evolving definitions, doctrine, practice, and case law. New York University, Stern School of Business. Unpublished manuscript.

Rubin, Robert. 1998. Strengthening the architecture of the international financial system. Remarks to the Brookings Institution, 14 April.

Sachs, Jeffrey. 1985. The dollar and the policy mix: 1985. *Brookings Papers on Economic Activity,* Issue no. 1:117–97. Washington, D.C.: Brookings Institution.

———. 1995. Do we need an international lender of last resort? Frank D. Graham lecture at Princeton University. 20 April. Available at [http://www2.cid.harvard.edu/cidpapers/intllr.pdf].

Schott, Jeffrey. 1998. The World Trade Organization: Progress to date and the road ahead. In *Launching new global trade talks: An action agenda,* ed. Jeffrey Schott, 3–24. Washington, D.C.: Institute for International Economics.

Schuler, Kurt. 1999. *Basics of dollarization.* Joint Economic Committee Staff Report, U.S. Congress. January (updated January 2000).

Schultz, George, William Simon, and Walter Wriston. 1998. Who needs the IMF? In *The International Monetary Fund: Financial Medic to the World?* ed. Lawrence McQuillan and Peter Montgomery, 197–200. Stanford, Calif.: Hoover Press. First published in *Wall Street Journal,* 3 February 1998.

Schwartz, Anna. 1998. Time to terminate the ESF and the IMF. *Cato Institute Foreign Policy Briefing,* no. 48, August, Washington, D.C.: Cato Institute.

Soros, George. 1998. *The crisis of global capitalism.* New York: Public Affairs Press.

Subramanian, Arvind. 1999. Intellectual property rights. Proceedings from Conference on Developing Countries and the New Round of Multilateral Trade Negotiations. 5–6 November, Harvard University.

Summers, Lawrence. 1999. The right kind of IMF for a stable global financial system. Paper presented to the London School of Business. 13 December. Available at [http://www.ustreas.gov/press/releases/ps294.htm].

———. 2000. International financial crises: Causes, prevention, and cures. *American Economic Review* 90 (May): 1–16.

U.S. Treasury. 2000. Response to the report of the International Financial Institution Advisory Commission. Washington, D.C.: United States Treasury Department, June.

Waldman, Michael. 2000. *POTUS speaks.* New York: Simon and Schuster.

Wang, Zhen Kun, and L. Alan Winters. 2000. Putting "Humpty" together again: Including developing countries in a consensus for the WTO. CEPR Policy Paper no. 4. London: Centre for Economic Policy Research.

Woodward, Bob. 2000. *Maestro: Greenspan's Fed and the American boom.* New York: Simon and Schuster.

Zettelmeyer, Jeromin. 2000. Can official crisis lending be counter-productive in the short run? *Economic Notes* 29 (February): 13–29.

2. Mervyn King

I am delighted to have this opportunity to comment on what can be done to reduce the risk of financial and currency crises and how to resolve those crises when they do occur. At the outset, I want to say that the large financial packages made available by the IMF in recent years cannot continue. They undermine the incentives of lenders to assess risks.

In addition, there is little political support among the major contributors to act as an effective lender of last resort. If you look at what countries have actually done—if you look at the attitude of the U.S. Congress and of the Group of Seven (G7)—there is no serious willingness to continue to put up large amounts of money on the scale of the packages seen in the late 1990s. Since there are de facto limits on official finance, we need a mechanism to enable countries to reschedule their sovereign debt payments where they are unwilling or unable to meet their liabilities, just as we have bankruptcy arrangements in domestic credit markets. We need a timeout mechanism of some kind to enable debtor countries to discuss a rescheduling—which may well involve no reduction in the present value of payments with their creditors.

First, however, I would like to discuss measures to prevent crises. Progress has been made in this area. There are, perhaps, six lessons for emerging markets from recent experience. The first is the desirability of policies that make equity investment more attractive, rather than a reliance on short-term debt finance. It is debt finance that creates the risk of financial crises.

The second is the need for self-insurance. One of the lessons that I think countries have learned is that if there is no international lender of last resort, then they must create their own by building up very large foreign exchange reserves. China now has over $160 billion of reserves; Korea has increased its reserves from $7 billion to over $90 billion. Now, there may be moral hazard involved, as was suggested this morning, in the existence of those reserves, but I still think you cannot blame countries for creating those reserves, given the cost to them of having to deal with rapid, short-term reversals of capital flows. At the multilateral level, we have put in place the International Monetary Fund (IMF) contingent credit line.

The third lesson is to monitor and manage the national balance sheet. This is perhaps the single most important analytical lesson of recent crises. It might be possible to devise some simple guidelines, such as ensuring that foreign exchange reserves are sufficient to meet liabilities over at least a one-year horizon. To eliminate the incentives to short-term capital flows requires not only measures in emerging markets but also measures in developed countries. Our own banking systems, and the implicit support we give to them, have created incentives for capital outflows to take the form of short-term debt finance.

Fourth, I think transparency is extremely important. A massive amount of work has in fact been done, and I think we should congratulate the IMF on progress in the difficult, and somewhat less glamorous, task of converting the agreements on transparency into practice. There are now some sixty-six standards and codes that have been developed, and these are being monitored. I do think, however, that there is one key point that is in danger of getting lost, namely, that transparency itself should not be compulsory. There should be no attempt to tell emerging markets that they should or should not follow a particular code. What is crucial, however, is that everyone should know whether or not a country is following a particular code. Therefore there should be transparency about transparency. That is the real role of the reports on standards and codes, the so-called ROSCs, which are now being implemented by the IMF. The heart of the surveillance process feeding into Article IV assessments would be these ROSCs and information about the degree of transparency about transparency.

Fifth, painful lessons have been learned in the area of relations with creditors. I think collective action clauses have a role to play, but the key is for debtor countries to work actively on their relations with creditors.

Finally, avoid fixed but adjustable exchange rate pegs. Many of these lessons are obvious, but they were ignored in recent years. Now they are widely accepted.

Where we have made much less progress is in crisis resolution. The two key principles here are the following. First, there are limits to official finance. There is no international lender of last resort. The choice is between either an orderly or disorderly process to reschedule payments. We need to think about this in advance and create some presumptions about an orderly process. Second, we need to give the private sector more clarity about exactly how the international community thinks about the principles that will guide it in dealing with crises.

Until the recent Fund annual meetings in Prague, there was a danger that this issue would not be addressed. If I may quote from the paper by Frankel and Roubini, they say, "the basic tension between the desire to limit official finance and the goal of having constructive and voluntary forms of PSI [private-sector involvement] has not been fully resolved in official doctrine and practice," and then in a footnote they say, "there is still a lot of room for fleshing out the G7 views on liquidity and systemic cases." How right they are. And I think until recently one could view official responses as lying on a spectrum between two extreme cases. One was to say that policy should be ad hoc, with each country treated on a purely case-by-case basis. The other was to say that we must have private-sector involvement and when asked to define private-sector involvement to respond by repeating the mantra over and over again. Following Prague, the G7 is now committed to discussing more fully what it means by private-sector involvement and to providing greater clarity to the private sector. These are significant steps forward.

What is needed is a regime of "constrained discretion," to use the phrase that has been applied to monetary policy. The question in coming months is how we are going to make this operational.

We will need to define more carefully what are the ex ante criteria for exceptional lending. Exceptional lending should not be frequent. There ought to be presumptions about the scale of IMF facilities. One useful idea might be to ask the new Independent Evaluation Office of the Fund to conduct an ex post audit in all cases of exceptional lending.

Second, we will need to spell out more clearly the nature of any timeout mechanism, including, if necessary, standstills. This is discussed in a very good paragraph of the Frankel-Roubini paper. I commend it to you; I won't go through those arguments, but they do suggest that any solution is likely to involve both the IMF and the private sector. We will need to give a clearer idea to the private sector about the scale of facilities that they should expect the Fund to provide to countries in difficulty. This is not a new issue. In the discussion leading up to the Bretton Woods meetings, a British representative wrote to the War Cabinet in February 1944, "in the course of discussion, the American representatives were persuaded of giving member countries as much certainty as possible about what they had to expect from the new institution and about the amount of facilities which would be at their full disposal." I also found very helpful a quotation from the briefing pack that the U.S. Treasury produced in 1944 after Bretton Woods. On page 83 of that document appears the statement, "it would be quite erroneous to assume that in the absence of the Fund, countries could permit uncontrolled capital outflow of any character at all times." So these issues were ones that people were aware of, but on which, until recently, discussion had lapsed.

Finally, on the governance of the international financial system, some have been tempted to ask, "do we need a new Bretton Woods?" The answer is clearly "no." As one of the U.K. representatives to Bretton Woods wrote, "the conference has become a madhouse. The most complete confusion now prevails." Moreover, in the Bank of England files, I found the most extraordinary report from a representative of the Bank of England to one of my predecessors. He wrote, "It has been an interesting experience to get onto friendly terms with the American press, but I think I've been reasonably successful. It has meant quite a considerable amount of hard drinking. Some little time ago a Miss Sylvia Porter wrote a number of scurrilous little articles about the BIS [Bank for International Settlements] and the governor of the Bank of England, and to my surprise I found that she was here as a representative of the *New York Evening Post*. I thought it my duty to make much of her, and succeeded fairly well, when I got a note from the *New York Times* man saying that she is known as Sylvia Hotpants." Naturally, the Bank of England official exercised constrained discretion. And that is surely the way to go. We need a framework of presumptive limits on IMF facilities that would provide greater clarity to debtors and creditors alike and make clear that debtors will need to negotiate with their creditors rather than asking for a bailout from the IMF. I am pleased that the IMF is committed to making progress on this subject.

3. Robert Rubin

What I would like to do is express a few views on a variety of subjects. I'm going to be much less organized than Mervyn King was and cover perhaps some broader ground in a much less systematic fashion. Let me also say that these are my views, and now that I'm finally out of the U.S. Treasury, I'm free to say what I want to say, and nobody should feel that people from the treasury identify with any of my views. Let me start by saying that this whole issue of crisis response, crisis management, and crisis prevention is enormously complicated. I read this whole paper, by the way, all 100 pages, and I thought it was very interesting; I thought in many ways it captured the debate and discussion we had at the treasury during the time that I was there. But it did strike me as I was reading it that however one may conceptualize about these issues, the fact is that when you are actually involved in having to deal with them, the reality is rather messy, and a lot of the conceptual constructs that one might think about from a greater remove lose a lot of their value once you actually have to deal with real situations.

In terms of crisis prevention, although clearly all these crises were a function of many factors within the developing countries, my own view—and I don't think this was a view widely shared at the treasury when I was there—was that they were at least equally due to excesses in capital flows from industrial-country financial institutions, whether as interbank lending or as investment. Moreover, having spent twenty-six years running trading operations, I think that there is an inherent tendency in markets to go to excess when times are good, that people reach for yield, and that there's an underweighting of risk and overestimation of the positive. I think there is an inherent tendency in markets to produce crisis, and when one focuses on what one does about crisis prevention, I at least would start from the question of whether there is any way to induce greater discipline and greater rigor on the part of those who provide interbank credit and those who invest in developing countries. I remember when the Korean crisis first became serious, calling people at a couple of the banks that had been extending credit to Korea, and it was absolutely astounding to me how little they knew about the country to which they had extended credit. I thought about that a little bit, and it reminded me of a lot of the experience I'd had when I was still on Wall Street. When times are good, people reach, and when they reach, sooner or later it leads to excesses, and excesses sooner or later lead to trouble. Transparency is useful, and, trying to put in place the kinds of things that I know we were talking about at the time I left the treasury and I gather have advanced since then is useful. To increase transparency in developing countries is very helpful, but if it's not used with discipline and rigor, it's not going to have the effect that is sought. Therefore, I think it would be exceedingly useful to try to think of ways to induce greater discipline and rigor on the part of those who extend credit and the part of those who invest. I believe in capital requirements for banks and I believe in margin requirement for investors, because I think they have at least some effect in terms of inducing people to focus on risk. I think we need to go far further, although I have no concrete suggestions to make, and it is a subject I've thought about. The process of trying to find devices that you think would actually induce greater rigor is, I think, a very difficult one. One of them is obviously greater disclosure on the part of the banks that extend credit and the investment institutions that invest. However, in the financial markets in the United States we have pretty highly developed disclosure on the part of banks and investors and all the rest; nevertheless, we have recurring crises that come either out of the banking system or out of overreaction to markets.

All of which suggests to me that it is very important to try to find further measures with respect to inducing discipline, but it's going to be very difficult to find them. The other thing I think we need to do is limit leverage, because I don't think we will ever find ways of inducing discipline and rigor that are anything even remotely close to a perfect system, so the answer to that is to limit leverage.

Let me go to a second subject: the question of private-sector involvement versus official-sector involvement versus reform. I thought the paper captured very well the kinds of debates that we used to have at the treasury and at the Federal Reserve. My own conclusion is roughly the conclusion of the paper, which is that some rough balance among them, on a case-by-case basis, is probably about the right place to be. I also think, as I said a moment ago, that people have conceptual models of all kinds, but once you get into the messy reality of dealing with actual crises, I think they lose most of their value. We used to have debates sometimes over whether something was an insolvency situation or liquidity problem. My personal view, although I don't think this was shared by everybody at the treasury, is that those two terms are approximately useless. I don't mean they're useless if you want to have interesting discussions; I just mean they're useless when you actually have to do something.

I think basically what you have is countries that are in trouble. Every country has all kinds of problems, including the United States. I remember a treasury official once saying that Brazil looked wonderful at one point, and then once it started to have problems, we all started to say, gee, there were a lot of problems. And there are plenty of problems in the United States. If we had a crisis tomorrow, people would say to us, look at their current account, personal saving rate, and a whole bunch of other things. So I think that basically what you've got to do is make a practical judgment in each case, on a case-by-case basis. And I don't agree that providing more certainty to the private sector is a step forward. I actually think it is a step backward. I think that in each one of these situations you're dealing with a very difficult question of how to restore confidence in the short run in order to stem a crisis, and confidence is obviously a psychological factor, and the psychology of markets is a messy, difficult, judgmental kind of matter. I think there are lessons we can learn that can help us think about the future, but I do think as a general matter you've got to make a practical judgment given the circumstances in each particular case.

I do believe very strongly that there should be some kind of presumption in favor of significant private-sector involvement because I think moral hazard is a very real issue. I remember during the Russian crisis when people were buying bonds at 50 and 60 and 70 percent yields, and I called a friend of mine at Wall Street and asked what people were doing. He said, well, everybody figures the International Monetary Fund (IMF) will bail them out because they've got 7000, 12,000, or whatever it was nuclear warheads, and I think it's the way people think—it's the way I would think, and I think that the answer to that is to make sure that people, based on their past experience, have an expectation that if there's trouble, they're going to have to pay part of the price.

Securitization obviously creates a whole set of new issues. Exchange offers have worked to a certain extent, or maybe even reasonably well, but my instinct is that the kinds of exchange offers that are available without a cram-down provision are not in fact the answer to this, and so I think we have a long way to go before we find an effective way of dealing with securitized debt.

Estimating the financing gap is another difficult issue. Some parts of it are pretty obvious. You can look at outstanding interbank credit or at debt outstanding, but there are other parts of it that are not so obvious: for example, how do you determine the potential for capital flight? So I think, once again, even if you think you've got your arms around the extent of the matter, I think that the answer is that it's very unlikely that you do, unless you're going to put in place capital controls. Therefore, it seems to me that what you've got to focus on, is getting the right mix of reform, official-sector money, and private-sector involvement, so that you can restore confidence, not only externally, but internally.

In terms of the structure of IMF programs themselves, my own view is that the IMF did an extraordinarily good job in the face of an extraordinarily difficult situation. The conditions in some respects were unprecedented; matters had to be decided very quickly, and you were dealing with the very complicated question of the psychology of markets.

I at least think that the IMF got it about right. It's very easy with hindsight, and if you don't have responsibility for the decisions in the face of collapsing economies, to be a critic of what was done. As I say, however, my instinct and judgment are that what was done was about the right balance. I'm not saying there shouldn't have been a little less fiscal policy in some cases; maybe in some cases there was a little too much structural reform, or maybe there wasn't, but I think that basically the judgments the IMF and the international community made were about right, and I think the proof is in the pudding, because I think in late December of 1997 and in the fall of 1998, we came very, very close to falling off a cliff in the global economy. It didn't happen, and I think it didn't happen because of what was done. Similarly, the countries that actually took ownership of reform, seemed to take ownership of reform, or at least were able to persuade people they had taken ownership of reform were able to reestablish confidence and, for the most part, to come back reasonably well, although there are certainly problems again in some of these countries.

On the question of whether or not structural reform should be part of a reform package, I guess you could make either argument on that in a conceptual, theoretical sense. But I think, as a practical matter, if structural issues are seen as having been part of what caused the problem in the first place, you're not going to reestablish confidence unless you address structural matters. My own view is that you could not have reestablished confidence in the international financial markets in Indonesia without doing something that gave people the feeling that you were addressing the issue of corruption, even though it was unlikely that whatever you were going to do was going to be more than moderately successful. Similarly, in almost all these situations, I don't think you would have been successful in reestablishing confidence unless the international capital markets felt that you were doing something to address structural issues. Now, as to where you draw that line, I don't have an answer. But I think, once again, it comes back to something I said in a slightly different context a moment ago, that *ex ante* rules are for the most part not an effective way of trying to deal with these kinds of problems. I think what you need to do in each individual situation is to make a practical judgment as to what is necessary to reestablish confidence.

What I'm about to say, I suspect, has a certain awkwardness about it. It seems to me, at least, having lived through several of these, that when crisis develops, and particularly in the world where all markets are interrelated so closely, that decisions made in each of the markets are almost instantaneously affected by what happens in other markets, that the following is so: Number one, crisis response has to be very quick. Number two, there is no assurance that any crisis response is going to work. That is to say, it's risky. Number three, politicians are risk-averse. If you accept those premises, and I think they're right, then it seems to me that this is almost surely only going to work if you have very strong leadership from the IMF, and I happen to think, as I said a moment ago, that the IMF under Camdessus, did a good job. I think you need a strong IMF, I think you need a strong leader who's willing to make gutsy decisions in full recognition that he may be criticized, and I think that you need a very small number of other countries that will be part of the process of dealing with these decisions. And I think the model we had over these last few years, of a group of G7 nations, with the United States having a particularly heavy involvement, is probably about right. You could choose a different group of nations if you want, but I think that kind of a structure is about right, because I think that as you start to get a larger number of countries and they start to debate with each other, you will not be able to move with the speed that you need to move with if you're going to deal with crisis. And the key industrial nations need to be at the core. Second, I think it has to be sheltered from a political system, because I don't think politicians for the most part are willing to take on the risks that are involved in these matters.

Another matter is industrial country macroeconomic and structural policies. One of the striking things about the Asian financial crisis was how concerned all of us were—at least, it was striking to me at the time—about whether anything would work in Asia as long as Japan was in an economic malaise. In the 1980s, as you all know better than I in many ways, the rest of the world was enormously critical of American economic policies, because of our fiscal situation and our trade imbalances. So the world is enormously affected by what happens in the major national economies or, in the case of Europe, perhaps, some collection of countries. But economic policy remains a sovereign matter. In the 1980s nobody could affect what the United States did, despite whatever damage we might be doing to the world, and in 1997–98, we were desperately concerned that if Japan didn't get back on track, it wouldn't be possible to reestablish confidence; nor would we have the import demand necessary to pull Asia out of this thing. There was no way to influence Japanese economic policy. I have no answer to that, except to say that this issue of the effect of the policies of the respective industrial countries on the rest of the world will probably become greater and greater as interdependence becomes greater and greater.

If you want to get a sense of how impossible the IMF's job is, just look at the paper's list of fifteen or so of the criticisms that were made of the IMF, and on each topic you can see they were criticized from diametrically opposed positions. At any event, I think there is also a tendency in these kinds of situations to come up with all kinds of ideas that are either dangerous or impractical or both. Because some of the people in this room were the sponsors of some of those ideas, I won't get into the specifics, but simply say that I do think one has to approach all suggested approaches with rigor, discipline, and a keen sensitivity to the messiness of what actually happens in these situations as opposed to what sounds attractive in some conceptual sense.

Let me conclude by saying that in my view, at least, crisis prevention is never going to be even close to perfect, but I think it can be better. I've suggested, at least in the jurisdiction of this panel, what I think should be the single most important focus of trying to make it better, although I think there are also a lot of things you could do in developing country policy as well. I also think it is inevitable that there will be future crises and I think it is possible that as we have them they will become more and more severe, because of the increases in capital flows, the increases in the speed of capital flows, the tendency of capital flows to go to larger and larger numbers of countries, with lower and lower credit quality, and also the vast increases in outstanding derivatives. And I think derivatives are an issue in the global economy that nobody's had to face yet because we haven't had a derivative-caused or substantially exacerbated crisis, but in my opinion it is likely that, sooner or later, we will have one.

With respect to crisis response, my own instinct, because I have lived through all this, is that the way these things were handled—on a case-by-case basis, and with the kinds of programs we had and the kind of mix of private-sector involvement, official-sector involvement, and reform—may be about as good as we're going to do, although it's certainly very, very important to keep looking for better ways. I also have an instinct, as I mentioned a moment ago, that we do not have effective ways of dealing with securitized debt obligations, and I think the kinds of exchange offers that have been used in the last two years (although to some extent I suppose they can be said to have worked) are unlikely to be an adequately effective mechanism, going forward. I guess the only other comment I would make is that I think there's probably more we can do on the prevention side; I'm sort of skeptical that there's a lot we can do on the response side, but I do think, as I said a moment ago, that we will almost surely have periodic crises and that they may well—on average, at least—tend to increase in severity. So I think it's enormously important that we not get complacent during good times but continue to focus on both prevention and response. Thank you.

4. George Soros

I should like to address some of the issues that were not addressed here today. The discussion of the international financial system has been framed in terms of the last crisis. The issues that have been addressed have been those that were raised by the last crisis: What went wrong? What can we do to prevent an occurrence of that crisis? In that context we have considered the behavior of the lenders, the behavior of the borrowing countries, and especially the behavior of the international financial institutions. Several reforms were introduced that are actually quite far-reaching, and they will be quite sufficient in my opinion to prevent a recurrence of the kind of crisis we had in 1997 and 1998. I believe the landscape has changed more radically than is generally recognized. The moral hazard inherent in International Monetary Fund (IMF) bailouts has been effectively eliminated because the private sector has suffered severe losses in countries like Indonesia and Russia. Even more importantly, it has been made very, very clear that bailouts are no longer politically acceptable. Instead of bailing out, we are now speaking of bailing in—and that means a shift of 180 degrees.

As a result of these changes, the power and influence of the IMF have been severely impaired. The emperor has no clothes as far as the markets are concerned. Because of that, the risks of investing in emerging markets have greatly increased, and the potential rewards have also diminished. The last crisis was caused by the excessive flow of capital to emerging markets. The next threat, as I see it, comes from the opposite direction—from the lack of adequate flows of capital to the capital-deficient countries at the periphery of the global capitalist system. The situation is reminiscent of the French construction of the Maginot Line after the First World War to prepare themselves for static trench warfare; but in the Second World War they were confronted by mobile warfare with tanks.

I am not so much making a prediction as I am making an observation, because the signs of inadequate capital flows are already visible. They do not show up in the published statistics about international capital movements, but they do show up in the persistent current account deficit of the United States. They are probably covered up by the large figure for errors and omissions. Since the United States has a negative saving rate, the deficit must be financed by the saving of foreigners. The international financial markets suck up the saving of the periphery countries into the center, but since the last crisis the financial markets no longer push out enough capital to the emerging markets. We can see this in the greatly widened margins that periphery countries have to pay for their borrowings and in the inferior performance of their stock markets. The emerging markets never recovered their losses from the last crisis, and they have turned down much before Wall Street. We can also see it in the substandard economic performance of periphery countries. I am thinking of countries like Bulgaria—a small country that few people pay attention to. They have actually done all the things that needed to be done, but there is no growth and people are discouraged. There is a danger that the government, which has been as good a reform government as any in the former Soviet Empire, will be rejected by the electorate at the next elections. Or take a country like South Africa, which, again, has had a really good government in terms of macroeconomic policy. Again, there is no growth, and you may well see a weakening of political will there. Countries like these could grow faster if they could attract investment, but the inflow of capital is missing. The situation is likely to get worse if and when there is an economic decline at the center. I think that the prospects of a hard landing in the United States have greatly increased in the last couple of months, so we shall see. It was quite unusual to have a crisis in the emerging markets that was not touched off by an adverse economic development at the center. If we now have such an adverse development, I believe it will aggravate the situation at the periphery. It will not necessarily manifest itself in the form of a crash, because a crash has already occurred. It is more likely to register as a depression, which could have negative political implications. So I think what is missing in our deliberations is an examination of the deficiencies of the global financial markets themselves.

The prevailing trend is to place ever greater reliance on market discipline. However, financial markets are inherently unstable, and global financial markets suffer from an additional element of instability from which the financial systems of developed countries are largely exempt. In the course of their development individual countries have learned to deal with the instability of their financial markets: they have established regulatory authorities and lenders of last resort. But the global financial system does not have a lender of last resort, and the prevailing regulatory environment is much more permissive than used to be the case before markets became globalized. Moreover, it is generally agreed that this is as it should be. The consensus among regulators is that markets are much better at regulating themselves than they themselves are at regulating markets. That is what they mean by imposing market discipline. Practically everybody is in favor of imposing market discipline. I feel very much like a lone voice in arguing that market discipline is not enough. I contend that greater reliance on market discipline will reveal certain deficiencies in the international financial system that are not currently recognized.

To understand these deficiencies, we must reexamine the prevailing paradigm that holds that financial markets have a built-in tendency toward equilibrium. This may be true of fish markets, but it is not true of financial markets because financial markets do not deal with known or knowable quantities: they are trying to discount a future that is contingent on how it is discounted at present. Financial markets are not just passively reflecting the so-called fundamentals; they are also actively creating them. Instead of rational expectations, market participants are confronted with a situation of radical uncertainty, in which their decisions shape the course of events. I have been told that modern economic theory has recognized this uncertainty in the form of multiple equilibria, but I am not convinced. In my view, financial markets do not necessarily tend toward equilibrium, and it is up to the financial authorities to preserve the stability of financial markets.

We have learned this lesson the hard way. Central banking and financial-market regulation have developed in response to financial crises, but under the influence of the prevailing paradigm, which I call market fundamentalism, we seem to have forgotten this hard-learned lesson. In the past, financial crises have usually led to a strengthening of our financial institutions. After the recent crisis, the tendency has been in the opposite direction: to downsize and reduce the influence of our international financial institutions. This can be seen in the reforms already undertaken and even more in the Meltzer Report, which is the only really incisive and coherent critique of the present situation and is likely to be very influential. The systemic breakdown that occurred in the 1997–99 crisis is attributed not to the inherent instability of international financial markets but to the moral hazard introduced by the IMF-led rescue programs. "Eliminate the moral hazard" became the battle cry of the market fundamentalists.

As I said earlier, the 180-degree turn that has occurred since the inception of the last crisis will be sufficient to eliminate the moral hazard. I also believe that this is basically a desirable development because the brunt of past IMF rescue programs had to be borne by the debtor countries. However, the correction of the moral hazard problem is revealing another problem that was hitherto obscured, and that is the built-in disparity in the position of the center and the periphery of the global financial system. I call this the problem of the uneven playing field.

The playing field is uneven not only because the center consists of well-developed economies and the periphery is less developed; the center is rich and the periphery is poor; the center is the provider of capital and the periphery is deficient in capital. Even more important is the fact that the center is in charge of managing the system. Make no mistake about it: the system needs to be managed. We have wonderful, well-functioning markets because they have been well-managed. And the management is in the hands of the Group of Seven (G7), of which the United States is by far the most influential member. The IMF is very much dominated by the G7. The system is managed with the interests of the center in mind. When those interests are truly in danger, we do have the means to preserve the system. We have lenders of last resort, we have regulatory authorities, and we have managers of monetary policy. This was clearly demonstrated in October 1998 when the default of Russia threatened to disrupt the international financial markets, and all the proper actions were taken to prevent the crisis from affecting us. Reducing interest rates and bailing out Long-Term Capital Management were the key measures, and they worked. We do not have similar institutional arrangements for intervening in the case of periphery countries—even if they threaten the stability of the international financial system—because the aim of the intervention is to preserve the stability of the system, not the stability of the country in trouble. As I mentioned before, the brunt of the IMF rescue operations has had to be borne by the countries that were being rescued.

The situation will not be corrected by replacing bailouts with bail-ins because the private sector is not a charitable institution, and if it is subjected to burden sharing, it is going to charge for it. That is why the next problem will be an inadequate supply of capital to the periphery countries. The reforms that have been introduced and the changes that have occurred have increased the risks of investing in those countries and diminished the rewards. With open capital markets, the periphery countries are not in charge of their own destiny. This puts them at an inherent disadvantage with regard to the center. For instance, if the center is threatened by recession it can lower interest rates or it can stimulate the economy by fiscal measures. But a periphery country cannot afford such luxuries. It must tighten its budget and raise interest rates in order to prevent the flight of capital. Thus, the insistence on market discipline and the elimination of moral hazard renders the playing field even more uneven than it was before.

To demonstrate how important who is in charge of the system is, I should like to invoke the case of the European Exchange Rate Mechanism (ERM). The member countries did not differ much in wealth or institutional development, but the exchange rate system was in charge of the Bundesbank. After the reunification of Germany, the role of the Bundesbank as the protector of domestic monetary stability and its role as the trendsetter of European monetary policy came into conflict. The domestic considerations took precedence, as they had to, and the ERM collapsed.

I do not think that it is possible to create a level playing field, just as it is not possible to eliminate the moral hazard associated with lenders of last resort. The United States and the G7 are not going to abdicate their power and responsibility, and it would be unrealistic to expect the Federal Reserve to give precedence to the needs of other countries over domestic consider-ations. However, it is not unrealistic to insist that we should take some steps to make the playing field less uneven. It can be justified on both moral and prudential grounds. If those who are in charge cannot bring some benefits to all the members who belong to the system, then the system cannot be considered just, nor is it likely to endure.

So what could be done to make the playing field somewhat more even? I'd like to introduce two very general concepts that are currently not part of the discourse. One is to provide some economic incentives for the countries at the periphery that follow sound economic policies. Because we have a sys-tem that combines a global economy with the sovereignty of state, you can't interfere with the internal affairs of a sovereign state through punitive mea-sures. You can do it only by offering incentives that they may voluntarily ac-cept. If you did that, you could help to overcome many of the internal, po-litical, and economic deficiencies that prevail in those countries. Going into the 1997–99 crisis, the IMF had practically no power to intervene until a cri-sis had actually occurred and a country had turned to the IMF for assis-tance. It is only by offering incentives that the IMF could play an active role in crisis prevention. This point has been recognized with the introduction of the Contingent Credit Line, but the emphasis on market discipline has militated against any concessions, and the Contingent Credit Line as it is currently constituted has had no takers. We need more elaborate arrange-ments according to which the kind of assistance that the IMF is willing to provide will vary according to the policies followed and the standards achieved by individual countries.

Second, an even more unacceptable idea is some kind of international wealth redistribution. We have a global economy, we need a global society and within a society there has to be some measure of social justice. At pres-ent, each country is supposed to pursue its own idea of social justice. But the development of global financial markets that allows capital to move around freely has impaired the capacity of individual countries to pursue their idea of social justice, because if they try to tax or regulate capital it will move elsewhere. This development has helped wealth creation but it has hindered the pursuit of social justice. Insofar as there is a need for social welfare, it can no longer be pursued on a national basis. Those who have persisted in their ideas of social justice as it could be practiced before the freedom of capital movements became universal have seen those policies fail in the new environment. That does not mean that the issues of social jus-tice and wealth redistribution are no longer relevant. It only means that they cannot be pursued on a purely national basis. Actually, countries at the center have a much greater degree of discretion in the matter than countries at the periphery. Even so, their discretion is limited. But wealth redistribu-tion on an international scale is simply not on the agenda. The only excep-tion is the proposal to provide debt relief to the highly indebted underdeveloped countries. The idea has received widespread support—it is even endorsed by the Meltzer Commission—but it amounts to charity, not a recognition of the problem of an uneven playing field, and it doesn't really address the problems of these countries.

I have some ideas on how these two very general concepts could be introduced into the international financial architecture, but I do not have the time to elaborate them. Nor do I have time to discuss the vexed question of exchange rates. The point I want to make is that the current discussion is too narrow and based on the wrong premise. The most far-reaching and incisive criticism of the international financial institutions comes from the Meltzer Report, which is a document imbued with market fundamentalism, although it is tempered by a dose of charity toward the highly indebted poor countries. There is an urgent need for a similarly comprehensive assessment based on the recognition that financial markets are inherently unstable and not designed to take care of social needs. We need institutions to serve those needs, and one of the primary needs is to curb the excesses of financial markets.

Discussion Summary

Jacob Frenkel remarked that it isn't possible to prevent all crises. Indeed, the expectation of future crises—some of which we will be familiar with and some of which we won't—is a logical corollary of the creativity of markets. The proper perspective to adopt is that of risk management rather than risk avoidance. As a practical matter, this means that we should focus on eliminating distortions in the pricing of risk, thereby moving away from volatility suppression and toward volatility reduction. Returning to the issue of desirable exchange rate regimes, he emphasized that as a rule speculative attacks on currencies came when governments tried to peg the exchange rate. In current conditions it is wrong to think of international reserves as the mechanism for self-insuring against a crisis. "[I]n the new world, the self-insurance mechanism is the development of financial markets that create the instruments to enable you to deal with [exchange rate] changes, and these markets will not develop if you insist on pegging the exchange rate," he said. On the issue of transparency, he said that "transparency about transparency"—that is, making it clear which countries publish information about the condition of the financial system—is one of the ways to encourage the development of self-insuring mechanisms.

Domingo F. Cavallo sought to clarify his statement from the session on exchange rate regimes, fearing that it was being misinterpreted. He said, "The currency system of Argentina is perfectly sustainable," and he pointed to the size of reserves, the ability of nationals to make deposits in foreign currencies, and the ability of banks to lend in foreign currencies as important elements in this sustainability. He went on, however, to say that we can't be sure that the current system is the final version. If Mexico had adopted the Argentine or Hong Kong system, he said, they would be converging to some kind of monetary association with the United States. He is not so sure that the Argentine system is converging to a monetary association, given that the euro and the yen are moving so much against the dollar. With Argentina's trade so diversified, at some time, possibly more than twenty years into the future, and when the Argentine exchange rate appreciates rather than depreciating, the country will move from a super-fixed to a floating regime, he said.

Regarding the problems being experienced by the Argentine economy, he said that they are not problems of overvaluation. Exports are actually growing faster than GDP. Rather, the problems are the result of destructive tax increases that have been closing off investment opportunities. This, he concluded, is not a situation you can come out of by devaluing the currency.

Andrew Crockett disagreed with Robert Rubin's pessimistic assessment that crises are inevitable and will probably become more common, finding it "profoundly gloomy in some respects." As interpreted by Crockett, Rubin's view is that this cycle of crises is inevitable because of the way markets "reach for yield and have excesses." He believes that one of the reasons for this reaching for yield is the way risk management is undertaken by institutions and reinforced by supervisors. The current practice assumes that risk falls in a boom and rises in a recession. However, it is more accurate to say that underlying risk rises in a boom and "crystallizes" in a recession. If risk management models could be made to reflect this, Crockett thought we might be able to break the trend of ever worsening crises.

Michael P. Dooley warned that he was going to be even gloomier. He said the discussion thus far had been based on the assumption that the real costs of crises come from the panic-induced breakdown of financial intermediation. He thinks that investors are smarter than that. Investors design contracts so that if they are not paid the renegotiation of the contract interferes with financial intermediation in the country. This, in turn, leads to output loss. This cost is what leads people to repay international debt, and so it is an important part of the system. If this interpretation is correct, Dooley said, involving the private sector is going to be much more difficult than suggested in models where its simply panic or bad luck that is driving the outcomes. Unless there is an alternative "enforcement mechanism," and he does not see what this might be, the threat of output loss is the one thing that makes international debt possible in the first place.

Dooley added that the ones to pay the price in the country are not the ones who have made the decisions. Residents of debtor countries suffer the loss in output while private debtors and creditors are bailed out. Referring to Richard Cooper's famous 1971 paper on devaluation, *Sebastian Edwards* interjected that the evidence is that government officials do pay the price. In the vast majority of crisis episodes Cooper studied, the finance minister or central bank governor was either fired or imprisoned, or maybe even executed. *Stanley Fischer* offered another calculation: of the six big recent crises the IMF has dealt with—Mexico, the three Asian cases, Russia, and Brazil—only two out of the twelve finance ministers and Central Bank governors involved survived in office following the crisis.

Edwards asked what mechanisms for preclassifying countries for preferential access to funds in times of crisis make sense. Based on the thinking of the Meltzer commission, he identified (without necessarily supporting) five: fiscal solvency, bank strength and supervision, participation of foreign banks, transparency, and avoiding pegged exchange rates.

Fischer responded to George Soros's call to reward countries with good policies in some way. He said that the recent changes to the IMF's Contingent Credit Line (CCL) bring it closer to what Soros suggests. However, Fischer thinks that standards and other reforms will only be effective if they affect spreads in the markets, and it is an open question how best to persuade market players to pay attention.

Arminio Fraga said that in designing any new facilities it has to be kept in mind that markets do not like discontinuities. It is fine to label countries when things are going well. But what, he asked, will be the response when a downturn comes? He favors something along the line of what Robert Rubin suggested—"some degree of ambiguity while the work is being done." He said this is not like the exchange rate regime debate, in which he supports the idea of extremes. The corner solutions are not practical when it comes to labeling countries. Fraga suggested that trade issues should receive more treatment in the Frankel and Roubini paper. He said the best thing that developed countries could do is to continue to work for global free trade, adding, "they should also practice what they preach."

Morris Goldstein said that Mervyn King had noted "with a tinge of pride" that the IMF now monitors sixty-six standards and codes. Recalling that in 1995 the number was zero, he said that if you want financial market participants to watch what countries are doing, they are not going to be able to watch sixty-six areas. A positive recent development is the decision by the G7 and the IMF to identify twelve as having some priority. It would have been even better, he thinks, if they had chosen six.

Yung Chul Park questioned the assertion in the paper that American capitalism has won and that the Japanese or Asian model has lost. He queried what faults they are referring to in the Japanese-Asian system. Do they mean, he asked, that relationship banking has deteriorated into crony capitalism? But this raises the question of whether the system is inherently defective or has been mismanaged by corrupt governments. He fears that "this game [of picking the superior system] will be played every four years like the

Olympic games." He added that trying to compare the Asian model with the Anglo-Saxon model is not very productive because all the East Asian economies have market-based systems. They do have bank-oriented financial systems, but Park recalled that just a few years ago the academic community recommended this system of developing and emerging market economies. He also complained that the East Asian economies feel that they are being left out of discussions relating to reform of the international financial system. And he noted that there is considerable support among East Asian countries—including China—for the idea of some sort of Asian Monetary Fund.

Nouriel Roubini raised the issue of how more internationally mobile capital and greater derivative-driven leverage have lead to greater systemic risk. We live in a world, he said, where everyone is a mark-to-market investor, there isn't the forbearance that existed in the 1980s, and everyone is using the same value-at-risk models. With everyone acting the same way, Roubini said, we must think about the systemic effects of another liquidity shock. Continuing on the leverage theme, he said it is not obvious that greater leverage is necessarily bad. Overall leverage has contracted along with the hedge funds. But the absence of leverage—or, more importantly, the absence of these market participants—might mean that liquidity is reduced. These and other issues that have a bearing on systemic risk need to receive much more attention, Roubini said.

Jeffrey Sachs said he wanted to come back to what he saw as a shared theme in King's, Rubin's, and Soros's presentations: that incentive problems existed on both sides of the market. Yet in the final analysis, he said, the system is run by (borrowing Soros's term) the core. "This is not an international system; this is a creditor-run system," he complained. The core has a fear that any standstill will break the system. Sachs said that he has always advised countries just to stop paying when they are in a crisis—and to do so unilaterally, without waiting for permission from the U.S. Treasury.

"When that happens," he said, "the crisis eases." Moreover, when we don't allow countries to do it, they often break into pieces, like Yugoslavia did when it was told that it wouldn't get a Paris agreement back in 1990. He added that there is no real lender of last resort in the world, and "there is very little money around." As an example he pointed to Africa, where net transfers are practically zero. U.S. aid to the least developed countries is now about $600 million, or less than six-tenths of 1 percent. Sachs ended by saying that the illusion has been created that there is little risk for the rich countries due to the fact that the imbalanced approach is being followed. But that illusion, and the bubble it may have given rise to, "is going to leave us most vulnerable ourselves."

4

IMF Stabilization Programs

1. Anne O. Krueger
2. Stanley Fischer
3. Jeffrey D. Sachs

1. Anne O. Krueger

IMF Stabilization Programs

The International Monetary Fund (IMF) was established after the Second World War at Bretton Woods (along with the International Bank for Reconstruction and Development, now referred to as the World Bank) as a multilateral institution to coordinate exchange rate arrangements among nations. The immediate concerns of the original IMF architects focused on avoiding the competitive devaluations of the 1930s, while at the same time encouraging liberalization of the world trading system.[1] It was anticipated that there would be a worldwide system of "fixed, but adjustable" exchange rates, with adjustments coming only when there was "fundamental disequilibrium."[2] In normal times, it was thought that there might be temporary financing problems for countries that could maintain their fixed exchange rates with the help of the IMF.

The preeminence of the American economy and the accompanying "dol-

The author is indebted to Jose Antonio Gonzalez, Nicholas Hope, Michael Michaely, T. N. Srinivasan, Jungho Yoo, and participants in the NBER Woodstock conference for helpful comments on the earlier draft of this paper, and to Marco Sorge for research assistance.

1. It was intended that there be an International Trade Organization (ITO) along with the IMF and World Bank. The ITO was to oversee trading arrangements. However, the ITO never came into being; instead of an international organization, the General Agreement on Tariffs and Trade (GATT) came into being by executive degree, and there was no international organization until the World Trade Organization (which incorporated the GATT) in 1995. For a brief history of the founding of the Bretton Woods institutions, see Krueger (1999).

2. The concept of "fundamental disequilibrium" was never well defined. In practice, most IMF stabilization programs have included an exchange rate adjustment.

lar shortage" in the international economy immediately after the Second World War was not anticipated, and there emerged a de facto ("fixed but adjustable") dollar standard, although the dollar itself was pegged to gold. The IMF functioned much as expected in occasional balance-of-payments crises among developed countries, such as the pound devaluations of 1949[3] and 1967 and the German appreciation of 1960. However, most Fund activity was with developing countries even in its initial decades, as the strength and resources of the American economy dwarfed those of the Fund, while the perceived needs for reconstruction support (which came in large part from the Marshall Plan) had been greatly underestimated.

Among the developing countries, balance-of-payments difficulties were sufficiently frequent that the Fund quickly came to be involved in several of these crises annually. During the 1950s and 1960s, the Fund dealt occasionally with developed countries' exchange rate or payments difficulties, but the bulk of its activities consisted of "stabilization programs" for developing countries.[4]

By 1973, the "Bretton Woods" system of fixed, but adjustable, exchange rates was abandoned, and the major developed countries adopted floating exchange rates.[5] With that, IMF stabilization programs became centered almost entirely on individual developing countries. The basic content of these programs remained much the same over the years, and this is discussed first in section 4.1.1. A key feature of the international financial system, as it interacted with these crises and subsequent programs, was that the trigger for a crisis usually took the form of an inability to continue servicing debt voluntarily. Most of that debt was either short-term trade credits or owed to official creditors.

With the 1980s, the first major change in Fund stabilization programs took place. By that time, some of the countries confronting crises had very large volumes of debt, both short and long term, outstanding to private creditors. The Fund's resources were often small relative to the size of outstanding private indebtedness, and it changed the nature of the way in which the Fund could support countries in crisis. Throughout the 1980s, most of these countries still maintained fairly severe and stringent capital controls, and many maintained quantitative restrictions on imports.[6]

---

3. The French, however, undertook an early devaluation and notified the IMF only after they had done so.

4. See Sturc (1968) for a description and analysis of early Fund stabilization programs.

5. Among the industrial countries, Canada had earlier adopted a floating exchange rate, and the United States had cut its tie to gold in 1971.

6. Many African countries were hard-hit by the debt crisis of the 1980s. Longer-term IMF programs (Extended Structural Adjustment Facilities) were established to support them. These programs differed in a number of ways from the programs discussed here, but their assessment would entail consideration of a number of different issues from those relevant to the Asian and other twin crises. At any event, the executive directors of the IMF voted in September 2000 to abolish these longer-term arrangements.

By the 1990s, however, some of the rapidly growing developing countries had greatly liberalized their trade regimes and opened their capital accounts to a considerable extent. In some instances, when crises arose, domestic financial systems were severely affected in ways that will be examined later. This changed both the time frame in which crises could erupt and be addressed and the nature of the impact of crises on the domestic economy.

Although Mexico confronted a balance-of-payments-cum-financial crisis (twin crisis) late in 1994, most observers of the world economy were alerted to these new-style twin crises with the Asian financial crises of 1997–98. The magnitude of the crises and the severity of the impact on the crisis-afflicted countries led many to question the role of the IMF both in failing to anticipate and prevent the difficulties and in overseeing programs intended to address the crisis situations.

The purpose of this paper is to examine the role of the IMF in the 1990s twin crises. Focus is on stabilization aspects of the program: Goldstein (2001) considers the extent to which these programs addressed areas other than those that were aimed at restoring viable financial and balance-of-payments situations, and those issues are not covered here. The starting point is with the more traditional IMF stabilization programs of the 1960s and 1970s. That is the subject of section 4.1.1. In section 4.1.2, the analysis is extended to cover situations in which balance-of-payments crises are accompanied by financial crises. A third section then considers the sorts of programs that must be developed when the financial and exchange rate crises occur simultaneously.

On the basis of that analysis, two of the IMF programs effected in the Asian crisis—Korea's and Indonesia's—will be examined in section 4.1.4. Section 4.1.5 then draws on the experience under these programs and contrasts them with the behavior of some other crisis countries and countries not subject to crisis.

4.1.1 Traditional Stabilization Programs

Consider a small open economy, initially in equilibrium at a fixed exchange rate, that experiences domestic inflation at a rate more rapid than is occurring in the rest of the world. As the demand for foreign goods grows more rapidly than the supply of foreign exchange,[7] there are several policy options. There is excess demand for foreign goods, so that the country initially incurs a current account deficit not offset by long-term capital in-

---

7. It is possible, of course, that favorable shifts in the terms of trade could offset the appreciation of the real exchange rate. However, this would be coincidence, and it is assumed here that there is no such offset. Without domestic inflation, the same excess demand for foreign exchange is likely to diminish as the demand for foreign exchange increases with an appreciating real exchange rate, because domestic demand for relatively cheaper exportables rises while the profitability of producing them falls.

flows.[8] In that event, the current account deficit can be financed in the short run by running down foreign exchange reserves or by borrowing from abroad. However, unless something else (such as the rate of inflation) changes, the deficit is unsustainable and some form of adjustment will be forced.

There are two alternatives if a fixed nominal exchange rate is to be maintained. A first is to let domestic monetary and fiscal policy be sufficiently deflationary so that domestic prices fall relative to those in the rest of the world (or fail to rise as rapidly as prices are rising in the rest of the world) or domestic incomes fall (and hence the domestic demand for foreign goods shifts downward while the domestic supply of exportables increases). The second alternative is to impose exchange controls, rationing the available foreign exchange through quantitative means across various demanders, and attempting to restrict foreign exchange usage to the available supply of foreign exchange. This can be achieved, at least to some degree, although over time private agents discover a number of ways in which to evade the regime.[9]

In the 1950s and 1960s, many developing countries chose to use quantitative restrictions (QRs) to keep their current account deficits from becoming larger than could be financed. These QRs were permitted on "balance of payments" grounds under General Agreement on Tariffs and Trade (GATT) rules. However, the costs of these QRs mounted over time, as export earnings failed to grow as rapidly as real gross domestic product (GDP; the real exchange rate was appreciating because the domestic inflation rate was greater than that in the rest of the world), while it was increasingly difficult to contain the growing excess demand for imports.

Even in the world of the 1950s and 1960s, a "crisis" eventually took place.[10] In some countries, the crisis was triggered when the lack of imports began severely restricting economic activity. This was the case in Turkey, for example, in 1958 when the crops (which were a major source of export earnings) could not be harvested: for lack of petroleum imports, farmers were unable to use farm machinery to harvest crops or to transport them to

---

8. More generally, the current account deficit simply needs to exceed the volume of voluntary net capital inflows. Hence, if a country is a recipient of some foreign direct investment (FDI; or foreign aid, or portfolio investment) and no other capital inflows, the relevant "deficit" is the current account balance less the net FDI (or other voluntary flows). However, it simplifies the exposition to assume no voluntary capital flows so that the entire current account deficit somehow must be financed.

9. As excess demand for foreign exchange builds up under a fixed nominal exchange rate and exchange control, various forms of evasion spring up. These illegal flows (smuggling, false invoicing, etc.) generally result in large "errors and omissions" items in the balance-of-payments statistics of countries attempting to contain excess demand for foreign exchange as the real exchange rate appreciates to more and more unrealistic levels. One of the extreme instances was in Ghana in the early 1980s, when the black market exchange rate reached a level more than 900 percent above the official exchange rate.

10. For a good documentary history of the IMF, see James (1996).

ports.[11] In other instances, the unavailability of sufficient foreign exchange to maintain voluntary debt service signaled the onset of the crisis. This was the more frequent trigger for change in regime in some Latin American countries where accelerating inflation at a fixed (or insufficiently adjusted) nominal exchange rate led to rapidly rising demand for foreign goods and services, which the authorities attempted to satisfy (in an effort to reduce inflationary pressures) until financing sources dried up. Excess demand for foreign exchange—usually expansionary fiscal and monetary policy—also led to accelerating inflation, which finally reached unacceptable levels. In these circumstances, real exchange rates had appreciated greatly by the time the crisis point was reached.

Regardless of the triggering mechanism, the underlying problems were similar in origin: excess demand for goods and services had resulted from fiscal deficits and expansionary monetary policy. At the point when the authorities deemed the situations sufficiently severe to warrant action[12] and approached the IMF, the usual situation was that current account expenditures exceeded current account revenues by a considerable margin (often with a large errors and omissions item in the balance of payments, as well, reflecting unrecorded outflows), the real exchange rate had appreciated substantially relative to other countries, the rate of inflation was unacceptably high, and all of these had been driven in large part by fiscal deficits. In many instances, there were capital outflows occurring through such mechanisms as underinvoicing of exports, overinvoicing of imports, inflated tourist expenses, and overstated factor payments abroad. Simultaneously, in anticipation of an exchange rate change, importers were attempting to accelerate imports and build up inventories, exporters were delaying exports, and so on. Despite capital controls, the number of devices people could find with which to speculate against a currency was remarkable.[13]

When the IMF was approached for support, the usual situation was one in which the problems mentioned above had to be addressed, and, in addition, the lack of imports was itself fueling inflation and restricting production. The term "stabilization" came about because these economies at times of balance-of-payments crisis were thought of as spiraling out of control, with inflation rising, efforts at capital flight intensifying, and debt-servicing difficulties mounting at increasing rates.[14] The essential IMF stabilization program, therefore, usually consisted of an agreed-upon set of ceilings on

11. By 1958, Turkey had accumulated considerable short-term debt in the form of suppliers' credits and could not obtain even trade financing for imports. Hence, the inability to borrow further (and creditors' demands for repayments) was the proximate cause of the difficulty.

12. Defining a crisis is difficult. One country's crisis is another country's everyday occurrence. See Little, Cooper, Corden, and Rajapatirana (1993) for a discussion.

13. It was even reported that the London *Times* carried advertisements offering to overinvoice shipments to countries with exchange control and stating its percentage fee.

14. See Sturc (1968) for a description and analysis of some early Fund stabilization programs.

fiscal deficits and domestic credit creation,[15] and a change to a new, fixed, nominal exchange rate.[16]

The altered exchange rate very often immediately reversed the speculative capital outflow, so that the recorded balance-of-payments position could improve very quickly. The fiscal and monetary tightening associated with the fiscal and domestic credit ceilings usually resulted in a slowdown in the rate of economic activity and in the rate of inflation, which in turn reduced the excess demand for imports and freed up the supply of exports. All of these measures then served to generate balance-of-payments improvement. Whether the improvement was long-lasting depended on a number of factors, chief among which was whether the key sources of inflationary pressure and excess demand had been satisfactorily addressed.[17]

For future reference, it is worth pointing out that, in some instances, IMF programs even in the 1950s and 1960s often imposed conditions on governmental behavior. In some cases, price controls on state economic enterprises (SEEs) insured that those SEEs would incur losses, which in turn were financed by loans from the central bank. In cases in which these SEE deficits were important and increasing, it was recognized that there could be no reduction in the pressures of excess demand unless the underlying problem—the controls on prices that led to SEE losses and central bank credit creation—were removed. The same sort of conditions applied on occasion when particular subsidies—such as that for Egyptian grain[18]—were so large that fiscal balance could not be achieved without reducing them. In the Dominican Republic in the early 1980s, the state-owned electric company was incurring a deficit equal to 11 percent of GDP! In that circumstance, it was evident that a major source of the fiscal deficit and inflationary pressure could not be removed until the underlying financial position of the electric company was addressed.

In addition to the circumstances in which changing a domestic policy was essential if the underlying factors that had led to crisis were not immediately to recur, there were cases in which a highly inefficient governmental policy could be replaced with a more rational one: such was the case with the Turk-

15. The independent ceiling on credit creation apparently was first initiated when IMF staff thought that there were off-budget expenditures being substituted for governmental expenditures.

16. For an assessment of IMF programs as of the late 1970s, before debts to private creditors had become important, see Cline and Weintraub (1981). Even at that time, there was considerable criticism of Fund stabilization programs. For some examples, see Williamson (1983).

17. See Edwards (1989) and Krueger (1978) for analyses of the paths of inflation, the real exchange rate, and current account balances after devaluations. It was not always true that economic contraction followed a fiscal or monetary tightening. Trade liberalization often permitted an expansion in the rate of economic activity. In Turkey in 1958, for example, real GDP expanded by 5 percent after the deflationary program of August 1958 was put into effect.

18. In the case of Egyptian grains, these were sold so cheaply in the domestic market that farmers found it profitable to feed bread to their chickens. Fund insistence on their reduction was followed by street riots, which led to a reimposition of the grain subsidies.

ish devaluation of 1958, after which the earlier chaotic trade regime under which everyone queued for unpredictable lengths of time for import licenses was replaced by a system in which designated imports were granted licenses virtually automatically, whereas other imports were subject to licensing through which maximums were set as to the quantity that would be permitted to be imported.

Usually, by the time the IMF was approached, countries had run down their foreign exchange reserves to very low levels and were incurring or had incurred considerable debts as they attempted to maintain imports and economic growth in the face of an increasingly overvalued exchange rate and worsening balance-of-payments position. Moreover, as already mentioned, imports had sometimes been greatly suppressed prior to the inauguration of the IMF program. For either or both of these reasons, governments typically sought debt rescheduling and IMF financing. Debt rescheduling spread out the overhang of debt to a more feasible repayment schedule. Typically, official debt (which was often the major portion of long-term financing) was rescheduled through a meeting of official creditors organized by the IMF but de jure carried out under the auspices of the French Treasury, and known as the Paris Club. Private debts—usually short-term credits from commercial banks—were rescheduled at a meeting of private creditors usually held in London and known as the London Club.

Often, countries' import flows had been severely restricted or reduced immediately preceding the crisis, while foreign exchange earnings had fallen sharply. In order to "restart" the economy, it was not sufficient to reschedule debt: new money was needed, and IMF financing was extended.[19] In many cases, IMF financing was supplemented by official credits from the World Bank and bilateral donors. This financing, at a minimum, enabled an inflow of imports which itself was deflationary and often also permitted a reduction in the restrictiveness of the QR regime for imports.

The mechanism by which the IMF program was adopted was straightforward. Once it was deemed that a proposed program was satisfactory, the head of government would sign a letter of intent (LOI) to the managing director of the IMF, requesting IMF financing and laying forth the govern-

---

19. Under the Articles of Agreement of the IMF, countries are entitled to draw down a certain amount from the IMF automatically. The more they have drawn down, the stricter are the criteria for drawing down further tranches. In most instances, countries embarking upon stabilization programs had already drawn down a considerable amount and were seeking higher tranches of lending. The Fund did not provide all financing at once; stabilization programs were usually for two years, and a typical program set six-month targets. At the end of each six-month period, fund staff reviewed performance under the program, and a next tranche was released when performance was deemed adequate. Evaluating performance was in some regards problematic: when countries fell short of some targets, issues arose as to whether the shortfall was the result of circumstances unforeseen at the time of the program negotiation and whether the shortfall was serious enough to warrant suspension of the program. There were frequent program suspensions, but also frequent compromises, and many instances in which governments simply did not abide by the terms of the program.

ment's plans as to the key macroeconomic indicators. Almost always, it was agreed that there would be a change in the nominal exchange rate, or in the exchange rate regime, as part of the program. Likewise, ceilings on fiscal deficits and domestic credit were almost always included. Proposed changes in other key parameters (such as the subsidy rate for Egyptian grain or the pricing of Dominican electricity) were also spelled out.

In some cases, the program had already been adopted in the borrowing country. This was the case in Turkey in 1980, for example, when the domestic authorities undertook sweeping reforms (which went far beyond what the Fund would have required in order to extend financial support) and then approached the Fund for a loan. In other cases, the program was devised jointly by IMF staff and government officials.[20] Often, this was because policymakers in the would-be borrower country were reluctant to alter policies; however, in the absence of any alteration, it was clear that Fund support would do no more than provide temporary breathing space and only postpone the onset of a similar crisis. And it is self-evident that it would do a disservice to a country to lend in support of a futile program: the outcome would be a renewed crisis at a later date, with more debt having accumulated because of the first program. However, since a program in most instances increased the probability that economic performance would improve, some programs were no doubt undertaken where chances of success were very limited.

The "joint" determination of the program was really an outcome of a negotiating effort between IMF officials and representatives of the government. Devising any stabilization program inevitably entailed judgment. Macroeconomic outcomes are uncertain: unforeseen or unpredictable future events (such as the prices of key exportable commodities or the weather), unpredictable or unanticipated (in terms of timing as well as of magnitude) responses of consumers and producers to altered relative prices, serious strikes, and changes in the government can all affect the speed of response. A "stronger" program carries a higher probability of success, but even a weak program could succeed with good fortune in terms of weather, external terms of trade changes, and appropriate changes in expectations and consumer and producer behavior.[21]

Moreover, a strong program is likely to entail more short-run adjustment

20. It is often forgotten that, in most developing countries especially in the 1950s and 1960s, the pool of available talent in key government ministries was very thin. Quite aside from the lessons of experience and changed economic thinking, one reason why developing countries' economic policies have been gradually becoming less inchoate over time has been the increased quality and breadth of able civil servants and policymakers.

21. It is probably true that consumer and producer responses are weaker and slower in countries where there is a history of past failed attempted stabilization programs. Since that variable is different for each country, to the extent that past history matters, it is clear that there is no "one size fits all" model of how much adjustment in the key variables is warranted. Moreover, since the outcome is in any event probabilistic, a key question concerns the probability of success that IMF and government officials should accept for programs, bearing in mind that "stronger" programs (with larger exchange rate changes and sharper tightening of monetary and fiscal policies) probably bring larger adjustment costs to politically vocal sections of society.

costs.[22] A cut of x percent in the fiscal deficit entails a larger increase in tax receipts or a greater reduction in government expenditures than a smaller percentage cut. Likewise, a larger increase in tariffs for electricity, bus fares, or other governmental services imposes more of a hardship on users than does a smaller increase.

Hence, there is reason to adopt no stronger a program than is deemed warranted in order to stabilize the economy and provide a sufficiently high probability that growth can be resumed. However, the fact that larger macroeconomic policy changes may impose hardships on particular groups in the economy is often used to oppose any changes at all. Hardships endured after the start of a Fund program are generally blamed on the program, without regard to the counterfactual trajectory of economic variables that would have occurred had there been no Fund program and the economy continued its downward spiral. Space does not permit a review of the evidence in this regard, but it is increasingly apparent that the very groups that are alleged to be most harmed by IMF stabilization programs are the groups that are most harmed by the unstable macroeconomic environment (especially inflation) that is generally the alternative.

However, in most instances, it could be expected that Fund programs with any credibility whatsoever would be followed by short-term increases in foreign exchange receipts and reductions in demand for foreign exchange. This is because these programs were usually adopted at a time when speculation against the currency had occurred and, with it, speculative withholding of exports, speculative prepayment of imports, and capital flight through whatever means were available. Thus, in the period immediately following the announcement of a Fund program and an associated devaluation, the foreign exchange situation could be expected to improve (both because of the reversal of speculative outflows anticipating the devaluation and because the receipt of Fund resources provided assurance in most instances that further exchange rate changes would not take place in the near future), and hence the crisis that brought the government to the Fund in the first place had passed and pressures to conform with the agreed-upon program were therefore much smaller.

---

22. There are two dimensions of "strong" and "weak." On one hand, there is the magnitude of the fiscal, monetary, exchange rate, and other adjustments. On the other hand, there is a question as to the period of time during which these adjustments are phased in. There is increasing, but by no means conclusive, evidence that changes in the key macroeconomic variables that are carried out quickly have smaller costs than those that are phased in over a longer time period, for a variety of reasons. First, a rapid change in macroeconomic signals sends a message that policymakers are serious in their determination to restore macroeconomic equilibrium. Second, those sectors of the economy (exportables, in particular) which benefit from reforms are likely to respond more rapidly when the adjustment is made at once than when it is phased in over time. Third, the political opposition faces a higher hurdle in its efforts to oppose and overturn reforms that have already been achieved than it does for those that are merely announced as intended at a future date. The above discussion, therefore, refers to the magnitude of the altered policies, not the speed. It should be noted, however, that some changes—such as in government expenditures or in tax structures—inevitably require time.

For this reason, there was obvious cause for concern that countries, once having received financial support and experienced a much-relaxed current account situation, would revert to their fiscal and monetary habits that had brought on the crisis in the first place. To avoid this, the Fund's programs typically imposed "conditionality," and Fund resources were extended only after staff reviewed the key macroeconomic performance indicators agreed upon. Thus, there was not a single domestic credit ceiling: there were ceilings specified for each six-month or one-year interval for the life of the program. Fiscal performance was also specified for a sequence of periods.

What this led to was the release of a tranche of funding once a Fund program was initially announced, with specified future dates at which further tranches would be released, assuming the country met its targets set forth in the LOI. It often happened that, on review for release of a later tranche, targets would not have been met. As already indicated, anticipating macroeconomic events is not a precise science, and the task of the IMF staff in the review was threefold: (a) to ascertain the extent to which the failure to meet targets threatened the success of the program; (b) to determine the extent to which failures to meet targets were a result of unanticipated macroeconomic shocks, of misestimation of the economy's response to the program, or, instead, of failure to implement the program; and (c) renegotiate targets for subsequent tranches in light of the findings with respect to the first two questions. When the failure to meet targets was the consequence of internal policy, the task was to ascertain whether it was feasible to get the program back to a place where there was a realistic chance of success, or whether to abandon the program.

Evidently, judgment had to be used. The first question—whether the failure to meet targets was of sufficient magnitude and likely duration[23]—is often a judgment call. Even when the cause of failure is clearly external (as, for example, an unanticipated increase in the price of oil leading to a larger fiscal and current account deficit than in the program), changes in targets may be warranted. Even when the cause of failure is governmental inaction (as happens, for example, when tax reforms are turned down by Parliament), a question is whether sufficient action could and would be taken in the immediate future to get the program back on track.

Needless to say, a number of fund programs have been canceled, and many others have had targets renegotiated.[24] Even in the initial program, it is always a difficult judgment call as to how much fiscal and monetary tightening and how much exchange rate change is the minimum that would have

23. Sometimes, unanticipated delays in fiscal expenditure reductions or increased tax receipts can occur that would be serious if sustained, but for which there is evidence that the delay was once and for all. And, of course, if the fiscal target is a deficit reduction of, say, 1 percent of GDP over a six-month period, there is a question as to whether 0.99 percent of GDP, 0.9 percent of GDP, 0.8 percent of GDP reduction, or some other number is sufficiently close as to warrant continuing support.

24. See Ergin (1999) for data on the number of cancellations and renegotiations over the years.

a significant chance for successful outcomes. There is also a question as to the ability and willingness of the relevant government officials in the program country to undertake the agreed-upon policies. Once the program is under way, information on terms of trade, weather, and other variables removes some uncertainties but increases others.

In fact, many IMF programs have failed to reverse the underlying economic trends.[25] Especially in the 1960s and 1970s, a typical experience was the "stop-go" cycle, in which the inauguration of a Fund program marked a period during which the government fiscal deficit and the rate of domestic credit creation were reduced, while the depreciated real exchange rate induced a reduced quantity demanded of imports and an increased flow of exports. These usually resulted in some degree of domestic recession (depending on whether the expansionary effects of import liberalization with the associated greater availability of intermediate goods and raw materials and of greater exports offset the contractionary effects of tighter monetary and fiscal policy). That, in turn, released further goods into export channels and reduced the demand for imports. Simultaneously, reduced domestic demand usually more than offset other effects, to result in—at least temporarily—a reduction in the rate of inflation.

However, once these effects had been taking hold for some time, governments typically began to increase expenditures and ease the monetary situation. As that happened, the real exchange rate began appreciating,[26] and, with it, the incipient current account deficit once again began increasing. Inflationary pressure accelerated, and, with it, the boom component of the cycle was once again under way. The boom ended when the next exchange rate or debt-servicing crisis became too costly, and once again the IMF was approached. This was referred to as developing countries' "stop-go" cycles.

Hence, even before 1973 and the first oil price increase,[27] a number of countries had had multiple IMF programs.[28] In some instances, they were

25. See Krueger (1978) for an early tabulation of the real exchange rates prevailing one, two, and three years after devaluations in ten developing countries in the 1950s, 1960s, and early 1970s. See Edwards (1989) for a review of the experience with a much larger number of countries over the 1970s and 1980s.

26. The index of dollar prices of tradable goods was virtually constant over the period from 1952 to 1969. As a consequence, any country with even a 5 percent rate of domestic inflation at a fixed exchange rate experienced real appreciation of its currency. Many developing countries had average inflation rates well in excess of that number, although the average rate of inflation across countries rose markedly after 1973.

27. After 1973, most developing countries continued to maintain fixed nominal exchange rates, or crawling pegs, which could lead to problems if the terms of trade deteriorated sharply. For this reason, they continued to call upon the IMF for support even after the industrialized countries' abandonment of fixed exchange rates had markedly diminished the fund's role with respect to their economies.

28. It is sometimes argued that finance ministers and other economic policymakers know that the IMF will support a program and that they therefore accept more risk than they would in the absence of the IMF. However, there is ample evidence that economic policy officials, and especially central bankers, who are in office at times of crisis quickly lose their jobs. See Cooper (1971).

almost continuous; in others, several years separated the resort to Fund support. In Chile, for example, there were Fund programs in 1956, 1959, and 1965 even prior to the inflation expansion set off under President Allende and the massive adjustment of the mid-1970s (see Behrman 1976). There were Fund programs in Turkey in 1958, 1970, and 1977, prior to the Turkish reforms of 1980. During the latter half of the 1970s, there were repeated renegotiations and abandonments of programs.

Before turning to the role of financial transactions in these crises and responses, I need to stress two final points. First, until the 1980s, the majority of developing countries used fixed nominal exchange rate regimes, so that a devaluation was an important part of their stabilization programs. Inappropriate real exchange rates led to retarded growth or depressed export earnings, increased imports or increasingly restrictive import licensing, depressed capital inflows, and encouraged various forms of illegal transactions to enable capital flight. By the 1970s, some of these costs were being recognized, and a few developing countries began experimenting with alternative exchange rate regimes. A few countries permitted their exchange rate to float during the crisis or in a period immediately afterward, prior to fixing a new nominal exchange rate. Some others, most notably Colombia and Brazil, began using a crawling peg exchange rate regime, under which the nominal exchange rate was altered at relatively frequent intervals according to a formula under which the adjustment was sufficient to compensate between the rate of inflation in the country in question and the average rate in its major trading partners.

The second point is that, although exchange controls certainly restricted the free flow of capital, and private capital flows were relatively small contrasted with official flows or their magnitudes in the 1990s, businesses and individuals found plenty of ways to evade exchange controls, and capital flight was often the trigger for a balance-of-payments crisis. Capital flight may be easier and more sensitive to small changes in macroeconomic magnitudes in the 1990s than it was in earlier decades, but it is not new.

4.1.2 Financial Crises

There have been a number of episodes of financial crisis with minimal balance-of-payments involvement over the years. The United States had many such crises in the nineteenth century, a major motive for establishing the Federal Reserve System. Sweden had a major financial crisis in 1992, which was again largely national and financial in origin, although the crown was also attacked (the overnight interest rate rose to an annual rate of over 400 percent at the peak of the crisis). And, of course, Japan's difficulties in the 1990s have had a weak banking system as a major underlying factor. Even the American savings and loan problem of the early 1980s represented a financial crisis, although it was relatively small scale contrasted with many others,[29] as measured by the percentage of the overall financial system affected or by the percentage of GDP of the ultimate bailout cost.

Because it has primarily been the banks that have been involved in the twin crises of the 1990s, I shall speak of banks as if they were the only important financial institution. Clearly, they are not, but since they are central and were major for the crises of concern here, it will simplify the exposition to refer to the "banks" rather than to "financial-sector institutions."

The business of financial intermediation is important for development and economic growth, because intermediation enables the resources savers make available for investment to be allocated to their best uses. By its nature, the finding of those best uses requires a skilled assessment of the likely future outcome of any given venture. That outcome is determined by several things: (a) the ability of the borrower; (b) the prospect that the proposed venture is technically feasible at a cost such that there will be sufficient demand in the market to make it pay; and (c) that the external environment does not change in ways that negatively impact the venture. All three of these components are better judged by trained professionals than others, but each of them is nonetheless subject to uncertainty.

Even the best of bank lending officers does not have a perfect record of forecasting which would-be borrowers will be successful and enabled to service their loans. In some instances, the debtor's plans simply do not work; in others, unforeseen circumstances (a deep recession, changing consumer tastes, development by a competitor of a superior substitute) can lead to the failure of a venture to yield a sufficient cash flow to enable debt servicing.

All banks have, and should have,[30] some nonperforming loans (NPLs) and reserves against NPLs. Moreover, since banks charge a higher interest rate on riskier loans, mechanisms must be devised to provide incentives and an environment in which bankers manage risk appropriately. If, for example, the owner of a bank has none of his own capital invested in it, he has nothing to lose if risky loans fail, and he will therefore have an incentive to have too risky a portfolio. It is for this reason that capital adequacy requirements are a part of reasonable banking regulation.

When the fraction of NPLs (recorded or not) increases, banks must charge higher interest rates on the rest of their portfolio to cover their costs and be profitable than would be the case with a smaller fraction of NPLs. In the extreme case when there are no performing loans, a bank's capacities to lend are entirely destroyed, but in fact that occurs long before NPLs absorb the entire portfolio.

Because of this, a bank that experiences above-average difficulty with its

29. It is not clear whether the savings and loan problem would have remained "small-scale" if it had not been handled reasonably quickly. One of the characteristics of weak financial institutions is that there is a tendency for problems to spread.

30. If a bank had no nonperforming loans (NPLs) on its books, it would either have been far too conservative in its lending policies or it would be failing to write down bad loans.

loan portfolio is highly vulnerable, because potential "sound" borrowers will be able to borrow at lower cost from other banks, leaving only riskier borrowers approaching the troubled bank, and depositors may attempt to shift their funds as information about the financial health of the institution becomes known. This, in turn, lowers the bank's reserve ratio. As these things happen, the fraction of NPLs is likely to rise still further.

When a number of banks experience an increasing fraction of NPLs simultaneously, the failure of any one or several of them results in losses to the depositors and shareholders. Those losses, in turn, weaken their asset position and can impair the ability of some of that group to service their obligations. As that happens, there is further weakening of the balance sheets. At some point, depositors recognize the danger to the banks and begin attempting to withdraw their funds, thus leading to the banking crisis. If banks are forced to refuse repayment, those depositors in turn become further handicapped in servicing their obligations, and, in addition, panic is likely to ensue.

When the banking system is so weak (i.e., when it has such a high fraction of NPLs in its portfolio) or is indeed under attack by depositors who have lost confidence in it, there are major risks in failure of the government to act. In particular, as individual financial institutions become unable to meet the demands for withdrawals, the liquidity of depositors falls, they fall behind or further behind on their debt-servicing obligations, and a downward spiral can occur in the absence of action.

To restore the banking system to economic health requires a number of measures. A first is to restore the banks' balance sheets. That may entail removing the bad paper from the banks, or it may entail forcing some healthy banks to consolidate with some that are impaired, or it may involve the government's acquiring the NPLs from the banks' portfolios in exchange for other assets.[31] Achieving that is difficult for a number of reasons: (a) resources must be raised, usually from taxpayers, to bail out the banks, which is inherently unpopular; (b) major questions arise and must be addressed regarding the valuation to be placed on NPLs; (c) without careful attention, borrowers who could repay a fraction, but not all, of their debt will have no incentives to repay at all, and hence the fraction of NPLs and associated losses is likely to rise; and (d) when businesses are heavily indebted to banks, restructuring the individual firms' finances and indeed replacing debt with equity in their portfolios may be an essential part of the workout process. As will be seen below, this has certainly been true in Korea.

31. As will be seen below, in Indonesia, the government bought up the bad paper in the banking system, giving the banks nonnegotiable treasury bills in exchange for these NPLs. Since nonnegotiable bills cannot be lent, there was little new credit available in the Indonesian banking system. That being the case, even borrowers who could have serviced their bank debts ceased doing so, knowing that if they repaid their loans, they would not receive new credits. This is one major reason why the recovery of the Indonesian economy is so slow.

Hence, "restoring banks' portfolios" is not a single activity. It requires valuation of the individual items in banks' portfolios, itself a lengthy process, as well as the development of arrangements for partially creditworthy borrowers to refinance their obligations. Further, it requires the development of incentives for banks to change their pattern of behavior, usually by raising capital adequacy standards and perhaps reevaluating the risk characteristics of various lending categories.[32] However, this latter procedure is tricky, especially at a time of financial crisis, when there are few potential domestic lenders.[33] Moreover, if foreign banks that do have the equity are permitted entry before the domestic banking system is restored to health, the fact that the new entrants are not carrying a significant fraction of NPLs on their books means that they can lend at a lower rate than the domestic banks to achieve the same profitability. If instead governments attempt to have healthy banks absorb less healthy ones, they must also insure equitable treatment for shareholders of the healthy banks, ensure that the newly merged banks are financially sound, and be willing to close banks with highly impaired balance sheets.

However, a government that undertook these actions and did nothing else would be failing to take any measures to prevent a recurrence of a banking crisis. If, for example, the weakness of the banking system came about because banks accepted too much risk, there is little point in restoring the banks' balance sheets without attempting to reduce the probability that they will once again develop an overly risky portfolio.[34] Hence comes the need for strengthening capital adequacy requirements and also, usually, for strengthening prudential supervision.

Strengthening prudential supervision requires both changes in the regulatory framework and improved capabilities of the regulatory authorities. Although changing the regulatory framework may meet political opposition (on behalf of those benefiting from the prior status of the banks), it is relatively simple to accomplish. However, strengthening prudential supervision requires more resources in the regulatory offices, and those resources

---

32. One of the precrisis "distortions" in the global financial system at the time of the Asian financial crisis was that the Bank for International Settlements capital adequacy standards assigned a lower risk category to short-term than to long-term lending, thus encouraging a shorter-term structure of debt than would otherwise have occurred. Since the focus here is on IMF programs, however, that issue is outside the scope of this paper.

33. Failure to achieve capital adequacy appears to have been a significant contributor to the difficulties the Mexican government faced over the refinancing of the banks. The private owners of banks, it is said, had to a considerable degree acquired the funds to purchase their banks by borrowing from each other! Thus, although there were individual "owners" of banks, these "owners" were in fact in debt to other banks and had little to lose if their banks went bankrupt.

34. There is considerable evidence that the banks were extending credit to risky endeavors in the years leading up to the Asian financial crises and in Mexico prior to the 1994 crisis. Rates of increase of domestic credit, and the increment of domestic credit as a percentage of GDP, were very high—going to over 20 percent annually in Indonesia (contrasted with domestic credit expansion of less than 3 percent of GDP per year in industrialized countries).

include trained bank examiners. Increasing the pool of qualified individuals is usually a drawn-out process.

Relating these considerations to developing countries, and to the financial crises of the 1990s, requires a step back to consider the role of banks in those countries. The importance of banks relative to the entire financial intermediation industry in developing countries is much greater than it is in wealthier countries. At very early stages of development, banks are virtually the only source of finance for enterprises with profitable investments they wish to pursue.[35] At that stage, most developing countries controlled the banks, imposing a ceiling both on the lending rate and on the deposit rate well below that that would have prevailed in a well-functioning financial market. For developing countries with appropriate policies, there were many profitable investment opportunities and consequent large excess demand for loans at the regulated rates. Governments typically oversaw credit rationing, requiring banks to give priority to particular activities at the expense of others.[36] For example, in Korea in the early years after the opening up of the economy and the encouragement of exports, banks were instructed to lend to exporters at preferential interest rates.[37] In other countries, credit to small farmers, to small businesses, or to other favored groups has been rationed at below-market interest rates. In other countries, however, preferential credit was directed to cronies or to politically influential individuals or groups.

When credit rationing prevails, the task of bank lending officers is simplified. In circumstances such as those that prevailed in Korea in the 1960s, almost any investment was bound to have a payoff in excess of the bank lending rate: Concerns with the creditworthiness of individual borrowers were very few, because the spectacular rate of economic growth (13 percent annual average) insured that almost anything would be profitable. The need for prudential supervision is much weaker than when there are competitive banking systems and market-determined lending practices, because banks under credit rationing are not really competing with each other but in effect

35. Almost by definition, the citizens of a poor country at the early stages of development have accumulated very little equity, and the ratio of bank loans outstanding to the value of capital stock, especially in the business sector, is very high. As development proceeds, that ratio can be expected to decline, but for countries that began rapid development within the past several decades, it is still well below that in industrial countries' markets.

36. In the 1960s, for example, the government of Korea regulated interest rates and directed credit allocations. The estimated real rate of interest on Korea Development Bank Loans in the period from 1962 to 1966, for example, ranged from –0.8 percent to –26 percent. During the rest of the decade, the real rate of interest was positive, but never exceeded 6.1 percent. By contrast, estimated real rates of return on investment ranged from 20 to 35 percent. The curb, or informal, market rate of interest for those seeking additional funding was well over 40 percent throughout the decade, whereas the nominal rate of interest on bank lending never reached 30 percent. See Hong (1981).

37. It is important to note that all exporters were entitled to preferential credit, which was allocated according to formulas based only on export performance. There was no commodity-specific differentiation among exports.

have a governmentally imposed monopoly. In those circumstances, to the extent that the interest rate is suppressed and banks have any choice among would-be borrowers, they naturally choose to lend to the safest borrowers, who will in effect be receiving a subsidy when they get loans at below-market interest rates.[38]

When a financial crisis occurs, the age-old prescription is to ease monetary policy generally and then for the central bank to follow the advice of Bagehot: lend freely at high interest rates to borrowers with good collateral. The point of this policy prescription is that healthy banks (or other financial institutions) that are illiquid because of the financial crisis need to be sorted out from those that are unhealthy and those that are (and would be even in the absence of crisis) insolvent. Simultaneously, a relatively easy money policy reduces the debt-servicing burden for borrowers, so that at the margin there are fewer NPLs. Indeed, a quick, but not necessarily desirable, way out of a financial crisis would be to inflate, especially if most loans have been made at fixed nominal interest rates. Inflation would ease the debt-servicing burden, although its other effects can have negative consequences and outweigh the benefits of reduced debt-servicing obligations.

4.1.3   Twin Crises

An economy afflicted with either a balance-of-payments crisis or a financial crisis presents the policymaker with serious challenges. To confront a balance-of-payments crisis, the appropriate policy responses entail an exchange rate change, tightening of monetary policy, and tightened fiscal policy. These measures, in turn, may require other supporting policy actions. To stem a financial crisis, by contrast, entails loosening of monetary policy, maintenance (or even appreciation) of the nominal exchange rate, and financial restructuring. Moreover, as is further elaborated below, an exchange rate adjustment as part of the response to a balance-of-payments or debt-servicing crisis can trigger a sufficient impairment of bank balance sheets to precipitate a simultaneous financial crisis. To a significant degree, in the presence of twin crises, whatever is done to address one will, in the short run, make the other worse.

In this section, I first address potential components of the policy package and their role, and later I address issues of sequencing and trade-offs across potential policy actions.

---

38. In some developing countries where import-substitution policies were followed, banks were directed to lend to them. Although they were often economically unsound, the firms producing import-substituting goods typically held sheltered and profitable positions in the domestic market and hence were financially profitable. However, in countries where much lending is directed toward "cronies" who have little intention to repay, a financial crisis can result from these practices.

Policies to Meet a Balance-of-Payments Crisis

Exchange Rate Change

An exchange rate change is necessary once foreign exchange reserves are being depleted in circumstances in which the prevailing real exchange rate is unrealistic. As has already been seen, when policymakers have chosen a fixed nominal exchange rate regime[39] and inflation rates have exceeded those in the rest of the world, the real appreciation of the currency gives speculators a one-sided bet: they can be reasonably confident that the currency will not appreciate in nominal terms, so they cannot lose (except for any forgone interest on holding foreign exchange relative to domestic currency), and they will gain in the event that there is a devaluation. In these circumstances, once capital outflows start increasing, there comes a point when only an exchange rate change of sufficient magnitude can deter further outflows.

The policymaker can choose to let the rate float or to announce and support a new, but more depreciated, fixed exchange rate. Three points need to be noted. A first one is that it is almost always domestic residents (who are closer to the scene and thus better informed) who are first to attempt to get out of local currency. Second, as already noted, there are many ways for domestic residents to move into foreign currency even under degrees of capital inconvertibility. Thus, it is not only the failure of foreign creditors to roll over loans or extend new financing that can place pressure on the foreign exchange rate; much of the domestic money supply can also do so.

Second, an exchange rate alteration may be inadequate to calm the markets. Indeed, there are numerous instances in which the announcement of a new exchange rate has not reduced pressures: this happened in Mexico after the initial devaluation in December 1994.[40] Even a devalued exchange rate may be deemed "inappropriate" by market participants. For that reason, many policymakers have chosen to let their exchange rate float, at least in the immediate aftermath of a currency crisis. In that way, speculators face a two-way bet, and the exchange rate is market determined.[41] When foreign exchange reserves are minimal, and no additional resources are available from other sources, there is no option but to float the exchange rate.

---

39. A crawling peg regime was also susceptible to speculative pressures when circumstances should have led to a change in the real exchange rate. Such was the case in Brazil on several occasions when Brazil had a crawling peg exchange rate policy. These exchange rate changes were referred to as "maxi-devaluations" to distinguish them from the ongoing adjustments to maintain purchasing power parity.

40. For a chronology of events immediately prior to, during, and after the crisis, see IMF (1995, 53–79).

41. There is another advantage to floating the exchange rate: during the period in which a fixed exchange rate is defended, the foreign exchange authority (usually the central bank) is usually selling foreign exchange at the old exchange rate; if success of the currency is unsuccessful, foreign exchange reserves are built up at the new, depreciated exchange rate. Consequently, a central bank can incur large losses in an unsuccessful defense of the exchange rate. Floating the rate guarantees that there will not be large central bank losses.

Third, although it is impossible to assert that there could *never* be a foreign exchange crisis under a floating exchange rate system, the probability of such a crisis is considerably reduced relative to that incurred under a fixed exchange rate when domestic monetary and fiscal policy are not targeted to the dictates of maintaining that rate.[42] Moreover, as will be argued shortly, a floating exchange rate regime would be less likely to have significant foreign currency–denominated unhedged debts and therefore would be considerably less vulnerable to a twin crisis.

Tightening Monetary Policy

People move out of domestic currency into foreign currency because they expect a higher (risk-adjusted) return on holding foreign exchange than on holding domestic currency. As domestic interest rates rise, the cost of moving into foreign currency rises. Indeed, when the interest rate is high enough and the time horizon in which devaluation might occur is long enough, the costs to investors of holding lower-yielding foreign assets can be made sufficiently high to induce them to hold (high-interest-yielding, short-term) domestic assets. Hence, a higher domestic interest rate deters—at least at the margin—investors from moving out of assets denominated in domestic currency into foreign currency.

Thus, the conventional prescription for a balance-of-payments crisis is to tighten monetary policy, in order to make holding of domestic assets more attractive. This must, of course, be part of a package including an exchange rate change, because if an exchange rate change is thought to be imminent, there is no realistic possibility of attracting foreign funds. Even if the expected devaluation were only 10 percent and were anticipated with a high probability to occur within a week, that would require an overnight rate of interest equivalent to an annual rate of over 50,000 percent plus the return on the foreign asset to equate the expected returns and hence leave investors indifferent between domestic and foreign assets. Obviously, such a rate would bring all domestic transactions to a virtual halt.[43]

42. The crisis would manifest itself differently, however: the government in a country with large debts denominated in foreign currency might find itself unwilling or unable to raise sufficient tax revenue to purchase foreign exchange in the market, thereby triggering heightened inflationary pressures in its efforts to repay debt. Moreover, the debt-servicing burden might be sufficiently large that a depreciating exchange rate resulted in a larger fiscal deficit, which in turn would lead to a higher rate of inflation. The need for macroeconomic stabilization would be every bit as great as in the crises of the 1990s, but it is likely that the magnitude of the debt-servicing obligations, relative to GDP and exports, would have to be considerably larger than it was in the countries experiencing twin crises in the 1990s.

43. In the 1950s and the 1960s when Chile confronted a balance-of-payments crisis, the authorities used to impose a 10,000 percent "guarantee deposit requirement." This was the amount of money, expressed as a percentage of the import cost plus insurance and freight price, that the would-be importer had to deposit, interest free (in the context of a three-digit annual rate of inflation) at the time of placing his order for foreign goods. The deposit would be returned after the goods had cleared customs. Because the lag between order and delivery in Chile was typically six months or longer, this was equivalent to a tax of many times the import cost of the good. Not surprisingly, imports ceased when the guarantee deposit requirement was imposed.

Adjusting Fiscal Policy

In order to avoid accelerating and finally hyperinflation, of course, fiscal deficits have to be held under control. In many developing countries, these deficits are large enough that the monetary authorities are virtually forced to buy up new issues of government debt and maintain relatively easy monetary policy in order that the burden of the domestic debt-service obligations not become so large that that becomes destabilizing. Hence, tightening fiscal policy so that government domestic debt will not increase—or at least not by more than can be financed—is also a necessary part of any stabilization program.[44]

Of course, the higher the ratio of government domestic debt to GDP, the more costly it is to the government to have increased interest rates. When interest rates rise by 10 percentage points or more, the increased financing needs of a government with outstanding debt equal to 50 percent of GDP are equivalent to 5 percent or more of GDP. Raising such a large additional sum without triggering inflation is exceptionally difficult. Hence, the degree to which monetary policy can be tightened is partly a function of the relative size of government debt. For that reason, the increase in domestic interest rates automatically increases the prospective fiscal deficit because interest-carrying costs of the debt will increase. Since it is also likely that economic activity will slow, tax collections are likely to be somewhat below prior estimates, whereas fiscal expenditures may—unless adjusted—be higher. As a result, some fiscal tightening is called for, even in the event that the fiscal situation going into the crisis was reasonably balanced.

Thus, the ideal combination of exchange rate adjustment, fiscal curtailment, and monetary tightening depends heavily on the relative magnitudes of foreign currency–denominated and domestic government debt at the time of crisis. A country with little internal and much external debt would find the increased fiscal cost lower with relatively tighter monetary policy and less exchange rate adjustment (because more devaluation means a higher local-currency cost of debt service); a country with a large domestic debt and few foreign currency–denominated obligations would find a package with a larger exchange rate adjustment and a smaller degree of monetary tightening to raise debt-servicing charges by a smaller amount more attractive.[45]

Policies to Meet a Financial Crisis

Just as quelling a balance-of-payments crisis requires restoration of the belief that the exchange rate is sustainable, or at least that the odds are even

44. It is also necessary because it is essential that expectations be altered. In the absence of fiscal tightening, the credibility of the stabilization program is at risk.

45. A strong case can be made that expansion of domestic credit under a fixed exchange rate regime is equivalent to increasing the contingent liabilities of the government, since the government is in fact implicitly guaranteeing that it will buy domestic currency at a specified rate.

as to whether it will appreciate or depreciate, a financial crisis requires restoration of confidence in the financial system. However, there is no "quick fix," parallel to floating or altering the exchange rate, that can achieve that result.

The measures mentioned in section 4.1.2—getting the bad paper out of the banking system while restructuring the debt of those who can pay part of their obligations, recapitalizing the banks, and providing incentives to avoid a repeat of the financial system's difficulties—all take time. Moreover, each one of these activities is contentious. Often, corporate restructuring to reduce the burden of debt is a necessary first step, entailing, for example, the exchange of debt of the companies for equity. However, the more favorable the terms are to the companies, the less favorable they are to the banks, and vice versa. Hence, it usually requires relatively strong oversight on the part of regulators or officials to push both parties to a division of the losses.

Determination of the value of the banks' assets is itself problematic. This is especially so because it is always tempting to assume that debtors will be able to increase their debt servicing once economic activity resumes, although experience suggests that economic activity does not fully resume until financial restructuring is achieved or at least well advanced.

Even when corporates (and the finances of other debtors) are restructured, however, there remains the problem of restoring the banks' balance sheets. This requires valuations of outstanding loans, and appropriate classification as to their risk category. Moreover, once these valuations—which are also contentious—take place, new owners, or at least new capital, must be found for the banks.[46] If an effort is made to merge weak banks with stronger ones, the terms on which this is done are also problematic.

At the point when these activities are advancing, which necessarily takes time, there is also a question as to how the losses will be financed. Governments can buy the bad paper from the banks' portfolios, but that shifts the burden to the taxpayers. Moreover, if they buy the paper from the banks, the banks have little incentive to collect even what they can from their debtors. Because these are key issues in the recovery of some of the Asian countries, these issues are discussed in more concrete form in section 4.1.4 below.

Interaction of Balance-of-Payments and Financial Crises

Enough has been said to give an indication of the difficulties entailed when either a balance-of-payments or a financial crisis takes place. Policymakers must take immediate action in circumstances in which the magnitudes of response of the affected parties are unpredictable and expectations are clearly of great importance.

---

46. In Mexico, it would appear that one of the problems was that new bank owners lent to each other to finance their acquisition of equity interests. This, in turn, meant that the new owners had nothing to lose by undertaking risky loans.

However, when there is a weak banking system and a balance-of-payments crisis occurs, the latter can trigger a financial crisis. There are several mechanisms by which this can happen:

1. When banks have been borrowing abroad at a fixed nominal exchange rate to fund their asset base, a devaluation necessarily increases the liability side of their balance sheet and leaves the asset side virtually unaffected. Hence, the banks' balance sheets deteriorate.

2. If borrowers from banks have either borrowed from the domestic banking system but incurred their liabilities in foreign exchange, or themselves borrowed offshore in addition to borrowing from the banks, a devaluation automatically results in a deteriorating of the borrowers' balance sheets. For firms that are engaged in exporting and importing, this effect is likely to be fairly small because export proceeds or domestic currency payments from imports rise pari passu with the devaluation. However, for firms whose costs are determined in the international market but whose receipts are determined in local currency, income and balance sheets are likely to deteriorate. If the banking system was weak prior to the crisis (as was true in most of the Asian crisis countries), the additional hits they take as a result of the devaluation result in further deterioration of their balance sheets.

3. When the monetary authority responds to a balance-of-payments crisis by tightening money with a consequent increase in interest rates, debt-servicing costs to individual borrowers necessarily increase. Again, outstanding loans of marginal borrowers are likely to be tipped into NPL status as interest-carrying costs on their outstanding indebtedness increase.

4. Insofar as fiscal and monetary tightening result in a (necessary) slackening in the pace of economic activity, that too affects borrowers' incomes and cash flows and hence impairs their ability to service their debts.

All of these effects weaken the banking system further. How important each of them is varies from country to country. In Mexico, it is thought that the increase in interest rates was the major factor that added significantly to the 8 percent of bank loans outstanding that were already nonperforming before the crisis.[47] In Korea, the banks' losses on their holdings of Russian and other securities combined with the inability of domestic firms to service debts to weaken the banking system.

---

47. See IMF (1995, 62). The IMF reports that about 8.5 percent of loans outstanding were past due before the crisis. Foreign currency loans were about one-third of the loans extended by Mexican banks, but many of them were to companies whose income was peso-denominated. As the IMF reports, "The sharp rise in interest rates also affected the peso-loan portfolio. . . . When interest rates reached levels as high as 80 percent in the first quarter of 1995, payments ceased on a large proportion of loans of all types. Banks generally chose to restructure these loans, or simply to suspend interest payments, rather than to be forced to recognize them as high-risk assets and write off a certain amount of their already declining capital by making provisions. Nevertheless, the deterioration in asset quality forced the risk-weighted capital ratios of several Mexican banks below the 8 percent minimum" (62–63).

The difficulty for policymakers is that when the banking system is very fragile or already in crisis, any actions that are taken to mitigate the balance-of-payments crisis are likely to weaken the banks still further, whereas any measures taken to shore up the domestic banking system (such as the easing of monetary conditions) will make the balance-of-payments crisis worse. Hence, policymakers both in the country and at the IMF are treading a fine line: too much reaction to the balance-of-payments crisis can result in a financial crisis if there is not one already or make it worse if there is one. Conversely, too much attention to the financial situation when the country is already vulnerable to external attack can invite that attack and destabilize the foreign exchange account.

These difficulties are clearly illustrated for the cases of Indonesia and Korea, discussed in the next section. Before that, however, there are two other points. First, countries with a sound banking system, such as Brazil in early 1998, have a much easier time of adjusting and resuming economic growth. In the Brazilian case, there was very little NPL paper in the banking system prior to the devaluation, and Brazilian banks had little or no foreign-currency debt, whereas their clients' debts were mostly denominated in domestic currency.

Second, and more relevant for understanding the policy response and the IMF packages in the case of the Asian crises, there is clearly a desirable or necessary sequencing for responses to crises. Although it is straightforward (and essential) to allow the exchange rate to depreciate immediately and to tighten money (at least to some extent, depending on the government's balance sheet), there are long time lags involved in financial restructuring. Fortunately, the job does not need to be done perfectly in order for economic activity to reverse its downward course, and there appears to be room for fine-tuning after the initial restructuring. Nonetheless, what does seem evident is that countries do not achieve a rebound and reversal of their difficulties after a twin crisis until such time as they are able to provide sufficient incentives for the banks to resume lending activity. When that does not happen, as for example in Japan in the 1990s, the crisis can transform itself into a long period of sluggish or negligible growth.

4.1.4   International Monetary Fund Stabilization Programs in Action

As the above discussion indicates, the number of factors that contribute to the onset of a crisis is large, and each crisis differs in some regards from others. Attempting to evaluate or assess stabilization programs in general is difficult precisely because these differences matter in program design. It is useful, therefore, to provide some case studies of IMF stabilization programs. Each twin crisis of the 1990s has been complex, and books could be and no doubt will be written about each of them. In what follows, emphasis is placed on those factors that seem most important (or that have generated most criticism) in evaluating IMF stabilization programs and on linkages between domestic economies and the international financial system.[48]

A first case to be examined is that of Korea, which is perhaps the best example for intensive analysis. Thereafter, features differentiating the financial crisis in Indonesia are discussed.

The Korean Crisis[49]

Background

As is well known, Korea was one of the poorest countries in the world in the late 1950s and was then widely regarded as a country without serious growth prospects. After economic policy reforms began in the early 1960s, Korea began growing at sustained rates previously unheard of in world history.[50] Real GDP grew an average 13 percent per annum in the decade starting 1963. High growth rates continued into the 1990s, and Korea's real per capita income in the mid-1990s was more than eight times what it had been in the early 1960s.

In general, economic liberalization proceeded throughout the first thirty-five years of Korea's rapid growth. In 1960, the country had had the usual developing-country mix of an overvalued exchange rate supported by quantitative restrictions on imports (and a black market in foreign exchange), consequent high walls of protection for domestic manufacturers, price controls on many key commodities, credit rationing, a large fiscal deficit, one of the highest rates of inflation in the world, and a huge (averaging around 10 percent of GDP over the period 1953–58) current account deficit financed largely by foreign aid inflows.[51] Indeed, when the government of

48. It should be recalled that focus here is on the extent to which stabilization programs enabled a cessation of capital flight and provided a basis for restoration of growth. One criticism of IMF programs have been that there were too many conditions attached which, while perhaps desirable in themselves or in the long run, were not essential to the stabilization effort. That concern is assessed in the paper by Goldstein (chap. 5 in this volume).

49. The IMF documents cited in this section may be found at [http://www.imf.org/external/country/KOR/index.htm].

50. Taiwan's rate of economic growth was equally rapid. There is truth to the frequently made assertion that policymakers in each country watched the evolution of the other's economy and policies, and that competition spurred each on. Prior to the crisis in the late 1990s, most observers would have claimed that the major difference between the Taiwanese and Korean economies was the relatively small scale of Taiwanese enterprises contrasted with the large share of the Korean *chaebol* in the Korean economy. There were other differences, however: perhaps because of greater strategic insecurity, the Taiwanese held very large foreign exchange reserves in relation to the size of their trade or their economy; the Taiwanese dollar showed no tendency for real appreciation; and Taiwan's current account had been consistently in surplus. The Taiwanese financial system also appears to have been considerably sounder than that of Korea, and the rate of expansion of domestic credit in the mid-1990s was much lower than that in Korea.

51. See Krueger (1979) and Frank, Kim, and Westphal (1975) for an account of the early period of Korea's rapid development.

Syngman Rhee was overthrown in 1960, one of the main sources of dissatisfaction was reported to be corruption.

First steps included moving to a more realistic (and constant real) exchange rate for exports, and the relaxation of restrictions on importing for exporters. Thereafter, imports were gradually liberalized and the exchange rate regime unified by the early 1970s. In 1964, a major fiscal and tax reform brought the government finances into a much-improved balance, and the rate of inflation fell.[52] Price controls were gradually removed, discrimination and price controls on key agricultural commodities were replaced with a protective regime for agriculture, and nominal interest rates were permitted to move to levels that at least made the real interest rate positive. However, credit rationing continued because it was below a market-clearing rate (see Hong 1981). Only in the late 1980s were interest rates freed.

When economic policy reform began, Korea's exports were only about 3 percent of GDP, whereas imports were about 13 percent. Policymakers therefore began focusing on measures to increase exports. They did so by encouraging all exports uniformly, but nonetheless they had something that might be regarded as being close to an "export theory of value." Any firm that could export was rewarded in proportion to the foreign exchange receipts from exporting. Many of the firms that were initially successful were *chaebol* (although they were very small at the time, and some Korean analysts today do not regard the Hyundais, Samsungs, and the like of the 1960s as *chaebol* at all). Because they were successful, they grew rapidly. They received new loans as their exports grew and as they expanded into new exporting activities.[53]

The *chaebol* were successful exporters and, for the first decade or more of Korean growth, were regarded almost as the heroes of Korean development. They were rewarded for export performance. In addition, when the authorities wanted a venture undertaken, they did so with the implicit guarantee of the government that credit, tax exemptions, and other support would be available to make the venture profitable.[54] However, the *chaebol*

52. The oil price increase of 1973 triggered a large increase in the rate of inflation, but the country rapidly returned to single-digit inflation. By the mid-1980s, there were even occasions when the domestic price level was falling.

53. Some of these activities were chosen by the *chaebol*. On occasion, however, the authorities suggested to *chaebol* owners that they should move into certain lines of production. This attempt to "pick winners" was not always successful; when it reached its height in the heavy and chemical industry (HCI) drive of the mid-1970s, the rate of economic growth and of export expansion slowed substantially, and policies were reversed by the late 1970s. When *chaebol* incurred losses while undertaking these mandated activities, the banks were directed to extend additional credit to the *chaebol,* thus setting a precedent for later difficulties.

54. It is important to underscore that these government "rewards" were there in the context of the export drive. When *chaebol* could not produce competitive exports, there was little support. Even in the HCI drive—the most industry-specific interventionist phase of Korean policy—the output from HCI industries was to be exported within a specified period. When it became clear that that performance test was not being passed, the entire thrust of the policy was reevaluated.

were on the whole remarkably profitable and had little difficulty in servicing their (subsidized) debt.

The extent to which the Korean economy changed structure is remarkable. Exports and export earnings (the dollar price index of traded goods being stable in the 1960s) grew at over 45 percent annually. Exports as a percentage of GDP rose from 3 percent in 1960 to 8.5 percent in 1970 to 35.2 percent in 1980; imports also rose, from their 10 percent level in 1960 to 43 percent of GDP in 1980. Hence, the Korean economy was much more open as growth progressed.[55]

In the early years, rationed credit financed a large fraction of new investment, especially in the manufacturing sector. The subsidies implicit in this credit served as a stimulus to industry and permitted much more rapid expansion than would have been possible had companies had to rely on reinvesting their own profits.[56] The real rate of return was so high that all the *chaebol* would happily have borrowed more had they been able to; most of them, as reported by Hong (1981), borrowed additional funds at the much higher curb market rates. That would imply that the lending at controlled interest rates was, at least in the early years, equivalent to an intramarginal subsidy to the *chaebol*. Estimates of their rates of return suggest that the *chaebol* were highly profitable at that time even without subsidies. Indeed, given the huge distortions in the economy that prevailed in the late 1950s, it is likely that in the 1960s, at least, almost any reasonably sensible venture into unskilled labor intensive exportable production had a high real rate of return.

As already mentioned, by 1964, the borrowing rate from the banks was positive in real terms. Over the following three decades, there were further liberalizations of the financial system as the real interest rate charged for loans rose, although credit was still rationed. At the same time, the real rate of return on investments naturally fell as the very high initial returns obviously could not be sustained. Hence, the implicit subsidy to the borrowers who received credit diminished sharply. When, in 1996 and 1997, gross profits of some of the large enterprises fell sharply, their ability to service their debt was impaired. However, in keeping with tradition, banks began "ever-

---

55. Some of the increase in imports was of course intermediate goods used in the production of exportables. However, the percentage import content of exports remained fairly stable at around 35 percent of the value of exports over the period of rapid growth. From 1960 onward, exporters were entitled to import virtually anything that they might use in producing exportables with little paperwork; in addition, they were permitted to import a "wastage" allowance, which they were free to sell on the domestic market. Thus, the de facto liberalization exceeded that which took place because of removal of quantitative restrictions and lowering of tariffs. With an average tariff rate in the tariff schedule of around 15 percent in 1970, average tariff collections as a percent of imports were about 6 percent.

56. In much of the public discussion of the reliance of firms in crisis countries on borrowing, what seems to be forgotten is that, starting from very low levels of income and development, there is very little equity, and a large fraction of investment must therefore be financed through other channels.

greening" the loans, lending additional funds to the borrowers to enable them to make interest payments. Hence, actual NPLs were building up in the banking system, although it is probable that it was thought that the decline in profits was temporary.

There is another aspect of Korean growth that is important in understanding the background to the crisis. That is, when rapid growth started in the early 1960s, the Korean saving rate was very low, and even negative by some estimates. With more rapid growth, domestic saving began growing rapidly, rising from around zero percent of GDP[57] in 1960 to 15 percent of GDP by 1970 and 25 percent of GDP by 1980. However, in the early years and until the late 1970s, profitable investment opportunities greatly exceeded domestic savings. As a result, domestic savings were supplemented by borrowing from abroad, equaling as much as 10 percent of GDP in years during the 1960s.[58]

The Korean government guaranteed loans and determined the maximum that could be borrowed, allocating borrowing rights among exporting firms. Because the foreign interest rate was well below the domestic interest rate (especially in the curb market) and the real exchange rate fairly stable for exporters, there was intense competition for foreign loans.

As domestic saving rose, the proportionate reliance on foreign resources for supplementing domestic saving to finance investment fell. By the 1980s, the domestic saving rate was in excess of 30 percent, and the current account went into surplus for several years in the mid-1980s.[59] Beginning at this time, the American government in bilateral trade negotiations began to pressure the Koreans to let the won appreciate in order to reduce the bilateral trade deficit with the United States.[60] Most Korean economists believed by the mid-1990s that it would be in Korea's best interests to have some real depreciation of the won, but the pressures not to do so prevented it. The

57. In 1960, it is estimated that private saving was a positive 3.2 percent of GDP, whereas government saving was a negative 2 percent of GDP. Foreign sources financed 78 percent of investment, which was 10 percent of GDP. See Krueger (1979, 206–07). In 1960, most foreign resources were foreign aid.

58. Most of the capital inflow was from the private sector—largely commercial bank lending—by the late 1960s. Foreign aid had peaked in 1958 and was less than 2 percent of GDP by the mid-1960s. The current account deficit was sustainable because of the profitability of investment and the declining debt-service ratio that resulted from such rapid growth of exports and of real GDP.

59. Korean policymakers viewed the emergence of the current account surplus as a transitory phenomenon explicable by "three blessings": the fall in oil prices in the mid-1980s, the drop in world interest rates (so that debt-servicing costs declined), and the boom in Korea's trading partners, especially Japan. The current account turned positive in 1986, rose to a peak of 8.0 percent of GDP in 1988, fell to 2.4 percent of GDP in 1989, turned negative (–0.8 percent) in 1990, and remained negative in the 1–2 percent range until 1997, when the deficit increased to 4.7 percent of GDP.

60. Korea was running a bilateral surplus with the United States and a bilateral deficit with Japan, and policymakers resisted as far as they could these pressures. One response was to ask the American authorities whether they should devalue with respect to the yen while they appreciated with respect to the U.S. dollar!

won exchange rate was not fixed, the range within which it fluctuated was relatively narrow: it appreciated from 890 won per dollar at the end of 1985 to 679 won per dollar in 1989, and thereafter it gradually depreciated to 808 won per dollar in 1993, appreciating again to 788 won per dollar in 1995. At the end of 1996 it stood at 844 won per dollar, and of course it depreciated almost 50 percent in 1997.[61] Thus, for the decade prior to the 1997 crisis, there had been little change in the real exchange rate.[62]

Events Prior to the Crisis

Thus, by the mid-1990s, Korea had sustained thirty-five years of rapid growth. Although there had been periods of difficulty—both slowdowns and overheating—Korean policymakers had met their challenges successfully. As noted by the Organization for Economic Cooperation and Development (OECD), the country had come from being one of the poorest developing countries in 1960 to having a per capita income equal to that of some OECD countries, with a higher rate of economic growth.[63]

The late 1980s had witnessed the introduction of a democratic process into Korea. The elected governments chose to liberalize further, including especially the financial sector and international capital flows.[64] In 1992–93 there was a "growth recession," as the growth rate slowed to just over 5 percent (contrasted with rates of over 9 percent in the preceding two years and an average rate above 8 percent in the preceding decade). One response was to ease monetary policy: domestic credit expanded by over 18 percent in 1994, 14 percent in 1995, and 21 percent in 1996.[65] Real GDP growth responded, exceeding 8 percent in 1994 and 1995.

However, there is ample evidence that, despite this cyclical recovery, the profitability of the *chaebol* was declining and the condition of the banks was deteriorating. Turning first to the *chaebol,* data for the thirty largest ones indicate that the return on assets, which stood at only 2.0 percent in 1994 and 2.5 percent in 1995, fell further to 0.8 percent in 1996 and was a negative 0.7 percent in 1997. Return on equity fell from 6.9 and 8.7 percent to 2.7 and minus 2.9 percent over the same years, while the rate of growth of operating income was minus 14.4 percent in 1996 (Hahm and Mishkin 1999, 60).

Even during the cyclical boom years of 1994 and 1995, the financial in-

61. Exchange rates, saving rates, and current account deficit data are all taken from various issues of the IMF's *International Financial Statistics* unless otherwise noted.
62. This may be somewhat misleading. The late 1980s was a time of the "three blessings" (low international interest rates, low oil prices, and a favorable international economy, especially Japan) for Korea.
63. For an account of the Korean economy in the mid-1990s reflecting this consensus view, see OECD (1994).
64. See the OECD (1994) description of the five-year financial liberalization plan.
65. This rate was not markedly faster, however, than it had been over the entire preceding decade. Hahm and Mishkin (1999, 21) reject the notion that liberalization of the capital account was responsible for the increase in domestic credit, but they note that it did play a role in permitting the banks to take on greater exposures to foreign exchange risk.

stitutions were borrowing abroad to finance their lending to the corporate sector (especially the *chaebol*). As a consequence of financial liberalization, twenty-four finance companies were transformed into merchant banks, which enabled them to enter into foreign exchange transactions. Thus, both the banks and the nonbank financial institutions increased their exposure heavily, and much of the onlending consisted of dollar-denominated obligations. According to Bank of Korea data reported in Hahm and Mishkin (62), foreign currency debt constituted 9.8 percent of total corporate debt in 1992, rising to 11.5 percent in 1996 and 16.4 percent in 1997. However, corporate debt itself rose from about 130 percent of GDP in 1991 to 150 percent in 1996 and 175 percent in 1997.

There were other signs that growth was not as solidly based as it had been. The incremental capital-output ratio, which had stayed around 4 for many years, had risen to 5 (often deemed to be the highest sound number) in 1991 and then rose to 6 and stayed fairly steady at that level until the crisis.

In 1996, the dollar value of exports of goods rose only 4 percent, contrasted with increases of 15 and 32 percent in the preceding two years. This very low rate reflected largely the faltering sales of semiconductors and the turnaround in the fortunes of Samsung: the terms of trade turned sharply against it, as the unit price of semiconductor chips fell by 70 percent, leading to a marked deterioration in Korea's terms of trade—about 13 percent based on unit value statistics.

External liabilities in foreign currency rose by 32 percent in 1994, 35 percent in 1995, and 37 percent in 1996. Of that total, short-term liabilities were 56 percent; these short-term liabilities were 2.79 times foreign exchange reserves at the end of 1996. The ratio of gross external liabilities to GDP (including the offshore borrowings of Korean banks and the overseas borrowings of their overseas branches) had risen from 0.20 in 1992 to 0.31 by the end of 1996.[66]

Hence, a close examination of the data on the Korean economy would have revealed that the economy's financial fundamentals had deteriorated quite substantially during the 1990s, especially if the short-term impact of the 1994–95 cyclical recovery was discounted. The macroeconomic aggregates, however, appeared fairly sound. The fiscal accounts were in balance, and, indeed, there had been fiscal surpluses equivalent to one-half of one percent of GDP or less in each year from 1993 through 1996. The current account deficit had, of course, increased sharply, as already noted, from 1.74 percent of GDP in 1995 to 4.42 percent of GDP in 1996. However, if the real exchange rate was examined only in the 1990s, it appeared to have remained fairly stable; the inflation rate was less than 5 percent per annum, and the saving rate was well over 30 percent. Moreover, as will be explored

66. Data are from Hahm and Mishkin (1999), table 2.

in more detail below, the condition of the banks was probably considerably weaker than the official numbers indicated.

The Crisis

A number of events took place early in 1997 that surely eroded confidence. One of the large *chaebol,* Hanbo, went bankrupt early in the year. Given that it had been widely believed that the large *chaebol* were "too big to fail," this in and of itself must have resulted in some loss of confidence and a reexamination of Korea's creditworthiness. Moreover, 1997 was an election year, with the presidential elections set to be held early in December. That the market anticipated difficulties is reflected in the fact that the Korean stock exchange index fell from 981 in April 1996 to 677 by the end of March 1997 and to 471 at the end of October, even before the outbreak of the currency crisis.

However, although the net and gross foreign (and especially short-term) liabilities of the banking and financial systems were continuing to increase, there was no visible evidence of crisis until the final quarter of the year. The Thai crisis had exploded in June, and the Indonesian crisis had begun during the summer of 1997, but most observers were confident, given Korea's past history, that Korea would not be affected.[67] Korea's offshore banks were holding paper from Indonesia, Russia, and other countries with dollar liabilities, which would further deteriorate the net foreign asset position, but that was not widely known at the time.

However, capital flight began early in the fourth quarter of the year. In many instances, it was simply a refusal to roll over short-term debt. However, other factors contributed: Korea's sovereign risk status was downgraded by Standard & Poor's in October; NPLs in the banking system doubled from the end of 1996 to fourth quarter 1997, reaching 7.5 percent of GDP by that time, owing largely to the bankruptcy of six *chaebol* and the sharp drop in the Korean stock exchange. However, once it became known that reserves were decreasing, others sought to get out of won, and the capital outflow intensified rapidly.[68] Total reserves less overseas branch deposits and other unusable foreign exchange were $22.3 billion at the end of October and had fallen to $7.3 billion by the end of November.[69] It is reported that, by the time the IMF was approached, gross reserves were being depleted at a rate so rapid that they would have approached zero within forty-eight hours. In the program presented to the IMF board, it was re-

---

67. The author was at a conference of Korean economic policymakers in August 1997 and the mood was one of deep gloom. Many of the participants were extremely pessimistic about the *chaebol,* the state of the financial system, and the potential for reforms of economic policy.

68. However, even in November, the finance ministry was issuing reassuring statements, and private forecasters were minimizing the likelihood that Korea would approach the IMF. For a representative account, see John Burton's "Korean Currency Slide Shakes Economy," in the *Financial Times,* 12 November 1997, 5.

69. Data are from Hahm and Mishkin (1999), table 11.

ported that usable reserves had dropped from $22.5 billion on October 31 to $13 billion on November 21 and $6 billion on December 2.[70]

The IMF Program

All three presidential candidates had declared repeatedly that under no circumstances would they approach the IMF. When the government did approach the IMF, the IMF's problem was complicated by several things: (a) it was not known who the new president would be and hence with whom the IMF would have to deal on the economics team; (b) there was very little time to put together a program, and, both because Korea had been viewed as sound until recently and because the candidates had all said they would not approach the Fund, there had been less preliminary work done than was usually the case;[71] (c) the exchange rate was depreciating sharply after the end of October, and when the band was widened to 10 percent on November 19, the rate of depreciation began accelerating rapidly; and (d) as already mentioned, the government was rapidly running out of foreign exchange reserves and would soon be forced to default on its obligations (see Boughton 1999). The high short-term indebtedness meant that foreigners could get out of won simply by refusing to roll over outstanding debt.[72]

The initial program was negotiated over the period November 26 to December 3. As stated in the memorandum to the executive directors as the staff sought approval of the program, "Owing to the critical situation in Korea, and the very short period in which program negotiations had to be completed, it was not possible to fully specify the program. Therefore, emphasis was placed on strong prior actions to demonstrate the government's seriousness to strictly implement its policy commitments." Even as the program was approved in December, the board was told that it would be reviewed in January 1998 (when, among other things, the new president and economics team would be known).

The initial program set forth as its objectives "building the conditions for an early return of confidence so as to limit the deceleration of real GDP

---

70. Other factors also contributed. A financial reform bill, proposed by a blue ribbon committee, had been turned down by parliament, and it was not clear whether the government had legally guaranteed the foreign exchange liabilities of the financial institutions. Although interest rates had risen by about 200 basis points, the Bank of Korea was nonetheless injecting liquidity into the system, which reversed the increase.

71. The fact that the Thai and Indonesian crises had already occurred no doubt diverted some of the attention that Korea otherwise might have received. At that time, too, it must have been anticipated that there would be Malaysian and Philippine programs.

72. Hahm and Mishkin (1999) point out that "the speculative attack was not in the usual form of direct currency attack to exploit expected depreciation. Due to the tight regulation on currency forwards which should be backed by corresponding current account transactions and the absence of currency futures markets inside Korea at the time, opportunities for direct speculative attack had been much limited. Rather, the drastic depreciation of Korean won was driven by foreign creditors' run on Korean financial institutions and chaebols to collect their loans, and by foreign investors to exit from the Korean stock market" (25).

growth to about 3 percent of GDP in 1998, followed by a recovery towards potential in 1999; containing inflation at or below 5 percent; and building international reserves to more than two months of imports by end-1998" (IMF 1997). The staff memorandum stated that there were three pillars to the government's program: the macroeconomic framework;[73] restructuring and recapitalizing the financial sector, and reducing the reliance of corporations and financial institutions on short-term debt.

The 5 percent inflation target looked ambitious in light of the large depreciation of the won (from the mid-800s per dollar to almost 1,800 per U.S. dollar at its peak) and the share of traded goods in GDP.[74] To achieve that objective, the liquidity that had been introduced into the system in prior weeks (in an effort to support the *chaebol*) was removed, and money market rates were raised sharply. In the words of the staff, these rates would "be maintained at as high a level as needed to stabilize markets" (5). Day-to-day monetary policy was to be geared to exchange rate and short-term interest rate movements, and exchange rate policy was to be flexible with intervention "limited to smoothing operations."

The 1998 budget as passed by the government had projected a surplus of about 0.25 percent of GDP. However, Fund staff estimated that lower growth and the altered exchange rate would reduce the balance by 0.8 percent of GDP and that it would require 5.5 percent of GDP to recapitalize the banks to meet the Basel minimum capital standards. It was assumed that these funds would have to be borrowed, and interest costs (0.8 percent of GDP) were therefore also included in the altered budget estimates. These factors would, on IMF estimates, have shifted the fiscal account into deficit to about 1.5 percent of GDP in 1998. As stated by staff, "In order to prevent such a deficit and alleviate the burden on monetary policy in the overall macroeconomic adjustment, fiscal policy will be tightened to achieve at least balance and, preferably, a small surplus." The program therefore called for fiscal changes approximately offsetting the negative anticipated changes and thus for maintenance of the fiscal stance as anticipated prior to the crisis, with the 1.5 percent of GDP cuts equally distributed between government expenditures and revenues. The government initially raised some taxes to yield about 0.5 percent of GDP.

The second leg of the program was financial restructuring. As already indicated, NPLs were large and increasing prior to the crisis. The deprecia-

---

73. Much of the controversy surrounding the Korean program centers on whether the program tightened fiscal policy too much. This is discussed below. It should be noted that the IMF staff's introduction of the macroeconomic program indicated that the program would involve "a tighter monetary stance and significant fiscal adjustment" (5).

74. As stated in the Request for Standby, "The inflation target reflects a very limited pass-through of the recent depreciation of the won to the aggregate price level. . . . In order to achieve the inflation objective, the government will aim to reduce broad money growth (M3) from an estimated 16.4 percent at end-September to 15.4 percent at end-December 1997, and to a rate consistent with the inflation objective in 1998" (5–6).

tion of the exchange rate increased debt-servicing obligations for *chaebol* and financial institutions, as did the increase in interest rates that came about with monetary tightening. The details of financial restructuring are intricate enough that they cannot be delved into here in any detail. Suffice it to say that an exit policy was to be adopted to close down weak financial institutions, recapitalizing the remaining banks (through mergers or other means). A deposit guarantee was to be phased out at the end of December 2000 and replaced with deposit insurance for small depositors only. Transparency was to be increased in a variety of ways. Large firms were to be audited by international accounting houses. Supervisory functions were to be reorganized, the Bank of Korea given much greater independence, and so on. Finally, the government undertook to withdraw from any influence over lending decisions, leaving those to the financial institutions.

One important point to note in terms of bank restructuring is that it required a prior, or at least concurrent, restructuring of the *chaebol* finances. Given their very high debt-equity ratios[75] (for one *chaebol* at the height of the crisis, the debt-equity ratio reached 12:1), financial viability, where feasible at all, would surely require swaps of debt by the *chaebol* to the banks, giving the banks equity in return.

The IMF standby also called for the Korean government to set a timetable to meet its World Trade Organization (WTO) trade-related commitments to remove restrictive import licensing and "diversification program" (which discriminated against Japanese imports). Equally, the program stipulated further capital account liberalization including, importantly, increasing the ceiling on aggregate foreign ownership of Korean shares from 26 to 50 percent by the end of 1997 and then to 55 percent by the end of 1998.[76] Remaining elements of capital account liberalization, which had already been agreed to with the OECD, were to be accelerated with the new program announced by the end of February 1998. In addition, restrictions on direct foreign borrowing by *chaebol* were to be eliminated. The first of these measures—permitting increased foreign ownership—encouraged foreign investment and enabled the possibility of foreign control of financial institutions, among other things.

The standby then addressed corporate governance and corporate financial structure issues, noting that the only scrutiny over *chaebol* investments, even of large scale, had been by bank managers "whose appointment has

75. These high debt-equity ratios were public knowledge. The *Financial Times* published data on debt-equity ratios for twenty *chaebol* on 8 August 1997. The highest was Sammi, with 33.3 times as much debt as equity; Jinro had 85 times as much debt as equity and Halla 20 times; Hyundai's debt was 4.4 times its equity, and so on. Profits were relatively small as a percentage of assets or sales. In Samsung's case, for example, net profits were 179.5 billion won on sales of 60 trillion won and total assets of 51 trillion won. Nine of the twenty *chaebol* listed in the *Financial Times* on that day had taken losses.

76. This measure—which some have criticized as being beyond the Fund's mandate—enabled a more rapid recapitalization of the banks than would otherwise have been possible.

traditionally been influenced by the government." It then anticipated that shareholders' and directors' oversight should improve, especially in conjunction with increased opportunity for foreign purchases of shares. One important element of these changes was to be the reform of bankruptcy laws, with governmental agreement that there would in future be no financial support, forced mergers, or tax privileges for individual firms.

The final components of the standby were those related to data provision and monitoring, which need not be of concern here. The staff then addressed the issue of the reasons for external support. It first noted that the current account deficit was expected to decline markedly in 1997 to about 3 percent of GDP, and then—with export growth and won depreciation—to about 0.5 percent of GDP in 1998. However, the very high level of short-term debt was seen to be worrisome. As stated in the standby, "It is difficult to estimate with any certainty the likely developments in capital flows . . . , given the uncertainty surrounding the rolling over of private sector short-term debt and the recent collapse in market confidence. . . . The working assumption is that, on the basis of the beneficial effects on market confidence. . . . The working assumption is that, on the basis of the beneficial effects on market confidence of the announced program and the large financing package, the bulk of the short-term debt will be rolled over. Under this scenario, the purpose of the exceptional financing would be largely to reconstitute reserves. For this outcome to materialize, it is critical that the financing package provided is adequately large and the program is perceived to be strong. . . . It is anticipated that a comprehensive financing package of about $55 billion will be provided on a multilateral and bilateral basis . . ."(12).

Aftermath of the Crisis

For at least two weeks after the announcement of the IMF program, questions remained as to whether the downward slide had been halted.[77] By late December, however, the exchange rate had stabilized, and by mid-January, foreign banks announced a $24 billion package of rollovers and new money (*Financial Times,* 30 January 1998, 11).

Domestic economic activity slowed markedly in 1998. For the year as a whole, real GDP fell by 5.8 percent, contrasted with the Fund's projected 3 percent. The unemployment rate, which had been 2.2 percent at the end of the third quarter of 1997, rose throughout 1998 and peaked in the first quarter of 1999 at 8.4 percent. The seasonally adjusted industrial production index fell by 15 percent from the end of 1997 to the second quarter of 1998.

---

77. Because of this, it is very difficult to accept the argument that the Fund program was "too stringent." Indeed, given those uncertainties, it is more plausible to argue that the program might have been even more restrictive initially.

Thereafter, it rose, reaching its precrisis level by the end of 1998 and 144.9 at the end of 1999.

The external accounts improved markedly. There was a sharp drop in imports in immediate response to the crisis, and a much-increased current account balance: whereas exports were slightly lower in dollar terms in 1998 than in 1997, imports fell 22.4 percent and the current account balance was equal to an astonishing 12.5 percent of GDP for the year. Foreign exchange reserves rose in response, reaching $74 billion by the end of 1999 and $83.5 billion by the end of the first quarter of 2000. The decline in real GDP ended in mid-1998, and by the end of the year, real GDP had exceeded its precrisis level. For 1999, real GDP growth exceeded 9 percent, and it was projected to attain that same rate for 2000.

After early 1998, the nominal exchange rate appreciated in dollar terms, entering the year 2000 at around 1,100 to the dollar, as contrasted with 1,800 to the dollar at the peak of the crisis. Moreover, prices at the end of 1998 were about 7 percent higher than at the end of 1997; in 1999 the rate of inflation was just 0.8 percent, as measured by the consumer price index.

Progress in restructuring the financial sector was necessarily considerably slower. Although interest rates had fallen below their precrisis levels by the end of 1999, restructuring of *chaebol* and financial institutions met considerable resistance.[78] Government policy pronouncements and actions have continued to push reforms, but the pace of reform has been much slower than with regard to the balance of payments and external finances.

By early 2000, it was certainly the case that the Korean recovery had been more rapid and more pronounced than had been anticipated by any. Although there was an underlying question as to whether the financial reforms had been effected in ways that would enable further financial development on a sound basis, there was no doubt that recovery had come, and come dramatically. Korea was regarded as the most successful country in pulling out of the crisis.

After the initial program of 3 December 1997, there were LOIs dated 24 December 1997, 7 February 1998, 2 May 1998, 24 July 1998, 9 December 1998, 10 March 1999, 2 November 1999, and 12 July 2000.[79] In each, targets were revised and the program was amended as judged appropriate. In general, the fiscal deficits achieved—especially in 1998—were smaller in magnitude than target, whereas foreign exchange reserves exceeded target. By 1999, fiscal objectives were once again to reduce the budget deficit as the recovery accelerated more rapidly than had been anticipated. The 12 July

78. See, for example, "Boxed into a Corner," by John Burton (*Financial Times,* 23 November 1998, 17), whose header read "South Korea's chaebol are fighting a stiff rearguard action against government reforms but the conglomerates are being forced to change their ways."
79. These are all available on the IMF's website: [http://www.imf.org/external/np].

2000 LOI was the final review under the standby, which was set to expire 3 December 2000.

How Good Was the Fund's Program?

There are three key issues on which the Fund has been criticized with respect to the Korean program after the East Asian financial crisis. The first pertains to the degree of monetary and fiscal tightening that accompanied the onset of the program, and the second is the extent to which issues such as corporate governance needed to be a part of the program.[80] The third is the size of the loan package, although on that issue there are criticisms both that it was too small and that it was too large.

Turning to the degree of monetary and fiscal tightening that took place, Stiglitz has been perhaps the foremost spokesman for the view that tightening interest rates may in fact have been counterproductive during the crisis phase. As was seen in section 4.1.3, there is a trade-off between tightening the money supply and letting the exchange rate depreciate more, and both of these measures have their dangers.[81] Given the rate at which reserves were dwindling and the exchange rate depreciating in November and early December 1997, it seems absolutely clear that monetary tightening had to take place. Its extent had to be such that a strong signal was provided (especially in light of the elections and the new government) that the government was serious about addressing the situation. Indeed, judging by the continued slide of the won in the first two weeks after announcement of the IMF program, a case could even be made that perhaps monetary policy should have been even tighter![82] Certainly, with respect to monetary policy, it seems evident that it was at the very beginning none too tight. One might question the rate at which it eased in 1998 once the exchange market had stabilized and the severity of the downturn in domestic economic activity

80. For criticisms of the Fund with respect to the monetary and fiscal tightening, see Jeffrey Sachs, "The Wrong Medicine for Asia," (*New York Times,* 3 November 1997) and Furman and Stiglitz (1998); for criticisms of the Fund with respect to the breadth of coverage of the program, see Feldstein (1998).

81. Stiglitz has argued that interest rate increases may have increased the degree of exchange rate depreciation and financial instability because only riskier investments would be undertaken at higher interest rates or borrowers had more difficulty servicing their debts. Tests of this hypothesis provide strong evidence that this was not the case in Korea. Cho and West (1999) tested the relationship between interest rates and exchange rates in Korea over the period December 1997 to mid-1999 and found that "the high interest rate policy after the crisis contributed to stabilizing the exchange rate in the short run." However, they found the recovery of the foreign currency liquidity position the longer-run determinant of the exchange rate. However, recovery in reserves came about because of the turnaround in the current account balance, itself a function both of the IMF loan and of the exchange rate.

82. See *Financial Times,* 12 December 1997, 17. John Burton, in "This is an Unusual Situation," wrote that "In the week since it signed up . . . , South Korea has seen its currency drop by nearly 30 percent against the dollar. Corporate bond yields are up nearly 5 percentage points to 23 percent, and the country's banks and companies seem as much in danger as ever of defaulting. . . . As the won dropped another 10 percent within four minutes of opening yesterday, some people began to fear that there might be a meltdown in financial markets."

became evident, but the criticism of the initial part of the program in that regard seems inappropriate.

Fiscal policy can, however, be questioned. As seen above, the first program took into account the impact on government expenditures of the stabilization program; although expenditures were to be reduced and taxes raised, these were intended to offset other increases in expenditure (e.g., larger interest payments at higher interest rates) and lower revenues (because of anticipated recession). There is no doubt that the first LOI did underestimate the extent of the downturn, anticipating 3 percent in contrast with the actual reduction of more than 5 percent of GDP. However, adjustments were made in subsequent reviews and LOIs. For example, the September 1998 original target was for a central government fiscal deficit of 7 trillion won; the revised target was 10 trillion won; the actual deficit for that period was 5.7 trillion won. Even for the March 1999 quarter, the target deficit was 23.5 trillion won and that achieved was 19.7 trillion won. Hence, although there can be questions about whether the original fiscal targets were too tight, subsequent IMF missions certainly assented to easier targets, and the actuals were smaller than the target deficits for most of the recession and recovery period.[83]

The second criticism—that the programs interfered more in internal economic policies than was necessary—is more difficult to evaluate. On one hand, financial restructuring was absolutely essential, first as a very credible intent, or capital outflows would have continued, and second as a prerequisite for economic recovery. Moreover, because the devaluation and higher interest rates would both weaken the financial sector in the short run (and this would be understood by the markets), failure to address the issue would clearly have increased the severity of the recession and delayed, if not aborted, the recovery. And financial restructuring could not be satisfactorily undertaken without addressing the very high debt-equity ratios of the *chaebol,* which immediately led into issues of corporate governance, supervision, and the like.

There is no doubt that financial restructuring is inherently domestic and politically difficult because it entails sorting out property rights among claimants and, perhaps even more important, allocating the losses among various groups—at least between shareholders, borrowers, and taxpayers. Were there an international institution or organization (such as the Bank for International Settlements [BIS]) that supported financial restructuring efforts, there would of necessity have to be close coordination between that agency and the IMF when twin crises arose. In the absence of such an agency, however, it would appear that the IMF cannot credibly support a

---

83. I have not been able to ascertain the extent to which this shortfall from deficit targets was the result of more rapid expansion of GDP than anticipated and the extent to which there were other factors.

stabilization program without being assured that appropriate financial restructuring will take place.

These issues would be much less pressing if countries' governments, financial institutions, and corporations did not take uncovered debtor positions in foreign exchange. However, as long as these positions are taken[84] and financial institutions are already weak at the outset of a crisis because of NPLs, financial restructuring will often be an essential part of stabilization programs.[85] Although improved incentives for financial institutions to manage risk appropriately and appropriate strengthening of prudential supervision would significantly reduce the incidence of twin crises, addressing these issues when they do arise is unavoidable.

There are also questions as to whether financial restructuring has gone far enough. As already mentioned, the Korean government has encountered major political resistance to efforts to restructure the finances of the *chaebol* and to attain arms'-length transactions between the *chaebol* and the financial institutions. The question, however, would be whether the international community should be *more* insistent upon rapid restructuring than it was; to the extent one can criticize the evolution of economic policy in Korea since the crisis, that criticism would be with respect to the slowness with which financial restructuring has occurred.[86]

The third issue (for all the Asian programs) was whether forthcoming support from the IMF and the other bilateral and multilateral institutions was of the appropriate size. Some argue that the financing should have been larger, at least enough to cover outstanding short-term indebtedness, and should have been available without conditions. To this proposal there are several responses. First, if a country does not adjust its policies, it is likely that capital outflows will continue, and capital flows are not limited to short-term debt. A larger size of program would then only result in larger capital outflows. A larger volume of foreign financial resources coupled with a smaller adjustment package would likely result in a greater capital outflow, and hence be self-defeating.

The other criticism—that the financial support should have been smaller—is based both on the outcome (not all resources were used) and on the proposition that there is moral hazard involved in IMF lending. Although there is no doubt moral hazard, those top policymakers who were

84. Hahm and Mishkin (1999) estimate that more than 60 percent of the foreign currency obligations were uncovered at the time of the crisis.
85. This is vividly illustrated by the contrast between Brazil's crisis in the early months of 1998 and the Asian crises. In Brazil, the financial system had few NPLs when the real was allowed to depreciate, and there appear to have been few foreign currency–denominated liabilities. The Brazilian recession was both short and shallow, and recovery was remarkably rapid, surprising most observers.
86. A great deal of the focus in the 12 July 2000 LOI, which is the last one, is on issues pertaining to further financial restructuring, including the need for reform of investment trusts and the corporate sector.

in office in the run-up to the crisis in Korea (as well as in Thailand, Mexico, Brazil, and Indonesia) lost their jobs very quickly in any event. Certainly, the risk to top economics officials must serve as at least a partial offset to moral hazard that would otherwise be entailed in their willingness to borrow and risk crises. Moreover, as noted, given conditions at the time of the IMF loan, it seems evident that the financial package should have been more than a "minimum" in order to reduce or eliminate expectations of a further free-fall of the exchange rate or of a financial crisis.

On most criteria, therefore, one can evaluate the IMF programs in Korea as having been successful: hindsight enables a clearer focus on the factors that contributed to the rapid emergence of the crisis,[87] and there are lessons for economic policy management for crisis avoidance, as well as areas where one can be critical at the margin of the stabilization program, but on balance, Koreans and the rest of the world are better off because of the fund's activities during the very difficult crisis period and its aftermath.

The Indonesian Crisis

The Korean stabilization program is of course of interest in itself; it is also of interest in analyzing the components of a Fund stabilization program and the reasons for them in light of conditions at the beginning of the crisis. By contrast, the Indonesian case is of more interest in understanding how political conditions or decisions can thwart an IMF program. I therefore very briefly sketch the background to the Indonesian crisis and the original Fund program, focusing instead on the factors that contributed to Indonesia's relatively poor performance after the initial crisis and Fund program.

Background

Indonesia had also experienced rapid growth over the preceding several decades, averaging about 7 percent annually. Indonesia started as a very populous (with little arable land per farmer and a large population, currently over 200 million) and poor country, but living standards and other indicators of well-being had risen markedly for most of the population, including that majority who were employed in agriculture. Indonesia's growth differed from that of the East Asian "tigers," however, in a number of respects. Growth of industry was spurred to a large extent by the internal market and had not been accompanied by a rapid growth of new manufacturing activity destined for exports; indeed, foreign exchange earnings to support growth originated largely in primary commodities—oil exports had accounted for more than half of foreign exchange earnings until the mid-1980s, when the price of oil fell sharply; agricultural commodity ex-

---

87. One can also raise issues about the incentives for foreign lending to emerging markets and ways that there might be incentives for a better balance between different forms of capital inflow.

ports were also important. Protection against foreign imports had remained relatively high, and many new projects (such as a national car plant; there were even plans to expand the uneconomic airplane factory to produce jets) were anticipated as import substitution ventures. Many viewed the Indonesian policymakers as schizophrenic between reliance on markets (and therefore presumably on growth of exports of industries with large inputs of unskilled labor) and retaining governmental controls and ownership over industry in order to develop high-technology import-substitution industries.[88]

Nonetheless, growth of agricultural output and productivity had been quite rapid, and rural standards of living, literacy rates, and health and nutrition indicators had risen significantly. The fraction of people living below the poverty line had been greatly reduced.

Hence, Indonesia was regarded as an economic success story, although visibility in the international economy was well below that of the East Asian tigers with their reliance upon manufactured exports and development of international markets for their output. Key differences were that living standards remained much lower than in East Asia, and politics were more suspect, especially after Korea moved toward more representative government in the mid-1980s, with Taiwan following suit.

President Sukarno, the independence leader and national hero, was in office until 1966. During his presidency, inflation had reached the thousands of percentage points annually, exports had dropped dramatically, and living standards had clearly not risen, although statistics were sparse and unreliable.

In 1966, Sukarno was overthrown in a bloody revolution,[89] and a general, Suharto, took power. He remained in office until early 1998. During his tenure, economic growth was rapid, as was already mentioned, and the Indonesian government was generally regarded as having done well in its economic policies, both for growth and for poverty alleviation. However, it was also widely recognized that President Suharto was the country's ruler, that his friends and cronies were benefiting enormously from the regime,[90] and that opposition was not tolerated. As his tenure in office got longer and as he aged, the regime appeared increasingly oppressive, and questions about succession were more pressing.[91]

88. See, for example, *Wall Street Journal,* 25 March 1993, A8: "Economic Roads: Indonesia is Divided on Whether to Compete on Low Labor Costs or Try High Tech."

89. The extreme violence in 1966 is one of the bases for nervousness about political instability in Indonesia.

90. See *The Economist,* 17 November 1990, 37. The subheading for the article read "The world's fifth most populous country may be on its way to producing another of those famous Asian economic miracles. Will politics ruin it?"

91. I was at a luncheon of bankers in Melbourne when the Indonesian rupiah was depreciating sharply. The Indonesian economy was the subject of discussion. One of the bankers present commented that he traveled all over the world for his bank and that he had visited Indonesia the preceding July. It was, he reported, the only country he had visited on business in which the first thing he heard about was the evacuation plans in the event of a political uprising.

The early 1990s were years of relatively successful growth: real GDP continued to grow at rates between 6 and 8 percent annually, inflation remained around 5 percent annually, and the government fiscal accounts were showing a small surplus. There were, however, a few worrisome signs. The current account deficit widened substantially from the $2 to $3 billion dollar range of the early 1990s to $6.4 billion in 1995, $7.3 billion in 1996, and $4.9 billion in 1997. Moreover, Indonesia's short-term debt had risen from $18 billion in 1992 and 1993 to $36 billion in 1997, while international reserves, which had equaled short-term debt in 1993, were only $20.3 billion at the end of 1997. The proximate source of this deterioration was a very rapid growth of domestic credit, which had increased by 21–22 percent in every year after 1993, and which then rose by 25 percent in 1997. It was well, but not officially, known that much bank credit was destined for the relatives and friends of the president and that many loans were on nonperforming status, or were at best "evergreen," in that additional credit was extended to enable the payment of debt-servicing obligations.

An election was scheduled for early 1998, and there was considerable speculation as to whether or not Suharto would run for another term in office. However, in the summer of 1997, capital flight began from Indonesia, and the rupiah began depreciating rapidly. The exchange rate had been 2,200 Rp per U.S. dollar at the end of 1994, and 2,380 Rp per dollar at the end of 1996. Even at the end of June 1997, it was 2,450. Then the rapid slide began. By the end of September, it was 4,471; by the end of December 6,274, reaching over 17,000 at its peak, and still 14,900 per dollar at the end of June 1998.

Of the various countries that were severely affected by the Asian financial crisis, it is probably Indonesia that caught people most by surprise.[92] In part, this was because of the relatively good economic performance of earlier years and, probably, a belief that the economic policies underlying this performance would continue independently of political events. Moreover, the Indonesian rupiah did not appear to be overvalued. Four sets of estimates have been made of the degree of real overvaluation of various Asian countries as of late 1996 or early 1997. One found the rupiah to have been undervalued, whereas the other three estimated overvaluation in the range of 4.2 to 9.6 percent.[93] Indonesia's incremental capital-output ratio remained at around 4 during the mid-1990s, while those of the other Asian countries were rising. Finally, Indonesian exports had continued growing reasonably rapidly—over 9 percent from the second half of 1995 to the second half of 1996—at a time when export growth in the rest of the region (except the Philippines) had been flagging. Hence, although observers had

92. To be sure, there were runs on the Hong Kong stock exchange and to some extent on the Taiwanese dollar and the Singapore dollar. In these instances, however, defenses were successful and the impact was far smaller than in Thailand, Korea, and Indonesia.

93. Estimates for the other Asian countries also indicated little evidence of overvaluation, with the largest estimates being for the Philippines. See Berg (1999, 8), table 2.

long recognized that Indonesia's political situation was potentially more volatile than that of the other rapidly growing Asian economies, there was less short-term concern about economic indicators.

However, the Indonesian banking system appears to have been much weaker than was generally appreciated. The official estimate of the percentage of NPLs in the banking system prior to the crisis, 8.8 percent for 1996,[94] was the highest in the region (Thailand's official estimate was 7.7 percent and Korea's 0.8 percent). However, JPMorgan and Goldman Sachs estimated actual NPLs as a share of total loans in 1998, and also the share at the peak of the crisis: their estimates were 11.0 and 9.0 percent respectively for Indonesia's total NPLs in 1998, and 30 to more than 40 percent at the peak of the crisis. These, too, were high relative even to other Asian countries.[95]

The corporate debt-equity ratio was put at 200 percent by 1996, and the estimated return on assets 4.7 percent. Thus, the financial sector was highly vulnerable and weak prior to the attack on the currency. When that attack came, the high ratio of short-term debt to international reserves was the proximate cause, but the weakness of the financial system clearly intensified it. There was no formal deposit insurance in Indonesia.[96] Once the closure of some insolvent financial institutions was announced, depositors questioned the dependability of other banks, and some fled to foreign currency rather than to the sounder domestic banks.[97]

The Crisis

The Indonesian rupiah began to depreciate in mid-1997, after the onset of the Thai crisis. Capital flight, if anything, intensified after that, even after the first IMF program was announced and begun early in November.[98] A key problem was that, once the downslide began, political instability followed. As already mentioned, there had been questions about the forthcoming election and whether President Suharto would run again early in

---

94. Data on Asian financial indicators of vulnerability prior to the crisis are from Berg (1999, 8), table 2, which seems to be as comparable a set of estimates across countries as is available.

95. Both sources put Korea's and Thailand's actual NPLs in 1998 above those of Indonesia in 1998, but Indonesia was still higher at the peak of the crisis by their estimates. It should be noted that the estimates for the Philippines were far below those of other Asian countries, which may explain why the Philippines was able to avoid the severe downturn that affected other Asian countries.

96. However, several banks had been closed earlier and small depositors had been compensated by the government.

97. Berg (1999, 23) points out that "After the announcement of the program at the end of October, foreign loans continued to be withdrawn. The exchange rate stayed reasonably stable until early December, when rumors of president Suharto's ill health . . . precipitated a sharp decline in the rupiah. Rollover rates on external credits fell to very low levels and fears of imminent default intensified."

98. The first LOI is dated 31 October 1997. All references to LOIs are referred to by dates. They may be found at [http://www.imf.org/external/country/IND/index.htm].

1998 even before the beginning of the crisis. Indeed, as late as December, the rupiah fell, partly due to the rumor that the president's health had deteriorated and that he would not seek reelection.[99] In the event, the economic downturn led to intensified political opposition, and President Suharto stepped down and was succeeded by one of his allies, President Habibie. Then, after elections were held in the middle of 1998 (for Parliament), a coalition government led by President Abdurrahman Wahid came into office. Some of the government's primary concerns were political,[100] and the problems of the economy seem to have been underestimated or at least not really fully understood by the leaders of the new government.

Either way, from October 1997 onward, political considerations dominated and led to considerable uncertainty as to what actions would be taken by the relevant economic officials; even when commitments were made, it was not apparent whether they would be carried out. This pattern started even under President Suharto, who declared in January 1998 that he would not necessarily follow IMF advice (despite the LOI of November). That episode ended with the famous photo of the IMF's managing director, arms folded, looking on as Suharto finally signed another agreement.

This state of things led to a number of renegotiations, cancellations of old agreements, signing of new ones, delays in approving second tranches, and so on. There were LOIs at frequent intervals; almost all restated earlier programs or had more urgent calls for actions that had been agreed upon in them.[101] The 15 January 1998 LOI, for example, set new and looser fiscal targets (in light of the severe deterioration of the Indonesian economy); the LOI of 19 October 1998 enumerated a large number of targets and set new dates for actions that had not been taken in accordance with the timetables in previous LOIs.[102] In January 2000, the earlier extended facility (of 25 August 1998) was canceled and a new extended arrangement entered into with the new government in place.

One of the manifestations of political instability was the apparent inability of the government itself to agree on a course of action. Announcements

---

99. Given President Suharto's age, observers were also keenly interested in his choice for a vice-presidential candidate, because his term of office if reelected would have been six years.

100. Chief among these was the role of the military. The president seems to have focused on this issue and was able to reduce the influence and power of the military significantly during the first part of 2000.

101. See Goldstein (chap. 5 in this volume) for further discussion of some of the conditions.

102. These included such items as introducing a law in Parliament to give Bank Indonesia autonomy; earlier LOIs had targeted this for 30 September 1998; in the October LOI, it was reported as being "in preparation." Likewise, there had been an intent to review the portfolios and finances of all the banks held by the Indonesian Bank Reconstruction Authority (IBRA), which had assumed control of the banks by 30 August 1998, and it was reported that twenty-seven banks had been reviewed, with the rest (twenty-seven) to be completed by November 15. A commitment to remove restrictions on debt-equity conversions—essential for corporate financial restructuring—had been made for 30 September 1998 and was reported in the LOI as "expected soon."

were repeatedly reversed, decisions taken were amended or not implemented, and inaction appeared to rule. Even as this paper was being written, the newly installed economy minister (who replaced his predecessor in order to bring "leadership" to the economics team) announced his open disagreement with the finance minister over the future of Bank Rakyat Indonesia.[103]

The decline in Indonesia's real GDP in 1998 was the severest of the crisis countries: it is recorded to have fallen by 13.7 percent, and preliminary estimates indicate a further drop of 0.8 percent in 1999. This compares with Thailand—the next hardest hit—which saw a decline in real GDP of 9.4 percent in 1998 and estimated growth in 1999 of 2.5 percent. Estimates for real GDP growth in Indonesia in 2000 center on 2–4 percent, which would not begin to reattain the precrisis level.

Evaluation of the Program

In an important sense, Indonesian economic growth has not resumed. The forecast growth in 2000 is expected to originate mostly in agriculture and other informal activities, and it reflects primarily a larger number of people in those activities. The important question is: what has gone wrong?

In a number of regards, the Indonesian situation as of mid-1997 appears not to have been dissimilar to that confronting Korea: each had political uncertainty (although Korea's election was sooner and it was quickly resolved); each had a high ratio of short-term foreign debt to international reserves; and each had a weak domestic banking system. Moreover, the initial IMF responses look similar. In both instances, programs called for financial restructuring and supporting measures for it as well as initial tightening of monetary and fiscal policy,[104] and they were implemented only after the currency had depreciated markedly.

The first difference between Korea and Indonesia seems to lie in the immediate aftermath. Neither Fund program provided (or could have provided) sufficient resources to enable private creditors to have been repaid: there had to be some debt rollover in addition to the support from the international community. In Korea's case, rollover of private-sector debt and the stretching-out of maturities started almost immediately with the restructuring of bank debt late in December, and $22 billion more was rolled over into medium-term debt in April 1999 (see Berg 1999, 21). By contrast,

---

103. *Indonesian Observer,* 13 September 2000. See also the editorial by Sadli, in *Bulletin Kadin,* September 2000, titled "Muddling Through of Economic Recovery Continuing, Amidst Political Uncertainties." As this paper was being revised in November 2000, Bank Indonesia officials were announcing that they could maintain monetary and exchange rate policies despite the resignation of many of the board members (*Jakarta Post,* 23 November 2000).

104. The Fund's later review of the programs in the crisis countries defended the initial monetary and fiscal stances in each country as set forth in the LOIs but recognized that relaxation of the fiscal stance might have come sooner. See the press conference of Jack Boorman, 19 January 1999, [http://www.imf.org/external/np/tr/1999/tr990120.htm].

in Indonesia's case, the capital outflow did not stop. Moreover, private firms and banks holding foreign currency–denominated debt found themselves with rupiah-denominated obligations increased by a considerably greater multiple than in Korea because of the larger proportionate rupiah depreciation. The already weak financial system was in imminent danger of collapse.

The government of Indonesia did take over the banks and founded the Indonesian Bank Restructuring Agency (IBRA) to undertake restructuring. However, IBRA was very slow to commence work, and a year after its inauguration it had done very little. Moreover, IBRA compensated banks for the loans it assumed with nonnegotiable government bonds. Much as some sort of takeover was probably in order, banks could not and cannot (since they still hold them) lend nonnegotiable instruments. There was doubt about the soundness of the banks that were still functioning; IBRA was not recapitalizing and restructuring the banks, and the banks were not lending. In the words of Al Harberger in December 1998, fourteen months after the crisis had begun:

> At some point in time during the early months of the crisis, the Indonesian commercial banks, beset by demand from their own creditors, virtually shut their "new loans" window. Their determination was to collect on their "old loans" to the extent that these were amortized, and then to use the proceeds either to pay their own creditors or to strengthen their very precarious liquidity positions. The response of the commercial banks' customers to this new policy was simply to stop making amortization payments on their debts to the banks. Some customers continued to pay interest, others did not. Of those debtor companies that paid neither interest nor amortization, some were solvent and able to pay, simply choosing not to pay under the special circumstances of the moment. Others were truly unable to pay; their loans would be "bad loans" under any circumstances. Unfortunately it was not easy to discriminate among the non-payers, so that one did not have a clear idea of how many of them were in one category and how many in the other.
>
> The situation of a wholesale "borrowers' strike" against paying off existing loans came as something new to me. It adds new complications to the problem of bailing out the banks, and may greatly magnify the cost that ultimately has to be borne by the taxpayers. (Harberger 1999, 60–61)

Failure of IBRA to act more quickly and decisively and the failure of the domestic financial system explains much of the continuing difficulties of Indonesia. Those difficulties, in turn, are in large part a reflection of the political situation and its uncertainties.

The question arises, therefore, as to (a) whether the Fund should have initiated a program in the first place and (b) once it had done so and the authorities were moving slowly, whether it should have continued in its support. The first question is by far the easier. Clearly, the political events that transpired once the Indonesian crisis was under way could not have been anticipated. The Indonesian situation was not that dissimilar to those in the other Asian countries,[105] and uncertainties appeared to be no greater, and possibly even less, than those in Korea. Moreover, it is even conceivable that had the Fund program worked initially as well in Indonesia as it did in Korea, the political difficulties that transpired during the winter of 1998 might have been postponed, and an upturn might have taken place. Perhaps most telling of all, however, there was, as stated by Berg, an "imminent danger" of the complete collapse of the Indonesian financial system, and it seems a straightforward conclusion that anything that brought about a significantly positive probability that that eventuality would be averted was a worthwhile proposition. Moreover, Indonesia is a sufficiently large and strategically located country that many of the Fund's largest shareholders were determined that the Fund should act. If it is believed the IMF should not have done so, criticism should be directed at the large industrial countries that insisted on support for Indonesia.

The inability of the Indonesians to carry out commitments, even when backed by Fund pressure, that were obviously essential to the resolution of the crisis suggests that many of the secondary conditions set forth in the LOIs were well warranted. Indeed, much of the detail included in the successive LOIs was there precisely because steps earlier promised had not been taken. Clearly, measures to restructure the finances of the banks and the corporate sector had to be included as part of the program,[106] and failure to act on these matters evidently delayed recovery.

The issue then is whether the IMF should lend at all unless these measures are undertaken. To the extent that Fund conditionality on these issues increased the likelihood of their implementation or accelerated the rate at which they were implemented, a strong case can be made for their inclusion;

105. There is also an issue, not discussed here, that was raised at that time and that supports the Fund's actions. That is, there was concern about "contagion" from country to country during the crisis. Indeed, there have been two views of the Asian crisis, one focusing on fundamentals, and the other on "irrational markets and contagion." Although it is clear that creditors, when surprised in one situation, look around to ascertain their vulnerability to similar situations elsewhere, the prevailing view of the Asian crisis seems to have swung more and more toward fundamentals as more and more evidence emerges as to the weak and weakening states of the domestic financial systems in the crisis countries in 1996 and 1997.

106. There were conditions such as that calling for the end to the government's clove monopoly that, it can be argued, while desirable, were not essential to the program and probably should not have been imposed on a government whose implementation capacity was in any event weak. Another condition called for reduced tariffs, which was arguably defensible: The ideal time to reduce import duties is when devaluation is occurring, because it minimizes the costs to the domestic economy and at the same time cuts the inflationary pressure of the devaluation. In Indonesia's case, an argument can also be made that the country had probably exhausted its potential for growth through import substitution and that resumption of growth could not occur at anything like the earlier rates unless such a measure was taken. Careful reading of the conditions in the LOIs for Indonesia suggests that there were a few, but not very many, conditions imposed that could not be justified.

an argument against most of these conditions that were essential to financial restructuring would have to hold either that no loan should have been forthcoming until the conditions were met prior to the loan or that the Fund's imposition of conditions was counterproductive.

The second question—whether Fund support should have continued when implementation was so slow and so weak—is more difficult. The case for continued lending is probably best couched in consideration of the alternative: what would have happened, given the state of Indonesian politics, had the Fund withdrawn its support?[107] Given the inability of Indonesia to attract private capital in any event, it is almost certain that such a move would have triggered further capital outflows, further weakening the fragile financial system, and reducing real GDP even further. Conjectures as to what the political responses might have been are well beyond the scope of this paper, but it seems likely that the political consequences would have been sufficiently grave that a decision on more than postponement of a tranche would almost certainly have required the approval of the major shareholders in the Fund. As already noted, it is doubtful whether such approval would have been forthcoming.

As of late 2000, the Indonesian economy had still not achieved a situation in which growth could resume and normal capital flows could replace official finance. Finding fault with the Fund program, on that account, however, requires the further step of assuming that there was an alternative program that either would have resulted in a different political evolution of the country or would have worked even in the absence of better implementation on the part of the government. Those believing that the IMF programs were inappropriate should be asked to specify an alternative scenario: it is not evident that there is one.

4.1.5   Contrasts between Korea and Indonesia and Other Countries

Thailand's crisis had a great deal in common with those in Korea and Indonesia. Thailand had a long history of rapid economic growth based on a reasonably open economy and export growth at a fixed nominal exchange rate. However, the financial sector was very weak and deteriorating. In the mid-1990s, a real estate boom was accompanied by rapid expansion of bank credit (averaging 37 percent per year from 1992 to 1996), in turn financed by capital inflows. Nonperforming loans prior to the crisis are estimated to have been between 17 and 18 percent of all bank loans outstanding. Because many were secured by real estate as collateral, Thailand was highly vulnerable to any decline in real estate prices. Between 1991 and

---

107. On several occasions, disbursement of later tranches of Fund support were delayed pending improved implementation. This happened, for example, in April 2000. The Fund staff obviously had to make a judgment call as to how much action they would insist upon as a condition for additional support.

1996, in addition, the debt-equity ratio of Thailand's corporate sector had increased from 170 to 340 percent, which was the second highest among the crisis countries.

In the case of Thailand, IMF staff were reported to have been urging the Thai government to alter the exchange rate or the exchange rate regime for at least a year prior to the crisis. The current account deficit had averaged over 6 percent of GDP in the 1991–95 period and stood at 7.9 percent of GDP in 1996. Short-term external debt at the end of 1996 was almost exactly equal to reserves.

When the crisis unfolded, capital outflows from Thailand were a key culprit. Initially, several banks were closed, and immediate action was taken to begin to restore the financial system. New money associated with the inauguration of the IMF program and exchange rate change (with the rate floating) was sufficient to stem the capital outflow.[108] The Thai government appears to have followed the fund programs fairly faithfully, and Thailand's recovery has been second only to Korea's among the crisis countries. As in the other crisis countries, the fiscal stance was loosened as the severity of the crisis became evident.

An interesting contrast is with that of a noncrisis country: the Philippines. By most measures of the performance of the foreign sector, the Philippine economy had the most troublesome situation going into the crisis period. The country had had a lower overall rate of economic growth in the 1990s than any of the crisis countries. Its real exchange rate is estimated to have appreciated markedly from 1991 to 1995; the current account was in increasing deficit, reaching 4.7 percent of GDP in 1996 and 5.3 percent of GDP in 1997. Moreover, the government was incurring small fiscal deficits, and public debt was a higher percentage of GDP in 1997 than in any of the crisis countries.

However, its financial sector appears to have been considerably stronger than that of the crisis countries. JPMorgan and Goldman Sachs, respectively, estimate actual NPLs in the banking system in 1998 as 5.5 and 3.0 percent of outstanding loans, and the peak after the crisis was proportionately much lower than that of any of the crisis countries. The corporate sector's debt-equity ratio was put at 160, somewhat lower than that of the other crisis countries.

These differences are striking: the Philippines' external sector was in more severe disequilibrium than that of the crisis countries, but its financial sector was in considerably better shape. The Philippines' nominal exchange rate depreciated 32.2 percent. However, the fact that its banking system was

108. Berg (1999) credits the stemming of capital flight to the Fund program and the fact that "foreign banks based in Thailand accounted for more than half of Thailand's private external debt maturing in 1998. These banks, largely Japanese institutions borrowing from their own headquarters, were willing to agree to maintain their exposure" (25).

sound permitted it to lower the nominal interest rate in 1998, and real GDP fell by 0.5 percent—a much smaller magnitude than any of the other crisis countries.[109]

Based on other corroborating evidence (the ease of Brazil's recovery from the real crisis in the context of a relatively sound banking system) as well, the conclusion seems inescapable that the negative impact on real GDP and an economy of a financial crisis combined with an external crisis is much greater than the sum of the negative impacts of two separate crises: each feeds upon the other. It also seems evident that restructuring the financial sector—or at least putting in motion credible policies that will insure the rapid restructuring—is essential to the resolution of a crisis triggered by capital outflows. Delay does not appear to ease the negative effects but to prolong them and perhaps even to intensify them.

The international economy can be, and is being, restructured in ways that make a crisis, either financial or foreign exchange, less likely. Floating exchange rates, altered BIS capital adequacy rules so that short-term debt is not preferred on the part of lenders, and various steps that have been taken and are now being contemplated to strengthen financial systems and to redress the imbalances between the attractiveness of short-term lending and other forms of capital inflow will all contribute.

However, crises there will surely be. Lessons from the Asian crisis will certainly enable all analysts to appreciate the interactions between financial and foreign variables and their crucial roles in determining vulnerability for crisis and its aftermath. However, especially in a world in which capital outflows can magnify quickly, an institution such as the IMF seems absolutely essential for ensuring the world's ability to react in a timely fashion. Moreover, as long as there are weak financial systems negatively affected by exchange rate movements or capital outflows, it will continue to be necessary for the IMF to address financial restructuring as well as exchange rate issues.

References

Behrman, Jere. 1976. *Foreign trade regimes and economic development: Chile.* New York: Columbia University Press.

Berg, Andrew. 1999. The Asia crisis: Causes, policy responses, and outcomes. IMF Working Paper no. WP/99/138. Washington, D.C.: International Monetary Fund, October.

Boughton, James M. 1999. From Suez to Tequila: The IMF as crisis manager. *Economic Journal* 110 (460): 273–91.

---

109. The shift in the Philippines' current account balance in 1998 was 6.7 percent of GDP, contrasted with 7.2 percent in Indonesia, 16.9 percent in Korea, and 20.3 percent in Thailand.

Cho, Dongchul, and Kenneth D. West. 1999. The effect of monetary policy in exchange rate stabilization in post-crisis Korea. Paper presented at the Korea Development Institute conference on The Korean Crisis: Before and After. 15 October, Seoul, Korea.

Cline, William R., and Sidney Weintraub, eds. 1981. *Economic stabilization in developing countries.* Washington, D.C.: Brookings Institution.

Cooper, Richard N. 1971. An assessment of currency devaluation in developing countries. In *Government and economic development,* ed. Gustav Ranis, 472–513. New Haven, Conn.: Yale University Press.

Edwards, Sebastian. 1989. Real exchange rates, devaluation, and adjustment. Cambridge: MIT Press.

Ergin, Evren. 1999. Timing of IMF programs. Ph.D. diss., Stanford University.

Feldstein, Martin. 1998. Refocusing the IMF. *Foreign Affairs* 77 (March/April): 20–33.

Frank, Charles R. Jr., Kwang Suk Kim, and Larry Westphal. 1975. *Foreign trade regimes and economic development: South Korea.* New York: Columbia University Press.

Furman, Jason, and Joseph E. Stiglitz. 1998. Economic crises: Evidence and insights from East Asia. *Brookings Papers on Economic Activity,* Issue no. 2:1–114. Washington, D.C.: Brookings Institution.

Hahm, Joon-Ho, and Frederic S. Mishkin. 1999. Causes of the Korean financial crisis: Lessons for policy. In *The Korean crisis: Before and after,* Korea Development Institute, 55–144. Seoul: Korean Development Institute.

Harberger, Arnold C. 1999. The Indonesian crisis revisited. University of California, Los Angeles. Mimeograph, December.

Hong, Wontack. 1981. Export promotion and employment growth in South Korea. In *Trade and employment in developing countries,* vol. 1: Individual studies, ed. Anne O. Krueger, Hal B. Lary, Terry Monson, and Narongchai Akrasanee, 341–91. Chicago: University of Chicago Press.

International Monetary Fund (IMF). 1995. *International capital markets: Developments, prospects, and policy issues.* Washington, D.C.: IMF.

———. 1997. Request for standby, 3 December.

James, Harold. 1996. *International monetary cooperation since Bretton Woods.* New York: Oxford University Press.

Krueger, Anne O. 1978. Foreign trade regimes and economic development: Liberalization attempts and consequences. Lexington, Mass.: Ballinger Press.

———. 1979. *The developmental role of the foreign sector and aid.* Harvard University Press Studies in the Modernization of the Republic of Korea: 1948–1975. Cambridge, Mass.: Harvard University Press.

———. 1999. The founding of the Bretton Woods institutions: A view from the 1990s. In *The political economy of comparative development into the 21st century,* vol. 1. ed. Gustav Ranis, Sheng-Cheng Hu, and Yun-Peng, 335–54. Cheltenham, England: Edward Elgar.

Little, I. M. D., Richard N. Cooper, W. Max Corden, and Sarath Rajapatirana. 1993. *Boom, crisis, and adjustment: The macroeconomic experience of developing countries.* New York: Oxford University Press.

Organization for Economic Cooperation and Development (OECD). 1994. *OECD economic surveys: Korea 1994.* Paris: OECD.

Sturc, Ernest. 1968. Stabilization policies: Experience of some European countries in the 1950s. *IMF Staff Papers* 15 (2): 197–217.

Williamson, John, ed. 1983. *IMF conditionality.* Washington, D.C.: Institute for International Economics.

2. Stanley Fischer

Because the discussion at the conference has focused on International Monetary Fund (IMF)–supported stabilization programs in Asia, I will start by outlining some of the lessons the IMF has drawn from the programs in Asia during 1997–98. I will then take up five general issues that arise in all IMF-supported programs: when to lend; choosing an exchange rate regime; setting fiscal and monetary policy; determining structural policy conditions; and how much to lend.

First, let us consider Asia. Jack Boorman and other IMF colleagues have written a thoughtful paper on IMF-supported programs in Thailand, Indonesia, and Korea in 1997–98 (Boorman et al. 2000). Among the key conclusions are the following:

- First, fiscal policy was too tight at the start of each program, but it was loosened rapidly (especially in Indonesia and Korea) once the extent of the economic downturns became clear.
- Second, the bank closures in Indonesia should have been more wide-ranging (when the sixteen banks were closed, it was known that others would have to be closed, which reduced confidence in the remaining banks) and there should have been more comprehensive guarantees for depositors (deposits in the closed banks were guaranteed up to a level that provided coverage for small depositors), to help persuade them to leave their deposits in the banks that remained open.
- Third, the Fund was right to put the focus of structural conditionality on financial system and corporate debt restructuring, problems that lay at the heart of the crisis. However, there may well have been too many structural policy conditions at the margins of the Fund's areas of central competence and interest. In some cases, particularly that of Indonesia, this conditionality was included to try to improve governance.
- Fourth, our advice on monetary policy was broadly correct. If monetary policy mistakes were made in Indonesia, they were because policy was too loose, not too tight.
- The programs succeeded when they were implemented resolutely and consistently. In all three cases, this took a change of government. Indonesia was a special case. The course of the crisis was tied up with the uncertainties surrounding the Suharto succession. We believed—and were assured by important Asians—that the key to restoring market confidence was to get the president's public support for the economic program. However, it seemed that when he did express support for the program—for policies that were at odds with much of what he had been doing for decades—the markets simply took this as a signal that

his time was running out, and they had no idea what would follow his departure.

Now let me turn to some more general issues.

When to Lend

In an ideal world, the Fund would get involved with a country early in its difficulties, when there is still time to stop the drama turning into a crisis. However, this is easier said than done. For one thing, the IMF cannot force a country to have a program. The country has to ask, and then the program has to have a reasonable chance of success.

It is clear from our Article IV consultations that we were warning about financial weaknesses in Asia long before the crises came to a head. In Indonesia, we were approached by technocrats in the government in August and September 1997 who were well aware of many of the problems in the banking sector and of what needed to be done to fix them. The president was not on board, however, and we could not move to a program because we had no confidence that the necessary measures would be carried out.

We are often urged to support a particular policymaker, or group of policymakers, because they offer the best—sometimes, we are told, the only— hope of getting a country out of its economic mess. That may well be so, and in many cases our support makes it more likely that the right things will happen. However, we have to be realistic. We cannot ask our executive board to commit the Fund's resources to support even the best-intentioned of reformers if the program does not have a reasonable chance of success.

This is a tough call to make. The best programs are those to which the authorities, and ideally the society more widely, are committed—programs *owned* by the country. For instance, in the program with Colombia that began at the end of 1999, we were confident of the ability and commitment of the Colombian policymakers to the principles and design of the program, and the political support they had, even though the difficult conditions in Colombia meant their task would not be easy.

Cases in which the international community is in effect supporting a particular reformist policy line, which is opposed by important and powerful domestic factions, are much more difficult. However, if we took a purist approach and never supported any program in which ownership is less than complete, then we would not support a significant number of programs that succeed. In many such cases, this is a risk that the international community is probably right to take.

Choosing an Exchange Rate Regime

The crises of the last few years demonstrate that countries open to international capital flows are wise to have either floating exchange rates or, depending on their histories, hard pegs, by which I mean dollarization, a currency board, or membership of a currency union.[1] Intermediate regimes—adjustable pegs, crawls, and narrow bands—have generally proven unsustainable.

I do not mean by a floating rate regime one in which monetary policy is completely indifferent to the level of the exchange rate. Policymakers can influence the exchange rate through monetary policy actions or occasional intervention. What they should not do is allow the defense of a particular value for the exchange rate to become the central plank of the country's economic policy, unless that commitment is enshrined in some form of hard peg.

In accordance with the Articles of Agreement, which leave the choice of its exchange rate system to each country, the IMF generally avoids being doctrinaire on the exchange rate regime when deciding whether to support a country's program. We have taken different approaches in different situations. In Ecuador, early in 2000, we supported dollarization after the event, even though we would not have recommended it beforehand. In Colombia, a few months earlier, we did insist on a move to a flexible rate, because the currency had been pushing against the bottom of its band for some time and the regime was clearly unsustainable. In Turkey, we supported a crawling peg to stabilize triple-digit inflation to begin with, but with an exit strategy to a float built in, a strategy that did not succeed.

If the Fund is convinced—as it was in Colombia—that a given regime is unsustainable, then it would be irresponsible to support a program that incorporates that regime. However, where the outlook is less clear—as it was, for instance, in the case of the Brazilian peg in October 1998—we have generally given the country the benefit of the doubt. This has been controversial, for there are always some who are convinced that the currency is overvalued and should not be defended. In giving the country the benefit of the doubt, we are deeply aware that we are not the policymakers directly concerned and responsible to the voters in that country, and that responsibility for a decision on a change in exchange rate or exchange rate regime, which may have massively adverse consequences, must rest with those who will carry it out.

Exit from a pegged exchange rate system is always difficult. When the going is good and the peg is strong, the country sees no reason to change the system. However, if the peg is under pressure, the policymakers will insist on defending it, for fear of the consequences of devaluation. And sometimes—for instance, in the case of Jordan, which has defended its peg over the period since 1996—they do very well this way over sustained periods. In such cases, the Fund generally tries to persuade the country gradually to allow more flexibility in the rate.

---

1. This theme is developed in more detail in Fischer (2001).

Setting Fiscal and Monetary Policy

Three interrelated factors help determine the required degree of fiscal adjustment: the sources and extent of financing for the budget deficit; the sources and extent of financing for the balance of payments; and debt dynamics. In the Brazilian program formulated in early 1999, after the devaluation, the debt dynamics were the critical factor. The debt-GDP ratio was 33 percent at the start of the *plan real* in 1994; it was 47 percent and rising in early 1999. The question was: how much fiscal tightening was needed to turn this trend around, given cautious assumptions on the behavior of real interest rates?

In Thailand we called initially for fiscal tightening for three reasons: because the balance-of-payments deficit had been large before the program; because the implicit liabilities and debt that would be created by financial restructuring had to be dealt with; and because we believed that would strengthen market confidence. In Indonesia and Korea, the tightening was motivated by the last two factors. These were legitimate concerns, although it soon became clear that policy was initially set too tight, and fiscal policy was eased.

In setting monetary policy within a program, the concern is to avoid generating too much inflation. Typically, performance criteria for monetary policy in IMF programs are set in terms of specific quantitative limits on certain monetary variables, usually a floor for net international reserves and a ceiling on net domestic assets of the central bank. There are interesting analytical questions about how best to adapt this time-tested framework to countries where monetary policy is set in terms of an inflation target. In a case like that of Brazil, where there is confidence in the people carrying out the inflation-targeting framework, getting the technicalities right may not be terribly important. However, there will be other countries where the precise specification of the monetary policy conditions is much more important.

Determining Structural Policy Conditions

Structural policies rightly come within the purview of IMF-supported programs when tackling them is essential to solving the country's macroeconomic problems. The scope and detail required will therefore vary from country to country. In our 1999 program with Ecuador, for example, privatization was needed not only for efficiency reasons but also because the country needed the privatization revenues to reduce its debt significantly. Banking-sector problems are often the source of structural conditions. In some transition economies, restructuring of the energy sector is needed for both balance of payments and domestic macroeconomic reasons.

The scope and detail of structural policy conditions in IMF programs has increased in recent years, in part because there is greater recognition now of the importance of structural policies in creating the conditions for macroeconomic stability and strong growth. However, there are also two major concerns: first, that the Fund has been moving outside its areas of concentration and expertise; and, second, that demanding too many conditions may be an infringement of national sovereignty that risks undermining the authorities' commitment to the program. In response, the Fund is streamlining structural conditionality.

One of the hardest areas in which to do this is governance. It is an unavoidable fact that if the international community wants to help countries in trouble, then it will be hard to sustain public support for this activity if people believe that the money we lend ends up in the hands of crooks. So governance—in the sense of corruption—issues inevitably have to be addressed.

This is a defensive reason for tackling governance problems. However, doing so is also good for the country concerned and its citizens (it also happens, in my view, to be the right thing to do). Indeed, the IMF frequently finds civil society in borrowing countries strongly supportive of anticorruption measures in IMF programs in their country. How far you go in each case is a different matter. Whether we should have confronted the clove and plywood monopolies in Indonesia is a reasonable matter for debate. However, some measures were undoubtedly necessary to begin changing the ways in which business was being done in Indonesia, if the investment climate and the basis for investment decisions in Indonesia were to change.

In determining structural policy conditions, we also have to ask how we can cooperate most effectively with other agencies to deliver the international community's objectives. Many necessary structural reforms are the primary responsibility of the World Bank, for example, the creation of social safety nets, or privatizations. Including these elements in a program helps ensure that they get done, and in the past we often included them at the request of the World Bank for that reason. We are now examining, with the World Bank, whether there are better ways of achieving the desired outcome.

Deciding How Much to Lend

In deciding how much the Fund should lend, it is conceptually important to distinguish between liquidity and solvency crises—a distinction easier to make in theory than in practice. Essentially, we need to decide whether a country's balance-of-payments position is sustainable in the medium term. If it is not sustainable, then it will be necessary to restructure its debts. If it is sustainable, then we might be prepared to lend big sums to help countries through the crisis. That is the appropriate solution to a liquidity crisis. Other considerations of course come into play in deciding when "big" becomes "too big," including the perceived risk of moral hazard. These issues are hard to judge in the abstract and have to be dealt with largely crisis-by-crisis.

One clear lesson from the crises in Asia and subsequently is that the days of smoke-and-mirrors lending are gone. If the international community is going to promise money, then it had better be there and it had better be seen to be there. It also needs to be available quickly. These lessons from some of the Asian programs were applied successfully to the Brazilian program that began in 1998.

References

Boorman, Jack, Timothy Lane, Marianne Schulze-Ghattas, Ates Bulir, Atish R. Ghosh, and Ham. 2000. Managing financial crises: The experience in East Asia. IMF Working Paper no. WP/00/107. Washington, D.C.: IMF.
Fischer, Stanley. 2001. Exchange rate systems: Is the bipolar view correct? *Journal of Economic Perspectives* 15 (2): 3–24.

3. Jeffrey D. Sachs

Thanks very much, Marty, and thanks for the opportunity to review this issue yet again. As you might guess, I'm going to take a bit more critical view of what's happened. I want to say at the outset that it is not in any way a personal view of any of the people involved, because there could not have been, I think, a stronger group with greater integrity than the people that led this.

I'd like to start with one general point, which also follows our discussion this morning, about the way that our profession discusses the issues that we've been exploring. I thought the discussion was fabulous, but I would have liked one sentence arching over the discussion, and that is that we cannot and should not be searching for one solution or one policy prescription that's appropriate to everybody and to all circumstances. I think the most important thing in macroeconomic policy making is to undertake what doctors call a "differential diagnosis." The symptoms of any case can suggest *multiple* competing explanations and interpretations. The first job is to understand which of these alternative views applies in a given historical context. Only then can the correct treatment be prescribed.

Since macroeconomic crises are very nonlinear and path-dependent processes, the detailed decisions matter a lot in determining the outcomes over the course of a couple of years. I should also add that I would have little disagreement with anything the International Monetary Fund (IMF) did in Asia if we were looking at a horizon of five to ten years. My concern is about the specifics of IMF management in the heat of the crisis. Over the horizon of a few years, we all believe in open markets, currency convertibility, financial-sector reform, and fiscal prudence. There are few fundamental issues at stake regarding medium-term macroeconomic management. The problem, as Keynes famously observed, lies in the short run—when the patient is very sick, and when a proper diagnosis is essential. The wrong prescription can further weaken, if not kill, the patient.

I think the origins of the Asian crisis are now fairly much accepted, and I think they could have been fairly well understood back in the middle of 1997. To refresh my mind, I went back to see what I wrote in op-eds and policy memos even before the crisis got serious in the fall of 1997. The basic problems—of overvalued currencies pegged to a strong dollar, huge short-term capital inflows, underregulated banking sectors, and financial vulnerability as a result of all of these factors—were all rather apparent.

The real issue was, in my opinion, was how to handle events at three critical periods. First, during the summer and fall of 1997, the collapse of the Thai baht pushed the region into a period of high risk. Second, at the very end of 1997 and early 1998, the region was in fulminant financial panic, marked by the massive and intense flight of foreign and domestic capital. Third, as of mid-1998, the region needed to consider the long-term strategies for cleaning up the balance sheets and overcoming the collapse of the financial system. My quarrels with the IMF mainly involved the first two time periods.

In the summer and fall of 1997, the entire region got pulled into financial crisis following the collapse of the pegged exchange rate in Thailand. Was the crisis inevitable? Specifically, was it inevitable as of mid-1997 that the region would face a fall in gross national product (GNP) of 5 percent or more in 1998? I think that the answer is no. The steep downturn could have been avoided. There was nothing in the "fundamentals" of the productive sectors of the East Asian economies that warranted a fall in output of 5–10 percent of GNP in 1998 (especially considering trend growth rates of more than 5 percent per year in most of the region). The steep fall was the result of financial panic, and the panic, in my view, could still have been averted in mid-1997.

We now know, in retrospect, that the collapse of output was the result of a ferocious outflow of short-term capital from the region. The capital left, in my opinion, not because of fundamentals, but because of a self-fulfilling panic. Since short-term debts were so high relative to reserves, panicky short-term claimants came to believe that they needed to move their money out of Asia ahead of other short-term creditors, lest they get caught with illiquid assets when the region's foreign reserves were depleted (as of course actually happened to the slow-moving investors). This was a rational view assuming that others took the same point of view—in other words, a "rational panic," in which a nonpanic equilibrium could also have been achieved.

If nobody had panicked, the short-term debts could have been rolled over, as usual. Maturities could have been lengthened to reduce vulnerability. The economies were strong enough over the medium term to scale back their current accounts, and export their way out of debt crisis, with moderate currency depreciations eliminating the preceding overvaluations. Instead, however, there was panic, and the banks and the government could not redeem the short-term loans being pulled. The result was a default on debt repayments and a ferocious credit squeeze.

In short, the East Asian economies were vulnerable to panic (because of high short-term debts, overvalued currencies, and weak financial sectors), but they were not fatally ill. So what pushed the economies from a moderate slowdown into a full-fledged panic? I believe that the panic was due, at least in some part, to the behavior of the IMF itself. When the baht was devalued and other neighboring countries started to face withdrawals of credit, the IMF began demanding root-and-branch reforms. The rhetoric from Washington escalated. Suddenly, the Asian economies could do no right. What had been Asian-style capitalism suddenly turned into Asian-style cronyism. All this was fine and good, except that the rhetoric was part of the fuel of the panic itself.

There were three interlocking mistakes, in my mind. The first, and perhaps the most explosive, was the decision by the IMF, in the middle of a fragile situation, to force the widespread closure of weak financial institutions in Thailand, Indonesia, and Korea. Again, I don't think I'd have any disagreement on a three-year or five-year horizon with tightening up on financial standards, and even closing many banks, but this is a crucial matter of timing. Wisdom led the U.S. bank regulators not to close the major U.S. commercial banks in the middle and late 1980s when the banks had very weak balance sheets (following the Latin American debt crisis), or even to close Long-Term Capital Management in 1998, for fear of a major credit crunch. Yet the IMF pushed hard for massive bank closures in Asia, and this helped to instigate panic, in my opinion.

In Indonesia, which was the place I was following most closely, one economic advisory group, and I don't vouch for them, wrote on 28 October, two days before the bank closures, "Forcing problematic banks to liquidate in the midst of the ongoing monetary crisis would further deteriorate confidence in the monetary sector, and could spark a run on the banks. The government should not act hastily in forcing problem banks to liquidate. It's likely bank liquidation would be done discriminately with banks owned by politically well-connected business people escaping the ax. Such bias would cause uncertainty among people and might worsen the public's confidence in the banking industry. This would in turn start a massive bank run, where customers would move their funds to foreign banks." Regulatory forbearance makes a lot of sense when you're in such an explosive environment.

Second, I felt that the IMF was trying to prove its strength by stressing how much the Asian economies needed fundamental reforms. The IMF began to lecture the Asian economies incessantly about all that was wrong with crony capitalism. Deep and rapid reforms, it was argued, would restore confidence. However, this approach did the opposite, making investors feel that the sky was falling, when all that was needed was a modest 20 percent depreciation of formerly pegged exchange rates.

Third, I thought that the way that the packages were put together at the beginning added to the likelihood of panic (and said so repeatedly at the time, for whatever it's worth). The notion that raising interest rates sharply in this context, squeezing credit, closing banks, and cutting budgetary spending sharply would *raise* confidence rather than lowering confidence was something that I found profoundly doubtful. When the packages were introduced, they certainly did not stop the panic. This is important to understand because, again, we're not debating views on fundamentals, or whether Suharto was a creep or whether his son was a crook or anything like that. We're debating clinical approaches to an *incipient* (but still avoidable, perhaps) financial panic. When the packages were introduced, the currencies continued to slide, the bank run developed in Indonesia in November, and the Korean package failed to stop the flight of creditors from Korean banks in December.

The result is, in my view, a macro collapse in 1998 that was much deeper than was justified by the real economy. Moreover, I saw in many countries that the fall of output was the result of the ferocious liquidity squeeze that marked the financial panic. In Indonesia, for example, the shoe manufacturers' association came to see the government in January 1998 to complain that the industry had confirmed international orders for around $500 million of shoe exports, but no working capital to buy the inputs needed for highly profitable exports! Thus, even in the context of an incredibly weak currency, exports were falling, not rising, because of the intensity of the financial squeeze. This is a powerful sign (among many such signs) that output fell far more than was justified by fundamental factors.

The credit squeeze might not have been fully avoidable (i.e., the panic may indeed have been unstoppable in late 1997, despite my belief that indeed it could have been avoided), but it surely did not have to be met with massive budget cutting and interest rate increases. There is the problem of the second time horizon that I mentioned at the start of my remarks, the period from the very end of 1997 to early 1998, when the panic was already fulminant. In this period, the IMF really piled on, demanding massive structural reforms while also advocating fierce fiscal austerity in the midst of a massive credit squeeze.

The IMF fiscal and monetary package certainly didn't ease the crisis. What really stopped the fierce downturn was the end of the short-term capital outflows. This occurred throughout Asia in late 1997 and until mid-1998 for three reasons: some debts were finally rescheduled or rolled over (as in Korea just after Christmas); central banks ran out of reserves, leading to defaults by domestic banks and companies to foreign creditors; and, third, many of the short-term loans were simply repaid.

Is all well that ends well? After all, the economies have recovered. Our judgment on how things went depends on the standards that we use. I think that there has been a tremendous amount of unnecessary suffering and economic loss. The legacy of the financial panic will last for years, because governments took on enormous debt in order to bail out the collapsed financial sectors.

Final notes. First, prevention is essential. In the precrisis moment, when a spark can set off a conflagration, forbearance and subtlety, not shouting, are all really good pieces of policy wisdom. In the crisis itself, it's crucial not to overload macroeconomic austerity, not to exacerbate panic, and to understand panic as a real phenomenon, not just as a turn of phrase, but as an actual event in capital markets that squeezes real output from the supply side, not the demand side. Forcing rollovers or standstills on debt repayments should be a core part of how we handle these episodes. Finally, we had U.S. senators pressing the IMF to make sure that the Korean deal with the IMF included market-opening clauses or other specific trade measures reflecting U.S. interests rather than Korea's macroeconomic needs. We have to figure out ways to keep the IMF a truly international institution, and not a creditor institution of the major shareholders. Thanks.

Discussion Summary

Guillermo Ortiz complained about the publicity that sometimes surrounds IMF missions to crisis-afflicted countries. After the Mexican crisis, no one knew when an IMF official was in the country, he said, adding that this was very helpful. Responding to Jeffrey Sachs's comment on the need for clinical analysis of each crisis, Ortiz expressed doubt about the likely success of ex post counterfactual analysis of alternative policy responses. As an example, he recalled that interest rates rose to 80 percent in February and March of 1995. "Would 40 percent have been enough?" he asked, answering, "I really don't know." He said you have to overshoot in your policy response in the midst of a crisis, avoiding the greater danger of falling short and not reestablishing confidence.

Morris Goldstein said that an important difference between Asia and Brazil was the extent of currency mismatches—liabilities denominated in foreign currencies and assets denominated in domestic currency—on the balance sheets of banks and corporations. The devaluation in Brazil was not associated with large-scale bankruptcies. He noted various ways to limit the mismatch problem: moving to a floating rate (counting on currency movements to make people aware of exchange rate risk); putting a spotlight on the extent of the mismatches so that the market demands a premium for lending where such mismatches exist; and dollarization. On the question of whether large recessions could have been avoided if a different policy course had been followed, Goldstein thinks the answer is "No." If the IMF had come out and said that it was really just a liquidity crisis and there was nothing to worry about, the markets would not have been reassured, given the bad news that was coming out each day about the state of the financial systems. Lowering interest rates worked in Australia, Sweden, and the United Kingdom—but they are not emerging markets, he said.

Peter Garber commented on the use of the word "panic." What we saw was a kind of "cold panic" that followed from the way risk is managed in industrial-country banking systems, he said. Value-at-risk methods push almost automatic reductions in positions as returns become more correlated in a crisis. Managers are faced with the option of increasing the capital held against positions in emerging markets or reducing those positions. The positions are often unwound. He dislikes the word "panic" in this context because it suggests that two outcomes can occur, with psychology determining which one prevails. It is not psychology, he said, but the result of the way risk is managed.

Paul Keating highlighted how the ending of the cold war led to a major shift in the importance attached by the industrial countries to Indonesia. One implication of its fall from importance was that debt standstills were not tried and, indeed, were strongly objected to. The ultimate result was a dramatic shift in capital flows. Regarding what was needed to maintain Suharto's support for reforms, he said support was lost as the list of demands for structural reforms grew, and he blamed the IMF for saying things that undermined investor confidence in Indonesia. *Stanley Fischer* strongly objected to this characterization of the IMF's role, which he said reflected a common misperception in Australia. *Keating* went on to describe the huge political and economic difficulties that Indonesia now confronts and called for some humility on the question of how appropriate the international response to the crisis was. He said that Indonesia had a liquidity and credit crunch, adding that "countries that didn't get the IMF in, like Malaysia, did better, and this point has not gone unnoticed." Returning to the geopolitical significance of Indonesia, he said that the Asia Pacific Economic Cooperation (APEC) would not have been possible without Suharto and his government. And Keating doubts that China would be joining the World Trade Organization (WTO) if APEC did not exist. He closed by urging the IMF to focus on its core mission of dealing with balance-of-payments disequilibria—"standing up to the United States Treasury or whoever," if necessary.

Charles Dallara said that it is important to recognize that the IMF, like everyone else, was scrambling to understand the transmission mechanisms in the unfolding crisis. Mistakes were made, but these mistakes are related to the complexity of the underlying mechanisms. On the question of the Fund's fiscal emphasis, he agrees that too much stress was placed on correcting fiscal problems. But, again, the path to restoring confidence was unclear. He added that at this time of "noncrisis" he is actually more worried that the Fund is not putting enough emphasis on fundamental fiscal reform, such as establishing rational, broadly based tax systems.

On the question of corruption and governance, Dallara said the Fund's shareholders would not tolerate putting money into countries where there is a high probability of misappropriation. He added that the fund needs more help in grappling with governance issues, taking into account its lack of staff expertise in such areas as corporate governance. If the Fund is to avoid mission creep, he said that it is essential that the World Bank take on a larger role in these areas, adding that if the World Bank "continues to address the diagnosis and development of programs for structural reform at the pace it does today, and the pace it has for all the years I've known it, the Fund has little choice but to scramble to try to cope with these issues itself." If the Fund's shareholders want to avoid mission creep, "they have to develop a much more activist, fast-paced organization in the World Bank."

Nouriel Roubini commented on a number of issues in Jeffrey Sachs's presentation. First, he said that while most people agree that the initial fiscal policies were too tight, two caveats needed to be kept in mind: some countries (notably Russia and Brazil) did have serious fiscal problems, and the financial-sector bailouts had major fiscal implications. Second, he said that he does not agree that an easier monetary policy would have helped. Given the large amount of foreign debt on the balance sheets, and given the fact that a lower interest rate would have led to further devaluation, the balance sheet effects of a looser monetary policy "would have been disastrous." As evidence, he compared Indonesia, which he said pumped in huge amounts of liquidity to support the banking system, to Korea and Thailand, which followed a more restrictive monetary course. Third, he questioned the wisdom of substantial "forbearance" when dealing with the banks. In many cases—finance companies in Thailand, merchant banks in Korea, and so on—the institutions were insolvent rather than illiquid. This raised the traditional problem of the institutions' "gambling for redemption." Roubini added that the eventual costs are greater if you don't intervene. To avoid panic, care must be taken in closing down institutions—for example, putting in place appropriate deposit insurance—but forbearance is not a solution. Fourth, Roubini said he disagrees with those who claim that there weren't significant problems in the real economies of the Asian countries prior to the crises. In Korea, for example, seven out of the top thirty *chaebol* were already formally bankrupt in the middle of 1997. Finally, on the question of how to stem the outflow of capital, he expressed skepticism about the wisdom of debt standstills. He pointed to various unintended consequences: a "rush for the exit" when standstills are anticipated; the risk of contagion as investors fear standstills in other countries; movement down the slippery slope to exchange and capital controls; inducement to asset stripping; and costly litigation.

Larry Summers sought to correct what Jeffrey Sachs said about guaranteeing bank liabilities in Korea. He said the Korean government had given a guarantee to cover most of the liabilities during the summer of 1997 and believed it was important to stand by that guarantee. Although one can disagree about the wisdom of such a guarantee, the international community had supported the Korean government's efforts. The support was not the "craven kowtowing to international capital that Jeff suggests," he said. Summers then asked two questions.

First, was the international community right in forcing Thailand to disclose its true net reserve position in the summer of 1997 (when it had substantial forward positions that effectively depleted its foreign reserves)? *Jeffrey Sachs* thinks it probably was a mistake, pointing out that the markets misunderstood the disclosure. People thought $30 billion had been lost, instead of market losses on contracts worth $30 billion. *Fischer* said there was never going to be a good day to make the disclosure. "There was no good time; it was done at the least bad time," he said. On how it was presented, he thinks it might have been possible to explain it better, but they tried hard to show people the cash flow projections and to emphasize that they were not going to lose $30 billion.

Second, *Summers* asked those who dislike what the Fund did in Indonesia if it should employ more or less people who think about political and governance issues. More people would allow the Fund to be more sensitive to the nuances of the situation. Fewer people would make them less involved in the set of issues that surround governance, and thus less involved in structural issues. *Sachs* said that adding more political experts is not desirable for the world system, given its present lack of legitimacy. He said he would rather see the institution depoliticize to become the foremost crisis prevention and crisis management tool for financial markets.

Edwin Truman said that Jeffrey Sachs's prescription, which he sees as amounting to massive forbearance, creates moral hazard on the debtors' side. He then raised the question of how vocal the IMF should be, recounting that he used to be of the view that the IMF should go quietly into a country. However, he does not think that is realistic today, now that the IMF has to explain what it is doing. He added that the IMF had used all its leverage with Thailand in advance of the crisis but was largely ignored. Indeed, Thailand devalued without going to the Fund for a program—which he dubbed the "Mexican solution" (in 1994)—which put the Fund in a difficult situation. He concluded by saying that Fund officials "should be judicious, but the notion that they should be absolutely quiet seems to me to be just unrealistic."

Anne O. Krueger recounted meetings with Korean technocrats in August 1997, when everyone had used the words "impending crisis." She said they all talked about the interconnections between the *chaebol* financing, the state of the banks, the exchange rate, and capital flows. There was no confusion about what the problems were, and there was a consensus that government would not act until forced to by a crisis. On Sachs's attempt to separate short-term issues from medium- and long-term issues, she said that, given the insolvency of the *chaebol,* dealing with the situation as if it were just a liquidity crisis would just postpone the crisis. Moving on to the current situations in the financial systems of crisis-affected countries (as of October 2000), Krueger said that the situation in Indonesia is very bad. The banking system is in bad shape because banks are holding nonnegotiable government bonds in the place of nonperforming loans. The problem with nonnegotiable bonds is that you can't lend them, so that there is no domestic credit, she said. Turning to Korea, she said that all is not well there either, with financial restructuring only half completed. She thinks Korea has gone too fast with its recovery without addressing fundamental weaknesses and would have been better off with a slower recovery that didn't leave another crisis looming for the future.

Responding to Krueger on the issue of timing, *Sachs* said that he was not making a distinction between what to do now and what to do ten years from now, but between now and three months or six months. Closing or suspending fourteen banks in Korea in December 1997, or closing sixteen Indonesian banks in the middle of an incipient run, is a gamble that does not make sense, he said. Responding to Nouriel Roubini's earlier observation about liquidity injections in Indonesia, Sachs said that it was not because the government was attempting to pump-prime the economy. They were responding to massive runs by depositors, and they had to decide whether to formally suspend the banking system—as was done in the United States in 1933—or to provide liquidity.

Sachs said that Morris Goldstein might be right when he says the downturn was unavoidable, but he pointed out that no one was predicting at the time that the downturn was going to be –8 percent. Observing the contractionary policies that were being pursued, he said he believed at the time that the downturn would be very severe. He agreed that he is essentially calling for forbearance, but "not for years." Instead, he believes that you must pursue the policy course that does most to avoid a panic. Moreover, he said if Peter Garber is right, and it wasn't panic but rather the working of the value-at-risk models of the international commercial banks, then the situation is even worse, and suspensions of flows or other mechanisms for direct intervention become absolutely essential.

Remarking on the financial problems of the Korean *chaebol,* Sachs said that it is one thing for these groups to be going bankrupt, but it is something else for the economy to shrink by 7 percent. He said the financial and real sides are different for all sorts of reasons, and this explains why Korea was able to bounce back sharply, utilizing its capacity in some of the most important industries (e.g., semiconductors) in the world.

Fischer said he has little time for the charge that the IMF could have stemmed the capital outflows if it had expressed more confidence. He said he is more struck by the charge that the IMF "was asleep at the switch" and, with the possible exception of Thailand, never did get around to telling people that a disaster was coming. He thinks the Fund was late in Korea and missed some of the signals. However, he pointed out that the Koreans were hiding some of their reserves data. So, if anything, the Fund needs to answer to the charge that it was overly optimistic in its projections, not that it helped spread the panic.

On the issue of whether the output collapse could have been smaller, he said that an easier fiscal policy would have helped, but not substantially so. He also pointed out that the Mexican rescue went badly until there was a fiscal tightening. At the time, people criticized the IMF for not recognizing the contractionary impact of a tighter fiscal stance. However, there had to be a judgment on the relative sizes of Keynesian impact and the confidence impact, assuming these went in opposite directions. On dealing with the banking sector, he doesn't think forbearance is the right solution. A better solution would have been comprehensive guarantees, as happened in Thailand. It was important to get on with restructuring the banks as quickly as possible. The alternative model is Japan, which is what you get with very long forbearance, he said.

Regarding what was needed to restore confidence in Indonesia, Fischer said that no one was going to believe you were doing anything to solve the country's problems, unless you were seen to be doing something to solve the problems with the banks.

Finally, on the issue of IMF accountability, he noted that the heads of governments of leading industrial nations were closely involved in the Indonesian program, with many heads of government calling on Suharto to urge him to pursue the reforms. He stressed that IMF technocrats should not be making decisions that are at their core "political judgments," and he added that he feels immensely reassured that the Fund has to take its programs before its board and listen to what 182 governments think. It is essential that member governments support decisions. It is the IMF's job to get the technical side right, but "we cannot pretend that the technical things we do are purely technical and do not have political consequences," he said.

IMF Structural Programs

1. Morris Goldstein
2. Timothy F. Geithner
3. Paul Keating
4. Yung Chul Park

1. Morris Goldstein

IMF Structural Programs

5.1.1 Introduction

"Detailed conditionality (often including dozens of conditions) has burdened IMF programs in recent years and made such programs unwieldy, highly conflictive, time consuming to negotiate, and often ineffectual."

"The IMF [International Monetary Fund] should cease lending to countries for long-term development assistance (as in sub-Saharan Africa) and for long-term structural transformation (as in post-Communist transition economies). . . . The current practice of extending long-term loans in exchange for member countries' agreeing to conditions set by the IMF should end."
— *Meltzer Report* (International Financial Institution Advisory Commission 2000, 7, 8, and 43)

"Both the Fund and the Bank have tried to do too much in recent years, and they have lost sight of their respective strengths. They both need to return to basics . . . [The Fund] should focus on a leaner agenda of monetary, fiscal, and

The author is grateful to Masood Ahmed, Mark Allen, Caroline Atkinson, Fred Bergsten, Barry Eichengreen, Martin Feldstein, Timothy F. Geithner, Stefan Ingves, Paul Keating, Mohsin Khan, Robert Lafrance, Carl Lindgren, Robert Litan, Michael Mussa, Yung Chul Park, Jacques Polak, James Powell, Miguel Savastano, Todd Stewart, Ohno Wijnholds, John Williamson, and Yukio Yoshimura for helpful comments on an earlier draft, and to Trond Augdal for superb research assistance. He also wants to thank Stanley Fischer and his colleagues at the International Monetary Fund for sharing with him the fund's data on structural conditions in fund programs.

exchange rate policies, and of banking and financial-sector surveillance and reform."
—*Council on Foreign Relations Task Force* (1999, 18–19)

"The one common theme that runs through perceptions of ESAF [Enhanced Structural Adjustment Facility] at the country level is a feeling of a loss of control over the policy content and the pace of implementation of reform programs."[1]
—*External Evaluation of the ESAF* (Botchway et al. 1998, 20)

"The IMF should eschew the temptation to use currency crises as an opportunity to force fundamental structural and institutional reforms on countries, however useful they may be in the long term, unless they are absolutely necessary to revive access to international funds."
—Martin Feldstein (1998, 32)

"The IMF's activities are not related to those specified in its charter for the simple reason that the par-value system of exchange rates it was to monitor no longer exists. In the tradition of skilled bureaucracies, the IMF has turned to new areas and has managed to expand substantially its financial resources and, in the process, its influence."
—George Shultz (1995, 5)

"The IMF has not been established to give guidance on social and political priorities, nor has its voting system been designed to give it the moral authority to oversee priorities of a noneconomic nature. Its functions have to be kept narrowly technical . . . and the Fund has to accept that the authorities of a country are the sole judges of its social and political priorities."
—David Finch (1983, 77–78)[2]

"The IMF programs in East Asia are far from optimal for restoring financial market confidence in the short term. . . . [T]hey have covered a very wide range of policies beyond the immediate financial crisis. . . . Most of the structural reforms, however, simply detract attention from the financial crisis. They have taken government expertise, negotiating time, and political capital away from the core issues of financial markets, exchange rate policy, and the like."
—Steven Radelet and Jeffrey D. Sachs (1998, 67–68)

"In view of the size of the current deficits and the difficulties that may arise in private intermediation, the Fund must be prepared, when necessary, to lend in larger amounts than in the past. Also, the structural problems faced by many countries may require that adjustment take place over a longer period than has been typical in the framework of Fund programs in the past."
—International Monetary Fund (IMF), *World Economic Outlook* (1980)

1. ESAF is the Fund's Enhanced Structural Adjustment Facility, established in 1987 to provide long-term concessional assistance to low-income countries facing protracted balance-of-payments problems.
2. Mr. Finch was then the director of the IMF's Exchange and Trade Relations Department.

"The Fund approach to adjustment has had severe economic costs for many of these [developing] countries in terms of declines in the levels of output and growth rates, reductions in employment and adverse effects on income distribution."
—*Report by the Group of Twenty-Four* (1987, 9)

"Our prime objective is growth. In my view, there is no longer any ambiguity about this. It is towards growth that our programs and their conditionality are aimed."

"Only the pursuit of 'high-quality' growth is worth the effort. What is such growth? It is growth that can be sustained over time without causing domestic and external financial imbalance; growth that has the human person at its center . . . growth that, to be sustainable, is based on a continuous effort for more equity, poverty alleviation, and empowerment of poor people; and growth that promotes protection of the environment, and respect for national cultural values. This is what our programs are, more and more, and must aim for."
—From speeches by former IMF Managing Director Michel Camdessus (1990, 2000a, respectively)

"In recent years, some critics of the IMF have gone to the opposite extreme, arguing that the IFIs [international financial institutions] should have done more, especially in the context of the economies in transition to develop an appropriate framework of property rights in support of markets. . . . [I]n considering the future of the two institutions, their activities need to be geared to strengthening the private sector and the appropriate role of government in relation to it."
—Anne O. Krueger (1998, 2003)

"I do not accept the view that when it comes to our poorer member countries, we should not be lending to them, but should turn it over to someone else. . . . Is the poverty reduction and growth facility . . . which we are working on jointly with the World Bank . . . going to be an improvement in the way we deal with countries? Absolutely. Why? Because . . . it forces us, in cooperation with the World Bank, to make sure that the macroeconomic framework is consistent with what needs to be done for social reasons. Macroeconomic instability is bad for everyone everywhere. . . . That is why we should remain in these countries. . . . But we cannot do that in a way that ignores the fact that poverty is the main problem confronting these countries, and that there must be massive efforts, spearheaded by the World Bank, to reduce poverty in these countries."
—Stanley Fischer, IMF first deputy managing director (2000b)

"A changed IMF is needed for the changed world we now have. . . . As we look to the future we need to redouble our efforts to find better approaches if not answers to fundamental questions. . . . How do we balance concerns about intrusiveness in national affairs and a desire to promote national ownership of reform programs with a desire to see governments take bolder steps to, for example, build stronger social safety nets, implement core labor standards, em-

power civil society groups, reduce the role of government in the economy, and address critical issues related to governance, corruption, and crony capitalism?"
—U.S. Treasury Secretary Summers (1999)

"[T]he proposed eligibility criteria [for IMF lending in the Meltzer Report] are too narrow. Even where they are met, they would be unlikely to protect economies from the broad range of potential causes of crises. The criteria focus on the financial sector, and yet even problems that surface in the financial sector often have their roots in deeper economic and structural weaknesses. One simply cannot predict with confidence what the next generation of crises will be and therefore we need to preserve the IMF's ability to respond flexibly to changingcircumstances."
—U.S. Treasury *Response to the Meltzer Report* (2000b, 17)

"A central part of the programs in the Asian crisis countries was an unprecedented body of structural reforms. . . . The overriding question is whether it was appropriate to place so much emphasis on structural reform measures in the financial and corporate sectors. . . . The answer is clearly yes."
—*IMF Report* (Lane et al. 1999) on Fund Programs in Indonesia, Korea, and Thailand

"[T]he bottom line of the 'era of the IFIs,' despite obvious shortcomings, has been an unambiguous success of historic proportions in both economic and social terms."
—*Minority Dissent, Meltzer Report* (Bergsten et al. 2000, 111)

As suggested above, an active debate has long been under way—and has intensified in the wake of the Asian crisis—about the appropriate scope and intrusiveness of IMF policy conditionality. In this paper, I take up one key element of that debate, namely, the role of structural policies in IMF-supported adjustment programs. By "structural policies," I mean policies aimed not at the management of aggregate demand but rather at either improving the efficiency of resource use or increasing the economy's productive capacity. Structural policies are usually aimed at reducing or dismantling government-imposed distortions or putting in place various institutional features of a modern market economy. Such structural policies include, inter alia, financial-sector policies; liberalization of trade, capital markets, and the exchange rate system; privatization and public enterprise policies; tax and expenditure policies (apart from the overall fiscal stance); labor-market policies; pricing and marketing policies; transparency and disclosure policies; poverty reduction and social safety-net policies; pension policies; corporate governance policies (including anticorruption measures); and environmental policies.

To set the stage for what follows, it is worth summarizing the main concerns and criticisms that have been expressed about the IMF's existing approach to structural policy conditionality.[3] These typically take one or more of the following forms.

First, there is a worry that wide-ranging and micromanaged structural policy recommendations will be viewed by developing-country borrowers as so costly and intrusive as to discourage unduly the demand for Fund assistance during crises (see, e.g., Feldstein 1998). Even though the cost of borrowing from the Fund (the so-called rate of charge) is much lower than the cost of borrowing from private creditors—particularly during times of stress—we observe that developing countries usually come to the IMF "late in the day" when their balance-of-payments problems are already severe.[4] This suggests that developing countries place a nontrivial shadow price on the policy conditions associated with Fund borrowing. The concern is that if these conditions become too onerous, emerging economies will wait even longer to come to the Fund (as Thailand did in 1997) or will turn to regional official crisis lenders that offer easier policy conditionality (e.g., in 1998 Malaysia was one of the first beneficiaries of low-conditionality Miyazawa Initiative funds, and Asian countries could eventually decide to elevate the infant Chiang-Mai swap arrangements into a full-fledged Asian Monetary Fund).[5] The outcome—so the argument goes—would then be even more difficult initial crisis conditions, greater resort to the antisocial behavior that the Fund was established to prevent, and a tendency toward Gresham's Law of conditionality (according to which weak regional conditionality would drive out not only the unnecessary but also the necessary elements of Fund conditionality).

A second concern is that insistence on deep structural reforms in cases of illiquidity (rather than insolvency) will serve only to frighten private investors about the size of the problem, thereby rendering more difficult the restoration of confidence and the rollover of short-term capital flows that are the keys to resolving the liquidity crisis (see Radelet and Sachs 1998). No country (including the Group of Seven [G7] countries) is without some structural weaknesses, but it is argued that, however desirable structural policy reforms may be for the performance of the economy over the longer term, it is a mistake to suggest that such reforms are indispensable to resolving the crisis (when they are not). Among the Asian crisis countries, Korea is identified as a case in which solvency was never in question and less

---

3. Neither these concerns and criticisms, nor the counterarguments outlined later in this section, should be interpreted as my own views. I provide my own summary assessment of past fund structural conditionality in section 5.1.4.

4. The Fund's rate of charge averaged a little over 4 percent from 1997 through the first half of 2000; in contrast, emerging market bond spreads (relative to U.S. Treasuries) have fluctuated from 375 to 1,700 basis points since the outbreak of the Thai crisis in mid-1997.

5. See C. Fred Bergsten's "Towards a Tripartite World" (*The Economist,* 15 July 2000, 23–26) on regional financial initiatives in Asia.

emphasis on structural reform both in the diagnosis and the policy prescription would have produced a milder crisis.

Concern number three is with equal treatment of countries—one of the Fund's key operating principles. Here, the argument is that the Fund has been asking for sweeping structural reforms from developing countries that it would not ask of industrial countries were the latter in similar circumstances. As Paul Volcker put it, "When the Fund consults with a poor and weak country, the country gets in line. When it consults with a big and strong country, the Fund gets in line" (Volcker and Gyohten 1992). Although differences across countries in economic and political power are a fact of life, the argument is that requiring developing countries to undertake more structural remedies than would their industrial-country counterparts undermines local "ownership" of Fund programs. It also works at cross purposes from simultaneous efforts to forge a consensus on strengthening the international financial architecture in (mixed developing-country and industrial-country) groups like the Group of Twenty (G20) and the Financial Stability Forum (FSF).

Yet a fourth criticism is that permitting the Fund to stray from its core competence of macroeconomic and exchange rate policies into a host of structural policy areas results in poor crisis management, weakens the Fund's overall reputation for competent analysis and advice (with adverse spillovers for the credibility of its recommendations in core policy areas), and runs counter to a sensible division of labor and an application of comparative advantage among the various international financial institutions (IFIs). In this connection, critics have maintained that the Fund bungled bank closures in Indonesia and precipitated a credit crunch in the crisis countries by requiring an unduly rapid increase in bank capitalization (see, e.g., Stiglitz 1999); that the Fund lacks both the expertise and staff resources to make timely and sound policy recommendations in areas as diverse as corporate governance, trade policy, privatization, poverty reduction, and environmental management; and that "mission creep" on the part of both the Fund and the World Bank, in addition to a blurring of responsibilities between them, reduces the public and legislative support necessary to fund them adequately (see Council on Foreign Relations Task Force 1999). Long-term structural reforms (at least outside the financial sector) and poverty reduction should be the main business of the World Bank—not of the IMF.

A fifth charge is that the way the Fund has been managing its structural policy conditionality is flawed. Specifically, the argument is that multiplication of structural performance conditions, the specification of "micro" policy measures, and the increasing reliance on (qualitative) structural benchmarks and program reviews (as monitors of policy performance) have combined both to increase the uncertainty facing Fund borrowers and to lower the incentive to follow through with structural reform. Performance criteria were instituted not only to assure the Fund that its financial resources were being used for the purposes intended but also to assure the borrowing country that if it undertook certain prespecified policy actions it would be eligible to draw (see Guitian 1981; Polak 1991). Also, because performance criteria were relatively few in number, easily measured, and macro in their impact, they both conveyed a relatively clear message about which policy actions were deemed (by the Fund) to carry the highest priority and provided a fairly predictable link with bottom-line economic outcomes (e.g., improvement in the balance of payments). However, when a Fund program contains, say, on the order of fifty or more qualitative structural policy conditions, when many of these conditions are very micro in nature, and when both fulfillment of these conditions and eligibility to draw require judgmental calls by the Fund, signals, impacts, and incentives will be more muddled. Should meeting thirty of fifty structural policy conditions be interpreted as a "good overall effort" that merits Fund support, or should it be viewed as a significant noncompliance with the program?

Suffice to say that these criticisms of the Fund's structural policy conditionality have not gone unchallenged. Again, in the spirit of motivating the subsequent discussion, it is well to consider the following counterarguments.

Although the structural policy conditions the IMF attaches to its loans are often demanding and threaten vested interests within the country, emerging economies recognize that a Fund program represents their best chance to make real traction on the structural weaknesses that have underpinned their crisis vulnerability. Private capital markets, although they sometimes supply strong disciplining force, are not perfect substitutes for either the Fund's specific policy advice or its financing; indeed, in more than a few cases, private creditors will not extend credit in large amounts until the Fund has blessed a country's policies.[6] Turning the steering wheel over temporarily to an outside party is always costly, but better the Fund than one or two large G7 countries. Ironically, the structural policy measures that have drawn the most critical fire in several of the Asian crisis countries (Indonesia and Korea) were for a long time high on the priority list of domestic reformers, but they could not get those reforms implemented (over the opposition of the ruling elite) in a noncrisis situation.[7] At this point,

---

6. Fischer (2000b, 1) argues that the fundamental reason why one needs an institution like the IMF is that "the international financial system left to itself does not work perfectly, and it is possible to make it work better for the sake of the people who live in that system." Also, see Masson and Mussa (1995) and Krueger (1998). Rodrik (1995) notes that an experiment in which private creditors attempted to specify and monitor conditionality in Peru was soon discontinued.

7. See Haggard (2000). On the role of domestic reformers in the Asian crisis countries, he concludes as follows: "it is misguided to see the course of policy solely as a response to external political pressures from the international financial institutions and the United States. . . . At least in some important policy areas, domestic groups were reaching surprisingly similar conclusions on the need for reform" (12).

there is no plan to turn Asian swap or credit arrangements into a serious rival to the Fund with competing policy conditionality. Also, very few crisis countries (in Asia or elsewhere) have seen capital controls as the preferred mode of crisis management. Just as it is not optimal for a host country to establish the weakest regulatory and prudential regime simply because it gives market participants the most freedom of action, it is not optimal (from the viewpoint of developing countries) to make Fund structural policy conditionality too easy or flexible. Fund *gaiatsu*—warts and all—may still be the best option out there for jump-starting structural reform.

The distinction between illiquidity and insolvency is not regarded as particularly helpful in most crisis situations, because the dividing line between the two often rests on the quality of crisis management, and because countries differ from firms both in the nature of the relevant collateral and in their willingness (as opposed to ability) to pay (see Fischer 1999). Although investor panic was an important part of the Asian crisis story, so too were "bad fundamentals" that increased downside risk. For example, in the run-up to the Korean crisis, seven of the thirty largest *chaebol* were essentially bankrupt; there were large terms-of-trade losses in 1996 (especially for semiconductors); nonperforming loans in the banking system and leverage in the corporate sector were already high; there was a low return on invested capital; capital inflows were biased toward short-term capital and against foreign direct investment; there was a lack of transparency (including on the country's short-term foreign liabilities); and substantial political uncertainty exacerbated the government's credibility problem.[8] Yes, many of these structural problems were of long standing, and despite them Korea had shown impressive growth performance over several decades. And yes, Korea has staged an impressive V-shaped recovery without eliminating all these structural problems. Nevertheless, it does not follow that Korea could have regained market confidence without making a good "start" on structural reform in 1997–98. Fund financing–cum–debt rescheduling and an (eventual) turn to easier monetary and fiscal policies—without any structural policy reform—would not have turned the situation around. Treating only the symptoms and not the (structural) root of the problem is not the way to restore confidence. Looking at precrisis fiscal positions in the crisis countries without considering the contingent government liabilities associated with financial-sector restructuring provides a misleading picture of fundamentals (see Boorman et al. 2000). Moreover, the alleged negative effect of Fund public pronouncements on market confidence is said to be much exaggerated. Once Thailand's fall "woke up" market participants to the poor health of banks and corporates in the rest of Asia and every large

8. See Roubini's comments in McHale (2000b). Claessens et al. (1999) also found that (precrisis) the four countries most seriously affected by the Asian crisis ranked low on the quality of the regulatory environment in an international comparison of middle-income emerging economies in East Asia and Latin America.

Group of Ten (G10) bank and security house in the region was issuing weekly reports on the rising share of nonperforming loans in Asian financial systems, it is very unlikely that a Fund statement claiming it was only a short-term liquidity crisis would have turned the tide (after all, the IMF's then managing director was already telling all who would listen that the crisis was really "a blessing in disguise").[9]

Reflecting, inter alia, their less preferred access (in terms of maturity, currency, and predictability) to international capital markets, their weaker institutional framework (ranging from judicial systems to insolvency regimes), and their track record of higher political instability, developing countries *are* different from industrial countries. Recognizing this difference is not dispensing unequal treatment but seeing the world as it is. If the Asian crisis countries—despite their impressive performance on economic growth, inflation, and macro fundamentals over a long period—were regarded by private financial markets as being just like industrial countries, they could have "done an Australia" and got out of the crisis by lowering interest rates and letting their exchange rates depreciate moderately—and this without any Fund assistance.[10] In the event, they could not do that. Nor will the crisis countries be able to sustain their recoveries if they lapse back into the same structural weaknesses they had before. Consequently, it is not realistic to expect a developing country that gets into a crisis to live by the same structural policy conditionality as would a troubled industrial country.[11] For the foreseeable future, developing countries will have to contend with a history of banking, debt, and currency crises, and restoration of confidence will often require a different dose and mix of macroeconomic and structural policies than would be the case for industrial countries. There is no indication that disagreement over past Fund structural policy conditionality is hampering the work of groups like the G20 and the FSF; on the contrary, those groups are making real progress in areas like the application of international financial standards.

The IMF has developed considerable expertise in dealing with banking and financial-sector problems in developing countries. Over the past five years, more than forty-five specialists (including former bank supervisors) have been added to the staff of the Fund's Monetary and Exchange Affairs Department alone. Admittedly, bank closures in Indonesia did not go well. However, since deposit insurance arrangements were not in place, since the authorities were willing to close only a small share of the insolvent banks, and since there were concerns about the moral hazard effects of a blanket

9. See Goldstein (1998) and Ahluwalia (2000) on the "wake up" hypothesis as an explanation of the contagion in the Asian crisis.

10. See Krugman (1998) on what the "confidence game" means for monetary and fiscal policies in developing countries during a crisis versus what is asked from industrial countries.

11. See Eichengreen and Hausmann (1999) on financing differences between developing countries and industrial countries.

guarantee, there was no easy alternative to that action (see Lindgren et al. 1999). Likewise, if stricter bank capitalization requirements had not been instituted in the crisis countries, we would have seen rampant "double-or-nothing" lending behavior by insolvent lenders and an even higher fiscal bill for the bank cleanup. Evidence on the existence of a credit crunch in the crisis countries in 1997–98 is far from clear-cut (see Lane et al. 1999).

In areas outside the Fund's comparative advantage, the Fund draws heavily on other IFIs with the requisite expertise—and especially on the World Bank. This collaboration is particularly close on poverty reduction and social safety net issues but also applies increasingly to corporate governance, privatization, trade policy, and environmental impacts. Eliminating all overlap between the IMF and the World Bank (on fiscal and banking reform) is neither feasible nor desirable. The Fund's major focus in the poor countries remains on the macroeconomic framework—a specialization that no other IFI is as qualified to handle. A merger of the Fund and the World Bank is unappealing, both because it would sacrifice the speed and efficiency that come with a still rather small IMF and because a mega-IFI would have too much power across a wide spectrum of macro and microeconomic issues.

Yes, the Fund has given increased emphasis in recent years to economic growth and to social conditions in the design and implementation of its programs with developing countries, just as it was responsive to the unique opportunity and massive need for institution-building systems in the fledgling market economies and new democracies of Eastern Europe. The world has changed. If the Fund did not change with it, and if the Fund did not embrace the same objectives in its programs as its members pursue in their national economic policies, there would be little chance that IMF programs would be either agreed upon or implemented (see Camdessus 1999b).

Structural policies are not like macroeconomic policies, and indicators of policy compliance have to reflect those differences. Progress on banking supervision or privatization cannot be measured in the same way net domestic credit or international reserves are tracked. Performance benchmarks for structural policies have to be qualitative, and a measure of discretion is needed to evaluate the results. Also, because of the interdependencies among structural policies, a macroeconomic impact will come only if progress is made on many fronts simultaneously. Furthermore, the devil is in the details. It makes a big difference if the borrowing country responds to a Fund condition for a large cut in the budget deficit by slashing expenditure on health and education versus the curtailment of the national car project. Moreover, because both the implementation of and payoff from structural projects take longer than macroeconomic and exchange rate policies, it is necessary to measure progress along the way. All of this produces many detailed structural performance tests and some uncertainty about whether the overall effort will warrant Fund financial support, but there are no short-cuts that would work better.

The rest of the paper elaborates on these issues and sets out some additional arguments and factual material relevant for gauging what IMF structural policy conditionality should be like in the future. In section 5.1.2, I ask what, if any, guidance on structural policy involvement can be gleaned from the Fund's charter and guidance notes from its executive board. I then discuss three alternative mandates for Fund lending within which structural policy conditionality might operate—ranging from a narrow one based on correction of balance-of-payments problems and resolution of the current crisis, to broader ones that add avoidance of future crises and pursuit of "high-quality" economic growth to the agenda. Section 5.1.3 looks at various dimensions of Fund structural policy involvement and conditionality—both in the Asian crisis countries over the past three years and more broadly over the past several decades. It also offers some tentative conclusions on the effectiveness of that conditionality, with particular emphasis on the compliance with Fund conditionality. Because very little factual material has been published heretofore on fund structural policy conditionality, this section contains a number of tables and charts documenting the patterns in such conditionality. In section 5.1.4, I speculate on why the scope and micromanagement of Fund structural policy conditionality have increased in recent years. Section 5.1.5 lays out a set of potential approaches to streamlining Fund structural policy conditionality if, as seems increasingly likely, the international community and IMF management were to agree that such streamlining would be desirable. Finally, section 5.1.6 provides some brief concluding remarks that summarize my own views on Fund structural policy conditionality.

5.1.2 Structural Policies and the Mandate of the International Monetary Fund

Scripture and Field Manuals

One starting point for figuring out how involved the IMF should be in structural policies would be to look at the Fund's basic marching orders. These range from the IMF's charter (called the "Articles of Agreement") to specific guidance notes issued by the Fund's executive board to IMF staff.

List A reproduces (from Article I of the Articles of Agreement) the Fund's purposes. Although amendments have been made to other parts of the charter over the past fifty-five years, this is not so with the purposes. Two things are immediately obvious from even a casual reading. There are many purposes, not just one; and there are a number of terms and concepts—such as "confidence," "national and international prosperity," "temporary," and "exchange system"—that are (and indeed, have been) susceptible to multiple interpretations.

List A

Purposes of the IMF

1. To promote international monetary cooperation through a permanent institution that provides the machinery for consultation and collaboration on international monetary problems.

2. To facilitate the expansion and balanced growth of international trade, and to contribute thereby to the promotion and maintenance of high levels of employment and real income and to the development of the productive resources of all members as primary objectives of economic policy.

3. To promote exchange stability, to maintain orderly exchange arrangements among members, and to avoid competitive exchange depreciation.

4. To assist in the establishment of a multilateral system of payments in respect of current transactions between members and in the elimination of foreign exchange restrictions which hamper the growth of world trade.

5. To give confidence to members by making the general resources of the Fund temporarily available to them under adequate safeguards, thus providing them with opportunity to correct maladjustments in their balance of payments without resorting to measures destructive of national or international prosperity.

6. In accordance with the above, to shorten the duration and lessen the degree of disequilibrium in the international balance of payments of members.

The Fund shall be guided in all its policies and decisions by the purposes set forth in this article.

It is clear (at least to me) that a primary objective is not only to correct balance-of-payments disequilibria but also to do so in a particular way, that is, in a way that doesn't involve either excessive deflation or unemployment at home or beggar-thy-neighbor policies. This is how I interpret the phrases (in paragraph 5) "without resorting to measures destructive of national and international prosperity" and (in paragraph 3) "to avoid competitive exchange depreciation." Such an interpretation is of course also consistent with the Fund's establishment as a response to the beggar-thy-neighbor and Great Depression problems of the 1920s and 1930s.

There is also clear support for measures that promote openness to international trade and a multilateral system of payments, and opposition to measures that hamper this openness. Capital movements are not mentioned. Again, this is consistent with the perceived (trade-output vicious circle) lessons of the 1920s and 1930s and with the then popular view about the perils of destabilizing capital flows.

Although there is no denying that a key task of the IMF at the time of its creation was to oversee a system of fixed but adjustable exchange rates, I interpret the promotion of "exchange stability" (in paragraph 3) as going beyond any particular form of exchange arrangements (be it adjustable pegs, currency boards, floating rates, etc.). Put another way, I don't see the raison d'être of the Fund as having disappeared in the early 1970s along with the arrival of floating exchange rates. If the intention were otherwise, paragraph 3 would presumably have referred to "exchange rate" stability, and there be would no purposes other than that one.

Although Article I makes it plain that the framers regarded "high levels of employment and income" and "development of productive resources" as good things, it doesn't say that the Fund should pursue those objectives by whatever means available. Instead, they specify that the Fund should facilitate "the expansion and balanced growth of international trade" and "contribute *thereby*" to buoyant domestic economic activity.

Where else might one look in the Fund's charter for advice relevant to structural policy conditionality? Many would say the revised (in 1976) Article IV, which deals with general obligations of member countries and with the Fund's surveillance responsibilities. Here, economic growth and, to a lesser extent, international capital movements, get greater play than in the Fund's purposes. Specifically, the new Article IV recognizes specifically that the essential purpose of the international monetary system is to provide a framework that both "facilitates the exchange of goods, services, and *capital* among countries, and that sustains sound economic growth." More noteworthy, member countries assume the general obligation to "endeavor to direct . . . economic and financial policies toward the objective of fostering orderly economic *growth* with reasonable price stability," and the fund assumes the obligation to oversee the "compliance" of each member country with this obligation.

Since "economic and financial policies" directed toward orderly economic growth potentially covers a lot of ground, the practical upshot of the revised Article IV was that it gave the Fund a much broader license to conduct wide-ranging surveillance and annual consultations with members. Ever since then, the Fund's Article IV consultation reports have covered a host of policy areas, including many that would be designated as structural policies.[12] Even though Article IV carries the title "Obligations Regarding Exchange Arrangements," it embodied the view that you had to look at the

---

12. For a review and analysis of the content of Fund surveillance, see Crow, Arriazu, and Thygensen (1999).

underlying domestic policy determinants of a stable exchange rate system to see if countries were meeting their international obligations.[13] Yes, Article IV is about Fund surveillance, not about Fund policy conditionality. However, the fact that the former has been given much wider scope (since at least the mid-1970s) probably has contributed somewhat to a wider field of view in Fund lending arrangements as well (more on that in section 5.1.4).

But what about more specific directives relating to performance criteria agreed and issued by the Fund's executive board? In my view, the most relevant document is probably the conditionality guidelines for standby arrangements, issued in 1979; see list B. To make a long story short, although the guidelines permit the number and content of performance criteria to vary with a country's problems and institutional arrangements, guideline 9 specifies, inter alia, that performance criteria will "normally be confined to macroeconomic variables" and that "performance criteria may relate to other variables *only in exceptional cases when they are essential for the effectiveness of the member's program because of their macroeconomic impact*" (italics mine). My interpretation of all this is that, at least in Fund standby arrangements, the intention was to limit the number of structural-policy performance criteria and to avoid "micro" conditionality (that is, measures that don't have macroeconomic impact). Although these guidelines have been revisited many times during later board reviews of conditionality, they have been repeatedly endorsed.

List B

Conditionality Guidelines for Fund Standby Lending

1. Members should be encouraged to adopt corrective measures, which could be supported by use of the Fund's general resources in accordance with the Fund's policies, at an early stage of their balance-of-payments difficulties. The article IV consultations are among the occasions on which the Fund would be able to discuss with members adjustment programs, including corrective measures, that would enable the Fund to approve a stand-by arrangement.

2. The normal period for a stand-by arrangement will be one year. If, however, a longer period is requested by a member and considered necessary by the Fund to enable the member to implement its adjustment program successfully, the stand-by arrangement may extend beyond the period of one year. This period in appropriate cases may extend up to but not beyond three years.

---

13. Eichengreen (1999) has made a similar argument that the Fund cannot expect to be successful at promoting international financial stability without addressing sources of financial instability at the national level.

3. Stand-by arrangements are not international agreements and therefore language having a contractual connotation will be avoided in stand-by arrangements and letters of intent.

4. In helping members to devise adjustment programs, the Fund will pay due regard to domestic social and political objectives, the economic priorities, and the circumstances of members, including the causes of their balance-of-payments problems.

5. Appropriate consultation clauses will be incorporated in all stand-by arrangements. Such clauses will include provision for consultation from time to time during the whole period in which the member has outstanding purchases in the upper limit tranches. This provision will apply to whether the outstanding purchases were made under a stand-by arrangement or in other transactions in the upper credit tranches.

6. Phasing and performance clauses will be omitted in stand-by arrangements that do not go beyond the first credit tranche. They will be included in all other stand-by arrangements but these clauses will be applicable only to purchases beyond the first credit tranche.

7. The managing director will recommend that the executive board approve a member's request for the use of the Fund's general resources in the credit tranches when it is his or her judgment that the program is consistent with the Fund's provisions and policies and that it will be carried out. A member may be expected to adopt some corrective measures before a stand-by arrangement is approved by the Fund, but only if necessary to enable the member to adopt and carry out a program consistent with the Fund's provisions and policies. In these cases the managing director will keep executive directors informed in an appropriate manner of the progress of discussions with the member.

8. The managing director will ensure adequate coordination in the application of policies relating to the use of the Fund's general resources with a view to maintaining the nondiscriminatory treatment of members.

9. The number and content of performance criteria may vary because of the diversity of problems and institutional arrangements of members. Performance criteria will be limited to those that are necessary to evaluate implementation of the program with a view to ensuring that the achievement of its objectives. Performance criteria will normally be confined to (a) macroeconomic variables and (b) those necessary to implement specific provisions of the articles or policies adopted under them. Performance criteria may relate to other variables only in exceptional cases when they are essential for the effectiveness of the member's program because of their macroeconomic impact.

10. In programs extending beyond one year, or in circumstances in which a member is unable to establish in advance one or more performance criteria for all or part of the program period, provision will be made for a review in order to reach the necessary understandings with the member for

the remaining period. In addition, in those exceptional cases in which an essential feature of the program cannot be formulated as a performance criterion at the beginning of a program year because of substantial uncertainties concerning major economic trends, provision will be made for a review by the Fund to evaluate the current macroeconomic policies of the member, and to reach new understandings if necessary. In these exceptional cases the managing director will inform executive directors in an appropriate manner of the subject matter of a review.

11. The staff will prepare an analysis and assessment of the performance under programs supported by use of the Fund's general resources in the credit tranches in connection with article IV consultations and as appropriate in connection with further requests for use of the Fund's resources.

12. The staff will from time to time prepare, for review by the executive board, studies of programs supported by stand-by arrangements in order to evaluate and compare the appropriateness of the programs, the effectiveness of the policy instruments, and the observance of the programs, and the results achieved. Such reviews will enable the executive board to determine when it may be appropriate to have the next comprehensive review of conditionality.

However, one must also take note that a variety of other lending arrangements (besides standbys) has been created in the Fund with the support of the membership over the past thirty years (ranging from a facility to assist transition economies in coping with the shift away from state trading to multilateral market-based trading, to one that was to assist countries experiencing liquidity problems related to Y2K). More to the point of this paper, some of those lending windows are directly aimed at protracted balance-of-payments problems and at supporting comprehensive efforts at macroeconomic *and* structural reform. These include the Extended Fund Facility (EFF; established in 1974), and both the Structural Adjustment Facility (SAF; established in 1986) and Enhanced Structural Adjustment Facility (ESAF; established in 1987); eligibility for both the SAF and the ESAF is restricted to low-income countries.[14] For these lending windows, structural policy involvement is at the heart of the exercise, and there is little guidance on how many or what kinds of structural policy measures would be viewed as "out of bounds."

Given the prominence of governance issues in the Asian crisis, a final guidance note worth noting is the one issued in July 1997 by the Fund's executive board on "The Role of the IMF in Governance Issues." Although the note states right at the beginning that "the responsibility for governance issues lies first and foremost with the national authorities," it seems to give

14. In 1999, the ESAF was reorganized into the Poverty Reduction and Growth Facility (PRGF).

the Fund staff quite a wide berth to include governance and corruption measures in Fund conditionality if they can make the case that governance problems have some direct macroeconomic impact. In addition, although the note urges the Fund staff to rely on other institutions' expertise in areas of their purview, it states that the Fund could nevertheless recommend conditionality in those areas (outside the Fund's expertise) if the staff considered that such measures were "critical to the successful implementation of the program." Given the timing and context of this guidance note (just at the outset of the Asian crisis), some IMF staff have expressed the view (to me) that the Fund's board was sending them a signal that they would henceforth not support programs that ignored serious and widespread governance and corruption problems.

To sum up, the Fund's existing marching orders on structural policy conditionality are Janus-faced enough that both supporters of narrow conditionality and those of more comprehensive conditionality can find their own biblical passages to buttress their arguments. On the one side, I don't see in the Fund's charter a broad agenda aimed at high-quality growth. What I see instead is a focus on balance-of-payments adjustment, trade opening, elimination of payments restrictions, efforts to increase the stability of the exchange rate system, and a directive to avoid modes of external adjustment that make recession or deflation deeper than necessary and that impose undue costs on other countries.[15] This is not to deny that the Fund's membership may want to pursue high-quality growth (and poverty reduction) for a variety of reasons, including moral imperatives. It's just that I can't find that commandment on the original stone tablets. In a similar vein, the Fund's conditionality guidelines for standby arrangements appear to have had the intention of limiting the number of structural performance criteria, particularly if they are micro in nature. On the other side of the ledger, the Fund's overall surveillance responsibilities (under the revised Article IV) are quite wide-ranging: as regards structural policies, a succession of specific lending windows has been established over the past twenty-five years or so with an explicit structural policy orientation, and guidance notes on "new" structural policy issues like governance and corruption give the Fund staff considerable leeway to include such measures in conditionality as long as they can make a case that they are critical to the success of the program. Perhaps more telling, I could find no evidence of concern about the scope or intrusiveness of structural policy conditionality in the published summaries (so-called Public Information Notices, or PINs) of executive board meetings on the Thai, Indonesian, and Korean

---

15. It's also relevant to note that, unlike the charter of the EBRD, the Fund's charter says nothing about promoting "democracy"; see Polak (1991) for a discussion of political influences on IMF lending.

programs over the past three years—even though the number and detail of structural conditions in those three programs are extraordinary (see section 5.1.3 below).

Three Alternative Mandates

If there is relatively little guidance available about the appropriate intrusiveness of Fund structural policy conditionality from official sources, one might consider what different mandates for the Fund would imply about such conditionality. Here, I consider three possibilities, starting with the narrowest and ending with the broadest (and most ambitious).

Mandate I

The Fund's primary focus would be on macroeconomic and financial stability; its crisis management guideline would be to assist a country to get out of the current crisis as soon as possible (without imposing undue costs on itself or its neighbors).

An announced IMF focus on macroeconomic and financial stability would be similar to the increasing popular practice of national central banks to announce that their primary objective is price stability. It doesn't preclude giving some consideration to other objectives, but it makes clear which objective is king and where the authority's central responsibility lies. The emphasis on getting out of the current crisis would mean that crisis management and resolution—and not crisis prevention—should guide program design. Crisis prevention measures would presumably then be handled by the country on its own *after* the current crisis is resolved.

Would Mandate I preclude Fund structural policy conditionality during a crisis? The answer, I believe, is no. However, the extent of the structural conditions would be limited to measures directly related to resolution of the *current* crisis, and their form would depend on both the nature of the crisis and the institutional structure in place in the crisis country; in addition, the design of essential structural policy conditions outside the Fund's core competence (monetary, fiscal, exchange rate, and financial-sector policies) would need to be handled by other international financial institutions (IFIs). A few examples should suffice to illustrate the point.

Suppose that key contributory factors to a balance-of-payments crisis were an overvalued exchange rate and overly expansionary monetary and fiscal policies. Also assume that correction of relative prices was being thwarted by widespread indexation agreements in wage contracts. Assume that the alternatives to devaluation as an adjustment tool are a more draconian tightening of monetary or fiscal policy (which would drive the domestic economy into deep recession) and a large hike in tariff and nontariff barriers. In that case, reduction or elimination of those indexation provisions could be regarded as essential to external adjustment (without either excessive deflation or beggar-thy-neighbor effects), and a labor-market performance test could be part of conditionality.[16]

Next, consider a case in which the primary source of the external disequilibrium is a large budget deficit. Assume that the necessary fiscal adjustment needs to be large, that the economy is expected to undergo a serious contraction, that the incumbent government is quite unpopular at home (because there is a long history of cronyism and corruption), and that there is no social safety net to speak of. In that situation, it could be argued that the Fund program needs to contain a few structural measures (e.g., the closing of a government cartel or monopoly) to send a visible signal to the public that some patronage is being taken away from well-connected government cronies and therefore that the program will be even-handed—and this even if the structural measures themselves have no macroeconomic impact and lie outside the Fund's core competence.[17] Here, these structural measures might be defended as necessary to establish confidence. Similarly, the creation of an unemployment insurance scheme or some other form of social safety net could be viewed as necessary to sustain popular support for the fiscal correction effort over the one- or two-year program period.

Next, picture a situation in which a banking crisis is under way and no deposit insurance system is in place. Depositors are withdrawing deposits from a group of weak banks, and the government is supporting the weak banks' ability to meet withdrawals by providing liquidity assistance to those banks. The deposit run is spreading, and the liquidity injections are pumping up the monetary aggregates and driving down the exchange rate. It is also known that substantial funds will soon be needed to recapitalize insolvent banks and to increase capital at solvent but still weak banks. Because its debt burden is already high, the government cannot fund all the bank cleanup costs on its own. It will need help from private creditors abroad. Here, too, one could defend structural conditions relating to bank closures or to deposit insurance reform as being essential for resolving the current crisis; without them, the authorities will not be able to control monetary policy and to halt the free fall of the currency. If the *immediate* aim of raising funds from abroad is being hampered by restrictions on capital inflows or by poor disclosure that prevents foreign creditors from judging the worth of domestic banks, the removal or correction of restrictions or disclosure practices too might be defended as a legitimate element in conditionality.

---

16. Another example in which labor market policies could be considered essential to overcoming the current crisis is when a banking crisis cannot be overcome without financial-sector and corporate restructuring, and the latter cannot be accomplished without revision of restrictive laws governing employee layoffs.

17. Allen (1993, 18) takes such a view: "Structural policies can also help build and maintain the political consensus that will support macroeconomic stabilization—for example, by combating unproductive and politically unpopular rent-seeking activities."

In contrast to the above scenarios, consider a crisis situation brought on, say, by a large terms-of-trade shock or a shift in investor sentiment stemming from contagion in a neighboring country. Assume also that there are many structural-policy weaknesses and institutional gaps but that these are not serious enough or linked closely enough to monetary, fiscal, and exchange rate policies to prevent the crisis from being resolved with traditional macroeconomic instruments plus some Fund financing. Here, however desirable structural measures may be for longer-term performance, they would not be included as conditions for the program. A plain vanilla Fund program will do the job.

Another relevant question is whether Mandate I would still permit the Fund to make a contribution to poverty reduction in poor countries. The answer is yes, but only insofar as macroeconomic and financial stability itself contributes to poverty reduction, or because the Fund (in collaboration with the World Bank) sees the incorporation of social safety nets into crisis resolution programs as necessary for the successful implementation of those programs. Longer-term efforts (outside of crises) to fight poverty would then be handled by the World Bank and the regional development banks.

Mandate II

The Fund's primary focus would be (as in Mandate I) on macroeconomic and financial stability: its crisis guideline would be to assist a country not only to get out of the current crisis but also to minimize the chances of getting into another one down the road.

Although the Fund's core competence remains the same in Mandate II as in Mandate I, the big difference is that the fund now incorporates crisis *prevention* as well as crisis resolution in program design. An implicit judgment here is that the country needs to use the crisis as a mechanism to reduce its crisis vulnerability and that it would not be able to do this on its own (i.e., without a Fund program) after the current crisis is resolved. Better, then, to "make hay while the sun shines" and combine crisis resolution and crisis prevention in the current program. If confidence in the crisis economy is very low, the Fund might also argue that investors will not return unless there is evidence that the probability of another (near-term) crisis is low; this in turn requires proof that the old (crisis-prone) system is changing, and structural reform would be part and parcel of such proof.

Mandate II increases substantially the scope for structural policy conditionality, even without going into noncore areas of economic policy. Again, a few examples convey the flavor.

Assume that the country has a long-standing problem of undisciplined monetary policy and that monetary policy excesses are also a key factor in the current crisis. In that case, the Fund might argue that a performance criterion that simply says that monetary policy will be tightened within the existing regime will not be credible. In this situation, the program might contain structural policy conditionality that either specifies granting independence to the central bank or takes the monetary reins out of the central bank's hands by establishing a currency board or single currency.

One could tell a similar story about long-standing weaknesses in fiscal policy that lead a country to accumulate a very heavy external debt burden. When, say, a large negative shock occurs to the terms of trade (e.g., oil prices fall), foreign investors run for the exits and a debt crisis breaks out. Assume that the chronically weak fiscal position owes much to a narrow tax base, to a host of large loss-making public enterprises, and to the absence of proper expenditure-control and budgeting departments in the ministry of finance. In parallel with the immediately preceding example, the Fund might argue that a performance criterion that simply targets a lower fiscal deficit for the next year will not be credible. As such, the Fund program could contain structural conditions for widening the tax base, for privatizing state enterprises, and for establishing new administrative units in the ministry of finance.

Carrying forward the same theme, imagine a banking crisis whose proximate determinants are a sharp contraction of economic activity or a sharp rise in interest rates connected with a defense of a fixed exchange rate. However, assume also that there was a large backlog of nonperforming loans brought on by the following: state-owned banks that lent without any regard to creditworthiness of borrowers; commercial banks that had long demonstrated a proclivity toward "connected lending"; lax loan classification procedures that encouraged the "evergreening" of bad loans and that grossly overstated the true value of bank capital; a legal framework that made it difficult for banks to seize collateral from bankrupt borrowers; ineffective banking supervision from a bank supervisory agency that had neither the political independence nor the mandate or resources to do its job; and lender moral hazard, stoked by repeated episodes of bailing out bank depositors and creditors. Against such a background, the Fund might maintain that a program that merely specified closing insolvent banks and recapitalizing others to international standards would amount to flushing money down the drain. Even if the current banking crisis were resolved, it wouldn't be long before the same underlying vulnerabilities produced a repetition (thereby exacerbating the problem of "prolonged use" of Fund resources). Better then—so the argument would go—to require structural policy conditions that would change each of these poor banking and supervisory practices.

The same kind of argument could be made about the need for conditions (on bank bailouts and the like) to control moral hazard problems, which, by definition, relate to the effect of inappropriately priced insurance arrangements (extended this period) on the risk-taking behavior of policyholders *next period.* Put in other words, it is precisely the worry about avoiding the next crisis that makes it necessary to put additional conditions on the management of the current crisis.

Mandate III

The Fund's focus would be on macroeconomic and financial stability and on sustainable growth; its crisis guideline would be to assist the country not only to get out of the current crisis and to reduce its crisis vulnerability but also to put in place the conditions for sustainable high-quality growth.

The difference here with respect to Mandates I and II is that high-quality growth now occupies a more central role both in the Fund's overall mandate and in its crisis-fighting strategy. Under this more holistic approach, conditionality would likely encompass measures that are viewed as necessary to improve economic growth and protect the poor and the vulnerable, as well as measures to improve the country's resilience to future crises. A hypothetical country scenario can again help to illustrate the differences involved.

Consider a country that is suffering from persistently weak economic growth, a chronic budget deficit, a weak external position, pervasive state intervention, heavy public ownership, protectionism, and a host of governance and corruption problems. A large, negative terms-of-trade shock or a group of bank failures may have pushed this country into crisis, but for the last decade or more it may never have been very far away from crisis.

Reflecting the focus on economic growth (under Mandate III), the Fund and the country authorities might agree that the program ought to have a three-year rather than a one-year tenure, so that any aggregate demand reductions could be made more gradual and so that there would be more time for structural reform to take hold. In addition, the Fund might ask that the country only make good progress toward external payments viability during the program period rather than actually achieving such viability. In an effort to reduce distortions that create an anti-export bias and that hamper efficient resource allocation, the program might well call for the following: scaling back the extent of price controls and state intervention in marketing of exports, foodstuffs, fertilizer, and petroleum products; the reduction or elimination of surrender requirements and controls on foreign exchange allocation; reduced reliance on quantitative restrictions on imports and a reduction in the level and dispersion of tariff rates; privatization of selected public enterprises and the entering into of "performance contracts" with existing managers of public enterprises; liberalization of interest rates (and other measures to move from state to market allocation of credit); development of financial markets for interbank funds, government securities, and stocks; and the phasing-out of government-owned banks.

To protect the most vulnerable groups, such a program would probably also place conditions on the composition of government expenditure cuts, as well as an overall target for the budget deficit. Specifically, these structural conditions could call, inter alia, for a shift in government expenditure away from military and "showcase" expenditures toward expenditure on primary education and health care; severance pay and retraining for workers released from public enterprises that are being privatized; a gradual (rather than abrupt) reduction of price controls on commodities that loom large in poor people's budgets; and the creation of an unemployment insurance system. There might likewise be provisions for special credit arrangements for agricultural producers and for small and medium-sized businesses, and the differential impact of currency devaluation on urban consumers versus agricultural exporters might be subject to partial compensation. As part of efforts to combat corruption problems, audits and public disclosure of findings might be required of certain financial institutions and of government-sponsored monopolies, and employment practices in the civil service could be subject to review. Additionally, core labor standards might be put forward if there were strong evidence of significant departures from them.

To sum up, what gets included in Fund structural policy conditionality depends in good measure on the nature of the crisis and on the extent of interdependence between traditional Fund macroeconomic policy instruments and structural policies. *But the intrusiveness of conditionality also depends on how broad are the objectives of the Fund and the country authorities.* Trying to get out of the current crisis is one thing. Trying to ward off a future crisis is quite another. And trying to spur high-quality growth in a low-income country with a host of government-induced distortions and large institutional gaps is something else again. Yet another relevant factor, particularly as regards the intensity or degree of detail in Fund conditionality, is how much confidence the IMF and creditor governments have in the willingness of the crisis country to carry through on its policy commitments; the greater the skepticism on that score, the greater is likely to be the number of prior actions and other performance tests included in programs. However, that takes us into the next section.

5.1.3 The Structural Content of Fund Policy Conditionality and Its Effectiveness

Thus far, I have summarized arguments about Fund structural policy conditionality and discussed how the Fund's mandate might affect the scope and details of such conditionality. However, I have not discussed the available facts on Fund structural policy conditionality, nor the existing literature on the effectiveness of conditionality. That is the subject of this section. First, I ask how commonplace, wide-ranging, and detailed structural policy conditions have been in Fund programs; whether structural policy conditionality seems to be increasing over time; in what policy areas structural conditionality has been most intensive; and what performance tests have been used to monitor this conditionality. Second, I then ask what we know about the effectiveness of that structural policy conditionality, including the track record on compliance with Fund conditionality. Most of these questions are not entirely straightforward to answer, both because the relevant data are available only in pieces and because the counterfactual to Fund policy conditionality (that is, what would happen in the absence of a Fund program) is extremely difficult to know or to estimate.

Structural Policies in Fund Programs

Since there is no comprehensive index of Fund structural policy conditionality that is available over a long time period, one has to rely on a set of statistics to tell the story. In what follows, I review, in turn: (a) data on the number of total structural policy conditions per program year for a sample of twenty Stand-By Arrangements (SBAs) and twelve EFFs for the 1996–99 period; (b) data on the average number of structural performance criteria for all Fund programs over the 1993–99 period; (c) data on the number of structural policy conditions (overwhelmingly structural benchmarks) in recent (1997–2000) Fund programs with three Asian crisis countries (Indonesia, South Korea, and Thailand); (d) data on the average number of structural benchmarks per Fund program for thirty-three transition economies over the 1993–99 period; and (e) data on the number of structural benchmarks in earlier SAF programs. For each body of data, I am interested not only in the scope and intensity of structural policy conditionality, but also in the trend, the differences across different types of Fund programs (SBAs, EFFs, and SAF/ESAF/PRGF programs), and the distribution across structural policy areas.

Before getting to all that, a brief digression on the instruments that the Fund uses to monitor compliance with conditionality is warranted. For the purposes of this paper, four of these are of interest.

Performance criteria (PCs) are meant to provide a direct link between program implementation and disbursement of Fund resources. If the criterion is met on the agreed test date (typically set at quarterly intervals), the member country is assured of disbursement; if the criterion is not met, the country cannot draw unless a waiver is obtained. Waivers are granted when a country's noncompliance with performance criteria is viewed by the Fund as inconsequential or when it reflects significant exogenous developments not foreseen at the time the program was framed.[18] PCs are expected to be under the control of the borrower, capable of being precisely and objectively formulated and monitored, and subject to relatively short (usually less than forty-five days) reporting lags. In the structural area, a PC could, for example, specify that elimination of restriction x on current payments be accomplished by date y, or that three insolvent finance companies be closed by date z. *Prior actions* are policy measures that the country agrees to take before a Fund agreement goes into effect. They are apt to be employed when severe imbalances exist and the country is viewed as having had a poor track

18. Waivers also require that the authorities have taken the necessary action to bring the program back on track if this is necessary to meet its objectives.

record of implementation (in earlier Fund programs). *Structural benchmarks* (SBMs) are indicators that aim to delineate the expected path of reform for individual structural policy measures and that can facilitate the evaluation of progress for these actions. Because many structural policies cannot be expressed in quantitative form, structural benchmarks are usually expressed qualitatively; for example, if the program calls for privatization of the state-owned telephone company, submitting the privatization bill to the legislature by date x could be one structural benchmark. Failure to meet structural benchmarks conveys a negative signal but does not automatically render a country ineligible to draw; instead, a decision about eligibility would be judgmental and would likely be taken in a broader mid-year *program review*—itself an instrument of conditionality—with an eye toward the country's overall progress on the structural front. Program reviews, like SBMs, assess implementation of policies not amenable to monitoring via PCs (because of their imprecise or qualitative nature). Reviews are broader than individual SBMs and can be used, for example, to assess whether there needs to be a change in program design.[19]

Number of (Total) Structural Policy Conditions per Program Year

At this point, the most comprehensive measure of Fund structural policy conditionality is that produced by the Fund itself via its so-called MONA database (which stands for Monitoring Fund Arrangements). It is the only series available that combines information on all four types of structural conditions, namely, performance criteria, structural benchmarks, prior actions, and conditions for completion of program reviews. When only one of those structural policy conditions is used, there is a danger that you are seeing only one part of the elephant. The Fund's index of programmed structural policy measures is then divided by the length of the period to obtain figures on number of programmed structural policy measures per annum. The rub is that this comprehensive measure is so far available only for the twenty SBAs and twelve EFFs over the 1996–99 period. To my knowledge, this comprehensive measure of Fund structural policy conditions has not been published before.

Table 5.1 presents the goods. Three conclusions stand out. First, the number of structural policy conditions that would be typical for, say, a three-year EFF Fund program over the last few years is high; specifically, it would be more than fifty (three times the annual average of eighteen measures per annum).[20] For a typical one-year SBA, it would be somewhere be-

---

19. When conditionality includes a program review, the text of the arrangement specifies what elements are to be reviewed; the review also assesses whether or not the program's objectives are in jeopardy.

20. Because the data in table 5.1 are expressed as the number of conditions per annum rather than per program, I need to assume that the number of conditions varies proportionally with time to arrive at conclusions about the number in conditions in a "typical" three-year program.

Table 5.1   **Number of Programmed Structural Conditions Per Annum, 1996–99**

	SBAs	EFF
Median	9	18
Mean	15	18
Standard deviation	12	12

tween nine and fifteen (depending on whether we used the median or the mean). This is a far cry from the "only in exceptional cases" guideline called for in the (1979) conditionality guidelines for SBAs. Second, the median number of structural policy conditions is much higher (double) for EFFs than for SBAs. This is not surprising. As noted earlier, EFFs *must* have a structural policy orientation; SBAs may have structural conditionality, too, but don't necessarily have to (if structural problems are not viewed as serious or pressing). Note that the difference between SBAs and EFFs vanishes when one looks at the mean number of conditions—a finding that could well reflect the presence of a few SBAs with very high structural policy content. Third, there is quite a lot of variation across both SBAs and EFFs in the extent of structural policy conditionality. Because these data are thus far available only for the 1996–99 period as a whole, there is nothing that can be said here about trends.

The Fund has broken down its comprehensive measure of structural policy conditions into ten broad policy areas. The results are portrayed in figure 5.1. In short, what we see there is that about two-thirds of structural policy conditions are concentrated in three areas: financial-sector policies, tax and expenditure reforms, and public enterprises and privatizations. Since the Fund's core competence is often identified to be monetary, fiscal, exchange rate, and financial-sector policies (see, e.g., Council on Foreign Relations Task Force 1999), this would seem to belie the charge that, on average, most of the Fund's focus in structural policies is far afield from its main expertise—or, to put it in other words, that Fund structural policy conditionality is typically "a mile wide and an inch thick." At the same time, figure 5.1 does show that fund structural policy conditionality has reached into a number of "noncore" structural policy areas (e.g., labor markets, social safety nets).

Average Number of Structural Performance Criteria per Program

The Fund's MONA database also contains information on performance criteria (PCs) for the longer 1993–99 period. Tables 5.2, 5.3, and 5.4 present the average number of performance criteria per program for all Fund programs, for ESAF/PRGF programs, and for SBA and EFF programs, respectively; separate figures are also given for the transition economies and (in table 5.2) for the Asian economies. In these tables, "quantitative perfor-

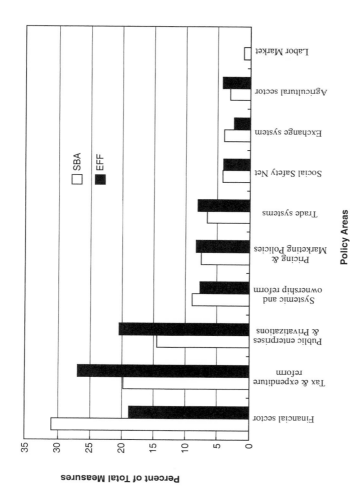

Fig. 5.1   Relative number of IMF structural conditions in different policy areas, 1996–99

Table 5.2   Summary of Performance Criteria in Fund-Supported Programs, 1993–99

	1993	1994	1995	1996	1997	1998	1999
A. Total Number of Arrangements							
Number of programs approved							
by year	22	35	30	32	21	21	20
Number of performance criteria	218	373	327	419	328	234	203
Quantitative	186	276	268	297	191	173	150
Structural	32	97	59	122	137	61	53
Number of performance criteria							
per program	10	11	11	13	16	11	10
Quantitative	8	8	9	9	9	8	8
Structural	1	3	2	4	7	3	3
B. Transition Economies							
Number of programs approved							
by year	9	8	12	12	7	6	4
Number of performance criteria	82	79	100	156	73	90	37
Quantitative	78	67	100	125	67	64	37
Structural	4	12	0	31	6	26	0
Number of performance criteria							
per program	9	10	8	13	10	15	9
Quantitative	9	8	8	10	10	11	9
Structural	0.4	2	0	3	1	4	0
C. Asian Economies							
Number of programs approved							
by year	0	0	0	0	3	1	0
Number of performance criteria	0	0	0	0	59	9	0
Quantitative	0	0	0	0	18	5	0
Structural	0	0	0	0	41	4	0
Number of performance criteria							
per program						20	9
Quantitative						6	5
Structural						14	4

Notes: Stand-by, extended facility, and SAF/ESAF/PRGF arrangements. Number of performance criteria refers to all performance criteria over the duration of the program. Performance criteria are classified by year of program approval, irrespective of test dates they applied to. Quantitative performance criteria applying to the same variable are counted only once, even if observance was required for more than one test date.

mance criteria" refers to macroeconomic variables (e.g., the nominal value of the fiscal deficit, net domestic credit of the central bank, the stock of net international reserves, etc.) that are used to track compliance with monetary, fiscal, exchange rate, and external debt policies. "Structural performance" criteria are meant to assess compliance with important structural policy commitments. Note that the data here are calculated per program, not per program year. This is more informative in some respects but also carries the disadvantage that the annual figures can be biased upward

Table 5.3   **Summary of Performance Criteria in ESAF/PRGF Arrangements, 1993–99**

	1993	1994	1995	1996	1997	1998	1999
	A. Total Number of Arrangements						
Number of programs approved							
by year	7	13	7	14	7	11	9
Number of performance criteria	86	183	116	227	134	132	106
Quantitative	61	102	81	118	72	97	68
Structural	25	81	35	109	62	35	38
Number of performance criteria							
per program	12	14	17	16	19	12	12
Quantitative	9	8	12	8	10	9	8
Structural	4	6	5	8	9	3	4
	B. Transition Economies						
Number of programs approved							
by year	1	1	0	3	1	3	0
Number of performance criteria	14	14	—	60	17	42	—
Quantitative	10	9	—	33	13	31	—
Structural	4	5	—	27	4	11	—
Number of performance criteria							
per program	14	14	—	20	17	14	—
Quantitative	10	9	—	11	13	10	—
Structural	4.0	5	—	9	4	4	—

Notes: Number of performance criteria refers to all performance criteria over the duration of the program. Performance criteria are classified by year of program approval, irrespective of test dates they applied to. Quantitative performance criteria applying to the same variable are counted only once, even if observance was required for more than one test date. Dashes indicate no program was assessed for that year.

(downward) if there are more (less) multiyear arrangements agreed in a given year. Note also that because we are dealing only with one component of structural policy conditionality in tables 5.2–5.4, we have to be careful about generalizing about the overall intrusiveness of Fund structural policy conditionality from these figures.

Five main conclusions emerge from tables 5.2–5.6. One is that "structural" PCs are on average less numerous than quantitative macroeconomic PCs—with the notable exception of the three programs for the Asian crisis economies in 1997 (see the upper two panels of table 5.2 versus the lowest one). A second conclusion is that the number of structural PCs in the programs with the three Asian crisis economies in 1997 (an average of 14.0 per program) was far above (roughly four times) both the average for all fund programs over the 1993–99 period (an average of 3.3 per program) and for 1997 alone (an average of 7.0 per program); in contrast, the average number of quantitative macroeconomic PCs was actually lower in the Asian economies than for all Fund programs. Finding number three is that the average number of structural PCs in programs with the transition economies was

Table 5.4   Summary of Performance Criteria in SBA/EFF Arrangements, 1993–99

	1993	1994	1995	1996	1997	1998	1999
A. Total Number of Arrangements							
Number of programs approved							
by year	15	22	23	18	14	10	11
Number of performance criteria	132	190	211	192	194	102	97
Quantitative	125	174	187	179	119	76	82
Structural	7	16	24	13	75	26	15
Number of performance criteria							
per program	9	9	9	11	14	10	9
Quantitative	8	8	8	10	9	8	7
Structural	0	1	1	1	5	3	1
B. Transition Economies							
Number of programs approved							
by year	8	7	12	9	6	3	4
Number of performance criteria	68	65	100	96	56	48	37
Quantitative	68	58	100	92	54	33	37
Structural	0	7	0	4	2	15	0
Number of performance criteria							
per program	9	9	8	11	9	16	9
Quantitative	9	8	8	10	9	11	9
Structural	0.0	1	0	0	0	5	0

Notes: Number of performance criteria refers to all performance criteria over the duration of the program. Performance criteria are classified by year of program approval, irrespective of test dates they applied to. Quantitative performance criteria applying to the same variable are counted only once, even if observance was required for more than one test date.

below (not above) the average for all Fund programs over this period. Fourth, there have on average been more structural PCs in ESAF/PRGF programs than in SBA and EFF arrangements (taken together).

A fifth finding—at least for all Fund arrangements taken together—is that we do observe some upward trend in the average number of structural PCs as we move from the earlier part of the period (2.0 in 1993–95) to the latter part (3.3 in 1996 and 98–99)—even if we exclude 1997; that being said, the straw that stirs the drink in the average of PC numbers is clearly the high figure (14.0 per program) for the three programs with Asian crisis countries in 1997.

Unfortunately, there are no directly comparable statistics on average number of structural PCs for earlier periods. An unpublished IMF (1987a) study on SBAs and EFFs during the 1979–97 period does show the breakdown of structural PCs by policy area; if I make the (risky) assumption that there was only one PC per policy area indicated for each country, I get an estimate of 1.3 structural PCs per program for that period—about one-third of the average figure (3.3) for 1993–99 (from table 5.2). Polak (1991) reports the average number of total PCs (presumably, quantitative macroeconomic PCs plus structural PCs) per program for some earlier periods. Specifically, his figures are less than 6.0 per arrangement for 1968–77, 7.0 in 1974–84, and 9.5 in 1984–87. The comparable figure taken from table 5.2 for average (total) PCs per program over 1993–99 would be 11.7. If other monitoring components of Fund policy conditionality (prior actions, SBMs, conditions for program reviews) moved in the same direction over this period—and Polak suggests they have—this would point to a significant increase in the monitoring of Fund conditionality over the past thirty years or so.

As regards the distribution of structural PCs across policy areas for earlier periods, the same 1987 IMF study found that the leading categories were the exchange system (12 percent) and the trade system (6 percent). The financial sector, which led the parade in figure 5.1, was in third place in 1979–87, and fiscal policy was yet further behind.

Number of Structural Policy Conditions in Recent Fund Programs
with Indonesia, South Korea, and Thailand

Since Fund structural policy conditionality in three Asian crisis countries has had a lot to do with reopening the debate on the appropriate scope and detail of conditionality, it makes sense to give those programs a separate look. In table 5.5, I provide a running count of the number of structural policy conditions—believed to be overwhelmingly made up of conditions for program reviews and structural benchmarks—contained in successive revisions of the Indonesian, Korean, and Thai programs over the 1997–2000 period. In figure 5.2, I present a rough breakdown of the three crisis programs by structural policy areas. In an effort to convey the flavor of the detail in those programs, I have also reproduced in list C the first half of the full SBM matrix for Indonesia as of June 1998. Perhaps it is a hint of one of the main conclusions that it was not practical to attach the full list of structural policy conditions for all three programs: as a group, they are much too long for a paper of this length. The reader should be cautioned that counting the number of structural policy commitments says nothing about which conditions are more important or are more intrusive. Nor does such a count tell us which commitments came at the initiative of the country authorities and which came from the Fund.[21] Moreover, such a count mixes together what might be called formal conditionality (monitored by specific performance criteria and structural benchmarks) and informal conditionality (monitored by program reviews).

---

21. Fund staff note that country authorities often use an IMF letter of intent to underline or to "advertise" policy reforms that have recently been made and those that are expected to be made in the near future—even if those reforms are predominantly "home grown."

Table 5.5   Number of Structural Policy Commitments in IMF Programs with Three Asian Crisis Countries, 1999–2000

Indonesia	10/97	01/98	04/98	06/98	07/98	09/98	10/98	11/98	03/99	05/99	07/99	01/00	07/00
	28	31	140	109	96	68	62	74	35	33	29	42	41
South Korea	12/08/97	12/05/97	12/24/97	02/98	05/98	07/98	11/98	08/99	11/99	07/00			
	29	33	50	53	51	39	53	83	94	68			
Thailand	08/97	11/97	02/98	05/98	08/98	12/98	08/99	09/99					
	26	24	21	73	50	69	8	9					

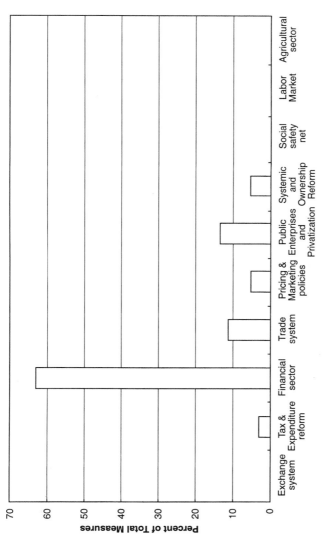

Fig. 5.2 The coverage of structural conditionality in stand-by and extended arrangements in Korea, Indonesia, and Thailand, 1996–99

List C

Indonesia: Excerpts from Structural Policy Conditions

Policy Action

Fiscal Issues

Remove VAT exemption arrangements.

Increase proportion of market value of land and buildings assessable for tax to 40 percent for plantation and forestry.

Introduce single-taxpayer registration number.

Increase non-oil tax revenue by raising annual audit coverage, developing improved VAT audit programs, and increasing recovery of tax arrears.

Increase in two stages excise taxes on alcohol and tobacco to reflect exchange rate and price developments.

Raise profit transfers to the budget from state enterprises, including Pertamina.

Raise prices on rice, sugar, wheat flour, corn, soybean meal, and fish meal.

Eliminate subsidies on sugar, wheat flour, corn, soybean meal, and fish meal.

Accelerate provisions under the Nontax Revenue Law of May 1997, to require all off-budget funds to be incorporated in budget within three years (instead of five years).

Incorporate accounts of Investment Fund and Reforestation Fund within budget.

Ensure reforestation funds used exclusively for financing reforestation programs.

Central government to bear cost of subsidizing credit to small-scale enterprises through state banks.

Cancel twelve infrastructure projects.

Discontinue special tax, customs, or credit privileges granted to the National Car.

Phase out local content program for motor vehicles.

Abolish compulsory 2 percent after-tax contribution to charity foundations.

Discontinue budgetary and extrabudgetary support and privileges to IPTN (Nusantara Aircraft Industry) projects.

Conduct revenue review with Fund assistance.

Monetary and Banking Issues

Provide autonomy to BI in formulation of monetary and interest rate policy.

Publish key monetary data on a weekly basis.

Submit to Parliament a draft law to institutionalize BI's autonomy.

Submit draft amendment to banking law to Parliament.

Provide autonomy to state banks to adjust interest rates on credit and deposit liabilities, within any guidelines applying to all banks.

Impose limits on and phase out BI credits to public agencies and public-sector enterprises.

Strengthen BI's bank supervision department and strengthen enforcement of regulations.

Upgrade the reporting and monitoring procedures for foreign exchange exposures of banks.

Appoint high-level foreign advisors to BI to assist in the conduct of monetary policy.

Set minimum capital requirements for banks of Rp 250 billion by end of 1998, after loan loss provisions.

Reduce the minimum capital requirements for existing banks.

Make loan loss provisions fully tax deductible, after tax verification.

Establish program for divestiture of BI's interests in private banks.

Require all banks to prepare audited financial statements.

Require banks to publish regularly more data on their operations.

Lift restrictions on branching of foreign banks.

Submit to Parliament a draft law to eliminate restrictions on foreign investments in listed banks and amend bank secrecy with regard to non-performing loans.

Eliminate all restrictions on bank lending except for prudential reasons or to support cooperatives or small-scale enterprises.

Bank Restructuring

Close sixteen nonviable banks.

Replace the closed banks' management with liquidation teams.

Compensate small depositors in the sixteen banks.

Place weak regional development banks under intensive supervision by BI.

Provide liquidity support to banks, subject to increasingly restrictive conditions.

Provide external guarantee to all depositors and creditors of all locally incorporated banks.

Establish Indonesia Bank Restructuring Agency (IBRA).

Determine uniform and transparent criteria for transferring weak banks to IBRA.

Transfer fifty-four weak banks to IBRA.

Transfer claims resulting from past liquidity support from BI to IBRA.

Transfer to IBRA control of seven banks accounting for more than 75 percent of past BI liquidity support and seven banks that have borrowed more than 500 percent of their capital.

IBRA will continue to take control of or freeze additional banks that fail to meet liquidity or solvency criteria. Where necessary, any such action will be accompanied by measures to protect depositors or creditors in line with the government guarantee.

Issue presidential decree to provide appropriate legal powers to IBRA, including its asset management unit.

Take action to freeze, merge, recapitalize, or liquidate the six banks for which audits have already been completed.

Establish independent review committee to enhance transparency and credibility of IBRA operations.

Conduct portfolio, systems, and financial reviews of all IBRA banks as well as major non-IBRA banks by internationally recognized audit firms.

Conduct portfolio, systems, and financial reviews of all other banks by internationally recognized audit firms.

Announce plan for restructuring state banks through mergers, transfers of assets and liabilities, or recapitalization prior to privatization.

Ensure that state banks sign performance contracts, prepared by the Ministry of Finance with World Bank assistance.

Merge two state-owned banks and conduct portfolio reviews of the two banks.

Draft legislation enabling state bank privatization.

Introduce private-sector ownership of at least 20 percent in at least one state bank.

Prepare state-owned banks for privatization.

Develop rules for the Jakarta Clearing House that will transfer settlement risk from BI to participants.

Introduce legislation to amend the banking law in order to remove the limit on private ownership of banks.

Introduce deposit insurance scheme.

Establish Financial Sector Advisory Committee to advise on bank restructuring.

Declare insolvency of six private banks intervened in April and write down shareholder equity.

Issue government bonds to Bank Negara Indonesia at market-related terms to finance transfer of deposits of banks frozen in April.

Initiate first case of an IBRA bank under the new bankruptcy law.

Foreign Trade

Reduce by 5 percentage points tariffs on items currently subject to tariffs of 15 to 25 percent.

Cut tariffs on all food items to a maximum of 5 percent.

Abolish local content regulations on dairy products.

Reduce tariffs on nonfood agricultural products by 5 percentage points.

Gradually reduce tariffs on nonfood agricultural products to a maximum of 10 percentage points.

Reduce by 5 percentage points tariffs on chemical products.

Reduce tariffs on steel/metal products by 5 percentage points.

Reduce tariffs on chemical, steel/metal, and fishery products to 5–10 percent.

Abolish import restrictions on all new and used ships.

Phase out remaining quantitative import restrictions and other nontariff barriers.

Abolish export taxes on leather, cork, ores, and waste aluminum products.

Reduce export taxes on logs, sawn timber, rattan, and minerals to a maximum of 30 percent by 15 April 1998; 20 percent by end of December 1998; 15 percent by end of December 1999; and 10 percent by end of December 2000.

Phase-in resource rent taxes on logs, sawn timber, and minerals.

Replace remaining export taxes and levies by resource rent taxes as appropriate.

Eliminate all other export restrictions.

Remove ban on palm oil exports and replace by export tax of 40 percent. The level of the export tax will be reviewed regularly for possible reduction, based on market prices and the exchange rate, and reduced to 10 percent by end of December 1999.

Investment and Deregulation

Remove the 49 percent limit on foreign investment in listed companies.

Issue a revised and shortened negative list of activities closed to foreign investors.

Remove restrictions on foreign investment in palm oil plantations.

Lift restrictions on foreign investment in retail trade.

Lift restrictions on foreign investment in wholesale trade.

Dissolve restrictive marketing arrangements for cement, paper, and plywood.

Eliminate price controls on cement.

Allow cement producers to export with only a general exporters license.

Free traders to buy sell and transfer all commodities across district and provincial boundaries, including cloves, cashew nuts, and vanilla.

Eliminate BPPC (Clove Marketing Board).

Abolish quotas limiting the sale of livestock.

Prohibit provincial governments from restricting trade within and between provinces.

Enforce prohibition of provincial and local export taxes.

Take effective action to allow free competition in the following:
1. importation of wheat, wheat flour, soybeans, and garlic
2. sale or distribution of flour
3. importation and marketing of sugar

Release farmers from requirements for forced planting of sugar cane.

The tale told by table 5.5 and by figure 5.2 can be summarized as follows. First, the number of structural policy conditions included in these programs with the three Asian crisis economies is very large (if not totally unprecedented)—many more than you can count using all your fingers and toes.[22] Without claiming any precision, my count from publicly available documents is that these structural policy commitments summed, at their peak, about 140 in Indonesia, over 90 in Korea, and over 70 in Thailand. Each of these totals is considerably above the average of about 50-plus for all Fund programs over the 1996–99 period. Second, in the programs with Korea and Thailand, the number of structural policy conditions was considerably smaller at the beginning of the program than at its peak—perhaps because the country authorities and the Fund first laid out the main elements of the structural reform package and then filled in the details as they went along, and because implementation of reforms was pretty good (see discussion below). In contrast, the number of structural policy conditions in the Fund program with Indonesia hits its peak pretty early on and then declines as the program period goes on, perhaps reflecting an initial effort to impress the markets with the extent of intended structural reform and then scaling that back as market reaction proved disappointing and as evidence accumulated that implementation capacity or willingness would be lower than anticipated. Third, although financial-sector restructuring and supervision is the dominant policy concentration in all three programs, additional data indicate that the scope of structural policy conditionality is much narrower in the Korean and Thai programs than in the Indonesian one. Putting aside the financial sector, Thai structural policies are mainly focused on tax and expenditure reform and on corporate debt restructuring. In Korea, the non-financial areas getting most attention are corporate governance and restructuring (and some trade and capital-account liberalization). In Indonesia, structural reforms outside the financial sector are more of a mixed bag, with significant commitment clusters appearing for privatization and reform of public enterprises, for trade systems, for pricing and marketing policies, for corporate restructuring, and for tax and expenditure reform; there are also minor clusters for energy and environmental policies and for social safety nets.

Turning to list C, what is striking is the number, scope, and detail of the structural policy commitments made by Indonesia, including in nontraditional areas of conditionality. There are, inter alia, measures dealing with reforestation programs; the phasing-out of local content programs for motor vehicles; discontinuation of support for a particular aircraft project and of special privileges granted to the National Car; abolition of the compul-

---

22. I hesitate to call the total number of structural policy conditions in even the Indonesian program "unprecedented" because I am told informally that there was a larger figure (close to 200) in one of Russia's programs with the Fund.

sory 2 percent after-tax contribution to charity foundations; appointment of high-level advisors for monetary policy; development of rules for the Jakarta Clearing House; the end of restrictive marketing agreements for cement, paper, and plywood; the elimination of the Clove Marketing Board; the termination of requirements on farmers for the forced planting of sugar cane; the introduction of a micro credit scheme to assist small businesses; and the raising of stumpage fees. Enough to say that the great bulk of such measures were *not* included because of their macroeconomic impact; they were presumably included instead for anticorruption reasons, to instill confidence in private investors that the system was changing, to facilitate monitoring of commitments, and (for some commitments) to reflect the structural policy agendas of either other IFIs (the World Bank and the Asian Development Bank) or certain creditor countries (see discussion in section 5.1.4).[23]

Number of Structural Benchmarks in Fund Programs
with the Transition Economies

Mercer-Blackman and Unigovskaya (2000) have analyzed the use of SBMs in Fund programs for twenty-five transition economies over the 1989–97 period. Their tally, also derived from the Fund's MONA database, is presented in table 5.6. Three observations merit explicit mention.

First, the average number of SBMs per program is roughly twice as high in ESAF (twenty-six) and EFF (twenty-three) arrangements and as it is for standby arrangements (thirteen). Second, although the data in table 5.7 are not directly comparable with those in table 5.1 (not only are the time periods different, but the latter include all structural conditions, whereas the former include only SBMs), the number of SBMs in standby arrangements for the transition economies do not seem far out of line (i.e., higher) with the recent averages for SBAs in all Fund programs—and they are clearly much lower than the averages on SBMs in the three Asian crisis economies. Third, there is more variation for SBAs in the number of SBMs (ranging from one in Bulgaria and Latvia to thirty-five in Armenia) than for either ESAF or EFF arrangements.

Figure 5.3, taken from Christiansen and Richter (1999), gives the breakdown by policy area of structural policy conditions for the fund's programs with the transition economies.[24] The main message is that the most frequently occurring structural conditions were in the area of public-sector management (institutional reform, tax and revenue policy, expenditure policy, and public wages and employment). Next in line were restructuring and

---

23. Haggard (2000) shares this view.
24. The data used to construct figure 5.3 are different from those used in table 5.8. The former cover (I think) all structural policy conditions (not just SBMs) and they also cover the Fund's initial programs with the transition economies under the (lower-conditionality) Systemic Transformation Facility. These differences, however, are not important for our purposes.

Table 5.6   **Number of Structural Benchmarks (SBs) According to Structural Benchmark Groups for Countries in Transition**

	Type of Fund Program	Number of Structural Benchmarks
Armenia	SBA	35
Azerbaijan	SBA	26
Belarus	SBA	21
Bulgaria	SBA	19
Macedonia	SBA	19
Romania	SBA	19
Estonia	SBA	18
Georgia	SBA	17
Hungary	SBA	15
Romania	SBA	15
Poland	SBA	14
Kazakhstan	SBA	13
Moldova	SBA	13
Ukraine	SBA	12
Uzbekistan	SBA	12
Croatia	SBA	11
Kazakhstan	SBA	11
Ukraine	SBA	11
Bulgaria	SBA	8
Kyrgyz Republic	SBA	6
Russia	SBA	6
Moldova	SBA	5
Poland	SBA	3
Latvia	SBA	2
Bulgaria	SBA	1
Latvia	SBA	1
Average		13
Kyrgyz Republic	ESAF	35
Albania	ESAF	34
Azerbaijan	ESAF	31
Georgia	ESAF	22
Armenia	ESAF	18
Macedonia	ESAF	17
Average		26
Azerbaijan	EFF	41
Russia	EFF	37
Kazakhstan	EFF	23
Moldova	EFF	16
Lithuania	EFF	11
Croatia	EFF	9
Average		23

Table 5.7   **Percentage of IMF Loan Actually Disbursed under Each Arrangement (distribution by quartiles)**

	$x < 0.25$ (1)	$0.25 \leq x < 0.50$ (2)	$0.50 \leq x < 0.75$ (3)	$0.75 \leq 1.0$ (4)	Fully Disbursed ($x = 1.0$) (5)	(4) + (5) $0.75 \leq x$ (6)	Number of Arrangements (7)
All arrangements							
1973–77	36.5	7.1	5.9	5.9	44.7	50.6	85
1978–82	19.4	16.1	10.5	12.9	41.1	54.0	124
1983–87	12.9	15.8	19.4	7.9	43.9	51.8	139
1988–92	17.5	15.1	20.6	14.3	32.5	46.8	126
1993–97	27.0	19.1	26.2	11.3	16.3	27.6	141
Full period (1973–97)	21.6	15.3	17.6	10.7	34.8	45.5	615
Stand-by	23.1	13.4	15.0	9.5	39.0	48.5	441
EFF	33.3	22.2	19.0	15.9	9.5	25.4	63
SAF/ESAF	9.0	18.9	27.0	12.6	32.4	45.0	111

Source: IMF, *Transactions of the Fund* (1998).

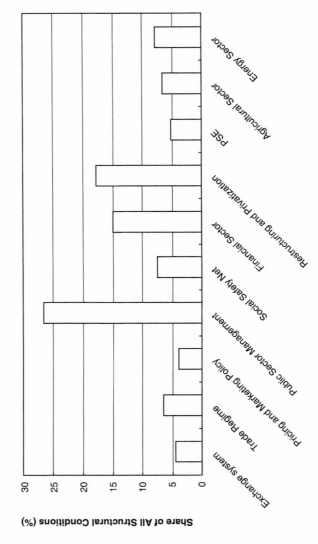

Fig. 5.3 Distribution of structural conditions in IMF-supported programs: Transition economies

privatizations, and financial-sector reforms. After that, we see a fairly even distribution across the remaining areas (energy sector, social safety net, agricultural sector, trade regime, exchange system, etc.). The top three categories accounted together for over two-thirds of structural conditions.

Scattered Evidence on Number of Structural Benchmarks in Earlier SAF Programs

An unpublished IMF study (1987) of seventeen SAF arrangements (for low-income countries) in 1986–87 also looked at the number and distribution of structural benchmarks. The main findings were that the average number of SBMs per SAF arrangement was about seven, that there was considerable variation around this average across programs (ranging from three in the program for Bolivia to fifteen for Uganda), and that structural conditions also ranged quite widely across policy areas (covering the exchange system, trade liberalization and tariff reform, public enterprises, tax and expenditure policy, producer pricing and agricultural marketing, and public-sector investment programs).

To sum up, structural policy conditionality is now a common and important element of Fund conditionality. When prior actions, performance criteria, structural benchmarks, and conditions for program reviews are combined, it has been typical (over the past few years) for a one-year standby arrangement to have on the order of, say, a dozen structural conditions and for a three-year EFF arrangement to have, say, fifty of them. About two-thirds of those structural conditions are apt to fall in the areas of fiscal policy, financial-sector reform, and privatization, with the remainder scattered across a fairly wide field. The structural conditions in the Fund's much-discussed programs with three Asian crisis economies (Indonesia, Korea, and Thailand) were much more numerous and detailed than is usually the case. Financial-sector conditions dominated in all three of those Asian programs, but detailed conditions in quite a few noncore structural policy areas were also evident, especially in the case of Indonesia. Although much of the external criticism of Fund structural conditionality has emphasized the wide scope of the Fund's involvement (e.g., some wonder what the Fund has to do with the clove monopoly), our review of the evidence suggests that the number and specificity of conditions in core areas ("micro management") are at least as important an issue.[25]

Those analyzing Fund structural policy conditionality, including researchers both inside and outside the Fund, are unanimous in concluding that there has been a pronounced upward trend in such conditionality over the past fifteen years, and this trend has probably become steeper in

25. Saying that the Fund has micromanaged some structural reforms is not the same as saying that such reforms necessarily lack macroeconomic impact. For example, a condition to reduce significantly the extent of wage indexation could be very detailed but might still carry macro impact.

the 1990s.[26] The evidence reported in this section (much of it previously unpublished) strongly corroborates this conclusion. Finally, there has also been a shift over time in the instruments used by the Fund to monitor structural conditionality, with resort to structural benchmarks, conditions for program reviews, and prior actions having risen faster than formal performance criteria. Prior to the 1980s, the Fund was hesitant to ask for prior actions, and performance reviews regarding structural policies were exceptional for standby arrangements (see Polak 1991; IMF 1987). Structural benchmarks were apparently not used prior to the establishment of the SAF in 1986. As demonstrated earlier, all this is no longer the case. For example, a comparison of the average number of structural conditions for standby arrangements in 1996–99 in table 5.1 with the figures on structural performance criteria in table 5.2 suggests that, taken together, structural benchmarks, prior conditions, and program reviews have recently been about five times as numerous as structural performance criteria.

Writing well before Fund programs with the Asian crisis countries, Polak (1991) contrasted the principles put forth in the 1979 Guidelines on Conditionality with actual practice:

> The guidelines do not attempt to change the structure of conditionality: their aim is limited to making that structure less intrusive by limiting the number of performance criteria, insisting on their macroeconomic character, circumscribing the cases for reviews, and keeping preconditions to a minimum. Yet these restraining provisions have not prevented the intensification of conditionality in every direction that the guidelines attempted to block. (61)

Nine years later, it's hard to disagree with that assessment.

The Effectiveness of Fund Structural Policy Conditionality

If we take it as given that the IMF has become more "grandmotherly" or intrusive with regard to its structural policy conditionality, the next question is how effective such conditionality has been.[27] Here, we address just two aspects of that question: the degree of compliance with Fund conditions and the quality of the Fund policy advice implicitly reflected in such structural policy conditionality. Again, much of the available evidence is often not in the form best suited to the focus of this paper (that is, it refers to compliance with, or the effectiveness of, *all* Fund policy conditions, not just structural policies, or when it deals only with structural policies, it covers only low-income or transition economies). Nevertheless, some conclusions

26. See, for example, Tanzi (1987), Polak (1991), Killick (1995), James (1998), Krueger (1998), Mussa and Savastano (1999), and Gupta et al. (2000).
27. The description of Fund conditionality as being "grandmotherly" is from Keynes; see James (1998).

can be put forward. In addition, some of the recent research on compliance with structural conditions in Fund programs with the transition economies is particularly interesting.

Compliance with Fund Policy Conditions

Clearly, Fund policy conditionality cannot have its intended effects if countries do not implement these policies. Two measures of compliance are typically found in the literature: the share of IMF loans actually disbursed, and the degree of compliance with particular Fund policies (e.g., credit ceilings, budget deficits, various structural benchmarks).[28]

Table 5.7, adopted from Mussa and Savastano (1999), shows the share of Fund lending actually disbursed for 615 Fund programs over the 1973–97 period. Although the authors caution that a low disbursement share could mean the program was so successful—or conditions improved so rapidly— that the country needed to use only a fraction of the committed IMF financing, they conclude that low disbursement cases mainly were ones in which the program went off track (because policies deviated significantly from those agreed upon and subsequent negotiations failed to reach agreement on a modified program).

Here, it is appropriate to highlight three of the Mussa-Savastano findings. First, if we take, say, disbursement of 75 percent or more of the total loan as implying close adherence to IMF policy conditionality, then less than half (45.5 percent) of all Fund arrangements over the entire 1973–97 period would have met that test; see column (6) in table 5.7. Second, again using the 75 percent or greater benchmark, the completion rate for standby arrangements (48.5 percent) was notably higher than that for EFF programs (25.4 percent) with higher average structural policy content; the completion rate for SAF/ESAF arrangements, which also have a relatively high structural policy content and deal exclusively with low-income countries, was much higher than for EFFs and only slightly below that for SBAs. Third, there is a suggestion that the completion rate for Fund programs is declining over time.[29]

A very similar exercise on completion rates was undertaken by Killick (1995) for 305 Fund programs over the 1979–93 period, with results quite close to those obtained by Mussa and Savastano (1999). Killick defines a "completed program" as one that disbursed 80 percent or more of the total Fund loan. He finds on this measure that 47 percent of Fund programs were completed, that the completion rate was higher for SBAs than for EFFs, that the completion rate was declining over time, and that completion rates

---

28. Another potential measure of compliance would be the share of programs that saw an early conversion of the program to a precautionary arrangement.

29. I use the term "suggestion," because Mussa and Savastano (1999) note that the results on completion rates for the 1993–97 period are biased downward due to the inclusion of arrangements with post-1997 expiration dates.

do not differ (in the expected way) on account of cross-country differences in either per capita income or type of export.[30]

Most earlier studies that looked at compliance with particular Fund policies were restricted to macro conditionality. In brief, Beveridge and Kelly (1980) and Edwards (1989) found that compliance with monetary or fiscal performance criteria was observed in approximately 48–62 percent of Fund programs. Polak (1991) updated these results for SBA, EFF, and SAF programs in the 1980s and found that compliance rates for the 1980s were below those for the 1970s. Killick (1995) cites one unpublished 1991 IMF study that looked at compliance with structural policies in SAF and ESAF programs: slightly over half of all structural benchmarks were observed on schedule (or two-thirds within a few months thereafter), and compliance was relatively high for agricultural producer pricing and marketing and for financial reforms, and relatively low for fiscal provisions (and especially for public enterprise reforms).

Two more recent studies of compliance with fund structural conditionality have been conducted for the transition economies by Christiansen and Richter (1999) and Mercer-Blackman and Unigovskaya (2000).[31] Four of their findings are of interest. First, the on-time compliance rate for structural benchmarks as a group averaged 42 percent, with an additional 16 percent of conditions met with delay; the remaining 42 percent of conditions were not met or no information was available. Second, the compliance rate for performance criteria (both macro and structural taken together) was higher than that for structural benchmarks. Third, the correlation between the number of structural benchmarks in a program and the completion rate for those structural policies was negative, although neither large nor statistically significant. Fourth, although there was sizable variation in the compliance rate across structural reform categories, the standard deviation of compliance across countries was more than twice as great as that for compliance by reform category.[32]

To sum up, existing studies suggest that obtaining compliance with Fund conditionality has been a serious problem, including the Fund's structural policy conditionality. The compliance problem has been getting more serious over time. Compliance has been lower for EFF programs than for standby arrangements (but not apparently for SAF/ESAF programs).

---

30. Killick (1995) did find some evidence that completion rates were lower for highly indebted countries and for those that received relatively low access to Fund resources.

31. A caveat should be noted with respect to studies of the transition economies. Because of the centrality of structural policies to their reform efforts in the 1990s, their experience with structural policy conditionality may be "special" and not necessarily transferable to economies where structural policies occupy a less central role.

32. The on-time compliance rate was highest (57 percent) for public wage and employment conditions and lowest (29 percent) for price and marketing conditions. Ukraine had the lowest overall compliance rate (14 percent of structural conditions met on time), while Lithuania had the highest (82 percent).

Compliance has also been lower for structural benchmarks than for performance criteria. Correlations between the compliance rate and the number of structural conditions, along with measures of the variability of compliance across program areas and countries, suggest that greater selectivity both in the countries approved for structurally oriented programs and in the structural measures included in such programs could have a high payoff in terms of compliance rates.[33] Further studies on a broader sample of countries would be useful in sharpening these conclusions, including the important issue of whether or not the product of the number of structural conditions and the compliance rate is approximately a constant.

Effectiveness of Structural Policy Conditionality

Even if countries consistently complied with Fund structural policy conditions, this would not necessarily constitute an endorsement for such conditionality unless it can be shown that these are "good" structural policy requirements that lead to "better" economic performance. Evidence relevant for answering that latter query can be gleaned from at least five sources: (a) econometric studies that estimate the effects of IMF programs (as a whole) by comparing program and nonprogram countries or periods; (b) studies that relate either structural policy action within a Fund program or structural policy action more generally (whether in Fund programs or otherwise) to economic growth; (c) studies that relate measures of corporate governance to the extent of exchange rate depreciation or stock market decline during the Asian crisis; (d) a comparison of Fund structural policy recommendations with the "consensus" of the economics profession on what structural policies are good; and (e) a review of the Fund's structural policy recommendations in the Asian crisis countries.

Studies on the Effects of IMF Programs as a Whole. By now, there is an extensive empirical literature on the effects of IMF programs.[34] If one defines "program effects" as the observed outcome (for growth, inflation, the balance of payments, etc.) relative to the counterfactual (that is, the outcome in the absence of an IMF program), then it is clear that most of the early literature had serious methodological flaws (see Goldstein and Montiel 1986). Before-and-after comparisons are not reliable because they attribute all the change in outcomes to a Fund program when exogenous shocks and other influences may really be causing that change. Comparison of program targets and outcomes will not be useful when program targets are set too ambitiously or not ambitiously enough. Simulations of economic models can

33. It is relevant to note that the 1979 "Conditionality Guidelines" suggest that the managing director of the IMF should only recommend that the Fund's executive board approve a program when it is his judgment that the program . . . will be carried out"; see Guideline Number 7 in appendix B.
34. For a recent survey of this literature, see Haque and Khan (1998).

tell us something about the effect of Fund-type policies but not about the effects of actual Fund programs, and comparisons of outcomes for program and nonprogram countries will not do the job if the two groups differ systematically in ways that matter for economic performance. Over time, most of these methodological problems have been addressed. Nowadays, studies typically seek to identify program effects after controlling both for nonprogram effects and for observed (precrisis) differences between program and nonprogram countries.

Still, even the best studies have only indirect implications for the effectiveness of Fund structural policy conditionality since they do not disaggregate the contents of a Fund program into its macro and structural policy components. In any case, what such studies usually find is that Fund programs have a favorable impact on the current account and overall balance of payments, that the effect on inflation is statistically insignificant, and that the effect on economic growth is initially (with the first year) negative but probably turns positive at longer time horizons (see Mussa and Savastano 1999; Fischer 2000a; Conway 1994); too little econometric work has been done on income distribution to say much.[35]

One possible explanation for why such studies do not generate large positive growth effects for Fund programs is that compliance with the policies that matter for medium- to long-run growth is far from complete (as demonstrated above); also, some countries that are in trouble implement their own policies that are not very different from those included in Fund programs. It has also been argued that even nonprogram countries have been influenced by the "silent revolution" in economic thinking on the importance of sound macroeconomic and structural policies and that the Fund has contributed importantly to this revolution (that is, nonprogram countries are not a good "control group" because they too are affected by the policy treatment; see, e.g., Krueger 1998). A second explanation is that the lags associated with the effects of structural policies on economic growth are long and, hence, may show up only after the country has left a Fund program. Yet a third explanation is that the results are right: despite all the rhetoric on "growth-oriented adjustment," Fund programs are still mainly about getting out of financial crises and don't much matter for growth in the medium to long run.

Links between Broad Measures of Structural Policy Reform and Growth. This is a more recent literature, much of it connected with understanding the economic performance of the transition economies.[36]

---

35. See, however, the recent study by Garuda (2000) who finds that Fund programs improve income distribution and poverty reduction for countries with relatively modest precrisis external disequilibria but worsen them for countries with severe precrisis external imbalances.

36. There is of course a much broader and older literature on effects of alternative structural-policy strategies (e.g., Balassa's [1983] work on outward-looking vs. inward-looking policy

One strand looks at whether greater compliance with Fund structural policy conditionality is associated with better growth performance. Here, the recent study by Mercer-Blackman and Unigovskaya (2000) is worth noting. They find that, after controlling for other factors, those transition economies that demonstrated higher compliance with IMF structural performance criteria had better records of sustained economic growth (defined as three consecutive years of positive real GDP growth); in contrast, they could find no significant association between compliance with Fund structural benchmarks and sustained growth. They also report that transition economies that did better on complying with Fund structural performance criteria also showed greater progress on implementing structural reform more generally.[37] One interpretation of their first finding is that the (relatively few) structural policies included as performance criteria are more important for growth than the larger number regarded as structural benchmarks. The authors concede that some of their results are also consistent with other views; for example, countries with better growth performance may find it easier to implement Fund structural conditions, and the unobserved "commitment to reform" may explain *both* Fund program implementation and progress on structural policy action more generally.

The other strand of this literature tests for an association between structural reform—whether achieved within the context of a Fund program or not—and economic growth. A good example is the recent study by Havrylyshyn et al. (1999), which examines the growth experience of twenty-five transition economies over the 1990–97 period. After attempting to hold other determinants of growth constant (including initial economic conditions, inflation, size of government, degree of openness, etc.), they find that the greater was progress on an index of overall structural reform, the higher was economic growth.[38] They also tested whether individual components of structural reform aided growth but found that only price liberalization had significant explanatory power when the overall reform index was also included—a finding that they interpret as suggesting that it is the combination of structural policies that is more critical for growth than any single type of policy.

---

strategies) and on the determinants of growth in developing countries more generally (e.g., Barro [1996]). In addition, there are many studies that take a nonquantitative approach to evaluating Fund structural policies; see, for example, Schadler et al. (1995a), who (looking at Fund programs during the 1988–92 period) concluded that "there was a broad measure of success in accomplishing structural reform" (29).

37. Progress on structural reform is measured using a structural reform index, derived from De Melo, Denizer, and Gelb [1996] and EBRD Transition reports. This index is meant to capture liberalization of prices and foreign exchange markets, small and large-scale privatization, governance and restructuring reforms, legal reforms, interest rate liberalization, and banking reforms; see Havrylyshyn et al. [1999].

38. Fischer, Sahay, and Vegh (1996) reached a similar conclusion in an earlier paper on the growth experience of the transition economies. Because there are very few transition economies that have not had a program with the IMF, a comparison of program and nonprogram countries is not a viable research strategy.

A similar growth exercise for eighty-four low- and middle-income countries during the 1981–95 period is summarized in IMF (1997). In these pooled, cross-section regressions, the authors find that after controlling for other determinants of per capita GDP growth, improved macroeconomic policies and improved structural policies both have significant effects on growth in the expected direction. They also conclude that behavior of growth in ESAF countries does not differ fundamentally from that in other developing countries.

Corporate Governance and the Asian Financial Crisis. As suggested earlier, there has been much discussion of the role that governance and corruption issues played in the Asian financial crisis. A new study by Johnson et al. (2000) provides some interesting empirical results and insights. The authors look at the behavior of nominal exchange rates and stock markets from the end of 1996 through January 1999 for twenty-five emerging economies. Their aim was to see if cross-country differences in measures of corporate governance (e.g., judicial efficiency, corruption, rule of law, protection for minority shareholders, creditor rights, etc.) could do a better job at explaining the extent of exchange rate depreciation and stock market decline than could standard macroeconomic measures (e.g., fiscal and monetary policy, current account imbalances, international reserves, foreign debt, etc.). In brief, they find that the corporate governance horse does better than the macroeconomic horse, particularly for stock market movements. They argue that institutions that protect investor rights are not important as long as growth lasts (because managers do not want to steal). However, when growth prospects decline and there is even a small loss of investor confidence, countries with only weakly enforceable minority shareholder rights become particularly vulnerable. This is because outside investors reassess the likely amount of expropriation by managers and adjust the amount of capital they are willing to provide (resulting in a fall of asset values and a collapse of the exchange rate). On some of Johnson et al.'s measures of corporate governance—particularly rights of minority shareholders—several Asian crisis countries (particularly Indonesia and Thailand) ranked low and hence were more vulnerable to the effects of a downturn.

Fund Structural Policy Conditionality and the "Consensus." In 1983 at a conference on IMF conditionality, Richard Cooper [1983] offered the following view: "we could choose any five people present and make a team to work up an economic adjustment program for a particular country other than our own . . . [and] the program we came up with would not differ greatly from a typical IMF program" (571).

I am more skeptical that we could make the same statement today, at least about Fund programs for the Asian crisis countries. Nevertheless, I would still maintain that the general thrust of the Fund's structural policy recommendations falls squarely in what my IIE colleague John Williamson (1990) has labeled "the Washington policy consensus." Whether it is interest rate deregulation, trade liberalization, tax reform, the currency regime, foreign direct investment, price liberalization, or banking reform, Fund structural policy advice is typically not far from the consensus. Writing fifteen years after Cooper, Anne O. Krueger (1998, p. 1998) offers a similar assessment:

> Many of the lending changes supported by the Bank and the Fund (in, for example, exchange rates, size of fiscal deficits, trade liberalization, agricultural and energy price reforms, privatization, and tax reform) are ones that would be endorsed in broad outline, if not in detail, by almost all economists.

But saying that the Fund's structural policy advice has generally reflected the profession's consensus view does not mean that this advice has not at times gone seriously astray. Three examples illustrate the point. First, along with several of its larger G7 shareholders (particularly the United States and the United Kingdom), the Fund often pushed hard on emerging economies to undertake capital account liberalization without due regard to the adequacy of the host country's regulatory and supervisory framework.[39] In Korea, for instance, the Fund apparently urged liberalization of both short-term and long-term flows. However, when the Koreans said they would only go for the former, the Fund apparently regarded this as better than nothing and accepted it.[40] A second example concerns Fund advice on privatization in transition economies. There, the IMF (2000) acknowledges that privatization runs the danger of producing perverse results in the absence of hard budget constraints, competition, and effective standards of corporate governance. As with capital account liberalization, a more selective approach to privatization with greater attention to sequencing would, with the benefit of hindsight, have been better. Yet a third example was the initial Fund recommendation in Indonesia to go with a limited deposit guarantee for banks rather than a blanket guarantee.[41] In drawing the lessons of the Asian crisis, the Fund (Lindgren et al. 1999) now concludes that in a systemic crisis a blanket guarantee is needed to restore confidence in the financial system.[42]

---

39. One of the few observers who stated publicly his concerns (before the crisis) about the magnitude of short-term capital inflows going into Asian emerging economies was Park (1996).

40. In appraising Fund structural policy recommendations made in the late 1980s, Schadler et al. (1995a, 31) similarly conclude: "Coordinated programs for structural reforms would have been desirable but were generally not politically or administratively feasible. It is appropriate, therefore, that programs supported the second-best strategy of seizing opportunities for reform on as broad a front as possible. This process cannot give a large role to sequencing considerations, but these are not unambiguous and could unduly slow the process."

41. A comprehensive guarantee was introduced in Indonesia two months later.

42. As suggested below, I do not share this view on the use of blanket guarantees, but I think most others do.

Fund Structural Policy Conditionality in the Asian Crisis Countries. Because
the heart of Fund structural policy conditionality in the Asian crisis countries dealt with the financial sector, and because there is already a separate
paper at this conference focused on financial policies in emerging economies, I will confine my remarks on the Fund's structural policy recommendations to four points.

First, I find the underlying rationale for dealing immediately with insolvent and weak banking and finance companies compelling. Without such
action, it probably would have been impossible to restore monetary and
currency stability (because large-scale liquidity support to insolvent institutions would have worked at cross purposes), and the fiscal tab for bank recapitalization would have been even higher than it has turned out to be (because managers of insolvent institutions would have engaged in more
"gambling for resurrection"). Moreover, I don't think confidence could
have been restored without some concrete evidence that financial-sector supervision (including transparency and disclosure) was going to be started
on a different path for the future than it had been on in the past. Similarly,
to show that cronyism and corruption would henceforth be less prevalent,
it was important (at least in Indonesia) to take a few visible privileges or
sweetheart deals away from those close to President Suharto. Once the crisis deepened and nonperforming loans of banks and corporate insolvencies
became larger and more widespread, it also became evident that banks and
corporates—particularly in Thailand and Indonesia—would not simply be
able to grow out of it without restructuring. Because of strong links between
banks and corporates (especially in Korea and Indonesia), as well as the
need to cushion somewhat the most vulnerable groups from the effects of
the crisis, there was a good case for including some corporate reforms (e.g.,
reduction of debt-equity ratios by the *chaebol*) and some social safety net
provisions in those programs.

Second, notwithstanding the above argument, there were elements of
structural conditionality in the three Fund programs with Indonesia, Korea,
and Thailand that seem superfluous. I don't find persuasive the argument
that trade liberalization measures in the Indonesian and Korean programs
were necessary to prevent a slide toward protectionism (see Hamann and
Schulze-Ghattas 1999). A better rationale would be that trade liberalization
was needed to increase competition and to help discipline inefficient domestic producers. However, that still doesn't explain why trade liberalization
needed to be done immediately rather than after the crisis. Likewise, I don't
see why the Indonesian program had to be so sweeping with respect to the
dismantling of state monopolies and cartels, elimination of restrictive marketing agreements, abolition of showcase projects, and the like, disagreeable
as those practices were. For confidence reasons, a few "candies" may have
had to be taken away from cronies at the outset, but the rest of the box (and,
admittedly, it was a very big box) could have waited for later. In the Korean

program, the tax reform and privatization conditions look like they could have waited until after the crisis. Additionally, in Thailand (which had the narrowest of the three programs), it's hard to see why privatization of state enterprises, removal of the real estate tax on foreign purchases of condominiums, and a new land act needed to be part of the Fund's conditions.

Moving from the width to the depth of conditionality, the level of detail reflected in the structural benchmarks for these three programs likewise seems excessive. For example, in Indonesia, was it necessary to have five commitments for reform of oil and gas policy, and eighteen commitments for follow-up actions to the findings of the audit of Bank Indonesia? In Korea, was it essential to have eleven commitments for restructuring, for investment guidelines, and for corporate governance of insurance companies? In Thailand, did six target dates have to be set up to guide the privatization of Bangkok Metropolitan and Siam City banks? More generally, did supervisory and prudential measures for financial institutions in the three crisis countries have to be specified so precisely? Wouldn't, say, a broader commitment to implement the Basel Core Principles of Effective Banking Supervision by date x, along with a few benchmark checks of good progress, be as effective (and less intrusive) and, in addition, carry the seal of approval of the world's key banking supervisors? Couldn't the Fund provide its very detailed views on ways of improving corporate governance as technical assistance, not as conditions in the Fund program? Yes, this would require more faith that the crisis country would want on its own to "do the right thing." However, if it doesn't really want to implement the reforms, then very detailed monitoring via a very large set of structural benchmarks may not push the ball much farther ahead. Besides, unlike performance criteria, failure to meet many of the structural benchmarks does not carry the automatic threat of interruption of fund financing.

Third, I don't agree with either the Fund or many of its critics that the Indonesian experience leads to the lesson that bank restructuring during a systemic banking crisis can only be accomplished successfully if blanket guarantees are issued by the government (see Lindgren et al. 1999). The closing of banks in Indonesia led to runs because the authorities were only willing to close a subset of a much wider group of insolvent banks, because high-level political support (from President Suharto and some others) for the initial bank closures was absent, and because the Fund agreed to a bad compromise. When there are widespread bank insolvencies, the key to restoring confidence is to convince the public that all the bad banks have been closed or resolved, that the remainder are solid, and that small retail depositors (not everybody) will be covered.[43] As a former colleague of mine put it, "people don't run banks that are closed; they run banks that are open

---

43. Ways to limit moral hazard without negating the benefits of deposit insurance are discussed in Financial Stability Forum (2000).

that they think will soon be closed." Also, when there is no deposit insurance in place or the insurance system is not viewed as credible, the necessity is for the bank supervisory authority to replace the old management of insolvent banks with a new one (so as to prevent "double-or-nothing" behavior and even larger credit losses), and to eventually dock the shareholders (so as to penalize the owners and to limit moral hazard); such insolvent banks can then be resolved in a variety of ways (even while they honor withdrawals and take deposits). What's not necessary—and can prompt runs— is to board up the teller cages of some banks (while other questionable banks remain open). The real lesson of the Indonesian experience is that a sensible, incentive-compatible deposit insurance system (along the lines of the Federal Deposit Insurance Corporation Improvement Act [FDICIA] in the United States) should be a permanent part of the financial infrastructure in all countries; without it, governments wind up providing ex post deposit insurance, but they do it at higher current cost and with moral hazard effects that increase the likelihood of future banking crises.

In much the same spirit, I disagree with those who say that bank capital requirements should have been phased in even more slowly in the Asian crisis countries so as to prevent a credit crunch. A cutback in lending exposure is an equilibrium response of a bank to a negative shock that reduces its capital. The relevant question is not whether one likes a credit crunch; it is whether one prefers some credit crunch to an expansion of lending—much of which is likely to go to the same insolvent borrowers that were at the root of the banks' difficulties (leading to even larger bank losses). To be sure, there was a fall-off in real credit supply in late 1997 and early 1998 in most of the crisis countries, and undoubtedly some "good" borrowers were also denied credit. However, there was also a fall in real credit demand that apparently was sharper than the fall in supply (at least in Korea and Thailand; see Ghosh and Ghosh 1999; Lane et al. 1999). In addition, there is some evidence that the allocation of bank credit improved (see Borenzstein and Lee 2000). In the end, I doubt we would have obtained a better combined score on economic activity and on bank losses if capital requirements had been less binding during 1998–2000.

Drawing on a sample of thirty-four countries (twenty-seven of them developing or transition economies) that have experienced significant fiscal costs from bank failures over the 1970–2000 period, Honohan and Klingebiel (2000) compare "regulatory forbearance" versus "strict" approaches to crisis resolution. They find that unlimited deposit guarantees, open-ended liquidity support, repeated recapitalizations, debtor bailouts, and regulatory forbearance add significantly and sizably to costs. One of their main conclusions bears repeating:

> Our findings clearly tilt the balance in favor of a "strict" approach to crisis resolution, rather than an accommodating one. At the very least, they

emphasize that regulatory authorities which [sic] choose an accommodating or gradualist approach to an emerging crisis need to be sure that
they have some other way of controlling risk. (19)

Fourth, compliance with the Fund's structural policy conditionality appears to have been much better than the average (for all Fund programs) in
Korea and in Thailand but not so in Indonesia. A good deal of progress has
been made on financial-sector rebuilding and reform, but much still remains to be done. Moreover, it is still too early to know whether the excessively close relationship between large business and government that has
been the source of so much inefficiency and favoritism has changed fundamentally for the better.

It's not easy (especially for an outsider) to measure compliance with structural policy conditions because the Fund programs with the three crisis
countries were revised often over the 1997–2000 period and because some
structural benchmarks have been dropped or added from one revision to the
next. Still, suppose we define "compliance" as having met a condition
within, say, three months of the target date. Then my ballpark estimate
would be that Korea has complied with about 90 percent of the structural
conditions laid out in the Fund's program.[44] The corresponding compliance
figure for Thailand would be about 70 percent. Two areas where compliance
was weak in Thailand were reform of state banks and privatization of public
enterprises. The calculation for Indonesia is subject to the largest margin of
error but probably falls in the 20–40 percent range. In Indonesia, compliance
with structural conditions has been seriously handicapped by prolonged
political instability and by a weak approach by the government toward debtors; compliance has been lower in noncore policy areas than in core areas.

The problem with looking only at the share of structural conditions met
is not only that some are more important than others: it is also that most
structural policy conditions capture *processes* that do not necessarily have
a tight link with outcomes. For example, if the structural benchmark says
you must have two outside directors appointed to a corporate board, that
can be done, but the outside appointees may not differ much from their
predecessors. Or a loan can be restructured, but in a way that doesn't much
reduce the present discounted value of the borrower's debt burden. For this
reason, it is useful to look at some other, less process-oriented benchmarks
for the financial and corporate sectors.

As background, we should recall that the three crisis countries (as a
group) experienced a sharp output recovery in 1999 and 2000; inflation is
mostly under control, and their current accounts are in surplus (albeit much

---

44. During a visit to South Korea in May 2000, I met with many Korean officials who had
been involved in the crisis negotiations with the Fund. My overall impression is that most of
the structural conditions included in the Fund program had been on the domestic reform
agenda for a long time and thus were not viewed as "imposed" on Korea. This may explain in
part why the compliance rate with structural conditions has been so high.

Table 5.8   Asian Crisis Countries: Real GDP, Consumer Prices, and Current
                   Account Balance

	Real GDP (annual % change)	Consumer Prices (annual % change)	Current Account Balances (as % of GDP)
Indonesia			
1998	−13.0	58.0	4.2
1999	0.3	20.8	3.7
2000[a]	4.5	3.3	6.5
2001[a]	4.2	5.6	5.3
Korea			
1998	−6.7	7.5	12.8
1999	10.7	0.8	6.1
2000[a]	9.0	2.4	2.6
2001[a]	5.0	3.5	1.7
Thailand			
1998	−10.2	8.1	12.7
1999	4.2	0.3	9.1
2000[a]	5.5	1.6	7.7
2001[a]	4.0	2.3	9.4

Sources: 1998 and 1999, IMF (2000); 2000 and 2001, Spencer (2000).
[a]Estimated.

reduced from the huge current-account surpluses of 1998); see table 5.8. In addition, they have much lower ratios of short-term external debt to international reserves than immediately preceding the crisis; they have abandoned publicly declared exchange rate targets; and both nonperforming loans in the banking system and corporate insolvencies are retreating from their peaks. They are moving in the right direction—albeit too slowly—on banking supervision and corporate governance. Additionally, in Korea, the debt-equity ratios for most of the largest *chaebol* have declined sharply. Turning to the negative side of the ledger, equity prices have declined sharply throughout emerging Asia (with the notable exception of China); the expected growth slowdown in the United States meant that export growth of the crisis countries was likely to be much lower (by roughly half) in 2001 than it was in 2000; volatile oil prices are a source of great uncertainty; the high public debt burden in Indonesia and the large fiscal deficit in Thailand limit the scope for countercyclical fiscal policy; bank lending to the private sector has been weak outside Korea; Japan's recovery remains both anemic and fragile; and there has been some political turbulence in the region (the Philippines and Taiwan).

Table 5.9, taken from Claessens, Djankov, and Klingebiel (1999), provides a summary of financial restructuring in the three crisis countries, at least as of mid-1999. Although there have been later developments, a number of their findings merit mention.

Korea has used a combination of recapitalizations, nationalizations,

Table 5.9   Financial Restructuring in Asian Crisis Countries

	Indonesia	Korea	Thailand
1. Initial liquidity support to banks	$21.7 billion (18% of GDP)	$23.3 billion (5% of GDP)	$24.1 billion (20% of GDP)
2. Bank shutdowns	64 of 237	None	1 of 15
3. Shutdowns of other financial institutions	n.a.	>117	57 of 91
4. Mergers of financial institutions	4 of 7 state banks	11 of 26 absorbed by other banks	3 banks and 12 finance companies
5. Nationalizations	12	4	4
6. Public funds for recapitalizations	Plan in place; some bonds issued	Government injected $8 billion into 9 commercial banks; 5 out of 6 major banks now 90% controlled by state	Plan in place; government injected $8.9 billion into private banks and $11.7 billion into public banks
7. Majority foreign ownership of banks	Allowed, 1 potentially	Allowed, 2 completed and 1 near finalization	Allowed, 2 completed and 4 pending
8. Weak financial institutions still in system	Many weak commercial banks	Many weak nonbank financial institutions	Some weak public and private commercial banks
9. Nonperforming loans remaining in banks (% of total loans)	22	18	50
10. Capital shortfall of banking system (% of banking system assets)	18	4	8
11. Corporate governance + management of banks			
a. independent outside directors	None	2/3 of board slots	19
b. changes in top management, majority-owned domestic banks	None	6 of 11 major banks	3 of 11 banks
12. Corporate restructuring (August 1999)			
a. out-of-court restructured debt/total debt (%)	13	40	22
b. in-court restructured debt/total debt (%)	4	8	7

(continued)

Table 5.9 (continued)

	Indonesia	Korea	Thailand
13. Interest difficulties of firms; percent that cannot cover interest expense from operational cash flows 2000–02 (assuming 1999 interest rates)	53	17	22
14. Public debt (% of GDP)			
a. 1997	48	11	7
b. 1999	98	37	40
15. Quality of financial-sector regulation index (4 = best practice, 1 = weakest)			
a. 1997	1.3	2.7	1.0
b. 1999	2.0	3.0	2.7
16. Ownership concentration + legal framework			
a. percent ownership of top 15 families	62	38	53
b. efficiency of judicial system, index (1 = worst, 10 = best)	2.5	6.0	3.2
c. rule of law, index (1 = worst, 10 = best)	4.0	5.4	6.3
d. corruption, index (1 = worst, 10 = top)	2.2	5.3	5.2
17. Market structure changes in financial sector			
a. number of commercial banks: taken over/sold to foreigners/nationalized	4/0/12	5/2/4	0/2/4
b. number of private domestic banks: market share (%)	122(21)	18(37)	13(48)
c. number of state banks: market share (%)	43(78)	10(58)	6(45)
d. number of nonbanks: market share (%)	245(1)	11(5)	22(7)

Source: Claessens, Djankov, and Klingebiel (1999).

Note: In a more recent World Bank [2000] report, it is estimated that nonperforming loans, as of June 2000, account for 30, 10, and 30 percent of total loans in Indonesia, Korea, and Thailand, respectively.

removal of bad debt, and mergers to strengthen its banking system.[45] However, it was much less active against weak nonbanks and has had to clean up a mess with those investment trusts that rushed in to finance the *chaebol* (especially Daewoo) after the banks cut back. Thailand has closed about two-thirds of its finance companies but has gone more slowly on bank restructuring, asking the banks to raise their own capital and making public money subject to stricter prudential and management changes. Indonesia, after a large, initial liquidity injection to banks, has gotten less far on bank restructuring than the others.

Banks are still undercapitalized—moderately in Korea, more so in Thailand, and extremely so in Indonesia. Nonperforming loans are still very high in Thailand and Indonesia. Korean banks may be able to cover their capital shortfalls from earnings; this is not so with either Thai or Indonesian banks. Korea and Thailand have made some governance and management changes in their banks, Indonesian banks much less so.

Korea and Thailand have restructured about one-half and one-third, respectively, of corporate debt, the bulk of it in out-of-court settlement; the corresponding figure for Indonesia is roughly one-sixth. Although corporations have benefited from the recovery, about one-quarter of Thai firms and over half of Indonesian ones cannot meet interest payments out of operational cash flows.

Despite quite significant increases in foreign direct investment, all three Asian economies have seen their public debt rise appreciably as a result of financial restructuring costs. Public debt is about equal to gross domestic product (GDP) in Indonesia and is more than one-third of it in both Korea and Thailand (having risen from very low precrisis ratios).

Gains have been made in the quality of financial regulation, but it still trails best international practice. So far, Korea and Thailand have come farther than Indonesia on this score. Corporate ownership is still very concentrated among the top fifteen families in all three countries. Corporate governance is changing, but a weak judicial system in Indonesia and a poor bankruptcy law in Thailand have limited the advances.[46]

Last but not least, because of heavy government intervention into the financial system during the crisis (nationalizations, purchase of bad assets, etc.) the government now owns a huge share—about 50 percent on average for the three countries—of total banking assets. Because governments do not do well owning and managing banks, there is a strong need for much larger divestitures (including sales to foreigners) than have occurred to date.[47]

---

45. In late September 2000, the Korean Government announced that it would be putting in an additional $44 billion of public funds to deal with bad loans of the banking system.

46. Other analysts (e.g., Root [2000] and Spencer [2000]) have pointed to the low number of affiliate sales by the *chaebol* and the recent rescue of Hyundai Engineering and Construction as disappointments in the Korean reform effort.

47. See Root (2000) on why a more decentralized approach to financial restructuring in Korea would yield better results than a government-dominated strategy.

To sum up, studies of the effects of Fund programs show that they have positive effects on the current account and overall balance of payments; effects on growth, inflation, and income distribution have proved to be much harder to pin down with any precision. Those transition economies that have done more on implementing Fund structural performance criteria appear to have done better on economic growth and structural policy reform more generally than those with weaker compliance records. Those emerging economies with better corporate governance structures in place prior to the outbreak of Asian crisis were, on average, hit less hard with currency and stock market declines during the crisis than those with a poorer track record on corporate governance. For the most part, Fund structural policy recommendations reflect the economics profession's consensus of what constitutes sensible structural policy reform, although some serious mistakes on the sequencing of reforms have sometimes taken place. The core of the Fund's structural policy conditionality in the three Asian crisis countries—which focused mainly on financial-sector crisis management and restructuring—was appropriate, with the exception of the bad compromise made on bank closures in Indonesia. That said, the Fund's structural conditionality in the Asian crisis countries (and especially in Indonesia) appears excessive—both in scope and in detail. Thus far, compliance with that conditionality has been high in Korea, above average in Thailand, and below average in Indonesia. Looking at a broader array of indicators, progress on restructuring in East Asia is evident but much more needs to be done to put banks and corporates on a sound footing. It is too early to tell whether the past close relationship between government and business has changed fundamentally for the better.

5.1.4   How Did Fund Structural Policy Conditionality Get to be This Way?

If one concludes that Fund structural policy conditionality has become more intrusive than necessary, it is relevant to speculate on how it might have gotten that way. In my view, nine factors have contributed to that trend.[48]

First, in the 1970s and early 1980s, IMF programs came under sharp criticism from many developing countries as being too demand-oriented and too short-run and as not paying enough attention to economic growth, to supply-side reforms, and to income distribution. The disappointing growth performance of developing countries in the early 1980s added to those concerns. Because developing countries increasingly constituted the demand for Fund resources, neither the Fund nor creditor governments could easily dismiss that criticism. New lending windows with higher structural policy content and with lending terms more favorable to low-income countries were created, and monitoring techniques for gauging compliance with structural policy conditions evolved.

48. Several of these factors are discussed in Allen (1993).

Second, the expansion of the IMF's surveillance responsibilities—agreed upon in the mid-1970s under the second amendment of the Fund's charter and given expression in the revised Article IV—permitted Fund Article IV country missions to take a wider field of view in evaluating economic developments and prospects. Structural problems thus came under greater scrutiny. This greater familiarity with structural problems may in turn have led to a greater readiness to include structural policy conditions in programs, at least in those cases in which structural weaknesses were perceived, rightly or wrongly, to have been linked to crisis vulnerability.

Third, the huge transformation task faced by the transition economies—especially in the first half of the 1990s—made structural policies and the building of a market infrastructure the name of the game in that region. And the IMF (along with the European Bank for Reconstruction and Development) was at the center of the technical assistance and policy lending to those transition economies. Again, structural benchmarks came to be relied upon as a way of monitoring structural policy conditionality across a wide front. When structural problems arose in later crises (such as that in Asia), the same monitoring techniques were applied.

Fourth, all the while, the Fund was more and more interpreting its mandate as broader than just promoting macroeconomic and financial stability and helping countries to manage financial crises. From the mid-1980s on, economic growth and, later, high-quality growth were given increased prominence. After the Mexican peso crisis of 1994–95, crisis prevention—with particular attention to strengthening financial systems at the national level and developing international standards and codes of good practice—too moved up on the agenda.

Fifth, crises that involve severe balance sheet problems of banks and private corporations lead to more structural policy intensive fund programs than do those that stem from traditional monetary and fiscal policy excesses—and the Asian crises of 1997–98 had those balance sheet problems in spades. The IMF's executive board also seems to have sent staff the message (in 1997) that lending into serious governance and corruption problems (without any measures to address them) would not receive board support. In the Indonesian program, a decision was made to try to impress the markets with the comprehensiveness of the reform effort.

Sixth, the long-standing and growing problem of obtaining good compliance with Fund programs led over time to greater reliance on prior actions and to more wide-ranging and detailed structural policy conditions, presumably in an effort to penalize poor earlier track records, to thwart evasion, and to detect slippage at an earlier stage.[49] If this broader and more detailed conditionality didn't produce higher compliance and the amount of

---

49. Failure to implement earlier Fund recommendations can over time push up structural conditionality even when some of those recommendations come in the form of technical assistance rather than as conditions in Fund programs.

structural reform hoped for, maybe the Fund concluded that it was still inducing more structural reform than would obtain with lesser Fund structural policy conditionality. The Fund's Guidelines for Conditionality—which might have reined in excessive structural policy conditionality—came to be viewed by the Fund's executive board as broad principles of intention, not as something to be monitored carefully and enforced.

Seventh, in the meantime, a wide array of legislative groups, nongovernmental organizations (NGOs), and even other international financial organizations came to see an IMF letter of intent as the preferred instrument of leverage for their own agendas in emerging economies. Yes, the International Labor Organization (ILO) might be the logical place to push core labor standards, but it doesn't have the teeth of an IMF program. Simultaneously, various G7 governments—and particularly the Fund's largest shareholder—were finding it increasingly difficult to get congressional support for "clean" IMF funding bills. Reflecting this congressional pressure from both major parties, the U.S. executive director at the Fund has been obliged to support with voice and vote a long list of structural policies (ranging from protection of the environment to promotion of economic deregulation and privatizing of industry), and the U.S. Treasury (2000a) is required to report annually to Congress on its compliance with relevant sections of the Foreign Operations, Export Financing, and Related Programs Appropriation Act of 1999. A reading of that report (U.S. Treasury 2000a) confirms that the United States frequently pushed for policies in fund programs that were far from the Fund's core competence. Likewise, in countries where there was prolonged use of Fund resources, IMF letters of intent sometimes became an instrument of leverage that the finance ministry could use in order to push structural reforms on other departments in the government that were opposed. In short, everybody has gotten in on the act.

Eighth, unlike other IFIs, the Fund and the World Bank have sufficient "ground troops" to make on-site visits to all countries. In addition, at least in official circles, the Fund has developed a reputation as being able to act quickly and efficiently. When new structural challenges have arisen, there has therefore been a tendency to say, "give it to the Fund; they go there anyway; have them just add a few specialists on problem x to the mission." The management of the Fund has apparently not said "no" very often to those demands.

Finally, there have been occasions—the Korean and Indonesian programs are important cases in point—when strong pressure from particular G7 governments (during program negotiations) resulted in the inclusion of specific structural policies in a Fund program, and this despite the provision in the Fund's charter (IMF 1988, 42, Article XII, section IV) for each member country of the Fund to "refrain from all attempts to influence any of the [Fund] staff in the discharge of [their] functions."

5.1.5   Approaches to Streamlining Fund Structural Policy Conditionality

The Fund's new managing director, Horst Kohler, has already indicated that he thinks that the Fund "has been overstretched in the past and needs to refocus" (Kohler 2000c, 3); he has also flagged his intention to end "mission creep," in large part by streamlining structural policy conditionality. To carry out that objective, there are at least eight approaches (not all of them mutually exclusive) worth mentioning.

Structural Preconditions

This radical approach, favored by the majority of the Meltzer Commission (see IFIAC 2000), would jettison ex post IMF conditionality in favor of a small number of preconditions, namely, freedom of entry and operation for foreign financial institutions, regular and timely publication of the maturity structure of outstanding sovereign and guaranteed debt and off–balance sheet liabilities, adequate capitalization of commercial banks, and a proper fiscal requirement.[50] Developing countries that met these preconditions would be eligible immediately for short-term liquidity assistance; those developing countries that did not meet them would not be eligible.

Objections to this approach have been registered on three counts (see Bergsten et al. 2000).

Although meeting these preconditions would reduce the risk of getting into a crisis, they would hardly be sufficient for crisis prevention. Although many currency and debt crises begin in the banking sector, quite a few others do not, and freedom of entry plus a capital requirement are not good substitutes for the broader range of measures outlined in the Basel Core Principles of Effective Banking Supervision.[51] The fiscal policy precondition is not defined in the report, and making it operational would be subject to the same kind of negotiation and intrusiveness as with present Fund conditionality.

More fundamentally, even if satisfied, these preconditions would not get a country out of a balance-of-payments crisis once it got into one. Without measures to reduce absorption and to switch expenditure from foreign to domestic goods, the crisis country's ability to repay would not improve. Moreover, giving large Fund loans to a country with a runaway inflation or a huge budget deficit would increase moral hazard, not reduce it.

Last but not least, it is highly questionable whether the international community would be willing to exclude completely from IMF financing countries that didn't meet these preconditions, particularly when a new gov-

---

50. At present, the only Fund lending window that uses prequalification is the Contingency Credit Line (CCL). However, since its inception in 1999, no country has yet come forward to use it.

51. Garber (2000) has argued that a subordinated debt requirement for banks a la the Meltzer Report could easily be manipulated and evaded.

ernment promised policies different from its predecessor.[52] For this reason, the Council on Foreign Relations Task Force (1999) rejected the "all-or-nothing" approach and opted instead to penalize (reward) countries that have followed poor (good) policies by charging them higher (lower) interest rates when they needed to borrow from the Fund.

Collateralized Fund Lending

Another radical approach to reducing or eliminating Fund structural policy conditionality would have the fund follow the Bagehot (1873) guideline and lend on good collateral (see Meltzer 1999; Feldstein 1999). Good collateral is meant to serve several purposes. It provides a test of whether the borrower is just illiquid rather than insolvent (a solvent borrower has good collateral to pledge; an insolvent one does not); it safeguards the solvency of the lender; and it reduces (borrower) moral hazard by discouraging the borrower from holding risky assets that would not be accepted as good collateral.

Opposition to the collateral proposal emanates from several arguments. If eligible collateral is defined narrowly and strictly (say, holdings of U.S. government securities), then it will not provide much additional advantage in crisis management (since countries so endowed wouldn't need to come to the Fund—they could borrow from private markets). Pledging collateral to the Fund might also run afoul of "negative pledge" clauses in existing loan agreements, and even if it didn't, its favorable impact would be limited because it would raise borrowing costs on the noncollateralized debt. Some would contend too that liquidating the collateral (say, export receipts) in the event of repayment problems (stemming either from bad luck or poor policy performance) would subject the Fund to even harsher criticism from developing-country borrowers than it receives when it interrupts disbursement under a Fund program. Would the United States, for example, have been able politically to cash in the collateral (oil receipts) pledged by Mexico during the 1994–95 peso crisis if things had not worked out so well for Mexico in 1995?

Define Conditionality in Terms of Outcomes,
Not Structural Policies or Benchmarks

The idea here would be for the Fund to leave the *process* by which countries respond to crises up to them and instead condition Fund assistance on positive changes in certain outcomes. For example, instead of making changes in the judicial system or the establishment of a new framework for

52. See Polak (1991). U.S. Treasury (2000b) argues that these preconditions would have precluded the IMF from responding to financial emergencies in the vast majority of its member countries, including all the Asian crisis countries.

corporate debt restructuring conditions of the program for Indonesia, the Fund could just say that half of the nonperforming corporate debt has to be rescheduled by date x. If the country meets the target, it gets the money; otherwise, it doesn't.

The rub here is that performance criteria are normally confined to variables that are under the control of the borrower. The difficulty with defining structural conditionality in terms of outcomes is that exogenous developments could affect the borrower's ability to meet the target. Consequently, there would be many demands for waivers. In addition, outcomes are often not easy to define for some structural policies (e.g., what is "good" banking supervision, or what constitutes a "restructured" loan). Finally, one of the main purposes of the Fund is to rule certain crisis management processes (e.g., increased resort to trade restrictions) as out of bounds.

Put Restrictions or Penalties on Foreign-Currency Borrowing

If much of structural policy conditionality comes from balance sheet problems of banks and corporates and the latter, in turn, often derive from the buildup of large currency mismatches, why not attack the problem at its source by seeking to discourage foreign-currency borrowing (see Krueger 2000; Dooley 1999)? Presumably, a key reason why Brazil has had a much milder crisis than the Asian countries is that currency mismatching in Brazil was better controlled; hence, when the real crashed, there were many fewer banking and corporate insolvencies. Although (enlightened) government borrowers ought to be able to internalize these externalities, this is not so for private borrowers, who may expect either a government bailout (if things go badly) or who may be driven to take up the cheaper foreign-currency loan because competitors are doing it. Although timely publication of aggregate data on currency and maturity mismatching may improve market discipline, some have proposed going much farther. Krueger, for example, has suggested that foreign-currency obligations incurred by domestic residents of emerging economies be made unenforceable in domestic courts. Others have argued that the currency mismatching problem is a powerful argument in favor of dollarization.

One counterargument is that such measures are too drastic for the problem at hand. If currency mismatching is the problem, why not have the government develop better hedging mechanisms (e.g., futures exchanges), as Mexico has been doing since it moved to a floating rate? Others might say that giving up (via dollarization) the potential advantage of access to easy monetary policy during a severe recession just to minimize the risk of one particular type of crisis is allowing the tail to wag the dog. Enforcement of currency-matching restrictions could also be a problem. In today's world of structured derivatives, what looks like a domestic-currency loan could well have embedded options that amount to an unhedged bet on the exchange rate.

Greater Resort to International Standards

Instead of custom-tailoring structural conditions to a particular crisis situation or particular financial institutions, the fund and its member countries could rely more on generic international standards. For example, if there was a serious problem with data disclosure, or with banking supervision, or with corporate governance, the crisis country could agree to meet international standards in these areas by date x. A potential appeal of the standards is that they represent the consensus on good practice in that area by a group of international experts—not the views of an individual mission chief or even of the Fund (see Eichengreen 2000). Since the fund is already engaged (on a voluntary basis) in evaluating countries' compliance with standards and codes, this approach might also afford more flexibility in the time frame for meeting these conditions.

The disadvantage of the standards approach is that the standards themselves may not be specific enough to address the pressing problems at hand. If the elements of the standards are too vague, monitoring would likely lead to frequent disagreements.

Leaner Structural Conditionality within Present Arrangements

Under this approach, the Fund's executive board would issue a new guidance note calling for "leaner" structural conditionality; henceforth, each structural condition included in a program would have to be directly related to financial stability and would have to carry a macroeconomic impact; in addition, the note might increase the use of formal performance criteria relative to more discretionary structural benchmarks and program reviews. The aim of this new guidance note would be not only to induce mission chiefs to be less wide-ranging and detailed in their structural policy recommendations but also to dissuade *both* creditor and debtor governments from pushing for structural conditions that did not fall within the Fund's core competence ("I'd like to help you, Mr. Deputy Minister, but that just isn't our job"). Associated with this leaner structural conditionality might also be an effort to increase the Fund's leverage for structural policy reform in nonprogram channels. For example, structural weaknesses could be given more attention in published Fund Article IV reports, leaving it more to the private markets to apply pressure for reform. Additionally, much of what now appears as detailed structural benchmarks (in a Fund program) on how to implement a given structural reform could be handled in Fund technical assistance.

Skeptics might argue that the existing guidance note on conditionality that has been around for twenty years or more is perfectly adequate. Why would a new one make much of a difference? To make a difference, management and the Fund's executive board would have to be much more committed to enforcing the new note than they were in enforcing the previous one. However, this would be unlikely to happen unless there was a clear understanding with the G7 and with emerging economies that greater restraint would be exercised than heretofore in assigning the fund new tasks. For example, just within the few months previous to the time of this writing, the G7 requested the IMF to step up its monitoring of money laundering. Questions would also arise on how many structural conditions and how much detail would be appropriate for such a leaner structural conditionality (that is, would it be a big change from prevailing practice, or only a small modification?).

Allowing the Fund to Borrow in the Private Capital Markets

If some G7 legislatures use the Fund's requests for funding (increases in quota, funding for new facilities and debt initiatives, etc.) as points of leverage to impose a variety of (counterproductive and superfluous) conditions on Fund lending practices, it might be argued that the Fund should be given authority to borrow in the private capital markets (thereby increasing its independence).[53] Those who oppose this proposal would contend that the Fund itself, not G7 legislatures, is the main source of excessive structural conditionality; thus, easier funding would reduce "accountability" to the Fund's shareholders and might just as well increase the scope of Fund conditionality as reduce it.

Clearer Division of Responsibility with the World Bank and More Outsourcing of Structural Conditionality in Noncore Areas

The aim here is to retain the advantages of a "comprehensive" approach to crisis prevention and management, sustainable growth, and poverty reduction, while improving the effectiveness of (total) structural policy conditionality by paying greater attention to the different comparative advantages of the various IFIs. Even if the number of structural conditions in Fund programs remained unchanged, the Fund would design and monitor only those conditions that fit within its defined "core competence" (say, monetary, fiscal, exchange rate, and financial-sector policies); anything else would be the responsibility of the World Bank or other IFIs. If one of the other IFIs was not moving fast enough in drafting a structural policy requirement, the Fund would not be permitted to take over. It would have to stay in its own yard. Under some proposals, the Fund would transfer primary responsibility for running the Poverty Reduction and Growth Facility (PRGF) to the World Bank, although the Fund would still have a sign-off on the adequacy of macroeconomic policies in such programs with low-income countries. Under other proposals (see Kohler and Wolfensohn

---

53. Another proposal for reducing political demands on the Fund is go to "independent" executive directors—much in the manner of national central banks; see De Gregorio et al. (1999).

2000), the World Bank would get its own new lending window (the Poverty Reduction Support Credit [PRSC]) to support poverty reduction in low-income countries, and the Fund would continue to run and fund the PGRF. Renewed efforts would also be made to improve Fund–World Bank cooperation.

Here, too, there are many potential objections and questions. If the problem is too much and too detailed structural policy conditionality as a whole, why would rearranging responsibilities among the IFIs solve it? If the PGRF is about poverty reduction and if that is supposed to be the main focus of the World Bank, why does the Fund run that facility? If it's true, as suggested by the U.S. Treasury (2000a), that unless the Fund's board has its own money at stake, Fund evaluation of macroeconomic policies in programs with low-income countries won't be done seriously (even with a formal sign-off in programs run by the World Bank), why should we expect other IFIs to be diligent in their evaluation of structural policies in Fund-led programs? Why do we need *two* lending facilities (the existing PGRF in the Fund, and the new PRSC in the World Bank) to support poverty reduction and macroeconomic stability in the low-income countries? Wouldn't one make more sense? How will the IMF and World Bank cooperate more closely with other international organizations (e.g., the Organization for Economic Cooperation and Development, the Bank for International Settlements, the World Trade Organization, the ILO, etc.) under the "contracting-out model" and still meet the demanding time requirements of crisis resolution?

5.1.6   Concluding Remarks

I agree with Stanley Fischer's (2000a, 2) assessment that "the IMF. . . . promotes good macroeconomic and financial-sector policies among its members." However, my reading of the record is that on structural policies the Fund has bitten off more—in both scope and detail—than either it or its member countries can chew. There are limits—no matter how numerous and detailed the Fund's monitoring techniques—to how far the Fund can push a country to undertake structural reforms that it itself is not strongly committed to. Consistent with this view, compliance with fund conditionality has been a serious and growing problem. International Monetary Fund mission chiefs have considerable knowledge and experience in macroeconomic and financial policies but not in structural policy areas beyond this core competence. Efforts to include in Fund conditionality everything but the kitchen sink under the loosely defined agenda of pursuing "high-quality" growth have taken the Fund too far from its comparative advantage and have elicited legitimate charges of mission creep.

Among the alternative crisis management guidelines discussed in section 5.1.2, the one (Mandate II) that would have the Fund focus on macroeconomic and financial stability and assist a country not only to get out of its current crisis but also to minimize the chances of getting into another one makes the most sense to me. Conditions that lie outside the core areas of monetary, fiscal, exchange rate, and financial-sector policies should be significantly fewer in Fund programs than the average of the past five years and should require strong justification in any program, including having a macroeconomic impact (as called for in the original conditionality guidelines for standby programs). I also read the record as suggesting that the effectiveness of Fund structural conditionality would be increased if a small number of structural performance criteria was substituted for the vast array of structural benchmarks that have characterized many past Fund programs. This would require IMF staff to think harder about which structural conditions merited the highest priority in the reform effort, and about which structural policy changes needed to be made now (during the crisis) and which could wait until somewhat later; putting more weight on a few structural performance criteria would also send a clearer signal to the borrower that failure to meet those performance criteria would likely result in a halt in Fund disbursements.

Last but not least, streamlining and improving Fund structural policy conditionality is about Fund management saying "no" more often than in the past—to requests for Fund assistance where the expectation is low that the country will actually implement Fund policy conditions, to G7 governments when they propose new tasks for the Fund that go beyond the Fund's core competence, to NGOs that seek to use a country's Letter of Intent with the Fund to advance agendas (even if desirable) that lie outside the Fund's mandate and comparative advantage, and to developing-country finance ministries that want to use micro conditions in Fund programs to impose spending discipline on other government ministries that could not be obtained via their national legislatures.

Mr. Kohler's intention to end mission creep at the Fund and to streamline the Fund's structural policy conditionality is welcome. However, it remains to be seen how he will pursue that objective and what the effects will be.

References

Ahluwalia, Pavan. 2000. Discriminating contagion: An alternative explanation of contagious currency crises in emerging markets. IMF Working Paper no. WP/00/14. Washington, D.C.: International Monetary Fund, February.

Allen, Mark. 1993. The link between structural reform and stabilization policies: An overview. In *Coordinating stabilization and structural reform,* ed. IMF Institute. Washington, D.C.: International Monetary Fund.

Bagehot, Walter. 1873. *Lombard Street: A description of the money market.* London: William Clowes and Sons.

Balassa, Bela. 1983. The adjustment experience of developing countries after 1973. In *IMF conditionality,* ed. John Williamson. Washington, D.C.: Institute for International Economics.

Barro, Robert. 1996. Democracy and growth. *Journal of Economic Growth* 1 (1): 1–28.

Bergsten, C. Fred, Richard Huber, Jerome Levinson, and E. Torres. 2000. Reforming the international financial institutions. Minority dissent to the report of the International Institution Advisory Commission. Allan H. Meltzer, Chairman. Washington, D.C.: March.

Beveridge, William A., and Margaret R. Kelly. 1980. Fiscal content of financial programs supported by stand-by arrangements in the upper credit tranches, 1969–78. *IMF Staff Papers* 27 (June): 205–49. Washington, D.C.: International Monetary Fund.

Boorman, Jack, Timothy Lane, Marianne Schulze-Ghattas, Ales Bulir, Atish R. Ghosh, Javier Hamann, Alexandros Mourmouras, and Steven Phillips. 2000. Managing financial crises: The experience of East Asia. Conference on Public Policy. 10–20 November, Pittsburgh, Penn.

Borenzstein, Eduardo, and Jong-Wha Lee. 2000. Financial crisis and credit crunch in Korea: Evidence from firm-level data. IMF Working Paper no. WP/00/25. Washington, D.C.: International Monetary Fund.

Botchway, Kwesi, Jan Willem Gunning, Yusuke Onitsuka, and Koichi Hamada. 1998. *External evaluation of ESAF.* Washington, D.C.: International Monetary Fund.

Camdessus, Michel. 1990. Remarks before the One-Asia assembly. February, Manila, the Philippines.

———. 1994. International cooperation for high-quality growth: The role of the IMF at 50. Washington, D.C.: International Monetary Fund. Available at [http://www.imf.org/external/np/sec/mds/1995/MDS9521.HTM]. 28 August 2000.

———. 1997. Good governance, the IMF's role. Washington, D.C.: International Monetary Fund. Available at [http://www.imf.org/external/pubs/ft/exrp/govern/govindex.htm]. 28 August 2000.

———. 1999a. Second generation reforms: Reflections and new challenges. Washington, D.C.: International Monetary Fund. Available at [http://www.imf.org/external/np/speeches/1999/110899.HTM]. 28 August 2000.

———. 1999b. Strengthening the link between economic and social policies within the framework of a globalized economy. Washington, D.C.: International Monetary Fund. Available at [http://www.imf.org/external/np/speeches/1999/102699.HTM]. 28 August 2000.

———. 2000a. Development and poverty reduction: A multilateral approach. Washington, D.C.: International Monetary Fund. Available at [http://www.imf.org/external/np/speeches/2000/021300.HTM]. 28 August 2000.

———. 2000b. The IMF and human development: A dialogue with civil society. Washington, D.C.: International Monetary Fund.

Christiansen, Robert E., and Andrea Richter. 1999. The pattern of structural conditionality in Fund programs with EU2 countries. Washington, D.C.: International Monetary Fund, August.

Claessens, Stijn, Simeon Djankov, and Daniela Klingebiel. 1999. Financial restructuring in East Asia: Halfway there? Financial Sector Discussion Paper no. 3. Washington, D.C.: The World Bank.

Claessens, Stijn, Daniela Klingebiel, and Luc Laeven. 2001. Financial restructuring in systemic crises: What policies to pursue? Washington, D.C.: The World Bank. Manuscript, February.

Conway, Patrick. 1994. IMF lending programs: Participation and impact. *Journal of Development Economics,* no. 45:365–91.

Council on Foreign Relations Task Force. 1999. *Safeguarding prosperity in a global financial system: The future international financial architecture.* Carla Hills and Peter Peterson, co-chairs; Morris Goldstein, project director. Washington, D.C.: Institute for International Economics.

Crow, John, Ricardo Arriazu, and Niels Thygensen. 1999. *External evaluation of IMF surveillance.* Washington, D.C.: International Monetary Fund.

De Gregorio, José, Barry Eichengreen, Takatoshi Ito, and Charles Wyplosz. 1999. *An independent and accountable IMF.* Geneva Reports on the World Economy, no. 1. London: Centre for Economic Policy Research Press.

De Melo, M., C. Denizer, and A. Gelb. 1996. Patterns of transition from plan to market. *World Bank Economic Review* 10 (September).

Dooley, Michael. 1999. Debt management in developing countries. University of California at Santa Cruz, Department of Economics. Unpublished manuscript.

Edwards, Sebastian. 1989. The International Monetary Fund and the developing countries: A critical evaluation. *Carnegie-Rochester Conference Series on Public Policy* 31:7–68.

Eichengreen, Barry. 1999. *Toward a new international financial architecture: A practical post-Asia agenda.* Washington, D.C.: Institute for International Economics.

———. 2000. Strengthening the international architecture: Where do we stand? In briefing book from Symposium on Building the Financial System of the 21st Century, 157–96. Bretton Woods, N.H.

Eichengreen, Barry, and Ricardo Hausmann. 1999. Exchange rates and financial fragility. In *New challenges for monetary policy,* 329–68. Kansas City, Mo.: Federal Reserve Bank of Kansas City.

Feldstein, Martin. 1998. Refocusing the IMF. *Foreign Affairs* 77 (March/April): 20–33.

———. 1999. A self-help guide for emerging markets. *Foreign Affairs* 78 (2): 93–109.

Financial Stability Forum, Working Group on Deposit Insurance. 2000. Background Paper. Basel, Switzerland: Financial Stability Forum, June.

Finch, C. David. 1983. Adjustment policies and conditionality. In *IMF conditionality,* ed. John Williamson, 75–86. Washington, D.C.: Institute for International Economics.

Fischer, Stanley. 1999. On the need for an international lender of last resort. *Journal of Economic Perspectives* 13 (4): 85–104.

———. 2000a. Presentation to the International Financial Institution Advisory Commission (Meltzer Commission). 28 August, Washington, D.C. Available at [http://www.imf.org/external/np/speeches/2000/020200.htm]. 28 August 2000.

———. 2000b. Remarks by Stanley Fischer, acting managing director. Remarks to the Bretton Woods Committee Meeting, 4 April 2000. Washington, D.C. Available at [http://www.imf.org/external/np/speeches/2000/040400.htm]. 17 July 2000.

Fischer, Stanley, Ratna Sahay, and Carlos A. Vegh. 1996. Stabilization and growth in transition economies: The early experience. *Journal of Economic Perspectives* 10 (2): 45–66.

Garber, Peter. 2000. Notes on market-based bank regulation. In *Global financial crises: Lessons from recent events,* ed. Joseph Bisignano et al. Boston: Klewer Academic.

Garuda, Gopal. 2000. The distributional effects of IMF programs: A cross-country analysis. *World Development* 28 (6): 1031–51.

Ghosh, Swati, and Atish Ghosh. 1999. East Asia in the aftermath: Was there a crunch? IMF Working Paper no. WP/99/38. Washington, D.C.: International Monetary Fund.

Goldstein, Morris. 1998. *The Asian financial crisis: Causes, cures, and systemic implications.* Policy Analyses in International Economics no. 55. Washington, D.C.: Institute for International Economics.

Goldstein, Morris, and Peter Montiel. 1986. Evaluating Fund stabilization programs with multicountry data: Some methodological pitfalls. *IMF Staff Papers* 33 (June): 304–344. Washington, D.C.: International Monetary Fund.

Group of Independent Experts. 1998. *External evaluation of the ESAF: Report by a group of independent experts.* Washington, D.C.: International Monetary Fund. Available at [http://www.imf.org/external/pubs/ft/extev/index.htm]. 13 September 2000.

Group of Twenty-Four. 1987. *The role of the IMF in adjustment with growth.* Washington, D.C.: Intergovernmental Group of Twenty-Four on International Monetary Affairs.

Guitian, Manuel. 1981. *Fund conditionality: Evolution of principles and practices.* Pamphlet Series no. 38. Washington, D.C.: International Monetary Fund.

———. 1995. Conditionality: Past, present, future. *IMF Staff Papers* 42 (4): 792–835. Washington, D.C.: International Monetary Fund.

Gupta, Sanjeev, Benedict Clements, Calvin McDonald, and Christian Schiller. 1998. *The IMF and the poor.* Pamphlet Series no. 52. Washington, D.C.: International Monetary Fund.

Gupta, Sanjeev, Louis Dicks-Mireaux, Ritha Khemani, Calvin McDonald, and Marijn Verhoeven. 2000. *Social issues in IMF-supported programs.* Occasional Paper no. 191. Washington, D.C.: International Monetary Fund.

Haggard, Stephan. 2000. *The political economy of the Asian financial crisis.* Washington, D.C.: Institute for International Economics.

Hamann, Javier, and Marianne Schulze-Ghattas. 1999. Structural reforms. In *IMF-supported programs in Indonesia, Korea, and Thailand,* ed. Timothy Lane, Atish Ghosh, Javier Hamann, Steven Phillips, Marianne Schulze-Ghattas, and Tsidi Tsikata. Occasional Paper no. 178. Washington, D.C.: International Monetary Fund.

Haque, Nadeem Ul, and Mohsin Khan. 1998. Do IMF-supported programs work? IMF Working Paper no. WP/98/169. Washington, D.C.: International Monetary Fund.

Havrylyshyn, Oleh, and Donal McGettigan. 2000. Privatization in transition countries. *Post-Soviet affairs* 16 (3): 257–86.

Havrylyshyn, Oleh, Thomas Wolf, Julian Berengaut, Marta Castello-Branco, Ron van Rooden, and Valerie Mercer-Blackman. 1999. *Growth experience in transition countries, 1990–98.* Occasional Paper no. 184. Washington, D.C.: International Monetary Fund.

Heller, Peter S., A. Lans Bovenberg, Thanos Catsambas, Ke-Young Chu, and Parthasarathi Shome. 1988. *The implication of Fund-supported adjustment programs for poverty: Experience in selected countries.* Occasional Paper no. 58. Washington, D.C.: International Monetary Fund.

Honohan, Patrick, and Daniela Klingebiel. 2000. Controlling fiscal costs of banking crises. Policy Research Working Paper no. 2441. Washington, D.C.: World Bank.

International Financial Institution Advisory Commission (IFIAC). 2000. Report of the International Financial Institution Advisory Commission (Meltzer report). Allan H. Meltzer, chairman. Washington, D.C.: March.

International Monetary Fund (IMF). 1980. *World economic outlook.* Washington, D.C.: IMF.

———. 1987a. Monitoring techniques and experience with their application to structural reform. Washington, D.C.: IMF. Unpublished manuscript.

———. 1987b. *Theoretical aspects of the design of Fund-supported adjustment programs.* Occasional Paper no. 55. Washington, D.C.: IMF.

————. 1988. *Articles of agreement*. Washington, D.C.: IMF.

————. 1993. *Articles of agreement*. Washington, D.C.: IMF.

————. 1995. *Financial organization and operation of the IMF*. Pamphlet Series no. 45, fourth ed. Washington, D.C.: IMF.

————. 1997. *The ESAF at ten years: Economics adjustment and reform in low-income countries*. Occasional Paper no. 156. Washington, D.C.: IMF. December.

————. 2000. *World Economic Outlook*. Washington, D.C.: IMF.

————. 2001a. Conditionality in Fund-supported programs: Overview. Washington, D.C.: IMF. Available at [http://www.imf.org/external/np/pdr/2001/eng/overview/index.htm]. 20 February.

————. 2001b. Conditionality in Fund-supported programs. Policy issues. Washington, D.C.: IMF.

————. 2001c. Structural conditionality in Fund-supported programs. Washington, D.C.: IMF.

————. 2001d. Trade policy conditionality in Fund-supported programs. Washington, D.C.: IMF. Available at [http://www.imf.org/external/np/pdr/cond/2001/eng/trade/index.htm]. 16 February.

————. 2001e. IMF executive board discusses conditionality. Public Information Notice (PIN) no. 01/28. Washington, D.C.: IMF. Available at [http://www.imf.org/external/np/sec/pn/2001/pn0128.htm]. 21 March.

James, Harold. 1998. From grandmotherliness to governance: The evolution of IMF conditionality. *Finance and Development* 35 (4). Available at [http://www.imf.org/external/pubs/ft/fandd/1998/12/james.htm]. 3 August 2000.

Johnson, Simon, Peter Boone, Alasdair Breach, and Eric Friedman. 2000. Corporate governance in the Asian financial crisis. *Journal of Financial Economics* 58 (1): 141–86. [http://www.jfe.rochester.edu/99362.pdf]. 13 September 2000.

Killick, Tony. 1995. *IMF programmes in developing countries: Design and impact*. London: Routledge.

Köhler, Horst. 2000a. The IMF in a changing world. Remarks to the National Press Club, 7 August. Washington, D.C.: International Monetary Fund.

————. 2000b. Streamlining structural conditionality in Fund-supported programs: Interim guidance note. In *Conditionality in Fund-supported programs*, International Monetary Fund (IMF). Washington, D.C.: IMF.

————. 2000c. Toward a more focused IMF. Address at the International Monetary Conference. 30 May, Washington, D.C.

Krueger, Anne. 1998. Whither the World Bank and the IMF? *Journal of Economic Literature*, December: 1983–2020.

————. 2000. Conflicting demands on the International Monetary Fund. *American Economic Review* 90 (2): 38–42.

Krugman, Paul. 1998. The confidence game. *New Republic* 219 (14): 23–25.

Lane, Timothy, Atish Ghosh, Javier Hamann, Steven Phillips, Marianne Schultze-Ghattas, and Tsidi Tsikata. 1999. IMF-supported programs in Indonesia, Korea, and Thailand. Occasional Paper no. 178. Washington, D.C.: International Monetary Fund.

Lindgren, Carl-Johan, Tomas J. T. Balino, Charles Enoch, Anne-Marie Gulde, Marc Quintyn, and Leslie Teo. 1999. *Financial sector crisis and restructuring: Lessons from Asia*. Occasional Paper no. 188. Washington, D.C.: International Monetary Fund.

Masson, Paul, and Michael Mussa. 1995. The role of the Fund: Financing and its interactions with adjustment and surveillance. Pamphlet Series. Washington, D.C.: International Monetary Fund.

McHale, John. 1998. Capital account convertibility and capital controls in emerging market countries: Some themes from the first meeting. Cambridge, Mass.: National Bureau of Economic Research. Available at [http://www.nber.org/crisis/capital.html]. 21 August 2000.

———. 1999. Currency and financial crises: The case of Thailand. A report on the first country meeting of the NBER project on exchange rate crises in emerging market economies. Cambridge, Mass.: National Bureau of Economic Research. Available at [http://www.nber.org/crisis/ThaiSum.html]. 21 August 2000.

———. 2000a. Brazil in the 1997–1999 financial turmoil. Fourth country meeting of the NBER project on exchange rate crises in emerging market economies. Cambridge, Mass.: National Bureau of Economic Research. Available at [http://www.nber.org/crisis/BrazilSum.html]. 21 August 2000.

———. 2000b. The Korean currency crisis. A report on the third country meeting of the NBER project on exchange rate crises in emerging market economies. Cambridge, Mass.: National Bureau of Economic Research. Available at [http://www.nber.org/crisis/KoreaSum.html]. 21 August 2000.

———. 2000c. The Indonesian crisis. A report of the fifth country meeting of the NBER project on exchange rate crises in emerging market economies. Cambridge, Mass.: National Bureau of Economic Research.

Meltzer, Allan. 1999. What's wrong with the IMF? What would be better? In *The Asian financial crisis,* ed. William Hunter, George G. Kaufman, and Thomas H. Krueger, 241–60. Boston: Kluwer Academic.

Mercer-Blackman, Valerie, and Anna Unigovskaya. 2000. Compliance with IMF program indicators and growth in transition economies. IMF Working Paper no. WP/00/47. Washington, D.C.: International Monetary Fund. Available at [http://www.imf.org/external/pubs/ft/wp/2000/wp0047.pdf]. 13 September 2000.

Mussa, Michael, and Miguel Savastano. 1999. The IMF approach to economic stabilization. IMF Working Paper no. WP/99/104. Washington, D.C.: International Monetary Fund. Available at [http://www.imf.org/external/pubs/ft/wp/1999/wp99104.pdf]. 13 September 2000.

Park, Yung Chul. 1996. East Asian liberalization, bubbles, and the challenge from China. *Brookings Papers on Economic Activity,* Issue no. 2:357–71.

Polak, Jacques J. 1991. The changing nature of IMF conditionality. Technical Paper no. 41. Paris: Organization for Economic Cooperation and Development, August. Available at [http://www.oecd.org//dev/PUBLICATION/tp/tp41.pdf]. 13 September 2000.

Radelet, Steven, and Jeffrey D. Sachs. 1998. The East Asian financial crisis: Diagnosis, remedies, prospects. *Brookings Papers on Economic Activity,* Issue no. 1:1–74.

Rodrik, Dani. 1995. Why is there multi-lateral lending? CEPR Discussion Paper no. 1207. London: Center for Economic Policy Research.

Root, Hilton. 2000. *Korea's recovery: Don't count on the government.* Miliken Institute Policy Brief no. 14. Santa Monica, Calif.: Miliken Institute, May.

Schadler, Susan, Adam Bennett, Maria Carkovic, Louis Dicks-Mireaux, Mauro Mecagni, James H. J. Morsink, and Miguel A. Savastano. 1995a. *IMF conditionality: Experience under stand-by and extended arrangements. Part I: Key issues and findings.* Occasional Paper no. 128. Washington, D.C.: International Monetary Fund, September.

———. 1995b. *IMF conditionality: Experience under stand-by and extended arrangements. Part II: Background papers.* Occasional Paper no. 129. Washington, D.C.: International Monetary Fund, September.

Schadler, Susan, Franek Rozwadowski, Siddharth Tiwari, and David O. Robinson. 1993. *Economic adjustment in low-income countries: Experience under the en-*

hanced structural adjustment facility. Occasional Paper no. 106. Washington, D.C.: International Monetary Fund, September.

Shultz, George. 1995. Economics in action: Ideas, institutions, policies. *The American Economic Review* 85 (2):1–8.

Spencer, Michael. 2000. Asia outlook for 2001. *Deutsche Bank Global Markets Research,* December.

———. 2001. Economics: Assessing the damage so far. *Deutsche Bank Asia Window,* April.

Stiglitz, Joseph E. 1999. Reforming the global economic architecture: Lessons from recent crises. *Journal of Finance* 54:1508–21.

Summers, Lawrence. 1999. Statement at meetings of IMF interim committee. September 1999 annual meeting of IMF and World Bank Group. 28–30 September, Washington, D.C.

Tanzi, Vito. 1987. Fiscal policy, growth, and the design of stabilization programs. ed. A. Martirena-Mantel, 35–40. In *External debt, savings, and the growth in Latin America*, Washington, D.C.: International Monetary Fund.

U.S. Treasury, 2000a. *Report on IMF reforms.* Washington, D.C.: U.S. Department of the Treasury, March. Available at [http://www.treas.gov/press/releases/docs/imfrefor.pdf]. 13 September.

———. 2000b. *Response to the report of the International Financial Institution Advisory Commission.* Washington, D.C.: U.S. Department of the Treasury, 8 June. Available at [http://www.ustreas.gov/press/releases/docs/response.pdf]. 13 September.

Volcker, Paul, and Toyoo Gyohten. 1992. *Changing fortunes.* New York: Times Books.

Williamson, John. 1990. What Washington means by policy reform. In *Latin American adjustment: How much has happened?* ed. J. Williamson, 5–20. Washington, D.C.: Institute for International Economics.

———. 2000. The role of the IMF: A guide to the reports. International Economics Policy Briefs no. 00-5. Washington, D.C.: Institute for International Economics, May.

World Bank. 2000. *East Asia: Recovery and beyond.* Washington, D.C.: World Bank.

2. Timothy F. Geithner

Structural Conditionality in IMF Programs

This is a good time for a broad reassessment of the appropriate scope of International Monetary Fund (IMF) conditionality.

The new conventional wisdom, fathered in part by Martin Feldstein, the thrust of which is that the fund has strayed far beyond its classic mandate to the point that it is gratuitously intrusive in a ridiculously expansive array of micro-level structural issues, is debilitating in its impact on the Fund's credibility. When the popular perceptions of the world's preeminent monetary institution are so dominated by small anecdotes of contestable judgements about cashews, sugar, cotton, or cloves, then you have a real problem, even if the judgments made were in fact fundamentally sensible. It is not a good sign when the debate about the Fund is framed by criticisms that echo the critique of U.S. diplomacy as foreign policy as social work or misguided nation building.

So this is a necessary debate, and, like the recent debate about facilities reform and pricing, it's a good way to reevaluate the basic mission of the institution.

Figuring out what to do about this potential problem of overreach is not easy, however. It is complicated by a few basic features of the present reality.

There is the basic reality that world has come over time to adopt a rather expansive definition of the range of policies and institutions that are important to economic success, to durable development, to reducing vulnerability to crises. The analytical judgments that led the Fund to conclude some time ago that there was a set of structural policies beyond the classic core of the monetary policy framework, the fiscal constraint, and the exchange rate regime that were in many cases necessary for successful programs remain valid today.

There is the basic reality that a cooperative institution structured like the Fund does not really have the luxury of not lending to its members, provided they are willing to promise to commit to some conditions. Moreover, in an institution of 182 members, many of which are what you might call weak states, governance challenged, and the like, a basic level of prudence or fiduciary responsibility will necessarily require broad, and sometimes intrusive, safeguards on how the resources of the Fund are used.

There is the basic reality that it will be untenable for the Fund to put substantial resources at risk in any country without seeking to address the problems that materially contributed to the crisis and without trying to reduce the sources of vulnerability to future crisis. If the Fund is denied this capacity, then you won't have a Fund with a meaningful capacity to intervene in crises.

There is the basic reality that the Fund does not have the capacity to apply meaningful conditionality ex ante, and thus much of the burden for important reforms falls on program conditionality ex post.

Finally, there is the basic political reality, most conspicuous in the United States, and fueled in part by the globalization anxiety, that has tended to support a progressively more expansive view of what the Fund should seek to achieve in terms of social equity, much less economic efficiency, using the leverage of its programs.

There is a fundamental danger in the new conventional critique of the Fund that its adherents shelter a diverse mix of motivations.

Some of the proponents of a return to some set of narrow, core, simple, old virtues of macroeconomic probity are moved primarily by opposition to or discomfort with the notion of conditionality itself. A simple requirement for collateral seems an appealing alternative to many.

Some of the critics are in the "ownership camp," which in its more extreme form has the strange circular logic that effective conditionality is possible only where it is fully owned, and where it is fully owned it is essentially unnecessary, and it is pushing the international financial institutions (IFIs) generally in directions that may produce simply less conditionality or weaker conditionality.

Some of the proponents of streamlining are moved by one critique of the Fund's prescriptions in Asia, a critique based on a not totally implausible view that the crisis was a liquidity crisis suffered by fundamentally quite healthy economies and that therefore recovery should not have required significant policy change. The truth, however, is that fundamentally healthy countries are not really vulnerable to sustained panics or runs that threaten a deeper crisis. Moreover, the countries in Asia each had a set of fundamental weaknesses that left them vulnerable to shifts in sentiment, and addressing those weaknesses was plausibly considered critical to a restoration of confidence and more durable recovery.

Some of the proponents of streamlining see a compelling virtue in simplicity for simplicity's sake, with the somewhat naive hope that the Fund can stay out of complex choices that are inescapable in dealing, for example, with a systemically insolvent financial system, where the government owns not just the banking system but much of the corporate assets of the country, and where there is no functioning legal system or other safeguards to prevent looting, or with a fiscal problem in a poor country where scarce resources are drained by state enterprises or subsidies for the urban class, or with an adjustment challenge in a country with a currency board where the structure of the labor market does not allow wages to adjust.

These motivations are not, I think, good reasons to favor streamlining, and they are not a good guide for how to refocus the Fund. To indulge them is in some respects dangerous, if you care about preserving the capacity of the fund to be engaged in creating a world less vulnerable to financial crisis, in promoting more durable transition in emerging market economies to capital-market access, and in addressing the development challenges in the poorest countries.

What is the right standard for determining what the Fund should and should not promote in its programs? There are three such approaches that I do not think make sense. The core/noncore distinction doesn't answer the question of what should be core. The critical/noncritical distinction doesn't help define what should be critical. The less-is-more minimalism doesn't define what minimalist core would actually be more effective than the broader alternatives.

The challenge is to define an affirmative standard for deciding what is important: core, critical, and so on. One way to do that is to think of a continuum, with the classic core macroeconomic framework at one extreme, with the financial system next, then other conditions necessary to restore confidence and capital market access and reduce the risk of future crisis, then governance issues, and then at the other end of the continuum a broader set of policies that are desirable from the standpoint of economic efficiency and social equity.

On this continuum, I think the right place for the Fund to start in the crisis context is in that middle area, with the presumption that, in addition to the macroeconomic policy framework and the financial system, you have to try to address credibly those other factors that are critical to restoring confidence and growth, to restoring capital-market access as soon as possible, and to reducing the risk of a future crisis. Moreover, it should be symmetrically hard to move too far in either direction on that continuum, either to the fundamentally more narrow extreme or to the more expansive realm of the simply desirable improvements in economic efficiency.

Under this standard, it would be appropriate to seek in the program to address, where they are material, fundamental problems in the insolvency regime, protections for minority shareholders, restrictions on capital inflows, and distortions in the capital account regime, the deposit insurance system, the social safety net, the legal regime governing privatization and asset disposal, conspicuous corruption problems.

This test, however, is still quite broad, and probably still too vulnerable to expansive interpretation. In order for it to work, it has to be supplemented by a set of other tests or filters to ensure a more selective approach.

- Forcing fewer conditions will help, because that will force prioritization, and sensible constraints on the quantity of measures can be effective discipline.
- There needs to be some credible test of scale and materiality in terms of economic impact.
- The Fund has to be prepared to forswear advocacy of the simply desirable, where it is not essential, or where the community of experts might disagree on the superiority of the proposed prescription.
- The Fund should be careful to agree to incorporate as a condition of the program policy requirements that do not meet the test of material or essentiality, simply because the reformers in the government want some leverage in promoting part of their broader agenda.
- It will be appropriate for the Fund to defer to the preferences of the government, if it has a record of credibility and competence and is democratically elected.
- Establishing a greater presumption against extensive structural benchmarks, and a presumption in favor of making core structural condi-

tions performance criteria, will also provide useful discipline in deciding what is really necessary to justify disbursement and worth suspending the program over if there is a failure to comply.

To support some evolution toward streamlining, I think there needs to be a complementary evolution towards a broader list of generalized conditions for access to IMF resources.

There is no reason why all IMF members should not be required to meet minimum standards for disclosure and for transparency of the fiscal accounts and monetary policy operation, to apply minimum safeguards such as the new requirement that central banks undertake annually and publish an external audit, and perhaps to meet some minimum standards relevant to the vulnerability of the financial system.

Adopting these as universal conditions will reduce the need for uncomfortably extensive lists of individualized conditions in specific programs. Shifting the burden of conditionality to disciplines that can be applied ex ante reduces the need for the ex post application of those conditions in program design.

In an institution where membership brings with it access to potentially large amounts of resources, it makes sense to have a greater set of ex ante constraints on potentially risky behavior. The Article IV process will never have sufficient traction to achieve this.

The corollary of this point is that we have to give the Fund the will to say "no" more often, to refuse to lend, or to suspend disbursements, in conditions that are untenable or in which justifying a program requires an excessive level of protections and therefore conditions.

It is hard to make this credible, in part because there will be cases in which the Fund will have no choice given the risk of broader economic damage to other economies. Also, it requires a greater willingness by the preferred creditors to accept the accumulation of arrears in situations in which the country at issue has large and immediate obligations to the IFIs that they may not have the resources available to meet.

Despite these difficulties, it is worth raising the bar for IMF engagement in conditions in which the level of corruption is truly systemic, the state is too weak to make credible commitments to deliver on the program conditions, governance problems are fundamental, the government is among the most extreme offenders on the money laundering or financial crime scale, and the government cannot make credible commitments in the program to address these problems.

A necessary condition for any meaningful withdrawal for the Fund from important structural conditions is a greater demonstrated capacity by the World Bank to design and apply meaningful conditionality for its program lending. This condition does not now exist. It may be in prospect, but the pressures now on the World Bank to reduce the scope and extent of conditionality, particularly on the middle-income countries, are formidable.

This is important, because part of the cause of the perceived expansion in the scope of IMF imposed structural conditions is a pragmatic conspiracy between World Bank and IMF staff and the reformers in borrowing governments to build conditions into Fund programs because of the absence of an effective vehicle in the World Bank for applying that conditionality with force.

It is important in this exploration of ways to streamline conditionality that we not lose sight of the probably more important substantive challenge of figuring out how to improve the design of policies and the content of whatever conditionality we decide is essential. The lack of consensus in the economic profession about the appropriate macro policy response to a confidence crisis in an economy with a healthy fiscal position but a terribly weak banking sector is fundamentally troubling. The extent of debate within the Fund, between the Fund and the World Bank, and among the experts in the supervisory community about the appropriate degree of forbearance and about strategies for intervention, recapitalization, resolution, and asset disposal in banking systems undergoing systemic failure is highly problematic and caused very damaging delays in the recent cases.

These problems of the substance of the economic strategy are in some ways more material and more important to try to resolve than the perceived imperative to simply streamline.

Moreover, any credible support by the United States for progress on this front will require an effort by the next administration to buy some room for maneuvering from Congress. The erosion of the traditional internationalist center in the U.S. political spectrum has left us more vulnerable to the demands of a coalition on the right and left, the price of whose support has been an escalating set of demands, on the one hand for market-oriented reforms and liberalization and on the other hand for social equity and core labor standards. The consensus shared by Congressman Barney Frank and Senator Phil Gramm requires us to advocate a particularly broad definition of desirable or core conditionality. It's possible they may each be more willing to cede ground in favor of a more narrow mandate overall.

Finally, I think it is important to ask ourselves whether the errors of the past have fundamentally been errors of excessive ambition for policy change or excessive indulgence of poor performance. The world is still a bit confused and divided on this point. Has the Fund been too tough or too accommodating? Or, as some have suggested, has it been both, by setting unrealistic aspirations for policy reform and then acquiescing to the inevitable failure of even relatively well intentioned governments to meet the bar? There is something to this. The right approach is some mix of greater realism in the initial level of conditionality established and greater force and will in holding governments to that more realistic standard.

3. Paul Keating

Morris Goldstein's paper is of such good quality that it is important to examine it, especially given his position as a former insider, somebody who is able to stand off and look at the International Monetary Fund. As you would expect from someone of Goldstein's experience, the paper is balanced, insightful, and knowledgeable. It is practically oriented, and above all else, it's important. This is the view of somebody who does know the Fund and has the objectivity of looking at it under stress.

From my point of view the great problem, apart from what the structural conditionality and the size of the program did to the Suharto regime and to other regimes during the crisis, was first and foremost the distractions these programs presented to the task at hand. In his paper, Goldstein distinguishes crisis management from crisis prevention, suggesting that crisis management should be the guide to the program. He says, "It doesn't preclude giving some consideration to other objectives, but it makes clear which objective is king, and where the authorities' central responsibility lies. The emphasis on getting out of the current crisis would mean that crisis management and resolution and not crisis prevention should guide program design. Crisis prevention measures would then presumably be handled by countries on their own, after the crisis is resolved."

He is attempting to address the Washington consensus on financial and structural improvement, which every finance minister and every finance ministry official worth his salt knows about: decent structural reform. However, what is the relevance of structural reforms of this nature in a crisis of this kind? Goldstein says, "The number of structural policy conditions included in these programs with the three Asian crisis economies was very large, if not totally unprecedented, many more than you can count using all your fingers and toes. At their peak there were 140 in Indonesia, over 90 in Korea, and over 70 in Thailand." Then he amplifies in table 5.5 a point I made yesterday, that in October 1997, when the crisis was really starting to boil, there were 28 structural policy conditions in Indonesia. By January 1998 there were 31, and by April 1998 there were 140. Even though Indonesia was in great trouble through this period, as the rupiah really started to collapse and as political strife started to set in, the conditionality went up. In other words, not only could the athlete not get over the bar at a certain height, but the bar, instead of being lowered to give him a chance to clear it, was actually raised. The tables make this point graphically. Goldstein, thanks to Stanley Fischer, who has given him access to the IMF, has listed the remedial programs, things like reducing tariffs on nonfood agricultural products by 5 percent and gradually reducing tariffs on nonagricultural products to a maximum of 10 percentage points. Well, these are all the things that I and people like me, in this room, hammered away at in the 1980s. We know how hard they are to do. They are important. But in a crisis like this, reducing tariffs by 5 percent on chemical products? Abolishing import restrictions on new and used ships? Phasing out remaining quantitative importing restrictions on other nontariff barriers? The list goes on. "Remove restrictions on foreign investments in palm oil plantations." "Release farmers from forced planting of sugar cane." It was these things and the breadth of the demands that, I believe, forced Suharto to give up and appoint his own cabinet, which included his own daughter and a number of the cronies. Of course, when that happened he put the wagons in a circle and decided to carry on independently. I do not mock these reforms—they are important in their own way—but I go back to Goldstein's point. The imperative issue was crisis management, not crisis prevention. These are crisis prevention issues: in fact, they are not even that. They're simply reforms that make an economy more open, more supple, and more productive. They're matters to attend to over time, that take time, that require dealing with the special interest groups. It takes a long time to achieve these things. In Australia's case, it took fifteen years to do these sorts of things. To demand these reforms instantaneously, in a crisis, is naive at best and wilful at worst.

Goldstein, in a very important note, says, "similarly, to show that cronyism and corruption would henceforth be less prevalent, it is important at least in Indonesia to take a few visible privileges and sweetheart deals away from those close to President Suharto." Well, the problem, for instance, with the bank closures in 1997, when the fund shut in one of the banks that belonged to Suharto's son, wasn't that the bank belonged to his son; it was the signal it sent to the Chinese community. You have to remember that all of the racial strife in Indonesia against the Chinese did not generate from the bottom; it always began at the top. The Chinese saw Suharto as their protector against detractors in the top ranks. He saw the Chinese as the people who could develop the economy. So essentially he was the one upon whom they relied. When they saw the Fund shutting in the son's bank, they said, "the old man is finished. The thirty years he's given us have ended." That is when the flight of Chinese capital began in earnest.

In the 1980s I nursed two banks in Australia with assets of 150 to 200 billion, as indeed did Paul Volcker during his time as governor of the Federal Reserve with banks in this country. Frankly, if we had cold-turkeyed them, they would have collapsed. There are in Australia lender-of-last-resort facilities, but in the end that is underwritten by the national budget. If you are worried about moral hazard, you'd have some real worries if you inculcate in a generation of bankers that they can be bailed out. So you nurse them through. I believe that shutting banks, for instance, in a crisis like this, was naive at least, and ill-advised—amateur hour stuff.

Goldstein makes many important points. He says that, for the most part, the Fund's structural policy recommendations reflect the economic profession's consensus on what constitutes sensible structural reform. Well, that's true. Although some serious mistakes in the sequencing of reforms have taken place, Goldstein goes on to say the core of the Fund's programs were appropriate, with the exception of the bad compromise made on bank closures in Indonesia. However, he says, "the Fund's structural conditionality in the Asian crisis and especially in Indonesia appears excessive both in scope and in detail." He goes on, "there were elements of the structural conditionality of the three Fund programs with Indonesia, Korea, and Thailand that seemed superfluous." He says, "I don't find persuasive the argument that trade liberalization measures in the Indonesian and Korean programs were necessary to prevent a slide toward protectionism." Let me underline that. The Bogor Declaration, which was the most ambitious trade declaration of any kind and which was in the course of being adopted at the end of 1992 and during 1993, at the Asia Pacific Economic Corporation (APEC) meeting in Indonesia, brought the Uruguay Round to a close. The Uruguay Round had been going for seven years. We'd had the Europeans fighting on agriculture for seven years against the Cairns group and other agricultural producers. It was only when it became obvious that the Asians and the United States could organize themselves into a trade grouping of some kind that the final impetus to getting the round signed came. At the 1993 meeting of APEC, where the Bogor Declaration was adopted, it was Suharto that championed it as the chair of the meeting. And right through the period, for any observer of Indonesia, his government was progressively deregulating. That cabinet of his was progressively deregulating the Indonesian economy. So the notion that they were going to slide back into protectionism was, of course, a self-serving notion by those designing the program. Moreover, if we look at the postcrisis situation, fortunately, with the exception of Malaysia, all of Asia has gone on to be open. So in other words, the inculcation of free-trade values has actually stuck, despite what's happened. Goldstein did not find persuasive the argument that we needed these things because of the likelihood of a slide toward protectionism. This conclusion is, I believe, correct.

I do not see why the Indonesian program needed to be so sweeping with respect to the dismantling of state monopolies and cartels, the elimination of restrictive marketing agreements, the abolition of showcase projects, and the like, disagreeable as some of these practices were. The car projects were Neanderthal. There is 50 percent more investment in car plants in Asia than the market can use. Again, however, this was trying to be done in the context of a crisis. For confidence reasons, a few candies may have had to be taken from cronies, Goldstein says, but the rest of the box, and admittedly it was a very big box, could have waited until later. He says, moving from the width to the depth of conditionality, the level of detail reflected in the structural benchmarks for these programs likewise seems excessive. For example, was it necessary in Indonesia to have five conditions to reform oil and gas policy? And eighteen conditions for follow-up actions to the findings of the Bank of Indonesia? Or in Korea, was it essential to have eleven conditions for investment guidelines and for corporate governance of insurance companies? He moves along in that vein.

I think this is the point of the triage list. Someone arrives at a hospital who's had an accident. He has a broken collarbone, a fractured ankle, and a punctured lung. What he doesn't need is a lecture about the evils of smoking. What he needs is a suture on the bleeding within the lung. Do that first. Then worry about the collarbone, and then the ankle. This is why these structural programs were so destructive to the task at hand.

Goldstein goes on to say—somewhat tongue in cheek, but let me quote him—"finally there have been occasions, the Korean and Indonesian programs are important cases in point, when strong pressure from particular G7 countries during the program negotiations resulted in the inclusion of specific structural policies in the Fund program, and this, despite the provisions of the Fund's charter, Article 12, Section 4, for each member country of the Fund, 'to refrain from all attempts to influence any of the Fund staff in the discharge of their functions.'" Now, from someone so knowledgeable, this is a pretty tough paragraph. What it's saying is that there was too much pressure applied to Fund staff for additions to conditionality.

Now I know Timothy F. Geithner made the point, perhaps validly, that people within Indonesia wanted to use the Fund as a battering ram to put structural conditions into the program, conditions that they thought they'd never get from the government, and the Fund says, "Oh yes, well, we'll put them in." Well, if you expect nothing of the Fund, you expect it to be wise. When you see people coming, pulling dirty postcards from their sleeves, for structural programs that they cannot secure through their own ministries, you should be wary. But not the U.S. Treasury or the Fund. The fact is, nobody is that naive. This was all happening for a reason.

I do believe, and this is where I disagree with a lot of people, I said yesterday, that at the end of the Cold War, Indonesia's importance faded. There was a view, particularly in the United States, that Suharto was too big a load to carry: okay in the Cold War, not okay now. This came particularly after Bishop Belo and Ramos Horta were given the Nobel Peace Prize. That Bishop Belo should have been given the prize was fine, but someone who had been an active guerilla on the part of Fretilin, the Timor branch of the Portuguese Communist Party, was of course one up the nose of every other person in Timor and the Indonesian government. From that moment on, Indonesia was in trouble, and somewhere along the way people said, it's time they were gone. The key point about Indonesia was that Suharto was already old, so the real issue was about the kind of country there would be after he left.

At any rate, we've been over these issues, and I don't see much product in going over them further. However, the paper is important in that it articulates the view that mission creep was on here in big doses. At its best, it was distracting, and at its worst, wilful, political, and damaging. As a result, the advised, which happened to be the member governments in the case of Indonesia, turned away from the advisor (the Fund) and decided to run their own policy, and that was of course the end. People may say that we've got an independent democratic structure from it. Well, we have a democratic structure, but whether it has appropriate economic and political authority is still a moot point. However, the cost to Indonesia and its population has been profound. The old families are still there, and frankly they much prefer to deal with the provincial governors than the central government, so this is not going to reduce corruption, I don't believe. I mean, out in the provinces, to where the power has now shifted, we're going to see more of this. We have not yet seen the kind of changes we looked for: we're not seeing assets freed up; we're seeing very crude debt-for-equity swaps. The old families are often still in charge, and instead of the debt, they hand banks a bag of equity, making them a minority equity holder in a business that is still controlled by the family.

None of this is changing much. The army, which has always been an integral part of Indonesia, is no longer in a position of unchallenged primacy. It's still there as an integral part, but it's no longer a decisive part of politics. It's now standing away from it, and it will again have to be dealt with by whoever's running the civilian authority. The problem with all of this is that if you live in Washington, Indonesia's a long way off. However, in our part of the world—Malaysia, Australia—we live with this. Indonesia is the epicenter of southeast Asia, and the importance of this conference is to get focused on some of these matters.

The Association of Southeast Asian Nations (ASEAN)+3 Summit, which is essentially the proposal that Prime Minister Mahartir had for the East Asia economic caucus, has now happened, and you have got ASEAN plus Korea plus Japan plus China looking at Asian solutions to problems. Australia is not there, and the United States is not there. The Chiang Mai initiative, the proposed swaps arrangement, and talk of some sort of Asian monetary fund are happening outside the U.S./IMF orbit.

Let me get a few other prejudices in the marketplace. I believe that if the IMF didn't exist, we'd have to invent it. So I'm not about seeing the IMF deteriorate. I attended my first Interim Committee meeting in 1983, and I attended it for ten years, so I know the Fund reasonably well. I think it's an important institution in this world. However, I don't think we should be unduly worried about other people doing other things. In other words, I think we should keep an open mind about whether there should or can be an Asian monetary facility. I think somebody made the point yesterday about the very high national reserves that countries are now accruing to protect themselves. The notion will occur to them, at some point, they should have a common reserve. We'll start to see something imitating an Asian monetary facility. The U.S. worry is that it would be dominated by Japan. If it were dominated by Japan, you wouldn't see the crassness we saw displayed in the conditionality programs in Indonesia. Whatever failings the Japanese have for negotiating from under the table and so on, the fact of the matter is that it would have a softer, more, if you like, Asian complexion, than anything that is operated by North Americans or Europeans. I'm not automatically for an Asian monetary fund, but I'm not for ruling it out. I don't think we ought to panic about the fact that people are talking about these things. If we have support facilities, which ease these crises, without adding to the moral hazard problem of making it easier for banks to withdraw, picking up Mervyn King's point from yesterday, about orderly versus disorderly exits, and about standstill and so on, it might be that the IMF doesn't have to carry the full load.

At any rate, the IMF's not getting the funding it needs. The United States has been employing a dog-in-the-manger policy here for years. The long run of all this may be that the Asian crisis brought on some rethinking about where we should go with a modern financial system and how we might deal with crises of this kind, crises that are probably going to occur in the future. A review of this, under Feldstein's leadership at the National Bureau of Economic Research, is, I think, terribly apposite—in fact, high time. The paper written by Morris Goldstein is a brave piece of work, one that is instructive to the rest of us who do not often have that inside knowledge but who worry about the future of countries that strategically are not always the center of attention.

4. Yung Chul Park

I have never spoken to an audience as distinguished as this one, so I have had some slight difficulties preparing this presentation. Instead of commenting on Morris Goldstein's paper, which is extremely well written and a good paper, I am going to talk about Korea's structural reform and restructuring of the financial institutions and corporations since the financial crisis in 1997. During my presentation I will use the terms "we" and "Korea" interchangeably.

I will make a start by talking about recent developments in Korea. As you have already noticed, the economy is slowing down considerably. At present people, including politicians, believe that Korea is still in a crisis, or, if not in a crisis, heading toward another crisis. Well, this perception is rather surprising. Since the financial crisis in 1997, Korea has increased foreign reserve by more than $90 billion, which is nearly 20 percent of Korea's gross domestic product (GDP). Korea's GDP grew 10 percent in 1999, and it is expected to grow more than 8 percent in 2000. The latest forecast, adjusted for the inflation, suggests that the economy will grow by 4–5 percent in 2001. Korea has spent more than $100 billion for restructuring financial institutions and corporations. Recently the government has appropriated another $50 billion to close down the insolvent financial institutions, not necessarily banks, but also to restructure corporate debt. Yet many people, especially the market participants—both domestic and foreign—believe that basically the major causes of the current looming crisis are due to the lack of progress in corporate and financial restructuring. The complacency among the policymakers who are responsible for the economic reform is another reason.

Now, it is time to think about what International Monetary Fund (IMF) structural policy has meant to a country like Korea. In my view, IMF structural policy had at least three or four fundamental problems.

The first problem was that the purpose and objectives of structural policy were not very clear from the beginning. In the case of Korea, the structural policy consisted of two elements. At the early stage of the crisis, the structural policy was to stabilize foreign exchange markets, domestic financial markets, and the payment systems. Stabilizing these markets required closing down a number of financial institutions and liquidating a large number of insolvent corporations. The second element of the structural policy was an institutional reform, covering the corporations, financial sector, public sector, and the labor market. Also, there was pressure on the further opening of the trade and financial regimes. However, what were the objectives of these policies? The objective of reform is basically to improve the efficiency of the country in the long run. For the reform to be successful, institutional reform must have very clear objectives in terms of time frame. As far as IMF structural policy is concerned, it is really hard to say that objectives were well defined, because many Koreans and market participants thought the structural policy was just designed to get the Korean economy out of the crisis. However, I strongly suspect that was the major objective.

The second problem was that the structural policy did not clearly state the targets of these policies and indicators. If the IMF could have identified it more clearly, it would have been much easier to carry out structural policies. For instance, as far as the corporate restructuring was concerned, we did not have a clear idea of the desired goal of corporate restructuring. For example, the debt-equity ratio: "Should the target be 200 percent? Or lower than that? If the 200 percent debt-equity ratio is the target, then why should it be the target?" There were not clear answers for these questions at that time. If we have to close down many insolvent financial institutions, then who will be responsible for the role performed by these major financial institutions to disappear? The other problem was that there were no indicators suggesting whether the structural policies were carried out according to the plan. It would be imperative to tell the market participants and other people interested in the structural reform process whether Korea was going in the right direction or not. In fact, Korea had difficulties in checking its performance because of unclear targets and the failure to provide appropriate indicators on structural reforms. Markets could not give clear answers to whether Korea's reform and restructuring were going in the right direction, either. At the same time, the markets were not very interested in understanding the thrust of the structural policies and the progress in Korea as a result of structural reforms.

When the economy is doing well with high growth, nobody raises structural problems. However, when the economy is stuck in a recession, as Korea is now, then people start doubting the economy. From my point of view, at the moment the problems are mainly caused by the adverse external developments: that is, the worsening of the terms of trade and the recession in Korea's major trading countries. Nevertheless, it is still believed that the structural problems are the major causes of the current economic recession and another possible crisis in the near future. I strongly disagree with this thought. If Korea is to step up with the reform and restructuring, then it would not be the right time. After two years of restructuring, labor unions and the politicians were tired of economic reform. As a result, they are not willing to spend any additional money on reform and restructuring, although another $50 to $70 billion would be needed to sort unprofitable financial institutions out.

In a democratic country like Korea, it is not easy to just order labor unions and politicians to go on with reform and restructuring. Politicians claim that the government is pushing too far with the reform program through the National Assembly. There is a heated debate going on about what further restructuring should be done in the future. In my point of view, $50 billion will not be enough to sort out a large portion of bad loans from financial institutions or to get rid of heavy corporate debt. The question is whether we should bail out a large number of financial institutions and corporations. Regretfully, in many cases, the structural policies can become a bailout operation. We should not pay for the cost of cleaning up unprofitable financial institutions. Instead, we should simply let the shareholders and the financial institutions bear the major burden of this restructuring cost. However, this will take a while (six months or one year). The market is unlikely to be patient enough to wait for another six months or a year. Pushed into a corner, the policymakers will have to bail them out. In other words, this restructuring is creating very serious moral hazard problems. Initially after spending $100 billion, the Korean policymakers felt that Korea was in a position to leave the restructuring process to the market force, to minimize the moral hazard problem. However, as soon as the market participants saw the deterioration in the macroeconomic figures, they started putting pressure on the government to do something about the restructuring. What they demanded was a bailout of many financial institutions and of corporations that should be liquidated or placed under court receivership. This is what was happening.

Finally, the IMF structural policy was not successful in Korea to minimize the chances of another crisis. Over the two-year period, Korea has introduced all sorts of institutional arrangements designed to deal with the structural problems. In any economy there are unprofitable corporations that should be liquidated. The market itself must take care of the restructuring process. In order for the market to do it, a large number of institutions has to be improved. For that purpose, we introduced these institutions, and we should give these institutions some tasks. However, Korea does not seem to have the time to let the institutions take care of these structural problems. It is always the case that the government is asked to jump into the process and spend quite a lot of money, and the problem creates very serious moral hazard problems.

There is one point that I would like to make about Goldstein's paper. It is that the article said the structural problems were the main causes of the crisis. I also believe that structural problems were significant, and they are still not negligible. Yet clearly the main causes of the crisis are not structural problems. These problems obviously deepened and exacerbated the crisis, but they are unlikely to have been the direct causes. On this question there are thousands and thousands of publications that Goldstein tends to ignore entirely. To be precise, he should refer to this growing literature on the precise causes of the East Asian crisis, particularly in the case of Korea. The causes are important because the IMF or any other international financial institutions would have to correctly understand causes if they were to design their structural policy. When Korea was heading toward the financial crisis in 1997, neither the World Bank nor the IMF fully understood the extent and severity of Korea's structural problems. We acknowledged these problems, but we did not imagine they were significant to put the whole economy down. At the same time, the IMF thought the economic fundamentals of Korea were strong enough to fend off the contagion from financial turmoil from Southeast Asian countries. Unfortunately, that was not the case.

Once we understood the causes of the crisis more precisely, it would be easier to develop more consistently structural policy framework, in terms of the objectives, targets, and time frame. Nobody believed at the time that Korea would be able to manage the reform and restructuring over a three-year period. I still wonder why Korea had to complete the structural reform within three years. In my point of view Korea ought to continue with the reform for another three or five years, depending on the targets and the objectives of the structural reform. Well, Korea may have to spend at least another $50 billion or more, in addition to the $50 billion they have appropriated for this purpose. We are keen on what could be done to improve IMF structural policy at this stage because we have not completely overcome the crisis and more reforms and restructuring have to be done. In this respect, I think Goldstein's paper is a very important contribution, and I am sure that many other countries, including a country like Korea, will learn a great deal from his paper. However, once again, it focused too much on East Asian countries and their structural problems. In my point of view, his argument is not fair as a generalization.

For the time being, we should give attention to some of the obvious problems in the international financial markets. For example, a large number of fund managers influence world capital flows and cross-border financial transactions. When they decide to invest in emerging markets, they are concerned about only three variables: (a) the growth rate as a benchmark for the rate of return on investment; (b) changes in the foreign reserve level, that is, current account balance to check the creditworthiness; and (c) other fund managers behavior to see if they should stay or they should move out of the country. In this state of affairs, we should pay a little more attention to problems of international financial markets and how the international financial system is able to address these problems.

Discussion Summary

Jack Boorman reported on internal IMF work on structural conditionality that adds to the information in Morris Goldstein's paper. He agreed that the number of structural conditions in IMF programs has increased substantially since the late 1980s, a fact that he attributes to the attention given to growth as an objective of fund-supported programs and to the concentration on transition economies. Although conditionality is most pronounced in programs designed to deal with structural problems, he said that it has also become more prevalent in standby agreements. He said it is important to keep in mind that structural conditionality is concentrated in a few areas, notably the financial sector, fiscal reforms, the trade system, and other areas in the direct mandate of the Fund. He also cautioned against judging the extent of conditionality by simply counting the conditions. Often the authorities want guidance on the specific steps needed to reach a particular goal. Even so, he admitted that within the Fund there is broad agreement that the institution went too far in certain cases. The hard question, however, is if the Fund is to "pull back," by what criteria it is going to do so. Boorman said that structural measures needed to be "macro-relevant": the financial sector is central to macroeconomic performance, but the performance of the corporate sector is key to the performance of the financial sector. The question is where to stop. He added that if the Fund is not going to go beyond its more narrowly defined core areas, some other institution, such as the World Bank, has to take responsibility.

On the issue of responding to pressure from domestic reformers to put things into programs that they otherwise would not be able to enact, Boorman said that Goldstein wants the Fund to "just say no." However, he asked if the Fund should say no to people when they believe the reforms being advocated move in the right direction. He gave an example of a prime minister in an Eastern European country that wanted accelerated privatization as part of a program. *Martin Feldstein* responded that the prime minister in a democratic country should be told that if privatization is not central to the technical problems that the IMF is dealing with, it would not subvert the democratic process by including it in the program.

Turning to the pressures put on the Fund by its major shareholders, *Boorman* reported that the U.S. Congress has put over forty mandates on the U.S. executive director in the Fund to go into all kinds of areas. He said that there should be a better mechanism for deciding "what that staff should be interested in and what the staff should be pressing." Here he picked up the much-commented-upon example of the clove monopoly in Indonesia. This monopoly diverted income from poor clove producers to those that had the monopoly on exports. Removing the monopoly led to an immediate increase in the price of cloves to the poor farmers. When Suharto reimposed the monopoly at the behest of the exporting monopoly, the price went back down. Taking this as an example of a contentious structural condition, he asked: "Is this something we should or shouldn't do? Do we care about poverty?" When poverty—and governance—can be affected so directly and substantially by this kind of measure, should that be ignored by the Fund? He added that similar questions arise when the Fund is dealing with marketing boards, the prices of other agricultural products, and the like. Finally, Boorman commented on what he sees as an inconsistency in the criticisms of the Fund from some quarters. He said that some—including the Meltzer commission—are pushing the Fund to move to "preconditioning," and it is doing this to a large extent with its Contingent Credit Line (CCL). In this, the Fund is told to look at a variety of things, including the soundness of the country's financial system, the relationships it has with its creditors, its adherence to certain standards, and so on. Yet when the country is in a crisis, the Fund is supposed to restrict itself to a much narrower focus.

Nicholas Stern addressed the evolving division of responsibility between the World Bank and the IMF. He said that whatever the division of responsibilities, we should be thinking of simplifying and streamlining conditionality rather than abandoning it. With so many crises having their source in structural problems—he gave Russia as an example—it would be negligent for the Fund to ignore structural issues. However, he added that the Fund must recognize that it often lacks competence in these areas. On the other hand, the World Bank has longstanding experience in such areas as rural agriculture and land reform issues that can be useful in advising on structural reforms.

Turning to concrete steps that have been taken, he pointed to the World Bank's new Poverty Reduction Support Credit (PRSC), which is to be used in conjunction with the Fund's Poverty Reduction and Growth Facility (PRGF). The PRSC is more social and institutional, whereas the PRGF is more macro and financial. The idea is that these facilities should move in parallel. Stern hopes that the new facility will allow the World Bank to overcome the problem of slow response that has plagued it in the past. Regarding other desirable changes that would make for more efficient response from the World Bank, Stern said that each country director should have a two-page description of structural and social conditionalities that would be required in the event of crisis lending. He added that if the director can't produce such a statement, "then it is hard to think of what he or she is actually doing there."

Finally, Stern addressed how to decide on the priorities for structural conditionalities. He said that the selection should be guided by two principles that follow from the objective of poverty reduction: (a) achieving growth, and (b) giving poor people a chance to participate in growth. The growth perspective draws attention to conditions that affect the investment climate—macro stability, governance issues including bureaucratic harassment, administrative issues, the financial sector, and so on. The participation perspective draws attention to issues such as education and public health. Together "these two ways of looking at [structural conditionality] should help us construct a focus that I think all of us would agree that the Bank could do with," said Stern. *Feldstein* asked Stern if he sees that social and institutional conditionality—for instance improving schools in a poor developing country—as helpful in resolving the current crisis, preventing future crises, or making the country in question a better place. *Stern* answered that this would help over the long term to reduce poverty. *Feldstein* followed up by asking if this condition would be in the two-page document held by the country director listing the conditions for getting assistance. To this *Stern* replied that the purpose of a condition would be made clear in the strategy document that lies behind the condition, adding that what should be in the two-page document is that social programs be protected in the adjustments that come in crises.

Larry Summers made three points. First, drawing on his experience with the Mexican rescue package, he said that he has reluctantly concluded that collateral for loans from the international financial institutions does not offer a workable substitute for conditionality. Arranging for collateral is a vastly more complicated business than almost anyone who writes about it supposes, he said. Moreover, if good collateral is available, it ought to be available to private-sector lenders. He said that the confusion on this issue reached its "apex in the Meltzer Commission's suggestion that local currency tax receipts of sovereign governments be used as a potion [of the collateral]."

Second, he sees a lot of "potential for mischief" in World Bank–IMF cooperation on conditionality. Those who like the idea of structural conditionality but dislike IMF mission creep support this idea, he said. However, he sees the potential for a proliferation of conditions and delay as both institutions seek to have their priorities included. The other possibility is that the World Bank won't provide much money in the time of a crisis because it doesn't want to be seen as a "money pump," with the result that the structural element will be lost from the program.

Finally, on Indonesia, he said that, although mistakes were made, it was not an obvious failure of wisdom to trust President Suharto's economic leader of thirty years for guidance on what to include in the program. Responding to Paul Keating's description of excessive and misplaced conditionality, Summers said that the hard question is what to do when the government leader is transferring substantial funds to his family and friends. This takes on special importance when one is transferring one's own taxpayers' money to the country. He said that the critics should set out a counterfactual history of what they would have had the Fund do and how they think things would have worked out.

Domingo F. Cavallo said the Fund and World Bank will never get good results if they try to impose structural policies. He said the only way to implement reforms in a country is to rely on the political and economic leadership in the country to carry them out, so the Fund and World Bank should be looking for opportunities to support good reforms.

John Crow said that consideration should also be given to the World Bank reviews and IMF consultation papers that come before a crisis. If an institution is to impose structural conditions at the time of a crisis, it needs to have been involved in consultations about the country beforehand.

Arminio Fraga said that in a crisis the Fund should worry about crisis management, and only crisis management. He said nothing should be done to hurt the main objective. On letting legitimate governments add things to the program, he said such additions should be allowed, but kept general.

Responding to the criticisms of Paul Keating and others, *Jeffrey Frankel* offered an additional defense of what he termed "enhanced conditionality." In Indonesia, Korea, and Thailand, there has been a movement toward democracy. He said we told civil-society types in the past that globalization would lead to growth and growth would lead to political liberalization.

However, it was not clear what the mechanism would be. The mechanism in East Asia in the 1990s turned out to be financial liberalization plus crisis plus conditionality. The IMF did not set out deliberately to overturn any governments, and to do so would of course have been an unacceptable violation of countries' sovereignty. However, in the Korean election of November 1997, due to the financial crisis, the incumbent president was defeated for the first time by an opposition party candidate, Kim Dae Jung, a man who was willing and able to accept the need for reform. President Suharto in Indonesia was arguably brought down in 1998 by the combination of structural conditionality in the IMF program and his own unwillingness to curb his family's economic interests. In each of these countries, a side effect of the crisis was a peaceful step in the direction of democracy. This political pattern is not in itself a good argument for undergoing a financial crisis. However, it belies the argument that IMF conditionality works to undermine the forces of democracy in the victim countries.

Charles Dallara pointed out that the inclusion of structural elements in IMF programs really began "gathering steam" in the 1980s. On the issue of the appropriateness of more recent conditionality, he said he agreed with Timothy F. Geithner that in today's world of free capital markets the international institutions must be concerned with issues such as strengthening financial sectors and addressing corporate governance. This follows from the Fund's fundamental concern with restoring a sustainable balance-of-payments position. In today's capital markets, restoring confidence requires that the international institutions address the concerns of international debt and equity investors. Confidence depends to a significant degree on issues such as the strength of the financial sector and minority shareholder rights. However, Dallara is not convinced that, just because there needs to be a comprehensive approach, it all should be part of Fund conditionality. He said the lack of an integrated approach utilizing the World Bank, the regional development banks, the Bank for International Settlements, and the Basel committee is one reason why there has been so much Fund mission creep. Bringing about this integration requires a "more brutal approach toward managing these institutions, and a more consistent shareholder attitude," he said. Without this, the Fund will be pushed to address issues fundamental to restoring confidence while being criticized for having too many conflicting objectives and lacking necessary staff expertise.

David Lipton argued that we need a realistic conception of program ownership. He said it is a mistake to think that there must be broad agreement across the political spectrum. "If we had settled for what the Korean government was interested in doing on December 2 [1997], we would have had no basis for going forward," he said. Regarding what should be part of a fund program, Lipton said that whatever is essential for restoring confidence has to be included. He recalled that the Korean government had resisted many of the demands for structural reform, including, for example, foreign ownership of banks. He added that we should judge these elements by whether they "helped to give a sense that Korea was going to head in a direction that would make it stable." Turning to Indonesia, he said that the Fund should not be criticized for including too many structural elements, but it should be criticized for "losing sight of the centrality of monetary policy." From November 1997 through February 1998 large liquidity credits were given in the name of stopping runs on banks, but it "was basically money being given away to cronies," Lipton explained. Lipton concluded by saying that the program has to "add up to be convincing, especially in a panic." Conditions should not be disqualified from consideration because they take a long time to have an effect or are fundamentally about efficiency. What is important, he said, is that these are seen as important first steps in useful directions.

On the issue of conditionality, *Edwin Truman* strongly agreed with David Lipton when he said that conditionality should be seen as a package. Truman said it is sometimes difficult to determine at the time what the "essential elements" of a credible package are. One reason is that the audience is varied: domestic residents, domestic leaders, foreign lenders, international financial markets, international institutions, and foreign officials who must authorize positive votes on programs in the international financial institutions. Truman noted that Guillermo Ortiz referred to U.S. insistence in early 1995 that the Bank of Mexico modify its previous practice of releasing information on its reserves only three times a year and adopt a policy of regular releases at least monthly. Larry Summers referred to the insistence that the Thai authorities reveal at the end of August 1997 the extent of their uncovered forward position. Truman was involved in both of these episodes. In the Mexican case, the Federal Reserve had long been troubled by the Bank of Mexico's policy. Along with the treasury, in early January 1995, the Federal Reserve conditioned access by the Bank of Mexico to the use of a drawing on the Federal Reserve's swap lines on such a commitment. It took the Bank of Mexico an entire weekend to agree. This agreement was important not only on substantive grounds (although some might argue that by itself it was trivial), but also because the action by the Bank of Mexico also helped to restore the Bank of Mexico's credibility in the eyes of the U.S. authorities. Essentially the same argument applied in the Thai situation. The central bank of Thailand had lost credibility with the Federal Reserve, and several other (but not all major) central banks, because of the way it had built up its forward exposure in secret. From this perspective, the credibility of the Thai package was enhanced by the central bank's reluctant agreement to reveal its forward position. These actions may not have been important to all observers or officials, but they were in each instance key to Federal Reserve support.

Creditor Relations

1. William R. Cline
2. Guillermo Ortiz
3. Roberto G. Mendoza
4. Ammar Siamwalla

1. William R. Cline

The Role of the Private Sector in Resolving Financial Crises in Emerging Markets

6.1.1 Introduction

Three years have passed since the outbreak of the East Asian financial crisis, and six since that of its Mexican precursor. Numerous official groupings and private analysts have sought to derive from these experiences appropriate lessons for international policy, including especially the manner in which private creditors can most fruitfully be involved in crisis resolution (G10 1996; G22 1998; IMF 1999b; G7 1999; IIF, 1996, 1999 b,c; Council on Foreign Relations 1999; Eichengreen 1999; Meltzer Commission 2000). Although there is considerable agreement on the central issues of crisis prevention, and although substantial improvement has occurred in this area (including heightened data transparency and a shift from fixed to floating exchange rates by a number of key economies), more significant divergences persist regarding how to involve private creditors in the resolution of those crises that do occur.

The principal divisions on the latter issue are on the questions of, first, whether official support on the relatively large scale of the key packages of

The views here were presented in the author's personal capacity and should not be interpreted as official positions of the Institute of International Finance. The author is grateful to Kevin Barnes, Bejoy Das Gupta, Martin Feldstein, and Lubomir Mitov for comments on an earlier draft.

the late 1990s is desirable (given evident success in the cases of Mexico, Korea, and Brazil) or undesirable (e.g., because of the risk of moral hazard), and, second, whether the nature of private-sector involvement should follow predetermined rules or should be determined on a case-by-case basis. On the latter question, some European officials have tended toward a rules basis, whereas U.S. officials have emphasized the need for case-by-case resolution of crises.

This paper will suggest that the approach most in keeping with an understanding of today's international capital markets is one that seeks to involve private creditors on as voluntary a basis as possible given the circumstances, and that, within the classic principles of financial crisis management (Bagehot [1873] 1917), temporary large official support can indeed be appropriate where the country is illiquid rather than insolvent and a prompt turnaround in private flows through adjustment and restoration of confidence is likely.

Section 6.1.2 reviews the differences between today's capital market and that of the 1980s, as a basis for inferring appropriate changes in crisis resolution strategy. Next the discussion considers what economic theory about sovereign lending would tend to counsel in the design of crisis resolution approaches. The paper then turns to actual experience in several of the recent country crisis cases. After evaluating one of the more prominent proposals for reform (inclusion of collective action clauses in bonds) and briefly considering the likely future composition of lending to emerging markets, the discussion concludes with a synthesis of policy implications.

6.1.2   The 1980s versus the 1990s

It is sobering that each of the past two decades has witnessed a widespread crisis in external financing for emerging market economies. The Latin America debt crisis of the 1980s was the more severe, precipitating a "lost decade" of growth there and ending up in debt forgiveness of about 35 percent for bank claims on much of the region (Cline 1995, 234). The spate of financial crises that began in 1995 with Mexico and was followed by East Asia in 1997–98, Russia in 1998, and Brazil in 1999 turns out to have been approximately comparable in scope although not (generally) in severity. Thus, as shown in table 6.1, the fraction of external debt to private creditors involved reached about 60 percent of the emerging markets total in both the 1980s and 1990s crises. The geographical pattern was sharply different, with concentration in Latin America in the 1980s but involvement of Asia and Russia in the 1990s.

The 1990s crises were more oriented toward collapses of currencies and domestic financial systems and less centered on excessive burdens of external debt. A severe mismatch of large short-term external debt against reduced external reserves was a typical precipitating factor (especially in Mex-

Table 6.1   Scope of Debt and Financial Crises in the 1980s and 1990s (Debt owed to private external creditors, $ billion)

	1984			1996		
	Bank	Other	Total	Bank	Other	Total
Latin America						
Argentina	32.7	8.1	40.8	—	—	—
Bolivia	1.1	0.1	1.2	—	—	—
Brazil	79.8	4.7	84.5	51.2	126.4	177.6
Chile	16.0	0.7	16.7	—	—	—
Ecuador	4.9	0.5	5.4	2.3	6.2	8.5
Mexico	81.2	5.7	86.9	30.1	79.4	109.5
Peru	4.5	1.1	5.6	—	—	—
Uruguay	2.9	1.0	3.9	—	—	—
Venezuela	31.8	3.2	35.0	—	—	—
Africa and Middle East						
Cote d'Ivoire	4.9	0.9	5.8	—	—	—
Morocco	3.5	0.1	3.6	—	—	—
Europe						
Poland	7.2	1.5	8.7	—	—	—
Russia	—	—	—	37.7	25.0	62.7
Asia and Pacific						
Indonesia	—	—	—	55.9	25.2	81.1
Korea	—	—	—	127.8	28.8	156.6
Pakistan	—	—	—	4.4	5.8	10.2
Malaysia	—	—	—	19.8	13.9	33.7
The Philippines	14.4	3.7	18.1	12.2	15.4	27.6
Thailand	—	—	—	68.8	13.5	82.3
Total	284.9	31.3	316.2	410.2	339.6	749.8
Percent of total for 37 major						
emerging market economies	65.7	41.5	62.1	57.4	54.4	56.0

Source: IIF (1994, 2000b)

Note: Dash indicates that country was not directly involved in the period's crisis.

ico, Korea, and Thailand), rather than a high ratio of total external debt to exports and gross domestic product (GDP), as was more typical in Latin America in the 1980s. Underlying economic structures and policies tended to be better in the 1990s (with the advent of trade liberalization, privatization, and fiscal adjustment). Stronger underlying conditions and the shorter-term nature of the financial squeeze meant that it was possible for the key economies involved in the 1990s crisis to return to economic growth much faster than those in the 1980s crisis, and to do so on a basis of return to normalized capital market access without debt forgiveness (excluding the cases of Russia and Indonesia, where political incoherence was far more severe).

One important difference between the 1980s and 1990s was the prevalence of capital controls in the former and capital mobility in the latter. This meant that when difficulties occurred in the 1980s, there was a tendency to go into arrears on official debt and to ration availability of foreign exchange for payment of external debt by private firms that otherwise were capable of servicing it. In contrast, under mobile capital regimes in the 1990s, the crises manifested themselves in plunging exchange rates rather than foreign exchange rationing, and in balance sheet shocks to domestic banks and corporations exposed in foreign currency–denominated obligations. The presence of capital quantity rationing in the 1980s in contrast to price clearing in the 1990s is one reason the latter crisis was shorter and much more front-loaded in its severity.[1]

Table 6.1 shows a crucial difference between the capital markets in the 1980s and the late 1990s. For the emerging markets in aggregate, in 1984 external debt to banks was nine times as large as that owed to nonbank private creditors. In contrast, in 1996 the debt owed to banks was approximately equal to that owed to nonbanks, the latter primarily in the form of bonds. These estimates confirm the by now widely recognized transformation of the emerging markets' debt composition from overwhelming dominance by international banks to approximate parity between bank and bond obligations.

Another key difference between the two decades is that for the banks, exposure to emerging markets was much larger relative to their total assets and capital in the 1980s than it is today. Thus, for U.S. banks, exposure to emerging market economies fell from 12 percent of total assets in 1982 to 2.5 percent in early 2000 (Dallara 2000). The sharp reduction in banks' vulnerability to emerging markets' debt, combined with the decline in their share of total debt, has meant that increasingly such 1980s-style solutions as "concerted lending" by banks have become outdated.

Finally, by the late 1990s the capital markets were much more heavily dominated by equity flows, especially direct investment, than in the 1980s, when bank lending was predominant. Thus, of total net foreign private capital flows to twenty-nine major emerging market economies, direct equity accounted for 31 percent in 1993–96 but rose to 68 percent in 1997–2000 (IIF 2000a,b). As a result, the impact of private-creditor participation in crisis resolution has become at least as important through its confidence effect on direct investment flows as through its direct capital impact through lending. The same point applies to portfolio equity flows, although these have held more steady (15 percent of net foreign capital flows in the first period and 13 percent in the second). In contrast, both direct and portfolio capital flows to emerging markets in the period 1980–84 accounted for only 11 percent of the total in that period, with net flows from banks accounting for 74 percent and nonbank private credits accounting for 15 percent (IIF database).

---

1. Thus, Korea's GDP fell 6.7 percent in 1998 but by 2000 was 13 percent above its 1997 level. In comparison, weighting by 1984–86 GDP, output fell only 1.6 percent in 1983 for Argentina, Brazil, and Mexico, but by 1986 it was still only 10 percent above the 1982 base (IMF 1999a).

Other contrasts between the 1980s and 1990s are also important. There has been a shift in lending away from sovereign borrowers toward private corporate and bank borrowers. Within bank lending, there has been a shift toward shorter-term (typically trade-related) credits, in part because banks considered long-term lending to Latin America to be vulnerable to restructuring after the 1980s experience. Finally, the shift away from bank toward bond and other nonbank lending has been especially pronounced when evaluated in terms of flows rather than outstanding stocks (cumulative new net flows from banks to twenty-nine major emerging market economies in 1997–2000 will have been –$61 billion, compared to $204 billion from nonbank lenders). As discussed below, there are reasons to expect the role of banks to remain reduced in the future, even though their net lending is likely to turn positive again.

The overall implication that emerges from consideration of today's composition of capital markets is that involvement of bank lending alone will usually be too small in potential to resolve crises directly. Instead, the principal impact will have to be through the general improvement in confidence that any such involvement will have for a much broader array of capital flows, especially in the form of direct investment. This inference is consistent with the premise that market-oriented, voluntary resolutions are desirable, because it is such outcomes that are most likely to preserve a capital-market atmosphere that is congenial to business as usual for direct investment, portfolio equity flows, and new bond issues.

6.1.3   Conceptual Framework[2]

Default Pain as Quasi-Collateral

It is crucial that policies toward crisis resolution be framed with an understanding of the underlying theory of sovereign lending. A seminal contribution to this theory is Eaton and Gersovitz (1981). They ask why anyone would lend to a foreign sovereign. There is no physical collateral. The tradition of sovereign immunity is a further deterrent. Their analysis appeals to consumption smoothing as the motive for sovereign borrowing. Countries borrow abroad when times are bad (e.g., because of an export price collapse) and repay when they are good. On the side of lending supply, the principal assurance lenders have that they will be repaid is the sovereign borrower's knowledge that if it defaults it will be locked out of capital markets in the future and will no longer have recourse to the opportunity to borrow for consumption smoothing.

This theory means that any international arrangements that convey the impression that default is painless will tend to depress capital flows to

2. Also see Cline (2000b).

emerging market economies. Essentially, a default-friendly international regime deprives international lenders of their quasi-collateral: heightened economic difficulty for the defaulter. The defaulting country may enjoy a one-time windfall gain of not having to repay its outstanding debt, but it will face a dearth of willing lenders in the future. Perhaps more important, there will be a negative externality of the defaulting country's actions for other emerging market borrowers. If it is blessed by an international regime seen as facilitating the default, the country's actions will increase the perceived risk of lending to all emerging market borrowers.

In such a conceptual framework, it is easy to see how good intentions by international policymakers could turn counterproductive. There are grounds for judging that this in fact happened during the course of 1999–2000. The seeming shift toward official international facilitation of default, most notably in the case of Ecuador, seems likely to bear some responsibility for the sluggishness of the return of capital flows to emerging markets three years after the onset of the East Asia crisis and the persistence of high lending spreads to many emerging market economies. Thus, for 2000 the net flow of bank and nonbank (mainly bond) lending to twenty-nine major emerging market economies is projected by the Institute of International Finance (IIF) at only $26 billion (IIF 2000a). Although this is up from the trough of –$17 billion in 1999, it remains minimal compared to the average of $157 billion annually in 1995–97.

Similarly, whereas spreads (above U.S. Treasury obligations) on long-term Eurobonds for Argentina and Brazil averaged 360 basis points at the end of 1996, by early September 2000 they were still as high as an average of 680 basis points, albeit below their peak average of 1,240 basis points at the end of August 1998 after the Russian default. A spread of 700 basis points on thirty-year paper implies a probability of default of two-thirds if the recovery rate is 50 percent (Cline and Barnes 1997, 40). This seems an exaggerated pessimism and is consistent with a capital market that remains poorly recovered from the crises of the late 1990s.

Moral Hazard

On the other side, the principal conceptual argument that has been invoked in favor of "bailing in" private creditors and leaning toward ensuring they take default losses has been that otherwise the public sector would be creating a moral hazard that would induce excessive lending and risk-taking by creditors anticipating high returns in the good-case outcome and public bailout in the bad.

The large headline figures for the official support packages of the late 1990s ($50 billion for Mexico, $17 billion for Thailand, $34 billion for Indonesia, $57 billion for Korea, $16 billion for Russia, and $42 billion for Brazil; IIF 1999c, 48) not surprisingly spurred critiques that such public support had created moral hazard (e.g., Meltzer Commission 2000). It is certainly likely that even the meager lending flows that have returned would have been smaller, and the still high spreads would have been higher yet, in the absence of these packages and the strong turnarounds they permitted in most of these crises (with Russia and Indonesia the exceptions, primarily for political reasons).

The more fundamental point, however, is that public-sector intervention that permits a large positive-sum-game outcome will often have some inevitable moral hazard side effect, just as the existence of automobile insurance and home theft insurance may at the margin make drivers a bit less cautious and homeowners a bit more willing to go on long trips. The central question is not whether there is moral hazard, but whether it is large and whether its costs exceed the social benefits provided by the intervention in question. There is no doubt that the impressive economic recoveries in Mexico, Korea, Brazil, and to a lesser extent Thailand would not have happened without the confidence supplied by the official support programs, so their social benefits appear to have been large.

As for moral hazard costs, in the large financial crises of the late 1990s private creditors and investors took large losses, so they are hardly likely to have learned the lesson that emerging markets' investments are risk-free because of official bailouts. Thus, realized or potential losses by foreign investors in emerging markets in 1997–98 from the East Asian and Russian crises amounted to about $240 billion in stock markets, $60 billion for banks, and $50 billion for other creditors including bondholders (IIF 1999c, 57–61). Specific econometric tests reject the hypothesis that the first of the packages, for Mexico in 1995, induced excessive lending at low spreads.[3] After the broader set of support programs in the late 1990s, the evidence shows that lending flows remain small and spreads remain high, strongly suggesting that any moral hazard was too small to induce excessive new lending at unduly low interest rates. In short, the critique that public support in resolving the major financial crises of the late 1990s involved moral hazard is true but trivial and misses the more relevant point that moral hazard costs were minor relative to recovery benefits.[4]

Burden Sharing

A general notion that the private sector should bear its share of the "burden" of resolving financial crises has also driven policy discussions. Here

---

3. Zhang (1999). The tests show instead that the large flows at low spreads by early 1997 were driven by global capital market conditions as proxied by spreads in the U.S. high-yield corporate market. Removing this influence and that of country-specific economic debt and economic indicators, emerging markets' spreads in the fourth quarter of 1995 through the second quarter of 1997 were not statistically significantly lower than before the Mexican support program.

4. It should be noted that the one country where moral hazard likely played a significant role in buoyant lending was Russia, where geopolitical importance was frequently assumed to ensure support if needed.

the key is to recognize the intertemporal pattern likely in well-managed crises. At the height of the crisis there may be temporary public-sector support even as private lending is low or even negative. Once forceful adjustment measures are taken and it becomes clear the country will not enter into protracted default, a strong renewed inflow of private flows can occur. Thus, in Korea, net private capital inflows (including equity) fell from $48 billion in 1996 to –$14 billion in 1997 and –$24 billion in 1998 but rebounded to $8 billion in 1999 and $24 billion in 2000. Net official flows were –$0.4 billion in 1996 and jumped to $18 billion in 1997 and $12 billion in 1998, but they dropped to –$9 billion in 1999 as Korea repaid International Monetary Fund (IMF) funding. Thus, although a snapshot of capital flows at the height of the crisis in 1998 would give the impression that the public sector was bearing the burden and the private sector was escaping, this interpretation would miss the more fundamental point of the balance-wheel role of official intervention and the dynamic picture of a return to private flows once adjustment measures have been taken and confidence restored. A similar U-shaped pattern for private flows, complemented by an inverted-U shape for public flows, depicts the resolution of the Mexican crisis in 1995 and the Brazilian crisis in 1998–99 (Cline 2000b).

It is also the case that for emerging markets as a whole, private capital flows have by far dominated the totals, casting further doubt on any broader impression that the burden of development finance is being borne by the public sector (even though the private flows are certainly not undertaken to shoulder any burden, but for profit). Even in 1997–98 at the height of the crises, net public capital flows to twenty-nine major emerging market economies were less than one-fourth private flows (a two-year total of $97 billion versus $409 billion, respectively). By 1999–2000, the relationship was back to its far more lopsided dominance by private flows, with a total of only $8 billion in net official flows versus $330 billion in net private flows (IIF 2000a).

The most narrow application of burden sharing is in the notion of "comparability" for private-sector treatment in Paris Club rescheduling of bilateral claims.[5] For example, if within the Paris Club official creditors reschedule for, say, a three-year period payments otherwise due to their export credit agencies, comparability would lead them to make it a condition of the rescheduling that the borrowing government seek rescheduling for a similar period from private creditors. Although unexceptionable in principle,

5. The Paris Club is an arrangement used by industrial-country governments when it becomes necessary to negotiate the restructuring of claims owed to their agencies by a government or private borrowers in a particular country. The term dates from 1956 when bilateral official creditors met in Paris to reschedule claims owed by Argentina (Rieffel 1985, 3). Principles of Paris Club rescheduling include the requirement that the country be engaged in an IMF adjustment program and that "comparable treatment" be granted to the debtor country by other creditors (traditionally commercial banks and, where relevant, bilateral creditors not normally in the Paris Club).

this concept has sometimes been applied in questionable ways. Apparent public-sector support for default on Ecuador's Brady bonds—which had already forgiven private claims, whereas bilateral claims had not been forgiven—is one example (although the Paris Club itself may not have formally requested Ecuador to default prior to the government's action). Paris Club relief for political purposes, as in the case of Poland in the early 1990s, is questionably appropriate for extension to the private sector, which does not enjoy the same political benefits as the industrial-country governments. Nor has the Paris Club typically accepted comparability when it could work in the opposite direction. A notable recent case is that of Russia, where private creditors gave substantial forgiveness in early 2000, but the Paris Club has resisted Russian government requests to grant comparable forgiveness.

The underlying point is that a rigid approach to burden sharing will be misguided when its effect is to damage the prospects of return to voluntary capital markets and thereby is more likely to harm than help the country in question over the medium term.

Market-Based Collective Action

An important concept for understanding the potential for private-sector involvement in crisis resolution is that of private-sector collective action on a voluntary or quasi-voluntary basis. Where a moderate number of relatively large financial institutions have short-term claims coming due, they may be able to carry out a joint action that is to their collective benefit by undertaking to maintain rather than run off their credit lines. This was the case in the Korean crisis (more formally through conversion of short-term to one- to three-year claims) and the Brazilian crisis (less formally through a pledge to maintain credit lines). The basic dynamic may be seen as a positive sum repeat game. Each institutional "player" knows the others, or most of them, and knows that its own adherence to the joint endeavor will affect the other players' future confidence in its reliability.

Voluntary club-based collective action is sharply different in effect from mandatory action imposed by the public sector, even though advocates of the latter also frequently cite the private creditors' own collective interest. It is noteworthy that in neither the Korean nor Brazilian case was there legal prohibition by the government of payment rather than rollover (or conversion) of short-term claims, and in fact a number of smaller institutions did elect to withdraw. A critical mass of support from larger firms was nonetheless successful. If instead there had been a comprehensive official freeze on payments, the results would have been radically different, with the return to capital markets greatly delayed.

It is also important to recognize that the positive impact on confidence from a voluntary collective action such as maintenance of credit lines can be far greater than might be expected by the share of total debt directly comprised by the initiative in question. Thus, in the case of Korea, a debt of $22 billion in short-term bank claims was converted, compared with Korea's total external debt of $159 billion at the end of 1997. Similarly, short-term trade and interbank claims of banks in Brazil were only about $25 billion by March 1999 when the banks entered into a voluntary arrangement to maintain credit lines (IIF 1999a), compared with total external debt of $259 billion at the end of 1998. However, in both cases the agreements to stem short-term outflows were crucial catalysts to the rapid rebuilding of confidence. In part this is because much of the rest of the debt was at longer term and could not immediately exit. The longer-term nature of bonds, in particular, means that they are rarely the proximate cause of a sudden liquidity crisis. More fundamentally, however, the initiatives, done on a quasi-voluntary rather than mandatory basis, sent a strong signal that key private-sector players had confidence in the country's longer-term prospects. This signal helped restore confidence more broadly.

Lender of Last Resort and Size of Official Support

Another key issue is whether the large official support programs of the late 1990s were appropriate. Here the most useful conceptual premise is Bagehot's ([1873] 1917) rule for a central bank: in a panic, lend in unlimited amounts to a solvent but illiquid bank; do not lend at all to an insolvent one. Cline (2000b) proposes a "Bagehot curve" as guidance for public policy in crisis resolution. On the vertical axis is the amount that can be provided in official support; on the horizontal axis is the probability that the country's situation is one of insolvency (ranging from zero to unity). Near the y-axis (near-zero probability of insolvency) official support can be extremely large (for example, many times the usual IMF quota) under the Bagehot lender-of-last-resort principle. As the probability of insolvency rises, the appropriate amount of official support drops rapidly.

By this gauge, the large official support programs in a quasi-lender-of-last-resort function were highly appropriate for Mexico, Korea, Thailand, and Brazil. They were arguably more doubtful for Russia and even Indonesia, although it warrants emphasis that neither IMF nor bilateral forgiveness has occurred even in these cases despite defaults on private claims (although in Indonesia defaults were only by private debtors). It should also be stressed that the country's underlying likelihood of assuring solvency, primarily by forceful policy action, should be the appropriate guide to whether relatively large official support is made available—not the criterion of systemic importance. The latter (for example, as proposed by Council on Foreign Relations [1999], which argues that in nonsystemic cases the IMF should "just say no" to large packages) would discriminate against small countries. In short, there is no room for financial acrophobia in international financial policy for crisis resolution, even though policymakers need thick skins to withstand the public backlash that typically accompanies big-ticket headline numbers.

A related question regarding the size of official support is whether it should be limited to traditional magnitudes relative to IMF quotas. The answer would seem "surely not," considering that these quotas were set at a time when trade imbalances were the primary determinant of financing needs rather than today's highly mobile capital flows. It became particularly evident in the case of Korea that the traditional IMF financing magnitudes of one to three times quota had become outdated, and the new Supplementary Reserve Facility (SRF) created in late 1997 made it possible for the IMF to lend $21 billion to Korea, or more than nineteen times Korea's quota. The SRF, with its much larger and front-loaded lending capacity with high and rising interest rates to encourage early repayment, is one of the most important concrete institutional changes to come out of the late 1990s' financial crises. The likelihood of prompt repayment to the SRF (as occurred in the cases of Korea and Brazil), moreover, means that the international financial community is likely to have available the resources to provide relatively large temporary financing in a crisis (except perhaps in a scenario in which massive contagion once again envelopes a number of the largest emerging market economies). Whether it will have the corresponding political will is unclear, although this would seem more problematic for the mounting of bilateral components of any future crisis management efforts than for the use in the IMF of the SRF and, perhaps, the Contingent Credit Line (CCL), both of which were designed specifically for this purpose.

Voluntary Approaches to Private-Sector Involvement

In view of the conceptual framework outlined here, the fundamental principle of private-sector involvement in crisis resolution is that it should be on as voluntary and market-oriented a basis as possible in view of the circumstances. This will maximize the chances of a prompt return to private-market access and limitation of public support to a temporary balance-wheel role for restoring confidence. Publicly mandated approaches, such as involuntary standstills enforced by exchange controls, should be avoided whenever possible, because they undermine the underlying dynamic of sovereign lending by facilitating default and not only delay return to market access but also risk adverse spillover to private lending to other countries through heightened perceived risk.

Along the spectrum from voluntary to involuntary approaches, the cases of Mexico in 1995, Korea in 1997–98, and Brazil in 1998–99 are toward (or, for Mexico, at) the voluntary end; those for such countries as Ukraine and Pakistan are toward the involuntary end; and the unilateral defaults of Russia and Ecuador are at the involuntary end. The discussion that follows reviews in summary fashion the course of private-sector involvement in crisis resolution in these and other cases.[6] The experience to date tends to confirm that more voluntary approaches generate more favorable outcomes for the country itself and arguably for the system as well.

---

6. For the cases of Thailand, Indonesia, and Korea, also see Cline (1998).

6.1.4   Resolving Liquidity Crises: Mexico, Thailand, Korea, Brazil

This section reviews the role of the private sector in achieving crisis resolution in four major country episodes that together represent a class of cases that involved potential systemic stakes and achieved relatively successful outcomes on the basis of voluntary or quasi-voluntary private-sector involvement. The discussion focuses primarily on how the private sector participated in each case. The treatment is chronological, because there was a learning-by-doing process at the international policy level, as well as a changing political environment for policy options.

Mexico

A large current account deficit (7 percent of GDP), two key political assassinations in an election year, adherence to a nearly-fixed exchange rate regime, heavy reliance on short-term obligations in the government debt structure, and considerable sterilization of capital outflows all played important roles in Mexico's end-1994 crisis. It is questionable whether more skilled management by the new economic team in December could have averted the collapse.

The U.S. Treasury led an international program of official support amounting to $50 billion. The decision to do so undoubtedly reflected recognition that otherwise the encouraging revival of emerging capital markets after the prolonged debt crisis of the 1980s and its tentative resolution by the Brady Plan would be in serious jeopardy of collapse. The magnitude of the package reflected the dimensions of the key variables capital markets were focusing on at the time: some $30 billion due in short-term dollar-indexed government obligations (*tesobonos*) against reserves that had eroded to only about $6 billion.

Direct private-sector involvement in initial resolution of the crisis is easy to describe in the Mexican case: there was none. U.S. Treasury Secretary Robert Rubin often stated in response to later critiques of the bailing out of the private sector that if he could have found some way to make private creditors pay some price without hurting Mexico, he would have done so. However, the obligations in question were dispersed capital market holdings, so the 1980s tactic of calling a London Club meeting of banks to reschedule claims was irrelevant.[7] Importantly, Mexican policymakers were

---

7. The London Club is an ad hoc arrangement of private creditors, historically primarily commercial banks, that coordinates the negotiation of external debt restructurings with developing-country governments. Participation varies depending on the composition of exposure in each case. Rieffel (1985, 4) identifies the first London Club rescheduling as that for Zaire in the mid-1970s. London Club activity was particularly important in the Latin American debt restructurings of the 1980s. Typically negotiations were led by an advisory committee of leading banks. Today, with the sharp ascendance of bond lending, a growing issue is whether the London Club process lends itself to extension to include representatives of bondholders.

loath to repeat the August 1982 measure of a unilateral suspension of principal payments. Mexico had simply paid too dearly in reestablishing its credit reputation in the intervening decade to make that an attractive option at the end of 1994.

Some private-sector investors believed they had been penalized, because they had held Mexican equities and peso-denominated government paper (*cetes*) only on government assurances that there would be no devaluation. Instead, the peso lost 35 percent of its value in December alone. Such private-sector complaints did not take account of the rich interest rates that had been earned on peso obligations (14–15 percent annually in 1993–94 while the peso had remained virtually unchanged against the dollar).

The private sector did eventually participate in Mexico's crisis resolution, by renewing inflows of capital after the devaluation and after tight monetary policies began to take hold. Private flows swung from –$4.8 billion in 1995 to $13.6 billion in 1996, primarily in direct investment and to some extent in bond flows. Mexico was thus the first case in the 1990s of successful balance-wheel official intervention that, along with forceful policy adjustment, revived confidence and a return of private capital.

Thailand

Thailand was the first of the East Asian financial crises of 1997–98. The region's crisis was marked by greater incidence of short-term bank claims than in Mexico, where nonbank holdings of short-term government obligations were the proximate problem. The relatively greater involvement of banks in Asia reflected the fact that after the Latin American debt crisis, banks had shied away from that region but had increasingly considered lending to Asia relatively safe and promising in view of the region's image of sustained high growth. Thailand was the first country where the growing strains of rampant expansion became evident, including an increasingly overextended domestic financial system. Rapid domestic credit expansion and an increasingly overvalued exchange rate (accompanied by a current account deficit of almost 8 percent of GDP) set the stage for a crisis.

By the second quarter of 1997 there was an increasing awareness that Thailand had undertaken forward currency commitments that made its effective reserves far lower than the reported totals. Facing increasing pressure on the baht, at the beginning of July the government allowed the currency to float, ending its thirteen-year peg to the dollar. Within the month the currency fell 22 percent, and it was destined to fall considerably further.

The crisis exposed the fragility of the domestic financial system. The greatest weakness was among some ninety finance companies, whose lending was concentrated in property, auto, and securities margin lending vulnerable to the sharp turnaround from rapid growth in the economy to recession. The central bank suspended operations of sixteen finance companies in June 1997 and of another forty in August.

Direct private-sector involvement in crisis resolution in the case of Thailand centered in the restructuring of claims on these finance institutions. These claims amounted to some $4 billion, only about 6 percent of total foreign claims (IIF 1999c, 65). The Thai government distinguished between financing companies, whose obligations were restructured, and commercial banks, for which the government guaranteed obligations. For claims on the sixteen finance companies closed in June, amounting to about half of affected foreign claims, creditors were entitled only to proceeds from auctions of assets. For claims on the forty finance companies subsequently closed, creditors were given five-year obligations on the main state bank at 2 percent interest.

In effect, then, a relatively limited restructuring of only a small portion of foreign claims—those on the suspended finance companies—was the only direct involvement of the private sector in resolution of the Thai crisis. In the case of Thailand, moreover, there continued to be a running down of foreign bank claims during 1998 through 2000, primarily from conscious deleveraging on the demand side rather than further contraction on that of lending supply. These repayments were facilitated by a massive swing of the current account from a deficit of about 8 percent of GDP in 1996 to a surplus of almost 13 percent in 1998.[8]

Because the Thai case involved only surgical rescheduling, it stands toward the voluntary end of the spectrum of private-sector involvement in crisis resolution. Although there is some support for a resulting reflow of voluntary capital in the fact that inflows of (mainly) direct and portfolio equity more than doubled from 1996 to a range of about $7 billion annually in 1997–99, the persistence of net debt repayments after the crisis leaves the case for renewed market access ambiguous so far.

For its part, the international official support for Thailand was complicated by the political backlash to the earlier U.S. official support for Mexico. The U.S. Congress had passed legislation prohibiting use of the treasury's Exchange Stabilization Fund for this purpose for a specified time period after the Mexican package, and this time limit had not yet expired by July 1997. In any event there appears to have been some official sentiment that whereas Mexico was primarily the United States' problem, Thailand was primarily that of Japan. By August, an international support program had been assembled involving a total of $17 billion, with $3.9 billion from the IMF, $1 billion each from the World Bank and Asian Development Bank, $4 billion from Japan, and $6 billion from other governments. The support and economic adjustment program contributed to economic recovery by 1999, but only after a severe recession (10 percent decline in GDP) in 1998.

8. Net bank flows to Thailand fell from $13.4 billion in 1996 to –$6.9 billion in 1997, –$9.7 billion in 1998, and –$12.1 billion in 1999 (IIF database).

Korea

By the time of the September 1997 IMF-World Bank meetings in Hong Kong, there was a nervous relief in international financial circles that Thailand's crisis was being managed with little damage to the international economy. There had been significant declines in regional exchange rates (by 20–25 percent from the end of June to the end of September for Indonesia, Malaysia, and the Philippines, albeit only 3 percent for Korea), but there was not yet a sense of severe regional crisis. Soon, however, the force of contagion was to prove far more virulent than anticipated, as the largest and most industrialized economy in the region was swept into the crisis.

Korea had already experienced signs of difficulty in the spring of 1997 as problems from excess capacity and high corporate debt began to surface. Some large corporate bankruptcies had begun to reveal the exposure of the banking system. Korea's earlier entry into the Organization for Economic Cooperation and Development (OECD), along with some financial-sector liberalization, had contributed to a sharp run-up in borrowing from foreign banks. Short-term debt, in particular, had soared (from $39 billion at the end of 1993 to $97 billion at the end of 1996; IIF 1999c, 89).

The incipient regional crisis brought an intensified focus of attention on Korea and other major borrowers in the region. Through most of 1997 foreign lenders took comfort from the broad notion that the government was capable of rendering support if needed, especially to the Korean banking system. By the fourth quarter the uncertainty associated with the presidential election contributed to more pressure on the capital account. The most severe blow, however, came in early December, when it was revealed that the central bank had already committed the bulk of its reserves to foreign branches of Korean banks. With usable official reserves below $10 billion and short-term external debt in the range of $100 billion, there was an acute market realization that even if the Korean government wanted to support external obligations of domestic banks or corporations, it might not have the resources to do so. In the final days of December there was thus an incipient financial meltdown even though the president-elect had committed to undertaking a far-reaching IMF adjustment program (involving structural changes such as deleveraging by the highly indebted *chaebol* conglomerates).

Korea's economy is so large, and its involvement in international trade and finance so substantial, that its crisis qualified as one potentially posing a systemic threat even under a stringent definition. Given the experience with international official support for Mexico, as well as that for Thailand, it is not surprising that international official support was thus soon mobilized for Korea (and by this time the restrictions on the U.S. Exchange Stabilization Fund had expired). The magnitude had to be large to be convincing, especially because financial markets were highly focused on the large gap between short-term external debt and usable reserves. A package of $57 billion in official support was thus assembled, with $21 billion from the IMF, $14 billion from other multilateral sources, and $22 billion in "second line of defense" funds available from U.S. and other bilateral sources. Notably, the IMF opened a new lending window (the Supplementary Reserve Fund) to permit such large lending relative to Korea's small IMF quota, and it incorporated sizable and rising interest rates to provide a strong incentive for prompt repayment.

Announcement of the program by mid-December did not suffice to stem capital market pressures, however, perhaps in part because only $14 billion was to be available immediately. Reported reserves fell from $31 billion at the end of October to $21 billion by the end of December, and usable reserves were much lower at some $6 billion. The government was no longer able to hold its daily limit to the decline in the currency, and the won lost 31 percent of its value from the end of November to the end of December after having already lost a cumulative 22 percent during October and November.

It was in this crisis environment that U.S. policymakers and their Group of Seven (G7) counterparts adopted a significant shift in the crisis management strategy of the late 1990s. They approached the major international banks and conveyed the message that it was essential to halt the rapid runoff in short-term bank claims, or otherwise the whole program would be in jeopardy.[9] By early January the banks had agreed to hold short-term credit lines for a period of three months, and discussions began on the conversion of these claims into longer-term obligations. The announcement of the short-term rollover initiative, combined with a surge in the monthly trade balance from near zero in October-November to a surplus of $2 billion in December, broke the momentum of the crisis, and as some measure of calm returned the exchange rate partially reversed its sharp descent to appreciate by 12 percent from the end of December to the end of January 1998.

By March the exchange of short-term claims was in place. Some $22 billion in short-term international bank claims on Korean banks was exchanged into one- to three-year bonds guaranteed by the government and bearing spreads above U.S. Treasury interest rates for comparable maturities of 225 to 275 basis points above the London interbank offer rate (LIBOR), considerably higher than the original terms but below market rates at the time of the crisis. In effect, this coordinated conversion of short-term claims came the closest of any crisis management episode in the late 1990s to the London Club reschedulings of bank claims on Latin America in the 1980s. This outcome was in part possible because much of Korea's external

9. It is not clear, however, that officials told banks there would be no more official support without a bank package, and indeed the official package had already been constructed. Such conditioning was much more explicit in the Latin American reschedulings with IMF support in the 1980s.

debt was to banks. At the end of 1996, 78 percent of external debt was owed to banks and only 17 percent to bondholders and other nonbank private creditors (IIF 2000b), making Korea something of a throwback to earlier debt profiles in comparison with many other emerging market economies by the late 1990s.

The conversion deal was de jure voluntary, because there was no legal restriction against running down rather than converting credit lines, and there was no control limiting foreign exchange availability to repay short-term loans. Some smaller banks did indeed run down lines rather than convert them. The Korean negotiating position was viewed by the banks as tough, although the government guarantee was an enhancement and by 1999 the interest spreads on the conversion bonds again looked attractive. Overall, the outcome was relatively balanced and, if not fully voluntary, at least quasi-voluntary.

Brazil

In 1994 Brazil ended decades of increasingly high inflation by adopting a successful stabilization program built around the anchor of a quasi-fixed exchange rate, the real.[10] Underpinned by privatization, high real interest rates, and some fiscal adjustment, the Real Plan succeeded in halting inflation but left Brazil by 1998 with an arguably overvalued exchange rate and a relatively large current account deficit (4.3 percent of GDP in a large economy with a relatively modest export base). The strategy counted heavily on increased productivity to validate the exchange rate. Whether this would have worked in normal times is unclear, but in a context of global contagion from East Asia and then from the Russian crisis in August 1998, the strategy proved infeasible. From the end of June to the end of September reserves had fallen from $71 billion to $46 billion, and by January the exchange rate had collapsed despite the mounting of a large official support program.

Like Korea, Brazil was clearly one of the emerging market economies large enough to have a systemic impact. As market pressures mounted on Brazil following the Russia shock, and once the presidential election was safely won, the Cardoso government finally turned to the IMF for support in October. Once again the international official community assembled a "show of force" package of $42 billion, comprising $18 billion from the IMF, $9 billion from other multilateral sources, and $15 billion from the bilateral sources. The G7 intervention to support Brazil was widely viewed as drawing a line in the sand to halt global contagion at the borders of a country too important to lose.

---

10. Initially set at parity to the dollar in June 1994 but without a fixed-rate commitment, the real promptly strengthened to 0.85 by September but in March depreciated to 0.90 under contagion pressure from Mexico. Thereafter it crawled slowly at an annual average of about 7 percent during 1996–98, within a minimal ±0.5 percent band.

The IMF-supported adjustment package was centered on fiscal adjustment and notably did not break the existing exchange rate anchor. Although the subsequent collapse of the real no doubt contributed to evolution in G7 policy against large interventions to support fixed exchange rates, it is easy to understand the rationale for the program at the time. Brazil's past experience had shown a large inflationary response to depreciation of the exchange rate, and there were reasonable grounds for fearing that floating the real would be an invitation to inflationary destabilization. It is just conceivable that the program might have worked, but the proximate cause of its demise was a domestic political unraveling in December when a renegade state governor threatened to default on state debt.

After a brief attempt in early January to devalue modestly (8 percent) and widen the band but slow the crawl, the government was forced to float the currency, and by the end of January it stood 40 percent below its end-December level. It is a remarkable indicator of the subsequent success of the Brazilian adjustment program that twenty months later the real was almost 15 percent stronger than at its trough at the end of February 1999. Currency overshooting was curbed by tight monetary policy and fiscal adjustment, rather than being allowed to explode into a spiral of domestic inflation and further depreciation, as many had forecast at the time. Moreover, in part because Brazil's domestic banking system was relatively strong (Brazilians insist with justification that they experienced a *currency* crisis, not a *financial* crisis), Brazil's economy did not plunge into deep recession like those in the East Asian crises, although it experienced a second year in a row of near-zero growth before rebounding to growth of about 4 percent in 2000 as real interest rates fell sharply.

The story of private-sector involvement in resolving Brazil's crisis is highly illuminating on the delicate balance of confidence and psychology that permeates capital market relationships. Perhaps the most remarkable aspect of this story is that Brazilian authorities from the start were extremely reluctant to become involved in any arrangement that had the appearance of a 1980s-type rescheduling or concerted lending operation. Like Mexico, Brazil had simply paid too dearly during the 1980s to rebuild its credit reputation and reenter capital markets to be willing to throw away the credibility it had built up by suddenly putting the squeeze on creditors.

A luncheon for senior representatives of major banks in New York in November 1998, illustrates the point. At this event, organized by Citigroup's William Rhodes, a key figure in the restructuring programs of the 1980s and early 1990s and in Korea's 1998 loan conversion program, Brazilian Finance Minister Pedro Malan, and IMF Deputy Managing Director Stanley Fischer set forth the new Brazilian program. At the end of the presentation, most participants expressed the willingness of their institutions to hold credit lines. However, there was no explicit request by the Brazilian authorities for them to do so in an organized fashion.

By late January and through February and early March, nonetheless, Brazil was in acute currency crisis. Many analysts were convinced that Brazil's public debt was spiraling out of control. Continued payments pressures had pushed currency overshooting even further (with the end-February rate about 5 percent below that at the end of January). The time had come when a crucial boost to confidence was needed in the form of a more organized response. In March, in conjunction with a revised IMF program and in an environment in which a congress shocked by the currency collapse had finally moved to take important fiscal measures, the international banks agreed to a voluntary arrangement providing for the maintenance of trade and interbank credit lines, amounting to some $25 billion.

There was some ambiguity in the extent of the arrangement, which some announcements specified as holding through July but which some individual bank participants instead emphasized was strictly contingent on Brazil's meeting its policy obligations. Nonetheless, there was a strong boost to confidence from the signal that the international banks would hold lines, and the currency began to regain some of its losses. Brazilian authorities coordinated with the IMF in maintaining updated data on exposure of international banks, information that was communicated to national banking authorities, but it would appear that this process at most played an informational role, giving some measure of assurance to banks in various countries that their counterparts in other countries were continuing to honor the initiative, rather than serving as a vehicle for heavy-handed enforcement by the official sector.[11] Once again there was no legal restriction against banks' running down their credit lines, nor any corresponding exchange controls. Once again, some of the smaller banks exited.

By April 1999 Brazil had begun a surprisingly prompt return to capital markets. Several large Brazilian firms had reentered the international bond market, and by the end of April the government had issued a sovereign Eurobond for $2 billion (at a spread of 675 basis points). Consider a counterfactual in which instead Brazil, the IMF, and the G7 had all decided in October of 1998 that Brazil should ask its bondholders and bank creditors to reschedule their claims, along the lines of 1980s debt reschedulings but this time embracing some rescheduling of bonds, or an exchange operation for them. It is almost inconceivable that if Brazil had chosen this course, it would have been back to the market by April of 1999. Brazil is perhaps the clearest case for the superiority of voluntary arrangements for private-sector involvement in crisis resolution over dirigiste alternatives. Brazil's authorities were right to be highly reluctant all along to be seen as seeking any type of a coercive rescheduling.

---

11. Such information sharing has the property of overcoming the key obstacle to collective action in the "prisoner's dilemma" negative-sum game, the fact that each prisoner questioned in isolation does not know whether his accomplice has confessed.

6.1.5   Debt Workouts in More Severe Cases

Mexico, Korea, Brazil, and to a lesser extent Thailand serve as the classic cases for successful adjustment and restoration of confidence and market access, made possible by large official intervention, forceful domestic policy corrections, and (in Korea and Brazil) some arrangement for voluntary or quasi-voluntary private-sector participation. Some other conspicuous cases have been less successful, largely because they were further to the right along the horizontal axis (insolvency probability) of the Bagehot curve. In some underlying sense the proper way to organize private-sector involvement is less interesting in such cases, because from the private creditor's viewpoint this is broadly a question of "choosing one's poison." Most of these cases involve some form of rescheduling or exchange of instruments, and these involve a discontinuous breach of a key threshold in terms of credit reputation rather than slightly more intense versions of the voluntary arrangements. Even so, there is interest in identifying what types of approaches may be less unfavorable than others. The common thread among the workout cases is a more profound domestic political incoherence than in the illiquidity cases discussed above, even though political strains played important roles in those crises as well.

Indonesia

Although Indonesia had many financial and macroeconomic distortions of its own, its financial crisis was sparked by contagion, as the country was forced to let the exchange rate fall 14 percent in August 1997 one month after Thailand devalued. The crisis was slower to develop, but ultimately much more profound than those of regional neighbors. Within a year the currency had lost 85 percent of its value. Although a modicum of stability had been restored by then, political disarray and recurrent bouts of currency instability have continued since. As an example of the salience of political factors, an exodus of capital of ethnic Chinese families and businesses as the Suharto era came to a close was a major source of pressure. Similarly, regional separatist strife, intense factionalism, and doubts about whether Suharto-related interests will cede power peacefully have hindered restoration of confidence.

A key feature of Indonesia's external debt was that the bulk of debt to private creditors was owed by the domestic private sector: banks and corporations.[12] This meant that when domestic firms faced extreme losses, as they did with the shocks from sharp currency devaluation and to some extent high interest rates, the question was not so much whether the Indone-

---

12. At the end of 1997 the government owed $60 billion in external debt, but this was almost all to official sources ($19 billion multilateral, $41 billion bilateral). In contrast, domestic corporations owed $66 billion, and banks owed $17 billion (IIF database).

sian government would orchestrate a special arrangement (even though it did) but whether foreign creditors could effectively realize what was left of their claims by pursuing domestic bankruptcy procedures. It soon became evident that lax bankruptcy laws and, especially, enforcement, meant that the latter course was not effective.

In October 1997 the government abandoned its longtime policy of avoiding IMF support and entered into an agreement providing a total of about $34 billion, of which $10 billion was from the IMF, $8 billion from the World Bank and Asian Development Bank (ADB), $5 billion from Japan and Singapore, and $3 billion from the United States. By early 1998 the government was widely seen as not delivering on its policy adjustment commitments, however, and instability intensified through May when Suharto resigned. The policy slippage meant that by mid-1998 only about $4 billion in official disbursements had actually occurred (IIF 1999c, 54). In 1998 GDP fell by 13 percent.

Private-sector involvement in resolving the crisis was unlikely on a voluntary basis under these circumstances. One key government decision was whether to guarantee domestic bank debt, including debt to foreign creditors. After severe capital flight following the closure of sixteen banks in November 1997 with minimal guarantee of depositors and creditors (a decision urged by the IMF, apparently in its concern to avoid the moral hazard seen to have occurred in Thailand), the government was forced to guarantee the rest of bank obligations.

Still, the bulk of private foreign claims was on corporations. Here, the government made the key decision that it would not socialize the debt (unlike the partial socialization of similar private obligations in Mexico in the early 1980s under Fideicomiso para la Cobertura de Riesgos Cambiarios [FICORCA]). Instead, it set up an umbrella organization for private debt workouts (Jakarta Initiative and the Indonesian Debt Restructuring Agency [INDRA]) offering only a minimal mechanism for hedging exchange risk on repayments. Although in principle this detached posture was unexceptionable and was consistent with minimizing moral hazard, when applied in a sociojuridical context of minimal capacity for creditor bankruptcy recovery, and following a government-sponsored temporary pause in debt servicing in early 1998, the result in practice was widespread default and prolonged arrears. Even so, about half of foreign claims on domestic corporations were on subsidiaries of multinational firms, and this half has largely been serviced. Of the other half, owed by Indonesian firms, the great bulk still remains in default, despite frameworks providing for mediation and some tax and other incentives for restructuring. The weakness of bankruptcy mechanisms, and hence the lack of debtor incentive to reach agreement, has been the basic reason.

With the eventual help of substantial foreign assistance, reduced political uncertainty after presidential elections in the third quarter of 1999, and higher oil prices, the Indonesian economy managed to halt the plunge of output by 1999 and returned to modest growth in 2000 (but with output still far below 1997 levels). The environment of lingering defaults means, however, that rather than returning quickly to normal capital market access, Indonesia has continued to face negative net flows of bank and nonbank lending (IIF 2000a).

Russia

Russia's crisis in August 1998 was much more the consequence of protracted failure to address structural economic distortions than a sudden liquidity crisis precipitated by external contagion. A succession of IMF programs of economic adjustment and reform starting in 1992 had failed to address the core problems of chronic fiscal weakness, large capital flight, weak property rights, and dominant influence of interest groups ("oligarchs"). Foreign investors had nonetheless pursued the high returns in ruble treasury bills (GKOs) and a surging stock market through mid-1997, in part because of the belief that G7 governments could not afford politically to let Russia fail. Increasingly these returns, and especially IMF programs premised on continued private foreign financing of large fiscal deficits, had "Ponzi scheme" characteristics of unsustainability. Thus, by mid-1998 treasury bills were yielding over 60 percent even though the official exchange rate crawl was minimal.

Pressure on Russia began to mount in the fourth quarter of 1997 as some contagion from East Asia did contribute to a decline in equity and government bond prices, and by the first half of 1998, a drop in oil prices aggravated prospects. It became increasingly doubtful that the government would be able to roll over its short-term external debt, which was more than twice as large as external reserves. In July a new IMF agreement was reached, providing for $17 billion in support, but even the first tranche was curtailed because the Duma had failed to pass key fiscal reforms. Some in private markets also doubted the seriousness of the program, in part because it delayed fiscal adjustment until the following year and was premised on continuation of private capital inflows. As capital market pressures continued, Russian authorities sought additional support, but G7 authorities were unprepared to do more because of the absence of a sufficient Russian political consensus for reform. In mid-August the government devalued the ruble, unilaterally restructured its domestic (GKO) debt, suspended payments (and soon defaulted) on former Soviet debt (which had already been rescheduled in 1997), and froze payments on private-sector external debt and forward exchange contracts.

The workout that followed was lengthy and often acrimonious. The government seemed to give preferential treatment to domestic holders of GKOs, for example, by allowing domestic banks to use them as collateral against new loans from the central bank. By mid-1999 negotiations had developed within a "London Club" framework, with the commercial bank structure from the past somewhat extended to include investment banks. Such financial institutions as asset managers and mutual funds, which held a sizable amount of the obligations, were not at the negotiating table.

Russia reached agreement with the London Club by early 2000, in a context of increased political cohesion with the replacement of Mr. Yeltsin by Mr. Putin, and on the strength of the sharp upswing in world oil prices and hence Russia's fiscal prospects. The present value of former Soviet debt was cut by about 30 percent (but upgraded to government debt instead of obligations by Sberbank). Critics of the process pointed to the lengthy negotiations that had been required. However, the negotiation process did require that the Russian authorities formally take into account the views of the creditors, or at least some of them. In contrast, the "unilateral exchange offers" in other recent cases (Ukraine, Ecuador) did not do so.

By the third quarter of 2000, Russia's economy had shown surprising strength, with GDP likely to grow 6 percent or more for the year. Spurred by import substitution, growth the previous year had reached 3 percent, following the economy's 5 percent decline in 1998. Russia also managed to avoid the hyperinflation some had feared in the event of devaluation and default, as a consequence of severe wage compression, a freeze in utility prices, tight economic policy, and the fact that a collapse of domestic banks contributed to curbing the money supply. The economy's recovery in 2000 was closely linked to that of oil prices, however. Large capital flight has continued (at rates of $20–25 billion annually in 1998–2000), and net private capital inflows—which reached a peak of $37 billion in 1997—collapsed to near zero by 1999 and less than $2 billion (mainly direct investment) in 2000. Although more fundamental factors such as insufficient enterprise restructuring would have constrained Russia's economic performance in any event, tougher conditions on earlier international support to prompt faster reform and—especially—a more cooperative approach to external debt restructuring might have left Russia in a much stronger economic position, and one much less dependent on strong oil prices.

There is little doubt that Russia's default in August 1998 marked a negative watershed for emerging markets more generally. For the first time in the decade, a major emerging market economy defaulted and sought sovereign debt forgiveness, rather than merely entering a period of illiquidity and taking forceful adjustment measures to restore confidence. The spillover is evident in lending spreads. Thus, the JPMorgan Emerging Markets Bond Index (EMBI+) index of spreads on Latin American bonds, which stood at about 500 basis points in mid-1998, surged to 1,500 basis points in August 1998 with Russia's crisis and did not fall below 1,000 basis points until November 1999 (IIF database).

As for lessons from Russia for private-sector involvement, the main one was that even geopolitical salience was no assurance against collapse. Any lessons about the optimal approach to postdefault workout are at best ambiguous. A more fundamental lesson is that the most certain way to assure private-sector involvement in crisis resolution—unilateral default—is also the worst way to do so, if the country seeks early reentry to capital markets.

Ecuador

Ecuador's persistent political problems were not unlike those of Indonesia and Russia. One president was ousted by the legislature in 1997 on grounds of "mental incapacity"; another was deposed in a brief military coup in early 1999. There have been sharp political divisions among interior ("altiplano"), coastal, and indigenous-group interests. In the past two years, there have been four different finance ministers.

Spillover from Russia in late 1998 compounded Ecuador's economic difficulties that year from El Niño weather damage as well as low commodity prices. A growing fiscal deficit and legislative resistance to fiscal correction added to the adverse investment climate. As external credit dried up, the currency depreciated sharply, external reserves fell about two-thirds from mid-1998 to early 1999, and interest rates reached 80 percent and more (compared to inflation that reached about 40 percent). With increasing problems in the banking sector, by March 1999 the government froze bank deposits.

It was in this environment of economic unraveling that the IMF appears to have chosen to make Ecuador a guinea pig[13] for a more aggressive approach to bailing in private creditors. There had been escalating political pressure within industrial countries to stop bailing out private creditors, and the public sector appears to have been tempted to try out new approaches on smaller countries where the systemic consequences would be limited if the outcome proved adverse.

Arguably, Ecuador might have been able to avoid default on Brady and Eurobonds. Out of $1.7 billion in principal due on public-sector external debt over 2000–01, only $38 million was payable on Brady bonds and none on Eurobonds (Ecuador 2000, 83). Of the $1.5 billion due in interest, $606 million was payable on Brady bonds and $110 million on Eurobonds. Thus, these two sources of private claims comprised only 23 percent of public external debt service due over this period. In contrast, principal and interest payments to the IMF and other multilaterals accounted for 54 percent, and those owed to governments represented 16 percent. Debt service to commercial banks and on suppliers' credits comprised the remaining 7 percent.

Public debt service due on Brady and Eurobonds in 2000–01 amounted to only about 6 percent of prospective earnings on exports of goods and services, and a forceful adjustment program coupled with IMF support and Paris Club relief might have sufficed to turn around private investor confidence. However, by the second quarter of 1999, Ecuadoran authorities ap-

---

13. This is the term one of the more senior members of the board of directors of the IMF used in private discussions more than a year later.

pear to have been under the impression that IMF and Paris Club support would only be forthcoming under circumstances in which Brady and Eurobond payments were also restructured.[14] In terms of what is on the public record, in effect the IMF blessed the concept by approving in principle a September 1999 standby agreement with Ecuador that was premised on the cash-flow outlook that included the restructuring of these instruments.

The notion of restructuring Brady bonds seemed curious at the time. It involved questions of equity, considering that holders had already forgiven 40 percent of their original claims when Ecuador reached a Brady deal with foreign banks in 1995. It also raised questions of public-sector memory, considering that the instrument itself had been designed to resolve the 1980s debt problem through a promise of exchanging a new secure instrument for earlier bank claims, trading off part of the claim in return for the reduced risk.[15] The official sector's decision to sanction Ecuador's default and restructuring of Bradies represented, consciously or otherwise, a decision to exterminate this type of instrument as a credible option for use in future crises.

At the end of August 1999 Ecuador did default on part of its Brady debt, and a prompt move by holders to "accelerate" quickly derailed the hope that this debt could for a time be serviced out of its rolling interest collateral, with the effect of escalating the default to all types of Brady debt as well as Eurobond debt. In part because Ecuador's economic policies were in disarray and the IMF program was delayed, far from enjoying a respite, the country experienced an intensifying economic crisis. By March, 2000 the new finance minister had declared the decision to default a "catastrophic error" (Reuters Market News Service, 28 March 2000).

The impact on emerging markets more broadly was modest at worst, although the default did appear to widen the spread between Brady bond spreads and those on other obligations. In broad terms, the capital markets treated Ecuador as a quarantined case rather than a harbinger for such countries as Brazil and Argentina. Nonetheless, the episode has left a sour taste among many in the private sector that has curbed the appetite for lending to countries where there could be "international financial institution risk" because of potential Paris Club pressure for comparability or IMF pressure for private rescheduling where multilateral claims bulk large.[16]

The particular workout modality eventually chosen by Ecuador, once it

14. Based on numerous discussions, including one with a ministerial-level Ecuadoran official.

15. Brady bonds typically forgave 35–40 percent of original claims, in exchange for a thirty-year bullet principal guarantee using U.S. Treasury zero-coupon bonds as collateral, along with collateral against twelve to eighteen months' interest due. The collateral has typically been in escrow with the New York Federal Reserve Bank.

16. Referring to the recent "bail-in risk," a representative of a major asset management company stated to the 2000 Annual Membership Meeting of the Institute of International Finance that his institution was no longer willing to undertake exposure in countries where IMF and Paris Club claims are relatively large, and observed that the heightened risk from official bail-in pressure had done major damage to second-tier emerging market economies.

had made the decision to default, was the unilateral exchange offer. In this approach, the country and its investment banking advisors informally take soundings of major holders of the bonds in question to arrive at an offer they consider to have a good chance of being accepted by a critical mass of, say, 85 percent or more. This "exchange of instruments" circumvents the array of difficulties likely to be involved in an attempt to enter into negotiations with bondholders on rescheduling the obligations due under the existing instruments.

In Ecuador's case, the exchange offer was designed "to provide participants with a significant pick-up in market value over the current trading prices of their Existing Bonds" (Ecuador 2000, 3).[17] It involved a 40 percent cut in the face value of Brady bonds, but with a significant offset of a partial immediate cash payment. Thus, $3.9 billion in new bonds (mostly thirty-year), plus cash payments of about $1 billion (of which about one-third was of arrears), were exchanged for $6.6 billion in (mainly) Brady and Eurobonds.

Although the exchange offer was well received, in that some 97 percent of holders accepted (well above the 85 percent threshold sought by the government), questions remain about this modality. Some substantial institutional holders of the bonds were not consulted in the preparation of the exchange offer. Like other exchange offers, it was essentially "preemptive" in nature, with only two weeks allowed for bondholders to respond to the offer. In such circumstances there is a take-it-or-leave-it dynamic that tends to make the high incidence of acceptance somewhat misleading as an indication of creditor attitude.

By the time of the exchange, Ecuador had made a somewhat more promising start on its program of dollarization than might have been expected, and a new IMF program had been adopted (in April). Including other multilateral lending, the support program amounted to $2 billion over three years, or 14 percent of one year's GDP. High oil prices have also helped the economy. However, unless the country's internal political environment shifts toward greater coherence, making possible more sustained fiscal adjustment and progress on banking-sector and other structural reforms, Ecuador could face renewed difficulties despite the debt restructuring and official support. For their part, private creditors would seem unlikely to return to the country soon, having been burned twice.

Pakistan, Romania, Ukraine

Three other recent cases warrant review as instances in which the public sector has pressed governments to restructure obligations to private creditors, or otherwise to press them to participate in crisis resolution.

---

17. In the event, market prices of Ecuador's Brady bonds rose on average by about 20 percent following announcement of the offer.

In early 1999 the Paris Club told Pakistan that its comparability of treatment principle would require that Pakistan restructure its sovereign bonds in order to obtain rescheduling of bilateral debt. These included a total of about $600 million in notes due in 1999 through 2000. At the time there was concern that this prospective first instance of Eurobond rescheduling would cast a severe pall on the international bond market. As it turned out, Ecuador's default preceded Pakistan's exchange offer. Although both probably had some adverse effect on international bond markets, the effect was at most modest.

In November 1999, Pakistan offered to exchange its bonds for others to mature in 2002–05, bearing 10 percent interest. More than 95 percent of holders accepted the exchange offer by the closing date in late December. One reason for the favorable response is likely to have been that the exchange did not seek forgiveness.

Pakistan's use of the exchange offer modality was informative, because its bonds were under U.K. law and so could have been rescheduled with consent of a qualified (high) majority of holders. In contrast, bonds under U.S. law typically require unanimous consent. As discussed below, the issue of requiring qualified majority rescheduling clauses in bonds has been one of the more prominent in the debate on involving the private sector; yet it seems to have been irrelevant in actual practice in the Pakistan case.

Romania managed with great effort (exchange rate depreciation and fiscal tightening that induced resident capital reflows) to pay off some $700 million in Eurobonds due in the second quarter of 1999. However, the IMF program that restarted in July of that year had as a condition that the country mobilize $450 million in new private-sector inflows. This was not in the context of Paris Club comparability, because Paris Club debt was small and there was no rescheduling in prospect. Instead, the condition reflected the intensifying pressure at the time for inducing private-sector "burden sharing."

After the release of an initial tranche of about $80 million, the IMF program was suspended in September because Romania only managed to arrange about $100 million in a one-year club loan from fourteen banks, far below the target, and also because of disagreement on the 2000 budget. However, by June 2000 the IMF agreement was renewed, with the IMF citing "the large reduction in the current account deficit [and] the sharp correction in the fiscal deficit" as grounds for the reinstatement of the $535 million standby program. At the same time, the government paid off the club loan of June 1999 and announced it would also pay off another club loan of $64 million dating from December 1999.[18] Repayment without announcement of other new initiatives for private support signaled that the new IMF agreement was no longer conditioned on a burden-sharing target for

---

18. Data from Reuters: Rompres news agency 13 June 2000; Rompres 27 June 2000.

private-sector involvement. This may have represented a straw in the wind indicating that the IMF considered its series of small-country experiments in this direction during the preceding year as less than successful.

In early 2000 in the face of a severe external payments problem reflecting in part persistent fiscal imbalance, Ukraine suspended payments on its external debt except that owed to multilateral institutions and announced its intention to restructure debt to private and bilateral creditors. In early February the government announced an exchange offer to convert $2.8 billion in bonds falling due in 2000–01 into new bonds with seven years' maturity and two years' grace and bearing 10–11 percent interest. The offer gave holders until mid-April to respond. The response was favorable and met the 85 percent threshold.

Workout Lessons

The first feature that stands out in the list of workout cases just reviewed is that, in contrast to the four success cases examined in the previous section, underlying economic strength and creditworthiness were generally far weaker. This amounts to an informal empirical verification of the Bagehot curve notion relating intervention policy to illiquidity versus insolvency: large, temporary official lending works to restore confidence when underlying creditworthiness is strong and the problem is a transitory shock; the opposite outcome of forced rescheduling is likely to be unavoidable where underlying creditworthiness is weak.

Table 6.2 provides evidence that supports the intuitive sense that the list of debt reschedulers and bond exchangers is populated by weaker

Table 6.2   **Institutional Investor Country Risk Rating**

Country	Date	Rating	Global average
Mexico	Sept. 1994	46.1	37.5
Thailand	Mar. 1997	61.1	40.1
Korea	Sept. 1997	69.7	41.0
Brazil	Sept. 1998	38.0	41.1
Average		53.7	n.a.
Indonesia	Mar. 1997	51.6	40.1
Russia	Mar. 1998	31.2	41.2
Ecuador	Mar. 1999	25.5	40.1
Pakistan	Mar. 1999	20.4	40.1
Romania	Mar. 1999	31.2	40.1
Ukraine	Sept. 1999	18.7	41.5
Average		29.8	n.a.

Source: Institutional Investor, various issues. Average rating for all countries included in *Institutional Investor* annual surveys.

Note: n.a. = not applicable.

economies than the list of countries that achieved a quick turnaround without major rescheduling. The table reports the country risk rating of the economy in question in the most recent semiannual compilation of the magazine *Institutional Investor* prior to the financial crisis in question. Running from zero to 100 (and with the United States rated typically at about 93), these ratings are based on a weighted survey of approximately 100 banks, asset management companies, and economists.

As expected, the average rating for the four success cases of major international support stands considerably higher, at 53.7, than that for the six workout cases,[19] at 29.8. The only anomaly is the case of Indonesia, whose relatively high rating probably represents the fact that many of the *Institutional Investor* survey respondents were referring to sovereign rather than general country risk, and Indonesia has not defaulted on its sovereign debt.

A crucial lesson from this dichotomy between two classes of country crises is that policymakers should not conflate workout-type solutions with market-resilient countries. Remedies that officials consider appropriate for an Ecuador would likely be inappropriate for a Brazil, because Ecuador's problem was much closer to insolvency than Brazil's, which was closer to illiquidity.

Among the workout experiences, an important pattern that seems to be emerging is the debtor preference for the "unilateral exchange offer" over rescheduling of the existing instrument, at least where the debt is primarily in bonds. In this approach the debtor "offers" to exchange a newly created obligation in exchange for the existing claims. At least in principle, the holder of the existing claim is not obliged to accept the new substitute instrument, but in practice the terms are set to make it likely that a large critical mass of existing claimholders will judge it prudent to accept the exchange instrument rather than holding out in hopes of forcing payment of the original claim instead. (This leaves ambiguity about whether a minority of holders refusing the exchange offer can collect on the original terms, and correspondingly leaves a risk of lawsuits by such holders.) Pakistan, Ecuador, and Ukraine used the approach of the exchange offer to swap new instruments for outstanding bonds. Russia used the alternative approach of a London Club negotiation, but much of its debt in question was to banks.

The remarkable speed with which the unilateral exchange offers have been completed shows that there is a major historical difference between dealing with bond defaults today and in the last major episode—the 1930s. Electronic communication today means it is easy to obtain prompt replies from thousands of bondholders, whereas lengthy delays were a problem in the 1930s.

---

19. Romania is not technically a workout case because it did not reschedule or exchange, but it is classed with the workout group here because it too was subject to an international official attempt at enforcement of private-sector burden sharing.

A potentially serious problem with the unilateral exchange offer, however, is that so far it does not seem to have been implemented in a manner that provided for widespread consultation with major holders. To some extent the risks associated with the lack of consultation have been mitigated by making the offer more attractive than terms consistent with the going secondary-market price. However, lack of consultation would seem to increase the eventual risk of lawsuits. It is too early to tell whether legal challenges will prove to be a drawback of the unilateral exchange offers.

One aspect of the rapid acceptance of the exchange offers has perhaps been that much of the debt in question had already been sold off to vulture funds and other speculative investors. For them, any increase in the terms from the secondary-market price equivalent might have been viewed as attractive. In terms of policy, however, it would be inappropriate to give much emphasis to this consideration as a basis for judging exchange offers (especially those involving forgiveness) as favorable outcomes. Essentially, the fulfillment of the obligation should be judged against its original value, not against the level to which it has fallen under distress.

Another pattern seems to be that the quarantine effect has dominated the contagion effect of small-country bond restructuring on the international capital market. There had been legitimate concern by mid-1999 that the official sector's seeming insistence on bond rescheduling in Pakistan and Ecuador would cause severe adverse spillover to the bond market generally for emerging market economies, because as a class bonds had not yet entered into significant restructurings. This de facto exempt status had reflected the small portion of debt owed in bonds in the Latin American debt crisis of the 1980s and, hence, the practice in that episode of rescheduling bank claims but not bonds. As it turned out, the Ecuadorian default and Pakistan's exchange did not cause a sudden and severe fallout for emerging market bonds globally. However, as suggested above, the persistence of relatively high bond spreads suggests that the official-sector pressure that contributed to the spread of restructuring to bonds may have slowed the pace of recovery in emerging capital markets.

The seeming ease of bond exchanges also contradicts the great concern in much of the debate on crisis resolution about the need for changes in official practice and even legal structure to deal with what had been perceived as severe obstacles to bond rescheduling, including such mechanisms as collective action clauses in bonds and "stay of litigation" powers for the IMF. These issues are addressed briefly below.

6.1.6   Rules, Case-by-Case Determination, and Principles

One of the central issues in international policy on private-sector involvement in crisis resolution has been the debate on whether there should be clearly codified rules about how the private sector should participate, what the public sector will be prepared to do, and whether each episode should be handled on a case-by-case basis. Broadly, the Canadians and Europeans have tended to favor a rules-based approach, and U.S. authorities have tended to favor the case-by-case approach.

The search for rules of crisis resolution seems primarily to reflect the political backlash against what appeared to be large public support programs that bailed out private creditors. The type of rules that some in the official sector seem to have in mind are of the following sort: IMF and official support should not exceed normal magnitudes of, say, two or three times IMF quota; private creditors should reschedule if the Paris Club reschedules; private creditors should somehow contribute new money, or at least not be receiving net repayments, when public lending is taking place; and so forth.

There is an inherent problem in spelling out rules for private- and public-sector involvement in crisis resolution, which is essentially the problem of "time inconsistency." The crux of the problem is that rigidly preannounced policies may adversely distort future behavior, even if those particular policies might be appropriate to apply in an actual contemporaneous event. In central banking, for example, authorities are loath to spell out in a precodified set of rules that they will (or will not) support banks that are "too big to fail." If they specifically say they will do so, the result will be a marginal distortion toward ever larger and fewer banks. If they specifically say they will not do so, they encounter a problem of credibility loss when and if they do so in practice. Thus, it is difficult to imagine an effective set of rules written in advance that would have authorized the Federal Reserve Bank of New York to press large institutions to support Long-Term Capital Management in 1998 lest its collapse severely destabilize markets.

In short, rules will tend to be unduly constraining or send potentially perverse signals affecting future behavior. In contrast, debt crisis resolution has traditionally been handled on a case-by-case basis. This was the watchword of debt strategy in the 1980s, even if de facto a great majority of the case outcomes wound up looking very much like each other. A case-by-case strategy meant nothing was guaranteed, but nothing was excluded. Its framework allows for the "constructive ambiguity" that is helpful in central banking intervention.

A rules-oriented strategy could also undermine the Eaton-Gersovitz conditions for sovereign lending. If the rules book turned out to look like a relatively accommodating official framework for sovereign default, the consequences might be a few rounds of relatively comfortable defaults followed by a long stretch of minimal capital flows to emerging markets.

The appropriate resolution of this policy debate would seem to lie in recognition that (a) the case-by-case approach is inescapable; (b) it should nonetheless be applied within a broad framework of principles; and (c) efforts to spell out "rules" applying these principles are likely to be subject to the time-inconsistency problem and should be avoided.

The principles for private- and public-sector involvement in crisis resolution that are most likely to be successful in restoring and maintaining capital market access would seem to include the following broad precepts.[20] First, private-sector participation should be on as voluntary and market-oriented a basis as possible given the circumstances. Second, optimal public-sector involvement may sometimes involve much larger, temporary support than traditionally envisioned in IMF programs and can appropriately be extended at higher lending prices (as in the IMF's new SRF). Third, a judgment of the country's position along a continuum between a pure liquidity problem, on the one hand, and a fundamental insolvency problem, on the other, should be the main determinant of whether large temporary official support is offered or whether instead primary reliance is placed on restructuring private-sector claims. Fourth, no one type of private claims (such as bonds) should automatically enjoy exempt or senior status, although such factors as whether the claims have already been restructured (e.g., Brady bonds) or whether their disruption would undermine economic activity (e.g., trade credits) should be taken into account in designing an equitable and effective restructuring package. Fifth, private creditors bear responsibility for their own risks and do not expect the public sector to make good their losses. Sixth, however, the public sector should act forcefully when it is in a position to orchestrate a positive-sum outcome that benefits the economies in question and helps minimize creditor losses (and maximize chances of return to voluntary capital markets) at no or minimal expected cost to taxpayers. Seventh, where debt restructuring is unavoidable, the sovereign obligor should consult fully with the creditors.

Other principles can no doubt be added. In evaluating either principles or more detailed rules, it is important to go through the counterfactual exercise of seeing whether the global economy (and that of the country in question) would have been well served if the proposed approaches had been enforced in each of the major crisis episodes of the recent years. It would be counterproductive to adopt for the future rules that would have made things worse in the past, because similar episodes could once again confront policymakers, who would then be forced to choose between disregarding the rules and causing suboptimal outcomes.

6.1.7 Further Considerations

This paper has outlined the evolving structure of emerging capital markets, set forth the conceptual framework for policy toward involvement of the private sector in crisis resolution, reviewed the major crisis episodes of the late 1990s as well as the spate of more recent small-country workouts,

---

20. Also see IIF (2001), issued subsequent to the preparation of this paper.

and considered patterns as well as implications for the debate on rules versus case-by-case approaches. A handful of specific issues warrant further comment to complement this review.

Future Evolution of Lending Structure

There are increasing signs that the shift in emerging markets lending from banks toward bonds will continue. It is telling that even if the crisis economies are excluded (five East Asian economies, Russia, and Brazil), net bank lending to the other emerging market economies plunged from about $30 billion annually in 1996–97 to close to zero in 1998–2000 (Cline 2000a). In contrast, net bond and other nonbank lending to the noncrisis economies held up well, at an average of about $35 billion annually in 1998–2000 compared to about $43 billion in 1996–97. Similarly, the most recent forecasts of the IIF (2000a) place nonbank flows to major emerging market economies still ahead of net bank flows in 2001 (at $36 billion versus $16 billion, respectively), even though the rebound of the latter will finally turn them positive after three years of negative net flows.

There are two structural reasons why this shift may continue. First, increasingly the large international banks appear to be concluding that shareholder value is better served by concentrating on fee-based income of an investment-bank nature (e.g., helping launch and sell securities) than by traditional balance sheet lending. Although not limited to emerging markets, this phenomenon contributes to the shift away from bank claims toward bonds in these markets. Second, the inherently high leverage of banks (whose Tier 1 equity capital is only 4 percent of risk-weighted assets under the existing Basel rules) makes them potentially more subject to retrenchment in sectors where risk is perceived to have increased than is the case for less leveraged investors. The interaction of the escalation of perceived risk in emerging markets lending with the degree of leverage may help explain why bank lending to the noncrisis emerging market economies fell off much more than did nonbank (mainly bond) lending in recent years. As the heightened perception of emerging markets risk seems unlikely to disappear soon, the leverage consideration could continue to constrain bank lending to these markets.

Despite this likely evolution, banks could continue to play a key role in helping resolve short-term liquidity crises through initiatives to maintain credit lines, as in the Korean and Brazilian cases. The share of banks in short-term debt (including trade credit) is likely to remain considerably higher than their share in longer-term debt, and, as noted, the longer-term repayments owed to bondholders do not tend to be the proximate problem in short-term liquidity crises. Continued evolution toward bonds would, however, increase their role in the resolution of more intransigent crises where longer-term restructuring is necessary.

Bond Clauses, Stay of Litigation

This in turn raises the by now familiar issue of whether public policy should require the inclusion of "collective action" or rescheduling clauses in bonds, to facilitate their restructuring if needed. Some (e.g., Portes 2000) have emphasized that this is the key reform needed in emerging markets lending.

Recent experience seems to suggest, however, that the traditional arguments for this reform may no longer be compelling. Prompt communication to numerous, dispersed holders has effectively been carried out in the bond exchanges, suggesting that technology has superseded some of the informational and organizational problems of the past in bond restructuring. The exchange offers have also not been held up by rogue bondholders, and the approach of providing a new instrument in exchange for the existing bond appears so far to have successfully circumvented the difficult challenges that would have to be overcome in formal rescheduling discussions even where a qualified majority rather than unanimity is required.

There thus would seem to remain considerable weight on the main reason to avoid an international regime of mandatory rescheduling clauses for emerging market bonds: Generalized adoption of such clauses could convey the impression that the international official community would lean toward facilitating default when difficulties arise. This would tend to undermine the Eaton-Gersovitz dynamic of default pain as quasi-collateral and hence curb flows of new bond lending and increase spreads.[21] Instead, the flexibility provided by qualified majority bond rescheduling clauses could be obtained by those sovereigns that chose to include such clauses, probably initially at a spreads premium.[22]

For the same conceptual reason, incorporation into the IMF's Articles the authority to impose a stay of litigation, as suggested by former IMF Managing Director Michel Camdessus, would tend to undermine emerging capital markets. This innovation too would send a signal that default could be facilitated by the official sector. The same problem is inherent in most proposals to create some type of international agency to provide at the international level bankruptcy workouts analogous to those present domestically. Such proposals typically fail to recognize the fundamental difference between bankruptcy recovery potential where there is tangible collateral and where there is not.

21. See Cline (2000b) for an interpretation of the results of Eichengreen and Mody (2000) that concludes their empirical tests on U.S.- versus U.K.-issued bonds should not alter this view.

22. The call to G7 countries to include rescheduling clauses in their own sovereign bonds as a means of removing any special stigma to emerging market governments' doing so seems highly unrealistic and would be especially troublesome for such countries as Japan, where public debt has escalated sharply relative to GDP.

Contingent Lending Arrangements

One of the instruments that at first looked promising as a mechanism for involving the private sector in crisis resolution has made little progress in the past three years: contingent lending arrangements. Under such arrangements, the country pays a commitment fee for assured access to credit up to an agreed amount in the event that the country wishes to draw on the credit. Mexico and Argentina have been the most conspicuous cases of such arrangements, but Mexico drew down its line of credit in September 1998 (to considerable acrimony from bank creditors, who felt that by then the terms were too generous; for a discussion see IIF 1999c, 35–36) and has not replaced it.

The underlying calculus of contingency financing would seem compellingly advantageous for a country that could thereby reduce the probability of a financial crisis, simply because small changes in that probability would be operating on a large economic base (GDP). It may nonetheless be difficult politically to enter into contingency financing arrangements in which creditors insist on particularly high spreads if the line is drawn upon. Perhaps a more fundamental reason why contingent credit lines have not thrived is that many countries have shifted from fixed to floating exchange rates and have run off the high short-term debt that was more typical prior to the crises of the late 1990s. An economy with a floating exchange rate and low short-term debt is less likely to need, or benefit from, additional liquidity from contingent credit lines. Correspondingly, it may be no accident that the principal such arrangement currently remains that of Argentina, which not only has a contingent line of about $7 billion with about a dozen banks, but also has a rigidly fixed exchange rate under its currency board.[23]

6.1.8   Conclusion

It has been said that farmers should know the difference between shearing their sheep and slaughtering them. Involving the private sector in crisis resolution is the art of knowing this type of difference. Too heavy a hand by the official sector to force private-sector involvement can transit quickly into a once-for-all zero sum transfer from the creditor to the debtor followed by a persistent cutoff in future credit. The opposite extreme of com-

---

23. For its part, the official-sector Contingent Credit Lines facility created in 1999 for prequalifying countries with strong policies has remained dormant. The central problem seems to be that even after qualifying and signing up for the facility, a country might subsequently not be able to receive funds from it because at the time of request its policies would be judged to have deteriorated; or, worse, the country might be disqualified from the facility, prompting heightened market concerns upon notice of the disqualification. It is unclear that changes adopted in the facility in September 2000 (making the degree of monitoring less intensive than under other IMF facilities and providing more automatic access in the event of a crisis) will suffice to attract entrants, because the risk of disqualification remains.

plete laissez-faire toward private creditors coupled with major official support invites public criticism that the official sector is bailing out private creditors.

Given the salient role of mobile capital in modern capital markets, it is crucial for authorities to distinguish between cases of transitory illiquidity and those of more protracted insolvency. In the former, the Bagehot principle of lending in large volume if necessary to stem a panic should be applied. It is encouraging that the IMF now has the SRF, which is designed to do just this. In such cases of illiquidity, it may be necessary to enlist private-creditor participation through such mechanisms as the arrangement of the international banks to maintain short-term credit lines in the second quarter of 1999 during Brazil's crisis. In general, the more voluntary and market-oriented this or other participation of private creditors, the better the chances for prompt reentry of the country into international capital markets. Where more severe debt problems make rescheduling or restructuring inescapable, more flexible arrangements such as exchange offers are likely to be preferable to mandatory reschedulings.

The cases of Mexico, Korea, Brazil, and to a lesser extent Thailand show that decisive international official support combined with adjustment of macroeconomic and structural policies and relatively voluntary mechanisms for private-sector involvement can restore confidence and market access. In a series of smaller-country defaults in 1999, however, the public sector seemed to be veering more toward mandatory approaches that could increasingly impose perceived "international financial institution risk" in these markets. Similarly, increasing calls for clear rules of action run the risk of a failure to recognize the inherent need for creative ambiguity in official intervention, a lesson well known under central banking principles.

Although the emerging capital markets have managed to begin a recovery from the sharp retrenchment of 1998–99, it will be essential that public policy move in a sophisticated manner on the issue of private-sector involvement in crisis resolution if these markets are to strengthen and provide the capital so crucial to global economic growth in the future.

References

Bagehot, Walter. [1873] 1917. *Lombard Street.* 14th ed. London: Kegan, Paul & Co.
Cline, William R. 1995. *International debt reexamined.* Washington, D.C.: Institute for International Economics.
———. 1998. *IMF-supported adjustment programs in the East Asian financial crisis.* IIF Research Papers series, no. 98-1. Washington, D.C.: Institute of International Finance, May.
———. 2000a. Ex-im, exports, and private capital: Will financial markets squeeze the ex-im bank? Paper presented at the Ex-Im Bank in the 21st Century: A New

Approach conference sponsored by the Institute for International Economics. 15–16 May, Washington, D.C.

———. 2000b. The management of financial crises. Paper presented at the Kiel Week Conference 2000 on The World's New Financial Landscape: Challenges for Economic Policy. 19–20 June, Kiel, Germany, Institute of World Economics.

Cline, William R., and Kevin J. S. Barnes. 1997. *Spreads and risk in emerging markets lending.* IIF Research Paper series, no. 97-1. Washington, D.C.: Institute of International Finance, December.

Council on Foreign Relations. 1999. Safeguarding Prosperity in a Global Financial System: the Future International Financial Architecture, Report of an Independent Task Force: Carla A. Hills and Peter G. Peterson, co-chairs; Morris Goldstein, project director. (Washington: Institute for International Economics, for Council on Foreign Relations).

Dallara, Charles. 2000. Letter to the chairman of the International Monetary and Financial Committee, International Monetary Fund. Washington, D.C.: Institute of International Finance. 14 September.

Eaton, Jonathan, and Mark Gersovitz. 1981. Debt with potential repudiation: Theoretical and empirical analysis. *Review of Economic Studies* 48 (April): 284–309.

Ecuador. 2000. Republic of Ecuador, "Offer to Exchange." (Prospectus: Salomon Smith Barney, 27 July.)

Eichengreen, Barry. 1999. *Toward a new international financial architecture: A practical post-Asia agenda.* Washington, D.C.: Institute for International Economics.

Eichengreen, Barry, and Ashoka Mody. 2000. Would collective action clauses raise borrowing costs? NBER Working Paper no. 7458. Cambridge, Mass.: National Bureau of Economic Research, January.

Group of Seven (G7). 1999. Report of the G7 Finance Ministers to the Köln Economic Summit. 18–20 June, Cologne, Germany.

Group of Ten (G10). 1996. *The Resolution of Sovereign Liquidity Crises: A Report to the ministers and governors prepared under the auspices of the deputies.* Washington, D.C.: International Monetary Fund, May.

Group of Twenty-two (G22). 1998. *Report of the working group on international financial crises.* Washington, D.C.: G22. October.

Institute of International Finance (IIF). 1994. *Comparative country statistics.* Washington, D.C.: IIF.

———. 1996. *Resolving sovereign financial crises.* Washington, D.C.: Institute of International Finance.

———. 1999a. *Capital flows to emerging market economies.* Washington, D.C.: Institute of International Finance.

———. Steering Committee on Emerging Markets Finance. 1999b. *Involving the private sector in the resolution of financial crises in emerging markets.* Washington, D.C.: Institute of International Finance, April.

———. 1999c. *Report of the working group on financial crises in emerging markets.* Washington, D.C.: Institute of International Finance.

———. 2000a. *Capital flows to emerging market economies.* Washington, D.C.: Institute of International Finance.

———. 2000b. *Comparative statistics for emerging market economies.* Washington, D.C.: Institute of International Finance.

———. 2001. *Principles for private sector involvement in crisis prevention and resolution.* Washington, D.C.: Institute of International Finance.

International Monetary Fund. (IMF). 1999a. *International financial statistics yearbook.* Washington, D.C.: IMF.

———. 1999b. *Involving the private sector in forestalling and resolving financial crises.* Washington, D.C.: International Monetary Fund.

Meltzer Commission. 2000. *Report of the International Financial Institution Advisory Commission ("Meltzer Commission").* Washington, D.C.: International Financial Institution Advisory Commission. March.

Portes, Richard. 2000. Sovereign debt restructuring: The role of institutions for collective action. Paper presented at World Bank-IMF-Brookings Institution conference on Emerging Markets in the New Financial System: Managing Financial and Corporate Distress. 30 March–1 April, Florham Park, New Jersey.

Rieffel, Alexis. 1985. *The role of the Paris Club in managing debt problems.* Essays In International Finance, no. 161. Princeton, N.J.: Princeton University. December.

Zhang, Xiaoming Alan. 1999. *Testing for "moral hazard" in emerging markets lending.* IIF Research Papers series, no. 98-1. Washington, D.C.: Institute of International Finance, August.

2. Guillermo Ortiz

Well, knowing that by this time pretty much everything that had to be said about financial crises in emerging markets has been said and repeated, Martin Feldstein asked me to say a few words about the experience of Mexico regarding the restoration of creditor relations. I would like to frame this in a more general discussion of restoring credibility after the crisis. As you may recall, Mexico maintained a very close relation with the investment community throughout the 1990s. In fact, it was the Mexican Brady Exchange of 1989 that really started a whole asset class of investment in emerging markets. A few years later, the privatization of Telmex around 1990–91 was a benchmark in developing interest among investors who were not previously engaged in lending to emerging markets. In fact, during the years 1990–94, between one-half and two-thirds of all portfolio flows to emerging markets went to Mexico.

As you may remember, the Mexican crisis of 1994–95 caught the financial community by surprise. Although there were certainly some ominous signs—all the events of 1994, the political assassination of Colosio, and so on—it was a real surprise. The timing was really bad: it was right before Christmas, so investors felt badly deceived by the authorities' decisions, first to raise the band, and then to float the currency. Thus, the immediate reaction of course was a complete loss of confidence in the authorities, and it soon became apparent that the situation that we were facing was very different from previous episodes of balance-of-payments problems.

It was the first of a new generation of crises that would reappear with a vengeance years later in Asia, Russia, Brazil, and other countries. In all these cases, as we discussed yesterday, there are common features, like the buildup of short-term obligations by the public sector and by the banking sector due to rapid credit creation; currency and duration mismatches in balance sheets; and, in general, a weakened situation of the banking system's regulation and supervision. In all these cases, as was amply discussed yesterday, fixed exchange rate regimes were subject to speculative attacks.

Another common feature of these cases, as I mentioned, was a loss of confidence in the financial authorities. In the case of Mexico, despite the fact that economic fundamentals were reasonably good, except perhaps for a large current account deficit, the magnitude of amortizations that we were facing in 1995 prompted what became eventually the worst crisis in the country's history.

It didn't take us very long to realize what was going on. In the first days of January, as I recall, we had a meeting—a huge meeting—in New York, at the Pierre hotel, to be precise. There was massive attendance, and I can tell you that people were extremely upset. We came out with a program that had been negotiated with the main sectors of the Mexican economy in the "pacto" system with the workers, entrepreneurs, and so on. The first reaction to the presentation of this program in 1995, surprisingly, was not very bad. In fact, following the presentation, we had a positive initial response from the markets; the exchange rate went up, and the stock market also responded favorably. I remember calling Larry Summers that night and thinking—this was 5 or 6 January—1995—that we had gone over the bridge, that we had had a very good start in the process of confidence restoration. Next morning, as I was leaving for Mexico City, I got a call on the phone and they told me the markets were in havoc again. Apparently, the interbank credit lines of some Mexican banks had been discontinued, the banks were buying in the foreign exchange markets, and the whole picture changed right away. So, instead of flying to Mexico, I flew to Washington. That afternoon, there was a meeting with the managing director of the International Monetary Fund (IMF); then there was a meeting at the U.S. Treasury. I don't know, David, if you remember those hours in which the Federal Reserve took stock with the treasury and ourselves. We started doing some rough back-of-the-envelope calculations of what was the amount of amortization due in 1995, and it came out to pretty staggering amounts. We were running a current account deficit of about 7 percent of gross domestic product (GDP)—that was about $40 billion. Plus we had another $35 billion worth of *tesobonos* and about $7–8 billion of sovereign debt due, and amortizations of private debt for another $40–45 billion. So the number was pretty big, as we sat there.

Anyway, I will not tell you the details of the meeting, but we realized that the strategy had to have two main elements. One was to put in place an adjustment program that would reduce the financing needs of Mexico in 1995 and cut the current account deficit. The other was to put sufficient money up front to reassure markets that Mexico would be liquid and would meet its obligations. This is what was done: In a matter of weeks we negotiated a program with the IMF, although at first there had been an initiative on the part of the United States to guarantee Mexican sovereign debt for $40 billion, which was shut down in the next few weeks in Congress when it came to committees. By the end of January, the whole package was pretty much finished, and in February we signed it with the treasury, the fund, everybody. We got commitments for about $50 billion at the time. Thus, the key, of course, was to restore confidence as soon as possible because, given the numbers I just mentioned to you, the $40 or 50 billion was insufficient to cover all the amortizations if we did not regain access to capital markets. The key was—the *bet* was—that strengthened economic fundamentals and sufficient money up front would do the trick. This is exactly what happened. We were able to re-access capital markets six months later, we repaid the U.S. Treasury fully in 1996–97 (several years ahead of schedule), and recently we finished paying the IMF.

However, there was a third element that was important in this whole story, and this element was that it took a lot of confidence of the markets in the authority. As I mentioned, investors felt betrayed because they felt that they had been assured by authorities in those early days that there would be no movement of the exchange rate. Thus, we had to put up a strategy, apart from the financial adjustment package, to try to regain market confidence. We hired an investment firm in those days and got advice from some friends, some of whom are sitting at this table, and we set up what was called an investor relations office at the Ministry of Finance. This investor relations office had as its main function to be a vehicle of communication with market participants, investors, analysts, and rating agencies. We started doing quarterly conferences, televised or telephone conferences, with the investor community. We designed a web page around mid-1995 and also organized several visits to be close to the investment community. This was essentially the effort that was undertaken by the Finance Ministry and that has been kept up. Every quarter, the minister of finance has to present a report to Congress on the state of public finances and the state of the economy. Also, a teleconference with investors around the world is held, and fact statistics are sent out. The funds and investors that have been active in Mexico get regular information and can access what they need through the Web. I think this is, in a nutshell, what was done after 1995.

Let me now make a few comments about what happened at the Bank of Mexico, because the Bank of Mexico also suffered a massive loss of confidence after the devaluation. The first task was to provide sufficient information to the markets. Mexico was accused after the devaluation of 1995 of hiding information and of not being sufficiently transparent. The Bank of Mexico was accused of publishing reserves information only three times a year. That was true, but the Bank of Mexico had been doing that for forty years, and it only became an issue after the crisis. We were accused of hiding information on the *tesobono*. However, the *tesobono* holdings data were published every week, but nobody seemed to look at it except after the crash in December. Nonetheless, the Bank of Mexico engaged immediately in a policy of transparency and started publishing on a weekly basis the main items of its balance sheet, the monetary base, the position of commercial banks at the central bank, and the open market operations intended for each day. That became another leg of the transparency effort on the part of the central bank.

The second important task was designing a monetary policy that would substitute for the loss of the exchange rate as an anchor when we started floating. In the first stage, what the Bank of Mexico did was to follow monetary aggregates and target the monetary base, which was the initial anchor chosen by the Bank of Mexico. However, as inflation started coming down, the relation between the narrow monetary aggregate, or even broader monetary aggregates, and inflation was pretty much lost, so in 1998 we started switching to inflation targeting. As Arminio Fraga said yesterday, inflation targeting is one of the only two games in town. In my view, when you are trying to substitute for a nominal anchor that used to be the exchange rate, inflation targeting is a very good marketing device that allows the central bank to communicate and, one hopes, to regain more credibility. The main elements of this inflation-targeting regime are, first, the annual objectives we have. We have been targeting an inflation of 3 percent for 2003, and last week we published intermediate targets for 2001 and 2002: 6.5 percent and 4.5 percent, respectively. It helps that, for two years running, we have been complying with our own targets. For example, this year the target was 10 percent, and we'll be hitting something like 8.8 or 8.7 percent.

There are other operational details of inflation targeting that I will not go over because I have only a few minutes left. Let me turn now to talk a little bit about the second part of the subject, which is the participation of the private sector, and I will be very, very brief and perhaps not very thorough in what I'm trying to say. I think that the way Mervyn King put it yesterday in terms of having two choices, either lender of last resort or some sort of workouts in the context of the discussions that we have been holding, is pretty much the right approach. In the cases of Mexico and other countries where we clearly had a run in the initial stages of the crisis, the crisis was provoked by the capital account, by the financial sector, and the like, all the elements that we can put together. The establishment of an up-front, very substantial package by the international community, especially including the United States, was fundamental to restoring confidence. This is true also of the situations in Brazil, Korea, and Thailand. The argument against this type of approach, of course, is the question of moral hazard. There is a common thread of thinking that says, for example, that the Asian crisis was caused to some extent by moral hazard deriving from the Mexico bailout four years earlier. However, there's absolutely no empirical evidence of this, and I don't think that this has been the case. For example, after the Mexican crisis, spreads for the Asian debt did not fall. I mean, this is something that we have been hearing all over, but I fail to see any hard evidence for this case. I think the Russian situation is totally different, and there we have political elements and so on that I don't want to discuss at length, but in my view this whole issue of moral hazard has been greatly exaggerated and has colored a lot the discussion of private-sector participation. I think George Soros was right in saying yesterday that the problem going forward is not excessive lending but too little lending, and I think there's a lot of evidence that investors are pulling out of emerging markets. The importance of dedicated funds and crossover investors has greatly diminished, in part due to this whole discussion of ways to try to bring in the private sector in some automatic way.

Let me conclude by saying that, notwithstanding the legitimate criticism of some aspects of IMF programs that were touched on yesterday by Jeffrey Sachs and others regarding specific actions in Indonesia and so on, the case-by-case approach that has been taken by the fund in the resolution of financial crises is probably right, and after two and a half years of discussing these issues—after two and a half years of discussing things like changes in financial architecture, international financial systems and so on—we have come up so far with two complete items. One is the Contingent Credit Line (CCL), and it has not even started: it's not operational yet. There has been a discussion for a year and a half. This was an American initiative that was shut down by the Europeans. Clearly: they put forth all the conditions so that it would not be utilized. The other item is the sixty-four codes that were mentioned yesterday. These are the only two complete things that we have today, so my conclusion is that the lessons that we have learned should serve to strengthen the internal workings of emerging markets. I think we have all been learning the lessons of working hard on fixing balance sheets, on making the economies more resilient, and all the things we've talked about, like moving to float the exchange rate and strengthening the financial sector because, frankly, I don't have much hope that anything will come out in terms of reforms in the international financial system that will be very helpful. Now, in the case of Mexico, and to conclude, is all well that ends well? Not exactly. Although Mexico has been growing by 5.5 percent over the last five years, real wages are 80 percent or 85 percent of what they were before the crisis. Income distribution has worsened substantially after the crisis, and, let me tell you, there's absolutely no enthusiasm on the part of the Mexican population for globalization and for the reforms needed to push forward this effort, which we all, in this day, think is worthwhile. So we have to reflect also on this last item: on the type of political support that is needed in our countries to continue the globalization process.

3. Roberto G. Mendoza

I would like to thank Martin Feldstein for giving me the opportunity to express a private-sector viewpoint on the papers that have been presented here, and in particular I'd like to congratulate William R. Cline on a cogent and compelling analysis.

The Cline paper largely addresses two issues: first, whether "big programs" are generally beneficial; and second, the relative merits of coercive rules-based systems and—at the other end of the spectrum—voluntary, market-based responses to crises. Cline analyzes clearly the theoretical justification for various forms of intervention. He concludes convincingly that a case-by-case, flexible, noncoercive approach, which explicitly recognizes the distinction between illiquidity and insolvency and can deal effectively with the messy, confusing situations that occur every time a crisis erupts. Cline lists seven principles that should govern crisis management; from a market participant's viewpoint, they appear very sound.

In my few minutes I will try to explain why I think that the natural tendencies of markets and the self-interest of market participants will serve to reinforce the conclusion that the Cline paper draws about the way to prevent, or at least diminish, the risk of emerging market crises and to reduce their cost when they do occur.

Three main points support this argument. First (and here I completely agree with Guillermo Ortiz's thesis), I think that the issue of moral hazard is of great theoretical interest and little practical import. Cline's paper argues that moral hazard represents a general, but frequently trivial, proposition. That seems about right to me. I don't believe that any serious creditor makes an investment decision on the basis that (a) it might go wrong and (b) if it goes wrong there will be some kind of official bailout that will protect him. In most so-called bailouts, creditors suffer large, explicit losses or implicit reputational losses. A price is paid.

I find the idea of debtor moral hazard even more difficult to understand. Default exacts a huge price on a country's government, its people, and its institutions. Avoidance of default through a bailout has lesser but nonetheless significant adverse consequences. The moral hazard issue requires consideration more (although not exclusively) as a theoretical rather than a practical matter; I do not believe that it influences behavior to the extent that the more extreme opponents of official support packages would argue.

Secondly, exchange offers *do* work. The strongest argument against exchange offers, as I understand it, is that in the absence of some type of legally enforceable cramdown mechanism that ensures completion, the borrower will be sued. However the suits are unlikely to derail the process. Analogously, many contested merger and acquisitions transactions that involve tender offers spawn lawsuits, which are usually a nuisance and can occasionally create friction costs. However, they do not often affect the outcome or materially influence the underlying economics of a transaction. In many tender offers, lawsuits are simply a fact of life.

Third, market participants, including official institutions, have a flexible toolkit of standstills, collective action clauses, litigation stays, and other mechanisms that can prove effective if voluntarily negotiated. The fundamental issue is whether it makes sense to impose mechanisms that interfere with, as opposed to reinforce, the workings of the market. In my opinion, the former would prove very damaging. Again, I would absolutely agree with Ortiz's point that the fear of market-distorting intervention by the official sector has contributed importantly to the reduction in size of the emerging markets asset class.

Three recommendations: first, policymakers and regulators should encourage—and eventually require—the adoption of fair market value accounting by banks. Arguably, one of the main causes of the crises of the 1990s was that certain market participants (and particularly insured depositories in the case of the Southeast Asian countries) lent money on terms and conditions that simply misjudged the risk-reward ratio involved. Banks would extend short-term, floating-rate, foreign currency financing (implicitly or explicitly government guaranteed) to borrowers who invested in illiquid projects that generated local currency cash flows. Leaving aside the issue of whether the underlying projects in and of themselves made any sense, the combination of all the classic mismatches led to the predictable result.

Why did the borrowers make those investments? Primarily because their riskiness was not reflected in the cost of the funding—a situation that can only end in tears. Commercial banks were prepared to make those loans in part because they could book assets at cost even though the assets were worth substantially less than cost on an economic basis. Moreover, there was a market, the derivatives market, that could have priced that risk reasonably accurately. Fair market value accounting would have forced the recognition of an immediate loss and therefore sharply inhibited the granting of such loans.

The systemic problem is even more serious than implied by this simple example because derivatives contracts are also booked effectively at cost rather than at fair market value. The historical cost accounting model permits banks to extend credit at below market rates without recognizing a loss and to sustain for some time equity price valuations that do not reflect their underlying cash flow–generating capabilities. This encourages inefficient capital allocation.

The widespread use of fair market value accounting would greatly reduce both the risk of crises and the cost of resolving them when they occur. However, there are two kinds of objections to this type of reform, the first being that fair market value accounting would increase systemic risk. Although this point is debatable, greater transparency in financial reporting, in my opinion, would decrease volatility over time. Market volatility is a reality. It is difficult—some might say impossible—to argue that a failure to recognize this reality in the financial statements of banks will decrease the risk inherent in the system.

Perhaps the more serious objection is that fair market value accounting would not in fact impose transparency, owing to the inability to price loans on a mark-to-market basis. Although this may have been true in the past, today's derivatives market for credit risk is broad and deep enough to price almost any item on or off a bank's balance sheet individually and in aggregate with a reasonable degree of accuracy—and certainly more usefully than historical cost.

My second recommendation is simply that policymakers should not fight the market view that, for most countries, the appropriate exchange rate policy is a responsible free float, that is, one that permits occasional "leaning against the wind" but does not attempt to maintain a band.

The third point relates to risk management procedures. The discussion last night highlighted the self-reinforcing characteristic of risk management methodologies. Market participants tend to use broadly similar models; when volatility increases, there is generalized pressure either to commit more capital or to reduce risk exposures. The latter approach represents the more natural tendency for publicly held firms (as opposed to hedge funds), with the result that volatility levels often increase further.

This view is largely accurate but is not an argument for downplaying the validity of the models. Rather, it simply suggests that the senior managements of financial firms must be quantitatively sophisticated enough to understand the subtleties of model outputs in order to have the confidence to override them when appropriate. This is a more complex responsibility than the traditional supervision of risk takers and places an added burden on the regulators to satisfy themselves that senior managements and boards are in a position to assume it.

The above three points suggest that, wherever possible, the regulators should seek to allow market discipline rather than official intervention to regulate the financial system. This would support the notion that governments should seek to reduce the distortions created by deposit insurance, possibly through the adoption of narrow banking models, although other, less radical market-oriented initiatives (such as mandatory subordinated debt issuance) may prove more realistic in the near term.

The debate in this conference has focused on the source of discipline to reduce the probability of crises and mitigate their impact when they do occur. The Cline paper argues persuasively that the market itself is the best source of that discipline. The removal of distortions such as coercive official intervention and opaque accounting practices that influence behavior will, over time, increase the effectiveness of market discipline and therefore reduce systemic risk. Advances in technology have made this possible for two fundamental reasons: (a) they have facilitated the development of the derivatives markets, which encourage a more efficient pricing, segmentation, and distribution of all types of risk; and (b) information has become a free good, seamlessly accessible by all market participants. Transparency of and access to information permit the market to act as an enlightened policy-maker. We heard last night that market participants should anticipate a regulatory and policy framework that combines "constructive ambiguity . . . with constrained discretion." This sounds like an intelligent complement to market discipline.

4. Ammar Siamwalla

It is amazing how much a change in perspective can affect the way one analyzes a given problem. Cline's paper starts from the private-sector lenders' perspective, and when there is a financial crisis, then the matter becomes a matter of "public-sector" concern, meaning by this, first, the borrowers' governments. Usually, it is the insufficiency of foreign exchange reserves to cope with a sudden exodus of the private creditors that ignites a financial crisis and the consequent arrival of the International Monetary Fund. The question that arises is how the private (lending) banks can be drawn in to minimize the attendant damage to the country and, perhaps, to the banks themselves.

For those of us living in the trenches, to ask how the private sector (both domestic and foreign) can be asked to bail the public sector out would appear quite odd (not wrong, but odd). The problem that Thailand and, I daresay, most other countries in Asia have been facing since 1997 is how to minimize the damage to our public finances from bailing out both our own private sector (banks and, in some cases, corporations as well) and the foreign banks. That the Thai crisis took place was due mostly to the heavy reliance on bank lending, notwithstanding the global shift in international investment toward equity and away from debt reported in Cline's paper. Most Thai borrowers depended heavily on borrowing from domestic banks (and their Bangkok International Banking Facility window), which in turn borrowed abroad for their dollar-denominated loans.

At the end of 1996, Thailand's total private external debt was $92 billion (its gross domestic product [GDP] at the then exchange rate was $180 billion); of this amount, the corporate sector (including the finance companies) owed directly to foreign lenders approximately $45 billion, the rest being owed by banks and finance companies, which had on-lent to the corporate sector in dollars. The rush to exit after the floating of the baht[1] by the foreign lenders led to the rapid depreciation of the currency, which in effect led a large proportion of the Thai private sector to become insolvent. In order to prevent the run on the domestic financial institutions by both depositors and foreign lenders, the government had to give a blanket guarantee for both depositors and lenders for all financial institutions, except the sixteen that closed before the issuance of the guarantee. This guarantee is turning out to be very costly for the taxpayers, with recent cost estimates for financial system restructuring running as high as 40 percent of GDP. Let it be noted that the cost of this bailout, including the cost to the foreign banks, is being borne almost entirely by the Thai taxpayers.

What could have been done to minimize the damage? One suggestion by Cline would have lessened it somewhat: to promote a private-sector collective action. At the very least, the sharp currency depreciation in the last quarter of 1997 and the first quarter of 1998 that follows from the exodus of the foreign banks would be limited. The open question in such a situation is the role of the government to nudge the various parties toward an agreement. In this respect, one thing the Thai government should have done was to make its guarantee of loans to financial institutions conditional upon an extension of the term of the loans.

In the event, the only thing that the Thai government did was to request the various banks to limit their withdrawals voluntarily. Only the Japanese banks appeared to have done so, but then Japanese banks were lending mostly to subsidiaries of Japanese multinationals.

By the middle of 1998, the rush to the exit door and the sharp currency depreciation came to an end. From that point on, the Thai government's central task has been to see to the restructuring the financial sector, which had been laid low by the fact that most of their loans have gone sour. Most of the smaller banks and many finance companies were taken over by the government, and the hole in their capital was or will be filled by the government. The larger banks were given time (approximately two and one-half years) to recapitalize themselves, with the government offering to provide part of the money. While this recapitalization process is going on, banks had to work out their problem loans with their debtors. With both lenders and borrowers starved of equity, it is unsurprising that there was a sharp fall of investment, and thence of output, which further accentuated the problem of nonperforming loans.

What the Thai government did not do at the time was to buy out the problem loans from the banks and park it somewhere, so as to let the banks re-

---

1. The attack on the baht in the last quarter of 1996 and the first half of 1997 was launched mostly by the speculators. This led to the depletion of the reserves and the floating of the currency. Relatively little outflow of bank money took place before the devaluation. The bulk of that outflow took place in the second half of 1997 and the first quarter of 1998.

sume lending. The main fear was that these problem loans, once parked, particularly in a government-owned parking lot, would sharply deteriorate. Indeed, the performance of the state banks since 1997 indicates very clearly that this route would have been unwise.

Discussion Summary

Anne O. Krueger suggested that we need a better theory of crisis. In addition to addressing the causes of crisis, the theory should help us understand when there are opportunities for reform. One issue here is how much you take advantage of short-term problems to address long-term problems such as chronic fiscal deficits or weak banking systems. Another issue is how far-reaching the reforms should be. Krueger said that this depends in part on whether you are trying to avoid crises in the short to medium term or trying to change the structure of the economy so that a crisis never happens again. The answer depends in part how often the country needed help in the past. Turkey, which has suffered repeated crises, might be treated differently from Korea, which has been relatively crisis-free. On the other hand, Krueger pointed out that Korea continues to have serious problems with nonperforming loans in its banking system and so remains vulnerable to a future crisis.

Krueger said that her implicit theory is that crises come along because governments did not pursue the necessary structural reforms, and they will continue to put them off until forced to do so. This leads her to believe that structural reforms such as banking reform and trade liberalization should be part of the crisis response. If, instead, you hold the view that governments will reform in good time, then it is sensible to concentrate on the immediate things necessary to overcome the crisis.

Martin Wolf agreed that crises lead countries to reform. Even so, this does not mean that crises are a good time to try to push through reforms. He thinks that having someone come in from outside de-legitimizes reform over the longer run. Turning to Cline's paper, he said he did not agree with the most important point—which he summed up as "give lots of money." He pointed out that the crises have imposed massive social costs both in terms of recessions and fiscal costs to taxpayers. The participants in the financial transactions did not internalize these costs. He concludes that the optimal flow of short-term capital to Asia may be zero and that it is wrong to insure investors fully against the risks.

Andrew Crockett agreed with Roberto Mendoza about the desirability of "fair value" or mark-to-market accounting in the financial sector. However, the case was not an open-and-shut one. There are both practical and conceptual difficulties in marking to market nonmarketable assets, such as loans. Moreover, other interested parties, such as securities supervisors and the tax authorities, have reservations about allowing provisions before a probability of loss has been established. Still others are concerned about the volatility that mark-to-market accounting would introduce into financial institutions' income streams. Nevertheless, despite all the obstacles, he felt that this approach was the best way of disciplining risk taking.

On the subject of risk management practices, Crockett argued that financial institutions were reasonably good at valuing what he called "relative risks," (i.e., the riskiness of different claims at a point in time) but less good at measuring absolute undiversifiable risks associated with the economic cycle. He said, "we all know the worst loans are made at the best times." The challenge in designing supervisory arrangements and risk management practices is to develop models that are better attuned to the movement of risk over the cycle.

Peter Garber pointed out that financial institutions use stress testing and event risk scenarios to go beyond value-at-risk modeling. These can be used to put quantitative limits on positions beyond what the value-at-risk models would dictate. Moreover, these methods are much more cyclically oriented, he said. Regarding the ease of marking to market, he agreed that credit derivatives could be very useful but said there is a lot of "magic" involved in their pricing as well, and he stressed the difficulties of pricing very long-term loans and illiquid credits. He agreed that asset-backed securities could be used to value packages of loans, but he again noted that it is not as easy as one might think to come up with accurate values.

Jacob Frenkel returned to the issue of reform "ownership." He remembered that it used to be the case that the IMF was comfortable with being "bashed" for the reforms they demanded. Governments often found it useful to be seen as coerced by the IMF in pushing through politically difficult reforms. However, this turned out to be an untenable situation, he said. The program does not have to be designed in the capital of the country. It can be designed by experts anywhere and negotiated. Wherever it is designed, once a program is agreed upon it must be under the ownership of the government if it is to have a chance of success.

Montek S. Ahluwalia raised the issue of what can be expected from the international community as lenders of last resort as opposed to reliance on private-sector involvement. Commenting on the phrase "constructive ambiguity" from Cline's paper, he said that constructive ambiguity is better than destructive ambiguity but added that what developing countries need is some constructive clarity. Developing countries would be better off knowing the limits to the official assistance they can get and, beyond that, what the rules for involving the private sector would be. Given Robert Rubin's prediction that there will be more crises in the future with more countries engaging with the international capital markets, Ahluwalia reiterated that countries such as India need to know better what lender-of-last-resort function exists. At present, the only way that the lender of last resort can do a credible job is if IMF resources are topped up with substantial bilateral resources, and this (perhaps unavoidably) introduces a great deal of political uncertainty. Ahluwalia is not sure this is "constructive."

William R. Cline said he understood the desire for clarity, but he sees a danger in a "very quick slide from clarity into essentially mandatory resolution." Cline believes it is much better to get toward what he called the voluntary end of private-sector involvement. The clearer you are, the more likely it is you go to capital controls. Moreover, the easier it is to default, the more likely it is that you shut down lending. He agreed with Roberto Mendoza and Guillermo Ortiz that the experiments in "bailing in" the private sector had contributed to the rising spreads and "sluggishness" that we have seen in some markets. Finally, he said he disagreed with Mervyn King that it will be impossible to come up with the large packages we have seen in the past. He asked: "If Chile goes down tomorrow, for example, is it impossible to come up with $7 billion—the same fraction of GNP we came up with for Brazil?" He understands why King is saying this, given the need to avoid the moral hazard problem that comes with large packages. He thinks that because of the good record of Chile or a comparable country, it is very likely that such a case would successfully be toward the voluntary end of private-sector involvement. Given this likely involvement, Cline thinks we need to be very careful in moving in the direction of too much coercion.

E. Gerald Corrigan said that a sizable majority of emerging market countries were making progress in most areas of crisis prevention—macro policy, debt management policy, risk management policy, and so on—but noted that progress has been very slow in banking reform. He expressed surprise that a better job had not been done through prudential supervisory practices at dealing with the problem of short-term unsecured credit. Given the progress that has been made, he said that the risk of systemic sovereign financial crisis has come down, but added that it is nowhere near zero. On the interbank restructuring in Korea in 1997–98, he pointed out that there had been a lot of comment that it was a bad idea and had been forced upon Korea by the IMF. He thinks both these claims are wrong and said there were a number of approaches on the table at that time that would have been rejected outright by the Korean government.

On the issue of what should be done in the future regarding private-sector involvement, Corrigan listed four alternatives: outright new money, unilateral suspension of payments, voluntary standstills, and voluntary restructuring. He thinks the first of these—new money—will not happen and the second—stopping payments—is a recipe for further instability. He thinks the emphasis should be put on the latter two options on the list, although he agrees with Mendoza that what is "voluntary" is sometimes in the eye of the beholder.

More generally, Corrigan thinks we should see that there is a menu of options, recognizing that there is no one thing that is going to solve the problem at the point of crisis. He added that the Fund's adjusted Contingent Credit Facility (CCF) should now be seen as part of the menu, and if it is made more flexible, it could be the basis for encouraging a greater use of appropriately priced private-sector standby-type facilities. Corrigan finished with the controversial opinion that, in "truly exceptional circumstances," there could be limited and partial official-sector credit enhancements. Although he expected that most people did not want to hear that, he reminded the audience that this was exactly what was done with Brady bonds. Thus, in shaping a menu, he said we "should never say never."

Paul Volcker disagreed that crises occurred primarily because of weak banking systems. Instead, he sees the problem in the nature of financial markets and their wide swings coming up against small and inherently vulnerable financial systems. Mexico didn't have a crisis because of its weak banking system but because of its rising *tesobono* debt. He said that financial markets ordinarily prosper from volatility, but he asked if industry can prosper in such an environment. Such volatility, he added, has a limited impact on the United States because it is a large, stable economy. It plays havoc, however, with smaller economies, in part because they are more vulnerable to exchange rate swings.

George Soros complained that there was no discussion of what had happened in Russia. He said that the G7 did not want to put up their own money, and the IMF was limited in what it could do since it signed a letter of intent with a government that could not produce. More generally, he said it would be useful to have a mechanism whereby a letter would be forthcoming from the Fund stating the conditions that were necessary for it to act as a lender of last resort.

On the question of what works and what doesn't in responding to a crisis, *Jeffrey Sachs* made two observations. First, he said that the "hemorrhaging" must be stopped. To do this, you need to understand where it is coming from—fiscal deficits or the financial sector. If the problem is fiscal, then the fiscal gap must be closed. If the problem is financial, there are three options: new money, a unilateral standstill, and a voluntary rollover. Sachs said that it is wrong to rule out any of these, adding that Mexico "worked" because of the United States, but often new money or a rollover will not be forthcoming.

Second, Sachs said that running things from Washington is not sustainable in today's world. Part of the problem is that "no money is brought to the table, only conditions," said Sachs, pointing to the negative net transfers to Africa. He said that he would not rule out considering issues of long-term management, but the current mix of conditions without money is failing. Moreover, he thinks that the current model we are using for development is fatally limited. The issues should not be limited to questions of governance and corruption but should extend to issues such as disease and clean water.

Frederic Mishkin said that we needed to think of the IMF as fighting a war. It needs to focus on two things: macro policy and getting the financial sector working again (which requires some structural reform). However, he said, "this is where it should stop." Referring to Nicholas Stern's suggestion from an earlier session, he said the World Bank should not have two-page plans for structural reform ready to implement at the time of the crisis but, rather, should focus on long-term thinking. In Mishkin's view the IMF has a high-quality staff, but it is overwhelmed. It is also in a political bind. On one side the Meltzer commission tells it to narrow its focus. However, the IMF's board has not strongly supported this.

Lin See Yan suggested that the Malaysian case is interesting in that it opted first for IMF advice (even though it was not eligible for financial assistance because the economy was judged to be "still strong" when entering the crisis), that is, tighten the fiscal budget (despite three previous years of large surpluses); tighten monetary policy (by raising interest rates to protect capital outflows); and reduce balance-of-payments current deficit (even though it was not in fundamental disequilibrium). This sent the economy into a tailspin that threatened political and social stability and led to further loss of confidence. The IMF's hungry "big eyes are much too wide for its narrow stomach," Lin said. Malaysia needed to change horses in midstream with worsening expectations regarding exchange rate volatility, portfolio capital outflows and stock market sentiment. The objective of public policy then turned its focus on the reestablishment of social and business stability through a number of pragmatic measures: (a) adopting Keynesian expansionary fiscal programs directed mainly at social (education and health) and poverty spending; (b) fixing the exchange rate to the US$ with the 40 percent devaluation (expectations pointing to 60 percent) to inject certainty in doing business; (c) introducing easy-to-implement selective capital controls directed mainly at temporarily stopping further portfolio outflows and denying speculators ready access to ringgit bank balances and currency; and (d) setting up the National Economic Action Council to take direct charge of crisis management, with full powers to implement effectively the "new" deal, including setting up new institutions to act on banking reform, bank recapitalization, and debt restructuring and resolution. Ironically, this option is not really unorthodox—indeed, it is a rather conventional Keynesian approach to reflate and reestablish confidence (after all, the IMF rules do allow temporary capital controls in a crisis). It introduced a modernized system of selected capital controls (designed to fit the occasion), a system that is highly focused, with rules precisely defined for effective implementation; well organized, leaving the banks' vast network with wide-ranging authority to approve; clearly decentralized, so that only large transactions need to be referred to the central bank; and subject to constant review, for effectiveness in practice. To date, the absence of any serious bureaucratic inefficiencies or black market in the ringgit reflects well on the appropriateness of the mechanisms that have been put in place. All in all, the prompt return of confidence and the early V-shaped economic recovery, with no adverse political and social fallout, appear to suggest that there may be something in the Malaysian way of managing its own type of crisis.

Timothy Geithner said that those who have been heavily critical of the Fund should temper their criticisms with some humility and ask themselves what they would have done, and how they would have performed, in similar circumstances with similar information and similar time pressures. Responding to Mervyn King's presentation on creditor relations, Geithner said he was troubled by King's enthusiasm for the broader use of standstills or suspensions of payments and in particular by establishing any presumption that a standstill would be invoked as a condition for access to large-scale financial assistance. Responding to Jeffrey Sachs, he said that the crucial issue is not necessarily whether net transfers to the poorest countries are too low, but that if you believe they are and want to see them increased you have to have a framework in place that will make that possible. The involvement in the IMF is likely to be critical to the willingness of donors to provide more concessional resources.

Paul Keating expressed the view that the world can no longer be run from the United States. The United States Congress has neither the internationalism nor the will to do it. The world's remaining superpower has become less generous over time, he said, and has downgraded the importance of India and China in the world. He said that India has to take nuclear actions to get noticed. In his view, the structure that followed the allied victory in 1945 is no longer adequate. The key question now is how we empower the Bretton Woods institutions, which are struggling with a world of integrated international markets and new communications technologies. He also questioned how representative the G7 is and blamed the Clinton administration for failing to create a more inclusive world order. He closed by saying the middle powers must be recognized and allowed to have a role in decision making, remarking, "the old political structure has had its day."

With respect to the issue of private-sector involvement, *Edwin Truman* said his sense is that this issue is often oversimplified as one involving bank or bond creditors on the one hand and a sovereign borrower on the other, or perhaps banks with the explicit or implicit guarantee of the sovereign. However, in the three major Asian cases and Brazil, although not Russia, this assumption about the dominant involvement of the sovereign did not hold. In those cases, broad-based private-sector involvement (i.e., a standstill) would have had two potentially troublesome consequences: First, it would have involved the extensive application of exchange and capital controls that, once imposed, are usually very difficult to dismantle and also can be very disruptive to trade. Second, it would have risked the socialization of many private-sector obligations, as both the creditors and the debtors would have looked to the government to guarantee the repayment of obligations that had been blocked. As we saw in the 1980s, such socialization of debt is very expensive and undesirable, given that it leads to a bailout of the private sector.

Biographies

Montek S. Ahluwalia is the first director of the newly created Independent Evaluation Office at the International Monetary Fund. At the time of the conference, Ahluwalia was a member of the Planning Commission in New Delhi as well as a member of the Economic Advisory Council to the prime minister.

Jack Boorman is counsellor and special advisor, and at the time of the conference was director of the Policy Development and Review Department, at the International Monetary Fund and one of the senior staff directly involved in the fund's response to the crises of the last five years.

Domingo F. Cavallo is honorary president of Fundación Mediterránea. He has been minister of foreign affairs and later minister of finance of Argentina (1989–96). He created his political party, Accion por la Republica, in 1997 and was elected national congressman until he was appointed to be minister of economy in March 2001, a position he resigned in December 2001.

William R. Cline is senior fellow jointly at the Institute for International Economics and the Center for Global Development in Washington, D.C. During 1996–2001, while on leave from the Institute, Cline was deputy managing director and chief economist of the Institute of International Finance in Washington, D.C.

E. Gerald Corrigan, former president of the Federal Reserve Bank of New York, is a managing director at Goldman Sachs & Co.

Andrew Crockett is general manager of the Bank for International Settlements, Basel, Switzerland, and chairman of the Financial Stability Forum.

John Crow is former governor of the Bank of Canada. In 1999 he chaired a committee of independent experts that evaluated International Monetary Fund surveillance.

Charles Dallara has been managing director of the Institute of International Finance since 1993 and was formerly a U.S. executive director of the International Monetary Fund.

Michael P. Dooley is professor of economics at the University of California, Santa Cruz, and a research associate of the National Bureau of Economic Research. He has been a staff member at the board of governors of the Federal Reserve and the International Monetary Fund.

Sebastian Edwards is the Henry Ford II Professor of International Business Economics at the Anderson Graduate School of Management at the University of California, Los Angeles, and a research associate of the National Bureau of Economic Research.

Martin Feldstein is the George F. Baker Professor of Economics at Harvard University and President of the National Bureau of Economic Research.

Stanley Fischer served as first deputy managing director of the International Monetary Fund from September 1994 to August 2001 and as special adviser to the managing director from 1 September 2001 until 31 January 2002. He is currently vice-chairman of Citigroup, Inc.

Arminio Fraga is governor of the Central Bank of Brazil.

Jeffrey A. Frankel is the Harpel Chair at Harvard University's Kennedy School of Government and directs the National Bureau of Economic Research program in International Finance and Macroeconomics. During the crises of 1997–99, he was a member of President Clinton's Council of Economic Advisers.

Jacob A. Frenkel is president of Merrill Lynch International, former governor of the Bank of Israel, and a research associate of the National Bureau of Economic Research.

Peter Garber is global strategist in Deutsche Bank's Global Markets Research.

Timothy F. Geithner is director of the Policy Development and Review Department at the International Monetary Fund. He was previously undersecretary for international affairs at the U.S. Department of the Treasury.

Morris Goldstein is the Dennis Weatherstone Senior Fellow at the Institute for International Economics and a former deputy director of research at the International Monetary Fund.

Takatoshi Ito is professor in the Institute of Economic Research at Hitotsubashi University, Tokyo, and a research associate of the National Bureau of Economic Research.

Karen Johnson is director of the Division of International Finance at the Federal Reserve board of governors.

Paul Keating is former prime minister of Australia.

Mervyn King is deputy governor of the Bank of England.

Anne O. Krueger is first deputy managing director of the International Monetary Fund and a research associate of the National Bureau of Economic Research.

John Langlois is professor of East Asian Studies at Princeton University. He is a member of the Council on Foreign Relations and the director of the Bank of Shanghai. He is also the president of the Center for International Political Economy (New York).

David Lipton is managing director at the Moore Capital Strategy Group in Washington, D.C. He served at the U.S. Treasury from 1993 to 1998, most recently as undersecretary for international affairs.

John McHale is associate professor of economics at Queen's University in Kingston, Ontario.

Roberto G. Mendoza is co-chief executive officer of Hancock, Mendoza, Dachille & Merton, Ltd. (HMDM). Mendoza joined JPMorgan & Co. in 1967 and served as vice-chairman of the board from 1990 to 2000. He joined Goldman Sachs & Co. in 2000 as a managing director and resigned in 2001 to cofound HMDM.

Frederic S. Mishkin is the Alfred Lerner Professor of Banking and Financial Institutions at the Graduate School of Business, Columbia University, and a research associate of the National Bureau of Economic Research.

Manuel Montes is a program officer at the Ford Foundation.

Guillermo Ortiz is governor of the Banco de Mexico, and during the period 1995–97 he was finance minister of Mexico.

Yung Chul Park is professor of economics at Korea University. He is currently serving as ambassador for International Economy and Trade, Ministry of Foreign Affairs and Trade, and also chairman of the board, the Korea Exchange Bank in Seoul, Korea.

Nouriel Roubini is associate professor of economics and international business at the Stern School of Business, New York University, and a research associate of the National Bureau of Economic Research.

Robert Rubin is the former secretary of the U.S. Treasury and is currently director, chairman of the executive committee, and member of the office of the chairman of Citigroup, Inc.

Jeffrey D. Sachs is director of the Center for International Development at Harvard University and a research associate of the National Bureau of Economic Research.

Ammar Siamwalla is distinguished scholar at the Thailand Development Research Institute.

George Soros is president and chairman of Soros Fund Management LLC, a private investment management firm, which serves as principal investment advisor to the Quantum Group of Funds, a series of international investment vehicles.

Nicholas Stern is chief economist and senior vice-president of Development Economics at the World Bank.

Lawrence Summers is president of Harvard University and former U.S. Treasury secretary.

Edwin Truman is a senior fellow at the Institute for International Economics in Washington, D.C. He served as assistant secretary of the U.S. Treasury for International Affairs from December 1998 to January 2001.

Paul Volcker is former chairman of the Federal Reserve board and chairman of the Group of Thirty.

Martin Wolf is associate editor and chief economics commentator of the *Financial Times,* London.

Lin See Yan is CEO of an independent strategic consultancy based in Malaysia. He is also pro-chancellor of Universiti Sains Malaysia and professor of economics at University Utara Malaysia. He was formerly deputy governor of Central Bank of Malaysia.

Contributors

Montek S. Ahluwalia
Director, Independent Evaluation
  Office
International Monetary Fund
700 19th Street, NW
Washington, DC 20431

Jack Boorman
Counsellor and Special Advisor
International Monetary Fund
700 19th Street, NW
Washington, DC 20431

Domingo F. Cavallo
Tagle 2810
C1425EEH Buenos Aires, Argentina

William R. Cline
Institute for International Economics
1750 Massachusetts Avenue, NW
Washington, DC 20036-1903

E. Gerald Corrigan
Managing Director
Goldman Sachs & Company
85 Broad Street
New York, NY 10004

Andrew Crockett
General Manager
Bank for International Settlements
CH-4002 Basel, Switzerland

John Crow
J&R Crow, Inc.
191 Ellis Avenue
Toronto, Ontario M6S 2X4, Canada

Charles Dallara
Managing Director
The Institute of International Finance,
  Inc.
2000 Pennsylvania Avenue, NW
Suite 8500
Washington, DC 20006-1812

Michael P. Dooley
Department of Economics
Social Sciences I
University of California, Santa Cruz
Santa Cruz, CA 95064

Sebastian Edwards
Graduate School of Business
University of California, Los Angeles
110 Westwood Plaza, Suite C508
Box 951481
Los Angeles, CA 90095

Martin Feldstein
President
National Bureau of Economic
  Research
1050 Massachusetts Avenue
Cambridge, MA 02138

Stanley Fischer
Vice Chairman
Citigroup Inc.
399 Park Avenue, 3rd floor
New York, NY 10043

Arminio Fraga
Governor
Central Bank of Brazil
SBS Quadra 3, Bloco, D-Ed. Sede
PO Box 08670
Brasilia DF 70074-900, Brazil

Jeffrey A. Frankel
Kennedy School of Government
Harvard University
79 JFK Street
Cambridge, MA 02138

Jacob A. Frenkel
President
Merrill Lynch International, Inc.
Ropemaker Place, 25 Ropemaker
    Street
London EC2Y 9LY, England

Peter Garber
Deutsche Bank
31 West 52nd Street
New York, NY 10019-6160

Timothy F. Geithner
Director, Policy Development and
    Review Department
International Monetary Fund
700 19th Street, NW
Washington, DC 20431

Morris Goldstein
Institute for International Economics
1750 Massachusetts Avenue, NW
Washington, DC 20036-1903

Takatoshi Ito
Institute for International Economics
Hitotsubashi University
Naka 2-1, Kunitachi, Tokyo 186-8603,
    Japan

Karen Johnson
Federal Reserve Board
20th Street and Constitution Avenue,
    NW
Washington, DC 20551

Paul Keating
GPO Box 2598
Sydney NSW 2001, Australia

Mervyn King
Deputy Governor
Bank of England
Threadneedle Street
London EC2R 8AH, England

Anne O. Krueger
First Deputy Managing Director
International Monetary Fund
700 19th Street, NW
Suite 12-300F
Washington, DC 20431

John Langlois
Department of East Asian Studies
Princeton University
Princeton, NJ 08544

David Lipton
Moore Capital Strategy Group
816 Connecticut Avenue, NW
Washington, DC 20006

John McHale
Department of Economics
Queen's School of Business
Queen's University
Kingston, Ontario K7L 3N6,
    Canada

Roberto G. Mendoza
Co-CEO
Hancock, Mendoza, Dachille &
    Merton, Ltd.
c/o Rhone Group
630 Fifth Avenue
Suite 2710
New York, NY 10111

Frederic S. Mishkin
Graduate School of Business
Uris Hall 619
Columbia University
New York, NY 10027

Manuel Montes
Program Officer
Human Rights and International
    Cooperation
The Ford Foundation
320 East 43rd Street
New York, NY 10017

Guillermo Ortiz
Governor
Banco de Mexico
Ave. Cinco de Mayo Num. 2, Piso 4
Col. Centro, Deleg. Cuauhtemoc,
Mexico D.F., CP 06059, Mexico

Yung Chul Park
Department of Economics
Korea University
1, 5-Ka, Anam-dong, Sungbuk-ku
Seoul 136-701, Korea

Nouriel Roubini
Department of Economics
Stern School of Business
New York University
44 West 4th Street, MEC7-83
New York, NY 10012-1126

Robert Rubin
Office of the Chairman
Citigroup Inc.
399 Park Avenue, 3rd Floor
New York, NY 10043

Jeffrey D. Sachs
Director
Center for International Development
79 JFK Street
Cambridge, MA 02138

Ammar Siamwalla
Office of the President
Thailand Development Research
    Institute
565 Soi Ramkhamhaeng 39
Wangthonglang, Bangkok 10310,
    Thailand

George Soros
Chairman
Soros Fund Management
888 7th Avenue
New York, NY 10106

Nicholas Stern
Chief Economist and Senior Vice-
    President, Development Economics
The World Bank
1818 H Street, NW
Washington, DC 20433

Lawrence Summers
President
Harvard University
Massachusetts Hall
Cambridge, MA 02138

Edwin Truman
Institute for International Economics
1750 Massachusetts Avenue, NW
Washington, DC 20036-1903

Paul Volcker
610 5th Avenue, Suite 420
New York, NY 10020

Martin Wolf
Financial Times
Number One Southwark Bridge
London SE1 9HL, England

Lin See Yan
LIN Associates Sdn. Bhd.
Veritas
23 Medan Setia 1
Plaza Damansara
Bukit Damansara
50490 Kuala Lumpur, Malaysia

Author Index

Subject Index